Glyndebourne

Spike Hughes

Glyndebourne

A HISTORY OF THE FESTIVAL OPERA

FOUNDED IN 1934 BY AUDREY AND JOHN CHRISTIE

DAVID & CHARLES

Newton Abbot   London   North Pomfret (Vt)

In memoriam Fritz Busch 1890-1951

First published 1965 by Methuen & Co Ltd
© Spike Hughes 1965

NEW EDITION BY DAVID & CHARLES 1981
© Spike Hughes 1981

British Library Cataloguing in Publication Data
Hughes, Spike
   Glyndebourne.—New ed.
   1. Glyndebourne Festival Opera—History
   I. Title
   782.1'07'942257   ML38.G63

   ISBN 0-7153-7891-0

Typeset by ABM Typographics Limited, Hull
and printed in Great Britain
by Redwood Burn Ltd, Trowbridge and Esher
for David & Charles (Publishers) Limited
Brunel House   Newton Abbot   Devon

Published in the United States of America
by David & Charles Inc
North Pomfret   Vermont 05053   USA

Contents

Illustrations

CHAPTER ONE

Roots and branches

ALL OPERA HOUSES ARE UNIQUE, but – as anyone who comes into contact with them soon discovers – some are more unique than others. It was clear from the very first, however, that Glyndebourne was the most unique of all. When in June 1933 a Captain John Christie told the Press that the following summer he would open the opera house he had built in the grounds of his country house in Sussex, with either *Don Giovanni* or *Die Walküre*, adding that 'in addition to the *Ring* we shall produce *Parsifal*, probably at Easter,' the whole idea was so alarmingly unique, so unlikely and puzzling that it seemed the only thing to do was to pretend it wasn't, by trying desperately to relate the idea to some familiar, rational and reassuringly recognizable aspect of everyday English life.

So it was that we came to read about the promise of a 'Manor House Opera', 'Opera in a Village Hall', 'Garden Opera House', 'Pocket Opera House', 'Village Opera', 'Opera in a Mansion'; even in 1935 – a lifetime afterwards by Fleet Street reckoning – my review of the famous *Figaro* recording was headed 'Opera on the Village Green'. It was clear that nobody really knew what it was all about. But then how or why should anybody have known? There was absolutely no precedent to go on. For all that the idea of Glyndebourne could be associated with such familiar and permanent features of English life as village greens, village halls, gardens, mansions and manor houses 'nestling' (always 'nestling') in the Downs, the truth was that it was the rural setting as much as anything that floored everybody in the end. Understandably – for ever since the Teatro San Cassiano was opened as the world's first public opera house in Venice in 1637, opera had always been an essentially urban form of entertainment. Opera houses, as every historian knows, have always been built on the sites either of demolished churches (particularly in Catholic countries) or of earlier theatres that have been burnt down. They had never, so far as anybody was aware, been built in the garden of an English gentleman's country house, and certainly never without a stage door.

Perhaps if in 1933 we had known about the absence of a stage door at Glyndebourne we might have had some clue to the nature of the whole project; or, if not, at any rate have been instinctively more suspicious of it. No stage door would mean no stage door keeper; and no stage door keeper would mean there were no autograph hunters to keep away, and – even more significant – none of those numberless, nameless, whispering conspiratorial figures with briefcases who haunt the doorways, anterooms and staircases of the rest of the world's opera houses. Here, we would have known at once, was uniqueness indeed. In spite of all these splendid displays of fierce nonconformity, however, Glyndebourne still had one thing conventionally in common with many other opera houses. We may have to go back 700 years into Sussex history to find it, but the fact is that, like La Scala, the San Carlo, the Carlo Felice, the Vienna Opera, Covent Garden, or the Teatro Regio at Parma, Glyndebourne would not have been what it was if it had not been for the Church.

The important difference was that where the other theatres were essentially secular institutions whose association with the Church was due to no more than the purely physical accident of their being built on sites where churches, monasteries and convents had stood, Glyndebourne might well never have existed at all if it hadn't been for the action of an Archbishop of Canterbury. Until the Reformation the Archbishops of Canterbury owned extensive property in the neighbourhood of Lewes, and there are still to be found in Sussex parishes known as 'Peculiars' whose churches, like those of the two villages closest to Glyndebourne, Ringmer and Glynde, for instance, while geographically in the diocese of Chichester, were in fact in the peculiar jurisdiction of the See of Canterbury. The Archbishop, indeed, is still patron of the living of Ringmer. At the time of the Domesday survey of 1086 the Hundred of Ringmer in the Rape of Pevensey included Archbishop Lanfranc's Manor of Mellinges, or Malling, a present day parish of Lewes through which all who come to Glyndebourne by train and Southdown bus pass on their way to and from Lewes station.[1]

The Manor of Malling is mentioned in Domesday; the Manor of Glynde is not, but it seems to have been established as part of the Manor of Malling not long after William the Conqueror's survey and in due course to have been conveyed by the Archbishop by sub-infeudation to a family who took their name from the village and were known as de Glynde. The next we hear of the de Glyndes is about 1300 when the heiress of the last male de Glynde, who rejoiced (as surely she must have) in the name of Dionysia, married Sir Richard Walleys. Glynde remained with the Walleys family until about 1490, when once again the property was inherited by a woman. Joane, daughter and heiress of Sir John Walleys, last male of his line, married Nicholas Morley who came, as the Rev T. W. Horsfield records in his *History and Antiquities of Lewes and its Vicinity*, published in 1824, 'of an ancient and respectable family which had its original seat at Morley in Lancashire'. By this marriage the Manor of Glynde passed into the Morley family, and it is with the Morleys that we first encounter Glynde Bourne itself. With its name indiscriminately written as one word or two, with and without a hyphen, until well into the nineteenth century and still pronounced locally as two separate words with an emphasis on the

---

[1] A Hundred was a division or part of a county supposed to have originally included a hundred families. A Rape is a term peculiar to Sussex and was applied to the six administrative divisions of the county – Arundel, Bramber, Lewes, Pevensey, Hastings and Chichester. The Concise Oxford Dictionary comments: '[since 1086: etym dub.]'.

second, the original house was a small affair built sometime in the early fifteenth century. It was built, like many Sussex houses, mainly of chalk, large blocks of which were used with great effect in the construction of walls and chimneys. The house was almost entirely rebuilt in Elizabethan times but some of the features of the original building are still visible. One of the chalk walls, for instance, may be seen on the right of the stairs leading to the private quarters of the house from an iron gateway in the passage at the west end of the Organ Room. At least, it would be more accurate to say that the wall is known to be made of chalk, but has unfortunately been covered with a thick layer of plaster. The characteristic grey cornerstones, however, can still be seen. At the back of the present building of Glyndebourne there are also some of the original walls made of flint and the soft white limestone known as 'clunch', mullioned windows, some panelled rooms, and a solid wide oak staircase which is the main stairs of the house.[1]

Glynde Bourne remained part of the manor of Glynde until the end of the sixteenth century when it is said to have been given as a dowry to Mary Morley on her marriage in 1589 to John Hay of Hurstmonceux. There is, however, a small doubt about this; whereas all the other Morley settlements have been preserved among the records from Glynde Place, there is nothing to show that William Morley made any settlement on his daughter Mary when she married. It is not even certain that during their married life she and her husband lived at Glyndebourne at all, for Mary Hay died in 1598 and was buried at Hurstmonceux, which suggests that that is where they lived. The Hays had five children. The eldest, Herbert, was 14 when his father died in 1605 and left him an orphan; he became the ward of his mother's brother, Herbert Morley of Glynde, and in 1616 was installed at Glyndebourne which Mr Richard Dell, the East Sussex County Archivist, tells me he believes was acquired by young Herbert Hay by purchase in 1616.

By whatever means he may have come by Glyndebourne, Herbert Hay lost little time in ensuring that it was fully occupied. He had thirteen children – eleven by his first wife, and two by his second. Of the eight who survived infancy, two played a sensible part in the history of Glyndebourne: John, the eldest son, who inherited the estate, and Sarah, who married Sir John Langham of Cottesbrooke, Northamptonshire, about 1650. John Hay was the first of four successive generations of Hays to enter Parliament. He himself was MP for Rye, his son William was Member for Seaford, his grandson William was also Member for Seaford, his great grandson Thomas was Member for Lewes. The first William Hay, who entered Parliament when he was 21 and died aged 24, had three children – John Hay, who died as an infant, a daughter Barbary, whose marriage to a William Tutté of Chichester was another union that affected the inheritance of Glyndebourne, and William, who was born at Glyndebourne the year his father died in 1695, and was a member of Parliament from 1733 until his death in 1755.

[1] There is a legend still current in Ringmer today that this staircase came originally from what was formerly Broyle Palace (now Broyle Place) on the Ringmer-Laughton road, built by an Archbishop of Canterbury in Norman times as one of the many country houses which lined the route to and from his Peculiars and so enabled him to travel from Canterbury to Lewes and further without ever leaving his own diocese. As far as John Christie knew the staircase had always been at Glyndebourne.

The second William Hay was one of the most colourful and endearing figures in the long history of the house described both cautiously and lyrically by Horsfield as 'a neat but unpretending edifice, once a favourite abode of the Muses'. The Muses, it is clear, had shared the house with William Hay, poet, politician and philosopher, at the close of whose descriptive poem entitled *Mount Caburn* Horsfield tells us 'the amiable writer thus delicately alludes to his own residence at the foot of the Mountain to which he had invoked the Muses':

> *Oh may some Bard, more favor'd of the Nine*
> *Thy Glories paint in an immortal Line;*
> *His Fancy bear resemblance to thy Clime,*
> *Rich as thy Vales, and as thy Hills sublime;*
> *His Strains more lasting than thy Oaks abide,*
> *And his smooth Numbers like thy Currents glide;*
> *Then all thy Deeds and Monuments of old,*
> *Which the Eye sees, or babbling Fame hath told,*
> *When sinking underneath the Weight of Time*
> *Again shall rise, and flourish in his Rhyme.*
> *   Perhaps he'll say, viewing my Cell beneath*
> *(Where I began and where will cease to breathe)*
> *Here liv'd the Man, who to these fair Retreats*
> *First drew the Muses from their ancient Seats;*
> *Tho' low his Thought, tho' impotent his Strain,*
> *Yet let me never of his Song complain;*
> *For this his fruitless Labour recommends,*
> *He lov'd his Country and his Friends.*

William Hay was survived by four of his five children. His talents, Horsfield records, 'were of a superior cast, and his mind was well stored with valuable information. He had much independence of spirit, and great decision of character; a playful imagination, and a cheerful and benignant disposition. He was generous without being prodigal; kind and indulgent to his children, domestics and tenants, and upright and just to all.'

With the death of William Hay's two surviving sons the male line of the Hays of Glynde Bourne came to an end. Thomas Hay, the elder, a much-travelled professional soldier who eventually became MP for Lewes and Lieut-Colonel of the Sussex Militia, died unmarried in 1786. William, the younger son, has this epitaph on a plate included in *The History and Antiquities of Lewes and Its Environs*: 'In 1763 being of the Supreme Council at Calcutta, he with one more was appointed to treat with Meer Cossim [Cassim], and remained a voluntary hostage, that his senior and other of his Countrymen might be allowed to leave Patna, where by the Tyrant's order he was murdered October the 5th 1763.' William was 28.

On the death of Thomas Hay, the estate went to his two sisters Henrietta and Frances, who moved into Glyndebourne from Ades, a house near Chailey which had been rented from the famous Dr Richard Russell, FRS, of Brighton, author of *A Dissertation concerning the use of Sea Water in Diseases of the Glands*, whose work on 'the efficacy of sea water, in glandular complaints, combined with his unwearied and successful attention to these disorders, under a marine course, brought numerous visitors to the neighbourhood; lodging-houses on the coast became a profitable speculation, and the town of Brighton began to flourish'.[1] (Part of Ades House is now occupied by Peter Ebert and his family.)

Henrietta Hay died in 1794, her sister Frances in 1803; between them they may be held to have been responsible for the Queen Anne windows added to the house at Glyndebourne about 1800 which John Christie referred to indignantly in his inaugural article in the first Programme Book of 1952. Both Hay sisters died unmarried and with their death the Hay family of Glynde Bourne became extinct. Their name is perpetuated locally, however, in the Hay Charity Trust still administered to this day.

The house and estate of Glyndebourne devolved on the death of Frances Hay upon her first cousin, Canon Francis Tutté, whose surname as well as many of whose personal characteristics strike a happily prophetic chord in view of what was to happen at Glyndebourne in due course. Tutté succeeded to Glyndebourne through his mother Barbary Hay, only sister of William Hay, the poet, politician and philosopher, who married William Tutté, a Chichester barrister. Like his uncle, Francis Tutté was an unusual and lovable figure, and indeed it is clear from the special mention he rates in Horsfield's chronicle that he inherited many of the characteristics of his mother's family. He was 74 when he moved into Glyndebourne. 'In this charming retreat he spent the last twenty years of his life; and here, in the ninety-fourth year of his age, he paid the debt of nature ... His disposition was amiable, cheerful and benevolent, and his love of society very great. Seldom was his house without visitors, whom he delighted by his uniform affability and playful humour. His benevolence was unobtrusive, but it was ever active. The unfortunate and distressed found in him a warm friend, and the poor a generous benefactor. What is particularly deserving of notice is that, although he himself was never married, a large portion of his humane intentions was devoted to the relief of widows and orphans in reduced circumstances. His charities were not known to the world at large; they were performed in secret, and were of the best and purest kind. During the twenty years he resided at Glynde Bourne he gave an annual entertainment to the poor of the parishes of Glynde and Ringmer. The plentiful repast was rendered more pleasing to his guests by the kindness which he manifested on these occasions, and the smiles of benevolence with which they were greeted. His appearance was prepossessing; his frame well made, and his aspect dignified, whilst the ruddy hue of health appeared to mantle in his countenance even to the last.'

Francis Tutté died in 1824, and the Glyndebourne estate, consisting of about 1,500 acres in the parishes of Glynde and Ringmer, passed to James Hay Langham, son and heir of Sir James Langham, Bt, of Langham Place, London, and Cottesbrooke Park, near

[1] The inscription on the family vault in St Michael's Church, South Malling, Lewes, where Dr Russell was buried in 1759, runs: *Admiring ages Russell's fame shall know,*
Till Oceans' healing waters cease to flow.

Northampton, and descendant of the Sarah Hay of Glyndebourne, who had married Sir John Langham in 1650.[1] On succeeding to the baronetcy in 1833 James Hay Langham moved to his family seat in Northamptonshire and in accordance with the wills of the last two Hay sisters Glyndebourne passed into the possession of Langham Christie, born 1789, and the eldest son of Daniel Beat Christie and his wife Elizabeth Langham. Langham Christie's father was born Daniel Béat Christin in 1745, a member of a Swiss family from the Canton of Vaud; he changed his name to Christie on entering the Bombay Engineers in the Honourable East India Company's Service, and in 1786 married as his second wife Elizabeth, eldest daughter of Captain Purbeck Langham.

When Langham Christie died in 1861, aged 72, Glyndebourne was inherited by his son, William Langham Christie, who sat as MP for Lewes from 1874 to 1885 and on its incorporation as a Borough in 1881 presented the ancient county town with the Gold Badge, Chain of Office and Ceremonial Mace that have been used by the mayors of Lewes ever since. William Langham Christie, who was born in 1830, married Agnes Hamilton Clevland, eldest daughter and co-heir of Colonel Augustus Saltran Clevland of Tapeley (or Tapley) in North Devon, a marriage which was in due course to bring large estates into the Christie family. Agnes Clevland's brother Archibald was a Cornet in the Seventeenth Lancers who came through the Charge of the Light Brigade at Balaclava in 1854 but was killed by a shell at Inkerman a few days later. Archibald Clevland was the last on the male side of the Clevlands, who had originally come from Lanarkshire to Devon in the first years of the eighteenth century, and so once more an inheritance ultimately to benefit the Christies passed through the female line. There is a picture of Archibald Clevland at Glyndebourne in the passage from the Organ Room to the garden.

At Glyndebourne, in addition to fathering six sons and three daughters, William Langham Christie made some startling alterations to the appearance of the house, decorating it with towers and castellation, covering the old flint walls with layers of Victorian brickwork and adding an Eton fives court. According to his grandson 'he had absolutely appalling taste; he knew so little about anything that he built the fives court with a rough brick floor and it was impossible to play in it'. This grandson, who in due course inherited Glyndebourne with the 'monstrous' Victorian brickwork and the useless fives court, was John Christie, born on 14 December 1882 at Eggesford in North Devon, the only child of Augustus Langham Christie and Lady Rosamond Alicia Wallop, sister of the eighth Earl of Portsmouth.

---

[1] The Langham baronetcy was created by Charles II in 1660, the year of the Restoration – a rather belated recognition by the Stuarts of services rendered by Sir John Langham who, when Sheriff of London in 1642, had been imprisoned 'with several other gentlemen' for refusing to publish 'An Act for the exheridation of the Royal Line, the abolishment of Monarchy in the Kingdom, and the setting up of a Commonwealth'.

CHAPTER TWO

Education of a landowner

JOHN CHRISTIE WOULD RELATE with pride that he had been born before the doctor arrived. It showed, he said, that right from the start he'd always had a certain amount of independence. His childhood was far from happy and the few pleasant memories he had in later life – such as swinging on the luggage rack of a railway carriage on a journey from South to North Devon when he was two and a half – were heavily outnumbered by the recollection of miserable experiences of early school life. He was just 6 years old when he went to his first private school where, he recalled, 'I was beaten my first term – I don't remember what for – and I'm sure every other term'. From this private school he went to a bigger one 'where we were beaten all the time'.

From the Squeersian atmosphere of his second school ('it was very well known'), John Christie went on to Eton, but since school of any sort was inseparably associated in his mind with being beaten, his principal memory of Eton was of a flogging he received from the headmaster in his last term there, when before leaving the room where it happened he stooped down to pick up some of the bits of the birch as a memento – and barely escaped being flogged again.

Christie's academic career as a boy at Eton does not seem to have been particularly distinguished. He had great mathematical gifts but little opportunity to exercise them in the limited intellectual world of the so-called Army Class which, as the name suggests, was designed for those intended for a military career. Christie's days as a boy at Eton were not followed, as was stated in a widely circulated newsagency obituary in 1962, by two years service in the Boer War. He was 18 years old and went to the Royal Military Academy at Woolwich, where for a year and a half he suffered 'a pretty boring and utterly useless and rotten education'. His stay was cut short by a riding accident; his horse slipped going over a jump and landed on its rider's ankle. Christie admitted it was his fault: 'I ought to have got clear.' He was taken to the Military Hospital, where his leg was put in a cradle and he was not examined for ten days by 'the criminally incompetent Army doctors'. Lady Rosamond Christie sent the carriage down from London for her son to be driven back to see Sir Thomas Barlow, physician successively to Queen Victoria, Edward VII and George V. The newly-invented x-rays disclosed that the whole of Christie's foot was crushed and out of joint. It was re-set and he was lame ever after.

Not that it mattered, he said. As a master of forty he boasted he could run faster than any boy at Eton – 'on the other leg'.

The permanent dashing of any prospects of an Army career was a great relief to John Christie and he was able to go up to Trinity College, Cambridge, where he read Natural Science. Because of his injury he was unhappily prevented from playing any games, and for much of his three years at the University he was still hobbling about on sticks; in addition, he injured and eventually lost the sight of an eye while there, though this did not stop him playing unserious cricket in later years or deny him the opportunity of developing into a first class shot. Not being able to play games at Cambridge must have been particularly frustrating, for Christie was by nature a physically active man whose stocky frame and broad shoulders contained all the strength and energy suggested by his fiercely determined chin, which in turn belied the gentleness and kindness of his nature.

John Christie's time as an undergraduate at Cambridge was the basis of one of the earliest of the innumerable legends that have grown up around modern Glyndebourne and its founder – a legend, that is, which if it was not the earliest to gain circulation at any rate concerns the earliest period of its subject's life to have developed into a legend. Only a few months before his death a Sussex lecturer was still telling the story that, while at Cambridge, John Christie was one of the team of scientists who worked with Lord Rutherford on splitting the atom. Christie did many things in his lifetime, but he did not do this; at the time he was an undergraduate Rutherford was Professor of Physics at McGill University, Montreal, and I believe did not work at Cambridge at all until 1919 or so. When one remembers his delight in pulling people's legs and making outrageous statements with almost the same straight face of his genuinely serious moments, it is obvious that most of the Glyndebourne legends were started by John Christie himself. But having started them it was another matter trying to stop them being universally accepted as true. The qualifying words 'Mr Christie told me that ...' have given an air of authenticity to numberless newspaper stories and oral accounts which down the years have disseminated as fact words spoken in characteristic jest and never intended to be taken seriously. The most persistent and indestructible legend of all was that Christie inherited a fortune left him by an aunt (or grandfather – it depended which paper you took) on condition that he 'did something useful', which is why he became a school-master. This was denied rather *sotto voce* in 1949, but was obviously not widely heard, for the legend was back in vigorous circulation shortly afterwards and inevitably cropped up again on Christie's death.

To be honest, however, there were one or two quite colourful Glyndebourne legends which, having been started by Christie, were so wholeheartedly maintained by their author that he convinced himself that they were absolutely true.

After taking his degree at Cambridge Christie returned to Eton in 1906 as an assistant master to teach science. He was then 24 and, except for an interruption of two years on active service during the first war, he spent the whole of the next sixteen years there in an atmosphere which he found sympathetic and stimulating. These, rather than the frustrated and unhappy years of his boyhood, were the truly formative years and he regarded them as probably the happiest period of his life. Chief among the many friends he made while a master at Eton was C. M. Wells, an outstanding athlete and scholar, and some eleven years Christie's senior. Those who knew the pre-war Glyndebourne will remember the Greek quotations that accompanied each item in the wine list. Some (but not all, as Christie proclaimed) of these were written by C. M. Wells, who took a first in classics at Cambridge, where he was in the University cricket and football teams; he played cricket for Surrey and Middlesex and rugby for England. He died in 1963 aged 92. Cyril Mowbray Wells was obviously something of an *Ich-ideal* to John Christie, who would have liked fewer things more than to have been a first-class cricketer and a classical scholar, and indeed his friendship with the older man caused him greatly to regret that he had not read classics at Cambridge.

His contribution to the Greek quotations in the early Glyndebourne wine lists was virtually the only association C. M. Wells had with Glyndebourne the opera house, as distinct from Glyndebourne the country house. He did not care for music, and would always make anxious enquiries on being invited to stay with Christie to ensure that there wouldn't be 'any singers or things about the place'. It was a long and firm friendship, not the least touching aspect of which was their annual reunion, which ended only with Christie's death, on Wells' birthday.

At Eton, John Christie also came to know 'Goatie' Lloyd. Dr Charles Harford Lloyd (his nickname derived from his beard), who founded the Oxford Musical Club as an undergraduate in 1872, had been precentor of Eton since 1892 and as musical instructor there had included among his pupils Edward J. Dent, whose classic *Mozart's Operas: A critical study*, first published in 1913, has for two generations played an important part in the appreciation of Mozart in this country.

The musical influence of Dr Lloyd on Christie, nearly forty years his junior, was obviously extensive. He took Christie to the Munich and Bayreuth Festivals, and I think one may deduce something of the nature of his influence from the preponderance in the Glyndebourne music library of half-morocco folio editions of Wagner's full scores. And, of course – *si monumentum requiris* – there is the Organ Room which came to be built in place of the useless fives court entirely because of Lloyd's refusal to stay at Glyndebourne where there was no organ for him to play on. Although he did not come into full legal possession of the estate until 1920, it was during these pre-1914-War years as an Eton master that Christie first came to spend such time at Glyndebourne as his work allowed, and he was clearly very unhappy at Lloyd's refusal to stay there. With a wonderfully characteristic gesture John Christie set out to put this state of affairs right. When he failed to find an organ to suit Dr Lloyd's requirements he bought the organ building firm of Norman and Beard and had an instrument made to the precentor's own design. Before the organ was completed, however, Dr Lloyd died – on his seventieth birthday in 1919 – and so never came to stay at Glyndebourne after all. But although Dr Lloyd never played on the organ he designed, the instrument itself and the Organ Room that housed it came to play a vital part in the evolution of the Glyndebourne Opera we know today.

Meanwhile, when war had broken out in 1914, John Christie had left Eton for a commission in the King's Royal Rifle Corps. He was invalided out in 1916 having been awarded the Military Cross and attained the rank of Captain. Little seems to be known of his experience as a soldier beyond the characteristic incident when, during the Battle of Loos, Christie and his detachment became separated from the rest of the company, and having to keep as still as possible in order to survive in the mine crater they were forced to shelter in, Christie took a copy of Spenser's *Faerie Queene* from his pocket and read it to an audience that grew increasingly absorbed in what they heard.

Christie himself recalled principally that he was quite irrationally fascinated by bombs and shells. He was frightened by neither; all he wanted, he said, was for them to burst just in front of him so that he could see them burst. 'They had nothing to do with me whatever,' he said. 'I was just made that way – nothing to do with bravery. I wasn't brave at all. I'm a complete coward if I look over a precipice.' While I have not met anybody who ever saw John Christie look over a precipice, there are many who count among their most terrifying experiences the occasions when he took them up and down ladders and along flimsy planks during the building and reconstruction of the Opera House roof. It was little consolation, they said, to be told to hang on to his broad shoulders when without warning he was likely to turn and point out some startling new feature of the building.

Christie told, too, of how during the war after a training exercise there was a discussion between the officers, and being a company commander ('and knowing nothing about it, of course'), he invented a lot of new military terms which very much interested his commanding officer. With great difficulty Christie managed not to laugh; but then his ability to keep a straight face was one of his greatest and – for those who didn't know him – most deceptive accomplishments.

On leaving the army Christie returned to Eton once more, where he resumed what the *Eton College Chronicle's* memoir of him described as his 'somewhat unconventional approach to his duties'. On the coldest days of the wartime winters he took Early School in the intimate warmth of his own house. ('Early School' at Eton are classes held before breakfast.) It is scarcely surprising that those he taught should remember him with affection – like Lord Donegall, for instance, who, when Glyndebourne first became news, recalled in his *Sunday Dispatch* column the famous incident of Christie's reply on being asked how he had arrived at the rapid solution of some mathematical proposition: 'Never mind, my boy. I did it by a dodge.' Or the frequent appearance, about a quarter of an hour after Early School should have started, of the butler Childs, who would announce: 'Captain Christie will be with you shortly, gentlemen.'

Joseph Roger Childs was as unusual a figure as any to be encountered in the history of Glyndebourne, and if John Christie's gifts had been directed towards literature instead of the creation of the Glyndebourne Festival Opera, he might well have taken his place in the national biography alongside the Sitwell family's immortal Henry Moat. Bearing in mind Christie's delight in exaggeration one is inclined to regard many of the things he said with suspicion, but there is certainly corroboration of the speech Childs once made in the 1930s at a dinner given to the employees and tenants of the Devon estates. As

Christie had seldom visited these estates since childhood he was introduced to his guests by Childs, who recalled how at Eton, 27 years before, he had interviewed Mr Christie ('a fair haired young gentleman who thought himself quite an important young person') with a view to obtaining the post of butler to him. Childs had found Mr Christie satisfactory and in turn had answered his employer's specification to the agency for a butler who, apart from the normal qualifications for the job, was 'very intelligent and very well read'. There followed a long and happy relationship between master and servant, which continued through the war when the butler became batman, and survived even what Childs called Mr Christie's 'lapse' in getting married in 1931, as well as such incidents as that of the Book of Ruth. For many years John Christie had read the lessons in church at Ringmer; one Sunday, however, he had trouble in finding the Book of Ruth and as he turned the leaves helplessly in his search for it a loud whisper came from Childs in the choir stalls: 'Try it in the earlier books, sir – try it earlier on!' Christie finally found Ruth; but after the service Childs said to him: 'I think, sir, it would be better if I read the lessons in future.' Childs read the lessons until he died in 1940.

After the war Christie found that the responsibilities of Glyndebourne and being a landowner were beginning to make increasingly heavy demands on his time; so when in 1922, and after 16 years as an assistant master, he was offered the chance of becoming a housemaster at Eton he decided to refuse – reluctantly, one feels, but it would have meant his spending another ten years there. It was clearly a difficult decision and, as it turned out, a decision which was a turning point in many people's lives besides his own.

To those to whom the name of John Christie means only the Glyndebourne Opera it may seem unlikely that there were people living within a mile or two of him who could ever have thought of him in any other way. But the truth is that when he died, there were many in the village of Ringmer who had never heard a note of the music ever played in the Opera House – even on the radio or television. To them his death was that of a man whose greatest work, as a local farmer put it to me, was that 'he brought employment to a whole district'.

It is natural to look back on John Christie as one of the great English eccentrics, for the very idea of the Glyndebourne Opera is in itself of monumental eccentricity. But in fact he was a man of quite prodigious determination and with a phenomenal ability to make into practical reality those ideals with which he was obsessed. There can be few people who, whether they knew him or not, were not aware of Christie's obsessions for they were regularly expressed in what I used to think of as his 'State of the Union' address published every year in the Festival Programme Book. These were not merely window-dressing or specially selected reiterations of faith and propaganda to keep his audiences aware of what Glyndebourne stood for and aimed at. Not long before his death he was repeating to me, with as much fervour as when I had first heard it nearly 30 years before, his strong views on the obligations of the wealthy and the aristocracy. How could anybody become an efficient landowner, he argued, if they hadn't any practical experience of their 'trade'? Building and repairs, forestry and the conversion of timber, garden-produce, garages, water-works, hotels, golf-courses – it was a landowner's job to enter every one of the trades connected with landowning and compete in the open market.

Christie blamed all the troubles of the modern world, from the Labour Party to opera at Covent Garden, on the failure of the Victorian aristocracy to lead in such matters. They were totally useless, inefficient, and intolerably pleased with themselves, he said. He himself had practised what he preached right from the beginning, and with such thoroughness and success that enterprises like the Ringmer Building Works, for instance, which had started out with a total weekly wages bill of £20, had developed from a small estate facility into one of the biggest building concerns in south-east England. And its managing director, Christie would repeatedly point out, had been a garden boy at Glyndebourne. This delegation of authority and responsibility to others whose judgment and experience he trusted was characteristic of Christie's administration of his estate from the first. He applied the principle to all his undertakings, from the Building Works, the garage, the forge and the electricity works at Ringmer, the hotels and golf courses in Devon, to the last and most ambitious and successful of them all – the Glyndebourne Festival Opera.

CHAPTER THREE

Marriage and a mission

IN ONE RESPECT JOHN CHRISTIE's departure from Eton came as a relief to his colleagues, for it meant that henceforward they would be able to travel by train to Glyndebourne instead of being driven there by their host in his Daimler. A motor car driven by Christie was as unmistakable a manifestation of character and personality as anything he ever did. There are people who (much to their surprise) are still alive today to recall the drives from Eton to Glyndebourne as probably the most hair-raising experiences of their lives. The driver's complete lack of fear, his sublime self-confidence, his unshakeable belief in the possession of a sixth sense which enabled him, every time he drove straight over a major road or overtook on a blind corner, to proclaim triumphantly (and turning his head right round towards his backseat passengers as he did so) that he *knew* there was nothing coming – these were qualities with which familiarity bred nothing but fear and panic.

Christie's philosophy of driving was expressed once in a letter to *The Times* from which it seemed that the safest way of motoring was to drive from A to B as fast as possible. This meant that less time was spent on the roads and that therefore there was less time in which to be involved in accidents.

Many tales have been told of John Christie's natural gregariousness, his hospitable nature and the childlike gift he possessed for making firm, immediate friends with complete strangers. A wayfarer stopping to look at the house from the road outside Glyndebourne would not only find himself suddenly taken inside by the owner to be conducted all over the house, gardens and theatre, but would as like as not end up in the Christie box for the evening listening to *Figaro*. This characteristic sociability was certainly not the least of the important elements from which Glyndebourne Opera eventually developed. In the years after Christie left Eton the house was constantly filled with people, and where many of the guests had been invited to shoot and enjoy the traditional pursuits of life in an English country house, there was an increasing number of visitors who came to sing and play music. Sometimes the company would include a professional string quartet, a professional singer or instrumentalist, but mainly the performers were amateurs, playing for their own and their host's amusement, and often, like Mrs Mounsey, the pianist wife of a well-known banker, with considerable skill. John Christie himself never played an instrument, but he did learn to read the notes and this certainly extended his experience and understanding of music during these years. Indeed, it is not exaggerating to say that in many ways Christie's genuinely formative years began in the latter part of the 1920s, when he himself was already over 40 years old and the performance of music in various forms became increasingly part of the everyday life of Glyndebourne.

He still went the rounds of the summer opera festivals at Munich, Bayreuth and Salzburg, enjoying musical holidays in place of those fishing holidays which he had had to abandon, he said, because there was 'always too much water or too little'; but there can be little doubt, I think, that the constant first-hand contact with music in his own home must have had a considerable influence on Christie's development and have widened his experience. The centre of all this was, of course, the Organ Room where what had once been music for the private enjoyment of those who played it was now shared to an increasing extent with an audience of estate employees and tenants, as well as house guests.

As these occasions thrived so, as one would expect, John Christie grew more ambitious, until in 1928 the scale and scope of the Organ Room performances were extended to include opera for the first time. On Sunday 3 June 1928, a complete and lengthy operatic scene was performed. The opera was not by Mozart, but by Wagner – a concert version of the first scene of Act III of *Die Meistersinger*. The printed programme, with its quaintly old-world lack of Christian names for the artists taking minor parts, is reproduced opposite as a document of a certain historical interest.

On the reverse of the programme was a synopsis of the action.

That Wagner should have been performed before Mozart at Glyndebourne may seem surprising, or even shocking, but it must be remembered that this particular priority was a clear reflection of John Christie's taste and preference at that time. The bulky full scores of *Parsifal* and the rest in the Glyndebourne Opera House music library today are a constant reminder of where Christie's first musical affections lay.

Mozart's turn, however, was not long in coming. On 5 and 6 January 1929, the first act of *Die Entführung aus dem Serail* was performed in the Organ Room. This time, in place of the Competitive Musical Festival form of score used for the *Meistersinger* scene, there was a nineteen-piece orchestra – strings, two flutes, but only one oboe, clarinet and bassoon, no horns and no trumpets. The orchestra, conducted by Arnold Goldsbrough, included several professional players whose names and faces will be familiar to many concert-goers, among them Cecil Bonvalot, the leader on this occasion, who was for a long time the violist in André Mangeot's famous International String Quartet, Helen Gaskell, for many years oboeist with the Queen's Hall and BBC Symphony Orchestras, Gilbert Vinter, who played the bassoon and is now conductor of one of the BBC's regional orchestras, and, as second flute, George Willoughby, now concert manager of the BBC. The clarinet, according to the programme, was played by that great all-rounder, A. N. Other.

Looking back at what has been written I find I have done an injustice to John Christie in saying that he played no musical instrument. This was not so. He played the cymbals in this *Entführung* orchestra, an instrument which, if it does not have to be played in tune, at any rate has to be played in time. In Mozart's opera this is often a feat of considerable physical endurance, for once the cymbals start the player has little time to call his own.

The formal use of 'Mr' and 'Mrs' in the programme credits was dispensed with for this second Glyndebourne opera enterprise. Except in the case of the Producer (an office not required in the *Meistersinger* performance), who was billed simply as 'Mrs Crichton', the artists' names were printed in accordance with modern custom. The plain 'Mr Biggs' of the earlier venture now became William Biggs (who sang Pedrillo), and we also discovered that like Margerie Harrison (Constanze) and Philip Warde (Belmonte), he was a member of the Johnstone Douglas Operatic School. Osmin was sung by Thornely Gibson, and the part of Pasha Selim was played by Mrs Mounsey's husband, J. E. Mounsey, who died a tragic death a few months later. Their son, Patrick Mounsey, played the

Glyndebourne.   Sunday, 3rd June, 1928.

" Die   Meistersinger "

Act III.————————————Scene 1.

By RICHARD WAGNER, 1866.

Characters in the order of their appearance :—

Hans Sachs, *the Shoemaker* - -	Mr. THORNELY GIBSON
David, *his Apprentice* - - - - - -	Mr. BIGGS
Walter von Stolzing, *a young Knight who has just arrived in Nürnberg*	Mr. STEUART WILSON
Sixtus Beckmesser, *the Town Clerk who hopes to win Eva* - - -	Mr. JOHN CHRISTIE
Eva, *the daughter of Pogner the rich Goldsmith* - - - -	Mrs. THORNELY GIBSON
Magdalene, *her maid, engaged to David* -	Mrs. ROBERTSON

At the Piano - - Mrs. LAMPSON.

At the Organ - - Mr. POTTER.

SCENE: The interior of the workshop in Sachs's house. The stairs on the right lead to Walter's bedroom, and the window on the left overlooks Pogner and Eva's house.   *Period 1550.*

29

triangle in the orchestra alongside his host. The chorus consisted of members of the Ringmer Singing Class.

On the back of the printed programme there was this time a synopsis of the whole of the opera the excerpt was taken from, not merely of the act being performed. In addition there were notes on the opera itself, written in that abrupt, austere, anonymous, unmistakable prose which we were to know so well in later years. What is probably John Christie's earliest essay in musical commentary to have survived in print, discusses the artists who appeared at the first performance of the opera in Vienna in 1782, and goes on to describe the characters they sang:

Constanze was first sung by a Viennese lady, Madame Cavalieri, who had a powerful voice, a wide compass and an amazing mastery of coloratura. Therese Teyber (Blonde) was a high soprano, with all the charm of freshness and youth. Belmonte was Adamsberger, a thorough artist, both as singer and actor. The part of Osmin was written for Fischer, a first rate actor, with a bass voice of remarkable quality and range. Osmin is, of course, the great creation of the Opera. He is the one personage who shows that wonderful power of individual characterization which (in his later operas at least) is Mozart's special gift. Every note he sings belongs to him and to him only. Belmonte, like Blonde, is a type, not an individual. Constanze is the great mistake of the Opera. She is not even a type, but merely a *prima donna*. The part of Selim Pasha is most ungrateful, as he does not sing at all and has too an unconvincing part to act. In Germany he always seems to me to be a complete failure.

The style is so characteristic of John Christie's writings that it is rather a shame to have to report that from the words 'who had a powerful voice' in the first sentence to 'merely a *prima donna*' in the last sentence but two, the entire passage was lifted, word for word and without acknowledgment from page 137 of the first (1913) edition of *Mozart's Operas: A critical study*, by John Christie's Old Etonian friend, Edward J. Dent. (The passage does not occur in the second edition published in 1947.)

It was some time before there was opera again in the Organ Room, but when it was resumed, at Christmas 1929, its effect on at least two of those most intimately concerned in it was what can only be described, with extravagant understatement, as far reaching.

John Christie was now about 47, the most eligible bachelor anybody could wish for, and it was beginning to be thought by his friends that he really ought to marry and 'settle down'. As though to oblige them, Christie fell in love with a young soprano in the Carl Rosa Opera Company called Audrey Mildmay. Old men's memories notoriously play curious tricks, and though he could remember clearly the incident of swinging on the luggage rack as a child of two and a half Christie had no idea when I asked him what part Miss Mildmay was singing when he first heard her. It would be pleasing to think that she sang Susanna, but *Figaro* was not then in the Carl Rosa repertoire. Miss Mildmay's roles at that time were Musetta, Gretel, Micaëla, Zerlina, the Doll in *The Tales of Hoffmann*, Lola in *Cav.* and Nedda in *Pag.*

In fact, John Christie first heard Audrey Mildmay singing Blonde in a performance of

Die Entführung in his own house. Originally it had been planned to repeat at Christmas 1929 the *Meistersinger* excerpt performed in the Organ Room in June 1928, but Mr and Mrs Thornely Gibson (Sachs and Eva) were not available and the project was dropped. Instead, Mrs Gibson suggested that Christie might do some more of *Die Entführung* and recommended that he engage her friend Audrey Mildmay to sing Blonde. This was done. Miss Mildmay came as a hired help, as it were, bringing (in company with a tenor colleague from the Carl Rosa) professional comfort and experience to an otherwise amateur enterprise. From Audrey Mildmay's own account it seems to have been a pretty hilarious affair with more than its quota of mishaps reducing the audience to such helpless laughter that many of them had to go out of the room.

On this occasion John Christie does not seem to have played the cymbals in the orchestra. It is said by some that he sang Osmin, but this is flatly denied by others. As I have found no documentary evidence either way I will have to content myself with the thought that, true or not, it was a nice idea anyway.

Audrey Mildmay's first visit to Glyndebourne lasted a week and she received £5 for her services. She was also shown over the house by John Christie, who opened the door of the bedroom named 'Broyle' (all the bedrooms have a name associated with the Christie family and estates) and announced abruptly: 'This is where we shall sleep when we're married.' Miss Mildmay rightly suspected this to be a proposal of marriage which, however, she did not take seriously and so did not accept – at least, not for some time.

Once having met her, John Christie followed Audrey Mildmay about the country, wherever the Carl Rosa's tours took her (including Belfast), sending her regularly a hamper of food from Fortnum and Mason as he considered she looked seriously undernourished. These hampers were enormous and most agreeably practical for they sustained the entire Carl Rosa company for nights on end.

Grace Audrey Louise St John Mildmay was born in Sussex only a few miles from Glyndebourne – at Hurstmonceux, on 19 December 1900. Her father, the Rev Aubrey St J. Mildmay, later tenth baronet, moved to Vancouver to become a vicar of Penticton, and it was there that she went to school and, inspired (the local papers claimed many years later) by the example of the famous Canadian singers Louise Edvina and Edward Johnson (alias 'Eduardo di Giovanni') whose photographs decorated her room, received the first part of her musical education. When she was 24 Audrey returned to England and studied singing with Johnstone Douglas, co-founder with Amherst Webber of the eventual Webber-Douglas opera school, an institution which was the only one of its kind and in its day did admirable work in the training of young opera singers. Quite astonishingly, neither Webber, Douglas, nor their school rates a mention in any of the usual reference books so far as I can discover.

At the end of this stage of her training Audrey Mildmay went on a long tour of Canada and the United States as Polly in *The Beggar's Opera*. This may strike those who know of the work only as a 'ballad opera' as being a rather modest assignment for an opera singer, and certainly less demanding than a modern 'musical'. Let it be said that nothing could be further from the truth. When Nigel Playfair staged his famous revival of *The Beggar's Opera* at Hammersmith in 1920 (it ran for 1,463 performances) Macheath was played by Frederick Ranalow and Peachum by Frederic Austin – two singers whose performances as Figaro and the Count respectively in Sir Thomas Beecham's wartime production of Mozart's opera are still remembered by all who saw them as among the very finest of their generation.

On her return to England after the Canadian and American tour of *The Beggar's Opera*, Audrey Mildmay joined the Carl Rosa Company at £2 10s a week. This indomitable concern, founded in 1873, is in danger nowadays of being forgotten as having been the first and often only source of operatic experience for thousands of people in this country for many, many years. The Carl Rosa, which never had a home of its own, gave opera on the frailest of shoestrings up and down the country, sending its scenery by canal barge when other forms of transport were too costly. It was not only audiences who learned about opera from the Carl Rosa; for a generation or more there was scarcely a British singer of any standing who did not have his first practical lessons in his trade with the Carl Rosa Company. Some, like Dame Eva Turner, who as a child heard her first opera at a Carl Rosa performance, began in the chorus of the company and graduated to leading roles which led her to La Scala to become one of the greatest of all Turandots. Not all who have travelled and toiled with the Carl Rosa have risen to such heights, but there have been few who have not been the better for having toured the hard way, lived in theatrical digs in No 3 towns, and become seasoned professionals in the process.

Audrey Mildmay and John Christie were married in the Somerset village of Queen Camel on 4 June 1931 – the best possible date for an Old Etonian to choose who wanted to make sure he never forgot his wedding anniversary. The Christies' wedding day was itself the first anniversary of a touching little incident recalled by Mrs Thornely Gibson, who tells how on 4 June 1930 Christie had taken Audrey Mildmay to Covent Garden to hear *Der Rosenkavalier* from a box and, at the exact moment in Act II when Oktavian presented Sophie with the silver rose, Christie had taken a miniature silver rose from his pocket and presented it to Miss Mildmay.

Childs, the butler, was best man at the wedding and, according to Christie, when asked later by Mrs Christie how he had managed to remember the ring, had replied: 'Well, I had had a grudge against Mr Christie for some time.' The honeymoon was spent in Germany, where first the bride and then – with a touching display of sympathy – the bridegroom had to be operated on for appendicitis.

It was in the months following the Christies' return to Glyndebourne that the idea of building a theatre first seems to have arisen. The project, however, was essentially an extension of the Organ Room entertainments. It was to be a small affair seating perhaps 150 people at the most; the performances would still be mainly amateur and the audiences non-paying guests – estate workers, tenants, and family friends as before.

The summer of 1931 was a period of recurrent political and economic crisis which culminated in the autumn in the abandonment by Britain of the Gold Standard. This action, taken by the recently formed National Government and not by a Labour Government as he often maintained in later years to make an ironic point, was the signal for Christie to start building his theatre. He foresaw the pound going the way of the franc and the mark, and decided that then or never was the time. Work was begun at once; in what had formerly been a kitchen garden the trenches were dug for the foundations of a building that was to be at right angles to the site now occupied by the Opera House.

Before the foundations could be laid, however, it struck Audrey Mildmay that this was not the way to do things at all. The historic moment came at dinner one evening when, during discussion of the subject by the Christies and their house guest Hamish Wilson, Audrey turned to her husband and said: 'If you're going to spend all that money, John, for God's sake do the thing properly.' From that point onwards the idea was seen on an altogether different scale and aimed at an altogether different target. Instead of semi-professional shows with free beer for the audiences there must be productions of an international festival standard – and higher. The trenches were quickly filled in and, as Christie later described it, 'in haste rather than in knowledge' the building was redesigned to seat 311 people and begun afresh on the new site.

One of the first people Audrey Mildmay got in touch with was Ernest Newman, an old and devoted friend, whose advice she sought on various aspects of the Glyndebourne idea, but particularly on the question of the architecture of the proposed theatre. Newman, who had not yet met him, suggested that if John Christie read German he should study all the books and periodicals concerned with German theatre design he could lay hands on. Otherwise he personally knew little of these things. In the course of a letter written on New Year's Day, 1932, in reply to one from Audrey Mildmay which had clearly been chock full of questions, Ernest Newman wrote that he was 'completely whacked' by her query about who could write her a good opera. He proposed Walton – who 'would do a good opera if he could get the right subject'.

Her question about a German singing teacher: Newman did not know any except Elena Gerhardt, who specialized in Lieder.

The letter ended with a characteristic postscript about a work for the opening of Audrey Mildmay's theatre. Why not, suggested Newman, try one of the lighter old works such as Pergolesi's *La serva padrona*? Either that, he said, or the *Götterdämmerung*.

Once their new aim was established neither Audrey Mildmay nor her husband was quite sure how it was to be achieved; she had had no experience of operatic management or organization, while Christie, although he had once owned the Opera House, Tunbridge Wells, for a short period some while before, knew even less of the practical business of presenting opera.[1]

---

[1] Christie was very reticent about his ownership of the Tunbridge Wells Opera House. He took it over, he said, 'to help a friend'. It was nevertheless a venture which played its part in the history of the Glyndebourne Opera, for while everything but opera was performed there, it was at Tunbridge Wells that Christie discovered, employed as a stage carpenter, 'Jock' Gough, whose ingenuity and professional experience were later indispensable to him and his Festival Opera. The Tunbridge Wells Opera House is still a going concern and at a recent Christmas offered Podrecca's Teatro dei Piccoli puppets and *La Dolce Vita*. Since then, however, I fear it has become almost exclusively a cinema.

What the Christies lacked in knowledge and experience they made up for in courage, determination, enthusiasm, an unshakeable belief in their ability to succeed in what was to become a sacred mission. Although she had retired from the stage when she married it was obvious that Audrey Mildmay did not mean her retirement to be permanent (her letter to Ernest Newman shows this clearly); once her idea of a festival opera had begun to be translated into bricks and mortar it was not long before she began to study again. She was still only 31 years old and it would have been too much to expect her not to want to take active part in an enterprise which was after all largely her own personal creation.

In the late autumn of 1932 Audrey Mildmay went to Vienna and in searching for a singing teacher was recommended a young Hungarian called Jani Strasser; she had a course of lessons with him, studying Lieder as well as arias. One day John Christie came to Strasser's studio – a burly figure, Strasser recalls, whose startling tweed suit, overcoat and cap, and stout country walking stick, caused something of a stir in the sober, respectably urban fashion world of Vienna. Telling him about the theatre that was being built at Glyndebourne Christie asked Strasser to suggest some short operas which could be performed there with a small orchestra and no chorus (it seems the idea of entertaining the tenants was still very much in his mind). The name of Mozart inevitably cropped up in the discussion as being the obvious composer for a small theatre; the subject of short operas was dropped and it was decided that Audrey Mildmay should turn her attention to studying Susanna and Zerlina with Strasser.

The night before the Christies were leaving Vienna John invited Strasser to pack his bags and come back to England with them. He expressed a little surprise that Strasser should have thought this rather short notice, but promised to let him know when to come. This was in late December. As nothing more was heard of it by the end of January Strasser presumed that the whole project had fallen through. Then suddenly one night there was a telephone call from Christie in England indignantly asking what had happened to Strasser and his wife Irene. Why hadn't they come to Glyndebourne? They'd been expected for weeks. The Strassers packed and arrived at Glyndebourne in February 1933; they stayed there five months.

Jani Strasser found the theatre much bigger than he had been led to expect from Christie's description of it; the roof was already on, but as anyone knows who has waited for a house to be built, that was no indication that the work was anywhere near finished. The spring and early summer months of 1933 were in their way probably the busiest in the whole history of Glyndebourne, for it was a period of incessant physical development. In addition to the structural work on the theatre itself, every stage of which was watched over by Christie, Hamish Wilson was already designing and building models for the operas it was intended to perform.

Wilson started life in a stockbroker's office where in the course of a career of 24 unwilling hours, he said, his complete ignorance of the trade all but undermined the entire economy of the nation. He was accordingly let out and so was able to go into the theatre, which is where he had always wanted to be. There he came to work as a designer, first with the British National Opera Company, and then with the Carl Rosa as a colleague of Audrey Mildmay who enrolled him in the Glyndebourne venture. Although his principal occupation was to design sets and costumes, Hamish Wilson's varied professional experience and the practical suggestions which were adopted while the Opera House was being built were invaluable.

John Christie, meanwhile, had recognized that stage lighting played an important part in the modern theatre. The theatre he was building was not only modern; it must be the most modern in Europe and must therefore have the most modern lighting system. He knew absolutely nothing about stage lighting, ancient or modern, but he learned the rudiments from Hamish Wilson who showed him where the lights had to be installed and why, and then set out to learn all there was to know about it himself. With that unique gift of application which he brought to his smallest undertaking he studied how such things were done in England and abroad. When he had made up his mind which method was the best he went about getting hold of the equipment. This, to his disgust, proved immensely difficult. Some of the firms he approached would not supply him with what he wanted; others could not; others again would suggest something quite different – at five times the price. Christie found some of the things he wanted in Vienna; the rest he had made in his own workshops.

It is obvious, from the energy and care he lavished on them, that the mechanics and general gadgetry of his theatre were what intrigued Christie most as work on the opera house proceeded. A complicated and ingenious system of steam pipes, for instance, was installed under the stage to produce special cloud effects. As he slowly built up his philosophy of presenting 'good opera at high prices rather than bad opera at low prices' Christie was oddly indifferent to the question of the orchestra. The orchestra pit was confidently expected, and indeed announced as able, to hold 100 musicians; it could never have done anything of the sort, for the simple reason that it had not been designed with any knowledge of the amount of room a hundred musicians need when they are bowing, blowing or banging their instruments in front of their music stands. A platform big enough for fifteen waiters to stand upright on in daylight has time and again been found by tone deaf architects to be an extremely tight fit for a three-piece dance band at night. The world, indeed, is strewn with concert halls and orchestra pits designed on this principle and without regard for the elbow room required by double bass players, and the enormous area occupied by a trombonist playing in the seventh position. The platform of the BBC Concert Hall at Broadcasting House and (as I saw it in 1933) the pit at Radio City Music Hall in New York are notorious examples of this kind of unskilled, over-optimistic planning.

Christie's initial intention, however, was not to fill his pit with 100 musicians, but to accompany his operas with a handful of amateur and semi-professional string players helped along by an organ supplying the wind parts – in other words, transferring what had more or less long been done in the Organ Room to the more convenient surroundings of the theatre.

When talk was first heard of an organ being used in the Glyndebourne orchestra pit it was not unnaturally taken for granted that the instrument would be a Christie Unit Organ. It was known that John Christie had an interest in organ building and the Christie Unit Organ had not long been installed in several British picture theatres where it had made a sensational contribution to the rather limited musical world of the cinema interlude. It would be pleasant to report that Christie invented the Christie Unit Organ, but in fact it was a product of his organ firm, William Hill and Son, Norman and Beard Ltd (Telegrams: 'Bassoonist', London), who merely named it in honour of their proprietor.

This remarkable instrument made its first public appearance in 1931 when one of its kind was installed at the Electric Theatre, Bournemouth.[1] One of the makers' preliminary specifications showed that a Christie Unit Organ could be bought in various forms at prices ranging from £1,145 cash (easy terms could be arranged) to £4,594 f.o.b. for instruments specially constructed for 'extreme climate conditions' in the East. The specification went on to announce under the heading 'Selective Stop Keys' that there were 'Twenty Selective Stop Keys producing special combinations of tone colour suitably labelled for various situations – Dramatic, Storm, Woodland, Dance, etc.'

But the pride and joy of the Christie Unit Organ was the startling variety of sounds it could produce which were mostly listed – a little incongruously sometimes – under 'Comedy Effects'. These included Bird Whistle, Boat Whistle, Train Whistle, Telephone Bell, Auto Horn, Syren, Fire Bell, Klaxon Horn, Surf, Rain, Hail, Sleigh Bells, Tolling Bell, Triangle, Cathedral Chimes, Muted Chimes, Tom Tom, Castanets, Xylophone, Chinese Block, Chinese Block (reiterating), Cymbal Tap, Fire Alarm, Glockenspiel, Aeroplane, Bass Gong, Saxophone (synthetic), Snare Drum roll, Bass Drum roll, Kettle Drum roll, Crash Cymbal, Orchestral Bells, Police Whistle, Crowd Cheering, Pistol Shot and Crockery Smash. It is doubtful whether, apart from the more conventional percussion noises, the unusual potentialities of the Christie Unit Organ would have been used to the full in the Glyndebourne orchestra pit, but there was surely no denying that an organ with Twenty Selective Stop Keys capable of producing special combinations of tone colour for Dramatic, Storm, Woodland, Dance, etc, situations had more than a touch of genius loci about it. A little disappointingly, the instrument which eventually found its way into the pit of Christie's theatre was of an altogether less spectacular and more conventional nature. It was also impossibly sharp pitched.

The story about the Captain John Christie who had built himself an opera house in Sussex first appeared with the date-line 'Glynde (Sussex) Thursday' in the London Evening News of 29 June 1933. The 'beautiful miniature opera house' we were told was intended to be 'the permanent home of international opera in England'. The fact that the central figure of all this was referred to as 'Captain' – a title more often encountered among racehorse trainers than impresarios – made the whole project sound even more

---

[1] I was going to suggest that those who had never heard what this machine was capable of might pay a worthwhile visit to the Odeon (formerly Regal) Cinema at Marble Arch, where there was a Christie Unit Organ for over 30 years. Unfortunately, it is now too late. The Odeon is being pulled down and after a 'wake' attended by 600 members of the Cinema Organists' Society to hear it played for the last time, the instrument has been dismantled.

unlikely and cockeyed. We were used to bearded baronets concocting and even taking part as conductors in ingenious operatic schemes, but to find an officer and a gentleman not only embarking on an operatic escapade but actually building his own opera house to do it with was carrying eccentricity too far. Not even Sir Thomas Beecham had ever gone as far as that. We gathered from what the *Evening News* told us, however, that the plan was quite definitely 'on' and that the first season would be held in 1934, opening with either *Don Giovanni* or *Die Walküre* (both good steam-pipe propositions) and following on, as I quoted in the opening paragraph of this history, with the *Ring* and *Parsifal*. After describing the unique lighting system of his theatre, Captain Christie told the *News* reporter 'English composers will be given every chance'.

These words were a popular bromide of the 1930s, expressed – because demanded – with monotonous regularity whenever a musical plan of any kind was projected. It was a form of meaningless formality like saying 'How do you do?' to a stranger; the last thing you want is an answer. Similarly, the last thing anybody wanted was English composers to be given 'every chance'; there was already enough English music that nobody wanted to hear as it was, without encouraging any more merely because it was English. Captain Christie also stated: 'We have asked Sir Thomas Beecham and his orchestra to come down here but that is not settled yet. We shall secure the services of two first-class singers from this country and from the Continent. My wife will take part.'

One would have thought that the announcement of an opera scheme of such originality and aspiration would have made a nation-wide sensation. In fact, apart from the syndication of the *Evening News* story in one or two of the provincial Northcliffe papers, there seems to have been scarcely any kind of follow-up at all. It was three weeks before the subject was mentioned in the Press again when H. E. Wortham went to visit Christie and elaborated on the original *Evening News* story at the luxurious length permitted in those days by the *Daily Telegraph*.

There were perhaps two good reasons for the meagre publicity which followed the original news story: the hoped-for association of Sir Thomas Beecham with the plan, and the announcement that Christie's wife would take part. Both these aspects of the venture were deeply suspect in the minds of news editors; Beecham was always involved in some opera scheme or other and so had little news-value, and the mention of Christie's wife singing in the operas brought the immediate reaction – 'another rich man trying to make his wife a star, I suppose'. There was rather a lot of this going on in London at that time. The fact that Audrey Mildmay had had considerable success with the Carl Rosa was hardly likely to cause much of a stir at the daily news conference. As far as Beecham's part in the affair was concerned, to say that nothing had yet been settled was a whopping understatement. He just never answered any of Christie's letters because he regarded the whole idea as too preposterous for a moment's serious consideration – and who should have known better than Thomas Beecham? Glyndebourne never became real news until it actually opened in May 1934. What went on there between Christie's announcement in June 1933 and the start of the first season was not generally considered in Fleet Street to be of much public interest.

37

Looking back at this date on Christie's first selection of operas – *Die Walküre*, *Don Giovanni*, then the whole of the *Ring*, with *Parsifal* as an Easter treat – one is inevitably struck by the heavy Teutonic nature of his choice which, with the exception of *Don Giovanni* (mentioned only as an alternative, not as a certainty), is quite astonishingly out of keeping with the surroundings and the whole spirit of Glyndebourne as we know it today. But in its way Christie's enthusiasm for Wagner, and his odd lack of protest against the description of Glyndebourne as 'the English Bayreuth', were typical of a social tendency of the time. The summer of 1933 was the climax of a great period at Glyndebourne when everybody was always dressing up in Austrian and Bavarian costumes. Male house guests were expected to follow their host in wearing *Lederhosen* – those unbecoming buckskin shorts with a flap instead of fly-buttons down the front – while the women wore *Dirndl* dresses. These gaily patterned cotton frocks, cut low at the bosom, tight-waisted and full-skirted, were regular summer wear for Viennese servant girls when I was a student in Vienna, and very pretty – to my adolescent eye – they looked. Just as the French Court dressed as shepherds and shepherdesses in their make-believe Arcadia immediately before the Revolution, so in England in the early 1930s it was the fashion among many to play at Austrians and Bavarians. The vogue reached its height at Salzburg Festivals where the only way you could tell a native Salzburger from an English tourist was by the fact that Salzburgers wore long trousers.

As the full significance of Hitler's rise to power began to be understood, however, the enthusiasm for Bavaria waned a little and Austria, already sensed by many to be in mortal danger, became the object of fashionable *Schwärmerei* among a noisy section of English society. So it was that when in October 1933 the *Daily Express* quite spontaneously took up the subject of Glyndebourne again and – more accurately than it knew – prophesied that the name of Glyndebourne might before long be famous all over the world, particular emphasis was put on Christie's expressed hope to get the Vienna Opera Orchestra as well as Beecham and the London Philharmonic Orchestra to his opera house. In passing, it was obvious that the subject of orchestras was still not Christie's strongest suit. He told the *Express* reporter: 'The people of this country do not know what really great orchestras are like. The BBC orchestra, when united, only numbers 110 players. The orchestra at the Vienna Theatre musters 225' – surely as misleading a series of *non sequiturs* as one can imagine.

There was no talk in this interview of repertoire beyond Christie having made up his mind that the season would open the following June with *Don Giovanni*. There was not even this much reference to the proposed repertoire in an article John Christie himself wrote in the November issue of the *Monthly Musical Record*. Once again the stress was on the stage equipment, the structure of the theatre, with a glancing reference to the high standards of singing in Germany and Austria (Italy was never mentioned), and an incidental mention of the ambience – the garden courts and lawns surrounding the building, and the proposed erection of a statue of Mozart to fill the central position in the largest court.

On one point, however, Christie was still surprisingly undecided. After reviewing the general operatic situation in England – 'Part of the public does not clamour for opera because it has not been well impressed, another part because it chooses, as long as it can, to remain ignorant, while the enthusiast, owing to the low English standard, goes abroad' – he declared:

Working on these lines, the Glyndebourne Opera House has two possibilities:
1 To offer superb performances to people who will regard them as the chief thing in the day or week to be looked forward to, and who will not try to sandwich them between business interviews and a society party.
2 To give educational performances for the ordinary public, with the best possible stage setting and only English orchestras and lesser known singers.
    I incline towards the superb performance, assisted by a marvellous holiday 'Festspiel' atmosphere, but expense would prevent the admission of the poorer portion of the public, and so it may be desirable to give local performances after the 'Festspiel' is over. We also hope to have Shakespeare festivals and fairly frequent concerts. At all performances the feeling of general happiness and benevolence should be conspicuous. The scenery and lighting, being designed anew for every opera, should be superb. There are no vested interests, no traditions in the way.

A few days after the appearance of this article, Richard Capell, who had earlier in 1933 succeeded my father as Music Editor of the *Daily Telegraph*, went down to Glyndebourne to see the place for himself. In a long feature, in the course of which he quoted John Christie's *Monthly Musical Record* manifesto at some length (Capell was also editor of this magazine and so could help himself, of course), he announced that when the 'John Christie Opera Festival' opened in the spring it would include *Die Walküre* and *Don Giovanni*. Capell had seen some of Hamish Wilson's sets for these two operas actually being made; he also saw, but didn't mention it, Wilson's models for the décor of a projected *Meistersinger* production. The article ended with the words: 'The Glyndebourne Theatre will be inaugurated early in the New Year by a private performance of the third act of *Die Walküre* for Mr Christie's friends and tenants.' This performance never took place, for by the time the New Year came round many things had changed at Glyndebourne. On 29 January 1934 the following appeared in *The Times*:

A SUSSEX OPERA HOUSE

Mr Christie's Plans at Glyndebourne

The opera house which Mr J. L. Christie is building on his estate at Glyndebourne in Sussex is nearing completion, and arrangements are in progress for its opening on May 28.
    Mr Christie proposes to give 12 performances of *Così fan tutte* and *Figaro*, conducted by Herr Fritz Busch, with the members of the Busch quartet as orchestral leaders, and a company of the best singers available. At a second Mozart festival in September it is hoped to add *Don Giovanni* and *Die Entführung* and that Sir Thomas Beecham will conduct. Further plans include a Christmas festival of Humperdinck's *Hänsel und Gretel* and *Königskinder*, but these later schemes will naturally depend somewhat on the success of the earlier ...

CHAPTER FOUR

'A man in Sussex'

THE NEWS THAT twelve performances would be given of Mozart operas, neither of which was likely to involve clouds of steam, came as something of a surprise to most and a relief to many, after the earlier threats of *Ring* cycles and vast orchestras. I remember that, like those of many of my colleagues at the time, my own reactions to John Christie's first proposals had not been particularly enthusiastic. There always seemed to be more than enough Wagner at the Covent Garden international seasons, where performances began before tea, without having to travel down to Sussex for more, where it would have to start before lunch if anybody was ever to get back to London at a civilized time. For the more sophisticated lover of opera, indeed, the prospect of what Christie told us proudly had been heralded in the German Press as a 'Privat-Bayreuth' was not madly attractive: Wagner had lost his charm for many and the Verdi revival was now getting well under way. In any case, Christie's whole presentation of his case, his hopes and intentions, had been depressingly unprofessional. What use was the world's most modern lighting system going to be if the only conductor who had been considered had regarded the proposition as not even worth acknowledging?

To me, at any rate, the Glyndebourne Festival Opera idea made sense for the first time only on seeing the name of Fritz Busch associated with it. I had first heard Busch conduct in Dresden in 1923, but as far as I remember he was hardly known in this country; he had conducted the concert in London at which the 9-year-old Yehudi Menuhin made his first appearance in England, and if the conductor derived comparatively little personal publicity from this occasion it was hardly surprising. In England, indeed, if Fritz Busch was known at all, it was more as the elder brother of the celebrated violinist Adolf Busch than as *Generalmusikdirektor* of the Dresden Opera where, in addition to his performance of Mozart's operas, his part in the great German Verdi revival had been outstanding.

How, between November 1933 and January 1934 the whole character of the Glyndebourne Festival Opera came to be changed and, in contradiction of all previous announcements, its first season came to consist of *Figaro* and *Così fan tutte* conducted by Fritz Busch, is a story that began on a foggy night at Eastbourne in the late autumn of 1933.

Adolf Busch had been playing at Eastbourne and after the concert was to have been driven back to London by Miss Frances Dakyns, a tiny, energetic Scotswoman in her late fifties, with her hair done in such a way that her most devoted admirers had to admit it looked like a bottle brush. Miss Dakyns, who died in 1960, was a kind of self-appointed chauffeuse, confidante, secretary and humble servant to the Busch String Quartet, and she considered it among her duties also to look after Adolf whenever he had solo violin engagements in this country. On the night of the Eastbourne concert, though the fog grew increasingly thick, Frances Dakyns was fully prepared to take Adolf Busch back to London by road. She was eventually dissuaded from doing so by Mrs Stutchbury, an amateur violoncellist of considerable skill and enthusiasm, who invited Adolf Busch and Miss Dakyns to spend the night at her house instead. Rosamund Stutchbury's house, Gayles, stands 350 feet up, surrounded by National Trust land with a spectacular and unspoilable view over the Channel, five miles or so to the west of Eastbourne. It was here, after Adolf Busch's concert, that Frances Dakyns began to talk of an article she had recently read in the paper about 'a man in Sussex who had a small theatre and wanted to turn it into an opera house'. Mention that the 'man in Sussex' proposed to perform *Don Giovanni* in his opera house led Adolf Busch to suggest that they ought to get his brother Fritz to conduct it. (Frances Dakyns' account many years later in a broadcast of what Adolf said of his brother included the delightfully schoolgirlish phrase: 'If anyone can conduct Mozart operas *he* can.') The 'man in Sussex' was identified by Mrs Stutchbury as John Christie; she knew him and his wife well and arranged to take Frances Dakyns over to Glyndebourne to meet them and to try to interest them in the idea of getting Fritz Busch.

John Christie had at this time never heard of Fritz Busch, though in later years he persuaded himself that he had thought of him all on his own – because 'the Dresden festivals were better than Munich's'. There were no Dresden festivals in Busch's time.

By the time Frances Dakyns had finished with him, however, John Christie had certainly heard of Fritz Busch. In late November 1933 she had done her work so well that she was able to write to Busch in Copenhagen the following letter, which in its original form, Mrs Grete Busch tells me, was written in a remarkable mixture of German and English:

Dear Fritz:
There is a Mr Christie who has built an opera house (stage about the size of the Residenztheater in Munich, but no revolving stage) in the country at his house in Sussex, Glyndebourne, near Lewes – he has lots of money and a pretty wife – a singer – Zerlina. He is a good businessman and thinks that *good* opera in England can be made to pay – he will pay all production costs and all building costs of the theatre – there is therefore no rent to pay – only fees, salaries and wages. He would like to open with a fortnight's Mozart festival at the end of June (the last two weeks) or three weeks – he spoke of *Don Giovanni* or *Entführung*. He has asked Sir Thomas Beecham whether he will conduct a few performances, but would very much like to have you, if possible ... If you could conduct and take things over it would be the beginning of opera in England.

(John Christie's decision to present an all-Mozart festival instead of the mixed Wagner-Mozart affair he had originally planned was the satisfactory result of some concentrated pressure recently exercised on him by Audrey Mildmay and Hamish Wilson. That two other Mozart operas were eventually chosen instead of *Don Giovanni* and *Die Entführung* did not matter; what was important was that he had been persuaded – for the time being, at least – to accept Mozart's operas as the best suited to the size and surroundings of the Glyndebourne Festival Opera House.)

Fritz Busch had to decline the invitation; he was too busy. A financial crisis in the Argentine shortly afterwards, however, led to a drastic shortening of his annual season at the Teatro Colón in Buenos Aires and he wrote to Frances Dakyns saying that there was a possibility of taking part in 'the beautiful opera project' after all.

Busch's musical activities were divided at this time largely between Copenhagen and Buenos Aires as he left Germany for good in early May 1933. He was not a Jew, but in the best sense a liberal who had found Nazi interference with his work intolerable. His artistic conscience, his loyalty to his Jewish colleagues, his fierce independence, were qualities that the pleas of Hitler and Goering had been unable to shake or corrupt; their blandishments – and threats – to persuade him to stay in Germany had left him unmoved. When Toscanini had cancelled his engagement to conduct at the Bayreuth Festival in 1933 as an immediate protest against Hitler's persecution of Jewish musicians, Busch was offered the job. His rejection of the offer was as emphatic as it was contemptuous. He met Goering's threat that he could be 'compelled' to conduct with 'Just try it! A compulsory performance of *Tannhäuser* conducted by me would be no pleasure to you. You haven't heard anything in your life so stinkingly boring.'[1]

Busch's fearless stand did not go unrewarded in his years of exile. The tragedy of it was that with his magnificent example before them so few of his fellow countrymen had the courage, the spirit and imagination to follow it.

Early in January 1934 Fritz Busch agreed to take charge of the first Glyndebourne Festival; it would consist of a fortnight's season of two Mozart operas, *Figaro* and *Così fan tutte*, and would start at the end of May or the beginning of June.

But although a great deal – including a repertoire – had been arranged between them, thanks to Frances Dakyns tirelessly bearing messages from one to the other, it was some time before Fritz Busch and John Christie ever met each other. A meeting was eventually fixed in Amsterdam where, Mrs Busch relates, she and her husband first set eyes on their 'unknown music-magnate – an imperturbable figure in rough, loosely hanging tweeds, whose unconventional appearance was accentuated further by the pug dog Tuppy which he brought to the interview under his arm'.

It is a charming and characteristic picture for Grete Busch to have cherished over the years of her first meeting with John Christie. Before it settles down as another Glyndebourne legend, however, it must be remembered that devoted to his pug dogs as he was, Christie would never have taken Tuppy for the night to Amsterdam knowing that on his return to England next day the animal would have to be put in quarantine for six months.

---

[1] *So etwas Stinklangweiliges haben Sie in Ihrem Leben noch nicht gehört!*

One can see how Mrs Busch got the idea, of course; to many people Christie always seemed to have a pug dog under his arm.

One of the most important consequences of Christie's visit to Amsterdam was his realization at last that his pet idea of a string quartet with an organ to fill in the wind parts would not do to accompany a Mozart opera – even if it did save money which could be spent on other items. Busch greeted this proposition with a sharp, stern echo of Audrey Mildmay's original admonition that either the thing must be done well or not at all. Christie decided it must be done well and no more was heard about organs in the orchestra pit at Glyndebourne until two of them were installed for the production of Monteverdi's *Incoronazione di Poppea* twenty-eight years later.

Meanwhile, a great deal more remained to be done before the first Glyndebourne Festival season could open than might have been gathered from the confident tone of the *Times* announcement quoted earlier. The question of a producer for the operas had occupied Busch's mind from the first moment he had realized what opportunities Glyndebourne offered for the performance of opera under ideal conditions.[1] Not long after he had accepted Christie's offer Busch was conducting in Vienna and happened to tell Max Reinhardt about the Glyndebourne project. Reinhardt, who had always wanted to collaborate with Busch in a Mozart production, offered his services so enthusiastically and with such conviction that Busch wrote to Frances Dakyns telling her how enraptured Reinhardt was with the idea, and recommending that Christie should do everything to bring this about: London society would flock to Glyndebourne and the highest prices could be charged for seats. When the question of money came to be considered seriously, however, Reinhardt's enthusiasm for producing Mozart in England weakened considerably. This – as Busch no doubt realized on reflection – was about the best thing that could have happened. Reinhardt's only previous experience of staging opera had produced two monstrously vulgar revue-like versions of *Die Fledermaus* and *The Tales of Hoffmann* in Berlin; to have let him loose on Mozart at Glyndebourne would have been a disaster.

Instead of Reinhardt, Busch recruited a Reinhardt disciple. This was Carl Ebert, who, like Busch and for the same reasons, was now a voluntary exile from Germany. Ebert, whom Busch described as 'a big man of handsome appearance, not unconscious of this quality', was then 47; he had enjoyed a successful career as an actor before his appointment in 1927 as Generalintendant of what one might call the 'dual purpose' Hessische Landestheater in Darmstadt had brought him into close professional contact with opera as well as drama. As an actor in 1922 his experience in the part of the Reciter in the first German production of Stravinsky's *L'Histoire du Soldat* had first made him think of becoming an opera producer, but it was not until he had been at Darmstadt for a couple of years – learning while earning, so to speak – that he finally had the chance to direct *Figaro* as his first opera production.

---

[1] It should be explained for the American reader that the term 'producer' is used throughout this study in its loose English sense – that is, to describe what in America is known as the 'director' of the stage production. 'Producers' in the American sense are so-called only in the film industry in this country.

In 1931 Ebert left Darmstadt and returned to his native Berlin, where in earlier days, having persuaded the Minister of Education to allow him to open a theatre school at the Hochschule für Musik, he had been given the title of 'Professor' which, the Minister insisted, was indispensable for the maintenance of discipline. On his eventual arrival at Glyndebourne it was inevitably shortened to 'Prof' and he has been known there as The Prof ever since. Ebert moved back to Berlin to become Generalintendant of the Charlottenburg Opera (its official name was the Städtische or Municipal Opera, but in my student days in Berlin, at any rate, we never thought of it as anything but the Charlottenburg Opera). During Ebert's first year there Busch saw his production of *Die Entführung*; he was deeply impressed by it – 'in spite of occasional over-subtleties' – and when he was asked to conduct this opera at the 1932 Salzburg Festival he agreed to do so only on condition that Ebert produced it. It was during their work together on *Die Entführung* at Salzburg that Busch and Ebert first discussed what was to prove a landmark in the growing Verdi renaissance – their production at Charlottenburg in September 1932 of *Un ballo in maschera*. Ebert had previously tried to persuade Busch to join him permanently in Berlin, but he had been unwilling to leave Dresden. He was able to come as a guest conductor, however, and so work for the first time as a member of the team which was later to bring Verdi to Glyndebourne; the others were Caspar Neher, the designer, and Rudolf Bing, Ebert's assistant producer, who had been with him at Darmstadt.

John Christie confessed that he found all Busch's talk about producers very bewildering. It was an operatic function of which he had had no experience; as far as he knew the staging of opera – especially at Covent Garden – was something which, like Topsy, 'just growed'. On Busch's advice, Christie wrote to Ebert inviting him to come over to England to discuss the question of building up the Glyndebourne Opera. The whole idea of a private opera struck Ebert as such a lunatic venture that, like Beecham, he did not bother to answer Christie's letter. Christie wrote several times more, and still Ebert did not reply. Since Christie, who had only just heard of producers and had certainly never heard of Ebert, must have mentioned that he was approaching him on Busch's recommendation it seems odd that Ebert should have shown so little confidence in his friend's judgment. However, after a desperate telegram from Christie, Ebert agreed to go; it was a good opportunity, he thought, to visit England for the first time.

On his arrival at Glyndebourne in the middle of February 1934 he found to his dismay that the theatre had already been built – with no way of flying the scenery, no dock to store it in, only a single tall door on the O.P. side through which every set would have to be moved when it was struck, before another lot of scenery could be brought through the door and set up for the next act.

Before Ebert could open his mouth to plead with 'this poor man' not to throw all his money away on an impossible project, Christie swept into a long discussion on the question of the bells in *Parsifal*. Where did Professor Ebert think was the best place for them backstage – on the prompt side, or the O.P. side? Ebert made embarrassed, non-committal replies and eventually changing the subject managed to ask his own questions: did Mr Christie really understand what a private opera involved, how much an orchestra, stage

44

staff, chorus, soloists, scenery, could cost? Christie retorted bluntly that none of this was Ebert's, or anybody's, business but his own. All he wanted to know was whether Busch and Ebert were willing to work at Glyndebourne. The Professor, realizing that nothing he said could possibly shake what he called Christie's 'stubbornness', replied that he and Busch would come to Glyndebourne on one condition: that they were given full responsibility for all artistic questions and that, while they would naturally discuss everything with Christie beforehand, the last word on such matters as the engagement of singers, the planning of the repertoire and the number of rehearsals needed, was to rest with them.

John Christie, who had been accustomed to delegate authority in all his enterprises since he first became a landowner, agreed to this without hesitation. As things worked out there were inevitably disagreements between the Christies and their artistic directors, but in the end the pact was kept – though sometimes when Christie involved himself and others deeply in plans which he imagined his artistic directors would certainly agree with, but didn't, it was a near thing.

At Christie's invitation, Ebert stayed on at Glyndebourne for a week or two and roughed out the kind of budget that was to be expected. It was a budget which, in the Professor's pet phrase, covered everything 'from usher to tenor', and in giving him his first close glimpse of the harsh economic facts of operatic life, it obviously came as something of a surprise to Christie. Ebert relates that Christie's immediate suggestion was to reduce the costs by having an organ and a string quartet in the orchestra pit, but this must surely be a case of memory telescoping events. Christie had already been given, and had agreed with, Busch's strong views on the subject at his first meeting with the conductor at Amsterdam. Indeed, so far from trying to cut down the orchestra, the growing problem at Glynde-bourne at this time was to build one up. The question of the engagement of singers and the day-to-day organization of an opera company had already been entrusted to Rudolf Bing by Busch, who had written to him in February 1934 suggesting he should join him as what can best be described as 'personal managerial assistant' at Glyndebourne. An English manager had already been appointed in Alfred Nightingale, a Brighton man who had been manager of the BNOC until its dissolution in 1929, when he went as manager to Covent Garden. The function of an English theatre manager, as Busch soon discovered, was not comparable to that of an impresario; though he might send out contracts for signature (in languages he didn't know a word of) he had nothing to do with artistic policy, his main job being literally the management of the theatre – beginning with the hiring and firing of cleaners, programme sellers and the rest.

Bing, an Austrian Jew who had been in charge of the *Künstlerbetrieb*, or artists' management, at Darmstadt under Ebert and had followed him as assistant to Charlottenburg, had had to leave Germany when the Nazis came to power. He had returned to his native Vienna where he had tried to take up his original career as impresario again. Bing had formerly been in charge of the concert and theatre agency of Hugo Heller-Bukum AG in Vienna and as assistant to Heller, a bookseller who was passionately interested in music, had played a considerable practical part in 1923 in the formation of the International Society for Contemporary Music and the arrangement of their first festival at Salzburg, when the Heller agency had collected and paid for all the artists the Society had needed. Rudolf Bing's return to his old job did not meet with much success, however; times were already becoming uneasy in the Austrian capital. Busch's letter to Bing ended with the encouraging and prophetic words: 'Even for a small sum of money it would be worth your while, particularly as, if it succeeds, it will mean work for you in the future.' Bing came for £100 including his travelling expenses.

The organization of an orchestra for the first Festival season proved to be a far from smooth operation. John Christie's announcement that the members of the Busch String Quartet would lead the string sections of the orchestra (a dream of Fritz Busch's) proved hopelessly premature. Not unexpectedly the Musicians' Union stamped sharply on what was a pretty ingenuously optimistic plan. The circumstances of the British orchestral player have never at any time been so happy that he could permit the luxury of import-ing an entire foreign string quartet, however distinguished, to help him with his work. Nor was the Busch Quartet to have been the end of the matter; between them John Christie and Frances Dakyns, who had made the organization of the orchestra her personal province, suggested half a dozen other foreign players to support the Busch group, among them two sisters called Honegger from Switzerland, a Professor Rebner who had recently been expelled from Frankfurt, and – Christie's personal choice – a pretty young Italian violinist with bright red hair who had been quoted in the Press by her sponsor as saying that in her opinion the acoustics of the Glyndebourne Opera House were perfect.

Fortunately, the highly skilled business of raising an orchestra received professional help and a contingent was recruited from what we later quickly recognized by the familiar faces and sounds in the pit to be the London Symphony Orchestra. For some reason, when the programmes eventually came to be printed, the thirty-three-piece orchestra for the first Glyndebourne season was given no kind of billing. All we were told was

'Leader of the Orchestra: GEORGE STRATTON'

with, underneath, the announcement that – rather like bottles of wine – 'Every Member of the Orchestra and of the Chorus has been personally selected'. Seated at the first desk with George Stratton was Andrew Brown, whose son James was first horn with the Royal Philharmonic Orchestra at Glyndebourne from 1960 until the end of the 1963 season. In 1961 Andrew Brown returned to Glyndebourne to play in the same orchestra as his son – this time in the second violins where, he said, he got a different view of the Mozart operas he had played in 1934. Also in that first Glyndebourne orchestra were Evelyn Rothwell, now Lady Barbirolli and first oboe of the Hallé Orchestra; George Eskdale, a brilliant trumpet player who died long before his time; Gordon Walker (flute); Anthony Collins, later founder of the London Mozart Orchestra and, until his death in 1963, a conductor in America, was among the violas with Alfred Hobday, who had led the LSO violas at the orchestra's foundation in 1904; the remarkable Draper family of woodwind players was represented by Mendelssohn Draper as second clarinet and Paul Draper as first bassoon (the second bassoon was Cecil James, who returned to Glynde-bourne as first bassoon with the RPO in 1961).

46

The corporately anonymous, but immediately identifiable, ladies and gentlemen of the LSO were not, however, to be the first orchestra to play in the pit of the Glyndebourne Festival Opera House. In March 1934, more than two months before the season opened, a trial run of three one-act operas was given in the Opera House primarily to test the acoustics. Christie had had the idea when, earlier in the winter, he had shown Boyd Neel over the theatre and suddenly decided the best way to find out what the sound was going to be like was to put on a proper performance and fill the auditorium with friends. Dr Neel supplied and conducted the Boyd Neel String Orchestra, with additional wind players, Hamish Wilson designed the scenery, and the Intimate Opera Company performed three items from their repertoire – Bach's *Coffee Cantata* in the operatic adaptation popular during the great English Bach craze of the 1920s and known as 'Love in a Coffee Cup', Mozart's *Bastien and Bastienne* and Pergolesi's *La serva padrona*. The operas, contrary to all subsequent Glyndebourne practice, were sung in the vernacular. Only one performance starting at 5 p.m. was originally planned ('tea will be served during the interval' the invitations stated), but so many people accepted the Christies' invitation that a second house had to be organized and the theatre was filled twice in one day. As a result of this try-out two important changes were made in the Opera House: the floor of the orchestra pit was raised by a foot and the walls surrounding the proscenium were darkened to cut down the reflection of the lights from the players' desks.

Although it was still being announced during this same March that the Busch String Quartet was to be the foundation of the Glyndebourne orchestra – at any rate for the two concerts to be played in the Opera House on Sunday afternoons, if not in the pit itself – John Christie had by now modified some of his earlier plans. For private reasons he had decided against a second season in September. He proposed in the summer of 1935, however, to do *Die Walküre*, *Siegfried*, *Der Rosenkavalier* and *Hansel and Gretel*.

'But this,' reported Francis Toye, then music critic of the *Morning Post*, 'is not the limit of Mr Christie's ambitions, for he confided in me his desire to produce the *Meistersinger* with a chorus of 200! I will confess that this seems to me to be exaggerated, for, even presuming he could get 200 people on the stage – which I very much doubt – a chorus of that size would be excessive for a theatre seating at most 320 people … Except in the matter of Mozart my personal operatic tastes scarcely coincide with Mr Christie's; for his enthusiasm seems to be exclusively confined to the Austro-German orbit.

'I would have preferred to hear Verdi's *Falstaff* or Purcell's *Fairy Queen* rather than *Walküre* or *Rosenkavalier* in such typically English surroundings as those of Glyndebourne. I like them better, to begin with, and I think the choice would be more interesting and appropriate.

'This, however, is an entirely personal matter. If Mr Christie's tastes are what they are, no one in the world has earned a better right to indulge them. Practical wisdom he can and will obtain with experience.

'He already possesses things that cannot be taught: imagination, enthusiasm, unflagging energy, and unbounded optimism. Such qualities have enabled men to win unexpected triumphs over seemingly insuperable objects before. Should they win through once again at Glyndebourne it will be a cause of rejoicing to anyone who appreciates the inestimable value of idealism.'

If Francis Toye was apprehensive about some of John Christie's ambitions it was understandable; an extraordinary man was likely to be able to achieve extraordinary things – perhaps even a production of a Glyndebourne *Meistersinger* with a chorus of 200. Fortunately, as Toye foresaw, Christie could and did acquire practical wisdom with experience. But where no more was heard in public of putting on *Meistersinger*, *Walküre*, *Siegfried*, or – until 1959 – *Der Rosenkavalier* at Glyndebourne, the dream of performing *Parsifal* did not seem to have faded. At the Lewes Petty Sessions held in April 1934 it was reported in the *Evening Argus* that Mr Eric Neve had applied for a theatre licence to be taken out in the name of Mr Alfred Nightingale, acting on behalf of Mr Christie:

'Mr Neve reminded the Magistrates that Mr Christie, at very great expense, had converted his house into one of the most up-to-date and modern opera houses in Europe. He was asking, he said, for a licence for one year, and at the Brewster Sessions he would ask for a Justices' licence to sell intoxicating liquor. The Mozart Festival to be given at the theatre this year, continued Mr Neve, would commence on 28 May and last until 10 June. It was primarily intended to run a season in September of the same year, but it would not be possible. However, there might be a Christmas season, and the following year it was intended to produce *Parsifal* at Easter. An unconditional licence was asked for, and with regard to *Parsifal* it was desired that this work should be performed on Good Friday and Easter Sunday ...

'The Chairman of the Magistrates said it was not in the power of the Bench to grant a licence for the performance of an opera on Sunday, but *Parsifal* might be performed on Good Friday. The application was otherwise granted.'

Two days after the granting of the licence there appeared the first announcements in the Press of the singers who had been engaged for *Figaro* and *Così fan tutte*. As it had been one of Christie's first declared principles that Glyndebourne was not interested in 'names', only in having singers who were the best possible for the roles they were to sing, the names we read were not at all familiar – Irene Eisinger, Luise Helletsgruber, Lucie Manén, Herta Csonka-Glatz, and a gentleman later identified as Willi Domgraf-Fassbaender who was particularly affected by printers' capers and was described variously as Dom Graf Fassbander, Domgraf-Fassbäinder, Domgraf-Fass-Bender, Fässbenderan and Fassba Ender (Edwin Evans suffered this one in the *Daily Mail*). Only *The Times* got it right first time. The same announcement also told us that the part of Figaro at one performance would be taken by Hans Strasser, of Budapest. (It never was.) The names of the British artists to appear in the list we knew better – Heddle Nash, Constance Willis, Audrey Mildmay, Ina Souez (born American, but a British subject by marriage), and Roy Henderson.

There now followed a busy period of what News Editors call 'prelims'. These are stories which, as the expression suggests, are intended to arouse the reader's interest in some important event shortly to come. As a young newspaperman I was a specialist in 'prelims'; the hours were reasonable and no expenses were queried, but it was a frustrating life for I was never by any chance sent to cover the story my 'prelim' was so carefully designed to lead up to. I was sent to write with 'a light touch' about Epsom on the day before the Derby, never about the Derby; to Lord's to watch the Australians at the nets, but never in a Test match. It was a case, indeed, of always being a bridesmaid and never a bride. (Occasionally by way of a good anti-climax I would be sent to do a follow-up – like talking to a Negro boxer sitting up in bed the morning after the big fight, or watching the Bertram Mills Circus pack up after its Christmas season at Olympia.)

As the opening date of the first season approached Glyndebourne inevitably became the subject of a series of 'prelims'. (I had fortunately been sent to Russia to cover the first Leningrad Music Festival during this period, so I was personally spared the Glyndebourne prelim assignment which, I am sure, would have disqualified me from ever actually hearing a proper performance there.) Reporters and special writers were sent down to study at first hand what News Editors hoped, and later sub-editors (to judge by their headings) were convinced, was to be 'Manor House Opera', 'Village Opera', 'Grand Opera in Sussex', 'Opera in Sussex Garden'. The headings were slightly different from those that had greeted the first Glyndebourne stories a year earlier, but the underlying bewilderment at the whole enterprise was still apparent. One heading, however, made good factual sense to the English reader. 'Grand Opera in Sussex' was a clear indication that instead of *Merrie England*, *The Rebel Maid* and *Iolanthe*, they would be putting on *Faust* (with ballet), *Cav.*, *Pag.*, or *The Tales of Hoffmann*.

The first batch of Glyndebourne prelims produced some colourful reading. Captain Christie, promoted to Major by the *Daily Mail*, had scarcely announced that he was prepared to lose £7,000 on his first season than it had been raised to £27,500 by 'Peterborough' in the *Daily Telegraph*. As though to provide added proof of that eccentricity which was already taxing readers' credulity to its utmost, careful mention was frequently made to John Christie's habit of wearing 'the oldest pair of tennis shoes I have ever seen'. What was intended as a touch of trivial local colour proved, in fact, to be the first public reference to one of the most important elements of what (for want of an alternative cliché) we would nowadays call the Christie 'image'. It is hardly surprising that Mrs Grete Busch should cherish indelible memories of John Christie in Amsterdam with a pug dog under his arm, when so many of the rest of us would swear that in all the years we saw him at Glyndebourne he never failed to wear tennis shoes with evening dress.

The most picturesque prelim of the season came from the *Morning Post* – the by-line stating without doubt that the author was not the paper's music critic but its Special Correspondent. The *Morning Post* story was something of a warning (which I don't think any of us heeded) of the trouble we were likely to get into over the foreign names and words involved in a Glyndebourne story dictated over the telephone to our offices. The *Morning Post* writer found his story of a *Figaro* rehearsal printed with references to the singing of Willi Domgraffassbaender, the 'Count Jerraviva' of Roy Henderson, and a character with a name like a soft drink who was called Cherribina and sang a song which began 'Voi eh sapeto'.

In view of what could happen even with a class paper like the *Morning Post* in 1934 one must admit that the convention of not letting the writer of prelims loose on the event itself was not altogether unreasonable.[1]

Even those prelims which appeared comparatively unmauled by wayward printers, and understandably perplexed shorthand-telephonists, did not really tell us what to expect, however. All the talk of an 'English Bayreuth' and an 'English Salzburg' proved to have been entirely misleading and beside the point. From the moment the very first member of the public set foot on John Christie's estate on the evening of 28 May 1934, it was clear that the Glyndebourne Festival Opera was unlike anything else in the world.

A drawing by Osbert Lancaster

[1] The hazards of telephoning stories from Glyndebourne have grown a little less over the years but still have not disappeared altogether. A couple of years ago in Andrew Porter's notice of *L'elisir d'amore* in the *Financial Times* the words 'Carlo Badioli plays Dulcamara' appeared as 'Carlo Badioli plays till tomorrow'. But perhaps Mr Porter is unluckier than most; his printers once had the Countess and Susanna singing 'the Lesser Duet' in *Figaro*.

CHAPTER FIVE

1934 Curtain up

THE PRELIMS HAD DONE their best to suggest to the general public something of the unique quality of Glyndebourne. A more positive picture, directed to the few, was of course contained in the printed throw-away prospectus. This, in addition to listing the times of the trains from Victoria and of 'The Glyndebourne Opera Special' back to London, and telling the reader, among other things, about the car park, dress, the food, the foyer, the gardens, the theatre, the orchestra, and the stage, set down for the first time (with an opening paragraph in prose worthy of early nineteenth-century English theatrical advertising) the intentions of the Glyndebourne Festival Opera's founders:

At the ancient Tudor Manor House of Glyndebourne, situated in a beautiful wooded stretch of the Sussex Downs near Lewes, has been erected an Opera House fully equipped for the worthy presentation of Opera, and designed on the most modern lines for the comfortable accommodation of the audience.

Here, from time to time, beginning with an opening season of two weeks from Monday, 28th May, to Sunday, 10th June, during which Mozart's *Figaro* and *Così fan tutte* will be performed, will be given Festival seasons of Opera which, it is hoped, will ultimately make of Glyndebourne an artistic and musical centre to which visitors will come from all parts of the world as they do to Salzburg and Bayreuth.

Two main intentions lie behind the enterprise. The first is to stage in this country productions of opera which, from the point of view of their singers and orchestra, of the beauty of costume and décor and of the care and finish of the presentation, can rank with the best that the European Opera Houses can offer. The second is to inspire in artists and audience alike by the charm and beauty of the theatre's surroundings something of that spirit of Festival which characterizes the famous musical and dramatic Festivals abroad.

After this superbly firm and confident statement of policy the prospectus turned to more mundane matters, announcing

Prices: on first nights

Box (seat nine) 20 gns   Stalls £2 0 0
Subsequently „   „   „   „ „   Stalls £2 0 0
    and £1 10 0
Sunday Orchestral Concerts   Stalls 12 6

We were then told of the 'roomy' car park (a long roundabout walk from the Opera House, as the lighted path which now leads to it was not built until 1935), and informed that there was 'an excellent landing ground for aeroplanes 100 yards from the Opera House' – an amenity which, strange to say, nobody made use of until 1962 when some friends of George Christie's arrived by helicopter.

The paragraph headed 'Dress' was abrupt and perhaps the most revolutionary of all: 'Evening Dress recommended.' Without the verb that gives it the air of a gentle hint in the modern Glyndebourne programme the phrase had the ferocity of a command that few would defy lightly – but in fact many did, though not for long.

In the section dealing with The Dining Hall (the only one, so it did not rate a distinguishing name) it was stated that, by giving twenty-four hours' notice, individuals or parties of any number could be served with dinner during an interval. If living memory can be trusted this was one of the things sorted out before the season got under way, just as there was some modification of the prospectus's original notice that on the second of the two Friday evenings in the season, when the performance would begin at 7 p.m., dinner would be served before the opera. As the 5.15 train from Victoria on this occasion would not have arrived at Lewes station before 6.20 at the earliest, to have to eat dinner before the curtain rose was obviously going to lead to group- and probably mass-dyspepsia.

The same section on The Dining Hall included one item of interest to the social historian: 'Patrons may also bring their own refreshments and consume them in the Dining Hall, and in this case may, if they wish, be waited on by their own servants.'

In order, one imagines, to make the public use it freely and feel at home in it, what is now customarily known as the Organ Room was referred to as The Foyer:

The lofty and spacious Foyer of the Opera House will be at the disposal of the public throughout the period of the Festivals. Built in Tudor style, with oak-panelled walls and great mullioned windows, it forms an ideal meeting place for discussion during the intervals, or a comfortable and restful resort for patrons of the Festivals who are staying in the neighbourhood for a few days.

This was perhaps the most puzzling passage in the whole prospectus. Was the Foyer intended to be open always, like a superior kind of hotel lounge with copies of the *Tatler* and *Country Life*, so that patrons staying in Lewes or Uckfield could drive over and put their feet up? Whatever John Christie had in mind it was clearly a most optimistic proposal, suggesting that he can never have reckoned with the number of rehearsals that would still be going on in the Organ Room even after a mere two-opera Glyndebourne repertoire was under way.

In the paragraph describing The Gardens, the author, for what must have been the first and last time in his long career as barker outside the Glyndebourne tent, became comparatively lyrical:

The Opera House is surrounded with beautiful lawns and gardens which will be at the disposal of the public. Within a quarter-of-a-mile's stroll of the house is a chain of woodland pools

Glyndebourne from the air. *(Gravett)*

(below, left) Audrey Mildmay (portrait by Kenneth Green). *(right) Pas de deux*: Carl Ebert and John Christie. *(Gravett)*

(left) Fritz Busch, Ina Souez, Salvatore Baccaloni, 1936.

(below) Left to right: Louise, George, Hector, Ptolemy, Mary and Augustus Christie, 1975. *(Gravett)*

following the course of a Downland stream, leading to coppices carpeted with wild flowers. The grounds are encircled by gracious hills and in whichever direction one looks the eye is met by views of unspoiled natural loveliness.

As experience showed, this brief travelogue was a misleadingly modest description of the charm and attractions of a site without parallel in theatrical history – for what are the paltry three urban acres occupied by the Paris Opera compared with the 640 acre site on which the Glyndebourne Festival Opera is set? The understatement of the prospectus, however, meant that the patron unfamiliar with the ambience of the place arrived at Glyndebourne not knowing the half of it, and in consequence having one of the most pleasant surprises of his life when he discovered that his ticket included the peaceful spectacle of Southdown sheep and Friesian cattle grazing in the meadows, in addition to an abundance of flowering shrubs, and luxuriant herbaceous borders, and a range of green in the trees as remarkable as the greens of Tuscany, where the colour goes from the black-green of the cypresses to the silvery grey-green of the olive leaves. At Glyndebourne the spectrum starts with the black-green of the yews and ilexes and ends in the pale yellow-green of the new beech leaves, a variety and richness of foliage that has been at its best in recent seasons when a late spring has held back the leaves and the brilliant late June light has intensified colours normally seen only in early May.

The manifesto ended with what were obviously the three most important items in the whole publication. The headings were in 14-point italic capitals and the text was printed across two folds of the paper. The section was headed The Stage, The Orchestra, The Opera House. But just to show that private printing was just as subject to the whims of compositors and sub-editors as any public newspaper prelim the paragraphs dealing with the comfort and appearance of the theatre were headed 'The Stage', while those describing the technical wonders of the stage were found under 'The Opera House'.

The first section, purporting to tell us about the stage, is interesting and worth quoting in full, I think, as a record of what the public's theatre, as distinct from the artists' theatre, was like when it was first opened:

The Opera House is a rectangular building designed in simple Tudor style, and built of materials already mellowed by time so that there is nothing to clash with the natural surroundings or the older architecture of the Manor House. All the seats are so arranged on one tier that a perfect view of the whole stage can be obtained from each one. The 300 stalls which form the capacity of the auditorium are specially designed with a view to comfort. Each seat is numbered and is allotted to a corresponding number in the roomy cloakrooms. There are also comfortable retiring rooms for ladies and gentlemen. At the back of the stalls is a box holding nine seats, approached by a separate entrance from an open terrace. While the seating throughout is roomy and comfortable ['roomy' was the writer's favourite word as Schikaneder's 'prächtig', or 'splendid', was in the stage directions of *The Magic Flute*] certain seats at the ends of the rows have been made specially wider for the benefit of patrons who wish for extra space, or for invalids. In a separate stage box are four seats which have been set aside for the free use of members of institutions for the Blind.

In the matter of audience comfort John Christie was speaking with an experience which he could not claim he had in other departments of the theatre. He was sick and tired, he said, of theatres 'where you can't leave your feet under the seat in front when its occupant gets up without one's ankle being crushed by the oak heel surrounding the rear of the seat as in most London theatres. Oak is harder than my feet.'

A feature of Glyndebourne at that time, though not mentioned in the prospectus, was the small circular lily pond and fountain which stood roughly between the steps up to the 'blue' side of the stalls and what is now the bar. It was featured regularly by the glossies of the day as an 'atmosphere' background to photographs of celebrities in conversation. When eventually the Covered Way was built the pond was removed – to the relief of many, for its picturesqueness was more than offset by its danger as an obstacle. More than one distinguished and sober visitor fell into it in the darkness before it was finally taken away.

Following a passage on The Orchestra, which consisted largely of a list of Fritz Busch's credentials and a few words assuring us that the orchestra would be so completely out of sight in their sunken 21-feet-wide well that they would not interfere with the spectator's concentration on the stage, the manifesto ended with the wrongly-titled section on The Stage:

It is no exaggeration to say that the technical equipment of the stage is second to none in this country. The dimensions permit the adequate mounting of elaborate and full-scale productions.[1] Every modern device for the rapid and easy change of the heaviest scenery has been installed, as well as equipment for the production of any stage effect or illusion for which Grand Opera calls.

Particular attention has been paid to the lighting installation, which is of the most complete and modern description, and contains many features still unknown in the theatres of this country. While the technical details of the improvements are highly interesting, it is enough to say here that the proper lighting of operatic productions, in which English opera-houses have hitherto lagged badly behind, will bring new and unsuspected beauties to the most veteran opera lover.

All the settings used in the operas have been made and painted in the Glyndebourne workshops. The setting of every opera is being viewed afresh, and the designs show a healthy disregard of some of the old tawdry conventions, while not sacrificing visual beauty to exaggerated modernism ...

On that final reassuring note, and a reference to Carl Ebert's credentials, the first Glyndebourne Festival Opera prospectus ended – an expression, as it were, of Glyndebourne's view of Glyndebourne.

How far these hopes and claims and optimistic declarations were to be fulfilled only Glyndebourne knew. Certainly right up to the first night the public had little faith in the success of the venture. Those who made the journey to Glyndebourne did so with hope, perhaps even with charity, in their hearts; but mostly it was to satisfy a feeling of curiosity

---

[1] The dimensions of the stage at this time were: back wall to footlights 37 ft 9 in, width 47 ft, proscenium opening 23 ft 8 in wide by 21 ft high. Stage roof 40 ft above stage level.

combined with a feeling that the idea of hearing opera at a Sussex country house was a bit of a lark. The full curiosity-value of Glyndebourne, however, was appreciated by nobody more deeply than the art-editors and gossip writers of the London evening papers whose later editions included the first pictures ever taken of the Glyndebourne-bound audience in evening dress catching the 3.10 p.m. train from Victoria to Lewes (10s 6d first class return, reduced in later years to 9s 9d). The idea of men and women in full evening dress at Victoria Station in the early afternoon has continued to astonish gossip writers and art-editors – but rarely the audiences – from that day to this. Those who today consider themselves hard done by to have to catch the 3.45 to Glyndebourne should remember that the pioneers of 1934 had relatively a much tougher time of it. In those days London theatre curtains rose at a civilized time and even opera at Covent Garden, unless it was Wagner or Richard Strauss, rarely began before 8 p.m. Operas like *La Bohème*, *Rigoletto* and *Tosca* began at 8.30. Since the war performances have started so early that on one occasion I was able to hear *Elektra* at Covent Garden so soon after tea that it was over in time for me to have a drink at the Nag's Head, take a tube to Oxford Circus and hear the whole of Danny Kaye's act at the second house of the Palladium.

The worst grumblers at the Glyndebourne routine were – as I fear they still are – the music critics, who would have us believe that for some reason they always have to change into evening dress in their own time. What sort of newspapers do they work for, that they don't do it in the office's time?[1] It was having to change into *tails* to go to the opera that seemed to rile them most in those days. Apart from a slight increase in one's laundry bill (nobody had yet dreamed up the so-called 'surcharge' and anyway it was an allowable tax expense), it never struck me, at any rate, that it was any more of a chore to wear tails than a dinner jacket, especially as in the 1930s one wore a white waistcoat with both. I never discovered the reason for my colleagues' reluctance to wear evening dress. Were they afraid of being mistaken for gentlemen of the orchestra? Or perhaps of losing their identity among the Friesians, in their formal black and white, the other side of the ha-ha? But for all their beefing it must be said that the critics who covered the first Glyndebourne season conformed more strictly to the management's recommendation that evening dress should be worn than many of the members of the public who attended the performances. Such Inveterate First Nighters (we never see that description in the gossip columns any more) and leaders of Fashion as Lady Diana Cooper and Princess Bismarck were notable non-dressers at the opening of Glyndebourne and were rewarded with special mention by the gossip-writers: 'Lady Diana Cooper ... wore a blue and white printed day dress and a straw hat', while the Princess Bismarck, 'who, with her husband, was in Baron Franckenstein's box, wore a blue and white printed chiffon afternoon dress', and – which the writer omitted to tell us but the photographs in the glossies showed – a straw hat.

'Baron Franckenstein's box' proved, in fact, to be John Christie's private box in which the Austrian Ambassador (and the Bismarcks) were guests. In spite of being offered for

---

[1] *The Times* was particularly cross in 1934: 'It would be to the comfort of all if it were recognized that evening dress is inappropriate in the circumstances.'

sale in the prospectus it was always used by the Christies and their guests. In 1935 it became officially a private box on the seating plan which, in practice, it had been all along.

According to contemporary accounts the theatre was 'packed' on the first night, and indeed in addition to the critics and a fairly liberal amount of inevitable 'paper', there were present far more people who had bought their seats than one has been led to suppose by the repetition over the years of the traditional Glyndebourne story that the house was almost empty. A list published in one of the papers showed that tickets for the two opening performances were taken by no fewer than 51 people, none of whom can surely have come alone – which makes at least 102 seats occupied by cash customers. The ticket holders included many names that were familiar in their generation as conscientious supporters of music and the theatre, whose enthusiasm and practical encouragement deserved wider publicity than the limited-circulation gushings of the social correspondents – 'Lady Snowden, who cannot resist opera' – 'Poor Lady Alice Mahon, who had to give up nightly attendance at Covent Garden' – 'Miss "Oggie" Lynn, who is working so hard for her concert on the 14th and never misses any worthwhile music'. It is interesting to recall John Christie's rather contemptuous reference in his *Monthly Musical Record* article to those who, he implied, went to the opera 'between business interviews and a society party', for Glyndebourne has depended right from the beginning on the support of Business and Society. They saved its life when the time came (for Society is now in Business) and have continued ever since to be well represented in the list of covenanters and donors to the Glyndebourne Arts Trust.

The published list of first night ticket-takers, which I reproduce here, still makes interesting reading, I feel, not only as a social document but also because it includes the names of many whose loyalty to Glyndebourne is as strong today as when it first started: The Duchess of Norfolk, Princess Hohenlohe, Lady Maud Warrender, Lady Diana Cooper, the Hon Lady Baring, Lady Rosamond Christie (John Christie's mother), Lady Boughey, Lady Norman, Lord Gage, the Hon Mrs Cecil, Lady Hood, Lady Sprigge, Lady Constance Milnes Gaskell, Lady Eckstein, the Hon Mrs R. Morgan-Grenville, Sir Robert Armstrong-Jones, Lady Alice Mahon, the Hon Mrs Lyell, Lady Monk Bretton, Lady Ponsonby of Shulbrede, the Hon Mrs Westmacott, Viscount Erleigh, Lady Pollock, the Hon Mrs Barnes, Lady Hutchison, Viscountess Snowden, Sir Oswald Stoll, Sir Anthony St John Mildmay, Lady Franklyn, Lady Dixon Hartland, Sir Harry Newton, Lady Gladstone of Hawarden, Lord Hollenden, Lady Dorothy Macmillan, Lady Gowers, Lady Lawrence, Lady Shiffner, Mrs Lois Nickerson, Mrs Bridgewater, Mme Conchita Supervia, Capt Baxendale, Mr Bruce Ottley, Mrs Stutchbury, Capt Malcolm Bullock, Mrs Bromley Martin, Capt J. B. Abbey, Mrs E. Prescige, Mrs R. Mathias, Mrs F. Ralli, the Hon Mrs Scully, and Mr T. Marchetti.

From the glossy weeklies that appeared a few days later (there were six in those days) we learned that also in the audience had been Cecil Beaton, Eduard Feuermann, 'the German tenor' (which was a fine way to insult one of the greatest violoncellists of the twentieth century), Geoffrey Toye, Maurice Baring, and 'Lord Hambleden's musician brother', as curious and oblique a way as can be imagined of referring to the Hon James

Smith, whose life has been one of endless and untiring devotion to the thankless task of organizing opera in England. The caption writers who turned Feuermann into a tenor also had trouble with Mr (now Sir) Robert Mayer whose name appeared variously as 'Herbert Meyers' and 'Robert Meager'.

Though a list of those present may seem irrelevant at this date, except to those who were there or knew those who were there, that first audience at Glyndebourne has its place in musical history; whether it went out of faith, hope, charity, curiosity, a sense of adventure, a personal loyalty and friendship for John Christie, or a desire to do the right social thing, it went – and it came back knowing that it had enjoyed a unique experience.

The impact made by Glyndebourne with the inaugural performance of *Figaro* was immediate and sensational. To begin with, most of the audience and critics were hearing the opera sung in the original Italian for the first time. The practice, which is common enough today, of singing Mozart's Italian operas in Italian was rarely encountered before the war outside Italy, where performances were infrequent, unpopular and for the most part distinguished by a congenital lack of understanding of Mozart's music. In most other countries they were sung in the vernacular, as of course were the two German operas, *The Magic Flute* and *Die Entführung aus dem Serail*, in Italy.

In adopting the policy of performing all operas in the language in which they were composed, Glyndebourne was well up among the leaders of fashion, if not actually ahead of them; for as far as I remember it was not in fact until 1936 when Ezio Pinza sang the lead that the Salzburg Festival ever played *Don Giovanni* in Italian. Hitherto at Salzburg the opera had always been called 'Don Juan' and sung in German, even though leading singers in the performances like Richard Tauber and Elisabeth Schumann had made classic recordings of arias from the opera in Italian. Toscanini's performance of *Falstaff* in 1935 was the first time Italian had been sung at Salzburg and it created a precedent for the use of the original language in festival performances there.

There had never at any time in the whole history of the enterprise been any question at Glyndebourne that *Figaro* should be performed in any language but Da Ponte's original Italian. The reason Fritz Busch, and after him, Carl Ebert, had accepted John Christie's proposition was that Glyndebourne seemed to offer ideal conditions in which to undertake the pursuit of an ideal. And to perform Mozart's operas as the composer intended was the highest ideal of all. Carl Ebert, as we have seen, had treated Christie's repeated invitations casually and, to begin with, incredulously. Fritz Busch, on the other hand, quickly realized that John Christie was a man of substance and invincible determination, and, after a brief skirmish over the question of an organ and a string quartet in the orchestra pit, had seen the possibilities of an opportunity which had never arisen before and would probably never arise again.

As Busch himself confessed, he accepted the invitation to take over the first Glyndebourne season because he never believed there would be a second.

CHAPTER SIX

1934 **The setting of a standard**

WHAT WAS IMMEDIATELY APPARENT to the first Glyndebourne audience was that Busch and Ebert had set a standard of performance and production made possible only by the complete reversal of normal British practice – by endless rehearsal and concentration on detail. There were, for instance, twenty-four full three-hour orchestral rehearsals for *Figaro*, which even at pre-war union rates amounted to a pretty penny. Busch had endeared himself to the players from the first moment when, on raising his baton to rehearse the overture to *Figaro* for the first time, he had dropped his arm and said 'Already is too loud!' The enthusiasm of an orchestra for its job is not a matter of union rates, to be bought at so-much-an-hour and double-double-time after midnight on Sundays. It is something which only a conductor – and very few conductors – can inspire and maintain. Fritz Busch had this gift, which he applied not only to the orchestra but to the principals and chorus as well whose work was also characterized by a unique and unshakeable, almost ferocious, determination to make Glyndebourne a success whatever happened. If 'They' said Glyndebourne couldn't succeed then 'They' had to be shown it could, with the same stubbornness and resolution of its stubborn and resolute founders. There was, in other words, a spirit and feeling of loyalty among those who first gathered to work at Glyndebourne which was peculiar to the circumstances and conditions of the time, when singers, choristers and stage staff worked until they dropped in what they regarded as almost a Sacred Cause.

In spite of changed times, much of that initial spirit is still to be found at Glyndebourne, though inevitably it lacks some of the original urgency. One thing that has not altered is the intense, obsessively thorough preparation of each production – an exhausting period of endless rehearsal which often strikes newcomers to the Glyndebourne company as excessive and unnecessary, until they discover from the public dress rehearsal onwards that their roles have become second nature to them. They understand them better, they sing them better, they act them better than ever they did anywhere else. The tradition was started by Busch; it has been rigidly continued by Jani Strasser.

It was this total immersion of the performers in their parts which impressed itself at once and so powerfully on the first Glyndebourne audience and critics. The English, who invented the term 'team spirit' and admire it, rightly or wrongly, above all things, encountered it in abundance at Glyndebourne where it was apparent from the first *pp* unison bars of the Overture to the last button and bow on the chorus's costumes. Even the much-publicized stage lighting apparatus took its place in the ensemble, receiving as far as I can discover no individual mention. This is as it should be, of course; one should only ever be aware of bad lighting, never of good.

At the inaugural performance of the Glyndebourne Festival Opera the programme of *Figaro* read as follows:

MOZART'S OPERA

LE NOZZE DI FIGARO

In Italian: the Original Text

By LORENZO da PONTE

Susanna	AUDREY MILDMAY (English)
Countess	AULIKKI RAUTAWAARA (Finnish) (Staatsopern: Helsingfors and Berlin)[1]
Cherubino	LUISE HELLETSGRUBER (Austrian)[2] (Staatsopern: Vienna and Berlin; Salzburg Festival)
Marcellina	CONSTANCE WILLIS (English) (Covent Garden)
Barberina [sic][3]	WINIFRED RADFORD (English)
Figaro	WILLI DOMGRAF-FASSBAENDER (German) (Staatsopern: Berlin and Vienna)
Count	ROY HENDERSON (Scotch)[4]
Bartolo	NORMAN ALLIN (English) (Covent Garden)
Basilio	HEDDLE NASH (English) (Covent Garden)
Antonio	FERGUS DUNLOP (English)
Curzio	MORGAN JONES (Welsh)

Conductor – **FRITZ BUSCH**

Producer – CARL EBERT   *Scenery* – HAMISH WILSON

[1] John Christie's obstinate delight in using German words where English would have done suggests that the State Opera at Helsingfors (now Helsinki) must have been German. It was not, of course. It would have been more to the point to have used the delightful Finnish name: Suomlainen Ooppera.
[2] Lucie Manén (German) (Städtische Oper, Leipzig) took over when Miss Helletsgruber had sung two Dorabellas in *Così fan tutte* and a Cherubino in a row.
[3] This was not a misprint, as may be thought, but the name as spelt when the opera is sung in German in Germany.
[4] This description of Mr Henderson as though he was a bottle of whisky was amended in 1935 to 'Scottish'.

The triumph of the first Glyndebourne *Figaro* was the triumph of a performance where the whole was immeasurably greater than the sum of its constituent parts. Credit was given to most, if not all, of these constituent parts in the 'Golden Book' programme. This was a twenty-page brochure, 7 in by 9½ in, with gold covers containing a photograph of Glyndebourne and the Opera House from the south; brief notes and synopses of the plots of *Figaro* and *Così fan tutte*; a photograph of the interior of the theatre with the curtain raised showing the scene Hamish Wilson had designed for *La serva padrona* containing the huge bed later used in Act II of *Figaro* with Mabel Ritchie in the costume of Serpina, sitting in the chair talking to Wilson who was wearing a sports jacket and flannel trousers; a page of brief notes on Mozart's life (with Handel carefully spelt by the author 'Händel', contrary to the composer's own practice in this country); the casts and other credits of the season's two operas spread across a couple of pages; the programmes of two Sunday concerts scheduled for the 3rd and 10th of June in the Opera House; a short essay on the acoustics of the theatre; two paragraphs of propaganda headed 'Where to Live'; a seating plan of the theatre; an Automobile Association map of the road from London to Glyndebourne; a map of the approaches to the house, the theatre and the car park; and two grateful acknowledgments for the loan of rehearsal rooms and grand pianos. On the back outside golden cover there was printed the date and the *personaggi ed interpreti* of the opera being performed on the night in question. It was a luxurious little booklet unlike anything one was accustomed to find at other English opera seasons, and had the added attraction of being distributed free to the audience at all performances.

In contrast to this, however, there was the oddly austere listing of the characters in the *Figaro* programme where, deprived of all rank, style and title, they were presented in a most informal manner. To make up for this the singers who interpreted the characters were given an elaborate display. Their nationality was shown in brackets – a practice which has been observed at Glyndebourne to this day in order to show the international nature of the casts and incidentally to draw careful attention to the number of British artists employed. Mention was also made in the first Glyndebourne programme of the singers' professional antecedents – in cases, that is, where in John Christie's opinion they had any.

The back outside cover of the Golden Book also included a Notice addressed to the public by the Management in the following oddly pessimistic terms:

Those unable to remain until the close of the last Act are requested to leave during the interval immediately preceding it, and thus avoid disturbing the Artists and the Audience while the performance is proceeding.

For the convenience of all attending the performance the Management request Visitors to attend punctually and to arrive in their seats at least five minutes before the commencement of each Act.

⁎ The Management earnestly desire that silence be observed during the performance.

That no such notice appears in present-day programmes is not so much because audiences at Glyndebourne are better behaved than they were thirty years ago as because the earnest desires and requests expressed by the Management to its first audiences were not really necessary in the first place anyway. The Management realized that it had perhaps misjudged its patrons' quality, and after a couple of seasons limited its appeal to the rather more striking: Patrons are earnestly requested not to flash TORCHES during the Performance.

The most significant detail in this programme was the typographical prominence given to Fritz Busch. It was significant because it rightly suggested that the conductor alone is ultimately responsible to the composer. Producers, lighting experts, scenery and costume designers, gardeners, cooks, wine merchants and car park attendants all contribute in their greater and lesser ways to the finished product, but in the end the composer's intentions and reputation depend entirely on the conductor and his musical staff. In an age when it is the fashion to give producers of opera billing over the composer this may sound heretical; but experience has taught one that in opera no amount of fancy lighting and production can ever save a musically second-rate performance, any more than a first-rate musical performance can altogether be destroyed by slipshod staging. Even a team bursting with team spirit still needs a captain, and at Glyndebourne the captain was Fritz Busch. Without him the team could never have taken the field.

Nevertheless, since the idea of opera 'production' was almost as unheard of in England as John Christie had insistently and contemptuously said it was, Press and public paid particular attention to the staging of the first *Figaro*. There was a superb sense of unity and co-operation between sight and sound in the production of *Figaro*, but in the end Ebert's contribution, like Hamish Wilson's striking but not obtrusive scenery, was always subservient to the music. It was a production which started with one great advantage, of course. As the opera was sung in Italian everybody in the cast (which included no Italians) had to study the work afresh and so was made to forget all the gestures and movements they had always used before when singing in German or English or Finnish. They were also made to learn the whole score without cuts, even though some cuts were made for the production.

Some of the Italian pronunciation heard from the stage at Glyndebourne in that first season was unbelievably bizarre, but somehow the performers all seemed to sing, as well as act, as if they understood what it was all about; and the use of the original Italian text speeded up the *secco* recitative, even when it was tackled by the German-speaking singers whose dexterity in the Italian language was far below their colleagues'.

The critics' reception of Glyndebourne's first opera was unanimously favourable, and there was not one of them who did not immediately sense the unique ensemble spirit of the performance and the idea which created it. Universal rejoicing among the critics at their evening's experience, however, did not prevent their equally universal criticism of the acoustics.

The Golden Book programme, in addition to the features already mentioned, included the first of those anonymous and inimitable proclamations which we quickly recognized as the true voice of Glyndebourne – didactic, stern, but kindly, a little reproachful, speaking as no opera management had ever spoken to any opera public in history. Page sixteen of the Programme consisted of a single long paragraph headed:

ACOUSTICS

This Festival Opera House has been built by the Ringmer Building Works who have, in con-junction with their architectural and acoustic advisers, undertaken to build a building where the *acoustics* are satisfactory. They have succeeded in producing a building where *the acoustics are supremely good*. Every whisper on the stage can be heard all over the auditorium. There is no echo to any sound made on the stage. The singers have never found any building so good to sing in. *This work is of National Importance*. The results are not accidental. At first the results were good; then, as the work progressed further, very good; then when the chairs were installed, as bad as they could be; and now the acoustics have been corrected (at a cost of a few pounds), so that, at last, they are marvellously good. The result has not been accidental, but is the result of the application of Science, of elementary Physics, and chiefly of commonsense. The balance of sound even in the front row is almost perfect. This is accidental, but 'it never rains but it pours'.

THE RINGMER BUILDING WORKS,
RINGMER, SUSSEX
(*Lewes* 300)

These confident claims, expressed with such conviction in their author's characteristic prose, were unfortunately not fulfilled. The acoustic conditions which had suited the strings, woodwind and pair of horns of the augmented Boyd Neel Orchestra and the performance of three pint-sized operas proved entirely unsuited to the concerted numbers and trumpets and drums of *Figaro*. There was a harshness and over-resonance about the acoustics which, as Ernest Newman put it, caused the singing to become, 'through no fault of the artists, sheer noise'. A certain amount was eventually done to alleviate if not completely to remedy this, but to this day a hard acoustic is one of the less pleasing fea-tures of opera at Glyndebourne – the result, one can only imagine, of the bareness and austerity of what must surely be one of the plainest opera house interiors ever built. Having unbent enough to allow Oliver Messel to design a decorative and warmly theatrical proscenium arch after the war it seems a pity that nothing was done at the same time to replace the oak panelling of the auditorium walls with something (damask perhaps?) which would not only have improved the look of the place but would almost certainly have helped to modify the acoustics without depriving them of brilliance. The acoustics of Glyndebourne, in other words, was a problem raised at the very beginning and which is still far from solved.

In addition to the acoustics several other details of the production and performance of the opening *Figaro* also came in for some fairly general criticism – among them Luise Helletsgruber's rough treatment of the Italian language and the boisterous Figaro of Willi Domgraf-Fassbaender, who too often failed to adapt his powerful voice to the scale of the theatre. Even the general acclamation of Audrey Mildmay's enchanting Susanna was tempered by observations that the range of 'Deh vieni, non tardar' was a bit wide for her voice, which was also a little lacking in power in the ensembles. The success of Audrey Mildmay was genuine nevertheless and consequently a great relief to all, for it spared us having to say the polite things we would otherwise have felt obliged to say about her as our hostess and co-founder with her husband of the Glyndebourne Festival. Not that she would ever have exploited her position as Mrs Christie to further the cause of Audrey Mildmay. She gave an audition to Busch like anybody else, and if she had not satisfied him as Susanna was prepared to sing Barbarina – but only if he thought her good enough. Audrey Mildmay's success as Susanna was not done justice to on the Glyndebourne recordings, for it was the result of a unique combination of charm of spirit and temperament and physical attraction which no record could possibly capture.

A factor which contributed most powerfully to the success of this first Glyndebourne opera, though I feel few people were consciously aware of it, was the presence on the stage of young women who were pretty to look at. In these days we have come to expect women in opera to be as presentable as their colleagues in the ballet or the legitimate theatre. But in the early 1930s the boards of the lyric stage were still groaning a little under the weight of prima donnas built on the barrel-shaped pattern of Tetrazzini and her contemporaries. Singers who did prove anything to write home about were generally such an exception that they were quickly snapped up by Hollywood – like Lily Pons, Grace Moore and Gladys Swarthout. But in 1934 none of these had been seen in the flesh at Covent Garden, so the new trend towards singers who could be seen as well as heard was still unfamiliar in this country. The sensational blonde beauty of Aulikki Rautawaara, the freshness and charm of Audrey Mildmay and Luise Helletsgruber at Glyndebourne were a novelty most of the audience had not encountered before, which added the penultimate touch of surprise to an evening that everybody agreed was a unique and ravishing experience. The final surprise, of course, was a sublime accident: the appearance of the bats in the last scene of *Figaro*. Not even John Christie could have arranged for this to have happened; but he took good care that nobody prevented it happening again. A young lady on the theatre staff, thinking to be of some help, asked the Public Health Officer of the local Council to come up and deal with the bats. When Mr George Kent arrived he was flatly forbidden by Christie to do anything about the bats; the creatures were accordingly left in peace to found a long line of Glyndebourne bats which have continued to this day to add colour not only to the last act of *Figaro*, but to the Dungeon in *Fidelio*, the midsummer night of the *Falstaff* finale, and to play the part of swallows in the sunlit piazza of *L'elisir d'amore*.

Though the success of the first Glyndebourne *Figaro* was immediate and sensational (the inclusion of the usually omitted arias for Basilio and Figaro in Act IV made a particular impression), there were nevertheless two features of the performance which became the subject of much controversy. Both, oddly enough, were to do with the music.

The first was Fritz Busch's use of an ordinary piano (which he played himself) to accompany the recitatives. To many ears this was a woolly, incongruous sound which somehow suggested that the singers were rehearsing; the orchestra would no doubt be back later. Ernest Newman, on the other hand, was in favour of the piano for recitatives;

a harpsichord, he maintained, 'strikes strangely after the orchestra' and most people found themselves 'suddenly wrenched into a world that was alien to them'. Busch stuck to the piano for *recitativo secco* until his dying day. When, after his death, Glyndebourne finally made the harpsichord a permanent feature of its Mozart performances the instrument, so far from wrenching the audience into an alien world, never for an instant struck them as anything but the right and only possible accompaniment to a Mozart recitative.

The other controversial issue was one on which Glyndebourne policy has never compromised and which is still one that divides musical opinion. This is the question of Mozart's appoggiaturas, which Dr Eric Blom, speaking for a great many of us, raised when he wrote: 'I have grave doubts whether he (Busch) has any historical justification in purging a Mozart score entirely of unwritten appoggiaturas.'

Just as the late Fats Waller, when asked by a lady what 'swing' was, replied: 'Lady, if you don't know, you aint got it', so the question of the presence or absence of appoggiaturas in Mozart's vocal writing may not seem of any great moment to those in the Glyndebourne audience who enjoy every bar of his operas without having the faintest idea what an appoggiatura might be. They would certainly notice one if they heard one, however, because the use, abuse and omission of the traditional Mozart appoggiatura can make all the difference to his tunes.

For the benefit of the lay reader whose technical knowledge of music may be limited, perhaps I may explain what an appoggiatura is and the part it plays – or should play – in the performance of Mozart's vocal music. The term is derived from the Italian verb *appoggiare*, meaning 'to lean'. In two of the most familiar arias in *Figaro* we encounter phrases in the score written:

Example 1
and
Example 2

Until Fritz Busch, first in Germany, then at Glyndebourne, suggested they should be done otherwise, these bars were sung as –

Example 3
and
Example 4

The reason for this convention and the absence of any indication in the score that it should be followed are too complicated and lengthy a subject to discuss in a book of this nature; but it is enough to recall that Mozart expected his Susanna, when confronted with the phrase in Example 1, to sing it as shown in Example 3. Exactly how Mozart himself observed the convention of his time in the matter of appoggiaturas was admirably demonstrated by Charles Mackerras in an article in *Records and Recording* of March 1963, in which he reproduced under the 'as-written' vocal line of an aria in *Lucio Silla* Mozart's own indications how the singer should perform it.[1] A great deal of the composer's decoration would certainly have been too florid for modern taste, even though in one instance Mozart substituted a single sustained note for the series of semi-quavers that appeared in the written version; but to cut the appoggiaturas altogether in Mozart's operas is not only without historical justification (a matter which in the end, of course, concerns only those interested in historical justification); in the opinion of many it destroys – or at best, alters – the character of the tunes. There is a gentleness and warmth in Susanna's phrase, 'o gioia bella', and a pathos in Cherubino's 'e se non ho chi m'oda' when sung with appoggiaturas that is entirely missing if the abrupt repeated notes of the printed score are sung. This ruthless attitude towards the appoggiatura has been one of Glyndebourne's most obstinate and puzzling habits ever since it started, and where there are occasions when the omission of an appoggiatura can accidentally add dramatic emphasis to a phrase (I am thinking particularly of the 'straight' performance by Glyndebourne of the last two syllables of Donna Anna's angry 'Or sai chi l'onore' in *Don Giovanni*), too often it results in a ravishing tune like 'Deh vieni' sounding flat and utterly charmless.

[1] Mr Mackerras wrote another and even more comprehensive article on the subject in *Opera*, October 1963.

This, at least, is my personal feeling; the abrupt end to the opening phrase Glynde-bourne's Susannas have been made to sing for the past thirty years has never failed to come as an unpleasant surprise. Were it not that during these thirty years most of my elder colleagues and contemporaries have felt the same way about it, I might have attributed to my musical upbringing my dislike of what is rapidly becoming a far more irritating con-vention than the one it originally replaced. The first Susanna I ever heard was Elisabeth Schumann; she sang her aria with the appoggiaturas and that, frankly, has always been good enough for me. But Elisabeth Schumann was at the Vienna Opera and sang accord-ing to the Viennese tradition, and the fact that the appoggiatura was associated in Fritz Busch's mind with Vienna may well have been his reason for abolishing it. It was the avowed intention of both Busch and Ebert to avoid any suggestion of what Ebert des-cribed to me with undisguised contempt as the 'velvet-and-chocolate' Mozart of Vienna, but in the course of their North German determination to be un-Viennese it seems to me they rather overdid it. It does not strike me as the right approach to Mozart to try to eliminate *all* his charm, just as a matter of principle; even at his grimmest – in the great G Minor Symphony and the G Minor Quintet – there are moments of charm which it would be entirely wrong to underplay or underestimate merely because in the twentieth century we have discovered Mozart to be a more 'serious' composer than our grand-fathers gave him credit for. For better or for worse, however, the Glyndebourne tradi-tion started by Fritz Busch persists and to this day Susanna's opening phrase, in perhaps the most sensual and perfect aria Mozart ever wrote, still ends in a prosaic bump.

CHAPTER SEVEN

1934 For the convenience of patrons

WHATEVER IT MIGHT HAVE BEEN led to expect by the newspaper prelims, the first night audience on the ideal summer evening of 28 May 1934 soon discovered it had not attended the birth of an 'English Salzburg', an 'English Bayreuth', or anything like it. Reduced to bare physical facts Glyndebourne was a theatre set in entirely pastoral surroundings and no more. It had none of the amenities associated with the older musical and theatrical festivals of Europe. There was no social life attached to it, no cafés, nowhere to go after the performances where one might mix with an international crowd of visitors and artists as one could at the Café Bazar in Salzburg. As far as the visitor to Glyndebourne was concerned it was a matter – to paraphrase the words of ITMA's immortal Aly Oop – of 'You go. You come back.'

Where in all other respects John Christie was a man of prodigious self-confidence and singleness of purpose, it is clear from the two paragraphs headed 'Where to Live', which occupied page 17 of the first Golden Book, that he was not altogether certain exactly what he wanted or expected Glyndebourne to develop into:

Why not come and live within reach of this Festival Opera? The Opera House needs your support so that its Festivals can be extended, so that there can be Shakespearean Festivals, so that there can be Lectures. If you come to this district you can help this scheme. You will have Downs, Sea-air, Woods and 'Kultur'. If you scatter yourselves over England you are too far away to support this enterprise. If you are near at hand you can enjoy superb intellectual food which you cannot get elsewhere. Make this an artistic and creative centre. You will then enjoy this marvellous country all the more.

There is an excellent service of comfortable express trains to London and there are good roads for motoring. The country contains many famous schools for those who bring a family to the district.

Whatever it was that Christie may have visualized in making this appeal it did not cause any noticeable rush on the part of patrons to move into the neighbourhood; on the other hand, any suggestion that this lack of enthusiasm for his invitation was in any way responsible for John Christie's eventual decision not to present Shakespearean Festivals and Lectures would be entirely false. If Christie had wanted us to have Shakespeare and

Lectures at that time it is quite certain he would have given us them. Fortunately he changed his mind and Glyndebourne, instead of becoming an all-the-year-round cultural centre, remained an opera house.

But although, reduced to its essential physical terms, a visit to Glyndebourne was merely a matter of going there and coming back, with only the long dinner interval to distinguish the experience from any other night at the opera, there is no doubt that from the very first moment it was not just an evening spent casually listening to music. John Christie's frequently expressed determination to make his audience 'take trouble' by wearing evening dress has over the years proved to be, in fact, the least of the efforts the audience is expected to make – although one would not think so from the way some of the Press still moan about it after thirty years. (It is interesting to note that it is always men, never women, who complain about having to dress up, although it is a far longer and more laborious business for a woman than ever it is for a man.) The very fact that Glyndebourne is where it is, that performances begin when they do, that attendance involves a complete break with daily routine, makes even the most experienced and frequent visitor 'take trouble' in a way that can be every bit as involved in its organization as a trip to Salzburg or Munich. There is not, and never has been, anything casual about going to Glyndebourne. You cannot 'drop in' on the spur of the moment as you can in Vienna or at Covent Garden. For those who, like my wife and me, live only a crow-flight mile and a hill called 'Old Hag' away from the Opera House, even a dress rehearsal is not something to be approached lightly. Like a regular public performance it still entails a change of linen, the planning of dinner or a picnic, a close study of the radio weather forecasts – and, in our comparatively experienced and sophisticated breasts, an inescapable feeling of excitement and anticipation, whether we are to hear an entirely new work or the revival of a familiar production.[1]

If those who today do not find their first visit to the Festival Opera House quite such a surprising experience as it might have been in 1934, then it is because there is less to be surprised about than there was 30 years ago. There is nothing, I mean, to match John Christie's still incurable Teutomania, for instance, which led him in that first season to label the lavatories simply 'Damen' and 'Herren'. There was not even a hieroglyph to help those who didn't know German; however, everybody seems to have guessed correctly which was which, for no incidents were reported.

The end of the dinner interval in 1934 was signalled by a trumpeter playing the famous call from *Fidelio* – a rather bewildering choice, when one thinks of it, for in Beethoven's opera it is a symbol of liberation, not a call to duty. (Perhaps the Retreat from *Carmen* might have been more appropriate.) Eventually, however, the *Fidelio* call sign was abandoned as it could not be clearly heard all over the grounds and there were frequent occasions when John Christie considered it necessary to round up dawdlers in person by

[1] The public dress rehearsal at Glyndebourne was instituted in 1935 and is even more difficult to get into than an ordinary performance – not because it costs less, but because there is only one dress rehearsal of each opera.

(left) Pelléas et Mélisande rehearsal, 1960: Henri Gui, Denise Duval, Carl Ebert. *(Gravett)*

(right) Pelléas et Mélisande première, 1960: Vittorio Gui and Denise Duval. *(Gravett)*

(left) Alceste, 1953: designer, Hugh Casson. *(Gravett)*

(below) Cosi fan tutte conference, 1969: (standing) Jane Berbié, John Pritchard, Myer Fredman, Jani Strasser; (seated) Hanneke van Bork, Martin Isepp, Franco Enriquez, Roger Brunyate. *(Gravett)*

knocking sharply on the doors marked 'Damen' and shouting at the occupants to hurry up or they would miss the best scene in the opera.

In place of the *Fidelio* trumpet Fritz Busch suggested an old bell – something with a rich, deep tone that could be rung with dignity and effect. Christie obviously misunderstood what Busch had in mind, and in his anxiety to avoid anything rung by hand that might sound like a country chapel or village school bell installed instead the hideous and piercingly functional electric burglar alarm that has shattered the peace of Glyndebourne for a generation.

The front-of-house amenities were found altogether satisfactory by the first Glyndebourne audience – once they had sorted out 'Damen' from 'Herren', that is. The single dining room (now called the Mildmay Hall) was large enough to accommodate the entire audience within its spacious school-gymnasium walls. The catering was done by a firm in Brighton, and though described in caterers' French on the roneo'd menu the food included such refreshingly English items as *pommes nouvelles de Jersey* and *agneau de South Down rôti*. (Towards the end of his life John Christie's memory telescoped many of the events of these early Glyndebourne days and I took his word for it in my article in the 1963 Programme Book that Glyndebourne did its own catering in the first season. In fact Glyndebourne did not take over the catering until a season or two later.) The now widely prevalent habit of picnicking in the Glyndebourne interval had not yet begun to develop (the first mention in the Press of sandwiches – a poor sort of picnic by modern Glyndebourne standards – being eaten in the car park was in 1935), and in consequence the audience, instead of bringing its own food and drink, was able to enjoy the Glyndebourne wine list. Here again John Christie's memory was confused; the wine lists with the Greek quotations did not appear until 1936. In 1934 the wine list seemed to be a modest typewritten affair consisting exclusively of the following German wines:

Schloss Reinhartshausener Cabinet 1920 Erbacher Brühl	6s
Deidesheimer Leinhöhle 1928 Wachstein	10s
Forster Jesuitengarten Riesling 1928 Bassermann-Jordan	10s
Hochheimer Domdecharny 1929 Auslese Abfüllung Geh. Commerzienrat	12s
Harzheimer Lachsteig 1921 Abfüllung der Stadt Mainz	15s
Niersteiner Rehbach Riesling Auslese 1925 Abfüllung Anton Balbach Erben	25s
Wachenheimer Rechbächel 1929 Abfüllung Bürklin-Wolf	35s
Deidesheimer Leinhöhle Riesling 1921 Reichsrat von Buhl	40s

This selection from the Glyndebourne cellars, though small, was of exceptionally high quality and not a little expensive. Certainly allowing for the change in the value of money in the past thirty years (£1 of 1939 is now said to be worth 5s) there is nothing in the modern Glyndebourne wine list comparable to the £2 asked for the 1921 Deidesheimer in 1934. John Christie's own figure, given at the time, of the number of bottles of wine sold in the course of the first season's twelve dinner intervals was 60 – an average of five bottles a night which, even after taking into account the small audiences in mid-week, is an estimate that can have been arrived at only as the result of a series of whopping clerical errors somewhere.

One way and another the front-of-house amenities enjoyed by the first Glyndebourne audiences were unique – largely because the Opera House was conceived as an extension of the house itself. The foyer was actually *in* the house, while the gardens – surely the most beautiful and 'roomy' precincts of any theatre in the world – gave the visitor an added feeling of being not only a 'patron' of the Christies' enterprise, but a guest in their home as well. Though the Southdown bus eventually whisked you back to the reality of Lewes Station, the Southern Railway and home, the four or five hours spent at Glyndebourne were hours spent in the enjoyment of a musical experience in surroundings which you felt somehow were yours for the evening. This feeling of being a privileged guest (albeit a paying guest) is nowhere more clearly expressed than in the complete absence of litter in the grounds of Glyndebourne on the morning after a performance. A cigarette butt is rare; a scrap of paper unheard of.

Backstage, on the other hand, while it could boast a superb lighting system and the latest in equipment to produce Wagnerian steam cloud effects, the Festival Opera House was sadly lacking in most of the more normal theatrical comforts. There was no scene dock, for instance; in spite of all Hamish Wilson's pleas Christie had refused to build one because it would have meant cutting down a large ilex tree. So all the flats, columns, steps, doors and backcloths of Wilson's sets were kept out on the lawn when they were 'struck' until they were put under cover in a marquee for the night. Backcloths could not be 'flown', so Jock Gough had to invent a method of moving them sideways. Jock's feats, in face of the difficulties which he might justifiably have considered had deliberately been put in his way to irk him, were miraculous. He recruited and trained as competent scene shifters a raw and mixed crew of artisans who had barely seen the outside, let alone the inside, of a theatre before and he prevailed on the Ringmer Building Works to build scenery and not 'real houses' for the stage.

There were only two dressing rooms – one for men, one for women, under the eaves on either side of the auditorium. It is a pity to have to spoil John Christie's time-honoured story that there were only two dressing rooms altogether. Certainly, there were only two dressing rooms for the *principals* when the theatre first opened; but there were, in fact, also two chorus dressing rooms under the stage. Nevertheless, the absence of individual dressing rooms for the principals ensured that right from the start the emphasis was on ensemble (what chance would the star system have had in a communal dressing room anyway?) and although accommodation for the artists was improved as soon as the first season was over, a principle that was born of necessity became a firm and lasting tradition.

Amid all the austerity, discomfort and lack of privacy that characterized living conditions backstage in 1934 there was one touch of luxury, however, which was John Christie's special pride. He had the women's lavatories constructed with doors wide enough to pass through in a crinoline.

Whatever was done for their comfort and convenience afterwards, the artists were

certainly not over-cossetted in Glyndebourne's opening season. In an admirably professional manner (one senses Audrey Mildmay's influence in this) first things were put first;
the public had to be spoilt and encouraged to come again; the artists were expected to
behave as troupers and put up with conditions which, while modest, were certainly not
as rough as they'd known in their time elsewhere, until the promise of public support
justified a little more luxury backstage. Not unreasonably, Audrey Mildmay had her own
dressing room; it was over the prompt side of the stage and had a door into the wardrobe. The room, with the name 'Miss Mildmay' still on the door, is now the conductor's
dressing room.

Though, apart from this, there were no individual dressing rooms in 1934 each artist
found a half-bottle of champagne on his dressing table on his first night – a characteristic
idea of Audrey Mildmay's who thought it would be more fun than the usual telegram or
bunch of flowers. The tradition continues to this day, each bottle bearing the label 'Mrs
Christie's Champagne' and accompanied by a personal message of good wishes from the
Management.

On the second night of the season, 29 May 1934, *Così fan tutte* was performed. It had
originally been intended to open the season with this opera, but as John Christie explained:
'It occurred to me that this was rather an affront to my wife, who had already been
selected by Fritz Busch for the part of Susanna in *Figaro*, so we reversed the order.' The
occasion has always had its special place in the history of Glyndebourne for, as Christie
never tired of reminding his public, on the first night of *Così fan tutte* only seven people
got out of the special train at Lewes and the total audience numbered no more than 54
altogether. It is impossible not to suspect a certain permissible exaggeration in this, in
spite of the story not having varied over the years by a single customer; nevertheless, even
with a full attendance by the critics (who, admittedly, came singly, for Press tickets were
limited to one per newspaper), and the presence with their guests of at any rate a percent-
age of those 51 original enthusiasts mentioned earlier who had brought tickets for the
two opening performances, the audience at the first *Così fan tutte* was certainly on the
small side.

Those who did have the courage and curiosity to go to the second night of the season,
however, so far from finding the occasion anything of an anti-climax, enjoyed an experience that proved even more exhilarating than the opening *Figaro*. There is little doubt, I
think, that the real ear-opener of the first season was *Così fan tutte*. To most people in the
audience Mozart's last Italian comedy came not only as a revelation but in many cases as
a complete novelty; the opera was by no means well known in this country at that time
and, though the overture was played often enough, it was generally supposed that the
opera itself (which so few were known ever to have heard) was dull and sub-standard.
Even when the Glyndebourne performance revealed this enchanting work in all its glory
there were still those who, while they enjoyed themselves, could seriously hold, like the
critic of *G. K.'s Weekly*, that 'the Opera as a whole is not in Mozart's happiest vein,
despite the glorious music'.

So unfamiliar was *Così fan tutte*, indeed, that the misprinted name 'Guglielno', which appeared in the programme (and was not corrected until 1936), was faithfully reproduced in this form by several critics, while the title of the opera itself was given with heterosexual impartiality as 'Così fan tutte' and 'Così fan tutti' – the distinction depending, one supposes, on the writers' personal view of the plot. One critic, with a rush of accents to the head, produced the admirable variant 'Cósi fan tuttî', and another constantly referred to the work as 'Così fan' – an abbreviation which, let us admit, is no sillier than the modern 'Così'.

Where the success of *Figaro* had been more or less entirely a matter of ensemble, the personal triumph of Ina Souez as Fiordiligi in *Così fan tutte* was the first instance of Glyndebourne's peculiar ability to tolerate and absorb the considerable detail of an outstanding individual performance in such a way that it did not disturb the balance of the whole.

Ina Souez was the first of Glyndebourne's striking discoveries. More accurately, she was a re-discovery, for five years previously this young Colorado-born soprano had made a sudden and sensational overnight hit at Covent Garden as an unknown, singing Liù in *Turandot*. But instead of making the most of her success and the publicity that went with it, she made the tactical mistake of going abroad – not for long, but long enough for her to have to start all over again as far as English managements were concerned. It was Hamish Wilson who brought her to the notice of Glyndebourne, where to most of the audience (*Turandot*, like *Otello*, was box office poison at Covent Garden in the 1930s) her name was as unfamiliar as everybody else's. Ina Souez's success in the 1934 *Così fan tutte* brought her a Covent Garden engagement the following year – the first, but by no means the last, time that the Royal Opera House cashed in on Glyndebourne's initiative and judgment.

The complete recording made in 1935 of the Glyndebourne *Così fan tutte* was for many years a convincing reminder of the quality of the first Glyndebourne Fiordiligi, the range and power of whose voice is still clearly apparent from the worn and scratched old 78s which are all most of us can lay hands on. In the United States RCA-Victor made an LP transfer of the recording about 1956; in this country a classic British recording is available as an LP to special order only from EMI Specialist Import Dealers, who will get it for you from Germany.[1]

After the care Glyndebourne took to show its contempt for bad contemporary habits by restoring the two arias customarily omitted from the last act of *Figaro*, it was a surprise to find that the same reformatory zeal did not apply to *Così fan tutte*. No fewer than four numbers were cut from the opera and the fact that this was usually done in those days for reasons of time did not seem a good enough excuse for leaving them out at Glyndebourne, where running time was of no great importance. The acceptance of

---

[1] The cast of the recording differs in only one respect from that of the first Glyndebourne production. John Brownlee sang the part of Don Alfonso in the records. The original Glyndebourne Don Alfonso was the fine Scala *buffo*, Vincenzo Bettoni, the first Italian to sing at Glyndebourne, the only Italian in the cast, and the only singer in the company who was not word-perfect in the Italian recitatives.

current convention in 1934 meant that Ferrando had no arias at all in Act II, for both 'Ah! io veggio quell'anima bella' (No 24) and 'Tradito, schernito, dal perfido cor' (No 28) were cut. The Duettino (No 7) between Guglielmo and Ferrando in Act I – 'Al fato dan legge quegli occhi vezzosi' – was also omitted, for no other reason surely than that it was the custom to do so. (In my edition of the full score the Duettino and Ferrando's aria No 24 are both marked with an asterisk and the comment 'Often omitted'.) In performance the Duettino plays little over a minute. Perhaps the greatest loss was the omission of Dorabella's 'È amore un ladroncello' in Act II, Scene 3. Apart from its refreshing and purely musical attraction, the aria is important as a stage in the development of Dorabella's character, and to cut it out is to obscure an important corner of Mozart's carefully drawn portrait of her.

For Heddle Nash, who sang Ferrando and was so ruthlessly deprived of two of his three arias, the first Glyndebourne season was very much a matter of making up on the swings what he lost on the roundabouts. On the nights he didn't appear in *Così fan tutte* he sang an outstandingly comic Don Basilio in *Figaro* where, thanks to the unexpected inclusion of 'In quegli anni, in cui val poco', he had a solo scene which he certainly did not anticipate when he joined the company.

In recent years the Glyndebourne production of *Così fan tutte* has been modified to include all the numbers originally cut in 1934 and the musical enjoyment of the opera has been greatly increased in consequence.

CHAPTER EIGHT

Ringmer

THE FIRST SEASON ENDED WITH a deficit of £7,000 and some healthy signs that the critics had fully recognized the purpose and potentialities of Glyndebourne. There was scarcely one of them who did not suggest that while its Mozart was a unique experience it would be a pity if Glyndebourne did not extend its repertoire to include works by other composers. Among the many helpful proposals were several which were later to be taken up at Glyndebourne – *Falstaff*, *Ariadne auf Naxos* (in its first form with *Le Bourgeois Gentilhomme*), Gluck's *Alceste* and *Orpheus*, *Il segreto di Susanna*, Berlioz's *Benvenuto Cellini*, *Beatrice and Benedict*, and part 2 of the *Trojans*, Gluck's *Iphigenia in Tauris*, Purcell's *Fairy Queen*, Rameau's *Castor and Pollux*, the second version of Richard Strauss's *Ariadne*, and Holst's *Savitri*. In addition, of course, there was the usual lunatic fringe of those who put forward operas they can clearly never have heard – like Hugo Wolf's *Der Corregidor*, for instance, which takes four long, unwitty acts to tell the same charming Spanish story of the Three-Cornered Hat that Falla and Massine told once and for all in a one-act ballet. The opera most frequently mentioned in the critics' lists was *Beatrice and Benedict*, although few of them could ever have seen the work on the stage. When the opera was performed for the first time in Britain, at Glasgow in 1936, the critics once more hopefully tried to draw Glyndebourne's attention to it, but their efforts have so far had no effect.

The critics, it will be seen from this, had the welfare and happiness of Glyndebourne very much at heart. They were clearly happy in their work, though the otherwise contented Mr Fox-Strangways of the *Observer* deplored that Glyndebourne had to be held at a time of year when there was so much music going on in London and it was difficult to find 'the nine hours on end that Mr Christie asks of one'. February would be more convenient, he thought.

There was, however, a certain uneasiness to be noted in what was written by one or two of the critics in their after-season summing up of Glyndebourne and its achievements. It was the fear that opera at Glyndebourne would become 'fashionable' and so attract 'society'. It is one of the strangest and oldest beliefs of music critics in this country that 'society', the aristocracy, or the plain downright rich have no taste in the arts and must be discouraged at any cost (usually at that of the arts) from occupying and paying for seats in the opera house or concert hall that would be better occupied by some state-aided student or £30-a-week factory hand.

This quaint intolerance of audiences which fail to pass the critic's test of cultural hepness still persists today; at least once a year we read a priggish reference to the 'debs' who are taken to Glyndebourne because it is the smart thing to do, with the thinly veiled implication that merely to be a deb is to have neither taste nor intelligence. Leaving aside the chance that the debs (and their delights) of today are often the Arts Trust donors of tomorrow, why shouldn't a deb go to Glyndebourne? How does she know whether she likes opera or not unless she hears some? She has to start somewhere, why not near the top? And what guarantee is there that if she likes it she won't come again? Equally, if she doesn't like it nothing on earth will induce her to come again, anyway.

Perhaps, to do my colleagues justice, these little petulances are a compulsory expression of proprietorial policy. I know when I was on the *Daily Herald* in the 1930s I had to bend over backwards every time I went to Glyndebourne to justify my undisguised enjoyment of good music, good food and good wine in thoroughly unproletarian surroundings by including some fatuous remark like 'the standards of Glyndebourne will be felt in the opera houses of the people'. It kept the comrades quiet, anyway.

In later years, John Christie used to have serious thoughts about letting the Press into Glyndebourne at all. There was £120,000 worth of sold out performances in the box office before the season began, he said, so what was the point? My own reply was that, although it was hard to believe it from what they wrote, the critics always enjoyed their Glyndebourne outings and we'd all miss it terribly. This didn't impress Christie as any sort of argument, but he was fortunately persuaded by closer and more influential advisers that in its way the Press had its uses – if only to help fill the artists' (and their agents') cuttings books.

One satisfactory result of the first Glyndebourne season as far as the Press was concerned was the acceptance by Editors of the suspiciously unanimous expenses of £10 claimed in print by gossip-writers as the cost of a night at Glyndebourne for two. Their editors, who apart from not realizing that the figure was meant to apply to paying customers and not gossip-writers (who got their £2 or 30s tickets for nothing, of course), had no precedent whatever to guide them, and so were happily unable to question the figure.

It should be remembered that £2 and 30s were regarded as a pretty stiff price for seats at Glyndebourne in 1934, especially in view of the travelling, dining and other incidentals involved in an evening's outing (the 5s dinner was also considered a bit exorbitant). Some idea of exactly how expensive may be deduced from the fact that the retail price of a whole bottle of gin in those days was 12s 6d, of which 8s 5d was tax.

Glyndebourne's first autumn and winter as a functioning opera house were passed, as these seasons seem to have been passed there ever since, in building and altering the theatre inside and out, front of house and backstage. Only the auditorium was left untouched after the 1934 season; no seats were added because as yet there seemed no need for them. The public had not been as quick as it was hoped in giving full support to any but the Friday and Saturday performances in the opening season. In spite of John Christie's classic assertion that after the third performance, when only 55 seats were sold, Glyndebourne had been 'sold out ever after', there was a noticeable sag in mid-week attendances. A contemporary report assessing the average audience at about 100, adding 'the public will come in time', may have been a little pessimistic, but it was obviously not wildly off the mark.

Most of the building that went on in the interval between the first and second seasons was rightly backstage. Hamish Wilson at last managed to persuade Christie to cut down the ilex tree and a scenery dock was built adjoining the stage. What had previously been shown on the map in the programme as a 'scenery shed' on the right of the road leading to the car park was renamed a 'scenery store' and a second scenery store was built a few yards away on the other side of the road.

The most spectacular piece of new building was also the most necessary: twenty-four dressing rooms and a green room were built in a quadrangle behind the stage. The block stretched from a row of yew trees, not to where the stage was at the time, but to where the stage would be when its depth was increased. The dressing rooms were connected with the theatre by temporary corridors.

For the comfort of patrons in the front of the house a lighted path was made from the theatre to the car park, and a kitchen, chauffeurs' room, and new dining room were built across the way from the original unnamed dining room, which now became the Christie Dining Hall. The new one was called the Mildmay Dining Hall. (As the Christie hall was eventually rechristened Mildmay, there is at present no room that commemorates the Festival Opera's co-founder.)

All this was, as usual, undertaken at cost by the Ringmer Building Works.

To most of those who visit Glyndebourne Ringmer is no more than a name on a signpost, the telephone exchange for the Box Office, or the last stage on the road down from London. In fact it is a village which, while it plays an active part in the day-to-day life of modern Glyndebourne and its opera house, has quite a history of its own. Architecturally it is frankly not alluring; it has none of the compactness of the typical English village, but sprawls inelegantly on both sides of the main road. In its time Ringmer seems to have been a pretty village. According to an eighteenth-century account it presented 'a cheerful and picturesque appearance, and an aspect of cleanliness and comfort truly inviting. The soil being particularly favourable for the culture of flowers and shrubs, the parterres and borders before the houses and cottages' could 'vie, in the beauty and variety of their productions, with any in the kingdom'. Much of this still applies, though I regret to have to report that in the spring of 1964 some of the parterres and borders were seen to be planted with plastic daffodils.

The motorist travelling to Glyndebourne from London perhaps sees the best of Ringmer, for his route takes him past the church, the Green, a group of sixteenth-century half-timbered cottages and, opposite them, the attractive Little Manor with its walled garden and a fine roof of Horsham slabs. At this point, at the corner of the main road and the one-way street leading back to London, there hangs the village sign. It was unveiled by the American Ambassador in 1923 to remind passers-by that Ringmer has two strong historical links with the United States. In 1636 Ann Sadler, daughter of the Rev John Sadler, Vicar of Ringmer from 1620 to 1640, married John Harvard, the clergyman son of a Southwark butcher; she emigrated with him in 1637 to New England, where he died the following year, aged only 31. Harvard bequeathed his library and half his estate to the college newly founded in Cambridge, Massachusetts, by the colony of Massachusetts Bay and in gratitude to his memory the college was renamed Harvard University.

The other link between Ringmer and America commemorated on the village sign is the marriage of William Penn, the Quaker founder of Pennsylvania, to Gulielma Springett in 1672. Gulielma, who is reputed to have been an exceptionally beautiful young woman, was the posthumous daughter of Sir William Springett of Broyle Place – a staunch Parliamentarian who died in the siege of Arundel Castle, aged 23. Broyle Place, the former Broyle Palace already mentioned, which stands back a little on the left hand side of the road from Ringmer to Laughton (A 273), was restored in 1955 at very great expense by its present owners, Mr and Mrs Eric Dawson, after a couple of centuries of neglect; for after the Springetts left it deteriorated into a not very interesting looking old farmhouse. The Dawsons' work was gratefully recognized by the people of Pennsylvania who sent them a replica of the statue of William Penn in Philadelphia. The road from Ringmer to Broyle Place is nowadays credit enough to the East Sussex County Council, but at the time of Gulielma's marriage it was notoriously one of the worst in a county famous as 'Sowseks ful of dyrt and myre' and to get to church on a Sunday the Springetts' coach had to be drawn by eight oxen.

The most prominent feature of the Ringmer village sign, however, is the picture of the tortoise made famous by the Rev Gilbert White, the great eighteenth-century naturalist, in his *Natural History of Selborne*. This creature, known as Timothy, belonged to White's aunt, Mrs Rebecca Snooke, whom he used to visit frequently in Ringmer. The Snookes, after the Rev Henry Snooke had retired from the living of Ringmer, lived at Delves House which, until it was pulled down and rebuilt as a Queen Anne house on the same site in 1937, was a pleasing white Sussex building of stucco and slate, in large grounds on the north side of the Green. On his aunt's death in 1780 Gilbert White inherited the tortoise and took it to Selborne, where it lived to a great age. Its shell is in the Natural History Museum at South Kensington.

Gilbert White and his tortoise, only one of whom, after all, was a resident there, have been given the status almost of patron saints in Ringmer. Not only is there a large marble relief of White, in a very *décolletée* toga with his tortoise, on the wall of the new Ringmer County Secondary School, but Timothy is incorporated in the arms worn on the school blazers – a curious symbol to choose, somehow.

Unless there is some law expressly forbidding people in evening dress to enter an English church, a look at the Ringmer Parish Church of St Mary the Virgin is well worth half an hour of any Glyndebourne visitor's time on the way to the Opera House.

Horsfield described Ringmer church as 'truly Sussex – rude, irregular and ancient', but like most English churches so much has been added and altered since it was rebuilt by the Normans on the site of a wooden Saxon church (to say nothing of what was destroyed by the Puritans in the seventeenth century) that it is difficult to place it in a hard and fast architectural category. There is everything from the Norman bases of the pillars and Early English pointed arches, to mid-Victorian perpendicular and late Ringmer Building Works Tudor.

Over the years the Christie family has contributed handsomely and frequently to the maintenance and improvement of Ringmer church. The tower, built in 1884, and the third in the building's history (the first was destroyed by fire in the middle 1500s, the second about 1800), was the gift of John's grandfather, William Langham Christie, and contains a peal of eight bells. (Bell ringing practice takes place in the late afternoons on Wednesdays and Saturdays throughout the year, and in the summer is often in full clang-our as motorists pass the church on their way to the opera. It is an impressive and peculi-arly English sound which the prevailing westerly winds make clearly audible in our house three-quarters of a mile away.) William Langham Christie also gave the East window in the Chancel when this part of the church was extended in the middle of the nineteenth century. The hatchments over the Chancel arch are those of members of the Christie family, two of whom, Archibald and Spencer Christie, uncles of John Christie's who died in their twenties, are commemorated by a window in the south aisle.

John Christie's own gifts to the church were on a characteristically generous scale – the gallery, built by the Ringmer Building Works in 1932, the panelling (some of which came from Glyndebourne and is over 250 years old) in the Vestry below it. And, of course, the organ. According to the new illustrated guide to the village of Ringmer and its church (copies costing a shilling can usually be found just inside the church, often next to a recent copy of the *Harvard Bulletin* which, however, is not for sale), the organ was built in 1922. 'The volume was so great that the congregation sometimes found it almost unbearable. About 1940, at the suggestion of Mr George Austin, FRCO, ARCM, who was organist at the time, the whole organ was revoiced with more pleasing results to every-one concerned ... The organ is one of the finest in the Diocese. Much of it consists of the best parts of old Continental organs. There are three manuals and 62 stops, and no less than 2,386 pipes.'

Finally, there is John Christie's touching personal memorial to his butler who died in 1940. This is an inscription in Latin on the floor where the ashes of Josephi Gulielmi Roger Childs are buried in the Lady Chapel or North Chapel. The inscription records that he was 'servant and friend at Glyndebourne, distinguished for his worth and greatly beloved'. It is a good piece of carving and in keeping with the many exquisitely carved seventeenth- and eighteenth-century memorials found in the church.

The Christie family's gifts to Ringmer church did not come to an end with John Christie's death. In 1962 George Christie presented the new oak doors leading to the Vestries in thanksgiving for his son, who had been christened Hector Thomas Clevland Christie at the church in October 1961.

One of the most interesting features of Ringmer church needs a certain amount of looking for. By comparison with the northern counties, where choral societies and the brass band movement have long flourished, Sussex has never had much of a reputation as a musical county. It was, however, at one time the home of the English village church orchestras which, with a small choir, were formed in the eighteenth century to lead the metrical psalms and perform simple anthems. (Organs had been banned in churches by a statute of 1644 which classed them under 'superstitious monuments'; but though the law was repealed at the Restoration in 1660 it was a long time before the organ was in general use again in the smaller parish churches.)

These orchestras (or 'musicianers') and choirs were placed in a gallery behind the congregation – that is, at the west end of the church. At Ringmer the western gallery was given by Gilbert White's uncle, the Rev Henry Snooke (presumably some time after he ceased to be vicar in 1729, for church orchestras were not common until much later), and was in regular use by choir and orchestra until 1865. The orchestras sometimes included violins and violoncellos, but usually consisted of a large complement of 'flewtes', clarinets, bassoons (the bassoon was known in Sussex as 'the horse's leg'), trombones and serpents – with a preponderance of bassoons to give what was considered the necessary bass support to the singing. (One orchestra of twenty-four players is reported to have included no fewer than nine bassoons which, considering the standard of amateur bassoonists, must have made the church sound like a beehive.)

The Sussex church orchestras in their heyday, from the end of the eighteenth century to the early 1830s, made use of a remarkable variety of usual and unusual instruments including banjos, barrel-organs, bass-horns (a form of upright serpent), bassoons, clarinets, concertinas, cornets, 'cornopeans' (two-pistoned cornets), fifes, flutes, 'flutinas', which were a cross between an accordion and a concertina, French horns (very rare and usually found only at Hailsham), kettle drums, side drums, oboes, pitchpipes, seraphines (or seraphims), which were the immediate precursors of the harmonium, serpents, triangles and trombones. In addition the orchestras also included vamp horns – a form of metal megaphone between three and seven feet long used to amplify the bass line supplied by the human voice. The double bass, it is intriguing to note, was always called a 'grandmother fiddle' in Sussex – an unexpected change of sex in an instrument usually known by such obstinately masculine names as 'bull fiddle' and the 'dog house'.

Snooke's 'musicianers' gallery was taken down in 1872 when the church at Ringmer was reseated, but there are preserved in a corner of the south wall of the South Chapel, and difficult to find, two instruments – a bassoon and a recorder – as a reminder of Ringmer's activity during the 'English village orchestral era'.[1]

Civilization marching in the direction it does, modern Ringmer, with a population of 3,000 or more, would be hard put to it to raise an orchestra of this nature today. But if

[1] The recorder is described as a flute on the notice beside it on the wall and technically it is a member of the flute family. But it is hardly recognizable as such, for this particular instrument was played with a long crook resembling a bassoon's.

Ringmer no longer produces its own music it has developed into a unique community of consumers of music. Thirty years' intimate connection with the backstage workings of the Glyndebourne Opera have had an inevitable influence on the tastes and musical habits of the inhabitants. I do not mean to suggest by this, of course, that every brick-layer employed by the Building Works is passionately interested in opera; there are many in Ringmer who will always prefer pops to *Poppea*. But the extent to which two generations have been intimately involved in opera, thanks to the accident of living in the village, is one of the peculiarly fascinating features of Ringmer. They have built the scenery and shifted it, dug in the gardens, installed and worked the lighting system, sewed costumes, made props, forged gates, acted as dressers, polished and swept the auditorium, controlled the traffic, sold the programmes and ushered the audience to their seats. They have never been brought up to look on opera as 'classical' music, and therefore not for the likes of them; in consequence, they regard a Glyndebourne dress rehearsal as an entirely normal form of entertainment, a good way of spending an evening in a theatre which, to many of them, is the only theatre they've ever been to in their lives. Before Glyndebourne was built the nearest theatre to Ringmer was in Brighton, twelve miles away. There had once been one in Lewes, but that was shut down in 1829 as a dead loss in a notoriously Puritan county town.

For nearly five months of the year Ringmer is also in close contact with many of the singers appearing at Glyndebourne who, with their families, become familiar figures in the village post office, in the shops, in the homes and kitchens of local residents with whom they lodge. To the garage these five months mean extra work servicing Opels and Fiats, Simcas and Alfa Romeos, Peugeots and Mercedes, and often frustrating hours spent in trying to get a spare part for a foreign car whose after-sales service in Britain is not at all what propaganda has cracked it up to be. Ringmer's personal contact with the artists naturally makes the problem of Glyndebourne dress rehearsal tickets as much of a headache for the villagers as getting tickets for ordinary performances is for the public supporter of the opera. As consolation there are, of course, the BBC's broadcasts of most of the season's operas and the televising of one – which may not be so much fun as the real thing, but shows in close-up many of the singers whom the village has come to know and like personally during the summer months.

In spite of its all-the-year-round association with one aspect of Glyndebourne or another, Ringmer's contribution to the opera has for the most part been manual. But if there have been no obvious signs of conductors' batons being carried in native knapsacks two local boys have made good on the musical side at Glyndebourne. Dennis and Howard Wicks, the sons of a Ringmer builder, were both in the choir of the parish church as boys and, as members of Joseph Roger Childs' local troop of Boy Scouts detailed to take a collection plate round after performances in the Organ Room, were able to hear many of the concerts given there before the war. Dennis Wicks, who started out as a bass in the chorus, first appeared in a solo part as Antonio the gardener in the 1950 production of *Figaro*. Since then he has taken increasingly bigger parts, including Truffaldino in *Ariadne* and Trulove in *The Rake's Progress*, as well as deputizing for Carlos Alexander in *Elegy for Young Lovers.* His brother Howard, who is also an accomplished organist, has been Glyndebourne's music librarian since 1951.

On the administrative side of the opera Janet Moores, daughter of a couple who keep the cycle shop and a grocery stores and now Assistant Manager, has been with the Glyndebourne Opera since it began in 1934. After leaving school Miss Moores went to work in the Glyndebourne Estate Office (which shares the same couple of floors as the Motor Works and the electricians) where she licked stamps and made cups of tea. She was then taken on as a general help in the office at Glyndebourne itself where – thoroughly involved in it all – she has been ever since. I'd like to claim that Janet Moores was a native of Ringmer but she isn't. Like her parents she comes from Yorkshire and was born in the same village as the Brontë sisters. But it was as a Ringmer girl that she joined Glyndebourne.

Though John Christie's connections with the village of Ringmer were largely in his capacity as employer and benefactor (he made a present to the Primary School of land for its playing fields, for instance), he was also Lord of the Manor of Ringmer, a position which touched on the lives also of those who did not work for him, go to church or play games as schoolchildren. The Manor of Ringmer was granted by James I (1603–25) to the fourth Earl of Worcester, whose home grounds were as far from Sussex as Raglan, Chepstow and Gower, and in the course of time came into the possession of the Christie family, by whose permission the village green is used for cricket and its medieval softball variant, stoolball, which women and girls all over Sussex play with skill and ferocious enthusiasm. That football is not played on Ringmer Green is not due to any fear that the cricket pitch might suffer, but to John Christie's belief that the game would bring in its wake charabancs, rattles and handbells, the scenes, sounds and crowds of a Wembley Cup Final. By the time the Lord of the Manor had been persuaded that such things were unlikely to accompany the inter-village football played by the local team, however, the Ringmer Football Club had been given a field by the village butcher, and on winter Saturday afternoons the peace of the Green remains undisturbed as before.

CHAPTER NINE

1935 **Trouble in paradise**

AS 1934 ENDED, ANY DOUBTS that Glyndebourne had 'arrived' were dispelled once and for all by the inclusion, in a glossy's annual review, of the inauguration of 'a lovely living British opera at Glyndebourne' as one of the four outstanding events of the year. The other three were Princess Marina's wedding, the cheerfulness of the Stock Exchange, and British victories in sport.

On the first day of the New Year, coinciding with the announcement of the birth at Glyndebourne of George William Langham Christie on 31 December 1934, the plans for the 1935 Festival were published. There would be 25 performances between 29 May and 30 June and in addition to *Figaro* and *Così fan tutte* there would be productions of Mozart's two German operas, *Die Zauberflöte* and *Die Entführung aus dem Serail*. And that is what in fact took place, except that, owing to the Silver Jubilee of King George v and Queen Mary, the opening night was later changed to 27 May ostensibly to enable Covent Garden to have its Gala Performance fixed for 29 May in peace – but also, of course, so as not to lose too many cash customers. It is said that John Christie still hoped to put on *Parsifal* at Easter, but if so he did not make his intention public. What was more significant than the absence of any hint of an Easter *Parsifal* was the complete lack for the first time of any proposal to hold a Christmas season at Glyndebourne. The practical experience of the first season had obviously convinced John Christie (if not Mr Fox-Strangways) that Glyndebourne and its opera were best enjoyed in the summer.

Meanwhile, preparations for the second season did not go altogether as smoothly as they had gone for the first – largely, I think, because so many of those concerned now knew what Glyndebourne was all about. Where in the early months of 1934 nobody had much idea where it was all leading to, and so kept their fingers crossed that the worst might not happen, scarcely had the curtain fallen on the last night of the opening Festival than Glyndebourne began to have its first mild experience of that distressing, endemic bloody-mindedness found behind the scenes of the rest of the world's opera houses. One would have expected Glyndebourne to have been immune from it, but to be truthful no opera house in the world is entirely free of this peculiar germ; it is in the very nature of opera itself. The only difference is that on the whole Glyndebourne has been lucky to be less affected by it over the years than probably any other operatic concern.

Fortunately in Busch and Rudolf Bing Glyndebourne had two men greatly experienced in the art of the hiring and firing of singers and they were able instantly to recognize the first signs of impending trouble and to deal with it effectively. There was the question, for instance, of Pamina in *The Magic Flute*.[1] In early December 1934, after Ina Souez's offer to sing Pamina and Constanze (a tone down) had been declined, Aulikki Rautawaara was contracted as Pamina (at £14 a performance); negotiations had begun some weeks before but had been delayed while Miss Rautawaara obtained permission from the German record company she was tied up with to record a complete Glyndebourne *Magic Flute* for HMV. (For some reason this plan never materialized. Without saying a word to Glyndebourne HMV had Sir Thomas Beecham record the opera in Berlin.) Scarcely had Aulikki Rautawaara signed her contract, however, than John Christie informed everybody that, within a week of giving birth to her son, his wife was feeling so well and full of spirits that she would sing Pamina. Bing did some rapid thinking and wrote immediately to Fritz Busch with the suggestion that in such awkward and unforeseen circumstances it would be best to have *two* Paminas, each of whom would sing the part of the Second Lady when the other was singing Pamina. But, added Bing, the idea must sound as if it came from Busch.

From Copenhagen, where he was engaged most of the winter, Busch replied: 'That Audrey is so well we are all delighted to hear. That she (or John) is considering Pamina is a little more problematic. Naturally Audrey would bring a great deal to the role. But whether her voice and vocal method have enough of that *repose* which is essential above all things to the part I rather doubt in view of her sensibility and nervous, highly strung nature. Rautawaara would be more phlegmatic, but "safer". Can one, at this date, deprive her of the première? I hardly think so ...'

As an additional pre-season problem Bing had to cope with the question of Luise Helletsgruber who had hoped to sing Pamina herself, but agreed to sing the First Lady *only* if Audrey Mildmay sang Pamina. If anybody else sang (Miss Mildmay, after all, was the host's wife), she begged to be excused. In the end, as everybody expected she would, Miss Helletsgruber sang the First Lady and Aulikki Rautawaara sang Pamina; Audrey Mildmay accepted Fritz Busch's judgment and retired from the cast of *The Magic Flute* altogether; the part of the Second Lady was taken by Sophie Schoenning, a Norwegian.

Luise Helletsgruber brightened the winter nights at Glyndebourne at this time by writing an article in her local Viennese paper, *Die Neue Freie Presse*. It was headed 'As a Mozart Singer in England' and described John Christie as 'one of England's most famous antique dealers'. Lewes was not only credited with no fewer than four first-class hotels, but on account of its 'old-time' architecture was popularly known as 'the English Nuremberg'. The article ended with a reference to 'Audrey Middlemay' and no mention whatever of Busch or Ebert.

---

[1] I hope I may be forgiven this vernacular title, but despite Glyndebourne's firm tradition of referring to it even in the most informal Programme Book articles as *Die Zauberflöte*, Mozart's opera has long passed into the English language as *The Magic Flute* and it is unnatural for most of us to think of it as anything else.

Where, in negotiating with artists for the first season, Glyndebourne had had little or no trouble about fees, the personal publicity and international prestige now enjoyed by some of the singers as a result of the Festival's enormous and unexpected success led to some pretty fancy wage claims for 1935. One gentleman's demand for a sum amounting to a 400 per cent increase in fees for a 60 per cent increase in working hours so surprised Bing that he suspected a typing error. No, the amount was correct; the artist had arrived in 1934 expecting to live in 'Glyndebourne-House' ('which would have been like a country holiday'); instead, he had had to stay at the 'Schelleys' Hotel in Lewes, where he had been obliged to pay for his own board and lodging. With considerable difficulty and after months of uncertainty a compromise was reached with the singer and he was eventually re-engaged. Approaches to artists who had not already sung at Glyndebourne, but who had learned of its reputation, were met by even more remarkable demands. A German tenor recommended for the secondary part of Pedrillo was unwilling to arrive before the dress rehearsal and expected £80 a performance (Walther Ludwig, who sang Belmonte, was content with £24 an evening).

Then there was the young soprano, just beginning her career in Germany and totally unknown in this country, who asked for more for appearing as Constanze and the Queen of the Night than Lotte Lehmann was paid at Covent Garden. (John Christie never thought the Queen of the Night justified much of a fee, since the part consisted only of 'five minutes' singing and no acting'.) When it was explained that the Glyndebourne Opera House held only 300 people and that the money came out of a private individual's pocket and not from the Government, the singer dropped her fee to a third of the original demand. Her offer was not accepted, however, and she never appeared in England.

The search for a singer for the two coloratura roles in *The Magic Flute* and *Die Entführung* went on endlessly throughout the winter of 1934–5. As news of one unsuccessful proposal followed another Fritz Busch wrote to Bing: 'Aren't there any English Queens of the Night? Disappointing! Whenever I walk down Regent Street I always see hundreds – but perhaps they can't sing?'

There were other anxieties also during this time, for Rudolf Bing and Hans Oppenheim, the chief of Busch's musical staff, had both heard of a project to start a new German opera house in London. It was to be built and run as a private enterprise by a Mr Nettlefold, the rich husband of a soprano called Vera de Villiers, who was later Mrs Albert Coates. How far Nettlefold's plan ever got I do not know; I cannot remember seeing any publicity about it at the time. If there had been any it would most certainly have been noticed, for obviously after the unpredictable success of Glyndebourne almost anything in English opera had to be taken seriously. Nettlefold had apparently consulted John Christie on how to put his scheme into practice, and Oppenheim and Bing had frankly asked Christie to put in a good word on their behalf. For Bing it would mean a rare chance to work again in the sort of job he had had in Germany with Ebert; at Glyndebourne he was little more than a kind of foreign agent who dealt with the contracts and working conditions of foreign artists whose language Alfred Nightingale couldn't speak.

Nothing came of Nettlefold's project, but to allay his understandable feeling of insecurity in a foreign country Rudolf Bing was officially appointed an Assistant Producer for the 1935 season. Busch's son, Hans Peter Busch, had been the sole occupant of this post during the first season, but with the extension of the repertoire to four operas it became necessary to have two men on the job. Bing was a little unhappy about his title. He would prefer, he said, to be described on the programme as 'Representative for the Continent', or 'Artistic Secretary'. He remained Assistant Producer for the very good reason that it was a title the Home Office could understand and would grant a permit for.

It is perhaps difficult for us at this date to imagine exactly how insecure Bing and his foreign colleagues felt during their first Glyndebourne seasons as refugees; or to understand the dismay with which they learned from John Christie that in the 1935 season it would be impossible to accommodate wives in the Christies' house. (The exception to this was to be Grete Busch.) The ban on wives was proposed by Audrey Mildmay, whose instincts as a hostess of something amounting to genius made her constitutionally incapable of not worrying about her guests. The only thing to do to cut down worry, therefore, was to cut down the number of guests. As Christie said when he explained the move: 'Audrey has already with her singing, responsibilities as hostess and anxieties over the troubles of the Festival, almost more than she can do.' The husbands were the Christies' colleagues; the wives, on the other hand, contributed nothing to the Festival, for they toiled not, neither did they sing. As it turned out things were not so alarming as was first feared by those concerned, who foresaw themselves having to abandon their wives for two long months to live alone in other parts of England, helpless and forlorn among a strange people whose language most of them hardly spoke at all. In the end it happened that everything was arranged quite happily and wives stayed in the house during the Festival after all. But there is no doubt that the crisis brought into unpleasantly sudden and sharp focus a problem which has been with Glyndebourne since the start and becomes increasingly difficult with the years: the problem of finding furnished houses, cottages, flats, digs and hotel accommodation in Lewes, Ringmer and the surrounding villages, not only for the opera staff but for the artists and their families, chorus and orchestra, although traditionally conductors, producers and most heads of departments have always stayed at the house, as guests of the Christies.

The preparations for the 1935 season were the subject of one of the most fascinating files of correspondence discovered – stacked away at the back of the butler's garage at Glyndebourne – at a late stage in the planning of this book; and it was not until I read it that I had any idea of the hazards, bombshells, near-misses, disappointments and general upheavals encountered during a period which the passage of time and ready acceptance of the Glyndebourne success story have always led us to believe was a peaceful, logical stage in the development and increasing prosperity of Glyndebourne.

There was, it is true, some intriguing and refreshingly unurgent correspondence in the folder, much of it made doubly intriguing by its very incompleteness. John Christie was notoriously bad at answering any questions put to him in a letter (Fritz Busch made a point of writing all his questions and declarations of fact to Frances Dakyns, who would then read the letter aloud to Christie and relay the answers or comments – if any – to

Busch). Equally, what might have been an interesting answer to one of Christie's questions is often not found in the file. There is a gap, for instance, that should have been filled by Bing's reply to a short letter written in January 1935 which consisted of three sentences: 'I have been recommended a young Singer – Huguès [*sic*] Cuenod, who is in the Geneva Opera. I don't know what his voice is. Is anything known of him?' John Christie's question was answered by M. Cuenod himself – 20 years later, when he sang for the first time at Glyndebourne in 1954, as Sellem in *The Rake's Progress*.

Rudolf Bing's early struggles with the syntax and spelling of the English language also bring welcome moments of charm and relief to a correspondence which in general makes for dramatic rather than diverting reading. On the subject of enlisting Thos Cook and Son to help with the 'propaganda', Bing had to report to Christie that Cook's 'easily could have made propaganda without charge in all continents if they would have got the particulars in December', adding that 'still now one could perhaps consider asking them to do a special London-propaganda, running perhaps special Cook-Couches to Glyndebourne and so on'. The idea of 'special Cook-Couches' has a delicious touch of luxury about it entirely in keeping with Glyndebourne's proud concern for its audience's welfare.

One lesson was learned the hard way in the months between these first two Glyndebourne seasons: the lesson that nothing can be taken for granted where the engagement of singers or orchestral players is concerned until the contract is signed, and even then it is as well to keep your fingers crossed. As Bing observed wryly to Busch at one point, John Christie was at this time so taken up with his plans and building projects for 1936 that the idea of having to settle 1935 first seemed to him an unnecessary distraction. As a consequence of what Busch called 'John's permanent holiday' it came as a shock to discover that Heddle Nash was not willing to repeat his Basilio and Ferrando, as everybody had gaily presumed, and still less to take on Monostatos and Pedrillo as well. Nobody had thought to send him a contract, and anyway Nash was now thinking in terms of Tamino and Belmonte, apart from being already committed to sing in *The Barber of Seville* at Covent Garden. Like a couple of Canadian Mounties, Bing and Oppenheim set out to get their man – 'a better Basilio I do not know', Busch had said – and things were eventually arranged so that Heddle Nash could fit in Covent Garden with Glyndebourne, where he was signed up to sing Pedrillo (but not Monostatos) and repeat his Basilio and Ferrando.[1]

The leisurely approach of John Christie and, taking his tempo from his employer, of Alfred Nightingale, to the drawing-up and final ratification of contracts with British performers all but brought final disaster to the whole Glyndebourne enterprise within a month of the date the 1935 season was due to open. It is obvious that behind this indifference to the basic principles of theatrical business procedure was not only Christie's lack of experience in the professional theatre, but his superb, but in this case misplaced, native inability to believe that anybody could possibly refuse the privilege of working at

---

[1] Among the candidates for Pedrillo was John Kentish. Bing had a very high opinion of him but was overruled by Hans Oppenheim, and Kentish had to wait until 1952 before he had a part at Glyndebourne.

Glyndebourne whenever they were offered it. If they happened to have a previous engagement elsewhere (but especially at Covent Garden) the Glyndebourne offer would naturally, and without question, take precedence. Christie was probably most astonished when he found that things didn't work out that way , and no doubt attributed it to the inherent wickedness of all other operatic organizations. Whatever his philosophy in the matter, however, it can have been little consolation when, six weeks before the start of the season, it was found that a third of the orchestra had had no Glyndebourne contracts and not unreasonably had taken jobs elsewhere (there was plenty of work for orchestral musicians in that Jubilee season).

The real crisis occurred over Ina Souez and her contract to sing Fiordiligi. Thanks to what Busch was beginning to find a maddening dilatoriness and unbusinesslike lack of urgency in negotiating contracts, Christie and Nightingale between them failed to send Ina Souez a contract until the middle of February 1935, a delay justified no doubt by the reflection that it had already been agreed at the end of the 1934 season that she would be wanted for the following year and so there was no hurry for the completion of a mere formality. When Miss Souez received the contract she did not answer for nearly a month. When she did, it was to ask for more money – the first of a long line of singers who have made their name at Glyndebourne and have then demanded fees which Glyndebourne could not possibly pay. In this case Glyndebourne was able to raise its offer; the contract was still unsigned, however, when it was found that Miss Souez had meanwhile agreed with Covent Garden to sing Micaëla in *Carmen* (Conchita Supervia was to be Carmen) – and at a smaller fee, it was later discovered, than Christie had offered her.

Fritz Busch, holidaying in Sorrento, seems to have heard nothing of what had been going on in the Souez case until, on 18 April, he received a cable from Frances Dakyns telling him that Ina Souez would not sing at Glyndebourne. Busch cabled back that if Souez was 'definitely lost' he himself would resign 'for certain'. He then sat down and wrote a couple of letters. To Frances Dakyns he wrote that his worst apprehensions had been confirmed by Ina Souez's crying off. Either the contracts, including Miss Souez's, had been concluded in time and in a binding form that would make it impossible for anybody to cry off, or the negotiations had not been properly concluded, in which case it was such an unheard of lack of responsibility that, as the only one answerable for the artistic success, he could not possibly be expected to work under such conditions. Who guaranteed that *all* the artistic preparations for Glyndebourne were being made according to his wishes? Ina Souez as Fiordiligi, continued Busch, cannot be replaced by anybody in the world, and losing her meant that even if an equally wonderful voice and appropriate personality could be found in the little time left, the whole plan of rehearsals would have to be changed. It was simply impossible for him as the conductor of all the rehearsals and performances to work thoroughly and successfully with a new Fiordiligi in the short time left. 'I know that Ebert will agree with me.'

To Bing, Busch wrote a stern and angry letter on the subject of contracts, reminding him that when a singer had had a great success like Souez there was nothing more natural in the theatre than to sign her up *at once*. This, Busch explained grimly at dictation speed, was usually done by a contract which *both* parties signed, but so long as the contract was signed by only one side it was worthless. It was sheer false pretences to put Souez's name in the prospectus and ridiculous, when an artist went to a rival concern, to sit there and complain afterwards that she had 'behaved badly'.

'That two people with years of experience of singers, like you and Oppenheim,' wrote Busch, 'can say *that*, I find astonishing. You must know that "bad behaviour" is the *rule* among singers, and for that reason Souez is quite right in my opinion to go where she can get more publicity and more money.' For Glyndebourne to say then that it had only been 'careless', he said, was ludicrous. 'Irresponsible' was putting it as mildly as possible.

John Christie and Frances Dakyns, Busch went on, were innocents ('Weltfremde') and *Theaterdiletanten* (Busch always spelt the word without the double 't'); the question he kept asking himself was how it could happen that professionals like Bing, Oppenheim and Nightingale could let a whole winter go by without asking whether *all* contracts were in order – that is, signed by *all* parties. Weren't they all employed at Glyndebourne to look after precisely *this* side of the whole undertaking? 'Where do I end up if my confidence is destroyed like this?' asked Busch. 'The thing has happened,' the letter went on. 'But the request: "telegraph whether you agree to the singer recommended by Erede" – no, dear people, that is *not* the end of the matter for me.[1] *I demand*, if my coming to Glyndebourne means anything, that the five guilty ones (i.e. Christie, Bing, Oppenheim, Nightingale and Souez herself) do *everything*, with, without or against Beecham, with the help of the King, or Parliament, of friend and foe, no matter *HOW*: that I have Souez at the necessary rehearsals and the 4–5 performances of "Così". Where there's a will there *is* a way. In the theatre altogether different things have been possible. This *IS* possible. That is my last word.'

This, then, was the perilous situation with less than five weeks to go before the opening night. Any sort of approach to Covent Garden in the hopes of coming to some kind of amicable arrangement was out of the question. From the first moment that Glyndebourne became an operatic reality John Christie had lost no opportunity to abuse and denigrate Covent Garden, more often than not as a matter of deep-rooted principle than as an expression of personal opinion on artistic matters. It was difficult to get Christie to go to Covent Garden at any time and Bing was to spend anxious years trying to persuade him to do the polite thing and put in at least a token appearance at the Royal Opera House from time to time. It was hardly surprising, therefore, that in the great Souez crisis, circumstances made it impossible for Christie to discuss things with Beecham. Bing did his best to encourage a meeting but felt it was hopeless because (taking a rather naïve view) 'the openly hostile Covent Garden' did '*everything* to harm Glyndebourne'. John Christie himself agreed that it was likely to be a fruitless gesture but was nevertheless willing to make an approach. In the end, however, Alfred Nightingale finally convinced him that

---

[1] This telegram had been sent by Bing the day before Busch wrote this letter, and referred to a singer whom Alberto Erede, then on Busch's musical staff, had found and more or less bespoken almost as soon as the seriousness of the Souez situation was recognized.

it was useless, and it was many years before Glyndebourne reached its present stage of friendly relations with its fellow enterprise.

Bing reported all this in a letter replying to Busch's ultimatum. He explained that as he was employed by Glyndebourne to deal only with the engagement of foreign artists it had been impossible for him to interfere with Nightingale, who dealt with the British artists (Ina Souez was a British citizen by marriage). So far as the foreign artists were concerned contracts had been signed and countersigned long ago. Everything had long been in order, Bing declared, and if a satisfactory situation had been reached it was more *in spite* of the Glyndebourne management than because of it. The most immediate problem, however, was still the question of a Fiordiligi. Another change of programme – this time a change of repertoire following the change of the opening date – would mean the death of Glyndebourne. Would Busch please arrange to hear Erede's recommended soprano Falconieri as soon as possible. An expensive option had been placed on her head and she couldn't escape until Busch had heard her.

Busch's reply was prompt and sympathetic, but he would give no definite decision on Falconieri as Fiordiligi until he had heard her himself (this was one case, he said, when he would not trust Erede's usually reliable judgment). Meanwhile, he would arrive at Glyndebourne on the 10th or 11th of May as he had originally planned; too much was obviously at stake to abandon Glyndebourne at this stage, as he had threatened.

By 30 April Signora Falconieri's option had been taken up and Bing sent to Italy for the personal particulars needed for her permit to work at Glyndebourne. The following day, however, Fritz Busch, who had now moved on to Rome, received a telegram from Ina Souez – the first word anybody had had of her for several weeks. It was in English, slightly the worse for the wear and tear of the Italian post office, and contained the important phrase: 'leave it with you.' Busch, puzzled at first by the unfamiliar American preposition, rightly interpreted it as meaning 'leave it to you'. He immediately instructed Bing – and only Bing – to get in touch with Miss Souez in person at once, and leaving aside all 'feeling' and moral indignation, to sign her up. If Bing could get her to agree to the conditions – *all* rehearsals and *all* performances – that would be good. If not – 'and I leave the decision to *you*, *ONLY* you and Oppenheim' – then they would take Falconieri.

Bing received this letter on 2 May. On 4 May the information appeared in the *Daily Telegraph* that the part of Fiordiligi in 'Così fan' would be sung at the Glyndebourne Festival by a new Italian soprano, Mme Falconieri. The announcement proved premature. On 5 May, Busch sent Bing a cable from Florence. It was in German, but not even the British Post Office's trouble with the proper names could disguise the spirit behind the simple message: DANK FUR ENGAGEMENT SONEZ HAB FALCONERI ABGESAGT – BUYCH. 'Thanks for Souez engagement have cancelled Falconieri.' With that telegram the pre-season correspondence for 1935 comes to a fitting and dramatic end. If Glyndebourne had not understood before, it certainly understood now what Fritz Busch had meant when he warned: 'The idyll of 1934 was once upon a time. It will not come again.'

The second Glyndebourne Festival Opera season opened, as advertised, with *The Magic Flute* on 27 May. With it Glyndebourne survived, but it had been a near thing.

CHAPTER TEN

1935 **The enchanted flute**

THE 1935 SEASON OPENED AT the new starting time of 6.30 p.m. with *The Magic Flute*. The later start pleased the critics, until they realized that a late start meant a late finish and a scramble for deadlines; but this year they did not grumble in public. If they made private representations to the Management, they were noted, although it was not until 1937 that the curtain regularly rose early on first nights for their convenience.

The evening of Monday 27 May was chilly and a cold spring had so delayed planting-out that Mr Harvey, the head gardener, was able to transfer the last of the plants from pot to bed only just in time for the dinner interval. For some reason *The Magic Flute* did not play to capacity on the first night; why this should have been so nobody now remembers. What is remembered by those who heard it is that this *Magic Flute* made a deeper impression than anything that had yet been experienced at Glyndebourne, or indeed anywhere else for many years.

When, after the first night of the new *Magic Flute* in 1963, George Christie asked how it had compared with the 1935 production, I found it difficult to answer; to discuss with anybody who hadn't heard it exactly what it was about the performance that made it an incomparable experience was an impossible task. It had a quality most of us had never encountered before and few of us, I believe, have ever encountered since. Between them Fritz Busch, Carl Ebert and Hamish Wilson created what one can only think of as an exceptionally *complete* performance; the pitfalls were avoided, the heights attained; what can so often sound silly in this opera sounded enchanting, what can so often sound dull was intensely moving. The scene changes were rapid, the costumes (the first to be designed by Wilson and not by his sister Ann Litherland) a pleasing mixture of fantasy and ceremonial splendour, and the staging of such scenes as the ordeals by fire and water imaginative and gripping.

But the greatest revelation was musical. Not all the parts were by any means ideally cast, but Busch's conception of the work was so panoramic, versatile and stimulating that the performance was one in which the whole was inevitably and immeasurably greater than the sum of its parts. Even so it was a performance which, like all good performances of *The Magic Flute*, revealed new aspects and new beauties, new ingenuities and new details of the music which one had somehow never noticed or been moved by before.

One moment in particular stands out in my own memory after nearly thirty years: Busch's heart-rending playing of the instrumental epilogue to Pamina's aria, which made a scene that had been pleasantly but not outstandingly sung into the high spot of the evening. Aulikki Rautawaara can never have known how much of the success she made with the audience was due to the way Busch performed the music played by the orchestra when she was no longer singing.

One other memorable detail of the first *Magic Flute* was the performance of Der Sprecher by Carl Ebert. Over the years Glyndebourne has confused us so much with its interpretation of exactly who and what Der Sprecher (Speaker or Orator) is supposed to be that I had better explain at once that Professor Ebert did not sing. He played the part of the character described in the programme of the first performance of the opera on 30 September 1791 as 'Sprecher' (with no definite article). In the first Glyndebourne production, however, Ebert was shown in the programme as playing the part of 'Ober-Priester', or High Priest, but the words he spoke were Der Sprecher's. 'Der Sprecher' was John Brownlee, who in fact was nothing of the sort. He sang the part shown on the original Vienna bill as 'Third Priest'.[1]

In the third scene of Act II Tamino finds himself in front of three temples. He goes to the one on the right, opens the door and is about to enter when a priest's voice warns 'Stand back!' He goes to the temple on the left and another priest's voice warns 'Stand back!' Tamino finally goes to the temple in the centre. This time he remembers to knock and there is no warning voice from within. Instead, in accordance with Schikaneder's stage directions 'an old Priest appears'. The notes the old Priest sings are allocated in the score to a bass described simply as 'Priest'. There is no hint, it will be noted, of the Speaker being anywhere in the neighbourhood.

When the Speaker does eventually appear, in the first scene of Act II, he does so in the company of the First, Second and Third Priests. The Third Priest has only one line and does not speak, sing or even appear again as a named individual. The practice of having whoever sings the 'Old Priest' double the speaking part of the Speaker is good theatrical economics, of course, though to have done so in the first Glyndebourne productions of *The Magic Flute* would have deprived us of Carl Ebert's impressive performance. What is confusing is to suggest that the Speaker and the Third Priest are the same person; the least we expect is that the singer in the first act who becomes an actor in the second should change the colour of his beard. In 1935 the confusion was made worse by having the so-called (singing) Speaker appear only in Act I, and what should have been the part of the (speaking) Speaker in Act II described as a High Priest.

---

[1] The 1935 Glyndebourne programme's presentation of the dramatis personae was waywardly bi-lingual. We had 'Der Sprecher', 'Ober-Priester' and 'Die Königin der Nacht' in German, and the other characters without proper names (like the Three Ladies, the Three Boys, the Two Priests and Two Armed Men) in English. In the synopsis of the plot all the characters were described in English – except for Der Sprecher, who remained Der Sprecher. The Ober-Priester was never mentioned at all, but by a quick mental process of elimination could be identified in Act II as being the same person as Der Sprecher.

In 1936 when, together with the Queen of the Night, the characters were described in English in the programme, they appeared (with a quaint economy of type) as:

The Speaker (Act I) .. George Hancock
    „   „   (Act II) .. Carl Ebert

This style was continued in 1937, after which *The Magic Flute* was dropped from the repertoire until 1956, since when matters have been simplified, if not rectified, and the part appears in the programme as a one-man job: 'The Speaker, *Priest of the Temple*.' The synopsis of the plot found in the 1963 programme and written by James Strachey for the 1936 production still kept the confusion going by telling us that Tamino 'is met by a Priest (the Speaker) ... ' In 1964, however, the whole matter was dropped and the synopsis didn't mention a Priest at all; only The Speaker.

The consistent inconsistency of this Glyndebourne idiosyncrasy seems hard to justify; one can only suppose it is something to do with the deliberate anti-Viennese policy adopted by Busch and Ebert at the start which made it impossible for them to observe *all* the instructions written in a libretto and score first performed at the Theater auf der Wieden. In fairness it must be said that the absence from Ebert's production of a Flying Machine for the Three Boys' entrance in Act II, scene 4, was not due to any anti-Viennese feelings. He wanted very much to introduce one but found it impossible in a theatre still without any means of flying the scenery.

Though the performance of the first Glyndebourne *Magic Flute* was a triumph of ensemble there were, in addition to Rautawaara's and Ebert's, two individual contributions which attracted attention – the entirely enchanting Papagena of Irene Eisinger (now described in the programme as 'Austrian' instead of 'Czech' as she had been in 1934), and the beautiful singing of Luise Helletsgruber as the First Lady. Willi Domgraf-Fassbaender was amusing enough as Papageno, but again often sang too loud for the theatre. So did Walther (mis-spelt 'Walter' in the programme) Ludwig as Tamino. The acoustics of the Opera House, indeed, were still harsh and unpredictable, and the orchestral balance was held responsible for obscuring Ivar Andrésen's low F in Sarastro's 'O Isis und Osiris'.

The vocal shortcomings of the Queen of the Night, however, could not be blamed on the acoustics. The months-long, continent-wide search for a singer to take this part, and later that of Constanze, had ended in the unhappy choice of Míla Kočová from Prague. She was not a success, and though critics at the first night sympathetically attributed her unsatisfactory performance to occasional nerves and being generally out-of-form, she did not last out the season. In the later performances of *The Magic Flute* and for the entire run of *Die Entführung* she was supplanted by another singer.

The only more-or-less unanimous criticism of Ebert's production was of his mistake in permitting Fassbaender to introduce gags in English. A characteristically emphatic anonymous note, unmistakably by John Christie, appeared in the programme to justify this:

[Schikaneder] was a clever actor and he himself took the part of Papageno, adapting his words to suit his audience. His purpose was to amuse his public and give them what they wanted. He would alter his words to suit the occasion and to suit his patrons. It is for this reason that Glyndebourne is introducing 'asides' in English in Papageno's dialogue, the essential object being to respect Schikaneder's atmosphere and to make his part a living part today.

In practice the idea flopped. Schikaneder's original jokes aren't terribly funny at the best of times; the 'asides' added in barely intelligible English sounded even sillier.[1]

This error of taste apart, however, the Glyndebourne *Magic Flute* delighted the critics even more than the *Figaro* and *Così fan tutte* of the year before – though one wonders exactly what kind of performances of *The Magic Flute* they had been used to in England when one of them – *The Times* – was so pleased by 'Papageno's happy *dénouement* following, instead of, as often happens, preceding the great scene of the ordeals which is Mozart's musical climax'.

After the fall of the curtain a few of us, who had telephoned our notices and were in no hurry to return to London, were invited to join the first party to be held after a Glyndebourne première in the new Green Room – the forerunner of nearly a hundred subsequent gatherings of the same kind at which artists and staff traditionally provide impromptu cabaret turns and take the mickey out of the management. It was at the party after *The Magic Flute* that Fritz Busch charmed his hearers by reading and misreading a speech in English in which he remarked: 'I used to divide the human race into three species: men, women and singers. Now I have found a fourth species: British singers.' Busch went on to sympathize with the understudies who learned the star parts but spent their life in the chorus just the same. 'No stars are ever away at Glyndebourne,' he said, 'because even work is more attractive than the night life of Lewes.'

The question of understudies at Glyndebourne has always been a favourite subject for ironic comment at these first night parties. At one of the most recent of them there was a sketch about the Glyndebourne understudy who at last got his chance after nearly 20 years of patient waiting and unfulfilled hope. His great moment came. He went in to the Covered Way and cried: 'Last bus for Lewes Station!'

Over the years these celebrations have grown too big for the Green Room and have been moved over to one of the dining halls or the artists' canteen. Here, after the last member of the public has left the grounds, and the Bar has closed – and when John Christie was still alive to walk around in tennis shoes to do it – every light in the place (including still-occupied lavatories) had been switched off according to nightly ritual, there is supper at tables lit by candles stuck in bottles and those who have been singing in the opera entertain the company with unaccompanied songs not in their usual way of

---

[1] The one English gag that seems to have registered was quoted by the *Daily Mirror* in a story headed 'Sunset Music in Buttercup Land' where, during the performance of 'Zaberflote' in 'the strangest opera house in the world' the audience was 'astonished' to hear Papageno say 'Why do you stare like that? You make my tummy feel gooey.' This 'set the audience laughing', and so confirmed once more that things too silly to raise a smile anywhere else will always make an opera house audience almost hysterical.

business. American singers come out with songs by Cole Porter and Richard Rodgers, and 'Smoke gets in Your Eyes' with *all* the appoggiaturas, the Italians with Neapolitan folk tunes, artists like Oralia Dominguez with racy Mexican tunes, Hugues Cuenod with rare little French songs and a moving and memorable performance of 'He never said a mumblin' word'. British singers contribute their Welsh and Scottish songs, but also show a gift for parody which goes down well, and a tendency to lengthy anecdote which – among their many non-English-speaking colleagues – does not. It is an occasion which preserves the peculiar indestructible family atmosphere which has been the strength of Glyndebourne, and the despair and discomfiture of its detractors, since the very beginning.

At the end of the Green Room party after the *Magic Flute* première I was given a lift back to London by Charles B. Cochran and his wife who, with Lilian Bayliss and Baron Franckenstein, the Austrian Minister, had been guests of the Christies in their box. It was Cochran's first visit to Glyndebourne and it had been a rich and stimulating experience. But, he confessed, it had also been a humiliating one. He was ashamed, he said, to think that the most modern and best equipped theatre in Western Europe was not in the West End of London where he could use it, but tucked away in Sussex, surrounded by sheep, cows, lakes and buttercups. On the other hand, he admitted, he was proud that it was in Sussex and not in some other county; he had been born at Lindfield and went to school in Lewes.

The sensational first production of *The Magic Flute* was followed three evenings later by a revival of *Così fan tutte* which, if anything, made an even deeper impression than it had the year before. The cast, with one exception, was the same and Ina Souez's performance, which was even better than her previous year's, showed forcibly how right Busch had been to raise hell about her contract. The newcomer to the cast was the Australian baritone John Brownlee, who sang Don Alfonso. Vincenzo Bettoni had been approached to sing the part again but had wanted more money than John Christie could afford; he spent the season at Covent Garden instead, where he sang the *buffo* parts in the memorable performances of *La Cenerentola* and *L'italiana in Algeri* with Conchita Supervia. As it happened Brownlee's fee was the highest paid to any singer in the 1935 season – a circumstance that delighted Rudolf Bing, who was constantly reproached for bringing in his 'overpaid foreigners'.

The revival of *Figaro* in 1935 took place in one of the busiest weeks the critics had had for years. On Monday 3 June Toscanini was conducting at Queen's Hall; Tuesday was the first night of *Carmen* at Covent Garden with Supervia in the lead and Ina Souez as Micaëla; on Wednesday Toscanini was at Queen's Hall again; Thursday was the first night at Covent Garden of *La Bohème* with the ill-starred Grace Moore as Mimi, and John Brownlee taking the night off from the Glyndebourne *Magic Flute* to sing Marcello (Ronald Stear deputized as the Speaker). On Friday there was a new Micaëla at Covent Garden as Ina Souez had been persuaded of her obligations to sing Fiordiligi at Glyndebourne that night.

The first night of the Covent Garden *Bohème* coincided with that of the Glyndebourne *Figaro* and, in the circumstances, naturally took priority over it. Critics accordingly sent their deputies to have, in many cases, their first experience of an evening at Glynde-bourne. These deputies seemed to enjoy themselves, though my own considered that since eight of the eleven principals in the opera were British (Stear was Bartolo in place of Bettoni) the work should have been sung in English (Helletsgruber singing in English would have really been something). He appeared to understand enough of the libretto, however, to enable the *Daily Herald* to produce the characteristic heading 'Class War as Opera Theme' and so justify an evening spent by its correspondent wearing tails and rubbing shoulders with the idle rich.

The last opera of the season, produced on 19 June, was something billed as *Die Entfüh-rung aus dem Serail*. This came as a pleasant surprise to many who recognized it (from the Overture, at least) as the Mozart opera they had long known by the popular Esperanto title of *Il Seraglio* (the Italian, after all, is *Il ratto dal serraglio*). That the opera ever went on at all was something of a miracle, for a new Constanze had to be brought in with only three days to go to the first performance. Míla Kočová was found to be even less satis-factory in the coloratura lead of *Die Entführung* than she had been as Queen of the Night, and in desperation Hamish Wilson suggested they should send for Noel Eadie, a Scottish soprano who had made her Covent Garden début in 1931 as the Queen of the Night under Bruno Walter (Andrésen had been the Sarastro in the same production). The sudden call to take over a part at a moment's notice was nothing new to Miss Eadie: the first time she had appeared on any stage at all she had gone on without rehearsal as the Queen of the Night in a BNOC production of *The Magic Flute*.

In the circumstances Noel Eadie's accurate account of 'Martern aller Arten' in the Glyndebourne *Entführung* was given an ovation. The rest of her performance was des-cribed as 'musicianly' – an ambiguous phrase used by critics to suggest that while a singer may not make a very beautiful noise at least she understands what she's supposed to be singing about. If Noel Eadie had not been musicianly in this case there might have been no performance at all, for she had to learn most of the music and all the German dialogue from scratch.

The first *Entführung* made a great hit with the audience. Walther Ludwig was a bit of a dull stick as Belmonte but Andrésen as Osmin and Irene Eisinger as Blonde stopped the show. Miss Eisinger had become a firm favourite with the Glyndebourne public with her Despina and Papagena; she completed a hat-trick of captivating performances with her appearance in this opera. Andrésen proved to be a superb comedian, particularly in the famous drunk scene, which Ebert treated brilliantly, with little of that exaggerated falling about most German producers think so funny.

Heddle Nash, as Pedrillo, was concerned with an exceptional musical detail that stays in the memory – Busch's beautifully conceived *pp* pizzicato accompaniment to the Serenade.

Finally there was Carl Ebert himself as Pasha Selim, a speaking part in which he exploited with great effect his familiar vocal charm and dignified appearance. His only action out of character, disapprovingly noticed by many of the critics, was the lapse of good manners which led him to walk off the stage during the orchestral introduction to 'Martern aller Arten' and so leave the unfortunate Constanze talking to herself instead of to the character to whom her defiant outburst is addressed. It is possible that in the first production of *Die Entführung* Ebert always had to see a man about the lights at this point, but even in the most recent revivals of the opera at Glyndebourne Pasha Selim still stayed only until half time. When the listener is holding tightly to his seat in his concern for the soprano's vocal safety in one of the most fiendishly difficult and spectacular arias ever written, there is nothing more maddening than to have one's attention distracted by a hitherto motionless figure suddenly and needlessly walking off into the wings. It is another of those curious Glyndebourne idiosyncrasies for which there seems to be no logical explanation.

In an enterprise so essentially private in its origins as the Glyndebourne Opera there has always been a tendency for all the family to join in, as it were. From the very beginning the fact that Audrey Mildmay was Mrs Christie inevitably made the borderline between house and theatre, private and public life, as narrow as the passage which divided the private residence from the Organ Room. It did not therefore come altogether as a surprise to those who knew or had heard tell of the Christies and their household to discover that the part of the Dumb Servant (shown in the programme only in German as 'Der Stumme') was taken by Joseph Roger Childs, the Glyndebourne butler. Childs gave a hilarious performance based, it is said, on close observation of the inmates of a deaf and dumb institution he once worked at. A contract in the archives of the Festival Opera House shows that J. R. Childs was paid 15 guineas for the season and subject to the same strict conditions of employment as other Glyndebourne artists. Among other things he undertook 'to replace other Artists at the request of The Company or their representative in all Operatic Performances, Concerts, Oratorios, Matinées or Soirées organized by The Company'.

Further help towards the enjoyment and appreciation of *Die Entführung* was given in the programme, where the commentary which had first appeared to accompany the famous Organ Room performance of Act 1 had now been considerably modified. Not only did the author no longer quote from Dent's book, but he seemed to have made up his own mind on several points, as well as implying how well Glyndebourne would be dealing with the problems raised by the opera and its characters:

OSMIN carries the opera on his shoulders. He is the central figure.
BELMONTE is the lyrical aristocrat and should be sung by a tenor of fine physique.
PEDRILLO ['pronounced Pedrillio as it is Spanish' the synopsis told us] is most difficult to cast. The first aria is too high for most tenors and the second is too low for high tenors ... This part requires a superb singer with a gift of humour and with physical activity. The combination is rare.
CONSTANZE has an aria of great difficulty to sing, 'Martern aller Arten' ('Tortures of all kinds'). This aria was added to the opera later by Mozart and is accompanied by orchestra and four solo instruments.[1]

[1] The author seemed to have misread something somewhere sometime. The aria was always in the opera from the first performance. The confusion seems to be with 'Mi tradì' in *Don Giovanni*, added at the Vienna production for Cavalieri who also sang the first Constanze.

BLONDE has arias which lie high and has in addition to be a character artist.

PASHA SELIM has no help from the Libretto and no music. He is handicapped by having to listen to a long orchestral introduction to the long and appallingly difficult aria 'Martern aller Arten', with nothing to do himself. This part can only succeed when taken by a great actor (and not, as is often the case, by a singer who has lost his voice).

Elsewhere in his notes John Christie gave the date of the first performance of *Die Entfüh-rung* correctly, but said it took place in Munich instead of Vienna. Why he should have changed his mind about this is not clear. He had got it right in his Organ Room pro-gramme, but perhaps by 1935 he had become too enthusiastic a disciple of the anti-Viennese teaching of his conductor and producer.

Except for the absence of manifestos on the Acoustics and appeals to live in Sussex, the lay-out of the Golden Book programme for 1935 was much the same as it had been the year before, including the references to 'Barberina' and 'Guglielno'. There were, how-ever, one or two puzzling changes – notably in John Christie's views on which singers qualified for a mention of their artistic antecedents. In 1934 Audrey Mildmay had appeared in the programme with none; now, in brackets, we read 'Carl Rosa' (one would have thought that 'Glyndebourne' might have been mentioned also). Aulikki Rautawaara, on the other hand, who had been introduced to us in 1934 with a long string of credentials, now had none at all. The Grand Opera, Paris, but not Covent Garden, was credited to John Brownlee, and then only when his name appeared in the *Magic Flute* cast. As Don Alfonso he was apparently unattached.

The list of Musical Staff had also grown longer in 1935. To the names of Hans Oppen-heim, Alberto Erede and Jani Strasser were added those of the first British-born musicians to join the opera company – Warwick Braithwaite, the New Zealand conductor who had been with the BNOC and more recently at Sadler's Wells; and Edward Renton, a gifted Scottish musician who had been a pupil of Fritz Busch in Germany. Neither Braithwaite nor Renton was allowed to conduct, of course, for they were employed solely as coaches. The first British conductor of a Glyndebourne opera was Sir Thomas Beecham, and that was at Edinburgh, in 1950; at Glyndebourne itself it was John Pritchard, in 1951.

Two minor items in the 1935 programme testified quietly to the growth of the Glyndebourne Opera. One was a grateful acknowledgment of Steinway's loan of six grand pianos for rehearsals (only four had been borrowed in the previous season). The other was the appearance on the plan of the Opera House and its surroundings, of the stage as it would be in 1936 – the fruit of John Christie's preoccupation with Glyndebourne's future which had so frustrated Bing during the darkest days of the Souez crisis.

Inevitably in one respect the 1935 season differed from its predecessor by including no fewer than eight days during the five weeks season when there were no performances of any kind. In 1934 both dress rehearsals had been held before the season opened and the two operas were played alternately for a fortnight with concerts on the two Sunday afternoons – which meant, of course, that some artists like Heddle Nash and Domgraf-Fassbaender were singing six nights a week. During the second season the extended repertoire not only gave one or two of the singers a breather, but necessitated the use of the theatre for dress rehearsals once the season was under way.

It is a little ironical that in the summer of 1935, just when a new dining hall had been built for visitors to the opera, the first case of picnicking at Glyndebourne should have been recorded in the Press. By present-day standards, as I have already suggested, it wasn't very much to write home about – sandwiches in the car park. But then the art of picnicking at Glyndebourne *à la française*, which has become so much a feature of a night at the Festival Opera since the war, had not yet been developed. Today *dîner* literally *sur l'herbe* is becoming less popular than it used to be; like the French, most of us have learned to do the things properly with chairs, tables, table-cloths, ice, proper napkins, china plates, glasses, pots of mustard and pepper mills. When it rains, of course, we revert to type and draw on our native skill in balancing plates of cold salmon, glasses of hock, and strawberries and cream on our knees in the car. But in fine weather the Glyndebourne picnic is a fine sight and an occasion which gives one a feeling of well-being and magnanimity towards the next act no Crush Bar sandwich scramble can ever provide. There are, inevitably, one or two visitors to Glyndebourne who have not yet caught up with recent international developments in the picnic world, and only recently I was saddened to see the occupants of one of those cars on which the loudest noise is the electric clock, drinking claret out of plastic mugs.

Speaking from my experiences as a critic in the 1935 season the prospect of eating even the most elaborate and sumptuous picnic in the car park was not one that would have appealed to me or any of my colleagues; for this was the year that Glyndebourne employed a firm of Press agents for the first time. On the recommendation of C. B. Cochran, who had used them for years, the firm of Leadley's took over the publicity, and one of their duties was to entertain the Press to dinner at first nights. It was a duty they discharged brilliantly and memorably.

It was in this season that the Glyndebourne wine list had a more ambitious look (the quality of its roneo'd contents in 1934 had never been in doubt, of course). In August 1934 John Christie and Hamish Wilson had gone to Germany and in the course of their journey had set aside an afternoon for wine-tasting with a view to stocking the Glyndebourne cellars. Christie did not hold with the *chichi* of professional wine tasting; he would spit out a mouthful of wine only if it was undrinkable. Adhering firmly to this principle Christie and Wilson sat down at a long table by themselves and together, methodically and critically, drank twenty-one bottles of Rhine, Moselle and Saar wine between them. They sat at a long table so that the empty bottles could be lined up on it for easy reference.

This pleasant afternoon's work produced five wines considered fit for the Glyndebourne Wine List, which was now printed and consisted of eleven items – five Rhine wines, one Moselle, one Saar wine, two Burgundies, a port and a champagne. The

German wines were annotated in a helpful, schoolmasterly manner mercifully free of any fancy wine writing.

The Wachenheimer Rechbächl Riesling Auslese 1929 which had cost 35s in 1934 was now top of the bill at 23s. We were told that it was 'A good wine of medium sweetness'. The note also explained: 'Riesling is the name of a particular grape variety. Auslese means that the wine is made from selected bunches.'

Of the 1931 Niersteiner-Fuchsloch: 'A very good rather sweet wine. This wine won the Prize of the Prussian Government.' The 1932 Forster Ungeheuer Gewürztraminer, originating at the Reichsrat von Buhl'sche Weingut Deidesheim, merited the longest comment of all: 'A good dry wine. von Buhl is one of the three most important names in the Pfälzer Weine. The other two important names are Basserman-Jordon and Bürklin-Wolf.' This Forster Ungeheuer (15s) was given to the Press at dinner and was excellent. I don't think it was intended as a bribe, but it was surprising how friendly it made us feel towards the management nevertheless.

The number of bottles of wine sold in the 1935 season showed an improvement on the year before. In the course of 25 dinner intervals 966 bottles were sold; this was an average of about 38 bottles a performance and an increase of more than 700 per cent over the alleged nightly average of the previous year; but still not a very impressive rate of consumption for an audience of between two and three hundred, even allowing for the car park picnic absentees.

What one might regard as a successful side show at Glyndebourne in 1935 was the issue of the first records by the cast of the inaugural *Figaro*. These records, made just after the 1934 season in the Festival Opera House itself, were issued by HMV as the first volume of the newly formed Mozart Opera Society and were available only to subscribers. The volume of six records consisted only of the concerted music from the opera. If the first volume proved a success the Mozart Opera Society intended to record the rest of the opera, which would be released in two further volumes. Fortunately the first instalment was successful and the second and third volumes were issued simultaneously later in the year – Volume II containing the Overture, arias and duets from Acts I and II, Volume III the arias and duets from Acts III and IV. One effect of this cock-eyed method of issuing the first 'complete' *Figaro* (no recitatives were included except those with orchestral accompaniment) was that it was impossible without six turntables and half a dozen sets of records to get a continuous reproduction of the Glyndebourne performance. If the reception of the first volume had not justified the recording of the sequels we would presumably never have known how the Glyndebourne principals sounded in their solo scenes. As things turned out, however, it wouldn't really have mattered so terribly (though it might have left a certain amount of curiosity unsatisfied), because the ensemble passages of Volume I were far and away more satisfactory than the rest of the recording. This first production had triumphed through the quality of its ensembles, whereas the individual performances, listened to in an atmosphere far removed from the friendly glow of an evening at Glyndebourne, were by no means outstanding. I have already mentioned how little these records told us of Audrey Mildmay's inimitable performance of Susanna; it may also be added that at no time during this period did Fritz Busch conduct *Figaro* so woodenly as – for some unexplained reason – he did in the second two volumes of this recording. Volumes II and III, it should be noted, were recorded after the end of the 1935 season, which explains how Italo Tajo came to sing the part of Dr Bartolo in Volume II. Tajo, who made his first big impression on the British public as Banquo in the Glyndebourne *Macbeth* in Edinburgh in 1947, was 20 years old at this time. Busch had auditioned him in Turin earlier in the year and had persuaded him to come to Glyndebourne and study Mozart roles while he sang in the chorus. In the volume of *Figaro* ensembles Norman Allin, as the Bartolo of 1934, had sung the part, but as he was not available for the later recording Tajo sang the first act aria, 'La vendetta'. Busch had a great admiration for Italo Tajo, who figures in much of the subsequent pre-war correspondence concerned with Glyndebourne casting.

Apart from the irritating manner and method of their issue, the Mozart Opera Society records of *Figaro* were distinguished by some pretty remarkable notes in the brochure that accompanied them. What got firmly under W. J. Turner's skin was the sentence:

The Countess' music has for its period an emotional truth comparable with the most expressive phrases of the best of Wagner and Strauss.

In his review in the *New Statesman* Turner commented that the 'Mozart Opera Society must be congratulated on having found somebody who could utter a dictum of such appalling impropriety'. My own reaction was to wonder who they thought Mozart was. 'For its period' is one of the classic inanities of all time. Thanks to the experience of Mozart provided in this country by Glyndebourne over the years, modern record annotations on Mozart's operas are now a little less gormless; though not always.

The 1935 season ended with a deficit of about £10,000 (£3,000 more than in 1934), and all underwritten of course by John Christie personally. He was convinced, however, that within a couple of years the losses could be turned into a small profit at any rate. Christie had already announced the alterations to the made to the theatre in time for the 1936 season in the plans printed in the programme. The repertoire for the following season was published in November, and proved to be less varied than newspaper specu-lation would have led us to expect. There had been confident predictions that either *Falstaff*, *Beatrice and Benedict*, or *Fidelio* would be produced at Glyndebourne. The anony-mous contributor to *Truth*, whose refreshingly vigorous anti-Wagnerian identity I have still not learned, forecast the addition of *Don Giovanni* to the programme. He proved to be correct. The 1936 season would begin on 29 May and last until 5 July. There would be 35 performances and the repertoire would consist of all five of the most famous Mozart operas – *Figaro*, *Così fan tutte*, *The Magic Flute*, *Die Entführung* and *Don Giovanni*. It was announced at the same time that a subscription scheme had been arranged which would include a seat and a 10s dinner at each of the operas for a total outlay of £13 5s (this was later reduced to £11). Those who did not wish to become subscribers were urged to buy the newly devised Glyndebourne Seat Tokens and give them as Christmas presents. The tokens were advertised in the Press and also on boards carried by sandwichmen hired by the Management to parade up and down outside Queen's Hall before and after the concerts. I don't know how effective this outdoor advertising was, but to most people Glyndebourne seemed impossibly remote on a wet November night.

Looking back on the general impression left by the second Glyndebourne season it seems that on the whole most people now knew what it was all about; we had no more vague chatter in the papers about 'Village Opera', and the like. In the course of twelve months the Festival Opera had established itself firmly on the international scene and it brought considerable satisfaction to all concerned to note the firm insistence by Jack Westrup and Francis Toye in their newspaper dispatches from the Salzburg Festival in August that any Mozart Salzburg could do, Glyndebourne could do better.

Only two newspaper stories were published during the season that suggested their writers had not done all their homework. One was a report that a party of enthusiastic Frenchmen had travelled from Dieppe to Folkstone and thence to Glyndebourne, returning by the same route after the final curtain – a method of going to Birmingham by way (almost literally) of Beachy Head if ever there was one. The other story told us that Aulikki Rautawaara was a New Zealander – which, when you think of it, is certainly a name with a Maori ring to it. Geography, however, as these two stories showed, has never been the English reporter's strong point. Upper Berkeley Street is still always described as Mayfair.

At the end of the season Rudolf Bing replaced Alfred Nightingale as General Manger.

CHAPTER ELEVEN

1936 **A strictly qualified success**

THE NEW YEAR OPENED QUIETLY for Glyndebourne. The public's curiosity about the coming season's plans had already been satisfied in November, and the most sparkling news item anybody could think of to lighten the winter darkness of the early days of 1936 was the announcement in the three 'serious' national newspapers that Alexander Kipnis had been engaged to sing Sarastro in *The Magic Flute* and that David Franklin would sing the Commendatore in *Don Giovanni*.

Nearer home the local Sussex papers reported an event which was to make life considerably easier for many of Glyndebourne's supporters – the formation of the Glyndebourne Sunday Opera Club. In order to 'air the matter', Mr Charles Adams, Christie's solicitor and a former pupil of his at Eton, while successfully applying at Lewes Petty Sessions for the renewal of the theatre's licence, publicly announced that the Sunday Opera Club was being formed. The Bench was assured that there was not the slightest intention of introducing 'what is known as the "Continental Sunday" '. The idea on which the Opera Club was founded was entirely different from that, counsel explained. This was received with relief all round, though if there is one feature more characteristic of Sunday on the Continent than horse racing it is surely the performance of opera. However, the Bench did not object; as it pointed out, private performances were none of its business anyway.

While the public waited patiently for the months to pass until the third Glyndebourne season opened, a welcome and diverting interlude was spontaneously provided by John Christie. In a speech in March delivered as guest of the Sussex Women Musicians' Club at the Old Ship in Brighton, Christie announced: 'If an English composer is prepared to write an opera which the staff at Glyndebourne regarded as really good, we shall be prepared to put it on.' He discussed his offer further in a letter sent a few days later to *The Times*, the *Telegraph* and the *Morning Post*. 'The opera must be suitable for our stage and our acoustics and the composer should make himself acquainted with these matters beforehand ... The casting of the chief parts should be arranged with us beforehand.' Christie also added that the works of British composers of opera had hitherto 'inevitably failed' because they had been produced under 'scratch conditions'.

Not unnaturally John Christie's letter got a poor reception from the correspondence columnists; conductors and singers were particularly annoyed at the suggestion that Beecham's successful promotion of English opera by Ethel Smyth, Stanford and Delius had been under 'scratch conditions'. But what riled most of all was Christie's tone of condescension. Sumner Austin, who was Lilian Bayliss's chief producer at Sadler's Wells, was heavily scornful in his reply to the *Daily Telegraph* of Christie's wish to give 'the poor composer a chance', and it was 'good to know that when Mr Christie, Herr Busch, Herr Oppenheim and Herr Ebert shall approve an English opera it will at last receive its due reward upon the miniature but gilded boards of the Festival Theatre in the Sussex Downs'.

Julius Harrison, conductor of the Hastings Municipal Orchestra, ended his letter: 'The organization at Glyndebourne is essentially German. Mr Christie models his whole scheme on Munich and Salzburg and glories in it. None of us mind that, and if Mr Christie can establish a musical pilgrimage to his beautiful little Sussex opera house it is all to the good. But if he imagines that British composers are going to rush in to submit their operas to his very un-British musical staff he is in for disillusionment ...'

That Julius Harrison, who had been associated with the old Beecham Opera Company, as well as with the BNOC throughout its five years' existence, should have been aroused by his attitude cannot really have surprised Christie, for not long before he had written to Harrison suggesting that he should get the Hastings Corporation to buy him tickets for Glyndebourne and so enable him 'to keep in touch with what can be done'.

Whether the cost of a seat prevented them from getting acquainted with the stage and acoustics of Glyndebourne, or whether they were just not greatly attracted by the idea anyway, no composer of any note is reported to have made any attempt to impress John Christie's musical staff. Nevertheless, in an address on British opera during the East Sussex and West Kent Music Festival at Tunbridge Wells not long after the first announcement of his offer, Christie stated that he refused to believe composers could not do the work. Since his new venture started, he continued, the postman had been groaning under the weight of manuscripts, the chief characteristic of which was not their excellence, but the complete disregard of the conditions with which the opera must comply. He believed it to be important that singers should sing what one actually said, and the librettist must understand what would 'come over' on the stage. In other words he must be a playwright.

After remarking that he did not think poets were paying attention to the problem, and that they had to be stirred up to do their part, John Christie was reported in the local paper as saying:

'I refuse to put on an opera with an unpleasant subject like *Salome*. It may be a great opera but if it is unpleasant, I will not put it on.' (Applause)

This seems a bit of a *non sequitur* in the context, but perhaps something got lost in the sub-editorial wash somewhere.

These words in the *Tunbridge Wells Advertiser* were virtually the last to appear on the subject of what was regarded – according to personal taste – as Christie's offer, challenge or insult to British composers.

It remained only for 'one of the best of our British composers' (he stayed obstinately unidentified) to make the final most reasonable comment to a *Daily Mail* columnist:

I very much doubt if Glyndebourne would make it worth while for any composer to expend the thought and immense labour of writing an opera, which in order to conform to the usual length would take from nine months to a year.

If the stage and acoustics are so unique at Glyndebourne, one can only conclude that a work written for that opera house will be unsuitable acoustically for any other. As this theatre is so exceptionally fine for Mozart operas, any work of Puccini or Wagner will be out of the question. Therefore the new British work will have to conform to the methods of Mozart, a difficult composer with whom to compete!

If the opera is to be written with special regard for the Glyndebourne singers' capabilities, then it will most likely be unsuitable for any other singers in any other opera house. Therefore, it seems that the opera would get too few performances to recompense the composer for his year of work.

If Mr Christie is really keen to add a British opera to his repertoire, the obvious thing would be to commission an opera from one of our composers who have been proved to have a flair necessary to good stage music.

With less than a couple of months to go to the start of the 1936 season public attention was now suddenly drawn to the announcement that Gaumont-British had signed up Aulikki Rautawaara as Britain's answer to Grace Moore. Miss Rautawaara, it was reported, had had the shape of her nose altered by a Harley Street plastic surgeon to conform to film industry standards; and she was looking for a new name, as her own was clearly unmanageable by the ninepennies. The film company also mentioned, as a kind of after-thought, that they were looking feverishly for a story in which to star their discovery. None of this affected Aulikki Rautawaara's commitments at Glyndebourne, of course; nor, apparently, did any of it affect the history of British films either. After its initial explosion the Gaumont-British story faded quietly away to sink without trace among a hundred thousand sensationally optimistic pronouncements of its kind.

Meanwhile, though there was nothing comparable to the Souez crisis of the previous year, preparations for the new season had not been going altogether smoothly at Glynde-bourne. Firstly, Charles B. Cochran had shown that it was not just the food, drink and the Glyndebourne lighting that had impressed him on his visit to *The Magic Flute* in 1935. He had been very struck by the charm and talent of Irene Eisinger and had signed her up for his Adelphi revue, *Follow the Sun*, in which she sang 'Love is a Dancing Thing', and Osbert Sitwell, William Walton and Cecil Beaton collaborated in a ballet. This left Glyndebourne without a Papagena, a Despina and a Blonde who had been one of the great personal successes of the first two seasons. There was, however, some consolation for Miss Eisinger's admirers in the issue in April of the Mozart Opera Society's records of *Così fan tutte* in which she sang Despina. The recording was complete inasmuch as it omitted only those numbers that were cut in performance at Glyndebourne; it included the recitatives (accompanied on the piano by Busch); and the records were released in the proper order instead of in the muddled form of the *Figaro* volumes. Vocally the *Così fan tutte* was incomparably better all round than the earlier venture, with Ina Souez repeating the brilliant performance she had given of Fiordiligi in the opera house.

Miss Eisinger did in fact make one brief appearance at Glyndebourne in 1936, but before the opera season opened. This was on the occasion of a Sunday afternoon concert given at the presentation to Mr and Mrs Christie of a George I silver mug to commemorate the birth of their son George on 31 December 1934. The gift was from 600 of Christie's employees and tenants whose signatures were in an album presented at the same time. Owing to the number of guests invited (they came from the Devonshire and Sussex estates as well as from Christie businesses as far away as Newcastle), the concert was given twice – once before and once after the presentation. Irene Eisinger sang one item on each occasion, opening the programme with the Aquarellen waltz of Josef Strauss. Audrey Mildmay, David Franklin and Roy Henderson sang groups of songs, Jani Strasser and Hans Oppenheim accompanied, and during the afternoon George Austin, organist of Ringmer Church, gave a short recital on the instrument in the Organ Room.

In addition to the abduction of Irene Eisinger from the Glyndebourne seraglio it was discovered in the middle of April that Willi Domgraf-Fassbaender would not be available. He had been seriously ill for several months and had not recovered in time to take the lead in *Don Giovanni* or to repeat his appearances as Figaro and Guglielmo. It was announced therefore that John Brownlee, who had been contracted to alternate in the part with Fassbaender, would sing Don Giovanni at all performances, Roy Henderson (already booked as Papageno) would sing Guglielmo, and Mariano Stabile would sing Figaro. The engagement of Stabile (by a person he referred to in all his correspondence as 'Signor Crysti') brought an artist of international repute to Glyndebourne for the first time, for he had appeared frequently at Covent Garden from 1926 to 1931. He had also, only the previous summer, sung Falstaff in Toscanini's unforgettable performances of Verdi's opera at Salzburg.

The 1936 season opened at 6.45 p.m. on the chilly evening of 29 May with *Don Giovanni*, and for the third time running the first night performance proved a startling ear-opener to audience and critics. The first *Figaro* had demonstrated the strength of the Glyndebourne ensemble; the first *Magic Flute* had been a unique experience of the musical greatness discovered in the opera by Fritz Busch. The first Glyndebourne *Don Giovanni* was a performance that left no corner unilluminated of this score's miraculous variety. Those singers whom we had already come to regard as the resident company at Glyndebourne all contributed memorable performances. Ina Souez was a superbly fiery and brilliant Donna Anna; Luise Helletsgruber made a touchingly human figure of the bewildered, illogical, lovable Donna Elvira; Audrey Mildmay was bewitching and unforgettable as Zerlina, a part which seemed to suit her better all round than Susanna whose great serious moment in the last act had been a little beyond her vocal and emotional grasp; Roy Henderson brought a new look to Masetto, who according to Mozart's characterization of him is young, sympathetic, determined and a little awkward, but never the half-witted oaf so many singers and producers have made of him. Henderson's was an exceptional performance.

John Brownlee, after a busy season at Covent Garden, where he had already sung Rigoletto, Scarpia and Amonasro before Glyndebourne opened, was a handsome, virile Don Giovanni, with a pretty leg but lacking the touch of evil which made Pinza so magnificent in the part at Salzburg later the same year. Don Ottavio was sung by Koloman von Pataky, who didn't make much of an impression, but David Franklin, making his first appearance on any stage, showed obvious and encouraging promise as the Commendatore.

The real hit of the show was the Leporello of Salvatore Baccaloni who, like Stabile, had been guided in his earlier career by Toscanini. Baccaloni was short, fat, with a round and naturally comic face, and gave a performance – reeking of garlic and olive oil, as somebody said – that was a classic of rich *buffo* singing such as had not been enjoyed in England for years. Not the least brilliant part of his playing, of course, was the speed and naturalness of his recitatives which inevitably showed up his non-Italian colleagues. (Both Audrey Mildmay and Roy Henderson came in for some criticism of their Italian pronunciation this time. Luise Helletsgruber, on the other hand, had improved since her first season.)

For the first time since Glyndebourne began in 1934 there was some general and sharp criticism in the Press of Carl Ebert's production. Two points were particularly and widely picked on. The first was at the end of Scene 4 of Act I when the curtain was brought down (for a scene change) before the trio of Masks had sung their 'Protegga il giusto cielo', thus forcing Anna, Elvira and Ottavio to sing it in front of the curtain as though they were asking the protection of the audience instead of invoking heaven's justice in the dark garden outside Don Giovanni's villa before entering the ballroom.

The other incident that jarred was the gratuitous introduction of a lot of near-naked courtesans at Don Giovanni's supper table in the last act – a bit of 'production' which was considered vulgar without being relevant. Richard Capell in the *Daily Telegraph* wrote: 'We had expected better of Ebert'; Eric Blom described it in the *Birmingham Post* as a typical 'wrong-headed German tradition'. (The *Times* critic concurred with his colleagues' judgment but alone among the critics of the national dailies did not tell his readers so until the Monday after the Friday of the first night. What appeared on the Saturday was a notice which, if not disgruntled, was, in P. G. Wodehouse's immortal phrase, far from gruntled; the 6.45 start of the opera had been much too late for *The Times* which in those days went to bed at a notoriously early hour – in this case, long before the end of the second act – and the greater part of the piece was taken up by telling us so.)

The two major blots on the original Glyndebourne *Don Giovanni* have now been removed, of course, but it took the interval of a world war and many years of what some call 're-thinking', but others regard as using ordinary commonsense, before they were got rid of.

Though their names were not mentioned in the programme an important contribution to this *Don Giovanni* was made by the amateur musicians who played on the stage in the ballroom scene. As funds would not run to a professional band the Musicians' Union, to its eternal credit, raised no objection to Glyndebourne's employment of amateurs, reasoning that it made better economic sense to keep a professional orchestra working in the pit and have amateurs on the stage than to demand a closed shop which John Christie couldn't afford and which, if insisted upon, could only result in no work for anybody.

The stage band amateurs were recruited largely from the National Physical Laboratory at Teddington, together with one or two students from the Royal College and Royal Academy of Music, and a few local musicians like Mrs Stutchbury, who put aside her violoncello on this occasion to play the double bass. Deputies were allowed, of course, but had to make do with the costumes originally made for those they were replacing. This led to some bizarre effects.

Life in the amateur stage band at this first *Don Giovanni* was not without its hazards and incidents, and there was a moment of panic one evening when, not long before the players were to appear, a professor from the National Physical Laboratory fainted from the heat. A lady in the orchestra went to his assistance and tried to loosen what she thought was his brightly patterned cretonne vest; she discovered he was not wearing a vest. The bright patterns were tattooed on his chest and she promptly fainted away as well. Both casualties were successfully brought round in time for their call.

The first act of the première of *Don Giovanni* was relayed by the BBC and with the broadcast there began an association which, though regarded with some suspicion by John Christie at first, quickly became a regular and important feature of British broadcasting. That there was no relay from Glyndebourne until the third season was not for want of trying by the Corporation. In 1934 the BBC had approached Christie but the money offered was too little and it was rejected. In 1935 the offer was raised, but not enough. In 1936 Christie suddenly took the initiative and told the BBC they could broadcast from Glyndebourne for nothing. This offer had to be refused, of course, for whatever its policy may be towards artists, speakers and writers, when the BBC is actually faced with something for nothing it finds its principles will not permit its acceptance. Money accordingly changed hands over the *Don Giovanni* broadcast, though how much it amounted to is not recorded. In addition to the first act of *Don Giovanni* the BBC also broadcast Acts I and II of *Figaro* (which were constantly disturbed by thunderstorms) and the second act of *The Magic Flute*, though neither of these transmissions was from a first night. For these relays the BBC engineers were given a dressing room as a control point and a great deal was made of the novelty of the surroundings by slinging microphones among the Glyndebourne trees to capture the authentic atmosphere of birds singing, sheep bleating and cows mooing before giving Fritz Busch his cue to go into the pit.

On the second night of the season *The Magic Flute* was given, conducted this time not by Busch, but by his assistant on the musical staff, Hans Oppenheim. It had been John Christie's express wish that Oppenheim should conduct and prepare *The Magic Flute* all on his own and Busch, with a repertoire now consisting of five operas, had agreed to it; Oppenheim, after all, had been coached in his coaching of the 1935 *Magic Flute* by Busch.

Unfortunately, another member of Busch's staff cut up rough at the apparent favouritism shown to Oppenheim, and protesting plainly that he considered himself just as worthy of being entrusted with the direction and preparation of an entire opera at Glyndebourne, refused to play the glockenspiel in the orchestra and behind the scenes in the opera for Oppenheim as he had done for Busch. It was an irritating situation that Busch dealt with in typical fashion.

'He is quite right to worry about his prestige and his future,' Busch wrote to Bing, 'although I don't understand this attitude and have never adopted it myself. However, I let him make his point and told him I would take his place at the glockenspiel and back-stage if Oppenheim can't find a good substitute.'

It is disappointing to have to record that, after all this, Hans Oppenheim was not a success as a conductor. He proved, according to one critic, 'too much of a time-keeper'; W. J. Turner, staunchest of Glyndebourne supporters, said bluntly that under Oppenheim the orchestral playing dropped quite perceptibly in intensity, in subtlety and in precision to something like the average level in a good opera house. 'This may be good, but it is not good enough for Glyndebourne.'

The performance as a whole, indeed, was not so well received as the year before. Noel Eadie as the Queen of the Night suffered from a punishing cold and had to ask the audience's indulgence for her omission of the top F's; Alexander Kipnis as Sarastro was disappointing to those who had heard him in Wagner; the Danish tenor, Thorkild Noval, was a personable young man but not at ease with Mozart's style. Aulikki Raut-awaara – perhaps as a result of her dealings with the film world? – brought a sudden sophistication to her playing of Pamina which deprived her performance of the spon-taneity and innocence which had been so touching in her first *Magic Flute* at Glynde-bourne. Lili Heinemann had the thankless task of following Irene Eisinger in the part of Papagena, and though she gave a competent performance did nothing to make the audience forget her enchanting predecessor. Roy Henderson, on the other hand, was most successful as Papageno but obviously embarrassed by the silly routine – now more pointless than ever – of having to interpolate English gags.

After two or three performances of *The Magic Flute* under Oppenheim, Busch (at the urgent request of John Christie) took over the direction of the opera once more.

Meanwhile, after the disappointments of *The Magic Flute*, in which only Carl Ebert, now shown as 'Speaker (Act II)', had given a first class performance, there had been a welcome return to familiar Glyndebourne standards with the revival of *Figaro*.[1] Once again it was a triumph of ensemble but with the difference this time that at least two of the links in the chain were much stronger than they had been before. Mariano Stabile's Figaro was an inspired performance – complete, subtle, polished, revealing with an unfailing touch the cunning, the bitterness, the wit, anger and good humour that com-bine to make Figaro one of the most complex and difficult of all Mozart's characters. For

[1] Not only *The Times* but also the *Daily Telegraph* was beaten by the deadline on this occasion. Notices of the Wednesday première did not appear in these papers until Friday morning.

the first time at Glyndebourne Figaro's *recitativo secco* was delivered with conviction. Stabile was not only singing in his own language; he sang with the authority and confidence of an artist to whom opera was an instinctive, instead of an acquired, means of expression.

The critics were ecstatically unanimous in their enjoyment of Stabile's performance; to most he was just plain 'magnificent'; to others he was the best Figaro they had ever seen anywhere; to Francis Toye he dominated the action throughout ('as Figaro should'), and it was difficult to look at anybody else when he was on the stage. 'In short,' Toye's notice concluded, 'Stabile's Figaro is not unworthy to rank with the Falstaff which so electrified Salzburg last year. No praise can be higher than that.'

Like Stabile, Salvatore Baccaloni as a superbly droll, gone-to-seed Doctor Bartolo, gave the same unmistakable impression that opera was his natural form of self-expression.

Whether or not it was a result of playing opposite Mariano Stabile, the other outstanding performance of the 1936 *Figaro* was undoubtedly Audrey Mildmay as Susanna. Her Zerlina certainly remained an enchanting study, but if it had seemed on first hearing to be a more satisfactory performance than her Susanna of 1934 and 1935, it was because nobody had yet heard her Susanna of 1936. In a curious way Audrey Mildmay had matured and acquired an air of self-confidence which, on recognizing it, one was rather surprised to realize had not always been there. True, she had gained further purely theatrical experience of the part by singing it at Sadler's Wells in February 1936, when she had shown her Glyndebourne 'breeding' in an unmistakable fashion.[1] But back on her home ground she gave us a Susanna whose comedy was even more infectious, and whose voice had grown richer and more varied in tone and wider in its emotional range in a remarkable manner. It is a regrettable accident in the history of Glyndebourne that its recording of *Figaro* had to be made with the original cast instead of with the cast that sang in the 1936 season. Apart from preserving the classic performance of Mariano Stabile, it would have told posterity far more than the 1934 records, or the memories of those who heard it can ever tell, how Audrey Mildmay sang at her best.

Opinions of John Brownlee's first Count Almaviva were sharply divided: he was aristocratic; he was not aristocratic enough; he was dignified; he was too schoolboyish; it was the best thing he had done at Glyndebourne; he was colourless; he was vivid; he lacked vigour and intensity. It was not an undistinguished performance, but there have certainly been better at Glyndebourne since then.

As had happened with the first Glyndebourne *Figaro*, the shortcomings of some of the rest of the cast – the rather humourless Countess of Aulikki Rautawaara and Luise Helletsgruber's losing battle with the Italian of Cherubino's recitatives – were redeemed by isolated moments of individual distinction but were generally forgotten in the excellence of the over-all success of the performance as a model of ensemble.

---

[1] This production, with sets by Rex Whistler, inspired a notice which must have come as a relief to everybody. It was in the *Catholic Times* and ended: 'Mr Braithwaite conducted, and the orchestra played Mozart's music.'

Between them *Don Giovanni* and *The Magic Flute* had more performances than the other three operas in the 1936 repertoire put together – *Don Giovanni*, with 10 performances, setting a new high in the number of times any opera had been performed in a single season at Glyndebourne. To make this possible *Così fan tutte* was performed fewer times than ever before; its meagre schedule of three performances was extended to four by the addition of an extra performance on a Monday, a day on which, except at Whitsun, there was now normally no performance. The demand for an extra *Così fan tutte* was understandable for, with *Figaro*, it was the opera above all others that had become associated in the public mind with a visit to Glyndebourne. This year was no exception. The public's affection for 'Così fan' was justified and increased by the high standard of performance of the opera described by Francis Toye as Glyndebourne's Star Turn. Ina Souez and Luise Helletsgruber again shone as the two sisters, with Miss Souez once more providing the best singing of the whole season; Heddle Nash sang the only aria he was allowed with skill and warmth; Roy Henderson, giving the most convincing performance of his career at Glyndebourne, was considered a marked improvement on Fassbaender as Guglielmo; John Brownlee repeated his smooth but oddly uncynical, unmalevolent Don Alfonso. Despina was Tatiana Menotti, later the wife of Juan Oncina, the Spanish tenor who sang at Glyndebourne for ten consecutive seasons between 1952 and 1961.

In only one of the three roles with which she had become associated was Miss Eisinger's absence not publicly regretted in the Press. This was in the performance of *Die Entführung* where the part of Blonde was so excellently sung and played by the young German soprano Irma Beilke, from Dresden, that no comparisons needed to be made. Except for Heddle Nash, who sang Pedrillo again, and of course Carl Ebert who repeated his beautifully conceived Pasha Selim, the principals were all new to the Glyndebourne production.[1] The search for the ideal Constanze was no more successful than before; Julia Moor, a Swiss coloratura soprano, attacked her big aria bravely but was just not well enough equipped to master it. (The same singer also took Noel Eadie's place as the Queen of the Night in one of the performances of *The Magic Flute* before the opening of *Die Entführung*, but there is no record of how she fared as apparently the change of cast did not rate an invitation of critical opinion. Julia Moor's most noticeable failing was an exaggerated vibrato – or, in plain English, a distressing wobble – which can hardly have suited the Queen of the Night any more than it suited Constanze.)

The casting of Salvatore Baccaloni as Osmin was also not an unqualified success. He naturally made the audience laugh; he had a wonderfully comic face anyway. But his struggles with the German language, while they were disarming enough, did not exactly help to establish the character of one of Mozart's most original creations. Nor was Baccaloni's voice really capable of the low notes which are such an impressive feature of the part. It is obvious, on reflection, that the engagement of Baccaloni as Osmin was largely

---

[1] For one evening during the run Ebert's part as Selim was played by a member of the chorus – Erich Kunz, who later became famous with the Vienna Opera and sang Guglielmo in two Glyndebourne productions of *Così fan tutte* after the war.

a matter of economics. The convenience of having the singer of Sarastro double the part of Osmin every time cannot always be counted on. It had worked in 1935, but it was clearly impracticable in 1936, for by no stretch of the imagination could Alexander Kipnis have been considered comedian enough to have sung Osmin as well. It was going a little far, I think, to say, as the *Observer* said, that the production of *Die Entführung* 'was in some respects as near to being genuinely bad as Glyndebourne has got so far'. But over the years it must certainly be admitted that the least satisfactory of all Glyndebourne's Mozart performances have been of this inspired, high spirited *Singspiel*. The reason for this is that in the absence of first-rate singing – and this deceptively simple score makes some spectacular demands on the singers – vocal shortcomings cannot be as easily disguised by an excellent ensemble as they can in *Figaro*, for instance. It is not an opera, in other words, in which the whole is greater than the sum of its parts, or which can leave a favourable 'over-all' impression. The individual artists must all be superlatively good, or *Die Entführung* is nothing.

The production of *Die Entführung* at last enabled *The Times* to print its notice in the next day's paper. This was because, for the first time in the history of Glyndebourne, the première of an opera was given for the exclusive benefit of the Glyndebourne Sunday Opera Club.

The deficit on the 1936 season at Glyndebourne was £4,000 – an encouraging figure compared with the losses of the year before and obviously helped along by the healthy increase in the wine sales to 2,500 bottles, an average nightly consumption of over 80 bottles per audience.

It was this summer that the famous wine list with the Greek quotations appeared at Glyndebourne. Most, if not all, of these quotations, which John Christie proudly and lovingly attributed to his great athletic and scholarly friend, C. M. Wells, were in fact supplied by Audrey Mildmay's father, the Rev Aubrey St John Mildmay. But Christie's detestation of his father-in-law was so violent and unrelenting that he refused to give him any credit for his homework or thanks for his help and insisted that C. M. Wells was responsible for the whole thing.

There was no crib for those students of the wine list who didn't understand Greek. Ignorance of Greek, however, did not mean that the diner got nothing to drink. An average knowledge of wine was enough to recognize the quality of the items in the first wine list compiled and supplied at Glyndebourne by Dr O. W. Loeb.

The Greek quotations (if you understood Greek) were neither more nor less fanciful than some of the purple prose thought up by the professional writers on wine, and in some cases were infinitely wittier. The ten German wines on the list were accompanied by some pretty lyrical passages. The 1934 Forster Jesuitengarten Riesling, Spätlese, Wein- gut Dr Deinhard Deidesheim at 23s a bottle brought forth Homer's 'It smells of violets and it smells of roses and it smells of hyacinth', while a 35s bottle of 1934 Wehlener Sonnenuhr feinste Auslese Weingut Pruem was considered to merit Diphilus's 'You persuade a sullen man to laugh'.

There were two champagnes, one of which was recommended by the words 'I like the widow most wonderfully', attributed to an author given as ('Who?'). Finally there was a solitary Burgundy listed at 10s a bottle and described in English as 'Unknown, Reputed to be 1924'. This, Dr Loeb noted on the copy of the wine list he sent me, was 'Definitely the "text" of Mr John Christie! !'

As the Glyndebourne season grew longer and the consumption of wine increased, the cellar in the house naturally became too small to hold the stock. To deal with this Christie constructed a huge cellar which can be seen by visitors as they drive the last hundred yards from Lewes to the Opera House. It is built into the side of the hill on the right and looks like a gun emplacement.

CHAPTER TWELVE

1937 **A change postponed**

NEITHER THE CORONATION NOR the Glyndebourne season for 1937 went quite according to original plans. The Abdication caused a change of cast in one, the refusal of a living composer to allow his opera to be performed at Glyndebourne upset the hopes of the other.

The third season had scarcely ended than Fritz Busch wrote a long letter to the Christies from the boat on his way to South America. It was written in English and began: 'The repertoire of the season 1937 at Glyndebourne is worrying me very much all the time so I thought a good deal about it on our voyage.' Busch then went on to suggest that another composer's work should be given beside Mozart's five operas. As these works had been played more or less by the same ensemble for three seasons there was a danger of routine taking the place of what Busch described as 'one of the most essential peculiarities of art: the artistical thrill'. Singers and orchestra, he insisted, now needed a change of atmosphere, and he went on to quote a passage by the anonymous critic of *Truth*, with which he said he completely agreed:

... but not a change merely for the sake of change. I mean that a festival of five operas by Mozart, if continued season after season without any other works, will be unfair to Mozart, especially as every one of these operas, with the possible exception of *Die Zauberflöte*, is a comic opera, no matter what its precise original designation may have been. Now, every great genius like Mozart has an individual style and outlook, and however great and universal he may be – and there is no composer greater than Mozart – we shall cease to respond fully to his work if we are given nothing else but it ...[1]

Fritz Busch's ambition was to produce Verdi's *Falstaff* as the ideal work to take its place alongside Mozart at Glyndebourne, but he feared that it would be 'the most expensive and most difficult' to put on. If, however, on account of Coronation Year and of 'John's

---

[1] There was much about the taste and forthright style of *Truth*'s anonymous critic that suggested W. J. Turner but I don't think it was Turner. At any rate, whoever it was he could produce pieces of advice like 'let him [Christie] eschew vigorously inferior composers such as Wagner ...' in the expression of a loathing of Wagner equalled in print in those days only by that of Constant Lambert, Cecil Gray and 'Mike' of the *Melody Maker*.

promises and speeches and words to the papers' it was proposed to stage an English opera there, drawing on his limited knowledge of British operatic literature, Busch suggested two works might be considered: *The Bride of Dionysus* by Sir Donald Tovey and *Sir John in Love* by Vaughan Williams. The opera by Tovey ('an old and very good friend of mine') was in Busch's opinion a more magnificent one and with 'a marvellous part for Audrey', but his music was unfortunately 'not at all yet very much estimated by his countrymen', so the work would have to wait.

Busch then enumerated the points for and against Vaughan Williams's opera. In its favour were the affection with which the composer was regarded in England and abroad, the fact that it was a 'real English' composer's work with a text by England's greatest dramatist, that it would be easy to produce with English singers only, and would fit in well with the Glyndebourne idea of the importance of ensemble; and it would not involve a larger orchestra like *Falstaff*. Against what he called 'the acception' of Vaughan Williams's opera Busch put forward the poor invention of the music, the great likeness to Verdi's masterpiece which would inevitably lead to unfavourable comparison, the lack of a part for Audrey Mildmay, and the weakness of the curtains compared with those in Verdi's opera. The work, Busch concluded, was not important enough to 'pass in a repertoire beside Mozart'. If, on the other hand, by putting on *Sir John in Love* Glyndebourne could get financial help from 'the BBC Corporation' then it might be worth while, but in the absence of this Busch was in favour of leaving the work alone.

As 'a last solution' Busch suggested they should do an opera by Gluck. He proposed *Orphée et Eurydice* in its second, French version; Eurydice would give Audrey Mildmay an excellent part and Aulikki Rautawaara would be Eros. As Orpheus Busch recommended Karin Branzell, a fine Swedish singer from the New York Metropolitan.

In due course Fritz Busch heard from Glyndebourne. Vaughan Williams had refused to allow *Sir John in Love* to be performed there; he had frequently criticized Glyndebourne and its policy, and the situation was ethically impossible; furthermore, he said, nobody would come to hear the opera anyway, and that would do *him* harm as well as Glyndebourne.

The idea of Gluck's *Orphée* was resolutely opposed by John Christie. He had heard the work at Salzburg and had been extremely bored by it, he said. The fact that he did not mind Gluck's opera being sung in Italian at Glyndebourne in 1947, although the score used then was of the French revision, suggests that it was not the music but the prospect of its being sung in French that appalled him about Busch's suggestion – although to be fair, when he had been so bored by the opera at Salzburg it had been sung in German. Christie's dislike of French opera was oddly deep-rooted, and though he accepted *Le Comte Ory* (one supposes because the composer was Italian) his prejudice was not finally broken down even in the year of his death, when he heard *Pelléas et Mélisande* and tried hard, but failed, to like it. Why he should have countenanced a French opera by Rossini, but not one by Gluck – who wasn't French either – has never been explained.

With Vaughan Williams's refusal to co-operate over *Sir John in Love* and his own flat rejection of Busch's proposal of *Orphée*, Christie continued to talk of a project which had now become dear to his heart: the idea of staging *Don Pasquale* and *La traviata* for Audrey Mildmay. When the autumn of 1936 came, however, it was decided that the 1937 repertoire would be entirely Mozart once again, but with the omission of *Die Entführung* which Busch considered was impossible without first-class singers and which he felt that neither John Christie nor his wife had liked in its previous year's production anyway. Christie argued that they must have at any rate three performances of *Die Entführung* in the Coronation Season, otherwise it would be thought Glyndebourne knew it wasn't good. Busch replied that he would accept responsibility for *Die Entführung* only with a first-class cast. He would agree to include the opera in the repertoire on condition that if it proved impossible to collect a first-rate company the three scheduled performances would be cancelled, the reason for their cancellation announced, and three extra performances of other operas given instead. It was Busch's view that only Irma Beilke had been hundred-per-cent successful; he considered her better than Irene Eisinger. As for Baccaloni, he should sing all the Leporellos and Bartolos in the 1937 season, but as Osmin, Busch emphasized, 'he is out for the rest of my life'.

Having persuaded Busch to include *Die Entführung*, Christie suggested that as it was the shortest of the five Mozart operas it might be preceded, as a curtain raiser, by Pergolesi's *La serva padrona* 'as a sop to the public in the nature of a new opera'. With quite startling unanimity and promptness Busch, Ebert and Bing slapped down on Christie's idea sharply. None of them liked the opera, nobody ever put on a curtain raiser to *Die Entführung* in any country they knew of, and since the performances of Mozart's opera would be sold out anyway, what was the point of spending money on *La serva padrona* which would add nothing either to Glyndebourne's reputation or box office takings? No more was heard of *La serva padrona* which, as far as the history of Glyndebourne is concerned, has remained a pre-historic incident. Obviously John Christie had a soft spot for this little opera; it seems sad that he should never have been allowed to hear it again in his own theatre after the Boyd Neel try-out.

But if Busch, Ebert and Christie were disappointed in their individual ways at the lack of novelty in the 1937 programme, at least Bing was satisfied by the prospect once more of an exclusively Mozart repertoire. It provided, he said, a great opportunity to remind the world by publicity 'that one may still say Glyndebourne is the only place in the world where Mozart's five masterpieces are presented at the same time'.

The period between the 1936–7 seasons at Glyndebourne was once again a time dominated by the endless and exhausting frustration of negotiating with singers. It was not just a question of trying to find the right singers, but also, once having found them, of getting them to sign agreements they had long ago orally greeted with shouts of joy and protestations of undying loyalty, or getting them out of trouble with other concerns with whom they had naïvely signed entirely invalid contracts after signing up with Glyndebourne.

The biggest headache this time was Erna Berger, whom Busch badly wanted as Queen of the Night and Constanze. Nothing in the world would give her greater pleasure than to sing at Glyndebourne, she said, and while agreeing to the Festival Opera's offer she must first get permission from the Berlin Opera for leave of absence. She was granted the leave she needed. Then it all depended on whether General Goering, who seemed to have a finger in the Berlin opera pie, would agree to continue her salary while she was at Glyndebourne. He would not agree, so Miss Berger, who had meanwhile got as far as arranging where she would lodge in Lewes, asked for more money from Glyndebourne. But as Glyndebourne hadn't got it to give her, she never signed the contract. All this took up three months of everybody's valuable time and left Glyndebourne without a Queen of the Night and a Constanze with only a few weeks to go.

John Christie himself was as furious as any of them and asked Bing what steps they should take to stop Berger and Giulio Tomei singing at Covent Garden. Bing had to reply that Berger wasn't singing there and what had Tomei done to Mr Christie? He himself had never been in touch with him in his life.

The Erna Berger affair dragged on for three maddening and uncertain months before ending in disaster. The Baccaloni affair of 1936–7, on the other hand, took very nearly six months to settle, but at least it had a happy ending. Salvatore Baccaloni, asked back for *Don Giovanni* and *Figaro*, had signed his contract with Glyndebourne but later committed himself to appear at the Colón in Buenos Aires on dates which conflicted hopelessly with those he had agreed to with Glyndebourne. Poor Baccaloni got himself into a real buffo's muddle and it took the threat of a law suit, the help of the British Consul-General in Milan, the intervention of the Italian Confederazione nazionale fascista dei lavoratori dello spettacolo and an admirable telegram from Bing to get him out of it. Baccaloni had cabled requesting Glyndebourne to save him 'serious troubles' and recommended Fernando Autori to them. Bing replied: 'Request you save us serious troubles and recommend Autori to Buenos Aires.'

John Christie, all this time, was having a very rough passage at the hands of his Artistic Directors and General Manager. Every time he suggested a singer he wanted to engage he was firmly corrected by one or other of them. It was a rather sad situation – like a small boy trying to play with his trains, which he not only owned but had bought out of his pocket money, and always having them taken away from him. With the Coronation Season ahead Christie, backed up by his wife, was extra keen to have as many British singers as possible. They wanted Heddle Nash for Ottavio, for instance, but Busch said no; he was more interested in Dino Borgioli who had just had a great success in the part at the Salzburg Festival. Noel Eadie would not do as the Queen of the Night again, Christie was told; nor would his proposal for an English Sarastro. In a very stern letter Bing reminded Christie that the artistic direction had been entrusted exclusively to Busch and Ebert, and it would be fatal to the whole conception of Glyndebourne if the judgment of the two Artistic Directors were questioned and British artists were engaged merely because they were British. Both Busch and Ebert as well as he himself, Bing continued, had found many of the Nazi German and Fascist Italian artists extremely unsympathetic as people, and so far from being prejudiced in favour of continental singers, if anything they went out of their way to use British artists where it was possible. The first consideration, however, was not just to maintain the Glyndebourne standard

The Rising of the Moon, 1970: designer, Osbert Lancaster. *(Gravett)*

Macbeth, 1965, banquet scene. Designer, Emanuele Luzzati. *(Gravett)*

(left) George Christie in the Organ Room. *(Gravett)*

(below) Figaro, 1974: Evelyn Mandac (Susanna), Helena Jungwirth (Cherubino), Kiri Te Kanawa (Countess). *(Gravett)*

but to improve it; the Glyndebourne audience, Bing insisted, 'which has for so many seasons been spoilt at Covent Garden and all over the world by international celebrities and doesn't care a bit what nationality singers are ... will refuse to pay £2 to hear artists they can normally hear for 6s at Sadler's Wells.'

Bing went on to point out that the Glyndebourne public would continue to support high-class productions, but that the Incorporated Society of Musicians, who had accused Christie of not employing enough British artists, would be the last to come to his support if the public stayed away on account of falling standards caused by the patriotic but artistically fatal 'protection' of what Bing called 'middle and lower class singers'. It was the Incorporated Society's job to protect them, not Glyndebourne's.

Busch supported all that Bing had said, and received in return a letter in which Christie, if not convinced of his errors or aware of how close he had come to ending a beautiful friendship, agreed to let his Artistic Directors take responsibility for who should sing what. The letter ended with the characteristic coda:

> Best wishes and love from Glyndebourne to you and your family,
>   The dog is well,
>   Yours ever ...

Within less than a month, however, Christie was in trouble again; Heddle Nash had motored down to Glyndebourne and, obviously finding it very difficult to refuse the singer's point-blank request, Christie had agreed to his singing two performances of Don Ottavio in addition to the Pedrillo and Basilio he had already been invited back for. Once more things had to be sorted out – as indeed they seem to have been since quite early in the winter months when Bing had first had to rebuke him over the way he approached Herbert Alsen. Alsen, Bing pointed out, 'did not mind at all your frankly telling him you did not like his Pogner. He did, however, mind your expecting him, after being chosen by Toscanini [in *Meistersinger*] and Bruno Walter [as Osmin] for leading parts in the Salzburg Festival, to approach a Mr Strasser – entirely unknown to him – to give an audition.' Alsen, said Bing, was very interested in coming to Glyndebourne and although he was one of the world's leading basses he was naturally prepared to sing for Busch and Ebert – preferably, of course, in a performance at the Vienna State Opera. Busch went to Vienna and confirmed his engagement.

The defection of Erna Berger left the choice of a Queen of the Night between two Russian sopranos – one was called Wischnevskaya, the other Lissitschkina. The second was eventually engaged. Her full name was Sinaida Silberschmidt-Lissitschkina, she had been born in Astrakhan and she was a Nicaraguan national. I don't think Fritz Busch ever managed to get her name right. In the letters he wrote by hand he gave up the struggle and called her Fräulein Lisipikituziwenska, while in his typewriting the name came out as Likitikimirikanusskawaska and would have been even longer if he had not come to the end of the line.

During the uncertainty of the Baccaloni episode Busch was prepared for the worst and made plans to have Italo Tajo sing Leporello. If by any chance Tajo fell through he was nevertheless insistent that only an Italian should sing the part at Glyndebourne. Busch found Ebert's suggestion that a German singer called Theo Hermann should take the part 'astonishing'. To begin with, no German was lively enough to sing Leporello; secondly, Hermann had been singing the part only recently during the Dresden Opera's visit to Covent Garden; and thirdly, if Hermann was all that good, how could Hamburg (where he was engaged) spare him for two whole months? (This, at any rate, is how Busch felt about things at the time. When he conducted *Don Giovanni* for Glyndebourne in 1951 his Leporello was shared by an Austrian and an Englishman. He was at least consistent about not having a German, even if he didn't have an Italian in the part.)

As if there were not enough to do to get the Festival Opera Season on as planned (or even not as planned), it seems to have been the lot of the General Manager ever since the beginning at Glyndebourne to find himself involved with projects, prospects and problems which, while not relevant to the immediate business in hand, nevertheless cannot be shelved. One of the major distractions during Bing's preparations for the 1937 season was the possibility of staging a Glyndebourne Festival Opera season in London. Sir Oswald Stoll, who had been to Glyndebourne and enjoyed himself, wanted to present a Glyndebourne season at his theatre referred to by Bing as the 'Colosseum', during which all the talents of the Festival Opera would unite in the production on a grand Coliseum scale of *Aida*. The idea fell through but not before there had been much serious discussion of it. Looking back, it is a pity Stoll's scheme never came off; the Coliseum, which had been the scene of several Diaghilev premières, was a superbly equipped theatre with an enormous revolving stage – the first in London – and would have been a wonderful place to mount a spectacular opera.

The final hitch in the preparations for the season at Glyndebourne was caused by the sudden illness of Audrey Mildmay. In the middle of April she was in a nursing home and so hoarse she could barely speak; it soon became obvious that she would not be able to sing at all in the coming Festival. For the first time since the Opera's foundation she ceased to lead two lives at Glyndebourne, and became wholly Mrs Christie. Even so she was not well enough to watch her two-year-old son George plant the Silver Jubilee Oak on Ringmer Green. The Jubilee of King George and Queen Mary had, of course, already been nationally celebrated in 1935, but as George Christie was at that time too small to plant commemorative oaks even with the help of Mr Harvey, the ceremony had understandably been postponed until he was old enough to perform it properly. The straggly ilex sapling planted in April 1937 has now grown into a sizeable tree; it stands about 20 ft high at the western end of the Green, opposite the Anchor and the Parish Hall, where it may be seen by visitors coming to the Opera from London or from the east along A 265.

The 1937 season opened at 5.15 p.m. on Wednesday 19 May with *Don Giovanni*. The curtain rose especially early, as it was to rise on all first nights during the Festival, in order to accommodate those critics whose papers otherwise went to bed too soon to carry a notice in the following morning's issue. There were three changes from the cast that had sung the opera in 1936. Norman Walker, the English bass who died not long ago, aged only 55, was impressive as the Commendatore, Marita Farell, a pretty young Czech, took the part of Zerlina, but as the normally heartless critics were rather sentimentally moved to point out, it was difficult for the Glyndebourne audience to accept her as a substitute for 'their own' Zerlina. Don Ottavio was sung with an instinctive elegance by Dino Borgioli, though John Christie remained unconvinced that he could 'beat' Nash in the part.[1] Otherwise, the strength and weaknesses of the production were much the same as before – with Busch and Baccaloni stealing the notices and the half-naked show girls sprawling about the supper scene coming in for severe criticism again.

The opening night revealed that the accommodation of the auditorium had been appreciably increased by a number of structural alterations made during the winter, and the Opera House now seated 433, not counting John Christie's box. (Both before and after the 1937 season Christie was quoted as saying that the theatre had been enlarged to hold 600, but it did not reach this figure until 1953.) The auditorium was widened by incorporating the areas used as dressing rooms in 1934 and side lobbies were added. At the back of the stalls, which now held 393, a balcony was built which seated 40 people in two blocks containing 20 seats each and flanking Christie's box which had been moved upstairs to the centre of the balcony. This box looked like a cross between a temple and a summer house; it had an acutely angled roof, back and side walls and an open gable end facing the stage.

In addition to the extra seats added in the stalls there were also ten rows of seats two deep across the stalls gangway against the side walls of the auditorium. These 40 seats were not shown on the official seating plan but were retained by the management to sell at 10s each to students and other deserving persons for whom Festival prices were out of the question. The view of the stage from these seats was not entirely uninterrupted but was patently better than nothing, and well worth the money.

The extension of the theatre meant the removal of the little fountain and round lily pond outside the 'Blue' entrance, but in its place the completed Covered Way provided welcome shelter for those wanting to get to their dinner on a rainy evening. The new Wallop Dining Halls, already mentioned in an earlier chapter, were opened this season; those named Over Wallop and Middle Wallop were ingeniously constructed to follow the lie of the land, so that Over Wallop was built on top of a bank and reached by steps instead of being on the same level as Middle Wallop, which would have involved excavation. Anybody who has ever owned a tree will understand why John Christie preferred to leave the ilex and the wych-elm standing and build the dining rooms round them. The two trees, which continued to grow quite healthily through the roof as though they were in Sieglinde's hut, are a whimsical and permanent reminder that the first opera John Christie ever intended to put on at Glyndebourne was *Die Walküre*.

---

[1] Christie's use of the word 'beat' in the sense it is used in sport ('Toscanini is doing *Die Zauberflöte* at Salzburg so we must beat him') was an endless joy to Fritz Busch who transported the word into German as a regular verb and formed out of it the past participle 'gebeatet'.

The 1937 wine list was expanded to match the increased number of dinners now being provided from a new kitchen and organized by Glyndebourne's own catering staff of 70 waiters and a kitchen staff of 30. The list was headed by a 1934 Zeltinger Sonnenuhr Feinste Beerenauslese, Original Abfüllung Joh. Jos. Prüm, which cost 50s a bottle – a tidy sum, even today – and was accompanied by Agathias's encouraging words: 'Drink old man and live.'

Four French wines made their first appearance in the Glyndebourne list. A 1906 Grand Vin de Beaune Grèves, Vigne de L'enfant Jésus (in 10s half-bottles only) took the place of the previous year's unknown Burgundy with its 'text' by Christie. Two clarets were listed – a château-bottled 1923 Gruaud Larose and a 1914 Château Grand La Lagune – and a white Bordeaux. This was a first-growth Sauternes, a 1913 Sigalas Rabaud, which alone among the French wines was honoured by a Greek quotation. Homer's words: 'Wine will give great strength to a weary man' had appeared among an assortment of quotations that had decorated the cover, but not the contents, of the 1936 list; they were now attached to reassure those who spent 25s on a bottle from Bin No 32 that it was money well spent.

New dressing rooms were also added to the theatre – this time, however, not for the artists but for such breathless City gentlemen who had not had time to change into evening dress before arriving at Glyndebourne. Behind the scenes a cyclorama wall had been newly built with a radius of approximately 22 ft 6 in; the space between this wall and the dressing room block behind it was now roofed over and used as a scenery park. By doing this the scene changes in *Don Giovanni*, which had not been very slick, were speeded up a little. (They would have been much faster if a whole set had not been thought necessary to provide a dressing table, attendants and general busybodiment as an accompaniment to the shortest scene in the opera – Don Giovanni's 'Finch' han dal vino'.)

The production of *The Magic Flute*, which followed on *Don Giovanni*, proved to be the last of this opera at Glyndebourne for nearly twenty years. It included several of the previous year's cast – Norval as Tamino, Rautawaara as Pamina, Henderson as Papageno and Carl Ebert as 'Speaker (Act II)' – but was not on the whole a success. For the third time running excuses had to be made for the Queen of the Night's lack of form (Mme Lissitschkina had a cold); David Franklin, singing Sarastro for the first four performances until Herbert Alsen arrived to sing the last four, made a splendid sound but was obviously too young to bring much suggestion of wisdom to the character. Irene Eisinger's return as Papagena, on the other hand, was warmly greeted. She did not sing every performance of the part, however; as the season progressed and she was singing Susanna, Despina and Blonde as well as Papagena, her place in *The Magic Flute* was taken on some evenings by Margaret Field-Hyde, an English singer whose appearances were for some reason not recorded either by the critics or (until 1964) in Glyndebourne's own published list of artists who have sung there. Miss Field-Hyde's name, which appeared formally on *The Magic Flute* programme and not on an inserted slip, was an unending orthographical problem for Fritz Busch. In the end, after struggling with Field-Hayd and Field-Heyd, he referred to her simply as 'Miss Hay-Field'.

The 1937 *Magic Flute* was also noted for the first appearance of a British artist, Ernest Frank, as Monostatos. This was at last in accordance with a policy Busch had long tried to put into practice. As he wrote to Bing: 'I am more and more of the opinion, and I say it now for the thousandth time, that for such parts as Monostatos we *must* and *can* find English singers.'

The chorus of Priests in this production of *The Magic Flute* included no fewer than ten Welshmen, most of whom were unemployed miners, tinplate workers and boilermakers. Their selection was naturally a source of great pride to the Press in South Wales where, it must be admitted, the exact nature of Glyndebourne was not altogether understood. The *Western Mail* wrote of John Christie having had the idea of 'enthroning Wagner in Sussex, which has proved so eminently successful', while *Reynolds*, the Sunday paper run by the Co-Op movement, spoke of the singers' engagement at 'the Wagner Festival centre near Lewes'.

The nightly programmes this year included for the first time a puff for the Salzburg Festival. This was in return for a mention of Glyndebourne in the Salzburg prospectuses, and announced that Arturo Toscanini would conduct *The Magic Flute, Fidelio, Die Meistersinger* and *Falstaff*, Bruno Walter would conduct *Don Giovanni, Figaro, Euryanthe* and *Orpheus and Eurydice*, and that Max Reinhardt would produce *Faust* and *Everyman*.

The revival of *Figaro* brought the inevitable regrets that 'Glyndebourne's own Susanna' was not in the cast, but Irene Eisinger proved, in a much used phrase of the day, a 'winsome' and witty substitute. Marita Farell was discovered to have a larger voice as Cherubino than her Zerlina had led everybody to expect and she made quite a hit with the public. As a critic remarked, 'All Glyndebourne Cherubinos are good' – a generalization which has remained remarkably valid to this day. Willi Domgraf-Fassbaender returned to sing Figaro, and either because the theatre had been enlarged or because he had learnt better, his singing was not nearly so overpowering as it had been at his earlier appearances. He did not cause anybody to forget Mariano Stabile in the part, however, and his sadistic, vehement way with 'Se vuol ballare' was now seen to be unnecessarily violent when compared with the subtlety of Stabile's conception of the episode.

Right from the start John Christie was justifiably proud, in his running of Glyndebourne, of being able, as he called it, to 'press into service' all the many business enterprises he had founded. During the 1937 run of *Figaro* he pressed the domestic amenities of the Manor House itself into service in an unexpected but fortunate manner. During one of the performances there was a complete electrical blackout 'when Gibraltar blew up' – this, at any rate, is how the incident is remembered and was described to me by Mr George Lincoln, the District Manager of what is now the South Eastern Electricity Board in Lewes, but was then the Ringmer Electricity Company. 'Gibraltar' is the name of the farm opposite Firle Park on the Eastbourne Road where the high voltage switch which 'tripped' was situated. When it was clear that the electricity was not going to come on again immediately Christie sent for all the available candles and silver candlesticks from the house and they were 'pressed into service' to light the stage and the orchestra pit. The opera continued by candlelight until the electricity was restored some time later.

The revival of *Così fan tutte* in 1937 was as successful as ever. The return of Irene Eisinger as Despina put everybody in a good mood for a start, and a touch of variety was given to the production by having Baccaloni alternate in the part of Don Alfonso with John Brownlee. In place of the dry cynicism of Brownlee's Alfonso Baccaloni brought a rich good humour to the part which was most infectious (he hardly had the figure for a cynic, anyway). Roy Henderson, after his success in the part the previous season, shared Guglielmo with Fassbaender whom he was obviously considered to have 'gebeatet' in the playing of Papageno, for he shared this part with nobody.

The score of *Così fan tutte* was still emaciated by cuts which prompted renewed critical appeals to the management to make the most of the ideal cast at its disposal and restore Ferrando's 'Ah lo veggio' (without which he had no wooing scene at all), and Dorabella's second act aria. There was also voices raised to get Busch to abandon the incongruous nineteenth-century sound of the piano to accompany eighteenth-century recitatives. Again, Busch took no notice.

The final production of the season was *Die Entführung* in which Herbert Alsen, who had meanwhile brought great dignity and a magnificent voice to the part of Sarastro, gave a superbly comic performance as Osmin marred only by the congenital tendency of Germans to overplay the drunk scene. Margherita Perras, the young Greek coloratura soprano whom Bing had tried to get for the first *Entführung* in 1935, sang Constanze with ease and skill but was thought to be rather limited in her gestures and acting generally. This in itself was a tribute to the impression Glyndebourne had made in the course of only four seasons. Before 1934 people might have commented on good acting in opera; it would never have entered their heads to regard poor acting as anything out of the way.

The part of Belmonte was sung by a young English tenor called Eric Starling, whom Busch had regarded as something of a discovery; but though he made a good impression (the critics were never more prejudiced in favour of British artists than at this period in English musical history) his lack of experience made his performance a little colourless.

The production of *Die Entführung* – Act II – was at last included among the BBC's broadcasts from Glyndebourne. An excerpt from *Così fan tutte* was also broadcast for the first time – a transmission of Act II which began at the civilized time of 9.45 p.m. The radio serialization of *Figaro* was continued; after the broadcasts of Acts I and II in 1936, Act III was relayed this time, together with Act II of *Don Giovanni* on the opening night and Act I of *The Magic Flute*.

The season of 1937, which included an extra performance of *Don Giovanni* to meet popular demand, ended with John Christie able to announce that, in accordance with his forecast in a newspaper interview at the beginning of May, the Glyndebourne Festival had ended with 'a little profit'. This amounted to £2,723 2s and was largely the result, one imagines, of presenting a repertoire which did not involve the orchestral rehearsal needed in earlier years. The wine sales were also encouraging, though for the first time in Glyndebourne's history no figures can be traced for the exact number of bottles consumed. Christie obviously expected to do well with his wine, for he had stocked up with 9,000 bottles from Germany before the season opened. For any operatic enterprise to show a final profit, by whatever means, is rare enough; John Christie achieved this in a season when, for the first time, there were wage increases at Glyndebourne. Fritz Busch, and I believe Carl Ebert as well, had his fee for the season raised by 50 per cent. The satisfactory financial situation at the end of the 1937 season, however, did not deter Christie from trying to get the orchestra to accept reduced rates for the following year. The orchestra refused to accept any such thing, of course, but Christie's concern was understandable. In August it was announced that in addition to the three familiar Italian Mozart operas, the repertoire for 1938 would not only include Donizetti's *Don Pasquale*, but another opera which demanded a far larger orchestra than anything hitherto heard at Glyndebourne. This was Verdi's *Macbeth*.

CHAPTER THIRTEEN

1938 First time in England

THOUGH IT WAS NOT DIFFICULT to agree in 1936 that the Glyndebourne repertoire should be extended, it had not been an easy matter to decide what form the extension should take. Still less, once having officially announced the plans, did it prove at all easy to adhere to them.

John Christie's determined proposal that *Don Pasquale* should be performed was accepted by the two Artistic Directors, but on strict conditions. Busch insisted that if they were to depart from an all-Mozart policy it was not enough to do so with *Don Pasquale*. Glyndebourne must offer something more important and unusual on its first excursion into a broader repertoire; by all means let *Don Pasquale* be included, but it must not be the principal feature of the Festival's new venture. The idea of Gluck's *Orpheus* sprang automatically to Busch's mind once more, but remembering Christie's earlier reaction to it had second thoughts and settled on Verdi's *Macbeth* – an opera on which Christie had no views since, like nearly everybody else in England, he knew nothing whatever about it. It had never yet been produced in this country although it was first performed in 1847.

Although the choice of *Macbeth*, originally suggested by Rudolf Bing, was to cause him many anxious moments later on, Busch's first consideration was Audrey Mildmay's competence to sing Norina in Donizetti's comedy. Singing Mozart was one thing; this was Italian opera and it was essential that she should study hard and long in Italy. This was agreed to but as late as January 1938, four or five months after the question had first been raised, Miss Mildmay had still not gone to Italy and Busch had to repeat that it was 'urgently necessary' she should go 'as soon and for as long as possible'.

If Busch was worried about her voice, Audrey Mildmay herself had suddenly and quite unjustifiably, at 37 years of age, begun to worry about her looks and strongly opposed the plan to have the part of Ernesto sung by a younger tenor than Dino Borgioli. She feared that a young singer would inevitably make her look old, whereas Borgioli's mature looks (he was 47) would emphasize her own youthful appearance. Carl Ebert disagreed with her argument; the danger, in his experience, was that exactly the opposite occurred. A young woman partnered by an older man usually appeared older than she really was. Nor did Audrey Mildmay's concern deter Busch either from his attempt to get Luigi Fort for Ernesto. That Fort was not finally engaged for the part was due entirely to contractual difficulties, for which there is little doubt that Miss Mildmay was privately more than thankful.

The casting of *Don Pasquale* and the task of preparing Audrey Mildmay for Norina soon became the least of Busch's preoccupations, however. Before he had encountered in earnest the troubles of finding anyone capable of singing Lady Macbeth he had serious misgivings about staging Verdi's opera at all. The problems, he felt, were formidable, and above all he doubted the wisdom of choosing such an unfamiliar work. The English public was not nearly so sympathetic or inquisitive about early and unknown Verdi as it is today, and there is no doubt that there was considerable risk attached to the idea of *Macbeth*. Should they go on with it, asked Busch, or had they the courage to change to something else? John Christie would not give up his precious *Don Pasquale* in any circumstances, nor did anybody want to persuade him to: *Don Pasquale* was accepted by Busch and Ebert as their first big concession to the Christies. In consequence, there was no prospect of being able to fall back in an emergency on an all-Mozart programme again. Busch suggested *Fidelio* instead of *Macbeth*, but Ebert was against this. He did not consider Beethoven's opera at all suitable to a 'Woods-and-Meadows Festival Programme' and indeed never came to do so. When *Fidelio* was finally done at Glyndebourne in 1959 it was produced by Günther Rennert, not Ebert. Busch then proposed they should perform *Idomeneo* which, although it was still a Mozart opera, was so unusual and unfamiliar, and in fact had never been performed professionally in England, that it almost rated as an important departure from the all-Mozart repertoire. The opposition to this proposal came largely from Rudolf Bing, who could see no box-office future for a work which, he had been advised by two musician friends, was almost unstageable.

It was Ebert who eventually reassured Fritz Busch that *Macbeth* was essential to the reputation and development of Glyndebourne. Perhaps 'die Snobs' in the audience (Ebert reckoned they constituted about 70 per cent of the Glyndebourne public) might not take to *Macbeth*, but to the remaining 30 per cent it would be an outstanding experience. With Busch finally convinced that the choice of *Macbeth* for Glyndebourne would be justified, the task of finding a soprano who could sing Lady Macbeth then became a full time occupation for everyone concerned. The search for a Queen of the Night had been comparatively simple. With Lady Macbeth it was a question of finding a singer whose voice, while spanning the exceptional range of the part, was not too powerful for the Glyndebourne acoustics. Many possibilities were considered – Gina Cigna, Maria Caniglia, Eva Turner, Florence Austral, Kerstin Thorborg, Gertrud Wettergren, Margery Lawrence, Germaine Lubin among them – but nothing came of them. Then, for two or three months, Dusolina Giannini was favourite – during which time, however, Busch changed his mind about her and was greatly relieved when she found she was unable to take on the engagement. Various outsiders were nominated, the most surprising of them being Ebe Stignani, who was suggested by a normally reliable contact in the United States.

In January 1938 Busch went to Italy and by the end of the month was beginning to wish that Shakespeare had never existed, 'or if he had, then that Verdi had never composed Macbetto'. Iva Pacetti, who had not long before actually sung the part in Italy, was recommended to him, but advice sought from Bruno Walter and Vittorio Gui suggested that she was past her best.[1] When Busch finally heard Pacetti sing in Italy he reported that she would do little towards solving the problem of finding a Lady Macbeth with a voice not out of scale for Glyndebourne.

No opera in his whole career, confessed Busch, had ever given him so much casting trouble as this Glyndebourne *Macbeth*. It was a work which seemed to bring with it all the traditional ill-luck associated with Shakespeare's play in the theatre. One of Busch's first choices for Lady Macbeth had been Marta Fuchs, who had sung the part with him when, at Dresden in 1928, his production of the opera had marked an important stage in the great German Verdi revival. But after nearly ten years the character of Marta Fuchs's voice had changed (she had lost the richness of her low and middle notes in her development as a dramatic soprano), and in any case she was now too busy to manage Glyndebourne at all.

It was during these early negotiations that Busch made an interesting observation when, on the subject of Pacetti, he wrote to Bing that in spite of her reputation her voice was very uneven and her intonation often affected by her mood and general disposition – 'an occurrence,' commented Busch, 'that is very common among dramatic singers who are used to giving everything they've got, but which is far too risky and unsuitable for Glyndebourne.'

Trying to find the right singer for Macbeth was almost as frustrating as the search for a Lady Macbeth. Ebert would suggest one baritone as 'an ideal type'; Busch would turn him down flat as 'out of the question'. It was obvious that when it came to preparing Verdi's opera the Artistic Directors did not see eye to eye (or ear to ear) nearly so closely as they had in the past – largely, I imagine, because Ebert the actor was on Shakespeare's side, Busch the musician on Verdi's. While he looked high and low for an Italian Macbeth, Busch always bore in mind the claims of John Brownlee to the part, until in January 1938 he heard what he called 'the most beautiful baritone voice I have heard for years'. Busch had found his own 'ideal type' in a young American-born singer, Francesco Valentino, who had been singing for some years at La Scala, the San Carlo and other Italian theatres. Valentino had an English wife which struck Busch as an advantage to any singer at Glyndebourne, even though the singer's native tongue was English. At the same time as he found Valentino, Busch picked on Franca Somigli for Lady Macbeth. She, too, was American-born and in addition to having sung at La Scala and the Florence Maggio Musicale had been the Alice in the *Falstaff* conducted by Toscanini at Salzburg.

With the question of the two leading parts of *Macbeth* apparently settled, preparations for the 1938 season at Glyndebourne continued with no more than the familiar quota of alarms and exertions common to most opera houses. However, on 16 February

---

[1] It was in this context that Gui's name appears in the Glyndebourne correspondence for the second time. In March 1937 Ebert had written to Bing suggesting that if Glyndebourne was going to include Italian *opera buffa* in its repertoire then Gui's was a name to remember. Ebert had first worked with Gui at the Florence Maggio in 1933.

Toscanini announced that he would not appear at the 1938 Salzburg Festival – a decision prompted by an uncanny anticipation of the disaster that was to overtake Austria less than a month later. The full significance of Toscanini's action was not understood by many of his colleagues until it was too late and the Anschluss had become a tragic reality. Fritz Busch, with a political instinct that equalled the Italian conductor's, immediately set about plans to get Toscanini to conduct at Glyndebourne. He suggested that the 1938 season should be extended for Toscanini to take over a revival of *The Magic Flute* in Ebert's production or, with Stabile, Somigli and Brownlee available, perhaps even to conduct a new production of *Falstaff* as well as one or two performances of *Don Pasquale*.

As discussion of the idea proceeded it was agreed that a revival of *The Magic Flute* was the most practicable and by the middle of March it was the only opera that any longer came into consideration – a curious choice, I feel, because Busch had been bitterly disappointed with Toscanini's performance of it at Salzburg the year before. Busch admitted that he had heard only a broadcast from Salzburg, but it had been enough to expose the shortcomings of Toscanini's interpretation of the work. Rudolf Bing was wholeheartedly against the project, his principal objection being to the cost of paying a large fee for Toscanini whose presence at Glyndebourne could not attract more people than already filled the house to capacity anyway. At best, argued Bing, Toscanini might attract *different* people, who could pay the inevitably increased prices, but since there was a limit to the prices that could be asked even for Toscanini the performances would still not pay their way. Nevertheless, having put in his two cents' worth, Bing drafted a plan for rehearsals of *The Magic Flute*, if and when ...

Whatever Toscanini may have divined of Hitler's plans for entering Austria, Bing had foreseen nothing and he found himself in Vienna at the very moment of the Nazi invasion on 12 March. He returned to England by way of Prague; he had no trouble entering Czecho-Slovakia but at the Austrian passport control point all Austrian passengers were ordered out of the train and sent back to Vienna. By an incredible stroke of luck Bing had in his possession a *Grenzempfehlung*, a document which had been issued in Vienna to facilitate the passage of an English Member of Parliament across the frontier and which he was taking back to England to give to the MP in person. Bing hid his Austrian passport and passing himself off as the person named in the *Grenzempfehlung* was able to leave Austria and enter Czecho-Slovakia without let or hindrance.

Bing returned to England to find that not only had Busch so far received no answer to the proposals he had cabled to Toscanini nearly six weeks earlier, but that there was a very strong rumour that Toscanini was to conduct at Covent Garden in 1939. It was therefore more urgent than ever for Glyndebourne to get in first. Another cable was sent, but this also remained unanswered, and it was only indirectly that Busch eventually learned that Toscanini had decided to conduct no opera performances in 1938.

The news was received by both Busch and Bing with obvious relief, though for different reasons. To Bing it meant a return to a comparatively quiet life; to Busch it meant that he could give his full attention to the solution of a Glyndebourne crisis that had arisen only three days before. On 21 March Miss Franca Somigli had cabled asking to be released from her contract; she had found the part of Lady Macbeth 'too difficult' and unsuited to her voice; she offered, however, to sing any other part from her repertoire that Glyndebourne might care to engage her for. Busch's anger at this defection was understandable, for he could not conceive how it could take anybody three months to discover that a part was too difficult. After a violent initial outburst, however, he shrugged his shoulders philosophically and remarked that worse things had been happening in the world than that during the last few weeks.

The choice now fell on Iva Pacetti who, in spite of the reservations expressed by Bruno Walter and Gui, was otherwise recommended on all sides. It was now April and everything in the operatic garden promised to be as lovely as its nature allowed. John Christie found time to write to Busch to tell him of his scheme for co-operating with Covent Garden the following year – a thought that will intrigue all those who recall Christie's views on the Royal Opera House so frequently and fiercely expressed in the Press, the programme and in end-of-term speeches from the stage of the Glyndebourne Festival Opera.

In April 1938, however, Christie wrote: 'I hope there may be a reasonable chance of managing Covent Garden as well as Glyndebourne, but I suppose it depends on whether Beecham makes a muddle and a loss again this year. This is in confidence, but I want Covent Garden to be combined with us. It is bound to be more efficient and more economical. It would mean I suppose thirty performances at Covent Garden followed by thirty performances at Glyndebourne – about twelve weeks ... '

Further discussion of this project and the air of deceptively placid contentment at Glyndebourne were rudely interrupted, however, when, entirely in keeping with the theatrical reputation of *Macbeth* as a bringer of ill-fortune, another disaster threatened. On 11 May, ten days before the opening night, it was announced that Iva Pacetti had suddenly been taken ill and once more Glyndebourne was without a Lady Macbeth. Eventually, on the suggestion of Bing, the part was given to Vera Schwarz, who learnt it at extremely short notice. Miss Schwarz was described in the programme as Yugoslavian, but her career had been made for the most part in Vienna and Berlin. She had been in the company of the Vienna Opera when I was a student there in 1923, but like several of her colleagues at that time she went off for a profitable spell on the operetta stage. With her striking head of bright blond hair and her success in such roles as Tosca, and Marietta in Korngold's *Die tote Stadt*, she was known to us in the Fourth Gallery as the Poor Man's Jeritza. Certainly if any of us had known Verdi's *Macbeth* at that time we would never have thought to hear Vera Schwarz in it.

Without further mishap the 1938 season opened with *Macbeth* on Saturday 21 May, the curtain again rising at 5.15 in accordance with the management's new and greatly appreciated policy to make first nights less of a rush for the critics with early deadlines. Once more the audience came to a theatre which had been considerably altered since the last time they had seen it. During the winter the capacity of the auditorium had been increased by 94 new seats. The balcony now held 64 as well as John Christie's box, and three public boxes with four seats in each had been built at the back of the stalls. (In the appeal brochure issued by the Glyndebourne Arts Trust in 1964 the section on

'Building at Glyndebourne' describes the addition of a single box seating 12. This is not quite correct. There were three small four-seater boxes labelled A, B and C.) There were now 451 seats in the stalls, including 52 against the side walls which were shown on the seating plan, but they were not numbered and were marked 'Reserved for the Management'; as before, they were sold to deserving cases at 10s a time. In addition, the entrances to the Opera House had been re-designed, there was a new cloakroom, the departure loggia had been lengthened to permit several cars to load up at once, and the approaches to the auditorium had been widened.

But the biggest alterations were those affecting the stage. A scenery tower had at last been built to enable the scenery to be 'flown' instead of pushed through doors and stacked against walls. The depth of the stage from footlights to the centre of the cyclorama had been extended to 59 ft; by removing the back wall of the stage an area 30 ft deep behind the cyclorama wall could now be used. The stage had also been enlarged and was now 140 ft wide – which, John Christie never hesitated to remind everybody, was 50 ft wider than the stage at Covent Garden.

As far as the critics were concerned there is no doubt that *Macbeth* made an unexpectedly deep impression. Francis Toye, who already knew the work, stated quite frankly that he had experienced an ideal performance. Others, with only a sketchy knowledge of the opera, had come in a doubtful frame of mind, but stayed to discover that Verdi in the theatre was an entirely different matter from Verdi in the pages of a vocal score. Only one critic actively disliked *Macbeth*. W. J. Turner, for whom Glyndebourne could hitherto do no wrong, considered it 'totally devoid of imaginative power' and called the whole thing 'this uninspired stuff'. Mr Turner was very put out.

The singers' performances, Busch's direction and Ebert's superbly effective and imaginative staging were received with almost universal praise. Vera Schwarz was clearly very exhausted by the time the first night arrived, but although her singing suffered in consequence her acting was outstandingly impressive. In accordance with what has become fairly frequently practice in the opera house nowadays the final *pianissimo* D Flat above the stave in Lady Macbeth's Sleep Walking aria was sung off-stage by another voice; at Glyndebourne in 1938 it was the voice of Barbara Beaumont, a member of the chorus. As everybody concerned realized all too well at Glyndebourne, the part of Lady Macbeth is a terror; the range is too high for a mezzo-soprano and too low for a soprano, and there are few who have sung the part who are not grateful at the end of a strenuous evening for the anonymous contribution of that high D Flat by another singer.

Only one point in the otherwise brilliant staging of *Macbeth* was regarded as unsatisfactory and that was Ebert's treatment of the death of Macbeth. In Verdi's opera, as in Shakespeare's play, Macbeth dies off stage. In his production of the opera in Berlin in 1931, however, Ebert felt that some sort of final aria was necessary for Macbeth before he died. Ebert got in touch with Ricordi's in Milan to see if some such aria existed – in the version first performed in 1847 but which had been cut in Verdi's revised version of the opera published in 1865 and universally followed today. Ricordi's laid hands on what Ebert was looking for. It proved to be an uninteresting, conventionally operatic death-aria which echoed several passages heard earlier in the opera and so lacking in distinction that one was inclined to believe it was spurious. Ebert included it in the Glyndebourne *Macbeth*, and in restoring a passage the composer had deliberately and carefully cut for (as he thought) all time, introduced an unnecessary element of comparative 'ham' which left Macbeth's corpse, in the words of the *Daily Telegraph*, 'lying disregarded on the stage while the chorus sang the concluding hymn as though the body had been merely that of the Second Murderer'. In the fine 1964 production of the opera by Franco Enriquez, however, the aria was cut and *Macbeth* at Glyndebourne is musically and dramatically the better for it.

The production of *Macbeth* not only introduced a new composer to Glyndebourne but also a new designer in Caspar Neher, who created some remarkable stage pictures marred only by the extraordinary hire-purchase look of the furniture in the Banquet Scene. Neher, who died at the age of 65 in 1962 and had collaborated in the famous Busch-Ebert production of *Un ballo in maschera* at the Charlottenburg Opera in 1932,[1] was not altogether unknown in England; his designs for *Don Giovanni* had been seen during the visit of the Dresden Opera to Covent Garden in 1936. In addition to being a designer, Caspar Neher was also a skilled librettist; he wrote the text of *Die Bürgschaft* in 1932, the last opera by Kurt Weill to be produced in Germany until after the war; he wrote four librettos for Wagner-Régeny, including one with Bert Brecht, and the libretto based on Kafka's *The Trial* for Gottfried von Einem's *Der Prozess*, produced in Salzburg in 1953.

There have been few seasons in its history when the Glyndebourne Festival Opera has not been able to claim a 'discovery' among its casts. In 1938 it was undoubtedly David Lloyd's singing of Macduff's 'Ah! la paterna mano' in the last act of *Macbeth*. Lloyd, a joiner by trade, and the son of a Welsh miner, had gained a scholarship to the Guildhall School of Music. He had an exceptionally beautiful tenor voice, but was a poor actor; in consequence his engagement became a subject of fierce argument between Busch and Ebert. Busch won. 'It is well known that Verdi attached the greatest importance to the part and the aria,' he said, 'and as it is a very beautiful piece of music I have no reason to sacrifice it to the whim of a producer. Finally, the aria is the number from *Macbeth* recorded by Caruso for the gramophone. For this reason the choice of a singer for this aria needs our greatest attention.' Busch's firmness was amply justified by results; David Lloyd was a great success with an audience which otherwise felt *Macbeth* to be generally lacking in 'typical' Verdi high spots.

The production of *Macbeth* at Glyndebourne presented many new problems, not the least of them the recruiting of a considerable complement of supers to appear as pages, Scottish and English soldiers. Quite early on in the preparatory stages – in October 1937 – Bing had half seriously, half jokingly, proposed that the restaurant waiters should be enlisted to appear as soldiers. They would not be needed until Act IV – that is, some time after the dinner interval. Carl Ebert was vastly amused by this suggestion and had hilarious visions of the hurried service it would involve towards the end of dinner with anxious

[1] See page 44.

waiters, determined not to miss their cue, dropping what he called *puddingsaucen* in the laps of the diners. As things turned out, what Ebert had understandably treated as a joke was seriously adopted as an ingenious solution to both the economic and theatrical problems involved. Further numbers were raised from among the staff of the Ringmer Building Works and the local troop of Boy Scouts.

The printed programmes for the 1938 season included for the first time the names of members of the chorus and the orchestra. Among the tenors in the chorus was the name of Peter Pears; among the horns in the orchestra the name of John Denison, later musical director of the Arts Council. It was in this season also that Harold Williams first sang in the chorus. His name did not appear in the programme, however, as he joined the basses after the list had gone to press. Mr Williams has been a member of the Glyndebourne Festival Chorus ever since and for many years past he has been its manager.

The *Macbeth* cast also included the name of Elisabeth Abercrombie as 'Gentlewoman, attending on Lady Macbeth'. Mrs Abercrombie had been associated with Glyndebourne almost from the beginning of the Festival Opera, understudying many of the important soprano parts and taking part in the frequent concerts and recitals which were given in the Organ Room and the theatre on numberless occasions out of season to entertain the Christies' guests and various commercial organizations who were lent Glyndebourne for conferences and conventions. When Elisabeth Abercrombie was first recommended to John Christie by a mutual friend, he had written to her husband Nigel Abercrombie, now Secretary General of the Arts Council, saying that she would be welcome at Glyndebourne, but warning him: 'We don't want any screechers here.' This was obviously a favourite phrase of Christie's at the time for he also used it in writing to thank Bruno Walter for recommending a possible singer for Glyndebourne. On both these occasions, at least, Audrey Mildmay prevented the letters actually being sent, but she was never certain how many of these blunt warnings may have got through without her knowledge.

The 1938 Salzburg Festival was, in view of many things, rather surprisingly advertised in the programme. Where we should have read the names of Toscanini, Bruno Walter and Max Reinhardt, we found those of Furtwängler, Knappertsbusch and Karajan, and the bald statement in colourless words that rang out like a passing bell: 'Performances of "Jedermann" have been cancelled.' It made uncomfortable reading.

Toscanini, who had come down to Glyndebourne to hear *The Magic Flute* and *Così fan tutte* in 1935, greatly admired Busch's performances of Verdi and paid another visit during the run of *Macbeth*. He complimented the chorus on being 'the best little chorus' he had ever heard and reassured John Christie that there was no better Verdi conductor in the world – Italy included – than Fritz Busch. After the performance, Mrs Busch recalls, Toscanini took the young Hans Peter Busch on one side and said of his father 'Lo dirige come viene diretto' – 'he conducts it as it must be conducted'.

In one respect, however, Toscanini's visit to *Macbeth* was something of a headache for the Glyndebourne management. It was only by much clever diplomatic manoeuvring that he was somehow kept from catching sight of Furtwängler who had come to the same performance and, as a Nazi musician, was the Italian conductor's particular *bête noire*. Whatever Furtwängler's political record Toscanini could never forgive him for failing to defy the Nazis as Busch had done, and as Toscanini himself had defied Mussolini. A gossip writer reported that at *Macbeth* 'Furtwängler applauded with a certain professional respect, Toscanini with an enthusiasm worthy of any amateur'.

Before the production of *Don Pasquale*, the second novelty of the 1938 season, the three familiar Italian operas of Mozart were revived. Audrey Mildmay returned as Susanna in *Figaro* and, obviously inspired and encouraged by playing opposite Mariano Stabile again, gave an even better performance than before. She also repeated her success as Zerlina in a production of *Don Giovanni* which gave Glyndebourne its first experience of what was only just beginning to be a feature of modern operatic life – airborne help in time of trouble. Luise Helletsgruber was suddenly taken ill and her place as Donna Elvira on the first night was filled by Hilde Konetzni who had flown from Prague (or Vienna or Berlin – according to the paper you read) in time for the dress rehearsal. Miss Konetzni had only a few days previously performed the same kind of service for Covent Garden by taking over Lotte Lehmann's part there in *Der Rosenkavalier*.[1]

Miss Helletsgruber recovered and in a short while was able to resume as Donna Elvira and to sing her usual part of Dorabella at the first night of the *Così fan tutte* revival, thus avoiding any disturbance of the balanced teamwork which had established this opera as such a *spécialité de la maison* from the very beginning.

Immediately after the end of the 1937 season John Christie had sent a note of almost Churchillian brevity to Rudolf Bing. It consisted of two sentences: 'Can you let me have the dates for next year? I am trying to fix up with the King and Queen.' Bing supplied the dates and in due course Christie 'fixed up' with the King and Queen to come to Glyndebourne. At first it was arranged that they should see *Figaro*, but later the opera was changed to *Macbeth*. The King had not been to Glyndebourne before, but as Duchess of York the Queen had paid two informal visits – on consecutive evenings in 1936 to see *Figaro* and *The Magic Flute*. The change to *Macbeth* not only provided a novelty but among other things offered the Queen the chance (not given to many) of spending an evening at an opera set in the house she was born in. Only a day or so before the visit was to take place, however, the Queen's mother, the Countess of Strathmore, died at Glamis Castle and all royal engagements were cancelled.

The Christies' understandable disappointment over the royal visit was undoubtedly a little mitigated the following week by the riotous success of *Don Pasquale*. Donizetti's comic opera, which had been excruciatingly performed at Covent Garden the year before, was undeniably another Glyndebourne revelation to many, and even those who looked down their noses in the Press and muttered the inevitable clichés about the 'base metal' of Donizetti's music had to agree with the public that a superb performance provided a most splendid evening's entertainment.

---

[1]During the week of all the excitement over *Don Giovanni* at Glyndebourne Vittorio Gui was conducting a performance of *Tosca* at Covent Garden in which the lead was sung by none other than Iva Pacetti.

(left) Il ritorno d'Ulisse in patria, 1972: designer, John Bury. (Gravett)

(below) La Calisto, 1970: Ileana Cotrubas, Ugo Trama. (Gravett)

(left) Peter Hall (foreground) learns from Benjamin Luxon how to string Ulysses's bow (*Ulisse*, 1972). *(Gravett)*

(right) John Pritchard and Moran Caplat. *(Gravett)*

The audience's uninhibited enjoyment of the Glyndebourne *Don Pasquale* was in one respect a little disconcerting to Christie; he was never quite sure whether he wanted people to laugh too much in his opera house in case the music couldn't be heard and, at this production, the *Times* critic observed, 'the audience roared and shouted like any shilling gallery'. As Busch and Ebert had recognized, *Don Pasquale* was the Christies' personal plaything and if they introduced what would nowadays be looked down upon as 'gimmicks' – well, all things considered, it didn't matter all that much. To those in the audience who were in the know it was quite fun to be able to recognize gamekeepers off the Estate among the supers, to admire Mrs Ashton, the Glyndebourne cook, in the part (non-vocal) of Don Pasquale's housekeeper and to marvel at the discipline of Tuppy, the first Christie pug dog to appear on the Glyndebourne stage, as he sat motionless and obedient by his mistress's side. Tuppy took a curtain call and, in a world where even more newspapers aimed for eye-catching headlines for stories about the arts than today (there were more newspapers then), earned the *Daily Herald*'s accolade with 'Pug Dog's "Hit" in Opera'.

'What has this got to do with Art?' Busch asked. But having asked the question he did not press for an answer; instead he turned his attention to other matters. To allow the founders to indulge in their little family whimsies occasionally was after all a small price to pay for all that Glyndebourne gave him.

Whatever Busch's private feelings about Glyndebourne's domestic contributions to the production they did not in any way affect his ability to turn *Don Pasquale* into an outstanding artistic success. The magnificently comic performances of Baccaloni as Don Pasquale and Stabile as Dr Malatesta brought the house down and gave most people a first unforgettable experience of the purest Italian *buffo* style at its very best. Their famous 'Cheti, cheti' duet in the last act was encored nightly, and so was the delicious little waltz sung by the chorus of servants. As Francis Toye so rightly pointed out – if 'Cheti, cheti' isn't encored it's a bad performance of *Don Pasquale*. Audrey Mildmay's Norina enchanted one and all and impressed many by the way her voice had developed and was capable of doing justice to a part quite unlike anything she had sung at Glyndebourne before. If Dino Borgioli's Ernesto struck anybody as 'elderly' they were too polite to say so; in any case the comment would have been irrelevant: Borgioli's singing of the lyric tenor parts in Donizetti and Rossini was surpassed at that time only by Tito Schipa.

One of the major surprises for the audience was certainly the discovery that not all comic operas were invariably set in the eighteenth century after all. In deciding to give *Don Pasquale* the costumes and décor of the 1840s Glyndebourne was in fact observing Donizetti's original intentions. The opera was first performed in Paris in 1843 and presented as a contemporary comedy; but soon afterwards the action was put back to the eighteenth century; opera audiences had then, as they have now, an unexpected resistance to opera in contemporary costume. It is only because they are more interested in the heroine who wears unreal fancy dress that audiences put up with the twentieth-century clothes of the Americans in *Madam Butterfly*.

Hamish Wilson had great fun with the scenery for *Don Pasquale* and revealed a nice and unsuspected touch of parody which was neatly matched by the costumes designed by Kenneth Green, a young artist whose admirable portrait of Baccaloni as Leporello hangs in the Blue Foyer, the gift of Lady Charlotte Bonham Carter to Glyndebourne Festival Opera on its twenty-first birthday in 1955. Green's portait of Jock is in the Red Foyer.

Audrey Mildmay's appearances as Norina meant that her place as Susanna in *Figaro* was taken from time to time by Irene Eisinger once *Don Pasquale* was in the repertoire. It was for this reason that Miss Eisinger was heard in the BBC's relay of *Figaro*, which took place on the evening following the first night of *Don Pasquale*. Having so far given us *Figaro* by instalments – Acts I and II in 1936, Act III in 1937 – it came as a great surprise that instead of the missing Act IV, which on form now seemed due for broadcasting, the BBC broadcast the *whole* of the opera from Glyndebourne. This was, of course, the first complete opera to be relayed from the Festival Opera House, and though a complete opera relay was a rarity at the time the BBC was most commendably unhurried and unapologetic in its presentation. After an ominous 20-minute talk on 'Agriculture in War-time' (we hadn't even had Munich yet), there was a 10-minute introduction to the relay proper which began at 6.50. There was a 10-minute interval between Acts I and II, which was filled by a talk. Act II began at 7.45 and lasted until 8.30 when the dinner interval was taken and the BBC passed the 75 minutes with a selection from *Tannhäuser* on a cinema organ, News, Weather, and a 30-minute play. At 9.30 the relay was resumed with Act III, followed by an interval of 15 minutes during which the listener could hear a talk by Wyndham Lewis, the painter and author of *The Apes of God*, on 'When John Bull Laughs'. Act IV was broadcast from 10.50 to 11.30 and the National Programme, continuing in its uncompromising vein of thorough minority-appeal, ended with half an hour of Swing Music on records.

In addition to the complete *Figaro* the BBC broadcast excerpts from each of the other operas in the repertoire – Acts III and IV of *Macbeth*, Act I of *Don Giovanni* (with Marita Farell as Zerlina), Act II of *Così fan tutte* and Acts I and II of *Don Pasquale*.

In a season of novelty at Glyndebourne one unusual experiment was tried: the institution of what the prospectus described as 'Two Popular Whitsun Performances'. On Whit Sunday *Figaro* was played, followed on Whit Monday by *Macbeth*. Both performances began at 5.30, the usual Sunday starting time at that period, and all seats were 30s. The experiment does not seem to have been successful for, as far as I know, Whit Sunday, when it has fallen in the season, has ever since been regarded as a normal Glyndebourne Sunday Opera Club occasion, while Whit Monday has always been regarded as an operatic holiday for management and public alike.

The twenty-page prospectus for 1938 was the first Glyndebourne publication on which the Christie arms appeared. The arms as they were shown in the rather rough line block printed on the title page were used on all Glyndebourne publicity matter until 1953 when a new version of the design was made. This differs quite considerably from the earlier form in which little conventional indication of heraldic colouring was given; the lamb passant with his flag stood on a field of what looked like a wallpaper pattern of quatre-foil. The new version is a much simpler and more rational design. The quatrefoil background has disappeared and the lamb passant (now clearly argent) stands on a gules field. The chief is shown to be azure, but in the course of acquiring a colour has been charged with three objects which have now altogether lost even that hazy identity they had in the earlier block. Since the arms of Glyndebourne are used much more exclusively than, say, the arms the Royal Opera House shares with magistrates' courts, the front page of *The Times*, the cover of the British passport and H.M.'s Appointed Organ Builders, it is surely high time that a new and accurate reproduction of the Christie blazon appeared at last on our programmes and prospectuses. The arms are described in Burke's Landed Gentry as follows, and it will be seen that they differ quite considerably from what we have been given all these years:

ARMS: Azure, a lamb passant the dexter leg supporting in bend sinister a banner argent, staff or, on a chief of the last [or] a tower with two turrets between as many gabions ppr [purpure]. CREST: a brown bear passant muzzled, the chain reflexed over the shoulder or, on the back a bezant charged with a cross sable, the dexter paw resting on an escutcheon per pale of the last and gu[les].

If the details of the arms have never been quite clear the Christie motto has always been legible. 'Integer vitae', like so many Latin mottos, is only the half of it – in this case literally so, for it comes from a line by Horace (Odes I. xxii. 1): 'Integer vitae scelerisque purus' – 'He that is unstained in life and pure from guilt.'[1]

The season of 1938, though it lacked the sublime experience of *The Magic Flute*, was undoubtedly the most exhilarating that Glyndebourne had so far presented. And there is equally little doubt, I think, that it was a year in which Fritz Busch's contribution was unusually large and in which his great gifts were fully recognized for the first time. With Mozart's operas it was very much a matter of his preaching to the converted; the difference was that Busch's sermons were infinitely better than his audience of converts had listened to before. But with Verdi and Donizetti he had the task of having to convert an almost entirely heretical congregation to the belief that *Macbeth* and *Don Pasquale* were worth listening to. Like Toscanini, Fritz Busch had the great gift of being able to see 'what is there' ('quello che c'è') in a score and so enable an audience to hear things it had never heard before; also, like Toscanini, he had the gift of showing an audience what it had long been quite *sure* wasn't there. Toscanini did this with his historic revival (there is no better word) of *Il trovatore* at La Scala in the 1920s; Busch did it with *Macbeth*, when he succeeded in opening the ears and breaking down the stubborn prejudices of English opera audiences against unfamiliar Verdi; he did it with *Don Pasquale* when he persuaded them that to be entertained by opera did not endanger their immortal souls.

[1] The most nearly correct reproduction of the Christie arms is on the car badge used by members of the Glyndebourne Festival Society. Except for the absence of any hint that the tower and gabions should be purpure, the colouring is heraldically right – or at least, better than we have seen it so far.

Shortly after the first performance of *Don Pasquale*, *The Times* printed a long and admirably reasoned article about Fritz Busch which paid an overdue tribute, in words many of us agreed with, but few of us had the opportunity (or the space) to echo:

GLYNDEBOURNE OPERA

The Conductor's Task

Some surprise was expressed at Glyndebourne on Tuesday on the discovery that Donizetti's *Don Pasquale* was treated as a classic. It was even suggested [by Richard Capell in the *Daily Telegraph*] that if the composer had known that a hundred years hence his comedy would be so treated he would have taken more pains to write a classic in the eighteen-forties.

It is difficult to see how the revival of any work, opera or symphony, can be otherwise treated. Presumably to play a work as a classic means that everything in it is treated as of importance in its degree. The relative importance of details is carefully gauged. The interpreter, be he singer, instrumentalist or conductor, does not pick out a tune he likes and exaggerate its significance to his audience; he does not pretend that trivial music is lofty music, but he gives it all for what it is worth and sees to it that its total worth shall be estimated at its highest by the hearers. That is all that a conductor can do with a symphony of Beethoven or a comic opera by Donizetti. The difference is that it may require greater qualities in himself to do that for Beethoven than for Donizetti. On the other hand, there are conductors who can give a truly classical performance of a great work and cannot give more than a decently competent one of a slight work just because, it being slight, they cannot bend their minds to it. That is what the term 'highbrow' in its derogatory sense suggests.

Mr Fritz Busch's ability to handle Donizetti consistently so that one felt it to be neither laboured nor belittled in his presentation of it showed him to be completely free from the limitations of highbrowism. His taste is impeccable, which cannot quite be said of the taste of his brilliant collaborator on the stage, much as we enjoyed Mr Carl Ebert's production as a whole. It is impossible to imagine a musical vulgarism comparable to the perambulator joke finding lodgment in the ranks of the orchestra.[1] Precision, neatness and refinement of phrasing even in the most blatant moments (and Donizetti is not without them) keep the musical atmosphere pure without lowering the vitality of the comedy. Everywhere he moulds the score so as to bring out the best qualities of the solo voices and get the maximum effect from the ensembles, including those in which the brilliant chorus participates. Above all, that indefinable characteristic called *élan* sweeps the work forward unflaggingly.

During the five Glyndebourne seasons we have now had the privilege of studying Mr Fritz Busch's methods in five operas by Mozart and in Verdi's *Macbeth* and Donizetti's *Don Pasquale*. Actually the last two have been the most illuminating, because neither the tragedy of Verdi nor the comedy of Donizetti possesses that quality of an unerring style which makes Mozart the one supreme composer of opera. Someone said after hearing *Macbeth*: 'Even the bad bits seem to fall into place; one realizes that they mean something.' It may be reasonably argued that a conductor shows himself the greater artist in making his audience perceive the essential greatness of

[1] Nobody can remember exactly what the toy perambulator business was. It met with pretty general disapproval and so deserves to be, as it has been, forgotten if not entirely forgiven by posterity.

an unequal work than in presenting a flawless one flawlessly. Mozart is an inspiration from first to last to a keen and sensitive musical nature; the other two are apt to disappoint such a one. *Macbeth* is a magnificent conception of a great tragedy marred in its execution because the composer was under the sway of certain trite conventions of operatic expression characteristic of his time. There is nothing magnificent about Donizetti's comedy, but his artistry is so facile that there are numerous points at which the music is no more than second best.

The two present therefore very different problems to the conductor who would treat them as classics in their several styles. Mr Busch's solution of each problem has shown his breadth of vision, his sure judgment, and his skill in ways which his beautiful performances of Mozart never put to the test. While everyone is talking of the wonders of the stage productions at Glyndebourne and while there is still a week in which these operas may be enjoyed, it seems desirable to pay a tribute to the masterly musical direction, the genius of which may be less conspicuous to the audience simply because the result is so manifestly right.

CHAPTER FOURTEEN

1939 **Disquiet before the storm**

NOT UNEXPECTEDLY THE 1938 season ended with a deficit. It could hardly have done otherwise, for *Macbeth* was an expensive production and it was only the last five of the ten scheduled performances of the opera that the public supported at all handsomely. Whatever his losses, however, John Christie did not consider them worth mentioning in public (they were in fact about £7,000) and told us instead that no fewer than 4,000 bottles of wine had been sold. This raised the average compared with previous years to roughly 108 bottles consumed during each dinner interval.

The programme for 1939 was decided on quite soon after the last performance of the 1938 Festival. The same five operas would be performed – *Macbeth, Don Pasquale, Don Giovanni, Figaro, Così fan tutte* – and the season would last from 1 June to 15 July, though none of this was officially announced until November. What went on before and after the publication of the prospectus demonstrated more clearly than ever that operatic practice and all it entails is like an iceberg: nine-tenths of it is below the surface, invisible and inconceivable to the casual observer and a constant danger to those who sail in its waters.

The question of Toscanini coming to Glyndebourne was raised once more and developed into a fierce contest between opposing factions, one of which attempted to persuade the Christies that it was a good thing, the other to persuade the Christies that it was a bad thing. The pro-Toscanini party consisted of Frances Dakyns, Adolf Busch and his wife, the anti-Toscanini party of Fritz Busch, Carl Ebert and Rudolf Bing. The suggestion this time was solely that Toscanini should be asked to do *Falstaff*.

The anti-Toscanini group won; it consisted, after all, of those most intimately concerned with the running of the Opera House and together they decided that the risk of things not going smoothly (such as disagreement over points of production, for instance – a laudable but none the less frustrating reason for not letting the English public hear Toscanini conduct *Falstaff*) was too great for Glyndebourne to take. Christie, who had been very enthusiastic about the Toscanini idea the second time it came up, accepted the opposition verdict. He recognized that while Miss Dakyns and Adolf Busch were fired by the highest ideals and had nothing but the welfare of Glyndebourne at heart, neither of them was in a position to accept any responsibility if the venture should fail. It was decided, therefore, that no invitation should be sent to Toscanini.

The early days of September 1938 were not, one would have thought, any time to be making ambitious plans for an opera house. But while the international situation got steadily worse, the thoughts of Glyndebourne were occupied not only with Toscanini, but with the possibilities of appearing at the Lucerne Festival the following summer, with the renewed prospects of co-operating with Covent Garden (Sir Thomas Beecham had offered Bing the job of managing the Royal Opera House as well as Glyndebourne), and with the invitation just received from America to appear at the New York World Fair in August 1939.

The Covent Garden project, for which Bing had roughed out a budget, would have been almost as much of an ear- and eye-opener as the inauguration of Glyndebourne itself, for it was planned to contribute to the Royal Opera House season eight perform-ances of *Carmen* conducted by Bruno Walter, and eight of *Un ballo in maschera* conducted by Fritz Busch. Both operas were to be directed by Ebert and so bring to London two productions which had already made operatic history: the Walter-Ebert *Carmen* at the Vienna Opera in 1937, the Busch-Ebert *Ballo in maschera* in Berlin in 1932.

But where the fulfilment of this particular dream depended on more than the normal quota of ifs and ans that plague the opera world, the New York Fair project was a more or less hard proposition and quickly became the principal talking point of all concerned. Not unnaturally, for Ebert and Bing saw it as a rare chance to get a foot in the door of the USA – a harder task for producers and managers, of course, than for a conductor like Busch. The offer had come from Olin Downes, musical director of the Fair and chief critic of the *New York Times*; it was a firm offer with no serious strings attached. It was up to Glyndebourne to decide whether they would accept, and if so what productions they would like to take. The one thing which prevented the immediate acceptance of the American offer was the question whether in the process of transplantation the Glynde-bourne performances could preserve their essential character. While *Macbeth* and *Don Giovanni* might come to no harm in a large theatre, it was out of the question to consider *Figaro* or *Così fan tutte* on anything but their original intimate scale.

All talk of New York, Lucerne, Covent Garden and the possibility of any 1939 season at all at Glyndebourne was put aside, however, as the events which led up to the Munich Agreement became more critical and alarming from one moment to the next. Although he now carried British identity papers and an unrestricted permit to work (Glyndebourne owed a great deal to the sympathetic presence in the Ministry of Labour of the poet Humbert Wolfe), Bing was desperately afraid he would be interned in the event of war which, he was sure, would lead to the destruction of Europe and a fascist dictatorship in England. He thought seriously of leaving for America. He was calmed down, however, by Ebert's assurance from Lugano that there would be no war just yet, and applied him-self instead to completing immediate plans for the possible evacuation to Glyndebourne of 260 London children.

Nevertheless, the situation did not improve and on 27 September the Glyndebourne office on the sixth floor of a building in Cockspur Street was evacuated to Ringmer. On 28 September the British Navy was mobilized; on 29 September the Munich Agreement was signed between Chamberlain, Hitler, Mussolini and Daladier; and on 5 October the Glyndebourne office returned to London.

It was not until 15 October, however, that there was a meeting of the directors of the Glyndebourne Opera Society Ltd and it was finally decided to hold a Festival in 1939. In view of the general international situation the policy was to observe the strictest economy; there must be no change of repertoire or alteration of productions (this put an end to the plan of having new scenery for *Don Pasquale* by the German designer Teo Otto). At about this time the management of Covent Garden also decided that the world was in too unreliable a frame of mind for them to start anything out of the ordinary either, and so the idea of Glyndebourne and the Royal Opera House collaborating was inevitably dropped.

As soon as he knew that the 1939 Glyndebourne season would definitely take place Busch wrote to Bing from Copenhagen urging him (now that his letter would reach him 'in the office and not in an air-raid shelter') to push on with every possible plan. Busch had no faith in Chamberlain's proclamation of 'peace in our time'; time was short and Glyndebourne should make the most of every moment before the inevitable catastrophe occurred. The New York project must be urgently pursued and so too must the idea of the visit to Australia which had not long before been proposed. Nothing came of the Australian idea, but in November it was officially announced that Glyndebourne had accepted the American invitation – a news item which inevitably produced a crop of syndicated headings like 'Village Opera for World Fair'. John Christie arranged to send Bing to New York to deal with the financial and practical details of the visit. Busch insisted, however, that the artistic direction of Glyndebourne should be represented as well, and as he hadn't the time to travel himself obviously Ebert must go. Christie explained that he could afford the expense of sending either Bing or Ebert, but not both. Busch replied that in that case he would be personally responsible for Ebert's expenses – his sole condition being that Glyndebourne should repay him the money if the visit had any material results.

Meanwhile a situation had arisen which was peculiar to Glyndebourne, whose strength and weakness lay in the unique domestic and family nature of the whole enterprise, and where those concerned solely with the artistic administration of the opera were often inevitably involved in the activities, and affected by the personal fancies, of the Opera's founders. Bing was horrified to learn that Audrey Mildmay had not only agreed to sing in Hamburg and Berlin in the early months of 1939, but had also shown herself more than willing to sing Susanna at the 1939 Salzburg Festival. In desperation Bing wrote to Busch and Ebert to back him in his protest to the Christies that this sort of thing would be the worst possible publicity for the Glyndebourne Opera – especially in America – and to persuade Audrey Mildmay that she would be doing her own reputation great harm if she visited a country where, as Bing expressed it, 'she would not just metaphorically but literally be shaking hands with murderers'. Fritz Busch wrote a fatherly letter of advice to Miss Mildmay, but it seems to have had no effect. The Christies' visit to Germany took place and Audrey Mildmay sang there.

John Christie's political innocence was a constant source of worry to his foreign collaborators at Glyndebourne who probably did not recognize it as characteristic of a section of English society at that time, many of whom unfortunately were just then ruling the country. It was a class which had been brought up to ignore Germany's criminal past because the Bavarians were such fine fellows – the Bavarians and the Austrians, of course. The fact that Nazism flourished more strongly in Bavaria and Austria than anywhere else did not occur to them, for they appeared to know nothing of the Brown House in Munich and had forgotten that the founder of the movement himself came from Austria.

Christie certainly had no idea what impression he made on many of his English supporters by his bland refusal to understand the seriousness of his attitude. In an address to the London Soroptimists he spoke proudly of how Hitler was constantly sending personal representatives to Glyndebourne to induce Fritz Busch and Carl Ebert to return to Germany.

'They are not Jews,' Christie is reported as saying in the *Star*, 'but left Germany because they refused to mix politics with art. They feel at present that they cannot go back.' He added that he did not feel quite as strongly as they did and he himself had been to Germany to discuss operas 'with the highest musical circles there'.

Least of all did Christie ever realize how all this affected the feelings of his artistic directors, so that Fritz Busch, for instance, could write to Bing after the Christies returned to England from Nazi Germany to ask bitterly if they had come back with the Dagger of Honour of the Party.

Ebert and Bing sailed for New York in the second week of January 1939 to give the World Fair project what *Variety* described as the 'o.o.' – that admirable ideogram for 'the once-over'. After a few days Bing reported that the Metropolitan would suit only *Macbeth* and *Don Giovanni* and that there was great difficulty in finding a suitable house for *Figaro* and *Così fan tutte*. Artistic points had been agreed upon, he said, but financial problems still had to be solved; it also appeared that since August was not an advisable date he was discussing the possibilities of September. Four days later, however, Bing had to cable that negotiations had come to nothing; there were, however, considerable future possibilities to be discussed. He added that he had been impressed by the singing of Risë Stevens at the Metropolitan and suggested her for Dorabella and Cherubino at Glyndebourne.

Once Bing was back in England at the beginning of February, with all such distractions as New York, Lucerne, Australia and Covent Garden put aside, it was possible to concentrate once more on the organization of the coming Glyndebourne season. Busch was delighted to hear that Risë Stevens was available; he insisted firmly that only 'pretty girls' (the phrase was always written in English) should be engaged at Glyndebourne and the prospect of an attractive new Cherubino and Dorabella pleased him very much. 'It would be frightful,' he said, 'to have the same ensemble as last year – boring for all concerned.'

These words were in a letter answering one from Bing in which he said he had been approached by a lady friend (*eine Freundin*) of Gigli's with the emphatic assurance that it was the famous Italian tenor's 'dream' to sing at Glyndebourne. Bing had replied that

Gigli could sing four Ottavios at £50 a time. Would Busch agree? Bing added that personally he didn't believe in any of it for a moment, but as Beecham was apparently going to put on *Don Giovanni* at Covent Garden with Ezio Pinza and Richard Tauber it would be 'quite nice' if Glyndebourne had Gigli. Fritz Busch replied that Bing could go up to £60 a performance and that it would be possible to cut down Gigli's rehearsals if need be. This seems to be the last that was heard of another of those intriguing ideas which flashed across the scene at Glyndebourne for a brief moment and then disappeared for ever.

The customary pre-season crisis occurred slightly earlier in 1939 than usual. It was found at the end of February that Aulikki Rautawaara would not be available. The crisis was caused not so much by the sudden necessity to find another Countess (that was something that would sort itself out, Busch considered), but by John Christie's embarrassing keenness to engage an English soprano for the part who was fine to listen to but quite exceptionally plain to look at. Christie went on about this lady so much that Busch had to read the riot act once more. As the owner of Glyndebourne, Busch said, Christie naturally had every right, especially as he had now had several years' experience, to express his wishes and to strive for their fulfilment. But when it came to the point of insisting on the engagement of a singer who, like the English soprano in question, was unacceptable to both Busch and Ebert, then Busch could no longer take responsibility for the artistic direction of the Opera. He knew Ebert felt the same way, and would agree that the greater part of the success of Glyndebourne had been due to the 'pretty girls' with talent. If Aulikki Rautawaara was to be replaced, Busch went on, then it must be by someone who sang better and was at least as good, and not worse, to look at. If this stern attitude did not immediately produce a tolerable Countess at least it prevented the engagement of a plain one. No more was heard of John Christie's English soprano.

Although she was not available for the Glyndebourne season Aulikki Rautawaara was among those engaged to take part in four curious one-night stands that had been arranged to take place in Belgium in April and May. Busch agreed to conduct *Figaro* and *Don Giovanni* at the Théâtre de la Monnaie in Brussels with a cast which, although the Belgians were quick to publicize it as 'la troupe des Festivals Mozart de Glyndebourne', was very much a second XI, some of whom wore clothes borrowed from the Glyndebourne wardrobe and all of whom appeared before scenery supplied from stock by the Monnaie. The casts included at least two singers whom Busch had refused to have at Glyndebourne at any price, the production was not by Ebert but by M. Fritz Busch's son, M. Hans Peter Busch, and M. Busch himself was associated with the excursion entirely for the sake of Audrey Mildmay-Christie (as she was described in the programme) to spare her, as he said, 'bad experiences with another conductor – as she may discover soon enough at Salzburg'.

Audrey Mildmay sang Zerlina in the company of her Glyndebourne colleagues, Ina Souez, and Messrs Brownlee, Henderson, David Lloyd and Franklin. Donna Elvira was sung by Margit Bokor who was also the Susanna in *Figaro*. The Leporello at La Monnaie was Virgilio Lazzari, who later sang with Pinza and Tauber at the Covent Garden performance of the opera. The cast of the Monnaie *Figaro* had only four Glyndebourne regulars – John Brownlee, Aulikki Rautawaara, Constance Willis as Marcellina, and Fergus Dunlop as the Gardener. It was altogether a quaint expedition which nevertheless seemed to impress the Bruxellois with the prowess of Glyndebourne. A visit by some of the Glyndebourne singers, Audrey Mildmay among them, to the Royal Flemish Opera in Antwerp on their way to Brussels landed them in single performances of the same two operas, in which Alexander Kipnis was the unlikely Figaro and Don Giovanni, and the Ottavio was Luigi Fort – the young tenor whom Audrey Mildmay had feared would make her look so old as Norina in *Don Pasquale*. The quasi-Glyndebourne contribution was part of an Antwerp Mozart Festival at which *Così fan tutte* was also performed, together with an opera with the evocative title of *De Tooverfluit*, which turned out to be *The Magic Flute* in Flemish.

Fritz Busch was not concerned with the Antwerp performances in any way, nor was his son. They were conducted by M. Eugen Szenkar, produced by M. Karel Schmitz, and the dances were arranged by M. Wlady Karnetzky – three names which suggest that the Koninklijke Vlaamsche Opera was as liberally cosmopolitan in its way as the Koninklijke Opera at Covent Garden.

Nearly two months before the Belgian trip, when Glyndebourne was still without a Countess for the Festival, Busch remembered that two years previously Audrey Mildmay had said she would like to sing the part when her voice was ready for it and that her husband had encouraged her in this ambition. Now, in March 1939, Busch wrote to Bing to say that he considered her voice had grown bigger and more mature and was most suitable for the Countess. If she could be persuaded to take it on it would solve two problems – the casting of the Countess and the still tricky matter of her visit to Salzburg. In learning the part of the Countess, Busch calculated, she would automatically find herself forgetting, or 'unlearning' (*verlernen*), Susanna and so be unable to go to Salzburg. The question was whether she could master the Countess in the fortnight or so left between the trip to Antwerp and Brussels and the first rehearsals of the Glyndebourne season which would open with *Figaro*. The really doubtful thing seemed to Busch to be whether she would do it at all, even though it had originally been her own wish.

Bing put the proposal to Audrey Mildmay but had to report that she was against doing the part; she was afraid her voice wasn't yet good enough. She had sung one of the Countess's arias to her husband and Jani Strasser and neither of them had liked it very much. In any case, she had said, she would definitely not like to accept the part without first singing it to Busch. 'She feels you might agree now,' Bing wrote to Busch, 'and then suddenly be disappointed if she didn't come up to your expectations. She would rather postpone it for another year.' The day he had written these words Bing received a letter from Miss Mildmay saying a definite no to the Countess.

While all this was happening yet another international crisis blew up. Hitler seized Czecho-Slovakia, the distant country which it will be remembered Mr Chamberlain told us nobody (including the Germans?) had ever heard of. 'Do you remember the lunch you had with Duff Cooper, and his prophecies?' Busch asked Bing ominously.

Between Chamberlain's warning to Germany on 17 March that Great Britain would resist domination by force 'to the utmost limit of her power' and the cession of Memel to Germany by Lithuania on 21 March, attention at Glyndebourne was pleasurably distracted for a moment by a cable from Busch in Copenhagen: 'Found Countess in Reykjavik Iceland letter following.'

In the letter which followed Busch said the young lady's name was Maria Markan; he was sending her to an Italian coach at the Stockholm Opera to learn the part in Italian as she had so far sung it only in German and Danish, and to compensate her for loss of work while on this course would Glyndebourne please send her £15. Where Aulikki Rauta-waara had had bow legs, continued Busch, Maria Markan's were a bit on the plump side; but as the Countess wore a crinoline the whole time it obviously didn't matter.

Bing was astonished to hear Busch say that Miss Rautawaara was bow-legged; person-ally he had never noticed her legs at all (skirts were worn long at the time). After working closely with Busch for five years Bing should not have been astonished, of course. It was exactly the sort of thing Busch *did* always notice and which was characteristic of Glynde-bourne's unique preoccupation with the look of opera as well as the sound of it

The fact that Maria Markan came from Iceland made her specially attractive to John Christie. 'We haven't had one before,' he said. There is no doubt that Christie derived the greatest possible pleasure from collecting exotic nationalities to show in the pro-gramme; certainly he would have been most disappointed if he had given way to the strong plea made by Bing in 1937 to omit all mention of them, and had in consequence been unable to claim an Icelandic artist at Glyndebourne to add to the collection which already included Nicaraguan, Finnish, Yugoslav and Greek singers.

To cap a singer from as far north on the map as Iceland, Christie was able to welcome one from as far south as Tasmania when Margherita Grandi was engaged to sing Lady Macbeth. The accident of Miss Grandi's birth in Hobart saved Glyndebourne a great many headaches, for though she was of Italian ancestry and had made her career in Italy, she bore a British passport and so made unnecessary all the usual doubts and delays of having to get a labour permit.

Except for an emphatic and refreshingly professional statement to reporters that she did not believe in 'mascots' Margherita Grandi was given oddly little publicity before the first performance of *Macbeth*. The principal topic of news editors' prelims for the year was the huge bass drum made for the 1939 production of Verdi's opera. 'The world's biggest drum', six feet in diameter, was to be used to give a more musical quality to the thunder in *Macbeth*. It had taken the firm of Henry Potter and Co a year to build as they had had to wait for two cow hides large enough to make the drum head out of. Even-tually the right sized cow died and the hide was used to complete what was said to be the largest drum in Great Britain for 155 years.[1]

---

[1] Except that it would have spoilt the rather meagre publicity value of the story I have often wondered why Glyndebourne didn't borrow the gigantic bass drum used by Toscanini in the Verdi Requiem at the Queen's Hall in 1938. This was a monster instrument and superbly worthy of Verdi's dramatic solo use of it on the

The only other prelim topic that gained any kind of circulation was Queen Mary's expressed intention to visit Glyndebourne. She had been shown over the Opera House during the winter (that part of East Sussex within easy motoring distance of Ringmer must hold the record for weekends spent there by royalty) and had said she would come and see *Macbeth* during the Festival. The high spot of the pre-season publicity was achieved when, with a neat journalistic stroke, an imaginative reporter decided to combine both the year's Glyndebourne stories into a piece which finished up with the heading:

Queen Mary
<u>Will Hear</u>
LARGEST
DRUM
IN WORLD

After that there was little anybody could say.

The audience which collected for the first night on 1 June to hear *Figaro* was met by fewer front-of-house changes than in recent years. The seating in the auditorium had been increased by ten seats altogether – six in the stalls and four in the balcony – to make a total capacity of 537, and the evening's programmes gave no sort of puff to the Nazis' Salzburg, but instead printed a generous selection of domestic credits including, for the first time, the acknowledgment never before thought of by any operatic organization: Head Gardener – F. Harvey. Mr Harvey's name appeared on the programme of every opera performed at Glyndebourne from that day until he retired in 1960.

The production of *Figaro* which opened the season marked what was virtually a break with Glyndebourne tradition: for the first time since the beginning of the Festival Opera there was a different Countess. Maria Markan started a little nervously, but as she gained confidence she played the part with great dignity; she had a beautiful voice and in spite of being a little pedestrian in the recitatives was considered to be an acquisition. It was something of a tribute to the effect she made that not one of the critics apparently made any comparison with her predecessor. Risë Stevens, on the other hand, survived frequent comparison with Luise Helletsgruber and was greeted as a charming discovery. She later enchanted a wider public when she starred in Metro-Goldwyn-Mayer's version of *The Chocolate Soldier* in which the story, for some reason (probably because MGM owned the film rights), was taken from Molnar's *The Guardsman*. Miss Stevens's co-star in this film was a singer who had once given an audition to Fritz Busch at Dresden. Busch described him as a young, good-looking man who sang 'without the usual stage fright, in such fine voice and with such beautiful expression' that he at once offered him an engagement. The singer was Nelson Eddy 'who, to our regret,' said Busch, 'did not accept the contract – a case that did not happen every day at Dresden'.

---

off-beats of the *Dies Irae*. It had been lent for Toscanini's performance by the Royal Academy of Music who had had it ever since Charles Stanford had it made for one of the earliest English performances of the work. I'm sure Glyndebourne could have had it for the asking in 1939.

On the second night of the season *Macbeth* was revived and made an even greater impact than on its first hearing. Margherita Grandi was found to have everything this almost impossible part required – a voice of enormous range and power, great gifts as an actress, and an impressive, noble appearance which caused Desmond Shawe-Taylor, who was not alone in doing so, to remark that she answered one's notion of Mrs Siddons. It was a classic performance, attended on one of those rare July nights when he was not announcing a new treaty or reaffirming a pledge to Poland, by Mr Neville Chamberlain. He was given an ovation by the audience few of whom were optimistic about the possibilities of peace lasting much longer in their time, but who nevertheless made the pretence that some good might come of his confidence in Hitler – for after all, the Prime Minister had said of him what Duncan had said of Cawdor –

> *He was a gentleman on whom I built*
> *An absolute trust.*

The cast of *Macbeth,* by coincidence, was entirely drawn from artists born in English-speaking countries – Tasmania, the United States, Wales, England and Australia. Indeed, Francesco Valentino was the only one of the principals who did not bear a British passport. Very much the same sort of record could be claimed in the case of the first performance of *Don Giovanni* in 1939, for with the exception of Salvatore Baccaloni's all the other seven names in the cast list were those of British subjects – either by birth, marriage, or (in the case of the Welsh and the Scots) by conquest. The two major changes from the previous year's production were the beautifully sung Don Ottavio of David Lloyd, and the Donna Elvira of Hella Toros, who came originally from Trieste but was British by marriage. For the first time Elvira's 'Mi tradì' was omitted, which led Richard Capell to suggest in the *Daily Telegraph* that Alfred Einstein's newly discovered Mozart recitative might be included as it helped to fit this aria (added by the composer for the first Vienna performance) into the scheme. Also, proposed Mr Capell, why not include the Zerlina-Leporello duet written for the same production, when it took the place of 'Il mio tesoro'? After all, it was argued, we always made a day of it at Glyndebourne so there was no point in saving time. It was pleasing to note how in so short a time Glyndebourne had come to be accepted as the only place we were ever likely to be given the luxury of a complete, if not always a correct, Mozart. In 1939 the question of recitatives accompanied on a piano and the absence of the customary appoggiaturas was still being raised as vigorously and unavailingly as ever.

Dino Borgioli joined the cast as Don Ottavio at the fifth of the year's seven performances of *Don Giovanni* when it was conducted for the first time by Alberto Erede, Busch's principal assistant and his chief, fluent German-speaking talent scout in Italy. Erede also conducted *Figaro* on a couple of occasions.

The names of the players in the stage bands in Act 1 of *Don Giovanni* were given for the first time in the programme of the 1939 production, and showed the three dance orchestras to be as mixed in their musical and their social constitution as ever – pros and semi-pros, with titled and other amateur ladies (including two bass-fiddlerettes) outnumbering the men in the total complement of twenty by no fewer than fourteen to six.

The revival of *Così fan tutte* introduced two newcomers to the production – Risë Stevens, who made as great a success of Dorabella as she had of Cherubino, and Gino del Signore, a young Italian tenor who was described, in the still prevailing prose style of the time, as having a 'winsome' way with him as Ferrando. The restoration of Ferrando's second-act aria, 'Tradito, schernito', which had hitherto always been cut at Glyndebourne, was welcomed with the natural and universal comment that nobody could understand why it had ever been left out in the first place. Ina Souez's Fiordiligi was as accomplished as ever and came in for special praise this year for the way she managed almost to distract us from the distraction of the elaborate stage business that had been added by the producer to accompany 'Come scoglio' since the previous production.

Finally, the revival of *Don Pasquale* was rapturously received once more, with the Stabile-Baccaloni duet and the Servants' Chorus encored every night and fully vindicating Fritz Busch's publicly expressed assertion that in the opera house it was 'absolutely absurd to forbid applause'.

Owing to the sudden illness of Gino del Signore the part of Ernesto was taken on the first night, and at very short notice, by Luigi Fort, who had arrived at Glyndebourne with only a few hours to spare after an urgent flight from Vienna. Or Italy. As with Hilde Konetzni's air-rescue operation, the papers were never quite sure exactly where these hired helps had flown from.

Audrey Mildmay, partnered by the young tenor she had originally protested so strongly against, was not made to look a day older as Norina by an Ernesto of considerable charm, with a small but attractive voice that led several writers to describe him as a *tenorino*. As in the previous year, once *Don Pasquale* was in the repertoire Miss Mildmay's part as Susanna was taken over on several occasions by Irene Eisinger. The success of Donizetti's little comedy with the Glyndebourne public was so great that an extra performance of the opera was announced 'owing to the demand for seats which cannot be met.' This plan was rather mysteriously cancelled by the announcement shortly afterwards that an extra performance of *Figaro* would be given 'in place of the extra performance of *Don Pasquale* previously advertised'. One result of the change was that John Brownlee had to sing two Don Giovannis, three Almavivas and one Don Alfonso in seven days.

While all this had been going on it had been decided to hold a ten-day Verdi Festival – *Falstaff* and *Macbeth* – at Glyndebourne in 1940 before the start of the normal season in June, and once again the idea of inviting Toscanini to conduct *Falstaff* was revived. This time, however, John Christie wrote to Toscanini right at the start:

9th July, 1939

Dear Maestro Toscanini,

The accompanying letter by Busch and Ebert, and the visit of our friend, Erede, will tell you of our idea of a Verdi Festival next year.

I would only like to add to their letter and to what Erede is going to tell you, that I, personally, should be delighted if you could see your way to accept: all of us would be more than pleased to welcome you and I hope that you would enjoy working here.

Alberto Erede, thoroughly briefed in every aspect of the proposal from the rehearsal schedules to the provision of a 'villa' at Ringmer, with all the servants, beds and luxuries the Maestro could possibly want, set off for Lucerne to discuss the proposition in detail. He reported that Toscanini had seemed extremely keen on conducting at Glyndebourne. The atmosphere of the place had pleased him very much, but it would be just impossible to find the time to rehearse and conduct five performances of *Falstaff*. The performance he had seen of *Macbeth* was wonderful, he said, and Busch could do *Falstaff* perfectly well – he couldn't do it better himself. In recalling this visit many years later Erede told how moved he had been to go from Busch to Toscanini and to sense the similarity between the two men who had in common a genuine feeling of humility towards music in which personal vanity played absolutely no part.

It is interesting to note that, according to Rudolf Bing's estimate, if Toscanini had accepted Glyndebourne's fee of £1,500 (which he certainly would have done if he had agreed to come) the Verdi Festival would have shown a profit of more than a thousand pounds.

As those who lived through those days will remember all too clearly the summer of 1939 seemed to be an endless succession of crisis weekends. Hitler always timed his moves for a Saturday and so made sure that nobody would do anything about it in England until Monday morning. So it was that when on the last night of the season – a Saturday – John Christie came on to the stage to report 'serious news' everybody feared the worst. With an inspired sense of anti-climax he announced that on that afternoon Harrow had beaten Eton at Lord's for the first time since 1908 – and by ten wickets, no less.

So ended Glyndebourne's sixth and, so far, longest season during which a small profit was made and the BBC broadcast two complete operas for the first time – the whole of *Macbeth*, the whole of *Don Giovanni*, together with the first two acts of *Don Pasquale*, the first act of *Così fan tutte* and the second act of *Figaro*.

When the curtain fell on *Così fan tutte* on 15 July it did not rise again on a normal Festival performance for another eleven years. The following day, however, at a reception given by the Music Club who entertained the entire Glyndebourne opera company at the May Fair Hotel, John Christie announced the programme for 1940. It would begin on 30 May and last until 17 July. The repertoire would consist of *Carmen*, *Figaro*, *Don Giovanni*, *Macbeth* and a revival of *The Magic Flute*. Christie went on to say that *Così fan tutte* had been left out because it had declined in popularity – a surprising revelation in view of its position as one of Glyndebourne's most exquisite and peculiar creations. Owing to lack of popular support in 1939 there would be only three performances of *Macbeth* in 1940; this was a rather puzzling show of pessimism because Christie had only just told everybody proudly that, after a slow start, the last three performances of Verdi's opera at Glyndebourne had been sold out. But obviously he hoped to get those three full houses back for certain.

The choice of *Carmen* did not seem so astonishing at the time as it must now appear to us. In 1939 many of John Christie's eccentricities and foibles were familiar enough, but few people knew of his innate prejudice against French operas; to find him agreeing to promote *Carmen*, the most popular French opera in history, suggests that Busch and Ebert must have been unusually persuasive in putting their case. Beyond the suggestion that Risë Stevens would play Carmen, however, no further details of the 1940 season were published.

Any doubts or hopes the executive of the Glyndebourne Festival Opera may have had, any dilemmas that may have still faced the Christies over a possible appearance at Salzburg, were soon dispelled, however. Within less than two months war had broken out and Glyndebourne had become a vast nursery school for 260 children evacuated from London.

CHAPTER FIFTEEN

Interval

ALTHOUGH THE HOLOCAUST H. G. Wells had led us to expect failed to take place on the declaration of war, there can have been few who held out much hope that the Glynde-bourne Festival Opera would survive. Few, that is, apart from the usual all-over-by-Christmas optimists and Glyndebourne itself. For the rest of us those first six Glynde-bourne seasons quickly took their place in past history as a phenomenon of their time – something unforgettable and probably too good ever to be experienced again.

John Christie had spent something like £100,000 of his own money in the creation of an institution which achieved world-wide fame in the course of its first brief season, not just because it offered its patrons a good dinner, a walk in somebody else's garden and a sight of the orchestra playing croquet, but because it set a standard of performance and artistic ensemble by which all other festivals were henceforth to be judged. Like La Scala in Milan, Glyndebourne was endowed from the start with the gift of keeping itself in the news without effort; even Christie's lamentable practice for many years of making his announcements only through *The Times* did not keep Glyndebourne's name out of the rest of the papers. The popular dailies merely lifted the stories from their low-circulation quality contemporary one day and ran them with larger headings the next.

The fact that for the first three months of the war no mention of the Glyndebourne Festival Opera appeared even in *The Times* did not mean that 'the emergency' (as some of our more idiotic public figures still called it) had driven opera out of Glyndebourne's mind. The plan for the 1940 Festival had been scrapped, of course, but in its place it was intended to present a War Season at Glyndebourne – a fortnight of *Figaro* and *Così fan tutte* (or *The Magic Flute*) in June. Bing wrote to both Busch and Ebert asking them to consider this possibility though, as he explained, the project depended largely on whether the BBC could be persuaded to subsidize it.

Since the outbreak of war, perhaps to make the British censor's job easier (or not), perhaps to save Bing embarrassment, Busch and Ebert began to write all their letters to Bing in English. Busch's answer from Stockholm to this particular letter contained the penetrating sentence: 'Everybody here is, however, rather disquiet on account of the Russians, whose mysterious intentions according to their nature seem completely impossible to look through' – as neat an observation of Russian foreign policy in September

1939 as one encountered anywhere. Until the War Season was definite, Bing explained, Glyndebourne's name would be kept before the public by a tour, and eventually a London run, of Gay's *Beggar's Opera*. (I emphasize that it was Gay's opera because in a German obituary notice of John Christie the writer was convinced it was the Brecht-Weill *Dreigroschenoper*. There are enough Glyndebourne legends already without allowing another to start unchallenged.) It was proposed that *The Beggar's Opera* should be produced by Ebert who had once mentioned it, with Marlowe's *Doctor Faustus*, as one of the pieces he wanted to stage in the open air at Glyndebourne and so extend the Festival Opera's activities.

Ebert was unable to accept, however, because the dates clashed with his commitments in Ankara where he was to spend the rest of the war building up a Turkish National Theatre. It is doubtful in any case whether he would have been given any sort of permit to work in England. When, a few weeks later, he accepted an offer from Gabriel Pascal to work as producer on films of *St Joan*, *Major Barbara* and Shakespeare's *Macbeth*, the Home Office refused to allow him to enter the country.

The Glyndebourne *Beggar's Opera* was in the end produced by John Gielgud, with Audrey Mildmay as Polly, Roy Henderson as Peachum and Michael Redgrave as Macheath. It might be thought that the production of an English classic of this nature with an all-British cast could scarcely involve the management in any trouble. In fact it did, and precisely because it was not all-British enough. A crisis arose when, under the Aliens Employment Order, Hans Oppenheim, by now working at Dartington, was refused a permit to conduct the show.

Fritz Busch, on receiving news of this from Bing, replied that he was absolutely delighted to hear it and, in the familiar paternal manner that had meant so much to the success of Glyndebourne, he remarked on the 'tactless stupidness' of an action directly contrary to John Christie's 'ancient principle' to give work to English artists. 'And now,' Busch went on, 'to choose a foreigner, by no means better and besides one living in satisfactory financial circumstances. This must have hurt the young English musicians who just now have to fight for their daily bread harder than ever before.'

An English conductor, or rather trio of conductors, was found easily enough – among them the man John Christie always referred to as 'old Austin'. Frederic Austin who, in today's fashionable phrase, had 'realized' (in other words, arranged) the music of *The Beggar's Opera* for the famous Playfair production of 1920 and whose score was used in the Glyndebourne production, was only 67 years old at the time and was obviously described as 'old' to distinguish him from George Austin, the Ringmer organist and Glyndebourne music librarian.

The *Beggar's Opera* tour of six weeks began at the Theatre Royal, Brighton, in January 1940. The printed programme contained instructions in what to do in an air raid and an announcement that the next production at the theatre would be the Wilton House Players in *Heil Cinderella*, 'A New Topical Christmas Pantomime by Cecil Beaton and John Sutro' which would be performed by a cast that read like a pre-war Glyndebourne visitors' list in the glossies – Lady Margaret Drummond Hay, the Lady Mayor of Wilton,

Cecil Beaton, Olga Lynn and, as the billing told us, 'Vivien and Poppet John, the daughters of Augustus John'.

After Brighton the *Beggar's Opera* tour of No 1 towns included Cardiff, Liverpool, Manchester, Glasgow and Edinburgh where, according to legend, Audrey Mildmay is said to have stood in the moonlight with Rudolf Bing and looking up at the castle have reflected once more on an idea she had first had a few years earlier in Salzburg: that the Scottish capital would make a wonderful setting for a Festival.

The London run of *The Beggar's Opera* began in March, reopening a newly-decorated Haymarket Theatre, which was the last London theatre to start up again after the general close-down ordered in September 1939. In several cases the first night was covered by the newspapers' dramatic critics who, being theatrically more sophisticated than their musical colleagues, did not hesitate to pan the fussiness of the production and the inappropriateness of Motley's pseudo-Cruikshank décor and costumes. The incongruous spectacle of Polly Peachum carrying a parasol led inevitably to the description of the show as 'genteel' and 'ladylike'. And when, within less than a week of the opening, Audrey Mildmay went down with German measles and Irene Eisinger took over, the effect of Polly Peachum with a strong Central European accent as well as a parasol was more incongruous still. On the whole *The Beggar's Opera* was not one of Glyndebourne's happiest conceptions; it was entirely lacking in style. However, in addition to making a profit, the company made a fairly good set of six records for HMV.

The Haymarket run ended on 25 May 1940, and though a second tour had been planned with Roy Henderson playing Macheath and Percy Heming as Peachum, this was cancelled. Within seven days the BEF had been evacuated from Dunkirk, and on 25 June France capitulated.

The fall of France also brought to an end an interesting plan which had been discussed to establish the Glyndebourne Festival Opera in a permanent home in the United States. The scheme had started in the early days of the war when Sir Robert Mayer was introduced to John D. Rockefeller Jnr. in America and had suggested the idea of adding Glyndebourne opera to the many things Rockefeller had already done in the course of spending $17,000,000 on the reconstruction and renovation of Williamsburg, Virginia. Rockefeller approved of the idea and agreed to build a small opera house in Williamsburg if the project proved feasible.

There were inevitable difficulties with the American Unions over the question of importing English electricians and scene shifters but these were eventually settled. Only with the Musicians' Union was no agreement possible; the local Virginia branch refused to consider allowing either the New York Philharmonic-Symphony, the Boston Symphony, or the Philadelphia Symphony Orchestra to be used for a projected season in April 1941. While this was all being argued, however, France fell and Rockefeller was forced to suspend the whole scheme, and the second, but by no means the last, attempt to introduce Glyndebourne to America came to an end.

In the summer of 1940 Audrey Mildmay and her children, Rosamond and George, were evacuated to Canada. There, and later in New York, they led the difficult, often humiliating and frustrating existence common to nearly all those English who were evacuated to dollar countries – unable, because of currency restrictions, to contribute a cent to their keep, and in Audrey Mildmay's case having often literally to sing for her supper. It was in Canada that Audrey Mildmay made her last stage appearance – as Susanna in 1943, at His Majesty's Theatre, Montreal, in a festival production of *Figaro* conducted by Sir Thomas Beecham, who brought her specially 3,000 miles across Canada from Vancouver to sing the part. From Canada Audrey Mildmay went to New York where conditions were even harder and she was discovered at one time to be living with her children in what is known in Manhattan as a 'cold-water walk-up' – an apartment with no central heating, constant hot water or lift. America seemed to offer even fewer opportunities than Canada for a singer whose gifts and personality were altogether too intimate and fragile to flourish in the rough and tumble of musical life in war-time America.

In the summer of 1944, after four disagreeable years away from home, Audrey Mildmay returned to England with her children and resumed the role of Audrey Christie.

During her absence neither her husband nor Rudolf Bing had been idle. Apart from having sold the contents of the Glyndebourne cellar of German wine for more than £17,000 (thereby leaving himself with nothing to drink and having to buy some of it back from the wine trade who had bought it – much of it at higher prices than the Glyndebourne Restaurant had charged, which as Dr Loeb has pointed out, were the highest prices for Hocks ever recorded at that time), Christie had also set out to buy the freehold of Covent Garden Opera House. He had employed a leading firm of property dealers and was prepared to pay up to £100,000 for it; he was told he could probably get it for a good deal less. 'But owing to the hostility which existed in certain quarters,' he said, 'I did not go on with it.'

Rudolf Bing had been given a job in the John Lewis Partnership after *The Beggar's Opera* folded and had risen to be a manager of Peter Jones in Sloane Square. He gave up being 'a draper', as he called it, in the autumn of 1944 to return to his job as General Manager of Glyndebourne, which by now was deeply involved in several enterprises. One of these did not come to anything; or rather, it did not come to anything in its original form. This was Bing's project to establish an annual international festival of Music and Drama at Oxford. It was an ambitious and brilliant scheme but though it was discussed in detail and various Oxford committees and councils were formed or planned, the necessary financial support was not found. On the other hand, Glyndebourne's creation of a professional Children's Theatre in London (an ambition of Audrey Mildmay's), and participation in the so-called 'Company of Four' at the Lyric Theatre, Hammersmith, were both realities – the second enterprise most harshly so, as the idea of presenting good and unusual straight plays for short runs performed by actors newly released from war service proved a financially fruitless experiment, and Glyndebourne had to pull out as soon as it could decently do so.

In the high summer of 1945 Glyndebourne's thoughts at last turned again to what it understood best – the question of opera at its own Festival Opera House. After Christie's failure to buy the freehold, Covent Garden had been leased to Boosey and Hawkes, the music publishers, and Christie's proposal that opera at the Royal Opera House should be a joint effort, to which Glyndebourne would contribute its experience and methods, had been turned down by one of the innumerable consultative committees that were formed in the later stages of the war. Christie, it is true, had been a little over-optimistic in believing that a repertory opera could really be run on Glyndebourne Festival lines, according to Glyndebourne standards based on his own congenital inability to consider any form of compromise. Nevertheless, Christie's plan and the idea that Bing might become General Manager of Covent Garden certainly did not warrant the rough and ill-mannered rejection they received from Lord Keynes, the Chairman of the Covent Garden Committee, and which inevitably led to a serious break in Christie's personal relationship with him.

Frank Howes, who was at that time music critic of *The Times* and had been a friend of Christie's for many years, has told me how twice in one week he heard the same story in identical terms from opposite sides: 'John Christie said: "I've known Keynes all my life, was at Eton with him and am a neighbour and ride up and down in the same train from Lewes with him, yet he won't see me." While somebody else [Mr Howes cannot remember exactly who] said: "Keynes says he's known Christie all his life, was at Eton with him and is a neighbour riding up and down in the same train from Lewes. But he says 'Mustn't waste one's time on – ' – and here unfortunately my memory fails – but 'cranks' (it wasn't 'fools') or some such word."' In the circumstances it was hardly surprising that Rudolf Bing was not appointed general manager of Covent Garden. Instead, the newly created position of General Administrator was given to Mr (now Sir) David Webster, who – like Bing – had also been connected with drapery in his time; and also, oddly enough, with a firm called Lewis's. But in Liverpool, not London.

Any hopes the musical public may have had that Sir Thomas Beecham would have anything to do with the new Covent Garden set-up were finally dispelled by the appointment of Karl Rankl as Musical Director after Covent Garden had failed to attract Eugène Goossens to the job.

Sir Thomas Beecham, however, had other plans. He turned to John Christie, his fellow Covent Garden reject, and offered to co-operate in putting on a Festival Opera season at Glyndebourne in 1946, and furthermore he would conduct without a fee. Beecham's offer was accepted and within a short time the repertoire had been decided upon, rehearsal dates discussed and the season planned to last from 12 June to 13 July. The repertoire would consist of *The Magic Flute* (in English) and *La Bohème*. If these two operas were not enough then, said Sir Thomas, 'We could knock together a third opera in no time' – a remark from a Bateman cartoon which shook Glyndebourne to its foundations. The third opera Beecham suggested was *Lucia di Lammermoor*, which appealed very much to Bing as being in the Glyndebourne tradition of 'discovering' an old masterpiece and presenting it in a new form as had been done with *Macbeth*. It was not long, however, before *La Bohème* and *Lucia* were no longer discussed and *Carmen* was adopted in their place. *Carmen* would be given in French in its original form – as *opéra comique* with dialogue – and the lead would be played by Kathleen Ferrier, a singer recommended by Roy Henderson and who had not yet appeared on any opera stage. When Sir Thomas Beecham heard of this he issued what can best be described as A Statement informing Christie in the third person that he was 'unwilling to take part in any representation of *Carmen* which is to be made the subject of experiments with comparatively raw and undeveloped material'. John Christie, in a series of abrupt four-word sentences, replied with an indignant re-affirmation of Glyndebourne's time-honoured and well-proven policy of doing exactly what Beecham objected to.

At this point, after Sir Thomas had made a number of irrelevant criticisms of Glynde-bourne's Mozart recordings, the Beechams decided to drop the whole idea (the extent of Betty Humby's participation in her husband's operatic affairs was astonishing for a con-cert pianist and an embarrassment to everybody). Instead, talk with the Christies turned to something vaguely called 'Week Ends of Music' at Glyndebourne which, it was thought, might be held in the summer of 1946.

As it turned out, the only form of Week Ends of Music which took place at Glynde-bourne in 1946 were the three Saturday night performances in the course of a fourteen-performance season of Benjamin Britten's *Rape of Lucretia*. Although it had its world première at the Festival Opera House on 12 July 1946, *The Rape of Lucretia* was not what is understood by a Glyndebourne production. Glyndebourne Productions Ltd sponsored and encouraged, but made no artistic contribution to, the season – unless it may take credit for having recommended Kathleen Ferrier to the composer. The fourteen per-formances were divided between two separate casts, Ernest Ansermet conducting the first team and Reginald Goodall the second. At the first night Kathleen Ferrier as Lucretia began her tragically short stage career, and a pre-war member of the Glyndebourne chorus, Peter Pears, sang the part of Male Chorus. As this was not a genuine Glynde-bourne occasion the nationalities of the singers were not shown on the programme; had they been it would have been noticed that the second-night cast of eight principals, performing for a company that was soon to be formed into the 'English Opera Group', included fewer British nationals than were found among the eight principals in per-formances of *Don Giovanni* and *Macbeth* at Glyndebourne before the war.

On the back page of the same programme, included among several references to current Glyndebourne interests and activities, there appeared the first guarded announcement: 'Plans are under consideration for the Edinburgh International Festival 1947 of Music and Drama.' This was followed by a short list of some of its more important features, though apart from telling us that the Vienna Philharmonic Orchestra would be appearing with Bruno Walter (Bing was understandably proud of having reunited conductor and orchestra for the first time since the Anschluss), the details were generally too vague to give us any idea of the class of festival it turned out to be – that, for instance, 'Chamber Music' would include the unique group consisting of Artur Schnabel, Joseph Szigeti, William Prim-rose and Pierre Fournier; that 'Foreign Drama Companies' would mean Louis Jouvet and his company; that Lotte Lehmann would be giving a Lieder recital with Bruno Walter accompanying her; and that Kathleen Ferrier, introduced to the conductor by Rudolf Bing, would be singing in Mahler's *Das Lied von der Erde* for the first time under Walter.

The financial losses on *The Rape of Lucretia* enterprise (the total of 126 performances included a tour of England and a visit to Holland) were described by John Christie as 'startling', and though he allowed an announcement to appear in the programme that the Glyndebourne Festival 1947 would include *The Rape of Lucretia* again, Purcell's *Dido and Aeneas*, edited by Benjamin Britten, 'together with a new Contemporary Opera', he made it quite clear that he had no intention of financing these contributions himself. The 'new contemporary opera' in fact turned out to be Benjamin Britten's *Albert Herring*, but it might equally have been something chosen and paid for by Glyndebourne, for Bing had been in touch with Gian Carlo Menotti over *The Medium* as a likely piece. Menotti, however, had been unable to let Bing have a score to look at as the only copy was at that time in Paris. This project had been discussed a month or so before the first performance of *The Rape of Lucretia* at Glyndebourne and was dropped, one suspects, as soon as John Christie had undergone his first modern chamber opera and did not relish the prospect of another – certainly not if he was expected to pay for it.

Christie did not at first greatly relish the idea of what he did come to pay for in the 1947 season: the production by Glyndebourne of Gluck's *Orpheus*.[1] Remembering that when Fritz Busch had suggested doing Gluck's opera before the war it was to have been in the French version, Christie naturally feared that the Paris edition of *Orpheus* would be used this time. 'I personally don't like the French language,' he wrote to Bing when the subject came up again at the end of the 1946 season. Bing for his part, though he may not have felt so strongly about spoken or sung French as Christie, treated French orthography in a pretty cavalier fashion. He constantly wrote 'Clodell' for 'Claudel' and, in the more detailed reference to the first Edinburgh Festival which appeared in the 1947 Glyndebourne programme, gave us 'Girodoux' for 'Giraudoux'. As though to play on Christie's well-known aversion to French music as well as French words, the serious alternative to *Orpheus* discussed for 1947 was *Pelléas et Mélisande*. Carl Ebert had by now become available to Glyndebourne again and, in the absence of Fritz Busch, had assumed sole artistic directorship of the Festival Opera. The idea of *Pelléas* was obviously his, but thinking that perhaps a work so essentially French would be trying John Christie's patience too much, decided to leave it for the moment – or at any rate, until 1962.

To Christie's great relief it was decided that *Orpheus* would not be sung in French. The opera had originally been written in Italian for Vienna in 1762, when the part of Orpheus had been sung by a castrato. In 1774 Gluck revised and enlarged it for performance with French words in Paris when Orpheus was sung by a tenor. In 1859 Berlioz made a version in which Orpheus was sung by a woman contralto. For Glyndebourne in 1947 elements of all three editions would be included – the fuller Paris score would be used with Berlioz's contralto singing the Italian words of the Viennese original. In this way Christie's objection to French was respected without affecting the Glyndebourne policy of performing all operas in what – in one edition or another – had been their original language.

---

[1] I have called Gluck's opera by this title rather than the 'Orfeo' by which it was billed at Glyndebourne in order to distinguish it in my own mind from the only work I can think of as *Orfeo* – the opera by Monteverdi which I trust will one day be heard at a Glyndebourne festival.

CHAPTER SIXTEEN

1946-7 **Edinburgh**

IN THE YEARS IMMEDIATELY following the war Glyndebourne was like a huge kitchen, where ideas, hopes, plans and proposals bubbled busily on the stove fired by the Christies' energy, ideals and ambitions. Some of these ideas, like Stravinsky's *Histoire du Soldat*, boiled over into nothing; some, like Mozart's *Schauspieldirektor* ('The Impresario') and Richard Strauss's *Ariadne auf Naxos*, were put on one side to simmer until they were needed; some, like Bing's suggestion of performing what Busch called Richard Strauss's 'exhibitionistic and embarrassing' *Intermezzo*, were declared unfit for human consumption; some were just impracticable, while a few were finally served up to the public.

It is perhaps a little eccentric in chronicling the achievements of the Glyndebourne Opera to discuss those things which never happened, but without them the study would be incomplete. In other words, the ones that got away from the Glyndebourne hook were no minnows, but often gigantic and formidable fish whose quality emphasized the stature of the fisherman. As soon as the prospect of Glyndebourne's offer to accept responsibility for the artistic organization of the first Edinburgh Festival became a reality both Toscanini and Bruno Walter were approached – Toscanini to conduct *Macbeth*, Walter to conduct *Figaro*. Although Toscanini no longer had the excuse that Fritz Busch was there to conduct Verdi as well as he could himself, he refused nevertheless; he was now 79 and had conducted for the last time in an opera house at the Salzburg Festival of 1937.[1] Bruno Walter, nine years Toscanini's junior, considered that he would be too fully occupied in conducting the Vienna Philharmonic Orchestra concerts at Edinburgh to be able to undertake an opera at the Festival; he was prepared, however, to conduct one or two operas at Covent Garden, but only if Bing and Ebert were in charge there.

After the disappointing outcome of his negotiations with Covent Garden, John Christie tried to find some way of joining up with Jay Pomeroy, whose two years of Italian opera at the Cambridge Theatre in London are said to have cost their sponsor £200,000. Had this scheme materialized Christie would have found a lot of old friends on Pomeroy's pay

---

[1] He did in fact conduct a stage performance of the third act of *Mefistofele* and the third and fourth acts of *Nerone* at La Scala in 1948 on the thirtieth anniversary of Boito's death, but his last performance of a complete opera in a theatre was in 1937.

sheet, including Mariano Stabile, Dino Borgioli, Alberto Erede and Carl Ebert, whose production of *Falstaff* with Stabile was a useful preliminary canter for his Glyndebourne version of the opera at Edinburgh in 1955.

One pot permanently simmering on the Glyndebourne stove and frequently stirred was the one filled with Christie's hopes of presenting Wagner. Early in 1947, when it was clear that nothing was going to come of the plan to associate with Pomeroy from January 1947 to August 1948 and to present a joint Festival at Glyndebourne in 1948, John Christie set out to form an organization for putting on an annual London Wagner Festival lasting a month. He was strongly supported in this by Ernest Newman who feared, however, that the new régime at Covent Garden might not be friendly. 'They seem dead set on British artists,' Newman wrote to Christie, 'some of whom are more British than artists. But Drury Lane might be possible.'

Almost the only idea during these early months of 1947 that came to anything was the plan by the present General Manager for re-numbering the seats at the Festival Opera House on the system that prevails today. In having his plan accepted Moran Caplat earned a reproach from Christie for using 'a dreadful word "finalized" in one of his letters recently (why not final?)', but the lasting gratitude of ushers and public. The introduction of this simple and familiar system, which apparently it had not occurred to anybody to adopt at Glyndebourne before, was Caplat's first contribution to the Festival Opera. Hitherto, as Bing's assistant (he had rated no better billing in the 1946 programme than the Catering Manager), he had been engaged, if not in menial tasks, at least in doing odd jobs not usually expected even of an assistant manager in an opera house, but unavoidable in the unique family atmosphere of Glyndebourne – such as taking up a new cook's references for Mrs Christie, and trying every Christmas to get her tickets to take the children to the Bertram Mills Circus at Olympia, and because she never let him know early enough, always having to settle for the circus at Harringay instead.

Moran Caplat had started out to be an actor; his father was an architect, his great grandfather, E. P. Hingston, ran the Opéra Comique in the Strand in the 1860s. The theatre stood on the site of what was later the Gaiety, destroyed, of course, in the peace. These hereditary and environmental influences had led Caplat, on his visits before the war to stay with his uncle Leslie Turner, who was Christie's land agent, to watch the building of the Festival Opera House with particular interest. Caplat did not become a very good actor, he says, but the money he earned enabled him to spend a great part of the summer doing what he really wanted to do, which was to go sailing. Thus when war broke out instead of joining ENSA (the Entertainment National Service Association) Moran Caplat joined the Royal Navy. He served in submarines until he was captured by the Italians when on Friday 13 of February 1942 his ship was sunk operating near Taranto. As a prisoner of war in Italy Caplat said he was able to complete his education in various ways and particularly to learn more about music than he had known before; it was one of the few things there were facilities and plenty of time for. After a little over a year as a prisoner of war and as a result of a characteristic pro-Allies fiddle by the Italians, Caplat was repatriated and joined in the war again with no idea of what he would do when it was over. He finished his naval career in the Second Sea Lord's Department where, in September 1945 as Lieut-Commander Moran V. H. Caplat, RNVR, he received a letter from Rudolf Bing who was looking for an assistant.

Caplat's name had been suggested by Mr W. E. Edwards, for many years John Christie's personal secretary and the real financial brain behind all his enterprises; it was a long shot for, as far as anybody at Glyndebourne knew, Caplat had never shown any managerial talent or ambitions; he was not even known to have any particular liking for opera. But as so often at Glyndebourne the long shot came off. Lieut-Commander Caplat, carrying a silver headed stick, made a favourable impression on the Christies at an interview held in the lounge of the Savoy Hotel and, with the priority in demobilization he had earned as a prisoner of war, was able to join the Glyndebourne Festival Opera in the position of Assistant Manager in November 1945.

When in due course he was told that Caplat was a French name John Christie refused to believe it. To the end of his life he maintained that Caplat was not even remotely French; he was much too nice, he said. On his father's side Moran Caplat could not have had a more typical French ancestry. The family was Norman and came from Alençon, where Caplat's grandfather and a great uncle were engaged in the two most important and typical of French export trades: his grandfather was a *viticulteur,* his great uncle a racehorse owner.

When the 1947 Festival opened at Glyndebourne on 19 June with Gluck's *Orpheus* Moran Caplat's name in the programme was in type as large as Bing's, Ebert's and the conductor's, Fritz Stiedry. Except in the matter of top seat prices, now £2 2s and 35s as against £2 and 30s pre-war, it was an austere and un-Festival-like season; petrol was still rationed, there were no special trains to or from Victoria, no reserved seats in the ordinary trains that did run, and in the circumstances the management wisely did not 'recommend' evening dress but declared it to be optional. The nine performances of Gluck's opera did not rate among the most inspiring achievements in Glyndebourne's history. The singing of Kathleen Ferrier as Orpheus was an historic performance, of course, and unforgettable by those who heard it, but as a Glyndebourne production it was woefully below pre-war standards. Ebert and Stiedry renewed in this *Orpheus* a producer-conductor partnership which had flourished between 1930 and 1932 at the Charlottenburg Opera, but on this occasion it was miserably unproductive. The production as a whole lacked style and was criticized by some of Glyndebourne's most faithful friends as 'tiresome', though in fairness it must be said that the *plus mauvais quarts d'heure* were provided not by Ebert but by the ballet, whose contribution was greeted with a vocabulary of epithets hitherto unknown at Glyndebourne – like 'tedious', 'deplorable', 'commonplace' and 'awful'.

On the second night of the season the English Opera Group who came, the programme told us, 'as visitors to Glyndebourne' gave the first performance of Britten's *Albert Herring,* another chamber opera with a twelve-piece orchestra in the pit. Relations between 'the Group' and the Glyndebourne management had now reached a difficult state which had not been improved by the advertising leaflet the English Opera Group had issued earlier in the year and was enclosed in the nightly programmes at Glyndebourne. To

Bing's dismay John Christie had approved it when it was first drafted, with the result that it had been published without a single reference to Glyndebourne – either to the assistance it had given to the Group the year before, or to the fact that Glyndebourne was to give them house-room during the 1947 season. Apart from the English Opera Group receiving a grant of £3,000 from the Arts Council while Glyndebourne got nothing, what riled Bing most was that in place of even the most begrudging bread-and-butter mention of Glyndebourne, the Group drew special attention to a possible short season at Covent Garden in the autumn, when their first consideration should have been to sell tickets for a definite season at Glyndebourne in the spring.

The run of nine performances of *Orpheus* came to an end and *The Rape of Lucretia* joined *Albert Herring* in an all-Britten, all-English-Opera-Group finale to the season. Kathleen Ferrier resumed her part as Lucretia in a cast that brought Richard Lewis to Glyndebourne for the first time. Lewis's name had first cropped up in the autumn of 1945 when an agent friend of Bing's had written from Brussels to say: 'I have a really excellent English tenor for you, who looks wonderful, has a very beautiful voice, is a superb musician and has absolute mastery of Mozart's style. I have not heard such beautiful Mozart singing for a long time ... He was stationed here in Brussels until last July when he was transferred to Oslo where he has found an ideal General who gives him every opportunity to sing and gain experience ...' It was a glowing recommendation which Glyndebourne, by nature suspicious of other people's fancies, did not ignore. Richard Lewis appeared as Don Ottavio in Edinburgh in 1948 and has sung with the Glyndebourne Opera every year except two from that day to this.

The nightly printed programme consisted of four pages and was the same size as before the war. In 1947 the editorial matter included what appeared to be a firm promise that the 1948 Festival would be held from 8 June to 10 July, and that the repertoire would be *Don Giovanni, Figaro, Orpheus* and *La traviata*. For reasons that will become apparent later the 1948 Festival never took place. *Orpheus* has never been revived and *La traviata*, mentioned for the first time so briefly and tantalizingly, one suspects is one of the ideas that has been placed on the side of the Glyndebourne stove to wait until the exact ingredients can be added to make it ready to serve.

The programme also included a rather sad little sentence: 'Glyndebourne wishes especially to express its gratitude to the Ringmer and District Electricity Co Ltd for the outstanding and exceptional help it has received ever since the opening night of 1934.' It was sad because it was a final salute to the local electricity company due to sink without trace when on 1 April 1948 the electricity industry was nationalized.

In early August, after a period of rehearsal in Sussex, the Glyndebourne Festival Opera company journeyed to Edinburgh, where the first International Festival of Music and Drama was scheduled to open on 24 August. Here, though certainly deprived of the home comforts of its native Sussex, but with financial losses not having to be met out of John Christie's personal pocket for the first time since its foundation, the Glyndebourne Festival Opera was able to function and contribute to the programme with at least some of its problems taken care of.

The arrival of the company in the Scottish capital caused a considerable stir among its inhabitants who had never before encountered such a polyglot crew and the local papers competed vigorously to run stories about Scottish-born or Scots-descended members of what was known as 'the Glyndebourne', as though it was a hunt like the Quorn or the Berkeley. The programmes at performances of *Macbeth* and *Figaro* at the King's Theatre, however, did not make such fine national distinctions. English, Irish, Scottish, Welsh and Anglo-Indian artists were all lumped together as British and left at that.

The Glyndebourne productions of *Macbeth* and *Figaro* at Edinburgh, directed by Carl Ebert in the appallingly cramped conditions of the King's Theatre, with the scenery and costumes seen before the war at the Festival Opera House, were sung by casts chosen from both familiar and unfamiliar singers who had been divided by six years of war into two distinct generations. Margherita Grandi and Francesco Valentino had been in the pre-war *Macbeth*, John Brownlee had sung the Count in *Figaro* in the last four seasons before the war, Tatiana Menotti, who had been the Despina of the 1936 *Così fan tutte*, now sang Susanna for the first time.[1] Giulietta Simionato as Cherubino, on the other hand, was brand new. Her first appearance outside Italy had been so long delayed that she was not surprisingly hailed as a discovery by British audiences hearing her for the first time, although she was already nearly 37 years old. Italo Tajo, who sang Figaro and Banquo, belonged in a way to both generations, for as a youth of 20 he had been in the Glyndebourne chorus and had sung some of the Bartolo music in the *Figaro* recording.

At Edinburgh, for the first time in Glyndebourne's history, there were flaps and frustrations, not about singers, but about conductors. Neither of the two conductors first announced to share the conducting of *Macbeth* in fact did anything of the sort. Georg Szell, the Hungarian conductor whose work had been familiar and admired in earlier days both in England and Scotland and who had recently been appointed to the Cleveland Symphony Orchestra (a post he still holds), was recommended by Bruno Walter, but came to disagree strongly with the management over something or other and left. Szell's direction of *Figaro*, for which he had also been engaged, was taken over by Walter Susskind, at that time conductor of the Scottish Orchestra, which played in the pit for the Glyndebourne operas. Tullio Serafin, also engaged for *Macbeth*, was frightened away by the spectre of the Inland Revenue and stayed at home. With both Szell and Serafin crying off, *Macbeth* was conducted throughout the season by Berthold Goldschmidt. One or two performances of *Figaro* were conducted by Renato Cellini who, until Szell's departure, had been one of the coaches now headed by Jani Strasser making his first appearance on a Glyndebourne programme since 1939.

Rudolf Bing, as General Manager of Glyndebourne, had acquired an assistant in Moran Caplat; as the awkwardly described 'Director of Festival Organization' at Edinburgh he had another assistant, Ian Hunter. Where Caplat had decided not to be an

---

[1] Audrey Mildmay had very much wanted to sing the part in four of the Edinburgh performances, sharing it, she had said in 1946, 'with Seefried (or whoever)'. But she changed her mind and her last Susanna remained the one she sang with Beecham in Montreal in 1943.

actor, Hunter, with a modesty and display of conscience as unheard of as it was exemplary, had decided not to be a conductor. Ian Hunter had been a pupil of Fritz Busch before the war and in the course of his studies had been with the conductor at Glyndebourne during the 1938 and 1939 seasons and rehearsal periods. After six years of war, however (he came out of the RASC a Lieut-Colonel, MBE), he felt that his chances of becoming a good conductor were too remote after the drastic interruption in his training, and he wrote to John Christie in the hopes of finding a job at the bottom of the ladder 'in the impressario [*sic*] line'. He had had some experience (none too easy, either) of organizing music and entertainment in the Army, running two symphony orchestras—one in Ravenna, the other in Klagenfurt, where he had also put on a couple of operas. Hunter wrote his letter in September 1945 and things didn't look hopeful until, some months after his demobilization in 1946, he was taken on by Bing at £10 a week to help with the Edinburgh Festival, which was now becoming something of a full-time job.

Like Caplat's, much of Ian Hunter's apprenticeship with Glyndebourne was taken up with the domestic chores of the Christies, answering Audrey Mildmay's requests to do what she always spelt as 'foreward' this-or-that enclosure to somebody or other, and booking sleeping berths to Scotland. Hunter's success in getting sleepers out of the London and North Eastern Railway for Mr and Mrs Christie was, in the winter of 1946–7, a feat of organizational skill and ingenuity which clearly qualified him to succeed Rudolf Bing as the second Artistic Director of the Edinburgh Festival when the time came.

In November 1947 John Christie went to the United States, where he made a rapid tour with Carleton Smith, a devoted American friend of Glyndebourne and the Christies, who was in those days a music critic of widely catholic taste and has been President of the National Arts Foundation of America since its inception in 1947. Together, in the space of twenty-four hours, the *New York Post* reported they heard Koussevitzky conduct in Boston, a rehearsal at the Metropolitan in New York, and a concert conducted by Arthur Rodzinski in Chicago. The purpose of Christie's visit, the paper continued, was to establish 'another opera house and music festival site in this country'. It was a short visit, but not so short that John Christie did not have time to go back stage in one or two New York theatres and tell them how badly all their lighting equipment compared with what there was at Glyndebourne.

When Christie returned home no sort of communiqué about his American visit was issued. He had nothing to say about Glyndebourne opera in the United States. What was worse, he had nothing to say about Glyndebourne opera at Glyndebourne.

CHAPTER SEVENTEEN

1948-9 **Projects and frustrations**

IN THE EARLY MONTHS OF 1948 it was obvious that there would be no opera season of any kind at Glyndebourne that year. This was put down by a rather rash gossip-writer to the abolition of the basic petrol ration, a suggestion which brought the immediate retort from Christie: 'If we put a barbed wire barrier round Glyndebourne they'd still get in!'

There was no season because there was no money. What Christie had warned Bing in 1939 would happen had now happened. The future of Glyndebourne, announced Christie, was in the balance and depended on whether it was backed by the State. Otherwise, he said, there was a possibility of Glyndebourne becoming what he described as 'Americanized'. The choice of the term 'Americanized' was most fortunate, because it was immediately and prominently interpreted in the Press as being a fate worse than death. What Christie went on to say was that he was planning to build new 'Glyndebournes' in the United States and Canada and hoped that the British Government would help so that it wouldn't be necessary to give up his work in England. So far from being the 'Americanization' of Glyndebourne the scheme sounded much more as if it would lead to the Glyndebournification of America; but looked at that way, of course, the situation would have lacked the appealing element of despair. The damsel in distress going to the rescue of the dragon might be news, but it wasn't romance. Either way it was now generally taken for granted that Glyndebourne was finished, and in May 1948 John Christie set off for the USA once more as if to confirm it.

Meanwhile, in addition to Edinburgh, Glyndebourne had started up what came to be known as the Bath Assembly. This festival, in one of the two cities Bing had feared would get in ahead of him when he was planning the Oxford Festival project in 1942 (the other was Edinburgh), was largely organized by Ian Hunter. It was an event of considerable charm and character with an all-English cast performing *Die Entführung* in English the main item of the ten days. When it was all over, however, the authorities at Bath decided they wanted a Popular Festival, saying that they already had 'a staff of full time people capable of dealing with that'. So Glyndebourne returned to its Southdown muttons and concentrated on other matters.

The Bath performance of *Die Entführung* seems to have turned Glyndebourne's thoughts once more to Sir Thomas Beecham who had arranged a Festival of Mozart Concerts (Manager: Moran Caplat) at Glyndebourne on four consecutive afternoons and evenings in July. (The afternoon concerts were chamber music, the evening concerts orchestral, with the two sessions divided by a 90-minute tea interval.) It was proposed that in April 1949 Beecham should conduct a new production of *Die Entführung* at Glyndebourne, the money for which, it was thought, would come from the Gramophone Company and the BBC. As Ebert was not likely to be available to produce the opera Sir Thomas suggested Frederic Austin as producer. Bing was appalled that the Beechams should have 'simply no idea of what we mean at Glyndebourne by "production"', and countered with Frederick Ashton. This, without further comment, the Beechams considered a good idea. (The notion of having Frederic Austin to produce was not really so wild as Bing seemed to think. 'Old' Austin, as Beecham knew at first hand and as his former occasional employer, had been a fine actor and opera singer in his time, as well as composer and conductor, and might well have produced *Die Entführung* extremely well, though Bing obviously did not know this.) The hoped-for aid from the Gramophone Company and the BBC was not forthcoming, however, and yet another Beecham brew on the Glyndebourne stove never came to the boil.

In August the Glyndebourne company journeyed up to Edinburgh for the second festival, now already so well established that an American newspaper referred enthusiastically and plausibly to the 'Edinburgh Festival at Clydeborne, Scotland'. Once again the inhabitants took the Glyndebourne singers to their hearts, this time with added warmth, perhaps because Ian Wallace, son of a former MP for Dunfermline, and singing with 'the Glyndebourne' for the first time, arrived at Waverley Station wearing the kilt. Whether as a result of this display of national pride or not, Wallace's name appeared in the programme as Scottish, not British; similar recognition of independence was made to other British singers in the company. Richard Lewis, born of Welsh parents in Manchester, was shown as 'Welsh', but in all subsequent seasons with Glyndebourne as 'English'. I can only think that when he became a neighbour of ours in Sussex Mr Lewis became naturalized.

Where in 1947 Glyndebourne brought two ready-made productions to Edinburgh with scenery and costumes from stock, their contribution in 1948 consisted of one old and one newly-designed opera. The familiar pre-war *Don Giovanni* with Hamish Wilson's sets and Hein Heckroth's dresses was paired with *Così fan tutte* with décor by Rolf Gérard. In two unpublicized details the performances of these operas were notable in the history of Glyndebourne. First, with *Così fan tutte* (in which Mariano Stabile sang with Glyndebourne for the last time), an artistic partnership was resumed between Carl Ebert and Vittorio Gui which, as I have already mentioned, had begun at the first Florence Maggio in 1933. Secondly, in *Don Giovanni*, the recitatives were accompanied by a harpsichord instead of a piano. It was at this Festival, too, that Sir Thomas Beecham's Royal Philharmonic Orchestra began an association with Glyndebourne which lasted until the end of the 1963 season.

Although he was still General Manager of the Glyndebourne Festival Opera, Rudolf

Bing's name did not appear on the opera programmes in Edinburgh. In Scotland his earlier clumsy title of 'Director of Festival Organization' had mercifully been dropped in favour of the tidier 'Artistic Director'. Credit for the management of Glyndebourne's personal appearance at the Festival was given for the first time in the programme solely to Moran Caplat, now 31 years old but looking so absurdly young that Audrey Mild-may insisted he should grow the beard he now wears and so give himself a look of greater authority.

During August 1948 Carleton Smith arrived in Edinburgh to discuss further the pro-ject of establishing in America what were to be called 'Glyndebourne Towers' – an im-posing name which Christie was advised would create the right impression in the United States. Two of these Glyndebourne 'towers' would be ready in the following year, one at Princeton, NJ, the other in California. 'Final details' were also settled of the Glynde-bourne Opera's own visit to the States which would take place in the autumn of 1949, immediately after the Edinburgh Festival. This would include a tour of American rural audiences.

In November 1948 there came an official announcement through Reuter's in New York that a 'three-week performance' (was John Christie doing the *Ring* at last?) had been arranged by Glyndebourne at Princeton University from 3 October to 22 October 1949. Sir Thomas Beecham would conduct and the Royal Philharmonic Orchestra would play. Carleton Smith followed this up with some near-details of the all-Mozart repertoire – *Don Giovanni* and (possibly) *Die Entführung*, interspersed with Mozart concerts by Beecham.

In March 1949 another official announcement told us that Glyndebourne's American visit had been postponed until the autumn of 1950. A couple of days later there was a paragraph in the London *Evening Standard* telling us there might be 'Opera Next Year at Glyndebourne'. A contemporary lifted the story the next day, again as a gossip item, but did not have the ethical grace to dish it up with even the mildest speculation. How opera at Glyndebourne was to be managed again, what was to be performed there, we were not told.

Glyndebourne did not get properly into the papers until the early spring of 1949 when the Great Hurdy-Gurdy Story broke. Sir Thomas Beecham, set up in style at Delves House in Ringmer for the summer (see page 77), conducted a series of weekend con-certs which took place twice daily on the last Saturdays and Sundays in April, May and June. The first weekend was Mozart, the second Haydn, the last Schubert, Schumann and Brahms. The Haydn programmes included a Divertimento for Two Hurdy-Gurdys, one of which would be played by John Christie making his first public appearance as an in-strumentalist. The Press was delighted by this news and ran endless stories explaining the difference between a hurdy-gurdy, a barrel organ and a street piano (which was invariably described as a barrel organ). There were several news stories about Sir Thomas' country-wide search first for a pair, then for a single example of these instruments. A Dutch teacher was flown (it was said) to this country to give Christie daily lessons in the instrument. All that was lacking was a good local bill, but wartime paper rationing had ended that pleasant practice apparently for good, and the nearest we got to it was the *Western Evening Herald*'s headline: 'Hurdy-Gurdy Will Be Played By Devon Man in Orchestra.'[1]

When the time came the Devon Man did not appear as hurdy-gurdyist after all. It was officially explained that he had poisoned his finger while gardening and could not play. The truth was that Christie found that playing a hurdy-gurdy was not just a matter of turning a handle; the strings had to be fingered. His part in the Haydn Divertimento, now adapted for one hurdy-gurdy (borrowed from the Royal College of Music), was in consequence taken by a deputy. The publicity came in useful, however, and there was obvious disappointment that John Christie did not perform.

Between the end of the Beecham concerts and the start of the 1949 Edinburgh Festival it was announced that Rudolf Bing had given up his position as General Manager of Glyndebourne and that Moran Caplat had been appointed in his place. This enabled Bing to concentrate more intensely on the Edinburgh Festival before leaving for the United States in October to become General Manager of the Metropolitan Opera House in New York. He was succeeded as Artistic Director of Edinburgh by Ian Hunter.

Whatever resentment the Christies felt at the time over Bing's departure for America (and they were understandably rather hurt), in later years John Christie characteristically put most of the blame on himself. 'Our own hesitation (for which we are to blame) in getting our funds has removed Rudolf Bing to the control of the Metropolitan Opera in New York,' he wrote in the 1952 Programme Book. And it was indeed his fear that neither private enterprise nor State support would come to the rescue which more than anything undermined Bing's confidence in the future of Glyndebourne and led him to feel (as he put it in a letter to Audrey Mildmay) that 'unfortunately somehow the happy atmosphere of pre-war days has vanished'. In the circumstances, chief among them obviously the complete and frustrating absence of genuine operatic activity at Glyndebourne, of Glyndebourne, by Glyndebourne and for Glyndebourne (and not for Edinburgh), it is hardly surprising that the old place should not have seemed the same.

Ironically, no sooner had Bing left the responsibilities of Glyndebourne behind him than the prospect of holding a proper slap-up Festival there again was suddenly brighter than at any time since the war. The authorities planning the Festival of Britain for 1951 had been persuaded by John Wilmot (then a Labour Member of Parliament and later Lord Wilmot) that they couldn't possibly have a festival worthy of the name without a Mozart Festival at Glyndebourne. As a result, a special Treasury vote for the Festival of Britain was made to enable Glyndebourne to run a Festival of four Mozart operas in 1951. This sounded fine, but it was quite obvious to Glyndebourne that it would be very difficult for them to mount four brand new productions in one season that would be up to the standard they wanted. So Glyndebourne suggested that if they could have half the

---

[1] For the information of a generation of newspaper readers that has been denied local bills, these were specially printed by the national dailies to interest local readers in some local news story. One of the classics among these was devised by my Night Editor on the *Daily Herald* when Sir Thomas More was canonized and a special set of local bills was sent to SW3 reading 'Chelsea Man Made Saint'.

money in 1950 they could put on two operas in that year, and revive those with another couple of new productions in 1951. This proved impossible, however; the money was there for 1951 only and Glyndebourne couldn't have any of it in 1950.

At this point Moran Caplat went to see John Spedan Lewis of the John Lewis Partnership. Mr Lewis was one of Glyndebourne's oldest and most generous supporters and before the war had given his employees (the 'partners' of the Partnership) £2 tickets for the Festival Opera when they were due for a bonus. Spedan Lewis's generosity towards Glyndebourne itself was also outstanding, so much so that when Bing was offered an 8 per cent discount with John Lewis's for the material of the *Beggar's Opera* costumes in 1940, John Christie refused to accept it: 'They have done so much for us that it would ease my conscience to pay in full.' Caplat returned from his visit to Spedan Lewis in Hampshire with the promise of a guarantee which would underwrite the likely deficit – £12,500 – of doing two operas in 1950.

The public, of course, knew nothing of any of this. No whisper of an announcement of a Festival at Glyndebourne was heard until the early days of the New Year, 1950. If we gave the subject any thought at all it was soon dismissed from our minds. The nebulous prospect of ever hearing opera in Sussex again was unimportant compared with the flesh-and-blood activities of Glyndebourne at Edinburgh where, in addition to *Così fan tutte*, Verdi's *Ballo in maschera* was performed in 1949. This was a near-replica of the famous Charlottenburg production of the opera in 1932 which had been directed by Ebert, conducted by Busch, with scenery designed by Caspar Neher. With its action transferred from Boston to an unspecified European country this version of *Un ballo in maschera* was as great a revelation to the British public as the pre-war *Macbeth* had been. Only one detail in an otherwise memorable production (the principal parts were sung by alternating casts) was not wholeheartedly accepted. Richard Capell considered in the *Daily Telegraph* that Ebert went 'to the questionable length of turning Ulrica's cave into an Italian port'. If the scene was strange to those who already knew the opera, at least it struck a chord in the memory of those who had known Glyndebourne. One of the most prominent props in the scene was the wreckage of the rowing boat that had been a familiar sight on the Glyndebourne lake before the war.[1]

I described the Edinburgh production of *Un ballo in maschera* as a 'near-replica' because it differed in one very important respect from the Charlottenburg original: it was not conducted by Fritz Busch, but by Vittorio Gui.

The absence of Fritz Busch from all Glyndebourne's activities in the years immediately after the war was due to one of those childish quarrels which can only happen in families – and in concerns run on such essentially intimate family lines as the Glyndebourne Festival Opera. What started it all, who was to blame and why, how far 'misunderstandings' were genuine or fabricated, the result of obstinacy, personal vanity or simple professional

---

[1] The experienced Glyndebourne patron visiting Edinburgh also encountered another reminder of pre-war days, though in far better shape than the boat; this was Aulikki Rautawaara, who gave a recital of songs by her countryman, Sibelius.

sulks and huffiness I do not propose to discuss. It is enough to say that it was a situation which was a credit to nobody concerned. And it was a situation which, in the end, could be resolved only by somebody who was not concerned.

The Christies, hesitating to make the first move themselves, eventually felt that something ought to be done and charged Moran Caplat with doing it. With the devoted support of Frances Dakyns, Caplat, as a complete neutral in the whole affair, invited Fritz Busch to return to conduct at the Glyndebourne Festival of 1950. Busch, who had little patience with what he considered a trivial squabble, agreed willingly; he was a man of strong principles, but as incapable of malice as he was devoid of personal vanity. When the time came his name did not appear in the Glyndebourne programme as Artistic Director, but as Conductor. It was characteristic of him that he accepted what others might have considered an insult to their prestige as of no account whatever. Busch knew his job and did it. He had given his views on prestige in the famous *Magic Flute* incident of 1936 and he had not changed them with the years.

In January 1950 it was announced that 'At last in 1950 Glyndebourne Opera is re-starting its own Festival at Glyndebourne.' It would consist of performances of *Die Entführung aus dem Serail* and *Così fan tutte*, and would last from 6 July to 23 July.

CHAPTER EIGHTEEN

1950-51 **Return to normal**

IT WAS OBVIOUS WHEN, like their predecessors, a new generation of gossip writers gasped with hysterical astonishment at the sight of people in evening dress catching the 3.45 from Victoria that the 1950 season was the real thing again. Seats were still £2 2s and 35s and it was unanimously calculated that for the purposes of newspaper expense accounts a night out for two at Glyndebourne now cost £12 – a puzzlingly modest increase, considering how the cost of living had risen in the previous ten years. Fashion writers told us of special two-way Glyndebourne dresses which would save the wearer 'from looking too conspicuous when she catches the 3.30 [*sic*] train from Victoria'. It was an ingenious garment to be worn as a cloak in London and as a long skirt at Glyndebourne. Or something. There were solemn prelims in the papers about cows in the flower beds, which suggested that the reporters did not know a Ranunculus acris from R. montanus (geranifolius) or even a Cephalaria tartarica. Best of all, there were once again in the glossies and the housemaids' dailies lists of those who had been 'among those who attended' – and, what is more, had attended in evening dress instead of the tweeds affected by all true, non-snob music lovers in the stalls at Covent Garden.

Backstage there were half bottles of 'Mrs Christie's Champagne' in the dressing rooms on first nights again, for the first time since 1939. And for the first time in the history of the Festival Opera House the artists were visited every evening before the curtain went up by a General Manager who himself had known life in a theatre dressing room. Moran Caplat's nightly round of the Glyndebourne dressing rooms is made to this day and is a characteristically sympathetic professional touch not often found among impresarios.

The critics, too, were back in their old form – from those who complained that Busch still stripped Mozart of all his appoggiaturas and accompanied the recitatives on a piano, to those who complained about dressing and, in a strangely militant prohibitionist mood, solemnly advocated that performances should begin at 6.30 with 'normal intervals for coffee and sandwiches'.

The printed programme, limited by the still prevailing paper shortage to eight pages, included the first signed example of those State-of-the-Union articles which have been an essential feature of all Glyndebourne programmes ever since. In this instance the manifesto was signed by John and Audrey Christie and introduced the Glyndebourne audience, as distinct from the newspaper reader who had known it for years, to the classic account of the seven people who got into the special train to return to London after the second night in 1934. The article was mostly devoted, however, to acknowledging gratefully the help of the John Lewis Partnership, and ended with a series of those forceful staccato sentences in which the Christie philosophy was so often and determinedly expressed.

The comparatively modest season itself, in its way one of the most important in the whole history of the enterprise, was also musically exceptionally stimulating and successful. The season opened with an *Entführung* distinguished by a magnificent Osmin by the Hungarian bass, Endre Koréh, who had all the notes and in addition, as Desmond Shawe-Taylor so vividly described it, that roguish look of the pop-eyed roué that used to decorate the cover of *Esquire* magazine. Ilse Hollweg's Constanze, after she had lost her first-night nervousness, was an accurate and assured performance of a part which, when it is not accurate and assured, can produce duodenal ulcers in an audience. Alda Noni as Blonde was surprisingly successful; the Italians do not as a rule shine in Mozart's German operas, as we remember sadly from Baccaloni's foray as Osmin, but Miss Noni gave the character a spitfire sharpness which was refreshingly astringent. She did not come any nearer to being an English Miss than a dozen Central European soubrettes, but then who has? And why should they? It made a nice change anyway.

The performance of the first post-war *Così fan tutte* at Glyndebourne, like the first before the war, was a triumph for the Fiordiligi – in this case Sena Jurinac, who had already sung the part of Dorabella at Edinburgh the year before. (Miss Jurinac, in the eight seasons she sang for Glyndebourne either in Sussex or at Edinburgh, showed exceptional versatility, singing not only Fiordiligi and Dorabella, but Donna Anna and Donna Elvira in *Don Giovanni*, and Cherubino and the Countess in *Figaro*.) The cast of the 1950 *Così fan tutte* also included Richard Lewis singing as a member of the Glyndebourne company in the Festival Opera House for the first time; he made an impressive début but, in accordance with one of the most puzzling and inconsistent Glyndebourne practices, was deprived of Ferrando's third aria, 'Tradito, schernito', like some, but not all, Ferrandos before him. The part of Guglielmo was shared by Erich Kunz, returning to Glyndebourne for the first time since his season there in the chorus in 1936, and Geraint Evans, who was making the first of a long sequence of successful appearances at Glyndebourne. Alda Noni was Despina and, like her Blonde, her performance made another nice change. Mr Shawe-Taylor, the most quotable critic of the year, welcomed her as a real Neapolitan soubrette instead of what he so aptly called 'the Viennese pre-incarnation of Johann Strauss's Adèle'–whom, I must confess, I find one of the most irritating characters in all opera.

For some reason the artists' nationalities were not shown in the 1950 programme. The omission was not deliberate; it was just a mistake caused, it is thought, by plain forgetfulness in the excitement of having the real thing again.

It was a short but extremely satisfactory season and could well have been extended but for Glyndebourne's commitments at Edinburgh where, however, Fritz Busch was not to conduct Glyndebourne opera but, returning to the city which had made him an honorary

Doctor of Music in 1934, a couple of concerts with the Statsradiofonen Orchestra of Copenhagen which he had trained and conducted since before the war. As it was, the fourteen performances in Sussex left everybody in a contented mood and looking forward eagerly to 1951 when, it was announced, the season would last from 20 June to 21 July and would consist of four Mozart operas – *Don Giovanni*, *Figaro*, *Così fan tutte* and *Idomeneo*. In only one respect was the 1950 season disappointing and that was the décor by Rolf Gérard. The scenery and dresses of *Die Entführung* were new; those for *Così fan tutte* had been commissioned (and paid for) by the Edinburgh Festival in 1948 and were borrowed for the Glyndebourne season. Apart from Sir Leigh Ashton, who raised a few eyebrows by doing an unexpected stint as music critic for the *Daily Mail*, no fewer than three regular music critics also commented on the deplorable travel-agent's-window taste of the designs. This in itself gives some indication of the low quality of the décor, for music critics are notoriously insensitive to the visual arts.

Rolf Gérard came in for more trouble at Edinburgh in August where he designed Glyndebourne's *Figaro* and caused one of the glossies to hope profoundly that what it referred to graphically as 'the Casa Pepe style of Mozart décor' would be dropped.[1] Although it was five years before he was allowed to design *Figaro*, the first appearance of Oliver Messel at the 1950 Edinburgh Festival, where he designed the Glyndebourne *Ariadne auf Naxos*, must have been a hopeful sign to regular patrons that a theatrical designer of taste and experience had been discovered. Messel's work elsewhere in the theatre had, of course, been well known to the rest of us (especially those who had worked with C. B. Cochran) for more than twenty years, but his introduction to Glyndebourne was a welcome indication that the circle of recruitment for designers was at last being extended beyond the inevitably narrow confines of the Christies' experience in such things.

It may seem a little lop-sided to mention the name of the designer of *Ariadne auf Naxos* before that of the conductor, but the arrival of Oliver Messel (literally) on the scene was in the long run of greater lasting importance to Glyndebourne than the conducting of Sir Thomas Beecham. Richard Strauss's *Ariadne* was given at Edinburgh in its original version – preceded, that is, by Molière's *Le Bourgeois Gentilhomme* instead of by the Prelude substituted when it was realized that the production of a play and an opera in the same bill was not a very practical or economic proposition. Under Festival conditions, however, the first version of *Ariadne* proved a practical though still far from economic proposition, and so at Edinburgh Miles Malleson appeared as Monsieur Jourdain in his own adaptation of Molière's play and Sir Thomas Beecham conducted the work he had originally introduced to London at His Majesty's Theatre in 1913, when Sir Herbert Beerbohm Tree played M. Jourdain in Somerset Maugham's version of the play. The 1950 Edinburgh Festival proved to be Beecham's only operatic association with Glyndebourne though he had been considered as a possible and welcome partner by John Christie in his venture from the earliest blue-print days right down to a few months before he died in 1961.

[1] The Casa Pepe is a well-known Spanish restaurant in London.

It was always rather difficult to decide whether Christie's constant and belligerent public reference to the lack of State support for Glyndebourne was due to pride in his independence or resentment that his work was given no official recognition; perhaps it was a bit of both. In 1951, and for the first and only time in its history, Glyndebourne Opera was given a Treasury grant. As a reward for its contribution of an all-Mozart Festival to the Festival of Britain the State gave a £25,000 guarantee against loss. Christie did not lose his independence, and although the money was for one year only and clearly did not set a precedent, it was very nice to have it. For one thing, it enabled the first structural alterations to be made to the Opera House since the war. The seating in the balcony was increased by 42 to 112, and Christie's own box was moved down to the back of the stalls where it had last been in 1936. The total seating of the house was now 592 – very nearly double that of the first season.

The opening performance of 1951 was a brand new production of Mozart's *Idomeneo*, an opera which was now being professionally staged in England for the first time since it was written in 1781. The operative word is 'professional', of course, for while *Idomeneo* had never been performed here in Italian, it had suddenly begun in the 1930s to appeal to inquisitive and enthusiastic amateurs, receiving several performances and quite a lot of interested attention from the critics once it had been produced at Glasgow in 1934 in an English version. Performances followed, in one order or another, at Falmouth, London, Oxford and Cambridge. In the Cambridge production of 1939 the four leading roles were, in fact, taken by professional artists from Glyndebourne – Irene Eisinger was Ilia, Elisabeth Abercrombie was Electra, Elizabeth Darbishire was Idamante and Eric Starling was Idomeneo. So it happened that the music of *Idomeneo* was not altogether unfamiliar to the critics, many of whom knew their scores well enough to recognize that cuts had been made by Hans Gal in the edition he prepared for Glyndebourne.

There are many operas which are what I call Prejudice Operas – operas one has been taught all through life are so full of faults, illogicalities, outmoded conventions and absurd dramatic situations that they are not worth another moment of the busy student's time even though they were written by a composer of genius. Verdi's *Macbeth* is one of these; so is *Idomeneo*. It has taken a long time for the modern public to be allowed to warm itself unselfconsciously at the blazing fire of *Macbeth* instead of being told repeatedly that there were one or two clinkers in the grate. And with *Idomeneo* it has taken almost as long for the critics to stop worrying about the formal virtues and shortcomings of *opera seria* and listen to the music. The public, not knowing *opera seria* from a bull's foot, enjoyed *Idomeneo* at Glyndebourne much sooner and much more than the professional opera-goers, among whom were two who considered the opera to be simply a 'colossal bore'.

For most people, however, *Idomeneo* was another typical Glyndebourne 'revelation' of music which Busch's fine performance, the imaginative production by Ebert (Ernest Newman and Eric Blom considered it his finest achievement), and the lovely sets and costumes of Oliver Messel showed to be a live opera and far from the museum piece it had hitherto been to most people.

The Opera House programme of *Idomeneo* (with singers' nationalities once more and headed with 'Under the artistic direction of Fritz Busch, conductor, and Carl Ebert, producer') bore the note: 'Glyndebourne has included "Idomeneo" in this year's Festival in memory of the late W. J. Turner (the distinguished critic of the *New Statesman*) who, before the war, continually besought us to perform this work.' It was a grateful gesture to the memory of one of Glyndebourne's most devoted champions (Walter Turner died in 1946), but perhaps rather a dangerous precedent to set when one considers what unsuitable works some of one's distinguished contemporaries are continually beseeching Glyndebourne to perform. So far, however, *Idomeneo* remains the only officially recognized Critic's Choice.

The outstanding performance among the singers was the Ilia of Sena Jurinac, whose understanding of Mozart's style grew more impressive with each new role she sang. The most disappointing – and, in retrospect, the most surprisingly so – was Birgit Nilsson as Electra. This Glyndebourne season was her first important appearance outside her native Sweden, where a couple of years before she had sung Lady Macbeth with Fritz Busch; realizing now, as we do, the kind of Turandot and Isolde she developed into it is even more puzzling that her Electra should have lacked those qualities of power and fury in which she nowadays excels.

Otherwise, apart from the objections raised by the two critics who were bored by the whole thing (both of them, I am unhappy to say, particular friends of mine), the only serious criticism of Glyndebourne's first *Idomeneo* was the purely constructive one made by Arthur Jacobs of the *Daily Express*, who pointed out the grammatical howler in the programme where the words 'dramma eroica' appeared. The criticism was noted and the gender of the adjective was corrected when the opera was revived the following year.

In one respect Busch's performance of *Idomeneo* caused some confusion. Why, asked the *Times* critic, did Busch consent to a harpsichord in *Idomeneo* when he was so obstinate about using a piano for *recitativo secco* in Mozart's other operas? As nobody has ever been able to answer this question except Fritz Busch himself, and nobody remembered to ask him, one can only suppose that he didn't mind the sound of a harpsichord in an opera like *Idomeneo* when it was played by somebody else (in this instance John Pritchard), and where in any case the continuo involved a solo violoncello as well and would have sounded like César Franck with a piano, whereas in the other Mozart operas Busch accompanied the recitatives himself and preferred to do so on a piano, an instrument over which he perhaps felt he had more control.

None of the other three Mozart operas in 1951 – *Così fan tutte*, *Figaro* and *Don Giovanni* – ever took wing in the same way as *Idomeneo*. Only *Così fan tutte*, dominated by the triumphant Fiordiligi of Sena Jurinac, had anything of the quality which had made this Glyndebourne's particular show-piece. (Sesto Bruscantini made his Glyndebourne début as Don Alfonso in this production.) Both *Figaro* and *Don Giovanni*, on the other hand, not only carried obvious passengers in their casts but suffered moments of uncharacteristic treatment from Fritz Busch whose conducting suddenly became disquietingly inflexible. For the first time in our experience we read of him as a 'drill sergeant', of arias 'hurried unfeelingly' and lacking in tenderness – puzzling and disturbing tendencies in a man whose conducting of Mozart's operas was equalled in his time only by Bruno Walter and Richard Strauss.

In performances where, owing to what one suspects was just plain unlucky casting, vocal teamwork and characterization were uneven in quality, only Alois Pernerstorfer and Lisa Della Casa as the Count and Countess met with general favour in *Figaro*; in *Don Giovanni* Suzanne Danco took over Donna Elvira at six hours' notice when Dorothy MacNeil fell ill, and scored an emphatic success with some lovely singing. Léopold Simoneau, in spite of Busch's rattling tempo for 'Il mio tesoro', sang Don Ottavio's part with charm and conviction and earned good marks all round.

With so much that was not quite right musically in the 1951 *Don Giovanni* it is perhaps not surprising that the décor by John Piper should have made a deep impression, and paradoxically, in casting a characteristic gloom over the stage proceedings, have thereby raised the spirits of the audience no end. Except for one scene in which he cramped the stage, Piper's designs fully justified Rudolf Bing's enthusiastic recommendation of the artist to the Christies as far back as 1945.

Looking back on the 1951 season at this distance it is easy to regard as ominous the incident of Fritz Busch's sudden illness during a performance of *Don Giovanni* when he could not continue after the first act. As it was it should have been regarded with suspicion, for Busch had never in the whole of his association with Glyndebourne been kept from his work by ill-health.

On this occasion Busch's place was taken by John Pritchard, after an unnerving sequence of events which began with a call for Pritchard, who was discovered to be bathing at Eastbourne, fifteen miles away. Driving as quickly as he could to Glyndebourne his car caught fire on the way; he managed to find a hire-car and arrived with little time to spare before the start of the second act. If ever the advantage of the traditional long dinner interval over the 'normal interval with coffee and sandwiches' was demonstrated it was on that evening.

It would be pleasant to relate that with this unheralded appearance on the rostrum John Pritchard, like Toscanini, became world-famous over night; but in fact he had already conducted *Don Giovanni* twice that same week in his official capacity as Assistant Conductor, a post which had previously involved him in the direction of two fully-credited performances each of *Così fan tutte* and *Figaro* earlier in the same season at Glyndebourne.

Like Kathleen Ferrier, John Pritchard had been strongly commended to the notice of the Christies by Roy Henderson, who, on a train journey in 1947 scribbled a letter to Audrey Mildmay in which he spoke highly of Pritchard with the words: 'He seems to me a boy worth training for further development.' In the same letter Henderson also hoped Glyndebourne would commission an English comic opera, adding his personal recommendation: 'Walton could write a marvellous comic opera.' With two of Roy Henderson's hopes for Glyndebourne successfully realized one looks forward to the completion of a unique hat-trick by the acceptance of his third recommendation. It is an idea that has crossed Glyndebourne's mind more than once.

The 1951 season ended with the first televising of an opera from Glyndebourne.[1] The BBC made a full three-hour broadcast of *Così fan tutte*; special trains were run to bring the invited audience to Sussex; the Director-General (Sir William Haley) was present, and although a black tie was now almost universally worn at Glyndebourne the BBC dressed its male guests in tails, including the camera crews who spent an uncomfortable evening wearing what by 1951 was virtually period costume supplied by the television wardrobe. The next day's public reaction was according to form. An 'Affront to Ordinary Viewers' was the least of the complaints by that peculiarly greedy and selfish section of our society – the television viewers and columnists who kick and scream unless their tastes are catered for every minute of the year. Serious television criticism had not yet been generally recognized as a specialized occupation and it was still the practice of many newspapers to use their film critics for the job. This led to some pretty confused conclusions, but in fairness it must be said it was not a film critic but 'our Show Biz reporter' whose notice was indignantly headed 'Three Hours in Italian' – as good a way as any other, I suppose, of describing *Così fan tutte*. But with that exemplary courage it shows from time to time the BBC ignored all philistine comment and has continued to televise from Glyndebourne annually ever since.

To mark the fiftieth anniversary of Verdi's death Glyndebourne staged *La forza del destino* at Edinburgh in August, also taking the production of *Don Giovanni* that had been running in Sussex. Both operas were conducted by Fritz Busch. The Verdi, given complete and lasting some three-and-a-half hours, was distinguished by a total absence of Italian singers from the cast; the tally of principals was one German, one Yugoslav, two Americans, four English, two Welsh and one Scot. The Italian accents were extremely variable and the singing lacked style. But even so Busch left the audience in no doubt of the qualities of the score of one of Verdi's most fascinating and musically attractive operas.

In the performances of *Don Giovanni* it was noted with relief that Fritz Busch's conducting was more relaxed and amiable than it had been at Glyndebourne earlier. That Busch was able to maintain this equanimity during the Edinburgh run of *Don Giovanni* is even more surprising, for the production seemed to have a jinx on it from the start. True, Dorothy MacNeil was able this time to open as Donna Elvira as advertised, but within a week she was invalided out and her part was sung once more by Suzanne Danco. Far more alarming, however, was the accident which befell Genevieve Warner, the young American who sang Zerlina. Miss Warner was walking back to her hotel in one of the most respectable but badly lit quarters of Edinburgh on a Sunday night when she was suddenly attacked by a man who pulled a rope tightly round her neck, dragged her down into an area and tried to steal her handbag; after a struggle he ran away. Genevieve Warner was found semiconscious and bleeding and taken to the Royal Infirmary with a suspected fracture of the jaw. Her injuries were not as serious as was feared at first, but she was kept in hospital to recover from her bruises, cuts and shock.

---

[1] It was not accurate to say, as some writers claimed at the time, that this was the first opera ever to be televised by the BBC. It was the first opera to be televised that had not been produced by the BBC itself.

Miss Warner's part in *Don Giovanni* was taken for one performance by her understudy, Roxane Houston, who was in the chorus, and then by Pierrette Alarie, a Canadian singer who happened to be in Edinburgh with her husband Léopold Simoneau, the Don Ottavio in the same opera. It was a grim, disturbing episode.

August, which marks the start of grouse shooting in Scotland, also seemed to be a popular month for American impresarios to visit the Edinburgh Festival and start negotiations with Glyndebourne. Earlier it had been Carleton Smith with the Princeton and California projects; in 1951 it was Sol Hurok come for further discussion of a plan already put to John Christie at Glyndebourne in June. This was to take the Glyndebourne Opera Company to the United States for a ten-week tour of *Idomeneo* and *Così fan tutte*. At Edinburgh it was stated that Mr Hurok's offer had been accepted and that the tour was fixed for October 1952.

No sooner had this subject been dealt with than what is usually described as a bombshell exploded; after a week of rumours, the Edinburgh Festival Society announced that the Glyndebourne Opera would not be invited back in 1952; they would be having the Hamburg Opera instead. The indignation this decision caused in Scotland was remarkable; there were leaders in the *Scotsman*, angry letters to the dailies and evenings in Edinburgh, Glasgow, Aberdeen and Dundee. Didn't they remember, they asked, that if it hadn't been for Glyndebourne there would have been no Edinburgh Festival? Wasn't Rudolf Bing, its founder, still 'Honorary Artistic Adviser' to the Festival? On the last day of the Festival the Edinburgh Festival Society rather shamefacedly announced that Glyndebourne had been invited to return in 1953. Glyndebourne did not commit themselves beyond the masterly statement issued by Moran Caplat: 'The more distant possibilities can only be evolved by further mutual discussion.'

All further speculation on the subject was sharply interrupted by the death in London, less than a week later, of Fritz Busch. He died suddenly, aged 61, in the Savoy Hotel on 14 September, ten days before he was to have conducted his Danish radio orchestra in London for the first time. He died of a heart attack, the victim of strain and the overwork of an exceptionally busy and concentrated season in which he had rehearsed and conducted six operas for Glyndebourne.

Two major strokes of luck stand out in the history of Glyndebourne. The first was John Christie's marriage to a woman capable of turning his half-formed dreams into professional reality. The second was the engagement of Fritz Busch. To find a conductor to perform Mozart's operas well is not easy at any time; to find one who also had the temperament to work so happily and successfully in the unique atmosphere and surroundings of Glyndebourne was little less than a miracle. Opera at Glyndebourne in the early years was prepared and performed in circumstances unlike those anywhere else in the world. The very physical peculiarities of the place and its working conditions concentrated musicians, producers, designers, singers, their wives and children under one domestic roof so that for the entire rehearsal period and the fortnight's season of the first Festival the Christies had no fewer than twenty people as guests in their house.

If it was Audrey Mildmay who designed Glyndebourne to be a functional machine and not a toy it was Fritz Busch who started it working, drove it and maintained it. It was he who introduced Carl Ebert, but in recognizing the indispensability of a producer made it quite clear that in opera, as he constantly pointed out, the conductor's contribution was the major one – 60 per cent he said, to the producer's 40 per cent. His insistence that operatic labour should be divided in these proportions was characteristic of an artistic integrity that had no time for the dubious glories of prestige or the luxury of personal vanity. Busch's physical energy and stamina were amazing, and like Toscanini he did not spare himself. He drove his singers and musicians hard, but no harder than was good for them, and certainly nowhere near as hard as he drove himself. John Christie placed a sense of humour high among the elements that contributed to the unprecedented success of Glyndebourne. It was a quality which Fritz Busch possessed in abundance. But where a sense of humour is essential to the relaxation of tension, Busch also had a unique good-humouredness which often prevented the creation of the tense situation in the first place. On these occasions at rehearsal, for instance, when Ebert's patience with the singers was beginning to show signs of cracking, Busch would deliberately take out his watch, place it on a table in front of him and tell the company they could have a five-minute free-for-all. When the five minutes were up, Busch said, he would resume his rehearsal. Some-times, when there was an argument between Busch and Ebert, order was not restored until John Christie appeared carrying a bowl of ice which he would place without a word between conductor and producer. No quarrel ever survived this silent intervention; the two Germans laughed and the dispute was forgotten.

What the death of Fritz Busch meant not only to Glyndebourne, or to the Vienna Opera which he was to have directed, but to the musical world in general it is impossible to estimate. As few had done in his generation he understood the unique position and responsibility of the conductor in the opera house and his duty to the composer. 'In opera,' he said, 'the heartbeat of the performance comes from the pit.' They are words which should be carved over the doors of every opera house in the world.

CHAPTER NINETEEN

1952-3 **Audience to the rescue**

FOR MANY REASONS IT IS NATURAL to regard the death of Fritz Busch as the end of a long chapter of Glyndebourne's history and the period which followed it as the start of a new era. But in fact he died at a moment of transition which was to lead in time to the complete reconstruction of the administrative and financial fabric of Glyndebourne.

It was more than ever apparent in 1951 that if Glyndebourne was to survive something drastic would have to be done about raising money. The Treasury grant was for the year of the Festival of Britain only, and while John Spedan Lewis's covenant provided welcome relief it was obviously too much to expect one man's contribution to subsidize the whole – as John Christie knew only too well. Assistance in kind, however, came during the 1951 season on a very handsome scale from a new figure who was to play an important part in the material welfare of Glyndebourne: N. T. Sekers, a Hungarian passionately devoted to music, whose firm, the West Cumberland Silk Mills, gave the fabrics (many of them specially made and dyed) for the costumes in *Don Giovanni*. The quality of the material in which the singers' costumes have always been made has been a characteristic feature of Glyndebourne's productions since the very beginning. Not only is this in keeping with the policy of the Festival Opera to 'do the thing properly', and necessary in a small theatre where a sophisticated audience would be certain to spot the use of second rate materials, but it has a valuable psychological effect on the singers – especially on newcomers who invariably comment on the exquisite quality of the velvets and silks such as they have never worn on the stage before.[1]

During the summer of 1951 Mr Sekers saw the big programme book of the Aix-en-Provence Festival, with its lavish colour advertisements, and had the idea that if the same sort of thing could be done for Glyndebourne it would be an important source of revenue for the Festival Opera. Mr Sekers was given the go-ahead to mobilize likely advertisers in British industry to buy space in what was designed to be a desirable 'prestige' medium. The target was forty advertisers bringing in £20,000 gross. The first acceptor was a

---

[1] Many singers arriving at Glyndebourne for the first time are surprised – and sometimes hurt – to discover that they are not allowed to wear the wigs and costumes they have brought with them and have worn for years, all over the world, in the part for which Glyndebourne has now engaged them.

visitor to the Sekers' house: Mr Geoffrey Herrington, director of High Duty Alloys, who agreed at once. The second was Gilbey's. Mr Sekers recalls that he went to see some of the senior partners of Gilbey's in the early afternoon; they gave him some excellent port and suggested it would be better if he saw Arthur Gilbey, who was very interested in music and had been a regular visitor to Glyndebourne since boyhood. They gave him some more port while he waited. 'By the time Arthur Gilbey arrived,' says Mr Sekers, 'I was nearly knocked out by the port, but a couple of minutes later Gilbey's joined as the second advertiser.' Arthur Gilbey, one of the first members of the committee of the Glyndebourne Festival Society and later a trustee of the Glyndebourne Arts Trust, died suddenly in May 1964, aged only 45.

The number of advertisers grew as each one in turn helped to find others until there were eighteen who were willing to take a full page in the first number of the Glyndebourne Festival Programme Book to be published in 1952. They were Yardley's, Marshall and Snelgrove, Floris, Sekers, Nuthalls (Caterers) Group, High Duty Alloys, Aristoc, the John Lewis Partnership, Abdulla, The Gramophone Company, Ringmer Building Works, S. G. Warburg and Co, Brandeis Goldschmidt and Co, Wm Hill and Son and Norman and Beard Ltd, Sir Thomas and Arthur Wardle Ltd, London Films, Saunton Sands Hotel and W. and A. Gilbey, whose design incorporated the first two bars of the flute part of the Minuet of Haydn's Surprise Symphony with, I am sorry to report, two wrong notes in it. By 1964 the number of advertisers had risen to thirty-nine, still one short of Mr Sekers's original aim, but satisfactory nevertheless.

It was as a result of this first encouraging response from advertisers that Lord Wilmot and Mr Sekers started the financial scheme which John Christie in his foreword to the 1953 Programme Book said 'led to the fundamental basis of our work in the future'. This was the formation of the Glyndebourne Festival Society, in principle a kind of supporters' club. Its chairman was Lord Wilmot of Selmeston, which Christie never tired of telling everybody – including Lord Wilmot – was pronounced 'Simpson' in Sussex. The rest of the committee consisted of Arthur Gilbey, H. G. Herrington, O. B. Miller of the John Lewis Partnership (John Spedan Lewis had had to decline owing to his ill-health), and N. T. Sekers. Lord Wilmot died in July 1964 and was succeeded as Chairman of the Glyndebourne Festival Society by O. B. Miller.

The object of the Society, it was announced in December 1951, was to raise £25,000 a year to cover the difference between the cost of running the Glyndebourne Festival and receipts. There would be three forms of membership:

1 Corporate membership for firms and industrial institutions; annual subscription £105, entitling each subscriber to four free seats a season.
2 Individual membership; annual subscription £26 5s, entitling the subscriber to two free seats and a free copy of the Festival Programme.
3 Associated membership; annual subscription £2 2s, entitling the subscriber to a free copy of the programme.
All memberships would ensure priority in booking.

By the time the 1952 season opened at Glyndebourne the Glyndebourne Festival Society had a total of 806 members, made up of 25 corporate members, 65 individual members and 716 associate members. It was a comforting start and apart from the good it did to Glyndebourne, of course, it also provided the ordinary visitor to the Festival Opera with the first of the annual Programme Books. This was a handsomely produced and illustrated 76-page brochure printed on art paper with a cover design by Oliver Messel, generously decorated with coloured pictures and costing 10s (the price was reduced to 5s the following year). It opened with the first grand-scale State-of-the-Union address by John Christie who covered the first 700 years of Glyndebourne's history, its philosophy, policy and achievements with enviable skill in just under 3,000 words. There followed an article by James Strachey on Fritz Busch, and informative essays on operas in the Festival repertoire – Desmond Shawe-Taylor on *La Cenerentola*, Frank Howes on *Idomeneo*, Dyneley Hussey on *Macbeth*, and Geoffrey Sharp on *Così fan tutte*. The contributions ended with a lighthearted piece on the wines at Glyndebourne by Dr O. W. Loeb.

Three days before the public opening of the Festival a special performance of *Idomeneo* was given in memory of Fritz Busch. It was conducted by John Pritchard, now no longer described as Assistant Conductor and Chorus Master but billed in his own right as Conductor, and performed by a cast which included only two major changes from that which had sung with Busch in 1951: Maria Kinasiewicz sang Electra, and John Cameron was Arbace.

During the interval of this *Idomeneo* the memorial bronze death mask of Fritz Busch was unveiled in the wall of the Covered Way, and at the end of the opera the curtain was raised again while the chorus sang the passage he is said to have loved most of all in the opera, the lovely 'Placido è il mar, andiamo'. It was an almost unbearably moving epilogue to the evening.

The official opening night on 18 June was altogether a less solemn occasion, although many were saddened by the absence from the theatre of Audrey Mildmay, who was in a nursing home for two months and had had to cancel her daughter Rosamond's coming-out dance. The first performance of the season introduced a new composer and a new conductor whose names had hitherto not appeared on the programme at Glyndebourne: Rossini's enchanting comedy, *La Cenerentola*, was conducted by Vittorio Gui. The prospect of hearing this opera at Glyndebourne was so pleasing and the demand for tickets so great in consequence that before the season started an extra performance had to be arranged. Gui's part in the great Rossini revival was well known, of course, to those who had been in Italy between the wars; but it would be less than fair to pretend that the business of successfully importing that revival into England would have been nearly so easy without the initiative of Sir Thomas Beecham. There is little doubt, I think, that the satisfactory advance booking for Glyndebourne's *Cenerentola* owed a great deal to the memory of the *Cenerentola* presented, but not conducted, by Beecham in his season at Covent Garden in 1934 with Conchita Supervia in the lead.

The arrival of Gui at Glyndebourne brought an unaccustomed and stimulating breath

(above) The Rake's Progress, 1977, Mother Goose's Brothel. Designer, David Hockney. *(Southern Television/Nutley)*

(left) The Rake's Progress, 1975: David Hockney (designer), John Cox (producer) with maquette. *(Gravett)*

(left) The Rake's Progress, 1977, Bedlam: Richard Van Allan, Felicity Lott, Leo Goëke. (Southern Television/ Nutley)

(below) The Cunning Little Vixen rehearsal, 1975. Left to right: Raymond Leppard, George Christie, Jonathan Miller. (Gravett)

of Italian air to the scene which, although familiar to those who had heard him conduct for Glyndebourne at Edinburgh, was new to audiences in Sussex. His performances of *La Cenerentola* in Ebert's often very funny production were immensely popular and started what was to become a Glyndebourne tradition of Rossini leading in the years that followed to *The Barber of Seville*, *L'italiana in Algeri*, *Le Comte Ory* and – though neither Gui nor Ebert was concerned in it – *La pietra del paragone*.

Gui made two departures from the exact text of *La Cenerentola*: he included the charming overture to Rossini's early opera *L'inganno felice* as an interlude while the scenery was being set up for the complicated final scene, and he scored for strings the accompaniment of Alidoro's recitative when the philosopher leads Cenerentola to her coach at the end of Act I, Scene I. Both Gui's modifications were effective; the interpolated overture spared us an intolerable wait, while the use of strings to accompany Alidoro made the scene most dramatic and affecting. For the rest of the recitatives in *Cenerentola* an early nineteenth-century piano was used which had been lent by Leon Goossens, who lived not far from Lewes at that time. When Mr Goossens left the district his piano was replaced by a harpsichord.

The first Glyndebourne *Cenerentola* was a riotous success. Sesto Bruscantini we knew already from the previous year's *Così fan tutte*; as Dandini in this Rossini opera he gave the first of a series of brilliant performances in a part which was to become one of the Glyndebourne classics during the ten seasons he sang there. Ian Wallace made a great hit as the *buffo* Don Magnifico, and was thereafter in constant demand to sing the part in Italy and elsewhere. Juan Oncina, the Spanish tenor, made his first appearance at Glyndebourne as the Prince and established himself as a specialist in the florid tenor roles which make the casting of Rossini's operas so tricky. According to the potted biography in the Programme Book, Juan Oncina 'made his professional début in Barcelona in 1946 as Des Grieux in *La traviata*' – which must have been a confusing evening for everybody.

Marina de Gabarain in the title part was thought by the critics to be disappointing; the fact that she was Spanish, like Conchita Supervia, was not enough, and her two sisters, sung by Alda Noni and Fernanda Cadoni, were considered more pleasing.

Vittorio Gui also conducted *Macbeth* in 1952 and appeared as a Mozart conductor at Glyndebourne for the first time with *Così fan tutte*, in which Sesto Bruscantini now played the optimist instead of the cynic – Guglielmo instead of Don Alfonso. Verdi's opera, still in Ebert's production and with Caspar Neher's scenery, made as deep an impression as ever and was rewarded by more satisfactory box-office returns than it had been before the war; the climate, as they say, was now more favourable for unfamiliar Verdi, thanks to one thing and another, including Sadler's Wells. The Lady Macbeth this time was Dorothy Dow, an American who sang splendidly but did not impress so much as an actress in a part which has so far only once been sung by an Italian at Glyndebourne, and she, it will be remembered, was born a British citizen in Tasmania.

The BBC chose *Macbeth* for its television relay from Glyndebourne and on this occasion adapted its own presentation of the complete opera to suit the medium. This meant that the invited, evening-dressed audience in the theatre missed a lot of what went on, but the domestic viewer got his money's worth. It was produced by Giorgio Foa who had been in the London office of Ricordi before the war and, apart from Vittorio Gui, was the only native Italian concerned in this *Macbeth* at all. After the reception of the first television relay from Glyndebourne in 1951 the Press notices of this two-and-a-half hour broadcast, though few, were surprisingly favourable; perhaps the name *Macbeth* in the programme did not suggest opera to the Show Biz reporters and their readers and so they missed the chance to lay about it. Thinking it was only Shakespeare they ignored it on principle.

Glyndebourne was handsomely featured in BBC programmes throughout the 1952 season. In addition to the televising of *Macbeth*, the Third Programme relayed *Macbeth* twice, and each of the other three operas once; the Home Service broadcast the second act of *Cenerentola*, and the Light Programme featured the Festival Opera House and some of its inhabitants in the Sunday feature, 'Down Your Way'. In this last programme it was Richard Dimbleby's custom to go to various parts of the country, talk to people and then have the BBC play a record for them. Mr Harvey, the gardener, chose an aria from the garden scene of *Figaro* – 'Deh vieni, non tardar' sung by Audrey Mildmay; Jock Gough, sternly and wildly patriotic, had Macduff's 'Ah! la paterna mano' from *Macbeth* sung by Caruso; Richard Lewis chose 'Dusk' by Armstrong Gibbs, Sena Jurinac a passage from Beethoven's Fourth Symphony played by the Vienna Philharmonic; Shirley Manger, from the chorus, asked for the Trio from *Der Rosenkavalier* sung by Lehmann, Schumann and Olczewska; Mr Jack Morris, from the catering staff, chose 'Alice Blue Gown' played by Glenn Miller's Orchestra; Rosemary Vercoe, manager of the wardrobe, chose four Beethoven Dances; Janet Moores, secretary to the General Manager, favoured the finale to the first act of *Così fan tutte*, Professor Ebert that to the second act. Jani Strasser provided the surprise item: he picked on 'St Louis Blues' played hot and loud by Louis Armstrong.

John Christie, having already taken part the year before when 'Down Your Way' had come to Lewes and he had chosen Kathleen Ferrier singing Orpheus's 'Che farò senza Euridice?', on this occasion shared a request with Moran Caplat, who carefully betrayed his French ancestry by picking on one of Bétove's 'Pastiches Musicaux' – the masterly parody of Wagner.

The 1952 season ended, as expected, with a deficit on the twenty-eight performances, but thanks to the formation of the Glyndebourne Festival Society and the eighteen advertisements in the Programme Book it was not so bad as it could have been. To give some idea of the money involved in this first season in which outside help was solicited it may be interesting to study the following extracts from a financial report made to the Executive Committee:

1 *Opera Festival*

Costs: £

(Artists' fees, production costs, publicity, etc).. 54,730

Less:

Receipts at Box Office 39,060

Excess of costs over receipts 15,670

Add costs:

Management overheads 5,070

Cost of maintenance of Glyndebourne garden, etc, say 5,000

10,070

Excess costs as above 15,670

Total costs to be met, therefore.. 25,740

2 *Glyndebourne Festival Society* £

Receipts from subscriptions 4,380

Less:

Cost of printing, postage, etc 230

4,150

Less:

Cost of seats allotted to Corporate and Individual Members .. 550

3,600

Less:

Cost of Festival Programme Books allotted to all Members.. .. 400

Total net credit, therefore 3,200

3 *Glyndebourne Festival Programme Book* £

Receipts from advertisements 6,950

Receipts from general sales 1,290

Receipts from allotment to Members of the Festival Society 400

8,640

Less:

Cost of production, distribution, etc 3,890

Total net credit, therefore 4,750

Analysis of receipts from Glyndebourne Festival Society and Festival Programme Book

		£		£
Glyndebourne Festival Society	Gross receipts	4,380	Net receipts	3,200
Festival Programme Book	,, ,,	8,640	,, ,,	4,750
Total	,, ,,	13,020	,, ,,	7,950

4 Summary

	£
Deficit on Opera Festival	15,670
Management and maintenance costs..	10,070
	25,740
Less:	
Net credit from Festival Society	3,200
	22,540
Less:	
Net credit from Programme Book	4,750
Leaving to be met by Mr Christie	17,790

The net assistance from the Glyndebourne Festival Society and the Programme Book of nearly £8,000 was encouraging, but even if the original object had been attained of raising an annual £25,000 by means of subscriptions and advertisements it would still not have been enough. It was this thought which inspired active discussion behind the Glyndebourne scenes of the possibilities of running the Festival Opera as a Trust. The idea had been in many people's minds for some time; John Christie himself had drafted a plan along these lines during the war. In the late summer of 1952 the question began to be studied in earnest and a first draft of a Memorandum of Association of The Glyndebourne Arts Trust Ltd was drawn up. In between whiles, as the Glyndebourne Opera had not been engaged there, Christie went on his own to Edinburgh where he spoke on 'The Problems of Artistic Standards' at the Institute of Public Administration. He was in characteristic form and among other things trounced the critics because 'they had never been trained in the opera houses', adding that 'some of them might be able to play the piano and might know what the composer wrote, but that was not enough'. It was a novel point of attack.

Almost as soon as the 1952 season was over the Ringmer Building Works set to work on major alterations to the Opera House. The auditorium roof was reconstructed, the supporting columns being moved outwards and the seating in the stalls increased to 507 with improved visibility. The proscenium opening was widened by five feet and heightened by six; the balcony was extended at the back over the Covered Way to provide a total of 178 seats; a new scenery dock was built to take back drops, and John Christie's box was moved once more from downstairs to upstairs where it was placed at the back between the producer's box and the newly-built permanent BBC control box. The accommodation in the three boxes at the back of the stalls was increased to 30 seats, to give the theatre a total capacity of 718 available to the public.

A seven-week season was announced for 1953 to begin on 7 June – a little earlier than usual, to give overseas visitors to the Coronation a chance to visit Glyndebourne. The Festival would open with Gluck's *Alceste*, followed by *La Cenerentola*, Richard Strauss's *Ariadne auf Naxos* (the second version, without the Molière play), *Così fan tutte* and *Die Entführung*. The choice of *Alceste* to begin the season assumed a special, unforeseen poignancy, for it followed within a few days of the death of Audrey Mildmay, who died on 31 May, after a long illness, aged only 52. She died at Glyndebourne, and her last wish – that the Festival should open as planned – was characteristic of that professional discipline which had tempered her husband's inspiration and made the Glyndebourne Opera not only unique, but successful. In the programme on that opening night there was a new name among the credits: that of George Christie, Producer's Assistant. It was a comforting sign of the strength of family tradition.

The preservation of that family tradition had deeply concerned Audrey Mildmay during the last months of her life and she had been uneasy about the idea of a Trust, fearing that if plans were made too hurriedly Glyndebourne might get into hands that would destroy its character and ignore its purpose. Her greatest anxiety was that the trustees might take Glyndebourne away from the Christie family and all that her children had been brought up to know and cherish would no longer exist. One Saturday afternoon in February 1953 Lord Wilmot and Mr Sekers went to Glyndebourne and by the time tea was finished had reassured her that the proposed Trust and its trustees could, in fact, be trusted.

In a letter to Mr Sekers written shortly after this meeting Audrey Mildmay put into words her own belief, which was in effect later adopted by the Glyndebourne Arts Trust as a basis of its policy: 'I think one does not want to hamper the growth of Glyndebourne by sticking to too old traditions – as D'Oyle Cart [*sic*] has done for Gilbert and Sullivan – but year by year to give it fresh "fertilization" yet always repolishing and improving the original idea.'

Audrey Mildmay did not live to see the Trust in action, but she died knowing that the future of Glyndebourne was secure and so would continue, as she put it, 'as long as there is any need for it'. Her wish that the 1953 season should open as planned was not just the natural reaction of the pro; it was also typical of her instinctive concern for other people's pleasures and welfare. As Audrey Mildmay the singer she never forgot her duties as Mrs Christie the hostess, and as Mrs Christie she never took advantage of her position to shirk any of the professional obligations of Audrey Mildmay the singer. Just how hard she worked and how thoroughly she absorbed what Busch and Jani Strasser and Ebert taught her was perhaps fully apparent only to those who had known her in her earlier Carl Rosa days – like Francis Toye, for instance, who wrote of her first appearance as Norina in *Don Pasquale* in 1938, that her performance reflected 'an immense amount of hard work and of striving after the highest ideals. I do not think that anywhere else a singer with the privileges enjoyed by Miss Mildmay at Glyndebourne would have been at such pains to improve and develop her technical resources.' Mr Toye ended his article: 'The infection of example is highly contagious – and I only hope that Glyndebourne will continue to exercise this beneficent influence on all the English singers fortunate enough to fall within its orbit' – a hope which has certainly been fulfilled year after year.

The effect of Audrey Mildmay's personal charm on all who met her was immediate and irresistible, but it can no more be described to those who didn't know her than the same elusive quality can be fully discerned and enjoyed in her records by those who never saw her.

My own first personal memory of Audrey Mildmay was at luncheon in a break between rehearsals before the 1935 season began, when I was being subjected by her husband to a splendidly magniloquent account of all the things he was proposing to do at Glyndebourne. From time to time she would interrupt John Christie's extravagant recital with a gentle, good-humoured 'Don't be silly, John', which, if it didn't stem the flow altogether at least diverted it temporarily into another channel – where, of course, an even more extravagant pool of ideas and plans would build up and burst its banks. Though I have long forgotten exactly what caused them I have remembered Audrey Mildmay's smiling reproaches clearly as typical of the sense of proportion she brought to everything connected with Glyndebourne – a sense of proportion which raised up, as it were, as well as kept down. John Christie's famous words, 'We should aim at the sky, but have our feet on the ground', were the expression of a principle that he can have learnt only from his wife. It was she, and nobody else, at Glyndebourne who realized from the start that a sense of proportion applied just as much to ensuring that the value of an idea, the importance of a situation, should not be underestimated, as it did to ensuring that they were not exaggerated. John Christie's opera house had to be developed into a proper professional concern, not a glorified village hall for amateurs; but once established it was essential that it should know its limitations as well as its potentialities.

In her unique position as Mrs Christie Audrey Mildmay's finely developed sense of proportion was an asset of inestimable value to Glyndebourne. Because she was a professional people came to her with complaints, troubles and fears which they felt she alone would understand. So it was that Rudolf Bing wrote to her, and not to John Christie, in his indignation at the way he considered he – and, as its representative, Glyndebourne – had been insulted by the English Opera Group on the Dutch tour of *The Rape of Lucretia*. Audrey Mildmay's reply was a masterpiece of sympathy and understanding and a persuasive plea for a sense of proportion, but at the same time she suggested to Bing that perhaps he tended to treat Mr Britten 'rather patronizingly'. Occasionally this sense of fairness and her exceptional kindness of heart could make things difficult for Bing, as when, for instance, in 1947 the English Opera Group Limited asked her to become a director of the company. Her natural inclination was to accept so that everybody might be happy – until Bing pointed out that this would enable 'the Group' to by-pass the Glyndebourne office and go to her direct in any dispute (and he foresaw plenty) which would obviously undermine his own position. Audrey Mildmay saw the wisdom of this and her acceptance of the Group's offer was tactfully left 'in abeyance'.

Where the bricks and mortar of Glyndebourne serve as a concrete memorial to her husband, like the bust in the walled garden, Audrey Mildmay's own memorial is intangible because it can be found only in the spirit of the Festival Opera and its faithful, unrelenting efforts to respect her famous dinner-table admonition: 'For God's sake do the thing properly.'

There is no record that John Christie raised any objection to the performance of the first opera to be sung in French on the Glyndebourne stage. The composer of *Alceste*, after all, was German (or Bohemian) and like Mozart could be forgiven for writing music to a foreign text because that was the way he had to earn a living. As far as his known dislike of the French language was concerned he could do little more than take the programme's word for it that the opera was sung 'In the Original French'. The cast was all-British, except for Magda Laszlo, as Alceste, who was Hungarian, and the words were sung in accents varying from Sussex and Scottish to Australian and Miss Laszlo's Hungarian view of a language which, like the English she was to sing later in Walton's *Troilus and Cressida*, it seemed she did not speak at all.

The first performance of *Alceste* was conducted by Vittorio Gui, and like *Idomeneo* the year before, was given for the benefit of members of the Glyndebourne Festival Society, and as in 1952 it was a memorial occasion; this time, however, the performance had not been planned as such; it became one owing to unhappy circumstances and the evening began with a spontaneous tribute of silence to the memory of Audrey Mildmay.

Gluck's opera did not rate as everybody's cup of tea, though it was generally admitted to be 'stately'. Magda Laszlo looked extremely beautiful and caught a number of people on the wrong foot by not bawling out 'Divinités du Styx' in the Wagnerian manner to which they were accustomed. The décor was all the work of newcomers. The scenery was designed by Sir Hugh Casson, who made his début as a stage designer with an impressive series of sets full of the rectangles which seem to have become his irremediable trade mark in the theatre; the imposing 20-ft-high statue of Apollo in the Temple was designed by Christopher Ironside; and Rosemary Vercoe, the Glyndebourne wardrobe manager, designed, as well as fitted, the costumes for the first time.

Apart from a *Cenerentola* which had exactly the same cast as the year before and so became the first, and I believe only, opera in Glyndebourne's history ever to have achieved this double, there was nothing about the rest of the season that could be regarded as exceptional – unless it was the début of Mattiwilda Dobbs, the young American Negro coloratura who sang what Richard Capell called a 'carefree' Zerbinetta in *Ariadne*, and was to sing a fine Constanze and Queen of the Night in later seasons.

The Constanze in the 1953 *Entführung* was sung by Sari Barabas, a pretty young Hungarian soprano (how well Busch's policy of 'pretty girls' has been continued!), who had to wait for her first sensational success at Glyndebourne, however, until her appearance as the Countess in Rossini's *Le Comte Ory* in 1955. Glyndebourne's first intentions, as expressed in the printed programme of *Die Entführung* in 1953, were not realized when the time came for performance. Alda Noni's part as Blonde was sung by Emmy Loose and April Cantelo, while Anton Walbrook's promised return engagement as Pasha Selim did not materialize. His place was taken on the opening night by Carl Ebert and later by David Franklin.

A Glyndebourne season has rarely been without a human interest story, and in 1953 it was provided by Sena Jurinac and Sesto Bruscantini, who got married in Lewes on 19 June and appeared together in the evening in *Così fan tutte*. Before the season was over the newly-weds were in the news once more: on the day before the last performance of the season, which ended with *Così fan tutte*, they had a motor accident. It was an all-theatrical crash at Offham on the London road just north of Lewes. Juan Oncina was driving with Sena Jurinac, Sesto Bruscantini and the German tenor, Helmut Krebs, and collided with a car driven by Rodney Millington. Mr Millington, who lives in another village near Lewes, was an original member of the company of the Festival Theatre, Cambridge, where they talked even more about their lighting than they did at Glyndebourne.[1] That was in 1926; since then Rodney Millington has been the proprietor of that fascinating theatrical directory *Spotlight*. After the crash Bruscantini was able to appear as Don Alfonso, but Sena Jurinac was shaken too badly to sing Fiordiligi and her place was taken by Rita McKerrow from the chorus, who had been her understudy for the past three years, and I believe was the first understudy ever called in for Fiordiligi in all the seventy performances of the opera given by Glyndebourne until then.

The BBC's choice for television this year was a complete *Entführung* which seemed to be enjoyed by most of the television columnists, including the *News of the World* and the *Daily Worker*. The inevitable dissentient was the critic of the *People*, an inveterate grumbler from way back who would have had us believe that the BBC, in transmitting two and a half hours of Glyndebourne once a year for the 'enlightened' few (his quotes), was guilty of 'rudely ignoring the masses who are the overwhelming majority'.

Later in the season Glyndebourne returned to Edinburgh, and included for the first

---

[1] The Festival Theatre at Cambridge was as unique in its way as Glyndebourne and anticipated the Festival Opera in several respects. It was started by a rich young Irishman called Terence Gray, who had been an amateur Egyptologist, drove an electric motor car, wrote plays and had a passion for theatrical lighting. The Festival, run as a weekly rep, was a converted mission hall converted from a theatre; it had a solid brick cyclorama, probably the most comfortable seats of any auditorium in Europe, caviar sandwiches at the bar, and in due course a grill room which had the best wine and food in Cambridge and was worth a journey on its own. An unusual and characteristic feature was the programme designed to be read in the dark. The typically Irish instructions read: 'To read this programme in the dark hold it up to the light.' Unfortunately, as in most theatres where lighting is an obsession, the stage was nearly always in pitch darkness. Terence Gray's Festival Theatre was a stimulating and memorable episode in the history of the English theatre (Ninette de Valois was director of dancing and Norman Marshall was producer), and it cost its founder a packet.

time a work by a living composer. Stravinsky's *The Rake's Progress*, sung in the original English of the libretto of Auden and Kallman (rapidly becoming the Meilhac and Halévy of our times), was given its first British performance and introduced a new designer to the Glyndebourne circle in Osbert Lancaster, who set the opera in the late eighteenth century instead of Hogarth's original period in order, he explained, not to clash with Rex Whistler's designs for the Sadler's Wells ballet of *The Rake's Progress* which was being performed later at the Edinburgh Festival. Richard Lewis created the part of Tom Rakewell and has sung it in every Glyndebourne performance of the opera since then.

Stravinsky's *Rake* became one of Glyndebourne's most popular operas until in its fourth season at the Festival Opera House in 1963 the management had to advertise in *The Times* that seats were 'still available' – which suggests that after about twenty performances in Sussex most of the people who wanted to see it had now seen it. When he first heard the opera at Edinburgh John Christie was quoted as saying: 'I don't like the music and I can't imagine hearing the overture played on a concert platform – and what use is an overture if it can't be played in a concert?' He added hopefully: 'I am told I may come round to it.'

In addition to *The Rake's Progress*, Glyndebourne took *Idomeneo* and *Cenerentola* to the Edinburgh Festival, the first time it had staged three productions there; thereafter the Glyndebourne contribution was never fewer than three operas, and on one occasion it was five.

Perhaps because of what Stravinsky and *The Rake's Progress* did to him, John Christie's thoughts in 1953 turned once more to his tireless ambition to perform Wagner at Glyndebourne. Shortly before the start of the 1952 season he had invited Wagner's grandsons, Wolfgang and Wieland, to the Glyndebourne Festival, but in a letter addressed – a little prematurely perhaps – to 'Mr St Christie', they had regretted that their work at Bayreuth prevented their accepting. Late in the following year the Wagners' sister Friedelind had visited Glyndebourne and in her bread-and-butter letter related how she had spoken to her brother Wieland about Christie's idea of bringing the Bayreuth production of *Parsifal* to Glyndebourne. Wieland had felt that the difficulties were insurmountable, however, apart from the Bayreuth tradition that no Bayreuth *Parsifal* must be performed anywhere else, even in another non-commercial theatre. 'Being the grandchildren,' wrote Miss Wagner, 'we have to adhere to our grandfather's will.'

If *Parsifal* was impractical Wieland Wagner was keen, nevertheless, to do something at Glyndebourne – *Tristan* perhaps. If Mr Christie was interested in this idea would he please be so kind as to let Wieland have all the stage measurements. Or better still, Friedelind Wagner added in her letter, Wieland was even more interested in doing something at Glyndebourne that had nothing to do with Bayreuth or Wagner – 'simply in his capacity as stage director'. Miss Wagner commented: 'I feel this would be the finest idea of all. Do consider it. To me the combination sounds perfect.'

And with those words the correspondence seems to have ended. The only Wagner Christie ever heard in his theatre was the *Siegfried Idyll* – once at a concert conducted by Busch in 1934, and once at a concert conducted by John Pritchard at Easter 1953.

CHAPTER TWENTY

1954 **The Arts Trust**

ON 31 MAY 1954 THE Glyndebourne Arts Trust, formed to ensure the financial future of Glyndebourne, was at last incorporated and the following announcement was made:

Mr John Christie has conveyed to the Trust, on a long lease at a peppercorn rent, the Opera House, the mansion house, the grounds and the gardens [in all about 100 acres], which together make up Glyndebourne.

The trustees will be responsible for the general supervision of these properties and of the Glyndebourne Festival Opera. They have made an agreement with Mr Christie that he and his colleagues, who have brought the Festival to its present high level of distinction, shall continue to be responsible for its direction and administration.

Glyndebourne does not receive any subsidy from public funds. It has to maintain itself out of its own receipts together with such resources as the trustees can create from the donations of persons and institutions who believe that it is of importance to preserve, at the highest international standard, this Festival of opera presented in the distinctive setting of an English country house. The trustees are anxious to emphasize that the formation of the Trust makes it no less essential for Glyndebourne's present friends to continue to give their increasing support.

The lease, which was for 66 years less one day, would be renewable in the year 2020 and was so framed that it contained no right of assignment – in other words, Glyndebourne could not be let to the wrong people and so become, in Audrey Mildmay's words, 'a useful side-kick to the everyday London entertainments – or even a Folies Bergère!'

One of the first to be approached to become a trustee was John Spedan Lewis, but after accepting he had had to cry off because of ill health. The first full team of trustees consisted of eleven members. Its chairman was Sir Wilfred Eady, a trustee of the Old Vic who, since his retirement from the Treasury in 1952, where he invented the Eady plan to help the British film industry, had come to live at Rodmell on the other side of the Ouse valley from Glyndebourne, about two miles from Lewes. The other members were Gerald Coke, Acting Chairman of the Trust and chairman of the Rio Tinto Company; Lady Violet Bonham Carter, also a trustee of the Old Vic; the Dowager Marchioness of Reading, who as Baroness Swanborough took her title from her house two miles on the same road from Rodmell to Lewes; Lieut-Colonel C. H. N. Adams, Christie's solicitor;

A. B. Barrie, a brilliant Scottish accountant who had suggested Sir William Eady as Chairman and had been Controller of Raw Materials Accountancy at the Ministry of Supply during the war; Viscount Duncannon, the present Earl of Bessborough, whose thirteenth-century religious drama, *Like Stars Appearing*, about the life and miracles of St Richard, Bishop of Chichester, had been performed for the first time at Glyndebourne at Easter 1954; the Hon Sir Geoffrey Gibbs, a banker, who had been in the Ministry of Economic Warfare during the war; Sir Mark Turner, another banker, who had also been in the Ministry of Economic Warfare – obviously the best possible training ground for anybody concerned with the finances of opera; N. T. Sekers and Lord Wilmot. The secretary of the Trust, as well as the Festival Society (he was also editor of the Programme Book), was Robert Ponsonby, who a year or two later succeeded Ian Hunter as Artistic Director of the Edinburgh Festival – the second Glyndebourne trainee in succession to occupy the post.

(Among the first people John Christie had approached to become trustees were Lord Salisbury and Sir Edward Bridges. Lord Salisbury had to decline because he had too much to do as Leader of the House of Lords and in the Cabinet. Sir Edward Bridges could not accept because he was still at the Treasury; as soon as he retired and became Lord Bridges, however, he became a trustee.)

With the formation of the Glyndebourne Arts Trust there came into being the set-up which, with a slight modification in 1958, has been responsible for the Festival Opera ever since. A body known as the Glyndebourne Executive, consisting of John Christie, Carl Ebert, Moran Caplat, with E. Scott Norman as the financial expert, and acting on behalf of the company known as Glyndebourne Productions Ltd, planned the artistic and financial details of the opera and then submitted its budget to the Arts Trust. The directors of Glyndebourne Productions Ltd, at the time the Trust was formed, were John Christie, Miss Rhona Byron, Lieut-Colonel Adams and E. Scott Norman; the General Manager was Moran Caplat, the Secretary Janet Moores. In 1958 the Glyndebourne Executive, which had never had any official existence, no longer got a credit in the programme; as Christie, Mr Caplat and Mr Scott Norman were already part of Glyndebourne Productions Ltd, it was obviously not necessary. That Carl Ebert still played a part in the planning of the Festival Opera was clear from his position in the hierarchy as sole Artistic Director.

Today, in 1964, there may be new names among the Trustees and the Directors of Glyndebourne Productions Ltd, but the method of artistic planning and general administration is much the same. During the winter months George Christie, Moran Caplat and Jani Strasser go off, 'generally, man by man', in search of talent; some of it they may fall upon by accident, some of it on the recommendation of Glyndebourne conductors, producers' friends and singers who have sung at Glyndebourne. The interest that singers take in all this may seem a little unexpected perhaps; but in fact they often show a genuine and touching generosity to their fellow artists and a chance postcard sent by one of them to the management will recommend a promising colleague with whom the writer has just been singing in Chicago or Buenos Aires. It goes without saying, of course, that a coloratura soprano will rarely draw attention to another singer in exactly the same line of business, but a baritone or contralto will put in a good word for a tenor or even a conductor.

The 1954 season opened on 10 June with another Rossini opera: *The Barber of Seville* was added to the repertoire in a performance produced by Carl Ebert and conducted by Gui which introduced Graziella Sciutti to English audiences. Miss Sciutti, one of the prettiest of all Glyndebourne's 'pretty girls', was universally hailed as a rare discovery, and nobody bothered to mention that she was a soprano singing Rosina instead of Rossini's prescribed mezzo-soprano. Like all good purists Vittorio Gui is just as purist as it suits him. At one moment he complains that *The Barber of Seville* has come down to us 'with a thick coating of impurities like the carbon on a motor engine, which many are still pleased to call "tradition" '; at the next he claims that Glyndebourne 'follows the original edition of *The Barber of Seville* in every respect, with the exception of the part of Rosina which is sung by a soprano instead of the original mezzo-soprano'. Not only did Gui follow a 'tradition' with a soprano Rosina, but he was not above introducing a glockenspiel with a recognizable tonic and dominant in place of the 'neutral' sound of the famous triangle *ostinato* in the finale of Act I and so appreciably alter the instrumental colour of the whole movement. Inconsistency such as this, however, is disarming, usually harmless and, of course, essential in distinguishing healthy purism from mere pedantry. Purism may benefit a composer; pedantry, never.

As far as Graziella Sciutti's Rosina was concerned she could have sung it with Don Basilio's voice for all the public cared. For sheer enjoyment there had never been anything quite like this *Barber* at Glyndebourne before. Sesto Bruscantini was an ebullient Figaro; Juan Oncina, like a good Spaniard, accompanied himself on the guitar in Almaviva's serenade – an impressively confidant temptation of providence if we remember at all superstitiously that it was Garcia's guitar playing which contributed so heavily to the fiasco of the very first performance of the *Barber*. Ian Wallace was commended most favourably for the excellence of his Italian and his sense of style as Dr Bartolo. In the Lesson Scene Gui's preference for the 'traditional' soprano made any puristic use of Rossini's original music impracticable, so in its place he interpolated the aria which has been performed there in two of the three productions of the opera at Glyndebourne – Mozart's lovely concert aria 'Voi che avete un cor fedele' (K. 217). The only trouble about using this particular aria is that it takes one suddenly into another world which even Rossini never inhabited, and after a brief sojourn there one is returned abruptly to the metallic brilliance of *The Barber*. But to hear this particular Mozart aria during a performance of *The Barber of Seville* at Glyndebourne is certainly to hear it in the best possible surroundings.

Finally there was Oliver Messel's exuberant décor; the costumes had a touch of Goya about them and the scenery, gay and extravagant, introduced a quick change of scene in Act I which has had a cheer every time it has been seen since. Glyndebourne's first *Barber of Seville*, in short, was a most satisfying addition to the repertoire.

The season continued with *Alceste*, the leading role sung by Magda Laszlo again in a performance that was generally considered, like the production as a whole, to have developed and matured. Richard Strauss's *Ariadne* was repeated but this year with a curtain raiser for the first time. Most German theatres have always considered *Ariadne* enough of an 'evening-filling' (*abendfüllende*) opera not to need anything in the way of hors d'oeuvre. Glyndebourne, on the other hand, with a timetable and performance schedule unlike any other opera house in the world, were always obviously uneasy about this and in their anxiety to give their patrons their money's worth had prefaced the 1953 production of *Ariadne* by the entire thirty-minute suite of Strauss's incidental music to *Le Bourgeois Gentilhomme* played in a darkened auditorium with the curtain raised on an empty twilit scene. This experiment was fortunately never repeated; it is one thing for critics to fall asleep during an opera, but another to encourage them to do so before the opera has started. Beginning with the 1954 production, therefore, the second version of *Ariadne* has always been preceded by an operatic outrider; in this case it was Busoni's one-act *Arlecchino*, first seen and heard in this country on BBC television before the war, but now given its first professional performance in a theatre. An excerpt from Vittorio Gui's memoirs *Battute d'aspetto*, subtitled *Meditazioni di un musicista militante*, appeared in the Programme Book to introduce Busoni and his opera (which Gui himself had first introduced to Italy in 1940), but at Glyndebourne the work itself was conducted by John Pritchard. It was produced by Peter Ebert, following in the footsteps of his father who had hitherto produced every Glyndebourne opera since the Festival began.

The casts of the 1954 repertoire were notable for the increasing number of American singers taking part – a tendency which has developed with every year since then, until in five out of the six 1964 operas the leading parts were scheduled to be taken by Americans, and there were an American Pamina, Papageno, Poppea, Pacuvio (in Rossini's *Pietra del paragone*), Count and Poet in *Capriccio*, and an American Lady Macbeth who came in as a late substitute for another American singer who had had to give up the part owing to ill health. The number and high quality of American singers at present in German opera houses alone, as well as in the United States, is so exceptional that when it comes to casting Glyndebourne nowadays often has no need to look further for what it wants than the Americans in Europe. The ascendancy of the American (and Canadian) opera singer since the war, its cause and effect, are a fascinating subject which has yet to be properly studied.

In the 1954 double bill of *Arlecchino* and *Ariadne* the principal women's roles were monopolized by American singers; Elaine Marbin sang Colombina, the only woman's part in Busoni's opera, while Mattiwilda Dobbs was Zerbinetta and Lucine Amara was Ariadne in the Strauss. Indeed, as Dorothy Dow had sung Ariadne the year before, and Lucine Amara sang it in the next two revivals of the opera in 1957 and 1958, the part did not pass out of American hands until Enriqueta Tarrés sang it in 1962, and then it was in the first version of the opera, not the second.

The 1954 production of *Don Giovanni* had an American Donna Anna in Margaret Harshaw, an American Giovanni in James Pease, and a Canadian Don Ottavio in Léopold Simoneau. On the other hand, *The Rake's Progress*, which had been sung at Edinburgh in its original English by an entirely Anglo-Saxon cast (including two Americans – Jerome Hines and Nan Merriman), was performed with no transatlantic singers when it reached Glyndebourne in 1954. In Sussex the cast once more assumed the kind of cosmopolitan look we had always been used to. Mr Hines' part as Nick Shadow was taken over by Marko Rothmüller from Jugoslavia, and Miss Merriman was replaced as Baba the Turk by Marina de Gabarain who, as we know, is Spanish. The third 'foreigner' in the Glyndebourne production was Swiss.

It should be explained that I use the term 'foreigner' here in its strict passport sense. The English language, teased and worried as it is by the Russian Stravinsky in *The Rake's Progress*, is the native tongue of no singer on earth. The composer's whimsical treatment of the stresses, accents, cadences and sense of English virtually forces all who sing it to tackle it from scratch as a language they have never known before. The Swiss singer was Hugues Cuenod, now making his first appearance at Glyndebourne in the part of Sellem and who, it will be remembered, had first come to John Christie's notice nearly twenty years before.[1] It is only recently that I learned from M. Cuenod the answer to the query Christie had raised. On having Hugues Cuenod recommended to him Christie had sent off Hans Oppenheim to see him in Paris in the hope that he would do for Monostatos in the first Glyndebourne *Magic Flute*. Unfortunately, M. Cuenod proved to be 6 ft 5 ins tall and the matter was dropped for, at that time in operatic history, at any rate, Monostatos was traditionally a small and bumptious figure. Hugues Cuenod himself, though disappointed at the time, now considers that things have turned out for the best. If he had sung at Glyndebourne before the war, he says, he would probably have been passed over afterwards; as it is he came to the Festival Opera in 1954 as a novelty and is now in his tenth season there.

For the first time at Glyndebourne there was only one Mozart opera on the bill. The BBC televised it, compressing the whole of *Don Giovanni* into 90 minutes and cutting three of the most popular arias – 'Batti, batti', 'Deh vieni alla finestra' and 'Dalla sua pace'. They also cut the final sextet; if they had included it the cameras might have had something better to do than linger so long on the final shot of Don Giovanni held in the grip of the Commendatore that the viewer was able to see the singers abandon their pose and slap each other heartily on the back in mutual congratulation while still in shot. The best Press notices of the following day were not surprisingly reserved for 'Sportsview', which had shown Sir Gordon Richards in a hospital bed.

In August Glyndebourne returned to the Edinburgh Festival where they staged Rossini's *Le Comte Ory* for the first time, revived *Così fan tutte* and repeated the summer's production of *Ariadne* (without *Arlecchino*). 'The Glyndebourne's' return was warmly greeted, though a prelim in the Scottish *Daily Express* on the morning of the opening night read a little ambiguously:

... but in the last two Festivals the second night was as brilliant as the first was disappointing.

[1] See page 86.

Let us hope that history will repeat itself when the Glyndebourne Opera revive Rossini's 'Le Comte Ory' tonight.

Whatever it was the writer was trying to say he obviously meant well and his good intentions were rewarded by a brilliant and hilarious performance of *Ory* which (on its first as well as second night) was perhaps an even greater all-round success than *The Barber of Seville* had been at Glyndebourne.[1] There was wit and charm in Carl Ebert's production and Oliver Messel's décor to match Vittorio Gui's exhilarating reading of the score, and the infectious performance of the firmly established Rossini Repertory Company of Mme Cadoni and Messrs Oncina, Bruscantini and Wallace, now adorned by Sari Barabas's enchanting Countess. The comedy and lyrical warmth of the masterly second act were presented with irresistible conviction and reassured those who had read them that Francis Toye and W. J. Turner had known what they were talking about – Toye in his book on Rossini, Turner in a *New Statesman* article in 1939 in which he had recommended *Le Comte Ory* to Glyndebourne's notice. It was a thoroughly stimulating experience to which Carl Ebert contributed an endlessly inventive and superbly timed production greeted by Ernest Newman as his finest achievement in any guise.

The *Così fan tutte*, also conducted by Gui, was as usual the biggest box-office draw of the three operas and introduced Magda Laszlo as a Mozart singer in the part of Dorabella, looking lovely and singing finely in a performance well up to Glyndebourne's traditional standard for this opera.

Glyndebourne had a finger in one other theatrical enterprise at the 1954 Edinburgh Festival. This was Stravinsky's *L'Histoire du Soldat* presented by the Edinburgh Festival Society 'in collaboration with Glyndebourne'; it was produced by Günther Rennert, conducted by Hans Schmidt-Isserstedt with costumes by Ita Maximovna – all of whom were later to become associated with Glyndebourne Opera in varying degrees of intimacy.

In September the Glyndebourne Festival Opera made its first visit abroad – not to America, or Holland, or Paris, or any of the possible places that had been talked about over the years, but to Germany to take part in the West Berlin Festival. There was irony and a most satisfying poetic justice in the acceptance of an invitation from the nation whose years of evil had unwittingly contributed so much to the good of Glyndebourne. At the Städtische Oper, where Carl Ebert was now returning after 21 years absence as the new Intendant, Glyndebourne gave two performances of *Cenerentola*. Rossini's opera was an even greater surprise to the Berliners than it had first been to the English at Covent Garden before the war. The Berlin Festival bill of the opera wisely included a translation of the title, but it was illustrated by a figure of Cinderella obviously derived from the German version of the story, for it showed birds feeding from her hand, which

---

[1] The opera had originally been announced in the Edinburgh prospectus as 'Il conte Ory', to be sung in Italian. In accordance with Glyndebourne policy and after much searching for copies of the right vocal scores, the opera was billed as *Le Comte Ory* and sung in the original French of the libretto set by Rossini for Paris in 1828.

as far as I remember was an important feature of *Das Aschenbrödel*. One of the critics, even when he had seen the opera, still thought the story was based on Grimm; which suggests to me that not only did he know nothing of Perrault but, owing to his Nazi childhood, he knew nothing about Grimm either.

The cast of *La Cenerentola* in Berlin was the same as it had been at Glyndebourne the year before – Marina de Gabarain, Fernanda Cadoni, Juan Oncina, Sesto Bruscantini, Ian Wallace, Hervey Alan, but with the part of Clorinda sung alternately by Alda Noni and Halinka de Taczynska, an Australian who had graduated earlier from the Glyndebourne chorus to sing Alice in *Le Comte Ory* at Edinburgh. Vittorio Gui did not go on the Berlin trip so the opera was conducted by John Pritchard. The success of the venture was phenomenal and its effect on the Berlin audience so staggering that it had the critics counting curtain calls – always a very important part of a critic's job in Germany where an exceptional success is concerned, for it makes more convincing reading to the German reader than anything else the critic can say about it. The general reception of the production, however, was summed up in the sort of heading all the company could understand: 'Perfekter Rossini aus England!'

Looking back on it 1954 was an outstanding year in many ways for Glyndebourne and not least in the public recognition of John Christie's work by making him a Companion of Honour in the New Year's Honours List. Christie, it is said, had been offered a title for his services to music before the war, but he had refused it. He had agreed to accept the CH, however, as he regarded it as much as anything as a tribute to his wife. He was also, in this same year, in addition to being given the Honorary Freedom of Lewes, where there are now a Christie Road and a Mildmay Road, the first Englishman ever to be awarded the Mozart Medal of the Vienna Mozart Society – an award which was made posthumously to Audrey Mildmay at the same time.

One other event, strictly concerned with the Glyndebourne Festival Opera, was noted with satisfaction in the summer of 1954 and that was the issue of the first recording since before the war of a complete Glyndebourne opera. In the two years when Busch was back excerpts had been recorded from *Idomeneo* and *Così fan tutte*; now Gui's performance of *La Cenerentola* was released as the first Glyndebourne LP with the cast that had first sung it at the Festival Opera House in 1952. For eight years it was the only available recording of the opera at all in Britain. Then, like too many of the Glyndebourne albums, it was withdrawn – it seems irrevocably. It is a depressing thought.

The Cunning Little Vixen, 1975. The Fox (Robert Hoyem), the Vixen (Norma Burrowes) and their cubs. Scenery, Patrick Robertson. Costumes, Rosemary Vercoe. *(Gravett)*

Idomeneo, 1974: Bozena Betley (Ilia), Leo Goeke (Idamante), Richard Lewis (Idomeneo), Josephine Barstow (Electra). *(Southern Television/Nutley)*

(above) Falstaff, 1976. Left to right: Elizabeth Gale (Nannetta), Kay Griffel (Alice), Reni Penkova (Meg), Nucci Condò (Quickly). *(Southern Television/ Nutley)*

(left) Falstaff, 1976: Windsor Forest. Donald Gramm as Falstaff. Designer, Jean-Pierre Ponnelle. *(Southern Television/Nutley)*

CHAPTER TWENTY-ONE

1955 The Festival comes of age

WITH THE SEASON OF 1955 Glyndebourne Opera came of age. In the 21 years that had passed since its foundation its activities had been interrupted by war and financial strife but, like a volcano, there had always been intense activity below the surface between one eruption and the next, however extinct it may have appeared to the onlooker.

The opening of the coming-of-age Festival coincided with a railway strike which, however, had no effect on attendances at Glyndebourne, since those who did not drive down from London by car climbed into evening dress earlier than ever in the day and caught special buses from Victoria at 2.30 (1.45 on Sundays). Like the first season in 1934 this one opened with *Figaro*. It was a new production shown first on 8 June to members of the Glyndebourne Festival Society. The décor (by Oliver Messel), the conductor (Vittorio Gui), and eleven of the twelve principals were either new to Glyndebourne or new to the part they now played at Glyndebourne. Sena Jurinac sang her first Countess, but was oddly disappointing; her husband, Sesto Bruscantini, sang his first Mozart Figaro, achieving a unique double by singing Rossini's Figaro as well later in the season; Franco Calabrese was the first, and so far the last, Italian ever to play the Count at Glyndebourne; Elena Rizzieri was the first Italian Susanna ever heard at Glyndebourne (Tatiana Menotti was in the 1947 Edinburgh production); Hugues Cuenod was the first foreigner – i.e. non-British singer – to sing Basilio at Glyndebourne. The American Frances Bible shared the part of Cherubino with her countrywoman, Risë Stevens, who alone of the cast had sung her part at Glyndebourne before – in this case, before the war.

With Italians as Susanna, the Count and Figaro, and an Italian conductor, it was not surprising that the performance took on a hard Italian brilliance which was unfamiliar. Busch's tradition of Mozart, while thoroughly masculine, had never lost sight of what have been called 'the shadows of human sadness cast by the sunlight of comedy' which make Mozart's operas unique; Gui and his countrymen dazzled and amused the audience, but somehow they didn't move it. The distinctive Italian quality of this production was clearly preserved in the recording of the complete *Figaro* made by the Glyndebourne company later in 1955. The ensemble was the same as during the Festival except in one detail, and that – the presence of Graziella Sciutti as Susanna – certainly did nothing to lessen the Italianate atmosphere of the performance (Risë Stevens sang Cherubino in the recording).

The Letter Duet from the 1955 *Figaro* production was featured in an unusual Glyndebourne by-product – the film directed for Rank by Anthony Asquith called *On Such a Night*. This was a rather whimsical semi-documentary about a young American who got caught up with the dressed-up crowds at Victoria Station and found himself at Glyndebourne, where he talked to John Christie and heard *Figaro*. The rights in the picture (the original working title was 'Puzzle – Find the Countess') were given to Glyndebourne as a present from the Rank Organisation.

The second (public) night of the season introduced what was a complete novelty to those in the Glyndebourne audience who had not been to Edinburgh the previous year – *Le Comte Ory*. Rossini's opera more than repeated its success; the Glyndebourne audience not only laughed at the jokes, but clapped them – 'like a Light Programme studio audience' as two critics noticed with some disquiet. But Ory's carousing nuns were as funny as ever and the stage picture of the Countess and her ladies at their embroidery was always greeted with applause as the curtain rose on Act II.

The family element, beginning with the Christies and in due course involving two generations of the Busch and Ebert families, has played so strong and essential a part in the development of Glyndebourne that it is natural that some of the operas performed there should have produced family associations of their own from time to time. In recent years Richard Strauss's daughter-in-law attended the first night of *Der Rosenkavalier* and Debussy's stepdaughter that of *Pelléas et Mélisande*. The first family connection of all with an opera at Glyndebourne (it would have been the second if Queen Elizabeth had not had to cancel her visit to *Macbeth* in 1938) was with *Le Comte Ory*, when there came as a guest to the first night Mrs Philiberte Ross, *née* Ory. Mrs Ross was the daughter of the last of the Ory family who had settled in England during the French Revolution and could trace their descent through many Counts Ory (including one who was Inquisitor General in the sixteenth century) from a Count Ory celebrated in a French Crusaders' ballad. If mention in a soldiers' song is regarded by the sceptical as unconvincing proof of existence, what about Mademoiselle from Armentieres who was a very real person? Whatever else one may think, to have a Rossini comic opera named after one's family is not an everyday distinction and it is pleasant to recall that Glyndebourne were well aware of it.

Peter Ebert made his début as a producer of a full-length opera with *Don Giovanni*, the third opera of the 1955 repertoire. The work obviously tested him more than *Arlecchino* had done, of course, but he came through with commendations for going his own way with an easy, fluent production and reducing the number of scene changes. Musically, however, this *Don Giovanni* was uneven largely owing to the obvious miscasting of the title role. Giuseppe Valdengo gave a rough, harsh performance which lacked charm and any suggestion that Don Giovanni was irresistible to women. Or was it miscasting? Perhaps it was that the musical resources of Glyndebourne were on this occasion not powerful enough to draw from Valdengo the convincing charm and smoothness which, when he sang in *Otello* under Toscanini's guidance, had contributed so much to his superb characterization of Iago. It would have been interesting to have heard what Busch might have made of Valdengo in a Glyndebourne *Don Giovanni*. What Busch in fact made of John Brownlee in the part we were reminded by the issue in 1955 of the original 1935 recording of *Don Giovanni*, now transferred to LP. This set was deleted in England in 1963, but the other Glyndebourne recording – *Arlecchino* – which was released in the spring of 1955 has lasted a little longer, though it is now available only as a tape.

On the credit side of the casting Geraint Evans's first Leporello was outstanding; it developed over the years into an increasingly witty, endearing interpretation which was so highly thought of by Carl Ebert (who did not in fact produce him in the part) that, according to a wry remark by Mr Evans: 'I believe the Prof thought he'd invented me.' Sena Jurinac, the Elvira of 1954, sang Donna Anna – some said tentatively, others said superbly, but all were inclined to feel that it was a better performance than her Countess had been.

The biggest disappointment was a purely negative one. According to the Programme Book we were to have heard Graziella Sciutti as Zerlina, as well as Rosina in the *Barber* later on. Not long before the first night of *Don Giovanni* Miss Sciutti was declared 'indisposed'; she was having a baby – or, as the critic of the *Scotsman* put it, had 'gone into another sort of production altogether' – and her part was taken by Genevieve Warner. In the *Barber* she was replaced by Gianna d'Angelo.

The change of cast in *The Barber of Seville* brought with it a change in the music used in the Lesson Scene. In place of the Mozart concert aria sung by Graziella Sciutti the year before, Gui chose a Rossini number for Miss Angelo. This was 'Bel raggio lusinghier' from *Semiramide*, an interpolation which, curiously, was identified – or, at least, mentioned – only by Andrew Porter in the *Financial Times*.

The last production of the Festival was a revival of *The Rake's Progress* and the season ended, as it had begun, with a performance for members of the Glyndebourne Festival Society and their guests only.

The Barber of Seville was chosen by the BBC for its annual television from Glyndebourne and, for a change, was not greeted by the usual philistine comment in the popular Press. Gianna d'Angelo's charm and looks made such an impression on the columnists that she was hailed with 60-point headings like 'Opera Finds a LA LOLLO'. (There was some unlikely talk at the time that Miss Gina Lollobrigida wanted to sing opera.)

During the Glyndebourne season it had been announced that Vittorio Gui would not be going to Edinburgh with the company. The inimitable American weekly, *Variety*, told us all we wanted to know with its customary clarity in its rubric 'Inside Stuff – Concerts':

Vittorio Gui, who was skedded to conduct the Glyndebourne Opera Co. in performances of 'Falstaff' and 'Barber of Seville' at the Edinburgh Festival, will obey his medico's advice and withdraw from the engagement. He will return to Italy after the last of his performances at Glyndebourne, Eng., July 16. 'Falstaff' will be taken over by Carlo Maria Giulini of La Scala, Milano (Giulini is making his U.S. début with Chicago Symph in the fall), Alberto Erede of the Metropolitan Opera will take over 'Barber' and John Pritchard will conduct 'La Forza del Destino'.

At Edinburgh Glyndebourne enjoyed their biggest artistic triumph for several years with their production of Verdi's *Falstaff*. Critical enthusiasm in one or two cases was inevitably tempered by memories of Mariano Stabile in the title role and comparison with the recently issued Toscanini recording of the opera, but it was generally acclaimed as an ensemble-performance of a standard hitherto unknown in England. Many of the details of Carl Ebert's production were familiar to those who had seen the performances he had directed at the Cambridge Theatre with Stabile, and those who had not seen them congratulated him on his restraint and (in their experience) his first treatment of a comedy without crossing all the 't's and dotting all the 'i's in a mistaken endeavour to underline everything that was already made clear to the audience by the music. In *Falstaff* the music was allowed to make its points (and there are plenty in this miraculous score) and everybody was grateful for it.

Fernando Corena, in what was surprisingly his only appearance with the Glyndebourne Opera, made a great hit as Falstaff ('surely he is Stabile's successor,' said the *Financial Times*); Oralia Dominguez, the superbly comic Mexican contralto, made her début as Mistress Quickly, a part she immediately claimed as her own and rightly monopolized in all subsequent Glyndebourne productions of the opera. Geraint Evans was originally intended to sing Ford, but cried off when he discovered the music was too high for him. At Edinburgh Walter Monachesi took over the part and so permitted Geraint Evans to develop into the magnificent Falstaff he eventually became.

Osbert Lancaster's scenery and costumes contributed a great deal to the success of a *Falstaff* which became the mould from which many first-class Glyndebourne performances were made. Mr Lancaster's costumes were full of fun and fanciful colour, though it goes almost without saying that some of the point of the scenery was missed. One criticism was that it all looked 'more like Slough than Tudor Windsor', as though 'Tudor Windsor' was not just as new in its time as Slough is in ours. The brightness of the new brick of Ford's and other newly-built houses (so new that nobody had ascribed them a 'period' yet) was a brilliant touch. Osbert Lancaster was not on the Editorial Board of the *Architectural Review* for nothing.

As the nature of Glyndebourne all along has been rather that of a private pleasure which the public may share, there was a private joke Osbert Lancaster was able to enjoy when he designed *Falstaff*. The ancestral portraits on the wall of Ford's house in the last scene of Act II bear a close resemblance to members of the Glyndebourne staff. Viewed from the auditorium, the first picture on the left of the balcony (it can be seen properly only by those sitting near the front, well over on the prompt side) shows a dark, bearded gentleman, sword in hand, a ship in full sail in the background, and is an unmistakable likeness of the General Manager, Moran Caplat. The centre panel of the triptych, with her red hair adding to her resemblance to Elizabeth I, is a portrait of the Assistant Manager, Miss Janet Moores. The third picture, a solemn bespectacled figure, is Dorothy Craig, secretary wife of Douglas Craig who at that time was Stage Director (he became Assistant General Manager the following year).

One detail of the *Falstaff* particularly pleased John Christie at Edinburgh and that was the introduction of a grotesque Lady Godiva on a hobby horse in the final masquerade of the opera. He took great delight in this as he claimed direct descent from Lady Godiva and her husband Leofric, Duke of Mercia. This genealogical tit-bit came as a surprise to most people, but a reporter on a Scottish newspaper was assured by Christie that it was true and, furthermore, that when *Falstaff* was produced at Glyndebourne Osbert Lancaster was going to have Lady Godiva wear a mask to look like John Christie. Unfortunately this little conceit never materialized – largely, Mr Lancaster tells me, because Christie neglected to tell him anything about it.

John Christie seems to have been generally in the highest spirits during the 1955 Edinburgh Festival, for he was widely reported to have arrived on the wrong day for a party given by the Scottish Arts Council. He returned on the right day wearing a clip-on curly moustache (in imitation of Osbert Lancaster's, it was said). He kept it on throughout the party, walked through the streets to the theatre wearing it, and continued to wear it during a performance of *The Barber of Seville*.

Glyndebourne's eighth Edinburgh Festival season, and the first which had included no opera by Mozart, ended with a revival of *La forza del destino* that contrasted unhappily with the brilliance and polish of the *Barber* and *Falstaff* which preceded it. Comparisons were inevitably made with the magnificent and enlightening performances of 1951, when Fritz Busch conducted and Carl Ebert produced. This time John Pritchard conducted and Peter Ebert produced, and the work never got off the ground. It lacked, as one critic wrote, 'fire in the belly'; while to one Scottish writer the tame, facing-the-audience presentation of the 'Rataplan' chorus was like nothing so much as the late famous Glasgow Orpheus Choir without its late famous conductor, Sir Hugh Roberton.

If the performance was redeemed at all it was by the Leonora of Sena Jurinac, who dominated a cast that almost perversely included no Italians at all. However, the occasion produced a brand new title-contraction in the papers: after 'Così fan', and the later 'Così', we were treated to Verdi's chummily familiar 'Del Destino'.

During the Festival Glyndebourne announced that it would not be returning to Edinburgh the following year. With six Mozart operas scheduled to celebrate the composer's bicentenary in 1956 at Glyndebourne it would be impossible to find time to prepare anything new for Edinburgh. This was accepted as a reasonable explanation and the Hamburg Opera was booked once more in Glyndebourne's place. As it turned out it was five years before Glyndebourne took part in another Edinburgh Festival.

CHAPTER TWENTY-TWO

1956-7 **Thirteen hits and a miss**

THE MOZART BICENTENARY YEAR began with the announcement in the New Year's Honours List of the award of the CBE to Rudolf Bing 'for services to music'. Why the penny of official recognition should apparently have taken so long to drop may be a little puzzling on first thoughts; Bing had left both Glyndebourne and Edinburgh all of seven years previously. But Bing was – and still is – a British citizen and his appointment to Commander of the Order of the British Empire suggested that his services to music had not altogether ceased when he took over the New York Metropolitan. In any case, Bing's award was following a precedent. His Canadian predecessor at the Metropolitan, Edward Johnson, had received the same honour from George v when he was General Manager.

The 1956 Festival established two records at Glyndebourne; the previous highest number of performances – thirty-eight in the 1939 season – was exceeded by ten, and for the first time the repertoire consisted of six full-length operas: *Figaro, Così fan tutte, Don Giovanni, Die Entführung aus dem Serail, The Magic Flute* and *Idomeneo*. The season began on 14 June, a cold windy evening, with a performance of *Idomeneo* for members of the Glyndebourne Festival Society and their guests. Except for Richard Lewis in the title part and Hervey Alan as the Voice of Neptune, there were no survivors from the 1953 production. Sena Jurinac was particularly missed as Ilia, but it seems she was too fully occupied with Donna Anna and Fiordiligi. Among the newcomers the strongest impression was made by William McAlpine, a young Scottish tenor from Stenhousemuir where he was known, owing to his former trade, as the Singing Bricklayer. It was this production of *Idomeneo* which finally drove the *Times* critic to blow his top on a subject he had obviously borne with superhuman patience for far too long: 'Only that awful Glyndebourne ballet, which year after year strikes a jarring note in every production, marred the visual scene.' They were sentiments with which his colleagues heartily agreed.

The performance on the following evening of *Die Entführung* caused almost universal satisfaction. It was a new production by Peter Ebert, in which the solo singing came in for more praise than the concerted numbers and Oliver Messel's designs for more than either. Andrew Porter perhaps summed up Mr Messel's contribution best, not only to *Die Entführung*, but to *Idomeneo* and *Figaro* as well, when he wrote: 'The great merit of his themes is that they impose nothing on the music, but seem to spring from it. Although intensely personal they reflect and decorate Mozart, whereas less sensitive designers try to interpret him.'

The cast, with the exception of Mattiwilda Dobbs as Constanze, was new to Glynde-bourne and gave one of the best performances of the opera in the history of the Festival. Lisa Otto as Blonde and Arnold Van Mill as Osmin were outstanding, and Ernst Haefliger distinguished himself by being the first Belmonte at Glyndebourne to be allowed to sing the aria, 'Ich baue ganz auf deine Stärke', at the beginning of Act III.[1] Kevin Miller, a young Australian who had joined the Glyndebourne chorus in 1954 and had deputized for the indisposed Juan Oncina as Fenton in the broadcast of *Falstaff* from Edinburgh in 1955, was given feature billing in the programme for the first time as Pedrillo. It was altogether a lively, cheerful occasion, and Peter Ebert was congratulated by one of the critics on avoiding the congenital busy-ness which has so often afflicted an Ebert production.

Towards the end of June John Christie journeyed to Oxford (what on earth was his own Alma Mater thinking about?) to receive the Honorary Degree of Doctor of Music. He was the last to receive his degree in a ceremony at which, among others Mr Harry S. Truman was made a Doctor of Civil Law and Sir Kenneth Clark a D. Litt. The Public Orator greeted Christie in that peculiar Latin *The Times* quotes and so thoughtfully trans-lates for us in its reports of these occasions, with: 'Finally, what could be more fitting than that we should honour the founder of Glyndebourne in the bicentenary of Mozart's birth?' (Sir Kenneth Clark, speaking at the Austrian Embassy's Mozart celebration in January, where Christie was also a guest, had said: 'It is, of course, an historical accident that Mozart was not born at Glyndebourne.')

Mr John Christie, the Public Orator continued, had a rare combination of gifts, for not many men could have built an opera house in the grounds of their ancestral country home and assembled there the pick of the world's singers and musicians. To plan on such a scale needed more than wealth. It needed business ability and foresight and the kind of tact that could soothe and pacify the easily ruffled musical temperament.

But, said the Public Orator, John Christie 'has besides an ever-present, all-absorbing picture in his mind of ideal or transcendant beauty; his great desire is to match it, and he turns all effort in each performance to that end.'

The announcement that a Michel Roux was to be in the 1956 *Figaro* at Glyndebourne raised at least two pairs of eyebrows. To those who knew French theatrical life the name was familiar as that of a well-known touring revue artist; only a few months ago, indeed, the posters advertising *Paris Volage* for one performance at the theatre in Bergerac billed his name below 'Les Sexy Girls' but above 'Les Mannequins Nus'. It came as a relief, therefore (with just a tinge of disappointment perhaps?), to discover that Glyndebourne's Michel Roux was somebody else of the same name. He came from the Paris Opera and proved to be one of the most convincing Count Almavivas we had ever seen. Elisabeth Grümmer was the new Countess in a performance which, like her Ilia in the earlier

---

[1] Scene 2 of Act II in Glyndebourne's two-act version.

Idomeneo, was disappointingly uneven. Joan Sutherland, making her first appearance at the Festival, took over the part for the last six of the nine scheduled performances – the first British singer ever to sing the Countess at Glyndebourne – and sang her two big arias beautifully.

The production of *Don Giovanni*, as seems to have happened so often with this opera at Glyndebourne, suffered from miscasting of the title role – in this case, of Kim Borg, of Finland, an excellent Pizarro in *Fidelio* in 1959, but not at all what one expects as Don Giovanni. The performance was otherwise redeemed by the high class Donna Anna of Sena Jurinac, in what was to prove her last season at Glyndebourne, and by the exceptional standard of the five British principals – Richard Lewis (Don Ottavio), Geraint Evans (Leporello), Elsie Morison (Zerlina), Thomas Hemsley (Masetto) and Hervey Alan (the Commendatore).

In July *The Magic Flute* was performed for the first time at Glyndebourne since 1937 – a curiously long time to have waited before reviving a work which had been perhaps the greatest experience of the Festival's early days. One can only suppose that the same difficulties of casting – especially the Queen of the Night – had prevailed until 1956 as they had in Busch's time. The engagement of Mattiwilda Dobbs as the Queen of the Night successfully allayed the anxiety which both management and public inevitably feel at most performances of this opera; she sang accurately, confidently and much better than she had recently done in the same part at Covent Garden. Although, according to John Christie's famous summing-up, the Queen of the Night's part consists of 'only two arias and no acting', it is surprising the general psychological effect its good or bad performance can have on an audience's temper for the rest of the evening. Miss Dobb's assurance encouraged freedom from fear and enabled the house to enjoy in comfort Oliver Messel's startlingly beautiful scenery, the first of Geraint Evans's many lovable performances of Papageno, a pretty and touching Pamina sung by Pilar Lorengar, a sonorous, dignified American Sarastro, Frederick Guthrie, who sang in the first three performances until Drago Bernadic, the original choice, had recovered from an indisposition. Vittorio Gui conducted – a lively, Italian interpretation which, while the greatest moments of the opera never had the moving intensity of Busch's performances (whose ever had, except Bruno Walter's?), was nevertheless a major factor in the successful revival of a work a whole new generation had grown up without ever having heard at Glyndebourne.

The last opera of the season was *Così fan tutte*, revived for the eighth time in nine years (including the three productions at Edinburgh). A happy blending of three new principals – Nan Merriman (Dorabella), Ivan Sardi (Don Alfonso) and Elena Rizzieri (Despina) – with four we already knew well – Sena Jurinac (Fiordiligi), Sesto Bruscantini (Guglielmo), Juan Oncina and Richard Lewis sharing Ferrando – resulted in a performance well up to the standard, so miraculously maintained through the years, of Glyndebourne's showpiece. On the last night of the season *Così fan tutte* was given for members of the Glyndebourne Festival Society and their guests, who spent the afternoon at a Members' Day gathering at Glyndebourne as the guests of John Christie. The Rank film, *On Such a Night*, was shown in the theatre, and in the evening they heard Sena Jurinac sing there for the last time. They didn't know it, but that is how things worked out.

The BBC's televising this time consisted of excerpts from each of the season's Mozart operas except *Idomeneo* – the duet from the finale of *Die Entführung*, the garden scene from *Così fan tutte*, the Catalogue Aria from *Don Giovanni*, part of Act I of *Figaro*, and the Queen of the Night's second aria in *The Magic Flute*. As the more disagreeable television columnists and their readers couldn't find anything bad to say about the programme this time, they said nothing at all.

In September, at the invitation of the Liverpool Philharmonic Society, Glyndebourne gave four performances each of *Figaro*, *Don Giovanni* and *La Cenerentola* in a fortnight's season at the Royal Court Theatre, Liverpool. This first visit to a provincial city was accompanied by some pretty metropolitan behaviour among the local spivs who were getting Cup Final prices for tickets – from those patrons, that is, who had not taken advantage of a hire-purchase scheme of buying tickets for 5s down and 5s a week. One person who did not have to bother about any of this was a young lady from Coulsdon, Surrey, who won a *Daily Mail* competition and as her prize was taken by chauffeur-driven Rolls-Royce from Coulsdon to Liverpool for the Glyndebourne Opera season and given a £50 cheque as well.

The company at Liverpool was no second XI. The Mozart operas were sung by the artists who had appeared in them in Sussex, the only difference being that Richard Lewis was replaced by Juan Oncina in *Don Giovanni* and Joan Sutherland was the only Countess. In *Cenerentola* only the two sisters were new; Tisbe was sung by Gianna d'Angelo and Clorinda by Cora Canne-Meijer. Otherwise it was the old firm of Mme De Gabarain, and Messrs Oncina, Bruscantini, Wallace and Alan, established 1952 and still going strong. The Liverpool Philharmonic Orchestra was in the pit; Gui and Pritchard conducted *Figaro* and *Cenerentola*, Pritchard and Bryan Balkwill *Don Giovanni*. The local Press were ecstatic and, unlike many of their London colleagues, were proud that so many of their fellow citizens should have had the grace to wear evening dress. It was obviously a unique experience for Liverpool and the season ended with loud demands that They should bring Glyndebourne to the city again as soon as They could. The trip also inspired a happy sub-editor on a national daily to give one a new view of *Figaro* when he headed the critic's notice: 'Mozart's Melodious Bedroom Farce.'

John Christie did not go to Liverpool; he was in a London nursing home. But in his absence Moran Caplat told a reporter of the *Liverpool Daily Post* of a scheme that was well worthy of Glyndebourne's founder. With the salty tang of a great seaport in his nostrils the ancient submariner told of his dream to buy up an old aircraft carrier, rip the trimmings out of the hangar deck and build a stage, a 350-seat auditorium and an orchestra pit for fifty – and, of course, luxurious restaurants to go with it.

The OS Glyndebourne (OS for Opera Ship), said Mr Caplat, would travel the world with its international company of singers and players aboard. Most of the great cities were accessible by, or within reach of, the sea, and though there might be trouble with the weather from time to time audiences could be ferried across to the ship by motor boat. The stage hands would be drawn from the crew.

I must admit the more one thinks of it the more appealing the idea of OS Glyndebourne becomes; the view of Venice or Nice, Naples or Palermo from the ship during the 75-minute dinner interval on a warm September evening is something that might run the Glyndebourne gardens pretty close as an attraction. But perhaps aircraft carriers are difficult to come by now that the Admiralty has gone out of business.

Encouraged by the success of the Mozart Festival, six full-length operas (and a curtain raiser) were planned for 1957: *Falstaff*, *The Magic Flute*, *Die Entführung*, *Comte Ory*, *Ariadne auf Naxos* (second version) with *Der Schauspieldirektor* to precede it, and Rossini's *L'italiana in Algeri*. The only doubt in people's minds – though not in Glyndebourne's – was whether anybody would be able to see any of them. The Suez adventure had led to petrol rationing and in the early months of the year, when thoughts were beginning to turn to booking for the season, it was still in force, and seemed likely to remain so for some time. We were assured that British Railways would see us through with extra trains, however, and with those words of comfort as their cue a number of people applied for membership of the Glyndebourne Festival Society, only to learn that they had to take their places in a queue. Since they had read the appeal for their support in the 1956 programme the limit of 3,000 individual members had been reached and a waiting list had been opened.

By the time the season opened in June petrol rationing had been abolished and the public arrived in the manner to which it was accustomed, to find that the Ringmer Building Works had been busy again during the winter months. This time the ceiling of the theatre had been rebuilt, a box added at the back of the balcony to hold another forty-four people at £1 11s 6d a seat, and John Christie's private box had been moved downstairs to the back of the stalls again.

The Festival opened with *L'italiana in Algeri*. For all the love Vittorio Gui lavished on it, and the splendid vivacity of Oralia Dominguez in the title part, it looked at the end of the first half as if Rossini's enchanting opera was going to amuse the Glyndebourne audience as little as I remember it had done when Beecham had put it on at Covent Garden with Conchita Supervia in 1935.

On the first night at Glyndebourne the verbal and musical jokes, all the gaiety and sparkle of one of the composer's most attractive scores were lost on an audience determined not only to take its pleasure sadly, but apparently to take no pleasure at all. The next day, indeed, even those critics who had not enjoyed themselves very much wrote more about the audience's behaviour than about the opera itself. Things were a little better after the dinner interval. It was a puzzling reception from which the production never really recovered; *L'italiana in Algeri* goes down in the records as one of the few operas the Glyndebourne audience has never clamoured to see again.

The antipathy was, I think, the result of unfavourable verbal report and gossip spread by members of the first night audience. Certainly the majority of the critics agreed on the merits and attractions of the performance of an opera which those who were old enough enjoyed hearing again, while those who weren't were pleased to hear for the first time.

It wasn't Gui's fault, or the cast's, or Peter Ebert's, who produced it; it wasn't the fault of Osbert Lancaster whose designs were witty, original and colourful. And it certainly wasn't the composer's fault. Perhaps it was just hearing the first act on an empty stomach that affected the audience. Operas have failed for more trivial reasons than this in their time. Even careful study of the Press notices doesn't help, for modern criticism too often cancels itself out. The *Scotsman* thought Mr Lancaster's décor was the only bright spot of the evening; the *Financial Times* thought it was the worst. Which paper do you read?

The production of *The Magic Flute* a day or two later, however, cheered everybody up. Paul Sacher, from Switzerland, conducted it this time in place of Gui and made musical history at Glyndebourne by allowing and encouraging the introduction of Mozart's conventionally implied grace notes by the singers. Sacher's innovation came as such a surprise after all the years spent by the critics vainly demanding their inclusion that when he finally did hear the appoggiaturas one critic actually found them 'most disturbing'. The outstanding performance of the evening was the Sarastro of Mihaly Szekely, a magnificent Hungarian bass who had in fact been considered for the production of *The Magic Flute* planned for 1940. The Tamino was David Lloyd – not the Welsh singer making, as some thought, a return to Glyndebourne after eighteen years, but an American tenor of the same name who had been the original choice for Rakewell in the Edinburgh *Rake's Progress* in 1953 and was now singing in Sussex for the first time. He was not very successful, I am afraid, either as Tamino or as Bacchus in *Ariadne*.

The part of Papageno was shared by Geraint Evans and the young American, Heinz Blankenburg, who made an impressive first appearance before an audience with whom he has become a particular favourite over the years. Margareta Hallin, from Sweden, threatened the audience's confidence in her Queen of the Night on the first night by singing nervously out of tune in parts of her first aria, but she recovered brilliantly for the fireworks of the second which she delivered with the angry dramatic attack it demands to establish herself thereafter as perhaps the best Queen of the Night ever on Glyndebourne's books.

There was a lot of work for coloraturas in the 1957 season, and the absence of Rita Streich, who had to be replaced because of a poisoned leg, was badly felt. Her place as Zerbinetta in *Ariadne* was taken by Mimi Coertse, a South African from Covent Garden, and Sari Barabas, and as Mlle Silberklang in Mozart's *Schauspieldirektor* by Naida Labay, who had been a member of the chorus the previous year. (Joan Sutherland sang the other leading part – Mme Herz.) Mozart's little one-act opera (better known in English as *The Impresario*) had had its story and spoken dialogue neatly fixed, or 'newly devised after G. Stephanie' by Hanns Hammelmann and Michael Rose, and its production was entrusted wholly to an assistant producer and an assistant conductor. Anthony Besch produced with taste and invention and Bryan Balkwill, after giving a helping hand to other conductors for so long, at last had an opera to conduct that he could call his own.

The *Ariadne* which followed this curtain-raiser was distinguished principally for the singing of the Swedish soprano Elisabeth Söderström as the Composer. She was making her first appearance at Glyndebourne and delighted audience and critics as much as Sena Jurinac had done before her.

Apart from *Le Comte Ory*, the other coloratura 'vehicle' for the year was *Die Entführung* which had the distinction of starting its run during a bus strike. British Railways, who had promised to cope with petrol rationing for us, was helpless to deal with this, and so a ferry service of taxis and private cars driven by Glyndebourne singers not appearing that night was organized between the Opera House and Lewes Station. The Constanze in this *Entführung* was Wilma Lipp, pretty, accurate, a little lacking in personality and making a less memorable impression than the very Austrian and – to revive an old phrase from way back – very 'winsome' Blonde of Rosl Schwaiger. The opera was conducted by Paul Sacher who, having put all the appoggiaturas back into *The Magic Flute*, took them all out again in *Die Entführung* where their use can add powerful dramatic emphasis to an aria like 'Martern aller Arten'. Oliver Messel's designs for *Die Entführung* were the subject this year of an art critic's enthusiastic attention – the first time this sort of thing had ever happened to the Festival Opera. Eric Newton wrote admiringly of them in his *Time and Tide* column, saying that the artist had 'a creative taste that goes far beyond pastiche, so that at each moment the stage picture resembles an Oriental miniature come to life, with the result that not only is the stage a delight to the eye but the music has more meaning for the ear'.

The major event of the 1957 season was undeniably the arrival at Glyndebourne of the Edinburgh production of *Falstaff*. Gui conducted and Geraint Evans made his first appearance in a part which, with increasing experience, he has come to sing with great and internationally recognized distinction. From my own memory of his performance it was characterized not only by that splendid clarity of diction possessed by all Welsh singers, but by a quality of pathos which is rare in the part but touchingly right. The moment which stood out particularly was in the last scene where, after all the teasing and torment, Falstaff is exhausted and begs to be left alone – 'Un poco di pausa. Sono stanco.' It was an unforgettable detail. Not the least remarkable achievement of the first night was Geraint Evans's survival in a temperature in the theatre that was almost unbearably hot. Oralia Dominguez was superb as Mistress Quickly again and inspired Desmond Shawe-Taylor, who has always been happy in his descriptions, to write of her face as 'a producer's gift: ripe, round and shining, like a melon that has just seen a joke'.

Curiously, where Carl Ebert's production had been accepted with little unfavourable comment at Edinburgh it met with a thorough pasting at Glyndebourne. Where at Edinburgh the producer had been commended for his restraint he was panned for the constant illustration of the most elementary lines with visual aids – such as 'dalle due alle tre' being counted on the fingers every time it occurred, as though the Glyndebourne audience could not even guess at the Italian words if it were unable to recognize the numerals from their recital in *Madam Butterfly*, Act I. But most of all the critics were embarrassed by the silly 'business' of having Oncina as Fenton fall flat on his face while pursuing Nanetta and making the chorus jump up and down in time to the music like a kindergarten singing game in the last scene of the opera. More than one critic concluded sadly that over the years the Professor was at his best in the serious operas he produced at Glyndebourne and at his worst in Italian comic opera.

The BBC's television from Glyndebourne for 1957 was the second act of *Le Comte Ory* which had been revived with its customary success and causing many to wonder once more whether this opera did not contain the most beautiful music Rossini ever wrote (Glyndebourne's LP recording of the complete work was issued to coincide with the revival). Unlike the première of *L'italiana in Algeri* the first night of *Ory* caused too many guffaws in the audience and at one point Gui had to stop the orchestra and wait until the clapping had died down before continuing with the orchestral introduction accompanying it. It was not, let's face it, the audience's year.

The season of 1957 saw the end of the custom, which had continued off and on since the Opera started, of offering diners at Glyndebourne a distinctive wine list. After the blunt informativeness of Christie's own annotations and the years with the Greek quotations, there was a short period until 1957 when the wine list was illumined with poetic descriptions by M. André Simon in the highest traditions of modern oinography:

An easy, friendly wine, which has no claim to greatness but is full of honest to Hessian goodness.
A young Rheingau Patrician with dry elegant appeal.
A princely wine in Gorgeous Court dress, a credit to the host, an honour to his guests.
A great aristocrat, mellowed but not bent by age.
A delicious Ruwer wine which possesses the grace of youth and the charm of breed.
A challenging athlete, muscular and sunburnt.
A true gentleman ... honest, courteous, and such good company.

As Dr Loeb would have said: 'Definitely the text of Mr James Thurber! !'

In what had been an eventful year at Glyndebourne the most dramatic incident there occurred, not on the stage, but as the result of some over-operatic behaviour in the kitchens of the restaurant. Not long after the curtain had fallen on the last night of the season a young Jamaican cook stabbed the chef with a broken wine glass.

1958-9 **Paris and a jubilee**

ALTHOUGH SHORTLY AFTER THE 1957 season Robert Ponsonby had said there was a chance of Glyndebourne returning to the Edinburgh Festival the following year with a repertoire including a Carl Ebert production of *Carmen* at last, the Edinburgh authorities eventually decided against it. Glyndebourne would cost too much. In 1954 they had cost £63,699 and the Edinburgh Festival Society had had to make good a loss of £35,622; in 1955 they had cost £67,303 and the loss had been £37,297. For 1958, Edinburgh said, the financial ceiling for opera would be between £48,000 and £50,000. So Glyndebourne concentrated on other things, the first of which was to visit Paris in the early May of 1958 to take part in the international *Théâtre des Nations* season at the Théâtre Sarah-Bernhardt where four performances each were given of *Le Comte Ory* and *Falstaff*.

While *Falstaff* was a rare enough experience for Paris, Rossini's French comedy had not been heard there for over thirty years (it had been revived for a few performances in 1926 at a small theatre), and to most of the audience the news that Rossini had written anything French at all, except *Guillaume Tell*, came as a complete surprise. Not, let it be said, that this discovery had much effect on Parisian taste. According to custom, the first night of *Ory* was preceded by a performance of the opera before an invited audience who did not pay for their seats but, according to Moran Caplat, sat on their hands – 'no laughs, no encouragement – we nearly went home again without opening'. The first night audience decided to enjoy themselves for their money and the evening was a great success; but even so, the third and fourth houses were only half full.

The production of *Falstaff*, on the other hand, was a triumph all along the line. The international nature of the company made a deep impression, and the fact that an Italian conductor, a German producer, an English designer, and Welsh, Italian, Spanish, Mexican, Swiss and English singers had combined to form such a perfect ensemble was a source of general astonishment and admiration. For some reason the eight different nationalities in *Le Comte Ory* did not cause so much comment as the six in *Falstaff*. The French critics, normally no less bilious than their English colleagues, were ecstatic about the whole thing; they hailed it as 'un *Falstaff* exemplaire', urged their readers 'for the honour of France and Parisian taste, to flock to hear it', and summed it up with resounding phrases like 'Mais quelle leçon, quelle leçon de mise en scène nous a donnée le "Festival de Glyndebourne"!'

A special issue of the Glyndebourne Festival Programme Book was published for the Paris season. It contained articles specially written for it and others which had already appeared in earlier years, all of them translated into French with one exception. The inimitable, untranslatable prose of John Christie's foreword was left in English. And rightly, for what translator could ever catch the rhythm and tone of voice of a sentence like 'There is no State jellyfish in our organization'?

Where much was done in it to help the French reader, the Paris Programme Book was magnificently perverse in describing the operas not in the usual Glyndebourne manner, with the full title of the work given as it appeared on the original score or libretto, but in English. Rossini's opera was not the familiar 'Opéra en deux actes' we knew at home, with 'Parôles de Scribe et de Lestre-Poirson' and 'Musique de Gioacchino Rossini'; but an 'Opera in two acts' with 'Libretto by Scribe and de Lestre-Poirson'.[1] The description of *Falstaff* was similarly in English. There was, it seems, a limit to fraternization, even in opera.

The advertisers in the Paris programme on the whole went out of their way to have copy translated. It was 'La voix de son maître', and 'Le Reader's Digest', 'Le Gore Hotel et ses restaurants', 'Les disques Philips', while Marks and Spencer and ICI told their stories in French. So did Black and White cigarettes ('la cigarette des Ambassades'). Coty, on the other hand, did not; they had bases in London and New York as well as Paris and used English. In addition to the English advertisers, some of whom were not to be found in the Glyndebourne edition, there were some evocative local contributions from Dior, Lanvin and Dubonnet.

The Glyndebourne Festival, with seats now £1 11s 6d to £4 4s, opened on 27 May to begin a season of fifty-one performances (the longest so far) with the *Falstaff* which had so delighted Paris. For those now seeing the 1958 production for the first time it was easy to understand its success at the *Théâtre des Nations*. It was a great improvement on the previous year. Geraint Evans's Falstaff had matured in every way; he had discarded some of the silly cissy gestures which had been quite out of character and gave an altogether more assured and rounded performance. Vittorio Gui was not just making a polite remark when he said – I believe it was to Noël Goodwin of the *Express* – that he considered Evans as good a Falstaff as any he'd known except Stabile. Carl Ebert's production, too, had been stripped of its fussier features and it was now possible to give the music the attention it deserved. For this was perhaps the strongest cast Glyndebourne ever collected for *Falstaff*. Oralia Dominguez repeated her splendid Mistress Quickly; Mario Boriello, who had not been to Glyndebourne since his Don Alfonso in the 1950 *Così fan tutte*, was a powerful Ford; Ilva Ligabue as Alice, recommended to Glyndebourne by Sena Jurinac, made her first appearance in England and was rightly greeted as a discovery; and Graziella Sciutti, last seen as Rosina, sang – and looked – an enchanting Nannetta. The Bardolph of Mario Carlin, the Pistol of Marco Stefanoni and the grotesque Dr Caius of Hugues Cuenod, made a menacing trio of ruffians.

[1] Scribe's collaborator's correct name was Delestre-Poirson.

The rest of the repertoire consisted of five operas already familiar at Glyndebourne – *Alceste*, *Figaro*, *The Rake's Progress*, *Comte Ory* and *Ariadne auf Naxos* (second version), which was accompanied by the only novelty of the season as a curtain-raiser: Wolf-Ferrari's *Il segreto di Susanna*.

The *Alceste* presented a new Spanish singer, Consuelo Rubio, whose singing in the title role was impressive but whose acting was a little elementary. The performance of *Figaro* was regarded as one of the best ever, due principally to the Susanna of Graziella Sciutti who stole the show with her immense charm and her ability (singing in her native tongue) to make the recitatives as convincing an expression of character as the arias and concerted numbers. That Geraint Evans as a first-time Figaro could keep up with her at all was an impressive indication of the fluency of his Italian diction. This was unfortunately the only Glyndebourne production of *Figaro* Miss Sciutti ever sang in. The opera was revived the following year but she was available only to sing Despina in *Così fan tutte*.

The most arresting newcomer of the year was another Spaniard, Teresa Berganza, who was singing in England for the first time. With a face like something out of a Murillo, her Cherubino was a complete joy.

Having a baby, which had delayed her original appearance at Glyndebourne by a year, interrupted Elisabeth Söderström's career once more in 1958; her part as Anne in *The Rake's Progress* was taken by Elsie Morison, who thus continued uninterrupted in the part she had created in 1954, and Helga Pilarczyk sang the Composer in *Ariadne*. In the Richard Strauss opera Rita Streich at last made her Glyndebourne début, but her Zerbinetta didn't come out as life-size as everyone had expected from her gramophone records.

The idea of *Il segreto di Susanna* to raise the curtain on *Ariadne* gave us a chance to hear the charming work that follows the overture everybody knows so well, and which the late Edwin Evans had suggested as long ago as 1935 was the sort of thing well suited to the scale and potentialities of Glyndebourne. And so it proved. It seems a pity that this production couldn't somehow have been televised, particularly as Mary Costa, the young American soprano who sang one of the two singing parts (Michel Roux sang the other and Heinz Blankenburg played the dumb servant), had come to opera by way of television. She had a small voice which would have been helped considerably by a microphone, and she was as pretty as a picture. Miss Costa came from Knoxville, Tennessee, and was familiar to millions of American viewers as the girl who got $1,000 a week for patting the bumpers of the latest shining car in the Chrysler commercials. When she arrived in England it was inevitable that at least one newspaper should publish her so-called 'vital statistics'. These, we were told, were 37 – 25 – 35 – which no doubt meant a lot to women readers, but absolutely nothing, of course, to men who cannot possibly assess desirability from a recital of figures. However, the BBC's choice for television in 1958 was *The Rake's Progress*. It had a good Press, except for a spoken prologue evidently introduced to try to make things easier for the viewer. So far from proving a help, it was considered pretentious and an unfortunate mistake. But then that's life all over.

One other event of the 1958 season should be recorded and that is the announcement on 4 June, Eton's particular festival and the twenty-seventh anniversary of his parent's wedding, of George Christie's engagement to Mary Nicholson. They were married on 8 August, a week after the end of the season, at Witley in Surrey.

This was followed not long afterwards by the announcement that George Christie, now 23 years old, had assumed the Chairmanship of Glyndebourne Productions Ltd in succession to his father, who had retired from the position but remained on the board of directors. The new Chairman had been uniquely trained from infancy for what is after all a unique position. It is one thing to inherit an opera house; it is another to understand, let alone like, what goes on inside it. For the first five years of his life he was surrounded by it in a way few children can ever have been. Though he complained to Fritz Busch from time to time that there was altogether too much 'mooky' (the 3-year-old child's word for music), Busch, who had a particular love for children, used to stand him on his knee and give him a stick to wag while the orchestra played at rehearsals. With a childhood spent in such a busy environment, George Christie finds that today he cannot remember which opera he heard first at Glyndebourne; but he knows he liked *Die Entführung* (he naturally couldn't understand *The Magic Flute*), and that *Macbeth*, with its soldiers and battles, impressed him most of all. As a small boy, when evacuated to Canada during the war, he learned the violin and played it until he was 17 years old. He now talks of taking it up again – a praiseworthy ambition, one feels, since the instrument he owns is a Nicolò Amati, given to him by a great friend of his parents, and it is a shame to let it lie idle in its case.

In accordance with a family tradition started by his great-grandfather (or perhaps even earlier) George Christie went to Eton and then to Trinity College, Cambridge, where he read German and Italian – the one degree, of course, that could make life with an opera house in your garden amusing, interesting or, at worst, at least just plain tolerable.

Institutions, unlike human beings, have barely come of age when they have a Silver Jubilee and from then on seem to celebrate every five years as though, like married couples, they were surprised things had lasted so long. Glyndebourne has not, so far as I can see, been noticeably affected by its subsequent quinquenniad, but in 1959 it certainly made the most of its chance to celebrate the first quarter of a century of its existence. The season started on 28 May, the exact twenty-fifth anniversary of the theatre's inauguration. But contrary to reasonable expectations the occasion was not marked by a revival of the first opera ever to be performed at Glyndebourne. Instead of *Figaro* the surprising choice for the gala opening was Richard Strauss's *Rosenkavalier*. Carl Ebert, now 72, had announced his retirement from the post of Artistic Director and had chosen *Der Rosenkavalier* as his farewell treat before leaving. The Professor, who had not unnaturally mocked John Christie's ambition to present *Parsifal* at Glyndebourne, now did some seam-bursting and precedent-breaking on his own account. The opera began at 5.15, intervals were reduced to two of almost coffee-and-sandwiches length, the stage was frequently overcrowded (as it had to be if the wishes of librettist and composer were to be respected), and in the hard acoustics and confined space of the Festival Opera House the orchestral din, in the words of *The Times*, on occasion 'seared the ears like a whiplash'. Only one critic, David Drew in the *New Statesman*, hinted at what surely everybody ought to have foreseen: that once you reduce the number of strings in a Richard Strauss orchestra, which had to be done at Glyndebourne, the mushy, uninteresting padding of the inside parts (particularly the wind) sticks out like a sore thumb. Cut the strings down in *Falstaff*, for instance, and you may alter the balance of the accompaniment, but you will still always have a musical sound.

At the end of the opening performance, for which members of the Glyndebourne Festival Society balloted for 6 guinea seats, John Christie went on to the stage to present his retiring Artistic Director with a silver rose-bowl, and made a highly characteristic speech lasting 25 minutes in which he did not once mention either Carl Ebert or the rose-bowl. He said plenty, however, about Covent Garden, the Arts Council, and other bodies whose representatives were his guests for the evening, but they appeared to take his abuse in good part. In the end, thanks to the intervention of the General Manager, Professor Ebert was presented with his rose-bowl.

Within the restrictions imposed upon it by the very nature of the theatre the Glynde-bourne *Rosenkavalier* was a fine achievement, with a cast – Régine Crespin as the Princess, Elisabeth Söderström (Oktavian), Anneliese Rothenberger (Sophie), and Oscar Czer-wenka (Baron Ochs) – which was generally considered as good as any seen in this country since the famous Lotte Lehmann–Elisabeth Schumann–Richard Mayr performances at Covent Garden in the 1920s. Mrs Franz Strauss, the composer's daughter-in-law who was at the first night of the opera at Glyndebourne, told John Christie (and he quoted her in an indignant but understandably unpublished protest he made to the Editor of *The Times* for its critic's lukewarm notice) that it was the best performance of the opera she had ever seen. She could hardly have said less to her host, of course, but as a boy I used to see her often with her husband in the artists' box at the Vienna Opera listening to *Rosenkavaliers* such as she certainly never heard elsewhere. They were sung by Lehmann, Schumann, Mayr and Marie Gutheil-Schoder – and conducted by her own father-in-law. (To the end of his days John Christie continued to write to editors about their critics. One can only suppose that he felt better after letting off steam in this way, for surely experience must have convinced him that no serious editor would ever take action against a member of his staff because Christie disagreed with the personal opinions expressed in an unfavourable notice. It was a practice which might well have done more harm than good had it not been for the personal affection felt by Fleet Street for their regular, indignant correspondent.)

One thing one had to give Glyndebourne, which Vienna never had, and that was the introduction of one of the famous Christie family pug dogs into Act I. Just to remind us that however cosmopolitan the Festival Opera can get, there is a corner of Glyndebourne that is forever England, the animal was of course given a credit in the programme as 'Master "Vino" Christie'.

The outstanding artistic success of the Silver Jubilee season was the opera Busch had so often wanted to do at Glyndebourne and Ebert had so often considered unsuitable – *Fidelio*. Performances of Beethoven's opera, in my experience, are either dreadful, and bore you to tears; or superb, and the experience of a lifetime. I have never seen a mediocre *Fidelio*. Glyndebourne's first *Fidelio* was superb and brought Vittorio Gui and Günther Rennert together as collaborators for the first time. Leonore was sung by Gré Brouwen-stijn, Richard Lewis was Florestan, the scenery and costumes (the splendid finale was a particularly lovely scene) were designed by Ita Maximowna who, like Rennert, was working at Glyndebourne for the first time; the Glyndebourne bats came on for the Prison Scene; and there was no Leonore Overture No 3.

The three Mozart operas chosen for the Silver Jubilee all had indissoluble associations with Glyndebourne's twenty-five-year history: *Figaro* and *Così fan tutte* had started the whole thing off, and *Idomeneo* had established a peculiar position in the artistic fabric of the Festival Opera ever since Busch had first introduced it to England. Both *Così fan tutte* and *Idomeneo* were well up to standard. In *Così fan tutte* Ilva Ligabue as Fiordiligi, Gloria Lane (Baba the Turk of the previous year's *Rake's Progress*) as Dorabella, and the entrancing Graziella Sciutti as Despina were a superb trio; and *Idomeneo*, with Richard Lewis still in the title role, was as moving and impressive as ever.

On the other hand, there seemed to be something of a jinx on the Jubilee *Figaro*. Instead, as one had hoped, of being the first production of this special season, it had to be the last because of the unavailability of artists for earlier performances. When the time came Geraint Evans had burnt himself badly in a domestic accident and was out of the cast as Figaro until the seventh of the ten performances; his place was taken by Carlos Feller from the Argentine. Teresa Berganza deprived us of her ravishing Cherubino by miscalculating the date of arrival of her baby and withdrew altogether. She was replaced by Josephine Veasey, who also had a baby later in the year. Glyndebourne still look on the engagement of two pregnant Cherubinos in one season as something of a record. Elisabeth Söderström, whose convincing Oktavian suggested she might have made a good Cherubino, appeared instead as Susanna – surely one of the most unusual 'doubles' in the repertoire. It was not happy casting, for Miss Söderström was a welterweight in a feather-weight part, and the impression her performance gave me was that she was wearing shoes a size too small for her. She sang 'Deh vieni, non tardar' beautifully, but she just never made the weight.

Peter Maag, a young Dutchman, conducted *Figaro* in place of Hans Schmidt-Isserstedt, who had retired for medical reasons. Maag came to Glyndebourne with a high reputa-tion as a Mozart conductor following a fanfare of rave notices for a Covent Garden *Magic Flute*. He left Glyndebourne having given one of the most bewilderingly eccentric interpretations of *Figaro* I have ever heard. His elaborate and noisy harpsichord accom-paniment of the recitatives was described by one of the orchestra as sounding like a parrot scraping his beak along the bars of his cage; his tempos were perplexingly wayward, all sorts of unauthorized effects and sforzandos crept into the overture, and in the case of the fandango the tempo was so sluggish that the flute's trills were reduced to a dismal burble.

Although she did not appear in *Figaro* we were not denied Teresa Berganza altogether in 1959. Earlier in the season she had sung in the first two of twelve performances of *La Cenerentola* and had a triumphant success, bringing to the part that peculiar Spanish quality of voice and personality which had characterized Conchita Supervia's classic performance of the part. Miss Berganza was succeeded by Anna Maria Rota, a young Italian singer making her first appearance outside Italy, whose performance had great assurance and whose rich velvety voice was every bit as agile as the part demanded. As the two sisters, both also new to Glyndebourne, Silvana Zanolli and Miti Truccato Pace were wonderfully contrasted. During what was our first full summer in Ringmer my wife and I had our maiden experience of one of the perennial hazards of living near Glyndebourne – trying to translate English music critics' notices for foreign singers. It is only when one attempts this that one realizes how much critics rely on jargon which cannot be convincingly translated. Miss Zanolli, for instance, took what was meant as a complimentary reference to the 'bell-like tones of her voice' as an insult. We reassured her by saying that music critics spoke a language all their own. 'Ah, just like in Italy,' she said, and returned to her knitting.

The male parts in *Cenerentola* were taken by the same singers as before – Bruscantini returning to Glyndebourne after an absence of two years and Ian Wallace resuming as Don Magnifico after an excursion into the world of The Musical, where he had taken the lead in *Fanny* at Drury Lane. The BBC's television relay for the year was of *Cenerentola* and it seemed to be generally acceptable, if not throughout England at least to those European countries who saw the transmission on Eurovision, the first Glyndebourne production to be broadcast in this way.

According to an announcement made in the Programme Book the year before, August 1959 should have been the occasion for a Handel–Haydn Festival of Concerts and Operas conducted by Sir Thomas Beecham. But once more – and not for the last time – a Beecham plan did not materialize at Glyndebourne; as a result of this the season was able to be extended into August and totalled a record number of sixty-eight performances (an extra *Cenerentola* had to be abandoned because Anna Maria Rota had to be in Naples or somewhere).

Late in the wonderful summer of the Jubilee year, when visitors had time and inclination to stand and admire the imposing new rehearsal stage which had been built on to the OP, or east, side of the Opera House and looked like a bank, we were made aware that a new era was about to begin at Glyndebourne. With Carl Ebert's retirement from his official position, though not from all professional association with the Festival Opera, the post of Artistic Director was abolished. In his place Vittorio Gui and Günther Rennert were appointed to the new positions of 'Artistic Counsellors', subtitled respectively 'Head of Music' and 'Head of Production'.

In recognition of his foundation's Jubilee, and in marked contrast to the blunt description of his Artistic Counsellors' functions, John Christie was awarded two medals of resounding splendour. The first, presented to him by the German Ambassador at a performance of *Cenerentola*, was the Bundesverdienstkreuz, or Cross of a Commander of the Federal Order of Merit. The second medal, the Great Silver Honorary Medal, awarded by the President of Austria to John Christie as well as to Sir Kenneth Clark and the Earl of Harewood, 'for services rendered to the Austrian Republic', came as a surprise to all three recipients who read about it in a Reuter's report from Vienna in the English papers before they heard an official word about it. John Christie's reported comment was: 'I don't think I've been given an Austrian award. I got one from the Germans a few months ago, but I haven't heard about an Austrian one. Perhaps there's been a mistake?' There hadn't, but as the medal (could it have been anything but Austrian?) was awarded in September there was no opportunity of presenting it to Christie on the stage of his opera house.

Honours and medals were much in the news in Glyndebourne's Jubilee Year, for in addition to Geraint Evans's CBE in the Birthday Honours, Carl Ebert received an Honorary CBE later in the winter from the British Ambassador in Berlin.

The continued international standing of Glyndebourne reflected in these awards to its founder by foreign governments was nowhere more apparent than in the German Press, where each production was reported at great length by the newspapers' London correspondents. Like their English colleagues many of these correspondents used the familiar evening-dress-at-Victoria gambit but, of course, with a highly national slant. It was in 1959, I believe, that the first of many regular and widely syndicated reports to the German Press was made by a writer with the admirably festive name of Dr Krug, whose annual Glyndebourne story has always borne the same heading and begun with the same 250-word introductory paragraph. The heading 'Festspiele im Grünen nur für Snobs?' ('Pastoral Festival only for Snobs?') is a question he has so far left unanswered – wisely, of course, for obviously if once it was answered it could never be asked again. The heading is always followed by a description, in exactly the same words every time, of the scene at Victoria where in the 'smoky atmosphere of the station' ladies in *grandes toilettes de soir* ('grossen Abendtoiletten') are accompanied by gentlemen 'in tails and top hats' who carry on their arms 'little picnic baskets containing the obligatory leg of chicken and bottle of champagne'. This prelude is usually followed by a brief recital (always in the same words) of the history of the Glyndebourne enterprise and concludes with a few words about the current repertoire. Dr Krug's annual piece, with its author's unshakeable illusion of tails and top hats at a smoky Victoria, has become a welcome and reassuring sign that all is still well at Glyndebourne.

CHAPTER TWENTY-FOUR

1960-2 Triumphs and tribulations

VITTORIO GUI HAD LONG WANTED to do an opera by Bellini at Glyndebourne and for some time the idea of *I Puritani* had been simmering on one side of the stove to await the availability of one or other of several pencilled-in sopranos to sing the lead. When it was seen that since she had last sung the Countess in *Figaro* with Glyndebourne in 1956, Joan Sutherland had developed a talent for early nineteenth-century *bel canto* opera, it was decided to produce *I Puritani* with Miss Sutherland as Elvira. The first announcement of this decision led to such triumphant claims by what *The Times* contemptuously called the 'canary-fanciers' that Glyndebourne were 'putting on *I Puritani* for Sutherland' that for the record it had better be stated that if anybody was doing anything for anybody else it was Miss Sutherland who was singing Elvira for Glyndebourne.

The introduction of a new composer to the repertoire brought a new producer and a new designer to the Festival Opera. Gianfranco (now billed as Franco) Enriquez, who produced *I Puritani*, was Gui's stepson; Desmond Heeley, who designed the opera, was a British artist used in accordance with Glyndebourne's recently-introduced policy of having British artists to design operas with an English setting – as Osbert Lancaster had done for *Falstaff* and *The Rake's Progress*. His credit for the décor of *I Puritani* was not the first time Desmond Heeley's name had appeared in the Glyndebourne programme. In 1953 he had made 'Properties, Decorations and Jewellery' for *Alceste*.

The production of *I Puritani* was announced as the first professional performance of the opera in England since 1887 and was hailed by one of the anniversary-conscious diarists in the Press as a fitting contribution by Glyndebourne with which to celebrate the 300th anniversary of the Restoration – though one wonders, if this anniversary was really so important, how it came to be missed by Covent Garden which, after all, owes its subsequent Royal status to this very event.

Vittorio Gui conducted the opera with great love and affection, Miss Sutherland's brilliance and accuracy delighted the canary-fanciers (*The Times* poured scorn on Bellini's 'tinkling tunes'), and allayed the audience's natural anxiety when confronted with vocal wire-walkers by her obvious inability to put a note wrong.

The season continued with the renewed success of *Falstaff*, sung with a new Ford (Sesto Bruscantini), a new Meg Page (Anna Maria Rota), and a new Nannetta (Mariella Adani).

The previous year's *Rosenkavalier* was revived with a new Oktavian, a charming young American singer called Regina Sarfaty, who radiated femininity which, while it was not entirely appropriate to the part, delighted the many male visitors who were beginning to find that without Graziella Sciutti the season's operas were a little short on sex appeal. It was the first time Miss Sarfaty had ever sung the role on the stage.

The novelty of the season, conducted by John Pritchard, was a new production by Günther Rennert (designs by Ita Maximowna) of *Don Giovanni*, which in a curious way never burst into flame. Ernest Blanc as Giovanni was dull and charmless, which laid a hand as heavy as the Statue's, and almost as fatal, on the performance. Fortunately, there was charm and to spare provided by the peasant couple Zerlina and Masetto. As Zerlina, Mirella Freni made her first Glyndebourne appearance and was quite enchanting; as Masetto, Leonardo Monreale (younger brother of Franco Calabrese) also made his Glyndebourne début and presented a portrait of Masetto, not as the usual middle-aged clod, but as an intelligent, likeable young man who – in this instance – earned extra sympathy for the treatment he received from an unattractive Don Giovanni.

Joan Sutherland, as Donna Anna, made a fleeting moment of Glyndebourne history when, at the dress rehearsal, with the connivance of the conductor and according to the intentions of the composer, she let fly a short cadenza during the silent pause in her aria, 'Or sai chi l'onore'. It goes without saying that this joyous moment was short-lived, for Glyndebourne, so lavish in so many ways, would not tolerate this departure from its austere, immovable observance of the letter of Mozart's scores. The cadenza was never allowed again. But there is no doubt that Miss Sutherland was absolutely right to introduce it and that Mr Pritchard was right to encourage it. It is no good anybody pretending that the silent pauses in Mozart's arias are pauses for 'dramatic effect'. What 'dramatic effect' is anybody supposed to be making in the silent pause before the return to the tune in 'Or sai chi l'onore', or in the silent pause before the reprise of the tune in the Countess's 'Dove sono ...'? These pauses were put in for the singer to fill up, and when Mozart didn't want them filled to overflowing he suggested moderation by writing into the part what he considered was enough – as one may see in the score of Don Ottavio's 'Dalla sua pace'. In the duets, trios and concerted numbers generally, on the other hand, the silent pauses are, so far as I know, always for dramatic effect. One has only to think of the pause after the Countess's astonished 'Susanna!' at the appearance of Susanna in the great Second Act finale of *Figaro*, or the pause a few pages later in the same movement which allows the bitterness of the Countess's reply to the Count to sink in when she says she is no longer the Rosina he first fell in love with, to realize that such moments of silence are to heighten the dramatic tension and not for the singer to decorate. It has always seemed a little illogical to me to permit the cadenzas in *Macbeth*, and even later operas of Verdi, merely because the composer wrote them down, but to forbid them in Mozart, who didn't write them down, because they were a flourishing convention which the composer expected his performers to observe and enjoy.

Following a revival of *La Cenerentola* with Anna Maria Rota in the lead and the rest of the cast the same as the year before, the last production of the season was *The Magic Flute*.

This was to have been conducted by Sir Thomas Beecham, but a relapse after a recent illness once more prevented his conducting an opera at Glyndebourne. This proved to be the last time, for he died the following March, aged 81. Beecham's place was taken by the 32-year-old English conductor Colin Davis who, like Peter Maag, came to Glyndebourne with a great reputation as a Mozart conductor. He took a fatally ponderous view of *The Magic Flute*, however, playing the Armed Men's fugato, for instance, like a funeral march, and failed to suggest even a flicker of the smile without which this opera is a dead duck. It was a disappointing début for a conductor who had been well spoken of.

On the last night of the season, when the artists had taken their final calls after *The Magic Flute*, the curtains parted again on an empty stage, the doors for the Ordeals by Fire and Water were thrown open to reveal, against the cyclorama, a more-than-life-size bust of John Christie. The head, sculpted by Oscar Nemon, was made of plaster (it was to be cast in bronze later) and it was presented to Christie by Mr Humphrey Whitbread on behalf of the Glyndebourne Festival Society who, with the staff and orchestra at Glyndebourne, had subscribed to the portrait. In its final bronze form the sculpture now stands in the walled garden behind the Covered Way.

The televised opera from Glyndebourne was later than usual this year; instead of following soon after the end of the Festival, *Falstaff* was not seen until the middle of September, when the company had returned to Sussex after a three weeks season at Edinburgh – the first time there for five years. (It had been the BBC's idea originally to televise only two acts of *Falstaff* but, as it proved quite impossible to decide *which* two acts, they came to their senses and relayed the whole opera.) The *Falstaff* relay, like the *Cenerentola* the year before, was seen on Eurovision, and one of the Italian papers went out of its way to remark that Geraint Evans had sung 'in perfetto italiano'.

The decision to invite Glyndebourne back to the Edinburgh Festival – the last that Robert Ponsonby had anything to do with before it was taken over by Lord Harewood – came as something of a surprise to the public. In the late summer of 1959 Eric Linklater had been raising the roof in Scotland to get Glyndebourne to return. He suggested a 2d rate in Edinburgh to do it. It was a 'woeful thing', he said, that Glyndebourne had disappeared from the programme. Edinburgh had derived enormous advantage from the Festival, and they should be willing to pay more to bring 'the Glyndebourne' back. Virtually the next that anybody knew about anything was that Glyndebourne *were* back at Edinburgh, and – without stinging Edinburgh for a 2d rate – were able to present *Falstaff*, *I Puritani*, and an unusual triple bill consisting of *Susanna's Secret* by Wolf-Ferrari, *La Voix Humaine* by Poulenc, and *Arlecchino* by Busoni. The Poulenc monologue, sung exquisitely by Denise Duval, was a setting of Jean Cocteau's famous *scena* which, in its original form, had been recorded by Berthe Bovy and frequently broadcast by the BBC Variety Department in the late 1920s when 'variety' had a far more literal meaning in British radio than it has now. Jean Cocteau himself came to Edinburgh to produce *La Voix Humaine* and so give a high gloss finish to the thin end of the wedge – the first purely French opera to be performed by Glyndebourne which was to prepare the way for the first purely French opera to be performed *at* Glyndebourne two years later.

Although in his later operatic life John Christie was undecided whether or not it was a good thing to invite the critics to his Opera House, he appreciated the interest the critics had shown right from the beginning in the potentialities of Glyndebourne, and their suggestions and hints and hopes for what should be performed there. And though he might pretend that he had had *Falstaff* and *Idomeneo* on his mind for years, when Glyndebourne did at length add these works to its repertoire Christie took an obvious delight in sharing their success with those who had so long been conscious of their suitability to his theatre.

During the season of 1960 Desmond Shawe-Taylor took time off in his *Sunday Times* column to consider 'Glyndebourne and the Future', and the kind of operas he would like to see performed there. He proposed four operas ideally suited by nature to Glyndebourne; each one of them has since been staged there – *Pelléas et Mélisande* ('above all'), *L'incoronazione di Poppea*, *Capriccio* and Rossini's *Pietra del paragone*. A fifth work, I believe, has been pencilled in for later on – Mozart's *La finta giardiniera*. Mr Shawe-Taylor's skill as an operatic tipster makes me feel that in due course his other confident selection – Monteverdi's *Orfeo* – will also turn up. It is really high time this had a first proper professional production in England after more than three and a half centuries.

The 1961 Festival, which ended with a final record tally of seventy-two performances, opened on 24 May when, before the first performance, Lady Violet Bonham Carter unveiled the bronze bust of John Christie on the lawn by the yew trees outside the Green Room. The sculpture, Lady Violet remarked, was 'a little larger than life, but the subject is a man whose personality has outgrown that of normal men'.

The new season, in a theatre now holding a total of 768 seats, was one of unusual experiments made with varying degrees of success. The choice of Franco Zeffirelli to produce Donizetti's *Elisir d'amore* as the year's first novelty on the opening night was received with excited anticipation by some, with gloomy apprehension by others. In a production described by Noël Goodwin in the *Daily Express* as 'precious and prissy', by Arthur Jacobs in *Reynolds* as symptomatic of the 'danger that the producer's art may be put over the singer's', by Andrew Porter in the *Financial Times* as 'enchanting' and by Adam Bell in the *Evening Standard* as searching out 'the universal human feelings that beat beneath [the opera's] formal trappings', we were asked to pretend that we were at a performance in a small provincial theatre in mid-nineteenth-century Italy. There were oil lamps for footlights and that sort of thing. Unfortunately, all Mr Zeffirelli's characteristic Italian passion for filling the stage with livestock and children, having the artists take their calls 'in character' (surely the corniest idea ever permitted at Glyndebourne), and distracting our attention with ceaseless, irrelevant, fidgety business in the crowd, could never convince us that the standard of singing we heard was in any way above that of a small provincial theatre in mid-nineteenth-century Italy. Only Luigi (alias Luis) Alva, the young Peruvian tenor making his first Glyndebourne appearance as Nemorino, ever began to sing as the opera deserves. Poor Eugenia Ratti, well below form anyway, was made to wear a top-knotted, scarecrow hair-do, and as Philip Hope-Wallace put it in the *Manchester Guardian*, made to go through 'contortions of complicated coquetry which far from seeming natural simply looked like over-acting on an inappropriate scale'. My own particular *non placet* I must confess went to the incident at the beginning of the second act when, after the long wedding feast sequence, the plot at last gets going again and a lot of children came on to take our minds off everything by moving the furniture. But perhaps, thinking to please his Glyndebourne audience, Mr Zeffirelli thought the less we heard of the recitative at this point the better. Maybe he was right.

The second experiment of the season was the world première at Glyndebourne of *Elegy for Young Lovers*, an uncompromisingly 'contemporary' opera by Hans Werner Henze in the original English of W. H. Auden and Chester Kallman. (The same opera with the libretto translated into German had already had a pre-world-première première, as it were, at Schwetzingen some weeks earlier.) The thing that was immediately apparent was that a theatre like Glyndebourne was far too small to tolerate a 'chamber' opera. The din was deafening at times. But then audiences, brought up the hard way, have long known what composers are always forgetting: that a chamber orchestra of nineteen soloists may cost less than a full orchestra, but it can never play as quietly, least of all in a confined space. Louis Armstrong's Hot Five always made more noise than Duke Ellington's loudest *tutti*. Henze's instrumentation was most eagerly modern and it was quite like old times to hear the flexatone again – an instrument surely not heard in public since the dance bands of the very early 1920s tired of it. The orchestra of course included a vibraphone. It was not used as Lionel Hampton or Milt Jackson can use it (for this requires a lot of skill and invention) but mostly to make those semi-ethereal noises, one rung higher on the ladder of musical taste than the cinema organist's vox humana (with tremulant), which were the last sounds heard in the coda of every commercial dance record for so many pre-war years. It is very touching, to me at any rate, to find the younger (and some of the older) generation of composers suddenly 'discovering' the long obsolete instruments of commercial dance music and so threaten to tread on the heels of Stravinsky who has now almost mastered the idiom of jazz he first heard in 1922.

There were some in the first night audience of *Elegy for Young Lovers* who felt strongly enough to boo at the end of the opera – a time-honoured welcome given to misunderstood masterpieces. Unfortunately, booing *Elegy for Young Lovers* didn't make it a *Pelléas*; or a *Traviata*; or a *Barber of Seville*; or even a *Wozzeck*. It was just booed and failed to convince even the ordinary non-booing Glyndebourne listener that it was of any world-shattering consequence. The personal column of *The Times* reflected this apathy almost immediately in the number of advertisers who had tickets for Henze's opera that they wanted to exchange for something, anything, else at Glyndebourne that season.

Unlike his opinion of *The Rake's Progress* there was no published account of what John Christie thought of *Elegy for Young Lovers*. But he is said to have met two strangers in the grounds and on asking them who they were, was told that they were Auden and Kallman. And what were they doing? They said they had written the libretto of *Elegy for Young Lovers*. 'Oh dear,' said Christie, 'you shouldn't have, really you shouldn't,' and walked sadly back into the house.

The remaining four operas in 1961 were revivals of long-established favourites – *Die*

Entführung, Don Giovanni, Fidelio, The Barber of Seville. In *Die Entführung*, conducted at every performance by Peter Gellhorn who left Glyndebourne at the end of the season to become chorus master at the BBC, Mattiwilda Dobbs made a popular return as Constanze, and Mihaly Szekely was so magnificent as Osmin that Desmond Shawe-Taylor asked whether he might not prove a splendid Baron Ochs. What Mr Shawe-Taylor did not know was that this idea also occurred to Glyndebourne when the *Rosenkavalier* production was first planned. Unhappily Szekely knew the part only in Hungarian and there was never any time for him to learn it in German.

Szekely's health tended to play him up during this Glyndebourne season, and there came a time during the run of *Fidelio* when his part as Rocco was taken over by Dennis Wicks, the Ringmer-born bass. A couple of nights earlier Wicks had sung the part from the wings while an ailing Szekely had spoken the dialogue and mimed the singing. Dennis Wicks was reported in the Press to have worn evening dress while singing in the wings – a matter of discipline, one imagines, like the dinner jackets worn by invisible announcers on duty at the BBC before the war.

The revival of *Don Giovanni* was the seventh of the opera by Glyndebourne since the war and introduced a seventh singer in the title role. After three Italians, an American, a Finn, and a Frenchman, Glyndebourne now tried out a Hungarian in György Melis, but he too came no nearer than his six immediate predecessors to finding the elegance and charm which are as essential as vitality to a part still not yet better sung at Glyndebourne than it was by the Australian John Brownlee in the seasons before the war. A colourless Donna Anna from Vienna did not help matters very much and Richard Lewis, so admirable the year before, was out of sorts as Don Ottavio on the first night. Fortunately there was plenty of compensation to be derived from the performances – all the better for a year's added maturity – of the other four survivors from the 1960 production. Ilva Ligabue's Donna Elvira, Geraint Evans's Leporello, the Zerlina of Mirella Freni, and particularly the Masetto of Leonardo Monreale ('a piece of operatic characterization for every collector to treasure,' said *The Times*) were as memorable and satisfying as any in post-war experience of the opera.

For the last production of the season Maestro Gui's Rossini Male Voice Repertory Company – Messrs Oncina, Bruscantini and Wallace – were joined by Alberta Valentini and Carlo Cava (in place of Franco Calabrese, originally announced) in a revival of *The Barber of Seville*. Miss Valentini was a rather shrill Rosina who sang the Mozart aria introduced into the Lesson Scene better than the music by Rossini. Carlo Cava, on the other hand, was a magnificent Basilio – unshaven, undarned, long-haired, oozing corruption and intrigue. His discovery proved a great asset to Glyndebourne in the years that followed. The *Barber of Seville* was chosen as the BBC Glyndebourne television for the year – the eleventh transmission of its kind from the Festival Opera House and now obviously such an unshakeable institution that even the most ill-educated telly-gossip columnists realized it was too late to do anything about it and left it in peace.

Apart from the birth of a son to George and Mary Christie on 10 July, the most important event of 1961, and the most original and successful of the year's experiments, did not take place at Glyndebourne but at the Royal Albert Hall in London where an entire evening of the Promenade Concerts was devoted to a concert performance of the season's *Don Giovanni*. This proved a quite astonishingly effective venture which owed a great deal to Moran Caplat's ingenious – *The Times* said 'brilliant' – idea of putting the singers on a small elevated platform behind the orchestra, where they were free to come and go as their cues dictated, instead of chaining them to a row of chairs at the front of the platform. It was an experiment that delighted everybody, not least the artists, who were astonished and gratified by the quickness of the Prom audience in laughing loudly at lines in the recitative which were usually received in silence at Glyndebourne. Either the audience had done its homework well or they had translations of the libretto; whatever it was they behaved as though it was the best 3s they'd ever spent in their lives.

There was one other, smaller sideshow by Glyndebourne during the summer and that was a concert given as part of the Sussex Festival Season in the Royal Pavilion, Brighton. The occasion was called 'Rossini and King George IV' and was described as 'An Entertainment of Italian Music suggested by the Recital given by Goiacchino [sic] Rossini before King George IV in the Music Room of the Royal Pavilion on 29 December 1823'. The idea was Jani Strasser's; he 'devised and arranged' the programme with admirable disregard of possible anachronisms (the items included several written by Rossini long after 1823) and it proved an enchanting evening. Eugenia Ratti, Luigi Alva and Enzo Sordello from the *Elisir d'amore* cast sang arias, duets and trios written by Mozart, Rossini, Haydn and Donizetti; Jani Strasser played 'A group of Piano Pieces written in Old Age' by Rossini, and the Overture to *La gazza ladra* for piano duet with Martin Isepp.

The last couple of weeks of the season were enlivened by a letter from Lady Bearsted putting the critic of one of the weeklies in his place on a subject which one was surprised to find anybody bothered to raise any more. Was the critic seriously suggesting, asked Lady Bearsted, that an ability to pay for one's seat at Glyndebourne prevented one being a music lover? She just did not believe, she went on, that musical audiences at Glyndebourne or anywhere else were chiefly composed of music critics and the frivolous ticket buyers so despised by the critic in question. This was all started, of course, by *Elegy for Young Lovers*. My own experience is that it is just as easy to be bored and discomfited by an opera for which – like a critic – one has not bought one's ticket, as it is by an opera one has paid to see.

After the season had finished and the repertoire for 1962 had been announced, the son of George and Mary Christie was christened at Ringmer Parish Church. Soon after the birth of his first grandchild John Christie had been asked by one of the Glyndebourne staff what the baby was going to be called. He replied without hesitation: 'Why, Sock, of course. After all his father was named after one of the pugs.' The story that his son George had been called after a pug was one John Christie insisted on even in print. In his memorial tribute in the Ringmer Parish Magazine to his butler, Childs, in 1940, he told it boldly, emphasizing that his son had 'not been named after the King', as some of us might have thought. As far as his father was concerned George was certainly named after a pug dog. To his mother, however, he bore the name of her favourite uncle George St

John Mildmay, who had died shortly before her marriage and with whom she had made her home in Somerset when she first returned from Canada.

When the time came for John Christie's grandchild to be christened he was called Hector Thomas Clevland Christie. Whether it was a pug or not I do not know, but in a dog's cemetery on the Christie estates in North Devon there is, I believe, a small tombstone to the memory of Hector.

After a couple of seasons' absence, following his retirement as Artistic Director in 1959, Carl Ebert returned to Glyndebourne in 1962 to direct one of the finest productions of his long association with the Festival Opera. Debussy's *Pelléas et Mélisande*, which opened the season, was put on ostensibly as a 'tribute' or what-have-you to the composer's centenary. Perhaps it was considered safer to tie it up with an occasion in this way; if so, it was an unnecessary precaution, because nothing ever had less need of a peg to be hung on than the Glyndebourne production of *Pelléas*, staged by Ebert, conducted by Gui, and beautifully designed by Beni Montresor. A stubborn, at times even arrogant, self-confidence characterized Glyndebourne from the very beginning, but the fact that John Christie eventually relinquished his one-man control of the opera did not in any way affect this typical quality. It needed this self-confidence to put on *Pelléas*. The opera, we know, is an acknowledged masterpiece; but it is not only 'different', it is also 'difficult'. It is unlike any other opera in history; it isn't even very like Debussy – or at any rate, the Debussy the public usually enjoys – who wrote *La Mer*, or *Fêtes* or *L'Après-midi d'un faune*. Its whole mood is dark, misty and elusive, and unless it is performed superlatively well it can be one of the most powerful soporifics in the repertoire. There is no doubt, I think, that the Glyndebourne public came knowing very little about *Pelléas*; it is not an opera that is performed every day of the week anywhere. But with its peculiar instinct it went away having immediately recognized the 'class' of Debussy's opera.

The first performance of *Pelléas et Mélisande* at Glyndebourne was made into something of a near-gala occasion with an audience that included Princess Marina, the French and Belgian Ambassadors (Maurice Maeterlinck was a Belgian, of course), Dame Maggie Teyte, who was chosen by Debussy to succeed Mary Garden as Mélisande at the Opéra-Comique when the opera was first heard, and Debussy's stepdaughter, Mme Dolly de Tinan. But the première of the first French opera to be heard at Glyndebourne was the first time since the foundation of the Festival Opera that John Christie was not in his box at the first night. He had had an operation for cataract on his only eye a few weeks before and was now blind. He heard the opera over a loudspeaker in his house. But during the dinner interval he was to be seen in the foyer as usual, a noble, patriarchal figure, his determined chin now hidden behind a white bushy beard that gave him the air of an Old Testament prophet. Christie had begun to grow the beard the previous autumn when he could no longer shave himself, and could not bear the idea of anybody else doing it for him.

Vittorio Gui's conducting of *Pelléas et Mélisande* was an outstanding performance – an authoritative and affectionate reading of a score he had known for sixty years by a composer he had known well. An unofficial feature of these Glyndebourne perform-ances of *Pelléas* was the small group of singers' children who collected in the wings to listen, fascinated and motionless, to the opera night after night. Gui was delighted by this; it proved, he said, that at last a generation was growing up that really appreciated Debussy's masterpiece.

The production of *Pelléas*, perhaps the finest thing Ebert had ever done at Glynde-bourne, was followed by a revival of *Figaro*, which was given an unusual kind of preview – or rather, pre-hearing, for the artists wore evening dress and there was no stage action – in the form of a concert version compèred by Moran Caplat before an audience support-ing the Jewish charity, British Ort.

The first night of *Figaro* followed a week later with no fewer than six principals mak-ing their first appearance in this opera at Glyndebourne, and three of them their first-ever appearance at the Festival Opera House. A new conductor was also in the pit – Silvio Varviso, a young Swiss, whose understanding of the score and refusal to try fancy frolics with the fandango came as a great relief. The 1962 *Figaro*, indeed, was worthy to rank among the best ever seen at Glyndebourne – on the second night, that is, for the new Countess, the Turkish Leyla Gencer, seemed to be a habitual sufferer from first-night nerves which invariably started her off below form. Gabriel Bacquier, from the Paris Opera, was another newcomer; he gave a brilliant performance as the Count – elegant, aristocratic and full of unexpected touches that showed a rare understanding of the charac-ter. Mirella Freni was the new Susanna, a part she was singing for the first time; she played it with great charm and above all with respect for Mozart's vocal writing – a much rarer accomplishment among Susannas than one might think. Susanna is no ordinary soubrette and Miss Freni recognized this in everything she did. There was another Murillo-like Cherubino who came, rather unexpectedly, from Switzerland. Edith Mathis brought her own peculiar charm to a performance that suffered little by comparison with Teresa Berganza's ('all Glyndebourne Cherubinos are good ...'). The new Figaro was Heinz Blankenburg – lively, witty but with so strong a streak of the dangerous social rebel about him that it seemed odd that an intelligent man like the Count shouldn't have spotted it. Carlo Cava, also new to *Figaro*, presented a convincing Bartolo.

An extra, unannounced performance of this *Figaro* was put on at six hours' notice when the season's last performance of *Pelléas* had to be cancelled because of an ankle injury to Michel Roux, who sang Golaud. There seemed to be no available understudy capable of acting the part; Roux was not a vocal casualty and so there was no question, of course, of anybody in a dinner jacket singing the part in the wings. Roux could sing all right; he just couldn't stand up. Gabriel Bacquier was asked if he knew the part; he did not. So for the first time in Glyndebourne's history a performance of an opera was cancelled and another put on in its place. Silvio Varviso and Edith Mathis had taken advantage of a four-day *relâche* between performances of *Figaro* to return to Switzerland and so were not available; the opera was accordingly conducted by John Pritchard and Cherubino was sung by Maureen Keetch.

The revival of *Così fan tutte* which came next was of really startling mediocrity. Only

Michel Roux, who was able to lean on a silver-handled stick as Don Alfonso and so remain in character as well as erect, and the little American coloured singer, Reri Grist, as Despina, made any sort of impression or suggested in any way that the opera had ever been Glyndebourne's perennial pride and joy. The four lovers, all newcomers to Glyndebourne, were quite astonishingly lacking in personality, and it was hard to believe that they could make such a hit with the Albert Hall audience when they gave their concert performance of the opera at the Proms. The difference was so marked, indeed, that it was almost as though the Glyndebourne run had been merely a rehearsal for the great, sold-out one-night stand in London.

The second novelty of the year was Monteverdi's *L'incoronazione di Poppea*, which a Nottingham paper, in a story about a local ex-collier who had joined the Glyndebourne chorus, delighted everybody by calling 'The Coronation of the Pope'. Originally the production was claimed by Glyndebourne as the first performance of the opera in Britain, but this was correctly modified to the 'first professional production' when it was pointed out that there had been a memorable week of seven or eight semi-professional performances of *Poppea* given by the Oxford University Opera Club in 1927, when the score was arranged by the recently graduated 23-year-old Jack Westrup, now Sir Jack and Professor of Music at Oxford.

To perform *Poppea* at Glyndebourne was in its way a greater challenge to its audience than the production of *Pelléas*. Debussy's opera had at least some idiomatic points of contact with everyday musical life; Monteverdi's, on the other hand, had none. It was unlike anything the great majority of the audience had ever heard in their lives before and I could find only one other critic who had also heard the Oxford performances, and he was an undergraduate at the time. The odds against *Poppea* making any sort of impact on the non-professional listener ought to have been overwhelming. It didn't even have the snob-appeal which we are always told makes people go to Glyndebourne. But once more the instinct which had sensed the quality of *Pelléas* recognized the genius of Monteverdi – to such effect, indeed, that for the first time an opera not by Mozart has been performed in three successive years at the Festival Opera House. Raymond Leppard's arrangement of the music of *Poppea* was most imaginative and dramatically effective. He was criticized for an allegedly anachronistic harp glissando at one point in his score; his reply was that nobody could tell him that in 1642 people didn't run their fingers up and down the strings in a glissando just for the joy of it – just as anybody still does today. This struck me as the best possible answer.

Mr Leppard's score, made specially for the Glyndebourne production, was given a fine send-off by an excellent cast. Magda Laszlo returned to Glyndebourne as Poppea, in place of Judith Raskin, whose name appeared in the programme but who had had to go into hospital in New York for an operation; Richard Lewis was Nero and so revived an operatic partnership with Miss Laszlo which had begun with *Alceste* at Glyndebourne and continued with *Troilus and Cressida* at Covent Garden. Carlo Cava, whom we had hitherto known only as a *buffo*, gave a most moving performance of the tragic Seneca; Oralia Dominguez, just surviving the most grotesquely silly head-dress ever seen on any stage, was comic, touching and generally splendid as Poppea's nurse, Arnalta. She sang her lullaby beautifully. Hugues Cuenod, as Lucano, had one short and brilliant scene with Richard Lewis which Rennert's production did its best to spoil by making the artists so over-act their drinking song and perform such contortions of staggering about that it was physically difficult for them to sing at all. Do German producers lead such sheltered lives that they have never seen a drunk in real life? Or even Charlie Chaplin? 'Somebody should explain to Herr Rennert,' commented one of the critics, 'that Lucan is not a court Booby, but the author of the "Pharsalia".'

The one serious piece of miscasting in *Poppea* was, to my mind, the choice of Sir Hugh Casson to design the scenery. Monteverdi's opera is Baroque opera; it cries out for curves and arches and decoration; and if this is considered to be carrying the idea of staging Monteverdi in the style of the theatre he wrote for too far, then it must still be remembered that the opera is set in ancient Rome, where there were curves and arches and decoration. Sir Hugh Casson, perhaps as a result of some premonition that she would be singing in the opera with Richard Lewis, produced the familiar rectangular slabs of scenery which had framed Magda Laszlo's previous appearances in his designs for *Alceste* and *Troilus*. To me anything less appropriate to Monteverdi's opera or duller to look at for two and a half hours than the designer's permanent set for *Poppea* it was difficult to imagine. The uncompromising angularity of the set was, to be fair, relieved by three circles in the form of three discs placed over the three doorways at the back of the stage. They looked exactly like the floor indicators over the lift doors of a German bank. It seemed to me that Glyndebourne did not give nearly enough thought beforehand to the visual implications of Monteverdi's opera. A first professional performance should, I feel, have erased all memories of a semi-pro performance at Oxford thirty-five years earlier, but they did not altogether. There had been the silhouette of ships waiting to take Ottavia into exile at the New Theatre; at Glyndebourne she obviously took the lift down to the basement.

These objections, of course, are all a matter of personal opinion, which only two of my colleagues in fact agreed with when they wrote of Glyndebourne's *Poppea*. However, as *Poppea* is likely, with any luck, to be revived constantly in the future no doubt these things will be put right.

On 4 July, a few days after the première of *Poppea* and an hour or so before the curtain went up on the evening's performance of *Così fan tutte*, John Christie died, aged 79. His death was not announced until later in the evening and it was not until the following night, before the performance of *Figaro* – the first opera ever produced at Glyndebourne – that the audience was able to pay its tribute of two minutes' silence to his memory.

Christie had grown progressively weaker since the season started, and in his last hours, with Jock and other old friends at his bedside, he talked not about Glyndebourne or the Festival Opera or even of the plans he had been making for their future, but about Eton. Christie had always looked back on his time there as a master as the happiest days of his life. On his deathbed the memory of them seems to have brought him final contentment.

By all everyday English standards John Christie was an eccentric; but this was only because he spent his money on opera. If, like other rich men, he had spent it on race-horses or yachts he would have been thought quite normal; he would have been doing something the man in the street understood, admired and wished he could do himself. To regard Christie as eccentric was, in fact, simply a Philistine misunderstanding of his whole character; for there was surely never a man so stubbornly and unwaveringly obsessed by the pursuit of an ideal. Osbert Lancaster tells the story of how, driving his car along the Mall in the evening rush hour, he caught sight of Christie standing motionless in the middle of the road; he stopped, Christie got in saying, 'I knew I'd see somebody I knew who was going to Victoria Station.' In fact, Mr Lancaster was not going to Victoria at all, but he took his passenger there just the same. The incident is recalled here because, though it is trivial enough, it epitomizes that characteristic singleness of purpose and unshakeable self-confidence which created and nourished the Glyndebourne Opera.

That John Christie occupied a unique position in operatic history we know well enough: by delegating authority entirely to others he instituted a form of constitutional monarchy which (except for one or two moments when human nature threatened the safety of the constitution) worked miraculously well – as, of course, it had to if the system was to succeed at all. It was a system which, nevertheless, preserved the essentially private and personal character of the Christies' foundation; Trusts and peppercorn rents notwithstanding, one was conscious that it was John Christie's theatre, his gardens and his enthusiasms that one was enjoying. And his company; for where else in the world could the owner and founder of an opera house be found in his theatre every night, talking to guests and strangers alike, even when illness forced him to attend in a wheeled chair? It was only in the last days of his total blindness that he was no longer seen in the auditorium. Today, more than two years after his death, it is reassuring to sense that this unique feeling not just of family participation, but of family responsibility, has not lessened. George and Mary Christie 'wear' the opera house, as it were, as a natural, permanent garment. George Christie was born into it; his wife has married into it and between them they are in every sense at home in it. It is a happy state of affairs which I sometimes think we take too casually for granted. Has anybody ever reflected what might have happened if George had preferred to be a sailor or a jazz drummer or something?

Because of his imperturbable optimism it is difficult to believe that John Christie was ever disappointed. Consequently one tends to be disappointed on his behalf when one hears that something one feels sure he would so much have liked to do in fact never came off. I will admit that his failure ever to hear a Wagner opera in the theatre he so hopefully, but vainly, designed for that purpose does not move me as much as I feel it ought to. But there was one scarcely known incident in his life which, because it never reached fulfilment, must strike all who knew him as unhappy and unjust. This was when Christie was asked by the King to advise him on the choice of German wine for the cellars of Buckingham Palace – a splendidly appropriate post, one feels, for one in whose theatre many had their first memorable encounter with Don Magnifico in *Cenerentola*. But before the appointment could take effect the 1939 war broke out and there was no longer any German wine to advise about.

Even for those who never knew him John Christie's death in 1962 was inevitably a sad occasion, for his bubbling personality and infectious friendliness were part of the fabric of his Opera House, and if he had been able to ask each member of the audience whether they were enjoying themselves he would have done so, because he was the host. The tributes that were paid to him when he died came from all over the world; but among them was one paid by Carl Ebert which, more than any other, defined the unique debt owed to John Christie by all who have ever worked at Glyndebourne. 'John Christie,' said Ebert, 'gave us time.'

A memorial service and commemoration in music for John Christie was held on 3 September 1962, in a crowded Westminster Abbey. Lord Hailsham (or, as he is now, Mr Quintin Hogg) read the Lesson; Vittorio Gui conducted Mozart's Requiem Mass sung by Elsie Morison, Pamela Bowden, Richard Lewis and Carlo Cava, with the Glyndebourne Festival Chorus and the Royal Philharmonic Orchestra. The service ended with the solemn march from Act III of *Idomeneo*, the Mozart opera which Glyndebourne had first brought to England. Before the service began Sir William McKie, Organist and Master of the Choristers at the Abbey, played four pieces by Bach, and the organ he played them on was built by William Hill and Son, Norman and Beard Ltd, the firm John Christie had bought so that he could have the instrument he wanted in the Organ Room where the Glyndebourne Festival Opera had its true beginning.

Meanwhile, the 1962 Festival had continued on its way with a revival of the first version of Richard Strauss's *Ariadne auf Naxos* with *Le Bourgeois Gentilhomme* preceding it. As at Edinburgh in 1950, the Molière prelude was produced, and the part of M. Jourdain in it played by Miles Malleson who had the support of a company from the Old Vic. The part of Ariadne was sung by an outstanding Spanish newcomer, Enriqueta Tarrés, and confirming Jourdain's final assurance before the curtain fell that there would be fireworks in five minutes, a short display ('Fireworks by Brock's' was the programme credit) was given after every performance of the opera as the visitors left the theatre. With most opera houses the police would have had to be consulted; at Glyndebourne George Christie had to consult his gamekeeper to make sure that the fireworks would not disturb the pheasants.

The season's last production was a revival of *L'elisir d'amore* with two changes of cast from the year before. Mirella Freni sang Adina and so began to emerge from the chrysalis of soubrette parts on her way to the more substantial roles she now sings; Sesto Bruscantini sang Dr Dulcamara. The visual distractions of Zeffirelli's production were nearly offset this year by having a pretty Adina to look at and to listen to (Miss Freni had obviously put her foot down about wearing her hair the way Miss Ratti had been made to), but Luigi Alva's white rabbit seemed as pointless a prop as ever. The BBC televised *L'elisir d'amore* and it was seen in seven countries in a Eurovision hook-up. The donkey that pulled Dr Dulcamara's cart was replaced in the television version by supers who did his work for him. This was to avoid any possible charge of cruelty to animals on the screen – the English being what they are about foreigners.

CHAPTER TWENTY-FIVE

1963-4 Transition

THE FORMATION OF THE Glyndebourne Arts Trust had ensured the continuity of the Christies' foundation, and with the death of John Christie the transition from what was inevitably regarded as the end of one chapter to the beginning of another went as smoothly as it had long been envisaged it would.

There were changes, of course. As a result of the new system of booking for members of the Glyndebourne Festival Society started in 1962 (with seats £2 and £4 17s 6d), the season for advertising in the agony column of *The Times*, for instance, began as early as 15 March with a member wanting to exchange the seats he'd been allotted for seats he'd prefer. Whether the Glyndebourne authorities had managed to stamp out the black market in tickets altogether I do not know, though clearly Moran Caplat's scheme begun in 1961 to keep back 30 per cent of the seats for the general public did quite a lot to help matters; it was certainly noticeable that the only seats mentioned in the personal advertisements from now on were for exchange, not sale. The sinister phrase 'Offers?' no longer appeared. One of these insertions incidentally produced a brand-new nickname for a Mozart opera to rival the familiar 'Così'. This was a reference to something called quite simply and without the definite article 'Marriage'; which must be the first time *Figaro* has ever been thought of in this way.

For perhaps the first time since its foundation the alterations and additions made during the winter at Glyndebourne did not directly affect the public. At the sides of the theatre, on the level of the front row of the balcony, five new boxes were constructed for the use of the Management and music staff. Three were made on the prompt, two on the OP side (increased to three on the OP side in 1964). The boxes on the prompt side, which included George and Mary Christie's and the General Manager's, are entered from a sound-proof corridor on a new floor constructed over the Red Foyer and containing offices looking out on to a terrace. These additions to the structure of the Opera House were the first signs of large-scale building operations which were later to be made in preparation for the removal of the Glyndebourne London Office to Glyndebourne itself on the expiry of the lease of the cramped premises at 23 Baker Street in 1964.

The 1963 season opened with a finely sung production of Richard Strauss's *Capriccio*, an opera intended by the composer to be played in one act without a break and lasting some two and a half hours. This was happily not permitted at Glyndebourne where a German precedent of dividing the work into two parts was followed. There had been a possibility, I believe, of performing *Capriccio* in one piece at Glyndebourne, with the audience having to wait until the fall of the curtain for its dinner. Second thoughts prevented what would surely have been a mistake. The prospect of trying to picnic in the dark afterwards without having enjoyed more than a glimpse of the gardens and the Downs the whole evening would make the expedition to Glyndebourne much less appealing. That this did not occur with *Capriccio* is something to be grateful for; that such a thing as dinner at the end of an opera – *anybody's* opera – at Glyndebourne should ever have been contemplated for a moment is nevertheless most disquieting.

The major disappointment of the 1963 season was the withdrawal of Vittorio Gui from *Fidelio* on medical orders to take things more easily. He still conducted *Pelléas* and the new production of *The Magic Flute* later in the season, but Beethoven's opera never really came to life without his wisdom and experience. The Glyndebourne Festival Chorus made a special hit of its own in the last scene of the work, when it sang with an attack and rhythmic bite instilled into it by its new Chorus Master, Myer Fredman, which was sadly lacking in the orchestra pit and elsewhere. There was a new Rocco, Victor de Narké, from the Argentine; Mihaly Szekely had died in Budapest in March, aged 62. In the part of Marzelline one conductor's wife succeeded another conductor's wife. April Cantelo (Mrs Colin Davis and a member of the Glyndebourne chorus in 1948) replaced Elsie Morison (Mrs Rafael Kubelik), who had originally been chosen to repeat the part she had sung in the two previous Glyndebourne productions, but was unable to take on this time as she was on tour with her husband.

The revival of *Pelléas et Mélisande* under Gui was an even more satisfactory experience than the original production had been. A new Dutch Pelléas, Hans Wilbrink, was an improvement on his predecessor, and Anna Reynolds as good a Geneviève in her way as Kerstin Meyer, who was absent from Glyndebourne altogether this season. Denise Duval again sang Mélisande and though I suppose, strictly speaking, she was no less sophisticated than she had been the year before (this had been the only criticism) her performance was so attractive, so musical and her singing of the French language so lovely that it was still a rare experience. Apart from anything else, she came nearer than many singers of the part to making us forget the greatest understatement in all opera – Mélisande's words, after she has been pushed and banged about by Golaud: 'Je ne suis pas heureuse!' Guus Hoekman, another Dutch singer and a fine Arkel, and Michel Roux, who went through the season this time without injury as Golaud, both gave admirable performances again.

The next two productions of the 1963 season, *Poppea* and *Figaro*, were both taken up to the Albert Hall for performance at the Proms and both, it was plain from anybody's loudspeaker at home, were riotous successes. The impact on the audience of the Monteverdi opera was as astonishing in its way as it had been originally at Glyndebourne the year before. Oralia Dominguez, who had sung seven of the ten performances during the Glyndebourne season, was the only principal unable to appear at the Proms. For the rest, the Nero-Lucan drinking scene heard over the radio was a great improvement on the stage production, as it at last allowed Monteverdi's music to make all the comic points that were necessary and so achieve twice the comic effect.

In the 1963 *Figaro* there were two changes from the 1962 cast – Michel Roux, returning as the Count, and Liliane Berton, a French singer of great charm who was unwisely put into a black wig as Susanna and so appeared much older than her voice. This, however, was put right during the run of the opera at Glyndebourne.

The Prom performance of *Figaro* was one of those almost chaotic affairs which only the grace of God and an abundance of sheer theatrical luck keep the audience from knowing about. The evening at the Albert Hall was one of the hottest of the whole summer. Liliane Berton had fainted from the heat during rehearsal; the rehearsal was abandoned and the evening's performance was presented with many of the stage gestures and movements still unmodified to suit the concert version. Silvio Varviso, who conducted, was in a panic until almost the last moment before the concert began because his dress trousers had been sent to the cleaners and not returned. The Glyndebourne Management sorted this out for him. Finally, Leyla Gencer, suffering from worse nerves than even on first nights at Glyndebourne, decided as she was about to go on to the platform that she had lost her voice. The Glyndebourne Management sorted this one out, too, by pushing Miss Gencer firmly through the entrance to the platform and leaving her there.

The first half of the performance was perhaps not unnaturally a little edgy, and I doubt if the first act trio between the Count, Basilio and Susanna has ever been taken faster by any conductor. But once this general nervousness had been mastered the performance was a credit to Glyndebourne and a constant joy to a sold-out Prom audience.

Back at Glyndebourne, the revivals of *Poppea* and *Figaro* had been followed by a new production of *The Magic Flute* – an all-Italian affair inasmuch as Vittorio Gui conducted, Franco Enriquez produced and the designer was Emanuele Luzzati. Opinions in the audience of this production were probably more sharply divided than on any Mozart production since the beginning of Glyndebourne. It was unusual, inventive, decorative and – to my taste anyway – very enjoyable. The most immediately striking feature were the designs by Mr Luzzati, who is surely the most original designer ever to have worked at Glyndebourne. True, the Queen of the Night's costume at first created the illusion that the singer was standing with raised, deformed arms, but when the lighting was favourable these 'arms' proved to be supports placed on her shoulders to hang a cloak on. The principal change from all other Glyndebourne productions of *The Magic Flute* was in the elimination of waits between the scenes. This was achieved by the use of ten tall decorated three-sided screens, each manipulated by a scene-shifter standing inside the screen, who moved about the stage according to individual instructions received from Geoffrey Gilbertson, the Stage Director, by radio on headphones. These mobile screens were most effective and though they were being used at Glyndebourne for the first time I remember having seen them in Vienna in the 1920s where they had been a feature of Stravinsky's ballet *Pulcinella* in the Redoutensaal. Vienna being what it always has been, of course, the idea was not new; in fact screens were often used in this way in the seventeenth-century theatre in France and Italy. The 1963 *Magic Flute* had only one serious fault in my view, and this came from a lack of musical understanding by the producer which I am surprised was not corrected by Gui. The first time the magic flute appeared in the story it was heard to play by itself. This was very magical and a charming idea – once. Unfortunately, Mr Enriquez was so struck by it that in the scenes of the ordeal by fire and water Tamino never once played the flute himself, and in consequence the dramatic tension so carefully created by the music was lost. At the end of the scene, which in any case was diffusely lit and so failed to concentrate the spectator's attention on what was happening to Pamina and Tamino, Pamina held the flute aloft as she led Tamino away – a piece of sexual symbolism which, if Mozart and Schikaneder ever thought of it, they were careful not to mention in front of Miss Brigid Brophy. All the libretto says, and which unfortunately the production did not pass on to us, is that during the scene, accompanied from time to time by muffled drums, 'Tamino plays his flute'. Carl Ebert's production never lost its power of creating tension at this point.

With any luck, however, this scene may get modified to make sense again over the years. Mr Enriquez's production was otherwise far too sensitive to spoil with a trick that was directly contrary to Mozart's – never mind Schikaneder's – expressed intentions.

The last opera of 1963 was a revival of *The Rake's Progress* which was disappointingly attended – something like eight per cent of the seats for the nine performances were unsold. This falling-off in box office appeal was attributed by one surprised and shocked writer to the unadventurousness of Glyndebourne audiences. I don't think unadventurousness had very much to do with it. It was surely just a matter of Stravinsky's opera having reached the limits of its restricted appeal. *The Rake's Progress*, after all, demands far less adventurousness from an audience than *Pelléas* or *Poppea*.

On the last night of the season George Christie announced the plans for the 1964 Festival which was to consist of six operas once more. The seven-opera repertoire in 1963 proved too complicated, not only in the matter of overlapping rehearsals, but in the sheer physical difficulty of finding accommodation to lodge the casts of two current productions and one, or even two more, in rehearsal at the same time. The repertoire, Mr Christie told us, would be *Macbeth*, Rossini's *Pietra del paragone*, *Capriccio*, *The Magic Flute*, *Idomeneo* and *L'incoronazione di Poppea*.

When the season was over *Figaro* was pre-recorded for BBC television in its complete Glyndebourne form, the first Mozart opera to be televised from the Festival Opera House for nine years. The pre-recording was made under more or less normal Glyndebourne conditions – that is, with a long dinner interval for the invited audience betweens Acts II and III and the bar open until 10.30 p.m.

This television performance marked the last appearance for Glyndebourne, after sixteen consecutive seasons, of the Royal Philharmonic Orchestra, many of whom had been with the orchestra when its association with the Festival Opera first began at Edinburgh in 1948. The breach (it was no less) between orchestra and management was unhappy and I am sure unnecessary. For me, at any rate, the departure of the RPO has been a sad parting from many friends in whose company my wife and I spent happy hours during the long opera intervals in the summer drinking and talking shop. Some of the players, like Andrew Brown, Terence MacDonagh, 'Tich' Pocock and Fred Harmer, I had long known as colleagues; two of them, Anthony Pini, the principal 'cellist, and Eddie Wilson, the bassoonist, have been friends all my adult life – for over 35 years. Only those who have mixed with orchestral players will properly understand how much one can miss their uniquely stimulating, good-humoured company.

As I write the 1964 season is a clutch of eggs yet to be finally hatched out. All that has so far any definite shape is the nest in which they have been laid – a Festival Opera House now fitted with new ventilation, a new stage lighting system (the old apparatus has been shared out between the National Theatre and the Wexford Festival), a widened proscenium opening from which Oliver Messel's modest velvet drapes have been removed, and offices for an ever-growing staff transplanted from Baker Street. And where in the past a Rolls-Royce was chartered for the season to fetch and carry the artists, Glyndebourne now has its own minibus.

The Programme Book for the year has thirty-nine advertisers, now only one short of the target Mr Sekers aimed at when he first evolved the idea in 1951. The Glyndebourne Arts Trust has been in existence for ten years and still numbers among its members some who were not only among the first trustees but were active supporters when the Glyndebourne Opera itself began thirty years ago.

The Glyndebourne Festival Opera begins its fourth decade with Jock's name absent from the programme credits for the first time since 1934. In the hard winter of 1962–3 Jock Gough was severely frost-bitten and, after a bad fall from a rostrum on to the stage before the 1963 season began, was taken to hospital for an operation which has forced him to retire. (It was only after Jock's retirement that I learned of his one particular, unfulfilled ambition: to have Glyndebourne stage Puccini's *Girl of the Golden West*. He had grown very fond of it during his time with the Beecham Opera Company; they had produced it at Drury Lane in 1917 and he had never heard it since.)

Carl Ebert's name also no longer appears among the institutional credits, even as a producer. His famous production of *Idomeneo* is now the responsibility of his son Peter with, however, the acknowledgment that it is 'Based on the original production by Carl Ebert'.

The retirement of Jock and Carl Ebert leaves Jani Strasser as the last founder member of the Glyndebourne theatrical staff (Miss Janet Moores is, of course, on the administrative side). As Director of Musical Preparation and Chief of Music Staff, Strasser's work is backroom work, whose value and indispensability the ordinary visitor to Glyndebourne is probably not aware of. But there is not a conductor, good, bad or indifferent (and Glyndebourne has had its fair share of them all in its time), whose work has not been made easier, and sometimes improved, by Jani Strasser's ceaseless, untiring musical disciplining of the singers in the weeks before the curtain first goes up.

The name of Vittorio Gui, now nearly 80, is another which, if not absent from the programme, appears in a different place in the list given under the heading 'Glyndebourne Festival Opera 1964'. It is found only among the season's conductors and no longer as that of one of the Artistic Counsellors. Günther Rennert is now sole Artistic Counsellor, and music is represented at the top table, as it were, by John Pritchard in the position of Music Counsellor. The occupation of this post by a conductor who owed much of his experience and opportunity to Fritz Busch will not, I hope, mean that Glyndebourne's tradition of omitting the appoggiaturas from Mozart's vocal parts is to be continued indefinitely. We have suffered this austere and virtually world-wide practice for thirty years now – for what is commonly regarded as a whole generation, that is. It is now surely the duty of another generation to take a lead which would be universally followed and enter wholeheartedly into the work of restoring the grace notes Mozart implied and expected. Mozart owes Glyndebourne a great deal. This is one thing Glyndebourne still owes Mozart.

What some inevitably regarded as the cuckoo's egg in the 1964 Glyndebourne clutch was the plan to present an Italian straight company in a short season of Shakespeare's *Taming of the Shrew* in Italian after the opera finished in August. As I have never looked on Glyndebourne as anything but an enterprise uniquely and exclusively concerned with the production of opera, what the management chooses to do out of operatic hours, so to speak, is really its own affair. All I hope, as a hint of theatrical superstition makes itself felt, is that Glyndebourne's association with the Compagnia dei Quattro will have proved happier and more profitable than its dismal association with the earlier Company of Four. As for Shakespeare at Glyndebourne, one can't say it is altogether a surprise. In the programme of the very first season in 1934 didn't John Christie plead with us to come to live within reach of this Festival Opera House, and support it so that its Festivals could be extended ... so that there could be Shakespeare?

We did; and there was.

Supplement 1964-79

In memoriam Vittorio Gui 1885-1975
Jani Strasser 1902-1978

1964

It is generally recognized that what the soldier said is not evidence. And neither, I discovered in writing the first part of this history, is living memory – only more so. Thus the story of John Christie's wooing of Audrey Mildmay told on page 32, for instance, proves to have been pure invention. Not only was *Rosenkavalier* never performed on 4 June at Covent Garden either in the late 1920s or early 1930s, but on 4 June 1930 the opera there was *Madam Butterfly* – a very different kettle of operatic fish, which includes no immediately obvious or suitable dramatic or musical cue for presenting a miniature silver rose to one's fiancée. Again (page 142) Audrey Mildmay did not sing in Brussels, as I had been told. She was taken ill and lost her voice at Antwerp a few days earlier; Zerlina was sung by Winifred Radford, whose name appeared in the programme without comment on her presence or Miss Mildmay's absence.

The clutch of eggs that finally hatched out as the 1964 Festival did so after a difficult period of incubation. The season opened with Verdi's *Macbeth* – a sure guarantee of the mishaps and frustration traditionally associated with Shakespeare's play in the theatre. Indeed, in this case the trouble had started in 1962, when Ebert flatly refused to accept Glyndebourne's choice of Beni Montresor as designer, in spite of his beautiful décor for Ebert's production of *Pelléas* which had been such a success. Ebert suggested two American designers instead; Glyndebourne would accept neither of them. So Ebert washed his hands of the entire project and never produced at Glyndebourne again. Gui's stepson, Franco Enriquez, agreed to do the production but rejected the designs as 'absolutely impossible'. (Gui himself had earlier also had 'serious reservations' about Montresor.) Then, at the end of October 1963, Glyndebourne cabled Gui to say that *Macbeth* was likely to be cancelled because of 'new difficulties'. This was for information only; Gui had already announced that he would not conduct *Macbeth*, nor indeed appear at Glyndebourne at all in 1964. How could he, he asked, when his suggestion in 1961 that Glyndebourne should sometime do Rossini's *Pietra del paragone*, had resulted in the travesty of the work that Rennert and a German collaborator had made being performed in 1964? Understandably, Gui was bitterly hurt by what he called 'la gaffe rossiniana', and appalled by the whole conception. Rossini opera, he wrote, 'cannot be well interpreted by the German people; even our old Ebert, indubitably a great producer, in the Barbiere and Cenerentola was not at all at his best. The sense of humour, the comicity [Gui's English for *comicità* – comic quality] of our great Rossini must never be "caricatura" – the style of our great genius, a Mediterranean genius, is immensely far from the comicity of the German races!'

No sooner had Gui been told that *Macbeth* was 'off' than it was on again. It would open the season, produced by Enriquez, designed by Luzzati, conducted by Lamberto Gardelli, and Lady Macbeth would be – well, they hadn't allowed for the *Macbeth* gremlin. Leyla Gencer was the first choice but was not available. Nor was the Russian, Galina Vishnevskaya. But the American soprano, Margherita Roberti, was free, approved and signed up, only to have to cry off exactly a month before the start of rehearsals because of influenza that had led to bronchitis and a total ban on singing for at least a month.

A Lady Macbeth, sound in wind and limb, was finally found and the part was sung by Marta Pender, another American, who lived and sang in Italy but had had little or no theatrical experience. But she knew the part, and the first night passed without disaster. Her dramatic inexperience and first-night nerves were obvious, but, as Andrew Porter bothered to tell us in the *Financial Times*, she later improved out of all recognition and was able 'to command her music and to command the scene'.

The Macbeth, Kostas Paskalis, a Greek baritone from the Vienna Opera, was outstanding in a staging which (except for the deliberate and unjustifiable omission of the visible ghost of Banquo specifically demanded by both Shakespeare and Verdi) was original and effective. The battle scene (with the fugue played in full – a welcome innovation) was particularly successful in its use of a cinematic quick-cutting by spotlights from one pair of combatants to another.

For the rest, it was a relief to hear Monteverdi's *Poppea* for the third year running, even though nothing had been done to modify the 'comicity' of the Nero-Lucan drunk scene. Raymond Leppard made his début in the Glyndebourne pit as conductor of his own 'realization' of the opera.

Vittorio Gui, now seventy-nine, was in the end persuaded to conduct six performances of *The Magic Flute* with much the same principals as he had directed in the initial production a year earlier.

The fifth revival of *Idomeneo* was the final opera of the 1964 season. Richard Lewis sang Idomeneo, as he had done in every Glyndebourne performance since the original Busch-Ebert production in 1951 (he was to sing the part again at Glyndebourne in 1974). The Idamante was a singer heard and engaged by Glyndebourne before he had been heard at the Scala or Covent Garden in 1963 – Luciano Pavarotti. The twelve performances of *Idomeneo* were all he ever sang at Glyndebourne, but years afterwards he remembered them when he said: 'What I learned there was to sing *piano* – from Jani Strasser.'

In 1964, for some contractual reason or other, the orchestra which succeeded the Royal Philharmonic in the pit was described as the "Glyndebourne Festival Orchestra".

In fact, as we have been able to read in the programme every year since 1965, the orchestra was the London Philharmonic whose principal conductor at the time was John Pritchard. Not since 1934 had Glyndebourne had an orchestra that had never played an opera before, but under its familiar director the LPO soon got the idiomatic hang of things, and with the ample rehearsal time available at Glyndebourne reached a high standard in under the seven-year par which Vittorio Gui once declared was the average time needed to train an opera orchestra.

1965

Though the revival of *Macbeth* in 1965 did inevitably bedevil the production of that opera itself, its notorious jinx this time also subtly affected virtually the whole season as originally planned several years earlier. The idea had been to open with *La traviata* (first proposed in 1936, then again confidently, but fruitlessly, announced for 1948), with Gui conducting and Mirella Freni singing her first Violetta. This most promising project came to nothing when it was found that performances had been so scheduled that Freni was expected to sing perhaps Verdi's most difficult role thirteen times in twenty-five days; this she understandably declined to do, and it was then too late to rearrange the dates.

So it happened that Mirella Freni made her début as Violetta elsewhere later in the year, and was found to be most disappointing in the part. One can't help feeling that if she had spent a month on the part with Jani Strasser at Glyndebourne, she would have developed into a far better Violetta than they made of her in Milan.

Four operas were inked in by Glyndebourne to follow *La traviata*, and had to be just as firmly inked out – *Don Giovanni*, produced by Peter Brook, a seventeenth-century double bill of Purcell's *Dido and Aeneas* and Monteverdi's *Il ballo delle ingrate*, and Cimarosa's *Le astuzie femminili*. The Mozart fell through because although he had accepted eagerly in December 1963, Peter Brook had had to change his mind five months later, when he found his other commitments too heavy. The Cimarosa ran into casting difficulties, *Dido* was postponed and with it the Monteverdi. As a result these five operas were replaced by six full-length works, which together contributed a record-breaking total of seventy-four performances during the season that lasted from 16 May to 15 August.

Cimarosa did, in fact, open the season as planned, but with the more famous *Il matrimonio segreto* introducing the composer to Glyndebourne for the first time. This should have been conducted by Gui, but on the journey by car from Italy his wife was suddenly taken ill with some form of food poisoning. 'I called the doctor,' Gui wrote to George Christie and Moran Caplat from a town in Jura, 'who found not only a serious trouble in the estomac with signs of intoxication, yet also a form of *allergie* . . .' (The Italians, like the French, commonly use the word intoxication in its strict medical sense of poisoning – and, of course, are as commonly misunderstood by the English.) After a rest at home in Florence, the Guis eventually reached Glyndebourne, where Vittorio conducted the last six of thirteen performances of *Il matrimonio segreto* (the first seven had been taken over by Myer Fredman). Frank Hauser's production, notable for the fact that for the first time in Glyndebourne's history the cast of six was entirely Italian, had a distinction and style that caused Desmond Shawe-Taylor to remark pointedly in the *Sunday Times* that 'by placing Frank Hauser's elegant *Matrimonio* in the same season as Rennert's crude travesty of *La pietra del paragone*, Glyndebourne invited a dangerous comparison'.

The other novelty of the season was Donizetti's *Anna Bolena*, an opera not only neglected in England, where it had not been heard for seventy-three years, but also in Italy, where there was no performance from the 1880s until its 1956 revival 'in the composer's native Bergamo. The following year it was put on at the Scala, its first time there since 1877, in an historic performance with Maria Callas as Anna Bolena and Giulietta Simionato as Jane Seymour. The conductor then, as at Glyndebourne, was Gianandrea Gavazzeni, a *bergamasco*, like Donizetti, and the author of a study of the composer.

Since her appearance as the Countess in *Figaro*, Leyla Gencer had been increasingly specializing in 'Callas roles' and she was impressive in the title part of *Anna Bolena*. That Giulietta Simionato did not repeat her Scala part was due entirely to the accidents of inconvenient dates and places; she had sung Cherubino for Glyndebourne in Edinburgh in 1947, and would have accepted the return engagement 'con grande entusiasmo'. Even more unexpected than Gencer's change from Mozart to dramatic soprano was the singing of an old favourite who had not been heard at Glyndebourne for four years, Juan Oncina, in the part of Percy. Oncina had been the principal *tenore di grazia* in all Gui's famous Rossini revivals, as well as in *Falstaff*, *Così fan tutte* and *Don Giovanni*. As Percy his voice had changed its character almost to that of a *Heldentenor* – indeed, he had recently sung Lohengrin. It was a fascinating and surprising transformation.

The performing edition of *Anna Bolena* followed at Glyndebourne was the same as Gavazzeni had used at the Scala revival, when few of the critics commented on the cuts in the score made by the conductor, and those who did were in favour of them. One of the Scala improvements had been the omission of the overture, which Desmond Shawe-Taylor had described as 'unworthy and trivial'. But when the same thing happened at Glyndebourne one of the London critics was highly indignant about the 'drastic cuts' made by Gavazzeni. 'We are told the overture is poor and banal,' he protested, 'but how can we judge unless we hear it?' How, indeed, except by doing what anyone else would have done – namely, look at the score?

The revival of *Der Rosenkavalier* was distinguished by the first appearance in England of the Spanish soprano Montserrat Caballé, who has since become one of the highest-paid singers in the world. Miss Caballé was ill during the first week of rehearsals, and having arrived at Glyndebourne without knowing a note of the part of the Marschallin at all – an unforgivable breach of traditional Glyndebourne discipline worthy of a Bateman cartoon – had to be taught the whole thing in six days by Gerald Gover of the music staff. Nevertheless, she was a great success and got some ecstatic notices.

Less ecstatic were the notices Miss Caballé received for her Countess in the revival of *Figaro* – the last appearance of the opera for another eight years. (Except for the war years and 1952-4, *Figaro* had never been out of the repertoire for longer than two years in all the Festival Opera's years of activity.) In 1965 the production seemed to suffer from a touch of the Macbeths. The cast, which promised well on paper, proved very disappointing in practice. Caballé's Countess was oddly clumsy and inelegant ('almost vulgar', said one critic). Gérard Souzay, as Almaviva, was strangely unsatisfactory, for while his performance had several moments of great personal, aristocratic charm, it lacked the ferocity which is such a subtle and important element in Mozart's characterization.

Except for Lydia Marimpietri's Susanna, it was altogether a rather colourless performance, for even Gui's direction lacked sparkle and tension. Daniel Leveugle's production showed little of the Gallic wit one expects from a Frenchman; instead, there was the now almost universal inability to resist fussy and distracting stage-business. Comparison with Carl Ebert's last *Figaro* (1962) was inevitable. In fact, Ebert had been urged to return for the 1965 production and for a time it seemed he would; but on reflection he decided that if he was to come back then it would have to be for an opera he had not produced before. There was no opportunity to do this, so his 1963 production of *Pelléas et Mélisande* remained, sadly, his last work for Glyndebourne.

Once the first night of *Figaro* was over, the Macbeth virus really took hold. Half an hour before the second performance of *Figaro*, Souzay suffered a sudden *crise de nerfs* and was totally unable to go on stage. The Count that night was sung by the understudy, John Kitchiner from the chorus. Michel Roux, due later at Glyndebourne for *La pietra del paragone*, was sent for after the second performance. At the next performance Caballé could not appear because of hay fever or something; she was away for two evenings, when her understudy, Lorna Elias from the chorus, appeared.

At this point Gui decided he had had enough for the moment, and took a rest from *Figaro* for a few performances. After three changes of cast, too much temperament, tension and tantrum, poor Maestro Gui was beginning to feel what he used to call 'desperated'. Once more, Myer Fredman (still, in his spare time, Chorus Master) took over, and in the course of seven days conducted three performances of *Figaro* and three of *Anna Bolena* (Gavazzeni had fulfilled his contract and returned to Italy). The reason Mr Fredman rested on the seventh day had nothing to do with working to Mosaic rule. There was just no performance that night.

The inclusion of *Macbeth* was inevitably accompanied by the traditional load of mischief that had affected all earlier productions of Verdi's opera at Glyndebourne. This time, however, the principal trouble – as always, the role of Lady Macbeth – occurred early enough not to cause havoc with normal preparation. True, the name of the Italian soprano, Linda Vajna, appeared in the programme, but that was because the programme had been printed and distributed well before *Macbeth* went into rehearsal. Miss Vajna withdrew before rehearsals began and her part was sung by Gunilla af Malmborg, a young Swedish soprano, who made a good impression as a singer of considerable promise, with a powerful voice and a striking appearance.

After the final performance of the season, George Christie made his annual end-of-term speech and announced several revolutionary changes in Glyndebourne policy for 1966. The season would be cut by twenty performances from thirteen weeks to nine; in place of the six operas performed in the season just ended, there would be a double bill, and three other operas – *Dido and Aeneas*, Ravel's *L'Heure espagnole*, *Werther*, *The Magic Flute* and Handel's *Jephtha*.

1966

Following the success of the 1956 bicentenary all-Mozart season at Glyndebourne, it was hoped that every tenth year thereafter would be a Mozart year – an ambition carefully cherished for seven or eight years. In 1966 there was to have been *Idomeneo*, *Die Entführung*, *Figaro*, *Don Giovanni*, *Così fan tutte* and *The Magic Flute*, with the addition of *La finta giardiniera*, which would have been new to the Glyndebourne repertoire.

The plan was reluctantly dropped when casting difficulties proved insuperable before the decision to shorten the 1966 season was made. Inevitably, the 1966 programme finally announced was not quite what was originally planned to suit the new economy. The double bill and *The Magic Flute* survived, but a proposed revival of *Alceste* did not. It was to have been the first of three new productions of Gluck operas conducted by Gui; *Iphigenia in Aulis* would follow in 1967 and *Iphigenia in Tauris* in 1968.

After the end of the 1965 Festival Glyndebourne produced three one-act operas in the theatre for BBC television – *Dido and Aeneas*, *L'Heure espagnole* and Busoni's *Arlecchino* (in English, with the original décor of the 1954 production). The Purcell and Ravel operas had never been performed by Glyndebourne before and so qualified for a useful subsidy from the BBC which helped the cost of staging the two new productions for its 1966 season.

The occasion was remarkable for the first appearance at Glyndebourne of Janet Baker as a principal (she had been a contralto in the chorus in 1956 and 1958), in a wonderfully moving performance as Dido. Rather unexpectedly the composition of the double bill came in for some public criticism. Purcell and Ravel were considered ill-assorted bedfellows. This doubt had also been felt by Gui who, some months before, had been very disturbed by the prospect of these two composers in one evening; even with the long dinner interval he thought the two works would not 'tune' together. 'By my long experience,' he wrote, 'I know that audiences, even unconsciously, are always [sic] sensible to the sense of style. Ravel with something more modern should be more fit than with Purcell.'

Incompatibility of styles, however, was less the reason for the critics' objections than the fact that *L'Heure espagnole* was in the repertoires of Covent Garden and Sadler's Wells. Personally, as I had never seen either opera on the stage, I was quite content. The seventy-five-minute dinner interval, with relaxed eating and drinking, was certainly as effective a buffer between Purcell and Ravel as any twenty-minute interval spent struggling at the bar of a concert hall ever provides between Vivaldi and Bartók. One thing was quite certain: even the very satisfactory all-francophone cast in Ravel's opera did nothing to erase the memory of Janet Baker's superb Dido and its final Lament.

Osbert Lancaster's designs for the Ravel made special demands on the ingenuity of the new Property Manager, Annabelle Hawtrey, who was asked to make nine different 'performing clocks', which struck the hours and quarters in a variety of ways. Some of these were specified in Ravel's score, others listed there simply as *automates*, with their precise nature left to the discretion of the designer. Ravel asked for a cock that crowed, a ballerina who danced and a man who played the trumpet. To these Osbert Lancaster added nine birds in a tree, a lady with a lyre, two men hitting a bell with a hammer, a church with a bishop coming out of it, a cuckoo clock and three men sitting on an elephant.

Miss Hawtrey, a grand-daughter of the great comedian Charles Hawtrey, well-endowed with Terry relations and the professional theatre-craftsman's ability to keep working against time and without sleep for days and nights on end, came to Glynde-bourne in 1964 to succeed Harry Kellard, who had joined the Festival Opera in 1947. The clocks she made for *L'Heure espagnole* were worked, not by clockwork or any electronic devices, but by hand, manipulated by wires and strings operated under the stage.

Massenet's *Werther*, the second production of the season, was full of Glyndebourne 'firsts' – the opera, the composer, the producer, the scene and costume designers, the four principal singers, were all new to the Festival Opera.

The choice of Sir Michael Redgrave as producer worked out well and if, with all his skill and knowledge of French, he could not do much with singers who, with a couple of exceptions, were no great shakes as actors, he was commended with comforting critical unanimity for his unobtrusive direction. 'Unobtrusiveness', in fact, was the term most frequently used and the quality that enabled Massenet to speak for himself in a musical language of peculiar charm and dramatic craftsmanship. As an opera *Werther* has an atmosphere all its own and for many people is one of the most attractive of all late-nineteenth-century Romantic operas.

The designers, Henry Bardon and David Walker, had been recommended as 'young English talented designers' by Lila de Nobili (the designer of *Elegy for Young Lovers*), who had been asked to do *Werther*, but had declined, writing 'You know how slow and disorganized I am . . . I can't find time to do it well. Let me suggest you an idea . . .' Which she proceeded to do.

The Paris *Figaro Littéraire* particularly praised the designs, describing them as 'des tableaux de puzzle. C'est idéal'. 'Un puzzle' is French for a jig-saw puzzle, and was a happy franglais description of the Glyndebourne scenery which, in its detail and colouring, was pleasantly reminiscent of the absorbing subjects of the typical jig-saws of one's youth.

Neither the Charlotte nor the Werther sang with much distinction, and a French critic was so ungallant as to describe the soprano as 'plus maternelle qu'amoureuse.' But there was some compensation in the discovery of the Czech-born Peter Gottlieb, at that time bearing a Brazilian passport, who sang Albert with a sense of style notably lacking in the two French performers; and another sympathetic performance came from the English Stafford Dean as the Bailiff. If, some time before, a French agent hadn't made a muddle with a timetable, Placido Domingo might have been singing Werther, but he was unable to reach Marseilles in time for Glyndebourne to hear him in the part. In spite of some vocal shortcomings, however, Glyndebourne's first excursion into nineteenth-century French music was a successful experiment and *Werther* was revived in 1969.

The only familiar production of the year was the Enriquez-Luzzati *Magic Flute*, with an unusually good cast headed by two Americans at Glyndebourne for the first time – George Shirley, as an attractively forthright Tamino, and Arlene Saunders, who developed into a sympathetic Pamina. The casting of Hugues Cuenod as Monostatos had a mixed critical reception. The first time M. Cuenod's name was mentioned in this book was on page 86, when, in 1935, Glyndebourne thought of him for Monostatos for its first-ever *Magic Flute*, but decided against him when they learned he was six foot five inches tall. In 1966 he was certainly no nearer the small, aggressive, chip-on-the-shoulder popular idea of the character than thirty-one years earlier; but Cuenod had a lean and hungry look that was at once droll, sinister and grotesque.

The outstanding newcomer to *The Magic Flute* was Peter-Christoph Runge, from Düsseldorf, who spent less than a week at Glyndebourne, having contracted to sing Papageno only at the first three performances. However, those three performances (with Sheila Armstrong as an enchanting Papagena) were enough to establish him as one of the most gifted Glyndebourne discoveries for many years – *Opera* magazine called him 'simply the Papageno of one's dreams; endearing yet never coy, funny but in a fresh way. His singing too was pure delight . . .' The critic of the *Financial Times*, for his part, described Sheila Armstrong as 'disturbingly attractive'. Perhaps he had hitherto always slept through Act II?

The last production of the season was the first to be sponsored by the Peter Stuyvesant Foundation, which had made a handsome present of £35,000, covenanted over seven years, to sponsor the staging of new productions. The production was of Handel's oratorio, *Jephtha*, substituted at short notice for *Alceste*. What amounted to little more than a concert in costume seemed to be carrying the new Glyndebourne policy of cutting-back a little too far. An oratorio for an opera seemed a poor exchange, even if – or rather, particularly because – the production and décor were the same as Rennert and the late Caspar Neher had been putting on with such success all over Germany since 1957.

The chorus was permanently tiered in a semi-circle to look like the Black and White Minstrels. (If producers are not aware of the physical strain and cramp that results from sitting still for so long they should ask the chorus – any chorus.) The soloists in this Handelian concert party sat on chairs downstage with their backs to the audience when they were not singing. This was to remind us that it was no ordinary oratorio.

I do not remember any Glyndebourne production having ever before been called 'dull', 'plodding', 'lethargic', 'painfully static' and just downright boring by the critics.

This was a 'first' in Glyndebourne's history we could have done without.

(above) *The Magic Flute*, 1978, Act I,
Scene I. Designer, David Hockney.
(Southern Television/Nutley)

(left) *Don Giovanni*, 1977, cemetery
scene: Benjamin Luxon, Pierre Thau,
Stafford Dean. Designer, John Bury.
(Southern Television/Nutley)

Fidelio, 1979, Prisoners' Chorus (Elizabeth Söderström, centre). Designer, John Bury. *(Southern Television/Nutley)*

Fidelio rehearsal, 1979. Left to right: Bernard Haitink (conductor), Peter Hall (producer), Guus Mostart (assistant producer), B. Hayes (stage management). *(Gravett)*

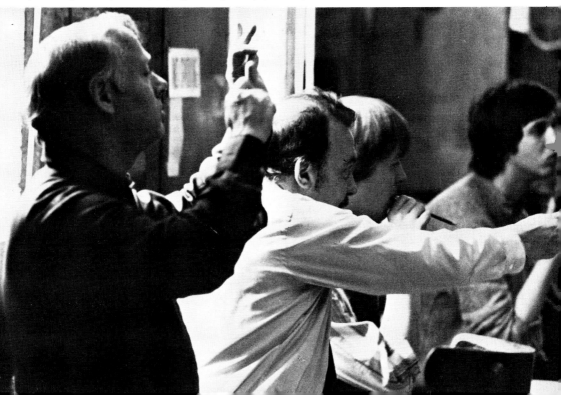

1967

The Festival of 1967 was eight days and six performances longer than 1966 and consisted of four operas: the first-ever production at Glyndebourne of a Puccini opera, a revival of Donizetti's *L'elisir d'amore*, Cavalli's *L'Ormindo*, arranged by Raymond Leppard, and a new production by Enriquez and Luzzati of *Don Giovanni*.

Reactions to the idea of *La Bohème* at Glyndebourne were not unexpected. Some people were plainly shocked at the very idea of a composer of Puccini's class darkening the doors of Glyndebourne's Sacred Halls; others looked forward to the experiment eagerly. The second category consisted mainly of those who, like myself, had always hoped that the Glyndebourne tradition of thorough preparation, imaginative presentation and the discovery of new young singers would be applied to some of the works which, although universally popular, are nonetheless masterpieces. As we know, *Carmen* and *La traviata* were several times proposed and dropped; the proposal to perform Puccini at his most popular survived, however, and *Bohème* opened the 1967 season.

Because one had expected so much, the occasion proved a sad disappointment. The singers, with the exception of the experienced Federico Davià, who was outstanding as Colline, were a very routine lot of all-Italian principals who nearly all sang too loud. The Rodolfo in particular was a dull stick, who addressed himself almost exclusively to the audience, and sang at the top of his voice.

The production did not do much to help, either. The same three who had produced *Werther* so imaginatively – Redgrave, Bardon and Walker – were assigned to *La Bohème*. When, early in February 1967, Michael Redgrave made his declaration of intent in a newspaper interview, one read with some foreboding that he had returned from Paris, 'where he had been doing some research on the opera'.

As one feared, this research inevitably affected the production in the wrong way. Act II was full of 'authenticity' that had everything to do with Mürger's novel, *Scènes de la Vie de Bohème*, but little with Puccini's opera. Puccini places Act II firmly in the Latin Quarter; Redgrave translated the Café Momus to its original site on the Right Bank. Puccini sets his scene outside his Café Momus; Redgrave, quite correctly according to Mürger's novel, set it inside, arguing that if the roofs were covered with snow throughout Act I, the Bohemians would hardly sit outside only a few minutes later.

Puccini's stage directions are specific. The Café Momus is on one side of the junction of the Rue Dauphine, the Rue Mazarine and the Rue de l'Ancienne Comédie, and is 'so crowded that some of the customers have to sit outside'. Colline, Marcello and Schaunard enter the Café, 'they come out carrying a table; a waiter follows with chairs; the customers at a nearby table, disturbed by the noise the three friends are making, get up and leave'.

None of this happened in the Redgrave production, because its design ensured it couldn't. Henry Bardon's original idea was to show both the inside and the outside of the Momus. This would have made sense, but the producer said he had 'talked him out of it'. As a result, Act II of Glyndebourne's *Bohème* has never made its most important theatrical point: the involvement of the audience as an extension of the Christmas Eve crowd on the stage, watching and hearing with them everything that is going on.

The 1961 production of *L'elisir d'amore* was revived with Zeffirelli's sets and costumes, but without his white rabbit. In spite of one or two irritating tricks added in re-production, the opera was allowed to make its full musical effect. The Nemorino of the young Ugo Benelli was a particular success; his performance had great charm and originality and would not have been out of place in the company of Mirella Freni and Sesto Bruscantini in 1962.

The first known performance anywhere since 1644 of *L'Ormindo* by Cavalli, arranged by Raymond Leppard, proved the season's outstanding experience. This enchanting opera, a remarkable medley of solemn, pathetic, bawdy and comic scenes, was a triumph of music and performance over production. What proved to be Rennert's last production for Glyndebourne suffered from a little too much German 'comicity', and Kondrak's designs were also censured for their heavy-handedness, one critic complaining that they 'misconceived the entire weight of the work', and another that as an essay in the exotic the scenery was strongly influenced by the old Leicester Square Turkish Baths school of building and decoration.

From the musical standpoint, however, a fascinatingly inventive and entertaining score received as satisfying a performance as anything at Glyndebourne for a long time. Without exception the cast was first-rate, Anne Howells making such an outstanding success of Erisbe that one critic was convinced that Rennert had obviously built his production 'round the warm, one might almost say sexy, Erisbe of Anne Howells' – which, considering that Miss Howells came into the production as a replacement so late that she didn't even get her name in the programme, was pretty fast production-building. It did not seem to occur to the writer that Anne Howells's own individuality might have had something to do with it. But that's a singer's life all over: it's your responsibility if you're bad, somebody else's if you're good. You can't win.

Perhaps fearing they were in for another *Jephtha*, the public was a little timid about booking for *L'Ormindo* to begin with, but once word got around that it provided an evening of beautiful and unusually entertaining music, the work settled down as one of the most popular operas in the Glyndebourne repertoire.

The new Enriquez-Luzzati production of *Don Giovanni*, the last opera of the season, was (let us say) 'interesting'. That is, much of it seemed to differ unnecessarily from long-established practice and just did not always come off. Luzzati's customary ingenuity with the scenery avoided long waits between scenes; the only trouble was that when the scenery was set up, a lot of it was seen to be in what was becoming known as Luzzati's 'toy-town' manner. Houses and practicable doors were less than man-size, and we had the spectacle of rather large ladies ducking their heads as they went into the houses and re-appearing, ridiculously out of proportion, at small first-floor doll's-house windows about six feet from the ground.

Some of the costumes and the decoration of the scenery were strikingly beautiful. I remember particularly the costumes of Donna Anna and the Commendatore in the opening scene, and the design of the cemetery, copied from the famous one in Genoa, with the sarcophagi stacked one above the other on shelves, like boxes in a shoe-shop.

The point of Leporello as a slovenly, ragamuffin double-ganger of his master wasn't quite clear, but Paolo Montarsolo, returning to Glyndebourne for the first time since his début there in 1957 (Mustafa in Gui's *Italiana in Algeri*), gave a splendid performance in the part, richly sung and funny. As Don Giovanni, Kostas Paskalis was elegant and dashing, though some of his comedy was rather plebeian at times – influenced perhaps by the infectious behaviour and strong personality of his towering servant.

Apart from Paskalis and Montarsolo, the two most satisfactory performances came from Sheila Armstrong and Leonardo Monreale as Zerlina and Masetto, who provided the human interest that was otherwise lacking in Enriquez's approach to Mozart's opera. One absolutely unexplained travesty of the words and music of *Don Giovanni* was the producer's eccentric treatment of the graveyard and final scenes of the opera. Desmond Shawe-Taylor described it in the *Sunday Times*: Any bright schoolboy, he wrote, knows that the Don invites the statue to supper – and the statue comes. But take the schoolboy as a reward to Glyndebourne, and what does he see?

Just the reverse. A rather poor-looking supper, with Don Giovanni, Leporello, little table and all, is whisked off to the churchyard. The statue, who hadn't even nodded his acceptance, stays motionless in his niche; the libertine's hand never feels the icy grip . . . Thus by one of those masterly strokes so frequent on the modern stage, two of the most thrilling moments in opera are sabotaged. What is the use of Mozart's shuddering drop from E major to C major in 'O statua gentilissima' if no supernatural movement has been seen? What is the point of all that build-up of tension in the final scene – first Elvira's scream, then Leporello's account of 'the man of stone, the white man' and his terrible tread ('ta, ta, ta, ta!') – if the statue hasn't budged an inch?

With thirteen years of hindsight to help me, it is now obvious that Enriquez was well ahead of his time. The whole action was taking place in the statue's mind.

As a final lunatic touch to the 1967 *Don Giovanni*, the BBC televised it, cutting the overture altogether – from *Don Giovanni*, of all operas! One imagines the Corporation must have known what it was doing. Nobody else did. Even the telly-show-biz reporters noticed it and complained.

1968

One of the most flattering, but frustrating, compliments constantly paid to Glyndebourne is the invitation to take its productions to other people's festivals. It is flattering because the invitations are extended in the belief that Glyndebourne's ensemble and artistic standards can have been achieved only by a permanent company performing together for months on end. It is frustrating because Glyndebourne has never had anything but an *ad hoc* company existing for one short season only, and so nearly always has to turn down attractive offers to perform in places like Athens, Seattle, New York (to open Lincoln Center), Paris (for the fiftieth anniversary of the Théâtre des Champs-Élysées), and Versailles, to open the 'Mai de Versailles' with *L'Ormindo*.

After the 1967 season, however, the circumstances, dates, artists and economics of an invitation had added up favourably: the Festival Opera made its first real foreign tour in Denmark, Norway and Sweden. (The visits to Berlin in 1954 and Paris in 1958 were limited seasons at one theatre in each city.) Two operas were taken – *Il matrimonio segreto*, with the same six Italian singers as in 1965, and *Don Giovanni*, with Luisa Bosabalien from Lebanon for Zylis-Gara in the otherwise intact cosmopolitan cast recently heard in Sussex. In nineteen days one performance of each opera was given at Gothenberg, and two of each at Oslo, Drottningholm and Copenhagen.

The tour was an enormous success in every way and neither Press nor audiences forgot that Glyndebourne had been started by a conductor with a long and close association with the Scandinavian countries. The *Svenska Dagbladet* headed its review with the words: ' "Don Giovanni" in the Spirit of Fritz Busch.'

After the Scandinavian tour, in the March and April before the start of the 1968 Festival, what was originally called the Glyndebourne Touring 'Group' and was now mercifully renamed the Glyndebourne Touring Opera, went on the road for the first time. The Arts Council had at last supplied some of the money still needed after the Gulbenkian Foundation and businessmen in the provinces had dug into their pockets – the first important grant from what John Christie always called contemptuously the 'State jellyfish'.

The touring company was formed simply because it would have been a terrible waste not to have done so. For years its understudies had provided Glyndebourne with more talent than it could ever use. This was frustrating enough both for the understudy and Glyndebourne, which saw its young discoveries, encouraged and trained to its own standards, constantly moving on after their apprenticeship to Covent Garden and Sadler's Wells, without a word of credit given to Glyndebourne for its part in their success. The formation of the Touring Opera at last enabled the understudies to appear under normal conditions instead of in the occasional emergency.

The first tour took *The Magic Flute*, *L'elisir d'amore*, *Don Giovanni* and *L'Ormindo* to Newcastle (the local Northern Sinfonia was appointed the company's orchestra), Liverpool, Manchester, Sheffield and Oxford. The operas were sung in their original languages, of course, and staged, as far as local theatre conditions would permit, with the scenery, costumes and production as at Glyndebourne. The immediate responsibility for running the Touring Opera was divided among three of the Glyndebourne staff: Myer Fredman had top billing as Musical Director; Brian Dickie, former assistant to Jani Strasser, was Administrator (he had recently also been made Director of the Wexford Festival); Geoffrey Gilbertson, general stage manager of the Festival Opera, was the Manager.

At Glyndebourne the 1968 Festival opened with Tchaikovsky's *Eugene Onegin*, sung in Russian. The title, to help the audience's pronunciation, was referred to in the publicity and the programme by an approximate phonetic equivalent of the Russian: 'Yevgeny Onyegin'. The orchestra, however, was not fooled by this. It recognized the waltz immediately and, in accordance with the custom of generations, continued to call it 'Eugene, One Gin'.

Originally Michael Redgrave was to have produced *Onegin* but he found himself too committed elsewhere. Instead, it was staged by Michael Hadjimischev, from the Sofia Opera, who spoke Russian and had spent much of his youth in London, where his father was Bulgarian Minister (Bulgaria did not then rate an ambassador).

Inevitably, Glyndebourne's tradition of singing opera in its original language was criticized when a Russian opera was sung in Russian with a non-Russian cast. It took an American critic, Henry Pleasants, to point out that the attitude taken by London critics seemed odd 'when one thinks of all the operas given in Italian without Italians, in German without Germans, and in French without French'. Russian words or not, the audience certainly had little to complain about, for it heard a superlative performance as Tatiana by the half-Russian, half-Swedish Elisabeth Söderström. (The rest of the cast included two Bulgarian, a Polish, a Swiss, an Austrian, a Finnish, and three English singers.) The production had great charm and atmosphere, much of it coming from the imaginative use of sepias and greys in Pier Luigi Pizzi's naturalistic sets.

Among those making their first appearances in this country, Assem Selimsky made a rather wooden figure of Onegin; Virginia Popova was a comfortable old nurse with that comfortable old wobble that is apparently endemic among Slavonic women singers. Wieslaw Ochman, the Polish tenor, was a sympathetic Lensky, particularly good in the soft opening phrases of the lovely finale of Act II, scene 1. He returned to Glyndebourne in 1969 to sing Mozart, and in 1970 for more Mozart and the revival of *Onegin*.

The two neatest performances, however, came from singers with no Slav blood in them. Hugues Cuenod's brilliant little study of Monsieur Triquet, the French tutor, was one; the other was the Larina of Pamela Bowden, whose agent recommended her for an entirely novel qualification – namely, that she had a Russian *au pair* girl.

The introduction of *Eugene Onegin* into the Glyndebourne repertoire was an adventurous experiment altogether; it came off splendidly, and left no doubt of the quality of Tchaikovsky's lyrical masterpiece.

The first revival of Mozart's *Entführung* since 1961 was given in a new production in 1968 by Enriquez and Luzzati. Their *Magic Flute* had been a delight, their *Don Giovanni* a little eccentric. Their new excursion into Mozart came somewhere between the two – charming and exasperating. I often wonder if producers realize what damage they do to one's memory of a whole production by a single ill-conceived gimmick. My recollection of Enriquez's *Entführung* is dominated, to the exclusion of almost everything else, by a trick of idiotic irrelevance that started Act II. This was a pair of intricate mechanical toy figures, constructed by Annabelle Hawtrey, representing one turbaned figure beheading another, to the sound of a recording of a Mozart piece for mechanical organ.

What remain in the memory of the performance itself are the Constanze of Margaret Price, whose acting Desmond Shawe-Taylor called 'elementary' but whose singing he regarded as 'brilliant, flexible and large-scale', and the first big part at Glyndebourne by Ryland Davies (like Miss Price, born in Monmouthshire), whose Belmonte was described by *The Times* as 'admirable' and commended for his Act III duet with Constanze and his duettino with Pedrillo in Act I, which 'were some of the major musical delights of the performance'. But the choice for Osmin of Paolo Montarsolo, a non-German-speaking Italian without the low notes which are the essence of this unique part, proved an odd bit of casting. Montarsolo was altogether too amiable and lacking in the comical frustration that gives the role its flavour and variety. A second Osmin, the Bulgarian, Dimiter Petkov, did no better, and for much the same reasons.

The two revivals of the season were *L'Ormindo* and *Anna Bolena*. In the first there was one important change from the original cast of 1967. Hanneke van Bork, a young Dutch soprano, supplanted Irmgard Stadler, who was ill, as Sicle. In the second, the indisposed Leyla Gencer had to cancel the five performances she had contracted to sing, and her place was taken by Milla Andrew, who had been due to sing the last seven performances and now sang all twelve. Which is how it happened that, with the exception of Marius Rintzler, the Rumanian bass, as Henry VIII, the whole of the 1968 *Anna Bolena* cast was English-speaking. Milla Andrew was Canadian, Patricia Johnson and Janet Coster (both in the original production) were English as was Stafford Dean, who sang Rochefort; George Shirley, the Percy, was American, and Hervey was sung by Peter Baillie from New Zealand.

The conductor was Italian. Gardelli restored many of the passages cut by Gavazzeni in 1965 – including the overture (whose quality, you will remember, a critical *analphabète* could not judge without hearing), which sounded just as trivial and tedious as Shawe-Taylor had said it would. When asked why he had put it back, Mr Gardelli replied: 'Because Donizetti wrote it.' An unanswerable answer, of course. But it didn't improve one's opinion of Donizetti.

1969

This was to have been Berlioz Year, commemorating the centenary of his birth by a production of *Beatrice and Benedict*. That it did not materialize was not surprising; it has always been a problem opera. It is in two short acts, which do not properly fill an evening, and most curtain-raisers involve a second cast and are, therefore, costly. There was, above all, the problem of finding a cast of singers capable of speaking the dialogue in a French less horrifying than the sort spoken in the 1978 *Carmen* at Edinburgh.

That singing French was an easier matter for foreigners than speaking it was shown by the cosmopolitan casting of the two French operas that shared the 1969 season with two by Mozart. *Werther* opened the Festival with a new Charlotte, sung by Josephine Veasey, an experienced and popular Glyndebourne artist since her 1957 début in *L'italiana in Algeri*. The new Sophie was the young Canadian, Annon Lee Silver, and Schmidt was sung by the francophone Hugues Cuenod.

The revival of *Pelléas et Mélisande* should have been directed by Denise Duval, who had been Glyndebourne's unforgettable first two Mélisandes, but she was not well enough. Instead, the opera was produced (still with the Montresor décor) by Pierre Médecin, a member of the famous Nice family whose distinguished part in the civic life of the city led to the Avenue de la Victoire, formerly the Avenue de la Gare, being recently renamed the Avenue J. Médecin.

Duval's successor as Mélisande was Ileana Cotrubas, an attractive Rumanian from Frankfurt, making her British début at the beginning of an international career that has so far (1980) allowed her to sing at Glyndebourne too seldom for the audience's taste. In the last four of nine performances of the 1969 *Pelléas*, Mélisande was sung by Jill Gomez in her first principal role at Glyndebourne, which she came to after joining the chorus in 1966 and singing Adina in *L'elisir d'amore* on the first tour in 1968.

With the two new Mélisandes, two new Genevièves (Jocelyne Taillon and Margaret Lensky), a new Golaud (the excellent Jacques Mars) and a new Yniold (Anne-Marie Blanzat), there was also a new Pelléas: Peter-Christoph Runge, the young German who left pleasanter memories than either his predecessors or successors in the part at Glyndebourne. The only member of the original 1962-3 casts who returned for this *Pelléas* was Guus Hoekman, the Dutch bass, whose recommendation for the part of Arkel had originally come from Pierre Fournier, the great French cellist. Or so the Glyndebourne files said. In fact, it turned out to have been the French conductor, Jean Fournet; distortion can occur in the best-kept archives.

John Pritchard, now described simply as Musical Director, conducted *Pelléas* for the first time and sent Gui a touching cable: 'On the occasion of the restoration of Pelléas to Glyndebourne Festival repertoire, we all send affectionate greetings with remembrances of its unforgettable impact under your direction.' Pritchard didn't let his master down.

While Gui returned to the Festival after his two famous *Pelléas* series, Debussy's opera was Carl Ebert's definite farewell to Glyndebourne as a producer. June Dandridge, who joined Glyndebourne as a stage manager in Busch's last season, 1951, and since 1956 has been Production Manager (except that until 1960 it was called Stage Director), had exceptional experience of Ebert at work. Whatever his faults, she said, he was one of the greatest of all producers: 'He had good taste (insofar as his German sense of humour allowed), *and he knew the music.* He was an actor and understood actors' problems, he was a musician and understood singers' problems. And he *rarely* misunderstood a composer's intention.'

Understanding the composer's intention was precisely what Jani Strasser had in mind when he once defined the difference between 'musical' and 'musicianly' as the difference between the gifted amateur and the competent professional:

The first [he said] enjoys music profoundly, distinguishes by instinct what he likes and dislikes without being able to give precise explanations; he becomes instinctively appreciative of some finer nuances – *when they are presented to him;* he will not be able to discover them otherwise, or from the score/orchestration and so pass them on to others.

A musicianly person can and should do this. I might use the simile of the difference between the student of Italian and the student of Italian literature. The former will be able to understand colloquial Italian, but the purport of Leopardi or Moravia will remain hidden to him, even if he grasps the literal meaning of the words. The latter will be able to explain and interpret the hidden meaning behind the words to the former.

For Strasser, Carl Ebert was 'by far the most musicianly, as distinct from musical producer I have ever known'. (A perfect instance of the 'un-musicianly' approach was seen in a later Glyndebourne production of *The Magic Flute*, when characters frequently left the stage in silence because the music so carefully prescribed for their exit had been allowed to run out. To the musicianly producer, Mozart's codas are stage directions.)

The Enriquez-Luzzati series continued – and, in fact, ended – with a new production of *Così fan tutte*, which will be remembered mostly for the youthful charm of Ryland Davies as Ferrando, his wife Anne Howells as Dorabella and Knut Skram, a young Norwegian making his début at Glyndebourne, as Guglielmo.

Looking back, I have wondered whether the reason *The Magic Flute* was the most satisfying of Enriquez's Mozart productions was that Gui was the conductor and his presence influenced his stepson's understanding of the opera. Unfortunately, Gui conducted none of the other productions, not even the *Così fan tutte*, the Mozart opera he had conducted most often for Glyndebourne.

The revival of *Don Giovanni* as the last opera of the season introduced on his first appearance outside his native country the twenty-seven-year-old Italian bass, Ruggero Raimondi, in the lead. A bass, instead of the baritone demanded by Mozart, tends to unbalance the ensemble, but if Raimondi's beautiful *basso cantante* wasn't the exact voice for the part, he had all the looks and vitality of a young Pinza in the part.

During the season, Southern Television made its first Glyndebourne programme, a sixty-minute documentary, directed by Wendy Toye and called 'A Goodly Manor for a Song . . .', in which the many stages in the production of *Così fan tutte*, from first rehearsal to first night were shown, including the building and painting of scenery, the making of wigs and costumes. We saw *Werther* rehearsals and singers relaxing at the local pub after work; and, dominating the preparation of both operas, the busy figure of Jani Strasser.

1970

The 1970 five-opera programme included three novelties: Cavalli's *La Calisto*, which had not been performed anywhere since its first production in Venice in 1651; Rossini's *Il turco in Italia*, gradually coming back into circulation after a century's neglect; and the world première of *The Rising of the Moon*, by Nicholas Maw (b. 1935), commissioned by Glyndebourne.

The Cavalli, arranged by Raymond Leppard, and produced by Peter Hall with designs by John Bury, proved to be an enchanting evening's entertainment, with a first-rate cast, imaginative use of machines and an atmosphere of baroque fantasy, extravagance and sheer magic, created by original, twentieth-century means without resort to the theatrical equivalent of reproduction furniture to suggest a seventeenth-century Venetian spectacle.

Janet Baker, who had not sung at Glyndebourne since her Dido in Purcell's opera in 1966, had a magnificent part as Diana, in which she appeared as the goddess, and as her father, Jove, disguised as the goddess, the one a lyrical role, touching and sad in the scenes with Endymion (a counter-tenor part beautifully sung by James Bowman), the other a thoroughly ambiguous comic part, which Miss Baker played expertly.

In the title role Ileana Cotrubas was thought by some to have suggested too much of the 'lost and dispirited Mélisande' in her performance; but then Calisto had a rather bewildering time, what with the way Jove treated her when he was disguised as Diana, and Juno turning her into a bear. The closing scene of the opera, where Calisto is taken up to heaven by Jove and transformed into the constellation Ursa Minor, had great pathos; but being a true baroque opera *Calisto* also had its fair Shakespearian share of bawdy comedy. There were thirteen strongly contrasted principal characters, all carefully drawn by Cavalli, and each of them a part worth singing. Hugues Cuenod, *en travesti* as the elderly nymph Linfea, inevitably brought the house down, and there were memorable performances by Ugo Trama as Jove, Peter Gottlieb as Mercury, Federico Davià as Pan and Janet Hughes as the mischievous little satyr. (After the run of *Calisto*, Cotrubas sang Pamina exquisitely in the last seven performances of the revived *Magic Flute*.)

For some reason, which nobody satisfactorily explained, Rossini's *Turco in Italia*, like the earlier *Italiana in Algeri* in 1957, just did not appeal to the Glyndebourne audience. If one did not know how successful the *Barber of Seville*, *Cenerentola* and *Comte Ory* had been, one might suspect that perhaps the audience no longer cared for Rossini unless it was 'processed' in Germany. As it was, the Glyndebourne version of the *Turco*, elegantly conducted by John Pritchard, was commendably correct (with fewer cuts than had been made by the Piccola Scala at the 1957 Edinburgh Festival), but in spi.e of the favourable reception given to the two Fiorillas (Graziella Sciutti, back at Glyndebourne for the first time since 1959, and Sheila Armstrong), the singing generally lacked distinction. The production was described variously as 'busy', 'fussy', 'fidgety, and often slapstick' and many found Luzzati's now too-familiar scenic mannerisms not only inappropriate but tiresome.

The third novelty of 1970 was a couple of years late reaching Glyndebourne because its composer, Nicholas Maw, had been held up by illness. Like any other composer, Maw had also had trouble finding a libretto. After considering the idea of 'originals' by Peter Shaffer, Anthony Burgess, N. F. Simpson and others, he thought of Pirandello's *Henry IV*, Cocteau's *The Eagle has Two Heads* and – most enthusiastically of all – Ingmar Bergman's *Smiles on a Summer Night*. Bergman, however, refused permission, without explaining that the musical rights had been granted to Stephen Sondheim who turned it into *A Little Night Music*. Finally, at the suggestion of Colin Graham (who was to stage the finished opera), Maw contacted Beverley Cross, who came up with the book of *The Rising of the Moon*.

At least one Irishman, hearing the title of the work, thought it must be based on the comedy of the same name by Lady Gregory, Desmond Shawe-Taylor's famous Aunt Augusta, but it proved to be nothing of the kind, though the subject of this 'operatic comedy' was Irish enough. It was a brilliant libretto, classical in its strict observance of the Aristotelian unities, witty, with moving and melancholy moments, and making the most of a genuinely comic situation that might have been invented by Boccaccio.

Musically, apart from a good rowdy English regimental chorus, the most memorable passages were lyrical, particularly a lullaby sung by Anne Howells in Act II. The work's principal fault was technical – the constant smothering of words by the orchestra too often playing at the wrong time. If the composer had looked at *Falstaff* first he would have noted that Verdi pointed his comic lines against a *sotto voce* orchestral background, or very often none at all, leaving the orchestra to make its comment before or after the line, never during it. Nicholas Maw toned down some of his orchestral boisterousness and the opera was revived in the same admirable production by Colin Graham in 1971.

Why the work has not been heard much more frequently since then, I do not know. It has been suggested that it's because it shows the English (the word 'British' is not in the libretto) in a bad light; but as the bad light was thrown by two *English* collaborators in an *English* comic opera, this hardly seems a good reason for ostracizing an entertaining piece of musical theatre. Or is caricature a form of bad-light shedding? The Victorian English officers looked and behaved like figures straight out of a cartoon by Osbert Lancaster (not surprisingly, since he did the décor), and I would have thought only the most naïve audience could really take their antics seriously.

However, as the Cross and Maw opera was to the taste of the Glyndebourne public, there should really be nothing to prevent the Welsh or Scottish National, and certainly not Australian or American, opera audiences also enjoying it, since all of them have relished seeing the English in a bad light for centuries.

1971

The popularity of *Eugene Onegin* encouraged Glyndebourne to perform Tchaikovsky's *Queen of Spades* in 1971 and, what's more, officially call it that and not *Pique-Dame* (which would probably have identified the work more readily to a whole older generation, which, for some reason, had never known it by any other name). Thus, this time we were spared the struggle of trying to introduce the Russian title into casual conversation and refer to 'Pikovaya Dama'. This was left to the singers since, of course, the opera was sung in Russian – by a cast of five Bulgarians, one Pole, one Frenchman, eight English and an Australian.

Compared with *Onegin*, the opera (also staged by Hadjimischev and Pizzi) proved to be a patchy experience – some of it the composer's fault, some of it the producer's, some of it the performers'. The performance was somehow never gripping; it lacked character and the dramatic tension essential to an opera with more than a touch of Grand Guignol about it. The most satisfying performances came from two Bulgarians in comparatively minor parts – Reni Penkova as Pauline, and the baritone, Pavel Guerdjikov, as Tomsky. Penkova was described by the critics as 'a joy throughout to look at and hear', 'charming and vivacious', 'vivacious and charming'; and evidently Glyndebourne agreed, for she was signed up to sing again for three more seasons, starting in 1975. (Where the admirable Guerdjikov disappeared to, I have no idea. There has been no mention of his singing anywhere at all that I can find in any of the comprehensive annual indexes to *Opera* magazine since 1971).

The Polish soprano, Teresa Kubiak, made her English début as Lisa with a beautiful voice but, like so many singers from behind the Iron Curtain, spoiled her performance by the exaggerated gestures and 'emoting' of silent films. Maurice Maievsky, French, but with a surname that was perhaps one good reason why he was a most impressive Hermann, sang 11·142 performances of the twelve he was due to sing; the one-seventh occurred on 24 June, when he was taken ill at the end of Act I, scene 1. While everybody was getting the understudy ready there was no way of telling the conductor what had happened, but John Pritchard took it so much in his stride that when a completely different Hermann appeared on Lisa's balcony in scene 2, there was no hint of a double-take. It was a moment worthy of *A Night at the Opera*.

The Tchaikovsky opera was the only novelty of the 1971 season, although a new production by John Cox of Richard Strauss's *Ariadne auf Naxos*, designed by Michael Annals, had a strikingly novel look to it. The scene of the Prologue, instead of being set back-stage of the rich man's private theatre, was set under its stage, among all the pulleys, capstans, wheels, ropes and other machinery found under an eighteenth-century stage. (The scene was taken from life, as it were, for the model was the Swedish court theatre at Drottningholm.) Except for a Swedish Bacchus (Helge Brilioth), a brilliant Hungarian Zerbinetta (Sylvia Geszty) and a warm, sympathetic American Ariadne (Helen Vanni), the other sixteen singers shown in the programme were either Canadian, Scots, Irish or English, with the four comedians – John Gibbs, Maurice Arthur, John Fryatt and Dennis Wicks – quite exceptional.

The Austrian Irmgard Stadler had to cancel all her Glyndebourne appearances because of illness, and her part as the Composer was taken by Anne Howells, a mezzo-soprano in a soprano part. Jani Strasser, who had retired from Glyndebourne at the end of 1970, had warned as recently as December 1969 that neither Miss Howells nor a Miss M. 'at this stage . . . has the right top for this part . . . But that may yet come.' It didn't, and Anne Howells was the first to admit that she wasn't right, which was a pity for she is a fine actress and had all the natural charm and youthful eagerness for the character.

Back in her old role as Cathleen in *The Rising of the Moon* (sharing the part with Delia Wallis), Anne Howells joined a cast that must have been relieved to find that Nicholas Maw had cut down some of his heavy orchestration since the previous season's production, and a lot more singers (and Beverley Cross's words) were now audible as a result.

Irmgard Stadler's absence also meant that she could not repeat her role of Juno in *Calisto*, although her name appeared in the programme (as it did in the cast of *Ariadne*). In her place the part was sung by Teresa Kubiak who, by the time she came to sing in the season's last production and obviously under the influence of Peter Hall, had learned not to overact as she had done as Lisa. It was now said by the critics that she 'looked superb and sang with real fire'.

In the revival of *Calisto* most of the original principals returned, and the opera was as enjoyable and beautifully sung as before. This time John Bury was credited with the lighting as well as with the designs.

1972

Three outstanding events occurred at Glyndebourne in 1972: the performance of Monteverdi's *Il ritorno d'Ulisse in patria*, the first engagement there of Bernard Haitink as conductor and an agreement with Southern Television to make regular recordings at Glyndebourne, including all Mozart productions. There was a fourth, less noticeable event: the introduction of a practice of dividing the number of performances of some operas into a 'Series I' and a 'Series II'. The programme showed that some singers appeared exclusively throughout one series, some singers exclusively throughout the other; that one singer would appear in the entire first series plus the first performance of the second, while another would sing the same part in the second series minus that one performance sung by his predecessor. Then there was the occasional singer who sang on only three evenings altogether, once in the first series and twice in the second. Finally, there would be a majority – as in the case of the opening production of *Ariadne* – who sang every one of the seventeen performances.

Trying to sort it all out was rather like reading a timetable, with the usual asterisks telling you when to change at East Croydon.

The first series of *Ariadne* introduced Gloria Lane as Ariadne and Maurice Maievsky as Bacchus, both singing their parts at Glyndebourne for the first time, like Irmgard Stadler who, we know, should have sung the Composer in 1971. Sylvia Geszty returned as Zerbinetta, but sang only the first four performances before devoting herself to Constanze in *Die Entführung*; Patricia Wise, a welcome American débutante, then took over Zerbinetta for the rest of the run.

The four *buffo* characters, the nymphs and the supporting cast of the Prologue all sang in every performance, in the first series under Myer Fredman and the second under Aldo Ceccato (who, *Opera* magazine considered, 'could not match Fredman's eloquence in the pit'). The second series, which was as well received as the first, had Helen Vanni back as Ariadne, with Delia Wallis as the Composer.

Meanwhile, alternating with *Ariadne* in the first weeks of the season, there was Peter Hall's superb production of Monteverdi's *Il ritorno d'Ulisse in patria*, the opera designed by John Bury and, as with Glyndebourne's other seventeenth-century Italian operas, the music arranged by Raymond Leppard, although this time Leppard's 'realization' entailed several pieces of restoration work in the form of music adapted from other Monteverdi sources inserted to fill gaps in the score left by original passages and scenes that had long been lost. As usual, Leppard's skill in reproducing much of the spirit of Monteverdi's music and less of the letter, pleased the public and annoyed the pedants.

Compared with his *Calisto*, which is a fairy story, John Bury's own brand of modern baroque was less decorative and less deliberately extravagant in *Ulisse*. Frills and fancy plumes gave way to shining armour and shields (with comparatively modest plumes on the helmets), and – a brilliant touch – Penelope's suitors and their hangers-on were dressed in the rich and colourful costumes of an Italian Renaissance painting. The machinery, on the other hand, was more elaborate and more impressively used than in *Calisto*, and it was not surprising to learn that 'some special effects' were the work of that same Kirby's Flying Ballet who created so much of the magic of *Peter Pan* in our childhood.

Peter Hall's unique contribution was his rare gift of restraint, allowing the music to speak for itself and so, by its very understatement, make its dramatic points often unbearably powerful and affecting. In this way I find my own memory of his productions over the years at Glyndebourne has always been musical. With *Ulisse* this memory was particularly vivid, for Janet Baker's Penelope revealed all the dignity, resolution and sadness of a part that Monteverdi, by his musical characterization, made one of the most sympathetic and convincing figures in the history of opera. As Ulysses, Benjamin Luxon, with what one of the critics called 'his burnished baritone voice', was in the same class, missing none of the subtlety of a character of great variety, ranging from the angry cunning of the early scenes to the immensely moving final scene of reunion with Penelope. The whole production, like the music indeed, was rich in well-defined characterizations, among them Anne Howells's most attractive and original conception of Minerva; the sympathetic old shepherd (according to the opera, but a swineherd to Homer and me) of Richard Lewis, singing at Glyndebourne for the first time since 1967; the forceful personality of Ugo Trama, doubling Time and the suitor Antinous; and the amusing panic-stricken glutton, Irus, played by Alexander Oliver, who in 1970 had graduated from the chorus to Monostatos in *The Magic Flute* and Brother Timothy in *The Rising of the Moon*.

The revival of *Die Entführung* was divided into two series, the first conducted by Bernard Haitink, the second by John Pritchard. The first series had Sylvia Geszty and Horst Laubenthal as Constanze and Belmonte, the second Margaret Price and Ryland Davies.

The engagement of Bernard Haitink came as something of a surprise, for he was not a conductor one associated with opera at all, but with such non-operatic composers as Brahms, Bruckner and Mahler. He was born in 1929 and did not conduct an opera until 1963, when, at the Holland Festival, he directed *The Flying Dutchman* (an appropriate enough opera and venue for a Dutch conductor's début). In 1966, again at the Holland Festival, he conducted *Don Carlos*, and then no more opera anywhere until he came to Glyndebourne six years later.

Thus he came to his first Mozart opera as an innocent, uninfluenced by bad traditions or experiences, and was able to approach the opera as though he were giving its first performance. Which is how it sounded – new, fresh and spontaneous, and described by *Opera* as a 'full-bodied, full-blooded interpretation based on perfectly judged tempos, refinement of detail and taut rhythms . . .'

Southern Television recorded both *Die Entführung* and the last opera in the programme, *Macbeth*, and in so doing David Heather, the director, and Humphrey Burton, the producer (who returned to the BBC in 1974), settled down at once to create a style and atmosphere of their own, by taking the viewer inside the opera house to join the audience in seeing, and almost smelling, a theatrical performance of which the television camera was the servant, occasionally the interpreter, but never the boss, of the show.

When, six years later, the BBC made what Clive James in the *Observer* called 'an assault' on *Macbeth*, he attacked the production as 'an example of how not to do it – i.e., re-create the work in "television terms".' Southern's Glyndebourne broadcasts, he reminded us, had the secret of good television opera: 'Find a good stage production and point a camera at it.' Certainly, over the years critics have come to regard Dave Heather's way as the most satisfying yet, combining the clarity of studio production with the feel and excitement of a real theatrical performance.

PS Richard Van Allan, winner of a John Christie award, appeared in two roles this season – both speaking parts. As a critic remarked, had Glyndebourne forgotten he could sing?

1973

This was the year of Peter Hall's first Mozart opera at Glyndebourne. His way with Cavalli and Monteverdi had been so successful and stimulating that for most people his *Figaro* was the most eagerly looked-forward-to event at Glyndebourne for many years. I don't think anybody was disappointed. Certainly for me, in all the fifty-five years I had known the opera, this was the production I had most enjoyed. It was also the first textually complete performances I had ever heard, for it has always been Hall's practice to make no cuts, least of all in the recitatives. In this way, many subtle points in the text which had been obscure now became clear. Not only were the recitatives complete, but they were sung, as they should be, in imitation of the fluctuations of speed and expression of natural conversation; they were no longer just gabbled in order to get on with the next number as quickly as possible.

The arias for Basilio and Marcellina in Act IV were both included (Marcellina's, I believe, for the first time at Glyndebourne); and so was the revised order of the scenes at the start of Act III, first commended to public notice in an article by Christopher Raeburn and R. B. Moberly in 1965. The adoption of this order has become increasingly common both in the theatre and recording studio, for by placing her aria 'Dove sono . . .' (No 19) *before* the sextet (No 18), the Countess's recitative beginning 'Susanna, not here? . . .' doesn't occur (as it does otherwise) when she has only just given Susanna the money to pay off Marcellina. Not only is the revised form more logical, but by shortening the interval between the Count's aria (No 17) and the Countess's, the emotional contrast between the arrogant jealousy of the one and the heart-breaking sadness of the other is even more emphatic. (The source of all this was the realization by Raeburn and Moberly that in the original production of *Figaro* the parts of Bartolo and Antonio, the gardener, were doubled by one singer, and that unless the sextet had been put earlier, Bartolo would never have had time to change and appear as Antonio with the Count in the short scene before the Letter Duet. Now that doubling of this kind is not practised – and certainly not encouraged by trades unions – the situation does not arise, of course. But 180-odd years still seems a long time to have taken to put it right.)

With Peter Hall's production, *Figaro* was at last all present and correct, a state of affairs Hall insisted on in his staging, in chronological order, of Mozart's three Da Ponte operas between 1973 and 1978. He went back to the original libretto so that he could eliminate the mass of stage directions that had grown like barnacles on the fabric of the numberless subsequent editions of the libretto, vocal and full scores. 'Tradition', especially the 'buffo tradition' (which the producer is not alone in thinking a most tiresome feature of so many comic opera performances), was jettisoned, and the comedy came where the *music* demanded it. The stress throughout was on what has been described as the unique quality of this opera – the shadows of human sadness cast by the sunlight of comedy.

Nobody played for laughs, any more than they played for tears. As much as anything this was the result of unusually close co-operation between producer and conductor, with Peter Hall constantly consulting John Pritchard about what was or was not implied by Mozart's music.

John Bury's sets were realistically solid to suit what Hall described as 'the first absolutely realistic opera'; the Almavivas' house was not a rococo museum but, in spite of being called a Palazzo, a thoroughly lived-in unostentatious villa. The Count did not hire a corps of professional dancers to entertain the wedding guests in Act III. The fandango was danced by the guests themselves, that is, the chorus of peasant girls and youths of the estate.

The cast was exceptionally good, and I'm not certain that, in the tradition that 'all Glyndebourne Cherubinos are good', the young American, Frederica von Stade, was not the best of them all – irresistible as the eager, amorous adolescent (as the Countess clearly showed), and infinitely touching in the lonely, rather tearful exit at the end of Act I, where, for a change, attention was focused on Cherubino's silent reaction to 'Non più andrai' instead of on Figaro's singing.

The part of the Countess was shared by Elizabeth Harwood and (making her Glyndebourne début) Kiri Te Kanawa – both of them lovely to look at and exquisite to hear. Their Count was Benjamin Luxon, unexpectedly a little gruff and lacking in elegance, but this served only to stress the dignity and nobility of the unhappy Countess. Ileana Cotrubas's Susanna and Knut Skram's Figaro were real, lively characterizations–a Susanna who was clearly the brains behind everything, and a Figaro who was young, agile and, in his brief hair-raising moment of confrontation with the Count (an unforgettable shot in close-up in the Southern Television recording of the production), a dangerous man to have as an enemy.

One quite brilliant performance was John Fryatt as Don Basilio, relishing every new development in the story and faultless in his timing – or, more precisely, in his timing of Mozart's timing – of his ecstatic 'Better and better!' at the Count's discovery in Act I of Cherubino hiding in the chair.

John Pritchard's contribution to this remarkable *Figaro* was evident in every bar of the music: for the first time in too many years he was conducting a work he knew intimately as though he was giving its first performance *every* night. His *Figaros*, *Don Giovannis* and *Così fan tuttes* had sometimes tended to sound a little routine and uncommitted, in spite of the excellence of the London Philharmonic Orchestra.

The two-series system was adopted in casting *The Magic Flute* this time, with only the Queen of the Night and Papagena singing in all eighteen performances. The first series was notable for the memorable first appearance as a principal at Glyndebourne of Thomas Allen as Papageno, Sheila Armstrong's first and charming Pamina and Bernard Haitink's first *Flute*. Allen was something of a Glyndebourne product, having studied with Hervey Alan (a regular Glyndebourne principal from 1949 to 1960) before joining the chorus in 1968. His Papageno was enchanting, his German good, and it was clear that he would develop into the fine acting-singer he soon became, with his warm, virile voice, excellent diction and strong stage presence. It was a good year for Papagenos, for the second series was sung by Peter-Christoph Runge.

The Magic Flute opened the season and was followed the next night by a complete novelty, an operatic version of Friedrich Dürenmatt's play, which was known in England as *The Visit* and in German as *Der Besuch der alten Dame*, but when set to music by the Austrian Gottfried von Einem (b. 1918) and translated into English, was known by the literal translation of the play's original German title, *The Visit of the Old Lady*. Long before the end of the evening I must admit I was wishing I had seen the Lunts' famous performance of the play in London instead, and that if it had to be an opera (which didn't seem necessary), the music had been by Kurt Weill, which would at least have had some tunes and some fun in it.

As it was, the opera was clearly not one that travelled. The Glyndebourne production was technically of a high standard – a real Ford motor car on the stage, a shop with life-size bottles of gin and packets of cigarettes and detergents on the shelves. There was also a train that roared through a station and a revolving stage used for characters to walk on (and so stay in one place while the background moved). Indeed, but for the absence of a real vacuum cleaner, a radio loudspeaker and a railway engine to come down stage and kill a violinist, it was all rather like seeing Křenek's *Jonny Spielt Auf* in Berlin in 1928 all over again.

Einem's score proved peculiarly faceless, making appropriate dramatic noises at appropriate dramatic moments, like film music. It was the composer's idea that the opera should be sung in English.

Richard Strauss's *Capriccio*, last heard in 1964, was revived in a completely transformed, overhauled and highly original production by John Cox, conducted by John Pritchard. The action was still set in the Countess's eighteenth-century house, but it took place in the 1920s, with contemporary furniture, costumes, manners, props and, on the walls, some witty paintings in imitation of Picasso, Braque, Marie Laurencin and others, which, like the elegantly designed, attractive 'period' dresses for the women, were done by Martin Battersby.

Most of the anomalies and anachronisms likely to occur in the text because of the up-dating of the action were avoided by simply changing the words, while the eighteenth-century ballet at the start of Act II was turned by Pauline Grant into an hilarious *pas de deux*. The cast was full of first-rate singers who could act, and so made sure that what John Cox set out to do was done brilliantly.

Il ritorno d'Ulisse in patria, 1979: Frederica von Stade, Richard Stilwell. *(Gravett)*

(left) Die Entführung aus dem Serail,
1980: Valerie Masterson (Constanze).
Designer, William Dudley. *(Gravett)*

(below) Der Rosenkavalier, 1980, Act II.
Designer, Erté. *(Gravett)*

The last three performances were directed by Andrew Davis, a young conductor not only making his Glyndebourne début, but in fact conducting an opera for the first time in his life. He did so with unusual authority and confidence and an instinctive sense of style that has served Glyndebourne well.

1974

This was the year when, for the first time in its history, the Glyndebourne programme did not give the nationalities of the singers in the cast lists but only under their pictures in the 'Photographs of Artists' section (known irreverently as the Rogues' Gallery). This, at least, was better than Rudolf Bing's suggestion in 1937, which John Christie flatly rejected, of abolishing *all* mention of nationalities; but the continuation of this new practice means that one can no longer take in the cosmopolitan character of the evening's cast at a glance.

The season opened with a revival of *Calisto*, as enchanting and colourful as before, but with two important changes of cast: Diana was sung by Anne Howells and Calisto by Barbara Hendricks, both of whom developed individual and charming character-izations, and compared well with their predecessors in the parts. There were three other changes: the first was Ugo Trama's doubling Jove and Pan; the second was the sub-stitution of John Fryatt, a tenor, for the baritone Peter Gottlieb as the crafty, cynical Mercury; the third was the first appearance on any stage of Louise, the eight-year-old daughter of George and Mary Christie, heavily disguised as the little bear that Calisto is turned into.

The revival of *Idomeneo*, last heard in 1964, now in a new production by John Cox, designed by Roger Butlin, was given with two sets of principals, of which the second set was by far the more successful. Series II introduced a pretty young Pole, Bozena Betley, to Glyndebourne where she has sung Mozart ever since; it also brought back Richard Lewis in the title role, which he had first sung in 1951 – almost before Miss Betley was born. When he returned for the second series, Richard Lewis was sixty years old.

Musically this *Idomeneo* was more nearly complete than it had been before. Several lovely arias, usually cut, were restored, adding to the riches of this fascinating score.

The hope that two new Mozart productions in consecutive seasons might lead to a more liberal restoration of appoggiaturas (see pp. 64-6) was unfortunately not realized. One or two crept into the recitatives of *Figaro* and one into Cherubino's first aria in the opera. (Frederica von Stade had sung two in the same aria broadcast from a Versailles production a month or so earlier.) *Idomeneo* fared a little better; in addition to quite a few appoggiaturas, John Pritchard, who had conducted every one of the five revivals of the opera in Fritz Busch's rather austere manner since 1952, actually encouraged little cadenza-like flourishes where pauses occur in arias for good musical, and not non-existent dramatic, reasons.

But though the example of *Idomeneo* was heartening, Glyndebourne still tends to regard Mozart's appoggiaturas with puritanical suspicion, as though they were a form of harlotry. When they *have* been heard it has all been rather like an elderly spinster dabbing on a little rouge and lipstick in a daring attempt to be in the fashion. It still doesn't come naturally.

The Southern Television recording of *Idomeneo* enabled the home viewer to see more of the action and production generally than the Glyndebourne audience, who had found some of the sight-lines of the scenery, with its steel hoops, pretty frustrating. The recording was made with the second cast, in which Josephine Barstow was gripping as Electra.

The idea of doing Richard Strauss's autobiographical *Intermezzo* at Glyndebourne was once put forward by Rudolf Bing before the war. Fritz Busch, who had conducted its world première at Dresden in 1924, rejected it firmly. He found the exhibitionism of its subject embarrassing. This was easy to understand (and I am surprised that Bing didn't find it so); for those of us who were around in Vienna when Strauss was co-director of the Opera and his wife was frequently seen at the theatre, the opera and its composer's libretto were a tasteless exercise. This opinion seems to have been shared widely in Germany and Austria during Strauss's lifetime. Since his death it seems there have been fewer people who feel strongly on the matter; though still not an international success, it has shown that, in Abraham Lincoln's words, people who like this sort of thing will find this the sort of thing they like. The Glyndebourne production was sung in an English translation by Andrew Porter, to make more clearly than ever the points of what its author rightly described as a 'bourgeois comedy'.

Peter Hall's production of *Figaro* was revived with Series-I-and-II casting. The part of Figaro this time was shared by Knut Skram and by Thomas Allen, making yet another advance in his development as a Mozart baritone. As the Count, Michael Devlin, a young American, made an immediately impressive and attractive Glyndebourne début, while Håkan Hagegård (the Count in *Capriccio*, 1973) sang his first Almaviva in Series II. Elizabeth Gale graduated from Barbarina to Susanna and back again during the run, to alternate with Evelyn Mandac, from the Philippines, who was considered by some a rather 'conventional' Susanna by comparison with Ileana Cotrubas, but was, in fact, very likeable, and attractive enough to be re-engaged as the 1975 Despina.

The Dutch conductor who should have directed all eighteen performances, Edo de Waart, had a breakdown in health too late to alter the billing in the programme, and his performances were taken over by John Pritchard, Kenneth Montgomery and Peter Gellhorn.

The day before the 1974 season opened, Southern Television's telerecording of *Figaro* was shown on all channels of the commercial network. The Glasgow *Sunday Mail* (circulation 760,438) headed its review with a five-column heart-cry: SAVE US FROM THESE TELLY SNOBS.

Southern Television had made its mark.

1975

This was the Year of the Slavs – one opera by a Czech, sung in English; one by a Russian, sung in Russian; another by a Russian, composed to an English text. The opening production, *The Cunning Little Vixen* by Janáček, conducted by Raymond Leppard and produced by Jonathan Miller, was an enchanting entertainment, but apparently a little difficult for the Glyndebourne audience, who complained that it contained no tunes (or at least, none they had heard before) and that it was too short for the money. Considering how familiar Janáček's highly personal music is in England, and how popular his operas are there, it was a puzzling reception. It was also sad to reflect that the outstanding performances of Norma Burrowes (the Vixen), Benjamin Luxon (the Forester), and a host of other well-cast characters should have failed to draw full houses.

If there were 'no tunes' in the *Vixen*, the audience didn't seem to mind that *The Rake's Progress* didn't have many either. But then the new production by John Cox of Stravinsky's opera had décor by David Hockney, a painter very much in fashion; and as this was his first essay in opera design, his work was widely publicized both before and after the première (the heading of one review even referred to 'Hockney's "Rake" '). The novelty of the whole occasion, indeed, was such that the quality of the actual performance accompanying the scenery and conducted by Bernard Haitink, tended to get forgotten.

While there was much humour in Mr Hockney's designs, there was nevertheless criticism that somehow the grotesque and evil side of the opera was missing in this production; certainly for people rather slow on the uptake, like me, the scene in Bedlam was a little bewildering. The composer and librettists wrote a scene that was closely based on the horror of Hogarth's picture, and expected it to look like it. With Osbert Lancaster's designs for Ebert's original production in 1953, the madmen included (as instructed) a blind man with a broken fiddle, a crippled soldier, a man with a telescope and three old hags. This time, in full stage lighting, the chorus, dressed in black with a variety of white masks, occupied a kind of egg-box (or jury-box?) which stretched from wall to wall of the set. The figures popped up into view from time to time, sang and popped down again. It was all very symmetrical and clinical, and was, I think, all going on in Tom Rakewell's head (or maybe the producer's). It certainly wasn't in the composer's, because he had also included a minuet in this scene to which he hoped the chorus of lunatics would dance before Tom 'with mocking gestures'. Nobody danced this time; there was no room to.

If visually this *Rake* was not always a help to the music, Bernard Haitink's powerful, uncompromising direction (several critics considered it his most impressive performance since he first started with Glyndebourne) made sure that Stravinsky's score was capable of helping itself. It was a thoroughly idiomatic, dramatically well-judged reading, with a cast in which Leo Goeke's Tom Rakewell stood out, and was superb in the pathos of the last scene. Some thought Donald Gramm as Nick Shadow not as evil as might be expected from the music, but there was little doubt of his position in the drama.

The third Slav opera of 1975 was *Eugene Onegin*, a revival of the seven-year-old, but still highly serviceable, production by Hadjimischev. Nothing about it had dated, least of all its straightforward, gimmickless honesty. Andrew Davis conducted it for the first time and showed a refreshing understanding of the romantic, tortured and seductive quality of Tchaikovsky's music (critics noticed that at last the LPO strings had let their horsehair down and played the tunes with the unashamed lushness and abandon the composer demanded). With Richard Stilwell as Onegin, Ryland Davies as Lensky and a Bulgarian Tatyana, Galia Yoncheva, who was making her début in this country, this was a first-rate musical experience. The Tatyana acted sympathetically and managed to suppress most of the wobbling that plagues Slavonic sopranos. (Has anybody ever explained the technical, physical or ethnic reason for this characteristic?)

In 1975 the first results of a change in fund-raising methods were beginning to be seen at Glyndebourne. During the universal decline of financial conditions over the past few years, George Christie had foreseen that it would be impossible to count any longer on box-office receipts to cover 80 per cent of costs without raising seat-prices to ridiculous heights, so he helped to organize a sub-committee of the Glyndebourne Arts Trust, which was designed to raise money in new ways and from new sources. The object was to encourage sponsorship and other forms of support by industry for new productions, a fund for vital repairs and maintenance, as well as the provision of new seating, a lighting system and rehearsal rooms. A substantial, undisclosed sum, for instance, was quietly, almost anonymously offered by W. D. and H. O. Wills to be spent on repair of the buildings (including those parts of Glyndebourne manor house itself concerned with the opera) and upkeep of the gardens. The sponsors and supporters I have included among the credits of the casts of the operas shown in Appendix D (page 339).

The financial genius behind this money-raising has been Sir Alex Alexander, then of Imperial Foods, a part-Hungarian refugee who first mobilized industry into giving money to Glyndebourne, as his compatriot, the late Sir Nicholas Sekers, had first persuaded them to become Corporate Members and advertise in the programme (see page 178).

Sir Alex (originally suggested by Brian Dickie, and today vice-chairman of the Trust and a director of Glyndebourne Productions) has also found industrial sponsors for the Chorus Scheme. This started in 1976 and concerns not bricks and mortar, but the people whose training and encouragement are essential to the artistic future of Glyndebourne. The scheme, generously sponsored by industry, bridges the gap between the end of a young singer's student days and the start of a career as a recognized soloist – a period of work in highly professional circumstances, during which the singer can develop from chorister and principal's understudy at the Festival, to a principal in the Touring Opera, before returning as a principal to the Festival.

1976

By a sad, ironic coincidence a photograph and short memoir of Vittorio Gui, who had died in October 1975, aged ninety, appeared in the programme facing the page where the synopsis of *Falstaff* began. As Mistress Quickly might have lamented, 'Povero maestro!', for Gui must have spun in his grave (to the tune of Verdi's 'Dies irae') at the self-indulgent display of 'comicity' of Jean-Pierre Ponnelle's production of Verdi's great comedy, which had not been heard at Glyndebourne since the last of Gui's unforgettable performances sixteen years before.

Nearly every critic found some gratuitous anti-musical trick in this new *Falstaff*. The catalogue of theatrical misdemeanours began when, for the first time in living memory (and probably in the history of the opera), we were to hear a Falstaff who could not sing falsetto, and so deprived Verdi of the musical effect he wanted and had so carefully judged. Then, instead of Falstaff's page Robin making the one fourteen-second appearance score and libretto demanded and then going home to mother, he was in and out of the action incessantly, like a puppy, distracting attention.

A member of the Glyndebourne staff advanced an interesting theory: M. Ponnelle was basically a designer who later became a producer as well, and that as a designer he has to give everybody a costume, which means that as a producer he wants everybody in a costume to have something to do, whether their actions help the music or not. This clearly explained a lot; but not why the designer-producer should introduce a character that Boito had carefully left out of his adaptation of *The Merry Wives of Windsor* – Mr Page. Not that the programme told you this; it was just the general buzz around the theatre. To the non-informed member of the audience Mrs Page seemed to be encumbered by a rather bald companion (her father perhaps?) who appeared to be mentally deficient. So the whole affair became even more pointlessly confusing.

M. Ponnelle's indifference to both score and libretto further caused serious damage to the music of what is the nearest Verdi gets to a full-blooded orchestral introduction in the opera. At the start of Act III, scene 1, the producer had Falstaff climb out of the orchestra pit, which represented the Thames; the curtain was already up, instead of rising to reveal him seated outside the Garter Inn, as Boito hoped. Scarcely a note was heard of the introduction (a wonderful, angry crescendo, from *ppp* to *ff*, lasting less than 30 seconds and intended to prepare us for the sight of an angry Falstaff), because the audience applauded through most of it – like a circus audience applauding during the more spectacular tricks of trapeze artists. (John Christie, as I recounted on page 133, was never quite sure whether he wanted people to laugh in his opera house, in case the music couldn't be heard. In that age of innocence the horrible possibility of *applauding* a visual joke during music had not crossed his or anybody else's mind.)

Like Shakespeare, Boito did not adhere to the unity of time in telling his story, so whether Falstaff is discovered an hour, or a day, after his ducking is not specified. It could be either. What *is* specified in the score is that the curtain rises on the twenty-seventh bar of the introduction and not before.

But the most unforgivable and unforgettable *bêtise* of the evening was both visual and musical. The twelve strokes of midnight in Windsor Forest, one of the most magical sounds in all opera, were sounded, not by a bell in the orchestra, but by a cracked, unsonorous frying pan, held in the hand and beaten on stage by Mistress Quickly. (In the 1980 revival, conducted by Andrew Davis, the bell was at last heard where the composer wanted it – in the orchestra pit.) But there was enough good in the production for Glyndebourne to put it on with increasing success for three seasons, with a third tour of the opera scheduled for 1981.

The second new production of 1976 was *Pelléas et Mélisande*, staged by René Terrasson, who, like Pierre Médecin before him in 1969, was never able to recapture anything of the peculiar atmosphere and mystical quality of the original Gui-Ebert-Montresor performances of 1962-3. A late replacement as Pelléas of the American Alan Titus (who was suffering from a real, not diplomatic illness) by André Jobin did not help matters; even though he was the son of Raoul Jobin, a famous French-Canadian Pelléas, this did not make André any more satisfactory. Michael Devlin, on the other hand, was superb as Golaud. If the rather solid, mundane scenery lacked the imaginative, dreamlike quality of Beni Montresor's, Bernard Haitink at least drew from the orchestra the sounds that suggested what we should have been seeing on stage.

The revival of *Capriccio* was conducted at all performances by Andrew Davis. The three Swedish principals (Söderström, Hagegård and Kerstin Meyer), Hugues Cuenod, Marius Rintzler and the two Italian singers repeated their 1973 successes; Ryland Davies as Flamand (his first Strauss role, apart from the tiny bit-part of the Major Domo in the 1965 *Rosenkavalier*) and Dale Duesing as Olivier were the only new-comers to the production, which was as rapturously received by lovers of Richard Strauss as before.

1977

Peter Hall's staging of the Mozart-Da Ponte triptych continued with what is probably the most difficult of them all: *Don Giovanni*. It opened the season with a dramatic force that had the critics and the too-often-lethargic pre-dinner-interval audience reeling by the end of Act I. As with *Figaro*, the producer went back to the earliest available edition of Da Ponte's libretto for his stage directions and included all the recitative. The opera, designed as usual by John Bury, was set in the Seville of Goya, a city of an oppressive black relieved only occasionally by a brightly coloured dress worn by Elvira or by the costumes of the peasants.

The unusual choice of period (no specific date is mentioned in the libretto) meant a sharp and healthy break with the tradition of a Don Giovanni in doublet and hose and bearded like Sir Thomas Beecham. Benjamin Luxon, as protagonist, shaved his own beard off and wore a moustache that made him look like Prince Albert. However, his behaviour soon dispelled this rather inappropriate impression and he presented a beautifully sung Giovanni. The Donna Anna was a young Australian, Joan Carden, encountered by Jani Strasser on one of his regular visits to Australia after his retirement, and recommended by him for Elvira. Unfortunately, the Elvira (in fact, both Elviras for the two series) had already been signed up for the production, and the Anna had not. So Miss Carden learnt Anna's part and sang that instead – and superbly. With Peter Hall's direction and her own unusual musical intelligence, Joan Carden showed in a remarkable way the nature and development of a character just as bewildering and complex in her way as Donna Elvira, notoriously the most complicated woman in all Mozart.

For Donna Anna's lover, Peter Hall conceived a middle-aged Don Ottavio, thereby giving rare point to the line in the libretto where Ottavio re-assures Anna that she will have a husband and a father in him. Leo Goeke made Ottavio more sympathetically human than the character usually appears, in a performance that was as musical and well acted as any he has given at Glyndebourne.

Apart from John Rawnsley (an excellent Masetto) and Pierre Thau as the Commendatore, who both stayed on, the cast after eleven of the scheduled eighteen performances was radically changed – a new Don Giovanni (Thomas Allen), a new Anna (Horiana Branisteanu), Elvira (Rachel Yakar), Ottavio (Philip Langridge), Leporello (Richard Van Allan for Stafford Dean) and Zerlina (Adrienne Csengery for Elizabeth Gale); and John Pritchard, after conducting with typical zest and understanding what was to be his last Mozart opera as Musical Director of Glyndebourne, gave way to his successor-elect, Bernard Haitink.

Series II, with a cast who were all good (and a couple of them quite exceptional), made an even greater impact – if possible – than Series I. Thomas Allen as Don Giovanni surprised everyone (and delighted the producer) by the unexpected strength and vitality of his performance – an irresistible portrayal of a sadistic, reckless but exhilaratingly fatalistic figure. In an opera that Mozart described as *buffa* and Da Ponte as a *dramma giocoso*, only Don Giovanni and Leporello found anything to laugh at – Giovanni laughed at his own jokes and escapades, while Leporello's laugh was often hollow, a laugh to keep up his apprehensive superstitious spirits. As Leporello, Richard Van Allan matched his master's violent actions with a display of physical resilience, acquired during his training in unarmed combat when he had been a policeman.

Where the first cast had included a superb Donna Anna, this one, in addition to a very good Anna, included a superb Donna Elvira. Rachel Yakar, a French soprano and for many years a member of the Düsseldorf Opera, was an Elvira in a hundred who, as one critic put it, 'plumbed the depths of Elvira's soul'. She also showed a nice sense of comedy during Leporello's Catalogue Song, which added a justifiably *giocoso* touch to the *dramma*.

Bernard Haitink had so far conducted only the two German operas of Mozart at Glyndebourne. His *Don Giovanni* came as a surprise to many people, for he had already conducted it at Covent Garden a few months earlier and got a bad Press for it. At Glyndebourne it was a different matter: Haitink gave a powerfully driven reading that matched, and was matched by, the dramatic strength of the production. The build-up of the finale of Act I was tremendous, though some of the critics were very upset that Don Giovanni did not escape at the end, in the traditional manner. As Peter Shaffer pointed out in a long letter to *The Times* in praise of the production, there is no mention whatever in the libretto of the libertine escaping. What Hall had done was to translate the words of the libretto into action – to introduce the tempests and the 'thunder of vengeance' that Giovanni's enemies call down on his head, and his own courageous defiance of it, while the music rose to its terrible and demonic climax. It was an unforgettable experience, which one critic admitted ruined the first half hour of his dinner interval and left him feeling that *Don Giovanni* would never be the same again.

Southern Television's recording of *Don Giovanni* proved to be its most successful production to date, a faithful re-creation of the theatrical excitement and atmosphere of the performance, with one or two subtle moments of 'pure' television technique – notably the grouped vignettes of the three maskers in their Act I trio – which Dave Heather introduced with taste and imagination.

When the season and the televising had finished, Glyndebourne took *Don Giovanni* with both casts to London to share six performances at the National Theatre (Peter Hall's home ground as it were), the first time the Festival Opera had had its name on a London theatre bill since its season of *The Beggar's Opera* at the Haymarket in 1940. The amenities of the Lyttelton auditorium proved more than a little cramped and inconvenient for conductor and orchestra; with most of the orchestra under the stage there were obvious moments when singers could not hear the accompaniment, and intonation was noticeably affected as a result. However, the season was a sell-out from the moment it was announced.

At Glyndebourne *Don Giovanni* was followed by the first production there of *La Voix humaine*, Poulenc's one-woman, one-act, *tragédie lyrique*, the curtain-raiser of a double bill completed by a revival of *The Cunning Little Vixen*. The British première of the Poulenc opera had been given by Glyndebourne at the Edinburgh Festival of 1960, with Denise Duval in the role she had created in Paris the year before. The Edinburgh production was directed and designed by Jean Cocteau (see page 220). In the 1977 performance, producer and protagonist was Graziella Sciutti, in a part one would hardly associate with one of the most brilliant soubrettes of her generation. Miss Sciutti's French was clear and idiomatic (she was born in Piedmont), and it was not her fault if the décor, set correctly in the 1920s (now a very voguish period among English theatre designers), had as much charm today as it had had for those of us who lived with it when it was new – which wasn't much.

The revival of Janáček's *Cunning Little Vixen*, coming as it did after the dinner interval, was received a little more hospitably by the audience than it had been on its first run in 1975. One or two points had been made clearer in the production, which was marked by some distinguished performances, notably by the young conductor, Simon Rattle, making his first appearance at the Festival after experience with the Touring Opera, and by the début of Eilene Hannan, an Australian soprano who shared the title role with Norma Burrowes. While Benjamin Luxon was singing Don Giovanni, the part of the Forester was sung by Thomas Allen, until it was his turn to take over Don Giovanni.

The long-delayed début at Glyndebourne of Renato Capecchi, a widely known, versatile and experienced singing actor, was at last made when he was fifty-three years old, and as the first Italian ever to sing Falstaff in a Glyndebourne production, brought with him an indefinable quality of authentic *italianità*, which was a great relief. (The first Glyndebourne Falstaff – at the Edinburgh Festival in 1955 – was Fernando Corena, who was Italian-trained on Gui's advice, but born in Geneva of Turkish parents.) In *Opera* magazine Renato Capecchi was welcomed as a 'fine musician and a superb actor', and it is comforting to know, as I write this, that he is due to return in the part in 1980.

The production of yet another unfamiliar opera by Richard Strauss, which even one of the composer's most enthusiastic admirers among the critics admitted was 'second-rate Strauss', was so skilfully jollied-up by the producer, John Cox, that *Die schweigsame Frau* (The Silent Woman) was transformed from a not-very-funny German joke into an amusing evening's entertainment, with its high spot a hilarious scene between Federico Davià and Ugo Trama as two members of the Italian opera troupe.

1978

Having the previous year presented a *Don Giovanni* that the critical jargonauts inevitably described as 'disturbing' (and, of course, 'challenging'), Peter Hall lost no time in completing his chronologically-arranged set of Mozart's Da Ponte operas with *Così fan tutte*. This was the high point of the whole 1978 season and of the producer's exhilarating view of the triptych. I was careful in the last chapter to describe *Don Giovanni* as 'probably' the most difficult of Mozart's three great Italian operas. I was right to be so careful. After hearing the new Glyndebourne performance of *Così fan tutte*, I was convinced that Hall had solved brilliantly the problems of what is certainly, not just 'probably', the most difficult opera of the lot.

It wasn't just a wind, but a tempest, of change that blew away the smog of slovenly tradition and left the atmosphere fresh, stimulating and clear enough to see the wood as well as the trees for perhaps the first time in one's experience.

As with his first two Mozart productions, Hall went back to the first available edition of Da Ponte's libretto of *Così fan tutte*. In this way we were spared a great deal of the sort of corny, uncalled-for 'comicity' that only an opera audience ever laughs at. The familiar exaggeration of the two young men's 'disguises' as Albanians was avoided; so was the introduction of the ridiculously enormous horseshoe-shaped magnet. (In this production Despina demonstrated the magnetic powers of two small pieces of metal, one held in either hand, which snapped together audibly as she held them a few inches apart. It was one of the most startlingly simple and convincing theatrical effects I can remember.)

Peter Hall missed nothing of the ambiguity in which the music and the ex-priest's libretto abound. He was blessed, in any case, with a first-rate cast of young acting singers, among them the American newcomer, Maria Ewing, whose Dorabella was a particular joy, with a natural gift of timing and an enchantingly comical face. Bozena Betley's Fiordiligi, by contrast, was a little solemn, perhaps because for too many previous productions she had been asked to sing her 'Come scoglio' as a serious number and was no longer able to change her ways and play the scene as the parody of a priggish young woman full of unconvincing the-very-idea-of-such-a-thing indignation that Mozart and Da Ponte intended.

Despina (sung by Nan Christie), on the other hand, was no longer seen as a cute soubrette, but as a member of what struck Desmond Shawe-Taylor as a very Irish household indeed. Although Despina is described as a maid, she is, in practice, a confidante who knows her mistresses better than they know themselves, and sees through their poses and tantrums. The two young officers, Max-René Cosotti and Håkan

Hagegård, disguised themselves as Albanians by using what was basically the simple device of having the fair lover wear a dark wig, and the dark one a fair wig. Stafford Dean was considered by some to look a little young for Don Alfonso, the 'vecchio filosofo', but cynicism isn't the prerogative of old age, and who knows that it isn't just what keeps you looking young, anyway? This Alfonso, whatever his age, relished every moment of his intrigue and – in accordance with his producer's principles – delivered his recitative with great conviction.

Ferrando (Cosotti) was allowed all his arias (even with a production that had to keep one eye more carefully than usual on the railway timetable, there was no question of giving way to the reprehensible custom of cutting his aria, 'Ah lo veggio . . .'). Hagegård made history by being the first Guglielmo at Glyndebourne to sing 'Rivolgete a lui lo sguardo', the long comic aria Mozart first wrote instead of the shorter 'Non siate ritrosi' that he later substituted for it. All in all, *Così fan tutte* was an excellent indication of why Peter Hall had recently been knighted.

In his first season as the new Musical Director Bernard Haitink conducted *Così fan tutte* with the same fire and understanding that had characterized his *Don Giovanni* the year before. The finale of Act I had a great drive and brilliance and one wondered once again what Rossini would have done without Mozart.

The season opened with a new production of *The Magic Flute* which, as it was designed by David Hockney, attracted much modish attention. The settings were aggressively Egyptian – as they should be, for the action is firmly laid in Ancient Egypt, or in Ancient Egypt as the librettist imagined it must have been like. Being a magic opera, John Cox's production made the most of all available trap doors and stage effects. There were moments, however, when some quite important details in Schikaneder's stage directions and dialogue were missed. At the very start of the opera, on his first appearance, Tamino was seen to shoot an arrow into the wings at the Serpent (in Hockney's version transformed into the Dragon from Uccello's picture of St George), which is chasing him. The libretto expressly says 'he has a bow, but no arrow', the reason being that, if the Prince, who is out hunting, had had an arrow, he would have slain the monster and there would have been no opera. (Princes with arrows never miss in fairy tales.) In the dialogue two important lines were dropped, both from Monostatos's part. The first was his realization for the first time that the Queen of the Night is Pamina's mother; the second, the words that explained why he joined up with the Queen. Perhaps, as they were spoken in German, only a few in the audience would have understood them; but they were not restored even for Southern Television, where they would have been understood from the English subtitles.

One moment stood out in the production, and that was when, for the first time since Carl Ebert's production of the opera was last seen in 1960, Tamino appeared to be playing the flute. But the moment didn't stand out for long. It proved to be a false alarm, for the instrument was merely being primed with a preliminary blow like bagpipes and had to play itself thereafter; the Prince wasn't quite as musical as we had expected.

As Pamina, the young and attractive Glasgow soprano Isobel Buchanan made her début at Glyndebourne, which she reached by way of Australia. Some critics considered she was still too inexperienced for the part (though admitting her beautiful voice and looks), which only shows how aural judgements can differ. To those who had known Miss Buchanan earlier (and not all that much earlier) in her career, her voice had developed much faster than they had expected, from a Mozart voice to almost a Verdi voice. Either way, there was no denying her lovely singing of Pamina's only aria (the heart-rending 'Ach, ich fühl's' in Act II), the exquisite *piano* of the high notes and the almost unbearable pathos of the closing phrases.

Leo Goeke's Tamino was full of character and conviction, like everything this singer does; he has a sympathetic voice and understands what he sings and acts. The American Queen of the Night (May Sandoz) hit all her top notes accurately, and the German Sarastro, Thomas Thomaschke, hit all his bottom ones in a sympathetic conception of the part.

So long as he sang, Benjamin Luxon's Papageno was warm and charming, but for some reason his spoken dialogue was oddly grumpy and surly in manner; *Opera* magazine described him as 'an aggressive Celtic type of bird-catcher'. Mr Luxon, of course, is Cornish, a Celtic tribe which does incline to xenophobia, so perhaps the critic had something there. However, Mr Luxon's initial mood regularly wore off in the course of each performance and by the time he met his delightful French Papagena, Elisabeth Conquet, we were relieved to find him more sympathetic. So was she, I should think.

Papageno's props were also a little unconventional. The magic silver bells, instead of being made in the form of a sistrum (than which nothing could be more Ancient, or more Egyptian), were apparently packed inside a most un-Egyptian-looking transistor radio and worked like a barrel-organ by Papageno turning a rather stiff handle. The most puzzling departure from the libretto, however, was Papageno's bird cage which was full of *dead* birds. Papageno's job was surely to catch birds for the Queen's aviary – not for her deep-freeze. This was not a happy conceit.

David Hockney's stage animals were great fun and the costumes as *prachtvoll* or 'splendid' (the librettist's favourite adjective) as Schikaneder could have hoped. Only the Three Boys were a disappointment. Being, in fact, Three Girls with rather plump knees, their gym tunics were not very becoming.

Andrew Davis, directing his first Mozart opera at Glyndebourne, was criticized for 'ponderous' conducting. So was Vittorio Gui when he last conducted the same opera. Mr Davis was much encouraged to hear this and kept to his unhurried ways.

John Cox's other new production for the year was *La Bohème* – in the same Redgrave setting that he had produced the work for the Touring Opera in 1972, and he did so again in as lively and authentic a manner as the perversely ridiculous inside-out scenery of Act II permitted. Bruno Bartoletti, who on Gui's recommendation had been pencilled-in to conduct at Glyndebourne a decade before, finally agreed to appear for Puccini's opera and was duly billed in the programme. But, because of one or other of the innumerable unforseeable, uncontrollable circumstances peculiar to opera houses, his place had to be taken at very short notice by Nicola Rescigno, the Italo-American conductor.

Rescigno, who had been a kind of 'conductor-in-residence' to Maria Callas for many of her busiest years in the States, had obviously learnt a great deal from her (she let many musicians hear a thing or two to their advantage); his performance of *La Bohème* was spirited, free of sentimental dawdling, and the music never lost its vitality or its warm sincerity. The cast was appropriately young for an opera that is about a quartet of young lovers and not – as so often presented – two couples, one of which is more important than the other. The improvement in status of Musetta and Marcello owed much to John Cox's direction, which rightly made the most of exceptionally good singers in the parts – Brent Ellis and John Rawnsley as Marcello, and Ashley Putnam as Musetta. The death of Mimì was beautifully done by the young American singer, Linda Zoghby.

1979

Sir Peter Hall had long wanted to do *Fidelio* with Bernard Haitink; this year it happened, and the season opened with a production that so impressed the Editor of *Opera* magazine that instead of waiting, as was customary, for the Festival issue published in mid-October to write about it, Mr Rosenthal made a feature of it in the July number. Though the notice appeared a few days after the run of the opera at Glyndebourne, it served to alert readers on the Glyndebourne Touring Opera circuit to what was coming their way, and remind those who were not that they would be able to see the production on ITV.

Once more Hall and his designer, John Bury, had read the libretto carefully and started from scratch to build up a dramatic experience that was different, not from what Beethoven and his librettist wanted, but from what the 'tradition' and stale custom of thousands of performances have too often tried to make us believe they wanted.

Understatement in a realistic setting, which characterized Hall's *Figaro*, *Così fan tutte* and, where it applied, *Don Giovanni*, was the basis of his production of *Fidelio*. The opening scene outside the jailer's house in the prison courtyard created an immediately convincing atmosphere by its careful attention to details, which were correct down to the clothes pegs and the type of iron Marzelline used on the family washing. Even the two hens busily pecking around in the courtyard fitted naturally into the scene, just as later (indulging further in a commendable Italianate love of stage livestock) the producer had a real live horse for Pizarro to arrive on. (The hens and horse were prudently not taken on tour.)

The element of understatement in the production was most marked in Hall's conception of Leonore. Elisabeth Söderström (according to the reference books, she had not sung the part before) was a slight boyish figure whose disguise as Fidelio was unusually convincing. The very matter-of-factness of the dialogue brought tension and pace to the drama, which was increased by the music so that Leonore's great cry of

'First kill his wife!' was an unforgettable moment. Vocally, Miss Söderström's performance was on a small scale (rightly, for Glyndebourne is a small-scale theatre), but she used her voice so intelligently and acted so movingly that it was precisely the physical limitations imposed on the interpretation that made her Leonore's devotion appear even more courageous. The Florestan, the Dutch tenor Anton de Ridder, did not erase memories of Richard Lewis in the great Gui performances of twenty years earlier, but the sustained intensity of Bernard Haitink's conducting of the long opening scene of Act II – the introduction and accompaniment to Florestan's aria – more than made up for what weaknesses the singer may have had (there were far fewer to worry about by the time the opera was broadcast, than on the first night when the critics were there).

Miss Söderström's compatriot, Curt Appelgren, made an outstanding début as Rocco, a most impressive and sympathetic performance of the part; their scenes together were exceptional. A novel, but logical, touch in the production was the careful way Peter Hall did not allow Marzelline and Jaquino to fall into each other's arms and so even hint at a conventional happy ending for them when Leonore's identity was disclosed and her reunion with Florestan achieved in the final scene.

Another unusual feature was the treatment of the chorus of prisoners in Act I. Instead of wearing the familiar prison uniform so beloved of German producers, they were kept in jail in the clothes they were committed in – an infinitely sad collection of highly individual, educated-looking men, afflicted by the illnesses and disabilities brought on by years in prison conditions of indescribable squalor and cruelty. This was an affecting scene which brought home more than ever the greatness and – unfortunately – continuing topicality of this opera.

In accordance with Glyndebourne practice, no Leonore No 3 Overture was played during the long scene change to the last scene of Act II. However, without conductor, music staff, producer or apparently anybody else noticing, the trumpet call played off-stage in the dungeon scene was not, as it should have been, the one written for *Fidelio*, but in fact the call from the third Leonore Overture. I don't think even Stan Woods, an old friend from the Royal Philharmonic's days at Glyndebourne, realized this; he played from memory, and on his cue instinctively played the version he had played so many times in concert halls.

Alternating with *Fidelio* was the revival of Peter Hall's production of Monteverdi's *Ulisse*. Remembering Janet Baker as Penelope, it seemed unlikely that any revival without her would be tolerable. Frederica von Stade, returning to Glyndebourne for the first time since her Cherubino in 1973, played the part differently and magnificently. Miss Stade has that rare gift, possessed only by great ballet dancers, a few actresses and very rarely by opera singers, of immobility. Not until her final scene, when at last she was convinced of Ulysses' identity and smiled, did she seem to make any gesture. It was a superbly sustained portrayal of heart-rending sadness.

The warmth and noble tenderness of Richard Stilwell's Ulysses matched perfectly the nobility of this Penelope. Richard Lewis, as Eumaeus, and the three suitors – Ugo

Trama, John Fryatt and Bernard Dickerson – repeated their sharply characterized performances of the original 1972 production; so, too, did Alexander Oliver as the gluttonous Irus – except that this time, as he had taken off so much weight, he no longer appeared topless, but had to wear a padded tunic to cover his new sylph-like look. As the new Minerva, Ann Murray was an endearing goddess and a pert, lively shepherd boy on her visit to earth. Another promising and sympathetic début was that of Patrick Power (from New Zealand *via* Oslo) as Telemachus.

The third Hall production of the season was the first revival of his *Così fan tutte*, faithfully reproduced by the young Dutch producer, Guus Mostart. Alan Titus, the American baritone, made a distinguished Glyndebourne début as Guglielmo, having recovered from the serious illness which had prevented what was expected to be a memorable appearance as Pelléas in 1976. His conspirator was John Aler, another American, whose Ferrando was beautifully sung. Patricia Parker, who had taken over as Dorabella for the last seven of the previous year's fifteen performances, sang the part throughout the revival, but was handicapped a little by having to act the part as it was originally designed to fit the looks and temperament of another artist.

The final opera was the first by Haydn at Glyndebourne – *La fedeltà premiata* (Fidelity Rewarded). When, in the early 1960s, I had once asked Glyndebourne why they didn't try some Haydn, I was told the operas were too undramatic. But they had, obviously, reckoned without John Cox, who took this first Haydn specimen to pieces, and by extensive but judicious manipulation made what was originally a long and complicated libretto with beautiful (but action-delaying) music, into a shorter and slightly less complicated libretto with beautiful music that still tended to delay the action, especially towards the end, when three lovely arias came in close succession. But the result was an entertainment that greatly pleased the public in spite (or because) of some rather elementary gags of the kind that sends opera audiences into fits, and delighted one of the critics so much that he had to describe the business of one of the hoariest of them all in detail. No matter; someone is always seeing a fat man slip on a banana skin for the first time.

The production had a really first-rate cast, among them some striking newcomers – Julia Hamari, Kathleen Battle, and James Atherton, whose song-and-dance experience on Broadway gave a rare sparkle to his characterization of Lindoro. The old-comers included Thomas Allen and Richard Van Allan (both superlatively assured in their versatility and interpretation) and Sylvia Lindenstrand.

The saddest thing about Glyndebourne's first Haydn opera was that a national strike of commercial television technicians prevented Southern Television recording it. It was possible eventually to record *Fidelio*, because the cast could be re-assembled at Glyndebourne in January, 1980, but the Haydn cast had just gone with the wind of industrial inaction, and the project had to be written off at a pretty formidable cost to Southern.

The *Fidelio* recording demonstrated what it would have been like if the serious suggestion, put forward by the critic of the *Observer* in 1934 that February, not May, would be a more convenient time to hold the Glyndebourne Festival, had been adopted (see page 74). Sunday, 13 January 1980 was a clear, very frosty night with a minimum temperature of –5° C. The heating in the auditorium failed, conditions in the long bar were arctic, and it was more or less pitch dark before the audience arrived in the afternoon. (February would in fact have been worse – very wet and the car park unusable.) Anyway, at least the idea of winter performances had now been tried out.

On 5 August, two days before the 1979 season ended, a touching and quite un-repeatable event took place at Glyndebourne. This was a memorial concert for Jani Strasser, who had died the previous September.

It was not a solemn occasion, but a tribute in affectionate memory of Jani's character, his mannerisms, eccentricities, prejudices and, above all, his devotion to Glyndebourne and his concern for its standards. In the large audience, the first generation of Glynde-bourne singers was represented by the eighty-year-old Roy Henderson, the first *Figaro* Count in 1934. Michel Roux, a later Count and the first Glyndebourne Golaud, who was one of Gui's generation of Glyndebourne singers between 1956 and 1970, came over especially from Paris; and Peter-Christoph Runge, one of the best of all the Papagenos, travelled from Germany.

On the stage, Richard Lewis sang Idomeneo's 'Vedrommi intorno . . .', which he had first sung in the original Busch-Ebert performances of the opera in 1951, and at sixty-five, was still singing as effortlessly as ever. The younger generation of singers was well represented by Teresa Cahill, Frederica von Stade, Thomas Allen, Ryland Davies, Stafford Dean and Richard Van Allan, who between them contributed solo scenes, duets, trios and a quintet. Miss Cahill was Elvira in the Act II trio of *Don Giovanni* with Thomas Allen and Richard Van Allan, Fiordiligi in the *Così fan tutte* trio (with Allen and Van Allen) and quintet (with Allen, Davies, Van Allan and Stade), and the Pamina-Papageno duet with Allen. Miss Stade sang the Cherubino aria, 'Non so più cosa son', that had introduced her to Glyndebourne, and Ryland Davies a scene from *Capriccio*. Two of the accompanists (Jean Mallandaine and John Pritchard were the others), Martin Isepp and Geoffrey Parsons, who was on the Music Staff in the early 1960s, played the slow movement from a Mozart piano sonata for four hands (K.497 in F). Moran Caplat introduced the items and reminisced wistfully and amusingly about Jani Strasser as his companion on numberless talent-digging journeys over the years. John Pritchard, who had written a fondly perceptive obituary memoir in *The Times* on Jani's death in 1978, came over from Cologne, where he is principal conductor, and made many new and hilarious contributions to the already large repertoire of Strasser anecdotes. Afterwards, he accompanied what proved to be a real show-stopper – Ryland Davies and Tom Allen as Almaviva and Figaro in the superb duet from Act I of the *Barber of Seville*; this was a virtuoso performance which made one regret that Rossini's opera could not have been planned for revival at Glyndebourne in 1981 with these two artists.

Having to follow that last item would have daunted almost anybody; but not Stafford Dean, who offered what could only be decribed as an aria (one of Osmin's from *Die Entführung*) followed by a *scena* that brought the house down. Not only was his mimicry of Jani Strasser's speech uncanny, but the parody of his whole manner, the caustic disparagement of all other operatic institutions, and the severe, but never wounding, things he said to singers (and their accompanists) in the course of coaching them was brilliant.

After seven numbers from opera and a piano duet, Frederica von Stade sang a song that was just a song. I don't know whether Jani ever knew it, though he may well have, for it was in Audrey Mildmay's library. But it made me feel that indirectly I was personally associated with a tribute to his memory. It was 'The Bard of Armagh', from the first volume of my father's collection of Irish Country Songs, which Miss Stade not only sang with the clarity of diction expected of a half-Irish, American-born singer of English words, but with an instinctive sense of idiom. Again her performance was distinguished by her command of stillness, never more necessary or difficult to sustain than between the verses of a song with unexpectedly long interludes for solo piano.

As a prelude to the finale of the programme, George Christie, who had known Jani all his own life, and as his parents' son had enjoyed a special family relationship with him, made a charming and affectionately appreciative speech. This led to his introduction of Jani's son, Imre, who had come from Canada and was obviously very touched by the occasion. The last music played was the incomparably sad and beautiful terzetto of farewell for Fiordiligi, Dorabella and Don Alfonso in *Così fan tutte* – 'Soave sia il vento . . .' ('Let the wind blow gently, and the sea be calm . . .'), sung by Teresa Cahill, Frederica von Stade and Stafford Dean.

There could have been no more fitting envoi to the lovable figure whose death left Glyndebourne a place that would never be the same again.

Looking back on the decade and a half covered in these chapters, the story begins in 1964 at a time when Glyndebourne's artistic fortunes were low. The precise year of the Festival's recovery from this comparative decline is difficult to pinpoint, but it coincided roughly with the start of the 1970s and could be attributable to what George Christie describes as the 'artistic consolidation' brought about by several notable events. These were the assumption by John Pritchard of the role of Musical Director in 1969; Peter Hall's arrival with *La Calisto* in 1970, followed by Bernard Haitink's succession as Musical Director; the treatment by John Cox (as Director of Production) of, among many other things, Richard Strauss's comedies; and Peter Hall's productions of Mozart's three Da Ponte operas.

Almost concurrently a social and political consolidation of particular significance occurred: the formation in 1968 of the Glyndebourne Touring Opera, which has taken Festival productions out to a far wider audience than could ever be reached at Glyndebourne itself. 'To this extent,' says Christie, 'the GTO is truly a Volksoper (though not performing exclusively in the vernacular).' For George Christie one of the many rewards of the Touring Opera has been the way it has made the 'image' of Glyndebourne more socially acceptable. Many thousands more people are now able to see

Glyndebourne at work and enjoy the results of that notorious 'élitism' – to say nothing of the millions who see its operas on television at home and abroad.

Finally, there is the matter of finance. During the 1970s the world's economy changed substantially, forcing on Glyndebourne the need for financial consolidation. 'This,' Christie explains, 'has been achieved firstly to the extent that a sizable programme of capital work has been carried out, and has to a major extent helped to ensure the future of Glyndebourne's physical context; and secondly to the extent that in far greater measure Glyndebourne's general operation has been underpinned.'

As for the future, George Christie is optimistic: 'The 1980s seem to hold a healthy prospect for Glyndebourne at a time when opera internationally is increasingly under fire economically and is therefore at risk of being undermined politically, socially and artistically.'

Ringmer
Sussex
1980

Appendix A *Operas and casts in chronological order 1934-64*

MUSICAL STAFF

FRITZ BUSCH formerly Head Conductor Staatsoper, Dresden. Festivals: Bayreuth, Salzburg, Buenos Aires

CARL EBERT formerly Intendant Städtische Oper, Berlin. Festivals: Salzburg, Buenos Aires

HANS OPPENHEIM formerly Head Conductor Deutsche Musikbühne, Berlin. Head Conductor Städtische Oper, Breslau

ALBERTO EREDE formerly Conductor Augusteum, Rome. Italian Opera den Haag

HANS STRASSER Professor of Singing Vienna, Budapest and Glyndebourne

GENERAL STAFF

Scenery Designer and Stage Manager HAMISH WILSON

Assistant Stage Manager B. HOWARD

Assistant Producer HANS PETER BUSCH

Manager ALFRED NIGHTINGALE

Costumes ANN LITHERLAND

Wardrobe Mistress JULIETTE MAGNY

Scenery Artist SIMPSON ROBINSON

Scenery Builders THE RINGMER BUILDING WORKS, Sussex

Engineer W. THORPE

Stage Foreman R. W. GOUGH

Wigs W. CLARKSON

Leader of the Orchestra GEORGE STRATTON

Le nozze di Figaro

MOZART   *6 performances*

Figaro	Willi Domgraf-Fassbaender (*German*)
Susanna	Audrey Mildmay (*English*)
Bartolo	Norman Allin (*English*)
Marcellina	Constance Willis (*English*)
Cherubino	Luise Helletsgruber (*Austrian*)
	Lucie Manén (*German*)
Count Almaviva	Roy Henderson (*Scottish*)
Don Basilio	Heddle Nash (*English*)
The Countess	Aulikki Rautawaara (*Finnish*)
Antonio	Fergus Dunlop (*English*)
Barbarina	Winifred Radford (*English*)
Don Curzio	Morgan Jones (*Welsh*)

Conductor FRITZ BUSCH

Producer CARL EBERT

Scenery HAMISH WILSON

Costumes ANN LITHERLAND

Così fan tutte

MOZART   *6 performances*

Ferrando	Heddle Nash (*English*)
Guglielmo	Willi Domgraf-Fassbaender (*German*)
Don Alfonso	Vincenzo Bettoni (*Italian*)
Fiordiligi	Ina Souez (*English*)
Dorabella	Luise Helletsgruber (*Austrian*)
Despina	Irene Eisinger (*Czech*)

Conductor FRITZ BUSCH

Producer CARL EBERT

Scenery HAMISH WILSON

Costumes ANN LITHERLAND

MUSICAL STAFF

As in 1934, with the addition of
WARWICK BRAITHWAITE, Conductor Sadler's Wells
EDWARD RENTON

GENERAL STAFF

Scenery Designer and Stage Director HAMISH WILSON
Assistant Producers RUDOLF BING and HANS PETER BUSCH
Leader of the Orchestra GEORGE STRATTON
Costumes ANN LITHERLAND and HAMISH WILSON
Wardrobe Mistress JULIETTE MAGNY
Scenery Artist G. SIMPSON ROBINSON
Engineer W. THORPE
Stage Foreman R. W. GOUGH
General Manager ALFRED NIGHTINGALE

The Magic Flute

MOZART　*8 performances*

Tamino	Walther Ludwig (*German*)
Three Ladies	Luise Helletsgruber (*Austrian*)
	Maria Selve (*English*)
	Sophie Schoenning (*Norwegian*)
Papageno	Willi Domgraf-Fassbaender (*German*)
	Roy Henderson (*Scottish*)
Queen of the Night	Mfla Kočová (*Czech*)
	Noel Eadie (*English*)
Three Boys	Winifred Radford (*English*)
	Jean Beckwith (*English*)
	Molly Mitchell (*English*)
Monostatos	Edwin Ziegler (*American*)
Pamina	Aulikki Rautawaara (*Finnish*)
The Speaker (Act I)	John Brownlee (*Australian*)
	Ronald Stear (*English*)
The Speaker (Act II)	Carl Ebert (*German*)
Sarastro	Ivar Andrésen (*Norwegian*)
Priests and Men in Armour	D. Morgan Jones (*Welsh*)
	Gerald Kassen (*South African*)
Papagena	Irene Eisinger (*Austrian*)

Conductor FRITZ BUSCH
Producer CARL EBERT
Designer HAMISH WILSON

Così fan tutte

MOZART　*5 performances*

Ferrando	Heddle Nash (*English*)
Guglielmo	Willi Domgraf-Fassbaender (*German*)
Don Alfonso	John Brownlee (*Australian*)
Fiordiligi	Ina Souez (*English*)
Dorabella	Luise Helletsgruber (*Austrian*)
Despina	Irene Eisinger (*Austrian*)

Conductor FRITZ BUSCH
Producer CARL EBERT
Scenery HAMISH WILSON
Costumes ANN LITHERLAND

Le nozze di Figaro

MOZART *7 performances*

Figaro Willi Domgraf-Fassbaender (*German*)
Susanna Audrey Mildmay (*English*)
Bartolo Ronald Stear (*English*)
Marcellina Constance Willis (*English*)
Cherubino Luise Helletsgruber (*Austrian*)
Count Almaviva Roy Henderson (*Scottish*)
Don Basilio Heddle Nash (*English*)
The Countess Aulikki Rautawaara (*Finnish*)
Antonio Fergus Dunlop (*English*)
Barbarina Winifred Radford (*English*)
Don Curzio Morgan Jones (*Welsh*)

Conductors FRITZ BUSCH
Hans Oppenheim
Producer CARL EBERT
Scenery HAMISH WILSON
Costumes ANN LITHERLAND

Die Entführung aus dem Serail

MOZART *5 performances*

Belmonte Walther Ludwig (*German*)
Osmin Ivar Andrésen (*Norwegian*)
Pedrillo Heddle Nash (*English*)
Pasha Selim Carl Ebert (*German*)
Willi Domgraf-Fassbaender (*German*)
Constanze Noel Eadie (*English*)
Blonde Irene Eisinger (*Austrian*)
Sailor Fergus Dunlop (*English*)
Dumb Slave Joseph Roger Childs (*English*)

Conductor FRITZ BUSCH
Producer CARL EBERT
Scenery HAMISH WILSON
Costumes ANN LITHERLAND

1936

Artistic Direction FRITZ BUSCH, CARL EBERT

General Manager RUDOLF BING

Stage Manager GODFREY BAXTER (*English*)
Chief Electrician B. PFLUG (*English*)
Assistant Producer HANS PETER BUSCH (*German*)
Engineer W. J. THORPE (*English*)
Wardrobe Mistress JULIETTE MAGNY (*English*)
Stage Foreman R. W. GOUGH (*Scottish*)

Glyndebourne 29 v - 5 vii: 32 performances

Don Giovanni

MOZART   *10 performances*

Leporello	Salvatore Baccaloni (*Italian*)
Donna Anna	Ina Souez (*British*)
Don Giovanni	John Brownlee (*Australian*)
The Commendatore	David Franklin (*English*)
Don Ottavio	Koloman von Pataky (*Hungarian*)
Donna Elvira	Luise Helletsgruber (*Austrian*)
Zerlina	Audrey Mildmay (*English*)
Masetto	Roy Henderson (*Scottish*)

Conductor	FRITZ BUSCH
Producer	CARL EBERT
Scenery	HAMISH WILSON
Costumes	HEIN HECKROTH (*German*)

The Magic Flute

MOZART   *8 performances*

Tamino	Thorkild Noval (*Danish*)
Three Ladies	Erika Storm (*German*)
	Sophie Schönning (*Norwegian*)
	Betsy de la Porte (*South African*)
Papageno	Roy Henderson (*Scottish*)
Queen of the Night	Noel Eadie (*English*)
	Julia Moor (*Swiss*)
Three Boys	Winifred Radford (*English*)
	Jean Beckwith (*English*)
	Molly Mitchell (*English*)
Monostatos	Paul Schwarz (*American*)
Pamina	Aulikki Rautawaara (*Finnish*)
The Speaker (Act I)	George Hancock (*English*)
The Speaker (Act II)	Carl Ebert (*German*)
Sarastro	Alexander Kipnis (*American*)
Priests and Men in Armour	D. Morgan Jones (*Welsh*)
	David Franklin (*English*)
Papagena	Lili Heinemann (*German*)

Conductors	FRITZ BUSCH
	Hans Oppenheim
Producer	CARL EBERT
Designer	HAMISH WILSON

Le nozze di Figaro

MOZART   *6 performances*

Figaro	Mariano Stabile (*Italian*)
Susanna	Audrey Mildmay (*English*)
Bartolo	Salvatore Baccaloni (*Italian*)
Marcellina	Constance Willis (*English*)
Cherubino	Luise Helletsgruber (*Austrian*)
Count Almaviva	John Brownlee (*Australian*)
Don Basilio	Heddle Nash (*English*)
The Countess	Aulikki Rautawaara (*Finnish*)
Antonio	Fergus Dunlop (*English*)
Barbarina	Winifred Radford (*English*)
Don Curzio	D. Morgan Jones (*Welsh*)

Conductor	FRITZ BUSCH
Producer	CARL EBERT
Scenery	HAMISH WILSON
Costumes	ANN LITHERLAND

Così fan tutte

MOZART   *4 performances*

Ferrando	Heddle Nash (*English*)
Guglielmo	Roy Henderson (*Scottish*)
Don Alfonso	John Brownlee (*Australian*)
Fiordiligi	Ina Souez (*British*)
Dorabella	Luise Helletsgruber (*Austrian*)
Despina	Tatiana Menotti (*Italian*)

Conductor	FRITZ BUSCH
Producer	CARL EBERT
Scenery	HAMISH WILSON
Costumes	ANN LITHERLAND

Die Entführung aus dem Serail

MOZART   *4 performances*

Belmonte	Koloman von Pataky (*Hungarian*)
Osmin	Salvatore Baccaloni (*Italian*)
Pedrillo	Heddle Nash (*English*)
Pasha Selim	Carl Ebert (*German*)
	Erich Kunz (*Austrian*)
Constanze	Julia Moor (*Swiss*)
Blonde	Irma Beilke (*German*)
Sailor	Fergus Dunlop (*English*)
Dumb Slave	Joseph Roger Childs (*English*)

Conductor	FRITZ BUSCH
Producer	CARL EBERT
Scenery	HAMISH WILSON
Costumes	ANN LITHERLAND

Artistic Direction FRITZ BUSCH, CARL EBERT

General Manager RUDOLF BING

Stage Manager GODFREY BAXTER
Chief Electrician B. PFLUG
Assistant Producer HANS PETER BUSCH
Engineer W. J. THORPE
Wardrobe Mistress JULIETTE MAGNY
Stage Foreman R. W. GOUGH

Don Giovanni

MOZART *10 performances*

Leporello	Salvatore Baccaloni (*Italian*)
Donna Anna	Ina Souez (*British*)
Don Giovanni	John Brownlee (*Australian*)
The Commendatore	Norman Walker (*English*)
Don Ottavio	Dino Borgioli (*Italian*)
Donna Elvira	Luise Helletsgruber (*Austrian*)
Zerlina	Marita Farell (*Czech*)
Masetto	Roy Henderson (*Scottish*)

Conductor FRITZ BUSCH
Producer CARL EBERT
Scenery HAMISH WILSON
Costumes HEIN HECKROTH

The Magic Flute

MOZART *8 performances*

Tamino	Thorkild Noval (*Danish*)
Three Ladies	Luise Helletsgruber (*Austrian*)
	Marita Farell (*Czech*)
	Joyce Newton (*English*)
Papageno	Roy Henderson (*Scottish*)
Queen of the Night	Sinaida Lissitschkina (*Nicaraguan*)
Three Boys	Winifred Radford (*English*)
	Jean Beckwith (*English*)
	Molly Mitchell (*English*)
Monostatos	Ernest Frank (*British Indian*)
Pamina	Aulikki Rautawaara (*Finnish*)
The Speaker (Act I)	Norman Walker (*English*)
The Speaker (Act II)	Carl Ebert (*German*)
Sarastro	Herbert Alsen (*German*)
	David Franklin (*English*)
Priests and Men in Armour	Eric Starling (*English*)
	Norman Walker (*English*)
Papagena	Irene Eisinger (*Austrian*)
	Margaret Field-Hyde (*English*)

Conductor FRITZ BUSCH
Producer CARL EBERT
Designer HAMISH WILSON

Le nozze di Figaro

MOZART *8 performances*

Figaro	Willi Domgraf-Fassbaender (*German*)
Susanna	Irene Eisinger (*Austrian*)
Bartolo	Salvatore Baccaloni (*Italian*)
Marcellina	Constance Willis (*English*)
Cherubino	Marita Farell (*Czech*)
Count Almaviva	John Brownlee (*Australian*)
Don Basilio	Heddle Nash (*English*)
The Countess	Aulikki Rautawaara (*Finnish*)
Antonio	Fergus Dunlop (*English*)
Barbarina	Winifred Radford (*English*)
Don Curzio	Eric Starling (*English*)

Conductor FRITZ BUSCH
Producer CARL EBERT
Scenery HAMISH WILSON
Costumes ANN LITHERLAND

Die Entführung aus dem Serail

MOZART *3 performances*

Belmonte	Eric Starling (*English*)
Osmin	Herbert Alsen (*German*)
Pedrillo	Heddle Nash (*English*)
Pasha Selim	Carl Ebert (*German*)
Constanze	Margherita Perras (*Greek*)
Blonde	Irene Eisinger (*Austrian*)
Sailor	Fergus Dunlop (*English*)
Dumb Slave	Joseph Roger Childs (*English*)

Conductor FRITZ BUSCH
Producer CARL EBERT
Scenery HAMISH WILSON
Costumes ANN LITHERLAND

Così fan tutte

MOZART *6 performances*

Ferrando	Heddle Nash (*English*)
Guglielmo	Willi Domgraf-Fassbaender (*German*)
	Roy Henderson (*Scottish*)
Don Alfonso	John Brownlee (*Australian*)
	Salvatore Baccaloni (*Italian*)
Fiordiligi	Ina Souez (*British*)
Dorabella	Luise Helletsgruber (*Austrian*)
Despina	Irene Eisinger (*Austrian*)

Conductor FRITZ BUSCH
Producer CARL EBERT
Scenery HAMISH WILSON
Costumes ANN LITHERLAND

Artistic Direction FRITZ BUSCH, CARL EBERT

General Manager RUDOLF BING

MUSICAL STAFF

ALBERTO EREDE (Conductor), JANI STRASSER,
JAMES ROBERTSON, GEORGE AUSTIN,
ALBERTO PEDRALOZZI, FRANK BURY

GENERAL STAFF

Stage Manager GODFREY BAXTER
Chief Electrician A. E. ROGERS
Assistant Producer HANS PETER BUSCH
Engineer W. J. THORPE
Wardrobe Mistress JULIETTE MAGNY
Assistant Stage Manager ERNEST FRANK
Stage Foreman R. W. GOUGH

Macbeth

VERDI *10 performances*

First professional production in England

Macbeth	Francesco Valentino (*American*)
Banquo	David Franklin (*English*)
Lady Macbeth	Vera Schwarz (*Yugoslavian*)
Gentlewoman	Elisabeth Abercrombie (*British*)
Macduff	David Lloyd (*Welsh*)
Malcolm	Eric Starling (*English*)
A Doctor	Fergus Dunlop (*Scottish*)
A Servant	Cuthbert Matthews (*Australian*)
A Murderer	Robert Rowell (*English*)

Conductor FRITZ BUSCH
Producer CARL EBERT
Designer CASPAR NEHER

Le nozze di Figaro

MOZART *9 performances*

Figaro	Mariano Stabile (*Italian*)
Susanna	Audrey Mildmay (*English*)
	Irene Eisinger (*Austrian*)
Bartolo	Salvatore Baccaloni (*Italian*)
Marcellina	Constance Willis (*English*)
Cherubino	Marita Farell (*Czech*)
Count Almaviva	John Brownlee (*Australian*)
Don Basilio	Heddle Nash (*English*)
The Countess	Aulikki Rautawaara (*Finnish*)
Antonio	Fergus Dunlop (*Scottish*)
Barbarina	Irene Eisinger (*Austrian*)
	Winifred Radford (*English*)
Don Curzio	Eric Starling (*English*)

Conductors FRITZ BUSCH
Alberto Erede
Producer CARL EBERT
Scenery HAMISH WILSON
Costumes ANN LITHERLAND

Don Giovanni

MOZART *7 performances*

Leporello	Salvatore Baccaloni (*Italian*)
Donna Anna	Ina Souez (*British*)
Don Giovanni	John Brownlee (*Australian*)
The Commendatore	David Franklin (*English*)
Don Ottavio	Dino Borgioli (*Italian*)
Donna Elvira	Luise Helletsgruber (*Austrian*)
	Hilde Konetzni (*Austrian*)
Zerlina	Marita Farell (*Czech*)
	Winifred Radford (*English*)
Masetto	Roy Henderson (*Scottish*)

Conductors FRITZ BUSCH
Alberto Erede
Producer CARL EBERT
Scenery HAMISH WILSON
Costumes ANN LITHERLAND

Don Pasquale

DONIZETTI *5 performances*

Don Pasquale	Salvatore Baccaloni (*Italian*)
Dr Malatesta	Mariano Stabile (*Italian*)
Ernesto	Dino Borgioli (*Italian*)
Norina	Audrey Mildmay (*English*)
Notary	Fergus Dunlop (*Scottish*)

Conductor FRITZ BUSCH
Producer CARL EBERT
Scenery HAMISH WILSON
Costumes KENNETH GREEN

Così fan tutte

MOZART *5 performances*

Ferrando	Heddle Nash (*English*)
Guglielmo	Roy Henderson (*Scottish*)
Don Alfonso	John Brownlee (*Australian*)
Fiordiligi	Ina Souez (*British*)
Dorabella	Luise Helletsgruber (*Austrian*)
Despina	Irene Eisinger (*Austrian*)

Conductor FRITZ BUSCH
Producer CARL EBERT
Scenery HAMISH WILSON
Costumes ANN LITHERLAND

Artistic Direction FRITZ BUSCH, CARL EBERT

General Manager RUDOLF BING

MUSICAL STAFF

ALBERTO EREDE (Conductor)
JANI STRASSER, JAMES ROBERTSON,
ARNALDO CATTANEO, GEORGE AUSTIN,
DENIS MULGAN

GENERAL STAFF

Assistant Producer HANS PETER BUSCH
Stage Manager GODFREY BAXTER
Chief Electrician A. E. ROGERS
Wardrobe Mistress JULIETTE MAGNY
Assistant Stage Manager ERNEST FRANK
Engineer W. J. THORPE
Assistant Manager L. H. TURNER
Secretary to General Manager E. M. LONG
Stage Foreman R. W. GOUGH
Head Gardener F. HARVEY

Le nozze di Figaro

MOZART　*10 performances*

Figaro	Mariano Stabile (*Italian*)
Susanna	Audrey Mildmay (*English*)
	Irene Eisinger (*Austrian*)
Bartolo	Salvatore Baccaloni (*Italian*)
Marcellina	Constance Willis (*English*)
Cherubino	Risë Stevens (*American*)
Count Almaviva	John Brownlee (*Australian*)
Don Basilio	Eric Starling (*English*)
The Countess	Maria Markan (*Icelandic*)
Antonio	Fergus Dunlop (*Scottish*)
Barbarina	Irene Eisinger (*Austrian*)
	Rose Hill (*English*)
Don Curzio	Maldwyn Thomas (*Welsh*)

Conductors	FRITZ BUSCH
	Alberto Erede
Producer	CARL EBERT
Scenery	HAMISH WILSON
Costumes	ANN LITHERLAND

Macbeth

VERDI　*10 performances*

Macbeth	Francesco Valentino (*American*)
Banquo	David Franklin (*English*)
Lady Macbeth	Margherita Grandi (*Tasmanian*)
Gentlewoman	Constance Willis (*English*)
Macduff	David Lloyd (*Welsh*)
Malcolm	Eric Starling (*English*)
Doctor	Robert Rowell (*English*)
Servant	Cuthbert Matthews (*Australian*)
Murderer	Nicholas Harrison (*English*)

Conductor	FRITZ BUSCH
Producer	CARL EBERT
Designer	CASPAR NEHER

Don Giovanni

MOZART *7 performances*

Leporello	Salvatore Baccaloni (*Italian*)
Donna Anna	Ina Souez (*British*)
Don Giovanni	John Brownlee (*Australian*)
The Commendatore	David Franklin (*English*)
Don Ottavio	David Lloyd (*Welsh*)
	Dino Borgioli (*Italian*)
Donna Elvira	Hella Toros (*British*)
Zerlina	Audrey Mildmay (*English*)
Masetto	Roy Henderson (*Scottish*)

Conductors	FRITZ BUSCH
	Alberto Erede
Producer	CARL EBERT
Scenery	HAMISH WILSON
Costumes	HEIN HECKROTH

Don Pasquale

DONIZETTI *4 performances*

Don Pasquale	Salvatore Baccaloni (*Italian*)
Dr Malatesta	Mariano Stabile (*Italian*)
Ernesto	Luigi Fort (*Italian*)
Norina	Audrey Mildmay (*English*)
Notary	David Franklin (*English*)

Conductor	FRITZ BUSCH
Producer	CARL EBERT
Scenery	HAMISH WILSON
Costumes	KENNETH GREEN

Così fan tutte

MOZART *7 performances*

Ferrando	Gino del Signore (*Italian*)
Guglielmo	Roy Henderson (*Scottish*)
Don Alfonso	John Brownlee (*Australian*)
Fiordiligi	Ina Souez (*British*)
Dorabella	Risë Stevens (*American*)
Despina	Irene Eisinger (*Austrian*)

Conductor	FRITZ BUSCH
Producer	CARL EBERT
Scenery	HAMISH WILSON
Costumes	ANN LITHERLAND

The Beggar's Opera

after tour of:
BRIGHTON
CARDIFF
LIVERPOOL
MANCHESTER
GLASGOW
EDINBURGH

JOHN GAY *arr.* FREDERIC AUSTIN

Peachum	Roy Henderson
Lockit	Joseph Farrington
Macheath	Michael Redgrave
Filch	Bruce Flegg
Mrs Peachum	Constance Willis
	Elsie French
Polly Peachum	Audrey Mildmay
	Irene Eisinger
Lucy Lockit	Linda Gray
Diana Trapes	Alys Brough

Conductors	FREDERIC AUSTIN
	Anthony Bernard
	Michael Mudie
Producer	JOHN GIELGUD
Décor	by MOTLEY

1946   *Glyndebourne 12 vii - 27 vii: 14 performances*

On Tour: 67 performances

Artistic Director CARL EBERT

General Manager RUDOLF BING

MUSICAL STAFF

Conductors ERNEST ANSERMET and REGINALD GOODALL

Associate Conductor and in charge of
Musical Studies HANS OPPENHEIM

Musical Assistant JAMES ILIFF

GENERAL STAFF

Assistant Manager MORAN CAPLAT
Catering Manager A. H. BROWN
Stage Director A. HUNTLY GORDON
Stage Manager P. D. MacCLELLAN
Engineer W. J. THORPE
Chief Electrician C. SALVAGE
Stage Foreman R. W. GOUGH
Head Gardener F. HARVEY

The Rape of Lucretia

BENJAMIN BRITTEN   *World Première*

Male Chorus	Peter Pears
	Aksel Schiötz
Female Chorus	Joan Cross
	Flora Nielsen
Collatinus	Norman Walker
	Owen Brannigan
Junius	Edmund Donlevy
	Frederick Sharp
Tarquinius	Otakar Kraus
	Frank Rogier
Lucretia	Kathleen Ferrier
	Nancy Evans
Bianca	Anna Pollak
	Catherine Lawson
Lucia	Margaret Ritchie
	Lesley Duff

Conductors	ERNEST ANSERMET
	Reginald Goodall
Producer	ERIC CROZIER
On Tour	HANS OPPENHEIM
	Benjamin Britten
Designer	JOHN PIPER

Artistic Director CARL EBERT

General Manager RUDOLF BING

Assistant Manager MORAN CAPLAT

MUSICAL STAFF

FRITZ STIEDRY (Conductor)

BERTHOLD GOLDSCHMIDT

RENATO CELLINI, JOHN PRITCHARD, JAMES ILIFF

GENERAL STAFF

Stage Manager HAROLD CHAPIN
Assistant Producer PETER EBERT
Stage Foreman R. W. GOUGH
Chief Electrician C. SALVAGE
Head Gardener F. HARVEY
Wardrobe Mistress NELLIE AYRE
Property Master CHARLIE MCCARTHY

MUSICAL STAFF AT EDINBURGH

Principal Coach JANI STRASSER

GEORGE AUSTIN, JOHN PRITCHARD, JAMES ILIFF

Orpheus

GLUCK *9 performances*

Orpheus	Kathleen Ferrier (*British*)
Eurydice	Ann Ayars (*American*)
Amor	Zoë Vlachopoulos (*Greek*)

THE SOUTHERN PHILHARMONIC ORCHESTRA

Conductor FRITZ STIEDRY
Producer CARL EBERT
Designer JOSEPH CARL

Edinburgh 24 viii - 13 ix: 18 performances

Macbeth

VERDI *9 performances*

Macbeth	Francesco Valentino (*American*)
Banquo	Italo Tajo (*Italian*)
	Owen Brannigan (*British*)
Lady Macbeth	Margherita Grandi (*Tasmanian*)
Gentlewoman	Vera Terry (*Australian*)
Macduff	Walter Midgley (*British*)
Malcolm	Andrew McKinley (*American*)
Doctor	André Orkin (*British*)
Servant	Robert Vivian (*British*)
Murderer	Edward Thomas (*British*)

THE SCOTTISH ORCHESTRA
Conductor BERTHOLD GOLDSCHMIDT
Producer CARL EBERT
Designer CASPAR NEHER

Le nozze de Figaro

MOZART *9 performances*

Figaro	Italo Tajo (*Italian*)
Susanna	Tatiana Menotti (*Italian*)
	Ayhan Alnar (*Turkish*)
Bartolo	Owen Brannigan (*British*)
Marcellina	Catherine Lawson (*British*)
Cherubino	Giulietta Simionato (*Italian*)
Count Almaviva	John Brownlee (*Australian*)
Don Basilio	Bruce Flegg (*British*)
The Countess	Eleanor Steber (*American*)
Antonio	Ernest Frank (*British*)
Barbarina	Barbara Trent (*British*)
Don Curzio	Gwent Lewis (*British*)

Conductors WALTER SUSSKIND
Renato Cellini
Producer CARL EBERT
Scenery HAMISH WILSON
Costumes ANN LITHERLAND

Artistic Director CARL EBERT

Manager MORAN CAPLAT

MUSICAL STAFF

GEORGE AUSTIN, JOHN PRITCHARD, GIUSEPPE RUISI,
MARY SHORE, JANI STRASSER (Principal Coach)

GENERAL STAFF

Assistant Producer PETER EBERT
Stage Manager HAROLD CHAPIN
Assistant Stage Manager RONALD PERRY
Wardrobe and Properties HARRY KELLARD
Stage Technician R. W. GOUGH
Wardrobe Mistress NELLIE AYRE
Electrician R. HATHAWAY

THE ROYAL PHILHARMONIC ORCHESTRA

Don Giovanni

MOZART *9 performances*

Leporello	Vito de Taranto (*Italian*)
Donna Anna	Ljuba Welitsch (*Bulgarian*)
Don Giovanni	Paolo Silveri (*Italian*)
The Commendatore	David Franklin (*English*)
Don Ottavio	Richard Lewis (*Welsh*)
Donna Elvira	Christina Carroll (*American*)
Zerlina	Ann Ayars (*American*)
	Hilde Güden (*Austrian*)
Masetto	Ian Wallace (*Scottish*)

Conductor RAFAEL KUBELIK
Producer CARL EBERT
Scenery HAMISH WILSON
Costumes HEIN HECKROTH

Così fan tutte

MOZART *9 performances*

Ferrando	Petre Munteanu (*Rumanian*)
Guglielmo	Erich Kunz (*Austrian*)
Don Alfonso	Mariano Stabile (*Italian*)
Fiordiligi	Suzanne Danco (*Belgian*)
Dorabella	Eugenia Zareska (*British*)
Despina	Hilde Güden (*Austrian*)

Conductor VITTORIO GUI
Producer CARL EBERT
Designer ROLF GÉRARD

Artistic Director CARL EBERT

General Manager MORAN CAPLAT

MUSICAL STAFF

Associate Conductor HANS OPPENHEIM

GEORGE AUSTIN, JOHN PRITCHARD (Chorus Master)

GIUSEPPE RUISI, MARY SHORE

JANI STRASSER (Principal Coach)

PRODUCTION STAFF

Assistant Producer PETER EBERT

Stage Technician R. W. GOUGH

Stage Director ANTHONY HUDSON

Electrician R. HATHAWAY

Stage Manager RONALD PERRY

Stage Assistant S. HUGGETT

Assistant Stage Manager JAMES SMITH

Wardrobe Mistress NELLIE AYRE

Wardrobe and Properties HARRY KELLARD

Wardrobe Assistant ELIZABETH FOX

Secretary JANET MOORES

THE ROYAL PHILHARMONIC ORCHESTRA

Un ballo in maschera

VERDI *11 performances*

Riccardo	Mirto Picchi	(*Italian*)
	William Horne	(*American*)
Renato	Paolo Silveri	(*Italian*)
Amelia	Ljuba Welitsch	(*Bulgarian*)
	Margherita Grandi	(*Tasmanian*)
Ulrica	Jean Watson	(*Canadian*)
	Amalia Pini	(*Italian*)
Oscar	Alda Noni	(*Italian*)
Samuele	Ian Wallace	(*Scottish*)
Tommaso	Hervey Alan	(*English*)
Silvio	Francis Loring	(*English*)

Conductors VITTORIO GUI

Hans Oppenheim

Producer CARL EBERT

Designer CASPAR NEHER

Così fan tutte

MOZART *7 performances*

Ferrando	Petre Munteanu	(*Rumanian*)
Guglielmo	Marko Rothmüller	(*Yugoslavian*)
Don Alfonso	John Brownlee	(*Australian*)
Fiordiligi	Suzanne Danco	(*Belgian*)
Dorabella	Sena Jurinac	(*Yugoslavian*)
Despina	Irene Eisinger	(*Austrian*)

Conductors VITTORIO GUI

Hans Oppenheim

Producer CARL EBERT

Designer ROLF GÉRARD

Artistic Director CARL EBERT

General Manager MORAN CAPLAT

Conductor FRITZ BUSCH

MUSICAL STAFF
Chief Coach in charge of Musical Studies JANI STRASSER
Assistant Conductor and Choir Master JOHN PRITCHARD
BRYAN BALKWILL, GEORGE COOP

TECHNICAL STAFF
Stage Director ANTHONY HUDSON
Assistant Producer ROBERT HERMAN
Stage Managers RONALD PERRY, ELIZABETH LATHAM
Wardrobe and Properties HARRY KELLARD
Chief Technician R. W. GOUGH
Producer's Assistant J. DALRYMPLE
Wardrobe Mistress NELLIE AYRE
Chief Electrican N. THORPE
Property Master E. DUFFY
Stage Assistant S. HUGGETT
Head Gardener F. HARVEY
Secretary to General Manager JANET MOORES
Press Officer RUTH LYNAM

THE ROYAL PHILHARMONIC ORCHESTRA

Die Entführung aus dem Serail

MOZART *7 performances*

Belmonte	Richard Holm (*German*)
Osmin	Endre Koréh (*Hungarian*)
Pedrillo	Murray Dickie (*Scottish*)
Pasha Selim	Anton Walbrook (*German*)
Constanze	Ilse Hollweg (*German*)
Blonde	Alda Noni (*Italian*)
Sailor	Michael Hayes (*English*)
Dumb Slave	David Ashley (*English*)

Conductor FRITZ BUSCH
Producer CARL EBERT
Designer ROLF GÉRARD

Così fan tutte

MOZART *7 performances*

Ferrando	Richard Lewis (*English*)
Guglielmo	Erich Kunz (*Austrian*)
	Geraint Evans (*Welsh*)
Don Alfonso	Mario Borriello (*Italian*)
Fiordiligi	Sena Jurinac (*Jugo-Slav*)
Dorabella	Blanche Thebom (*American*)
Despina	Alda Noni (*Italian*)

Conductor FRITZ BUSCH
Producer CARL EBERT
Designer ROLF GÉRARD

Le nozze di Figaro

MOZART *9 performances*

Figaro	George London (*American*)
Susanna	Elfride Troetschel (*German*)
Bartolo	Ian Wallace (*Scottish*)
Marcellina	Jean Watson (*Canadian*)
Cherubino	Sena Jurinac (*Jugo-Slav*)
Count Almaviva	Marko Rothmüller (*Jugo-Slav*)
Don Basilio	Murray Dickie (*Scottish*)
The Countess	Clara Ebers (*German*)
Antonio	Dennis Wicks (*English*)
Barbarina	April Cantelo (*English*)
Don Curzio	Leslie Fyson (*English*)

Conductor FERENÇ FRICSAY
Producer CARL EBERT
Designer ROLF GÉRARD

Ariadne auf Naxos

(First Version)

RICHARD STRAUSS *9 performances*

Le Bourgeois Gentilhomme

M. Jourdain	Miles Malleson
Dorante	David King-Wood
Dorimène	Tatiana Lieven
Professor of Philosophy	Harold Scott

Ariadne auf Naxos

Najade	Maureen Springer (*English*)
Dryade	Marjorie Thomas (*English*)
Echo	April Cantelo (*English*)
Ariadne	Hilde Zadek (*Austrian*)
Harlekin	Douglas Craig (*English*)
Zerbinetta	Ilse Hollweg (*German*)
Brighella	Murray Dickie (*Scottish*)
Truffaldin	Bruce Dargavel (*Welsh*)
Scaramuccio	Alexander Young (*English*)
Bacchus	Peter Anders (*German*)

Conductor SIR THOMAS BEECHAM
Producer CARL EBERT
Designer OLIVER MESSEL

Artistic Directors FRITZ BUSCH
and CARL EBERT

General Manager MORAN CAPLAT

MUSICAL STAFF

Chief coach in charge of Musical Studies JANI STRASSER

Assistant Conductor JOHN PRITCHARD

DAVID ANDREWS, GEORGE COOP, ERNA GAL, MARY SHORE

PRODUCTION STAFF

Assistant Producer PETER EBERT

Production Manager ELIZABETH LAYTON

Lighting Consultant MICHAEL NORTHERN

Assistant to Producer ANTHONY BESCH

Stage Managers LISTER WELCH, JUNE DANDRIDGE

Chief Technician R. W. GOUGH

Wardrobe Manager ROSEMARY VERCOE

Wardrobe Mistress NELLIE AYRE

Property Master HARRY KELLARD

Stage Assistant S. HUGGETT

Chief Electrician N. THORPE

Secretary to General Manager JANET MOORES

Press Officer RUTH LYNAM

Head Gardener F. HARVEY

THE ROYAL PHILHARMONIC ORCHESTRA

Idomeneo

MOZART   6 *performances*
First professional production in England
(*The original edited for performance by Hans Gal*)

Ilia	Sena Jurinac (*Jugo-Slav*)
Idamante	Léopold Simoneau (*Canadian*)
Arbace	Alfred Poell (*Austrian*)
Electra	Birgit Nilsson (*Swedish*)
Idomeneo	Richard Lewis (*English*)
High Priest of Neptune	Alexander Young (*English*)
Voice of Neptune	Bruce Dargavel (*Welsh*)

Conductor   FRITZ BUSCH
Producer   CARL EBERT
Designer   OLIVER MESSEL

Le nozze di Figaro

MOZART   7 *performances*

Figaro	Alois Pernerstorfer (*Austrian*)
Susanna	Genevieve Warner (*American*)
Bartolo	Owen Brannigan (*English*)
Marcellina	Janet Howe (*Scottish*)
Cherubino	Dorothy MacNeil (*American*)
Count Almaviva	Alfred Poell (*Austrian*)
Don Basilio	Murray Dickie (*Scottish*)
	Alexander Young (*English*)
The Countess	Lisa Della Casa (*Swiss*)
Antonio	Dennis Wicks (*English*)
Barbarina	April Cantelo (*English*)
Don Curzio	Leslie Fyson (*English*)

Conductors   FRITZ BUSCH
John Pritchard
Producer   CARL EBERT
Scenery   HUTCHINSON SCOTT
Costumes   ROLF GÉRARD

Così fan tutte

MOZART *6 performances*

Ferrando	Richard Lewis (*English*)
Guglielmo	Marko Rothmüller (*Jugo-Slav*)
Don Alfonso	Sesto Bruscantini (*Italian*)
Fiordiligi	Sena Jurinac (*Jugo-Slav*)
Dorabella	Alice Howland (*American*)
Despina	Isa Quensel (*Swedish*)

Conductors FRITZ BUSCH
John Pritchard
Producer CARL EBERT
Designer ROLF GÉRARD

La forza del destino

VERDI *9 performances*

Marquis	Stanley Mason (*English*)
Leonora	Walburga Wegner (*German*)
Curra	Bruna Maclean (*Scottish*)
Don Alvaro	David Poleri (*American*)
Don Carlo	Marko Rothmüller (*Jugo-Slav*)
An Alcade	Dennis Wicks (*English*)
Trabuco	Robert Thomas (*Welsh*)
Preziosilla	Mildred Miller (*American*)
Fra Melitone	Owen Brannigan (*English*)
The Padre Guardiano	Bruce Dargaval (*Welsh*)
Surgeon	Philip Lewtas (*English*)

Conductor FRITZ BUSCH
Producer CARL EBERT
Designer LESLIE HURRY

Don Giovanni

MOZART *6 performances*

Leporello	Alois Pernerstorfer (*Austrian*)
Donna Anna	Hilde Zadek (*Austrian*)
Don Giovanni	Mario Petri (*Italian*)
The Commendatore	Bruce Dargavel (*Welsh*)
Don Ottavio	Léopold Simoneau (*Canadian*)
Donna Elvira	Suzanne Danco (*Belgian*)
Zerlina	Genevieve Warner (*American*)
Masetto	Geraint Evans (*Welsh*)

Conductors FRITZ BUSCH
John Pritchard
Producer CARL EBERT
Designer JOHN PIPER

Don Giovanni

MOZART *9 performances*

Leporello	Alois Pernerstorfer (*Austrian*)
	Owen Brannigan (*English*)
Donna Anna	Hilde Zadek (*Austrian*)
Don Giovanni	Mario Petri (*Italian*)
The Commendatore	Bruce Dargavel (*Welsh*)
Don Ottavio	Léopold Simoneau (*Canadian*)
Donna Elvira	Dorothy MacNeil (*American*)
Zerlina	Genevieve Warner (*American*)
	Roxane Houston (*Irish*)
	Pierrette Alarie (*Canadian*)
Masetto	Geraint Evans (*Welsh*)

Conductors FRITZ BUSCH
John Pritchard
Producer CARL EBERT
Designer JOHN PIPER

Artistic Director CARL EBERT

General Manager MORAN CAPLAT

MUSICAL STAFF

Chief coach in charge of Musical Studies JANI STRASSER

Coaches ERNA GAL, ALFONSO GIBILARO,
ROMEO OLIVIERI, MAURITS SILLEM

PRODUCTION STAFF

Assistant Producer PETER EBERT

Stage Director DOUGLAS CRAIG

Assistant to Producer ANTHONY BESCH

Stage Managers JUNE DANDRIDGE, REGINALD CORNISH

Wardrobe Manager ROSEMARY VERCOE

Property Manager HARRY KELLARD

Assistant to Designers JOHN CLARIDGE

Chief Technician R. W. GOUGH

Chief Electrician N. THORPE

Head Gardener F. HARVEY

Secretary to General Manager JANET MOORES

Box Office Manager PHYLLIS MAULE

THE ROYAL PHILHARMONIC ORCHESTRA

Idomeneo

MOZART *8 performances*

Ilia	Sena Jurinac (*Jugo-Slav*)
Idamante	Léopold Simoneau (*Canadian*)
Arbace	John Cameron (*Australian*)
Electra	Maria Kinasiewicz (*Polish*)
Idomeneo	Richard Lewis (*English*)
High Priest of Neptune	Alexander Young (*English*)
Voice of Neptune	Hervey Alan (*English*)

Conductor JOHN PRITCHARD
Producer CARL EBERT
Designer OLIVER MESSEL

La Cenerentola

ROSSINI *9 performances*

Don Ramiro	Juan Oncina (*Spanish*)
Dandini	Sesto Bruscantini (*Italian*)
Don Magnifico	Ian Wallace (*Scottish*)
Clorinda	Alda Noni (*Italian*)
Tisbe	Fernanda Cadoni (*Italian*)
Cenerentola	Marina de Gabarain (*Spanish*)
Alidoro	Hervey Alan (*English*)

Conductor VITTORIO GUI
Producer CARL EBERT
Designer OLIVER MESSEL

Macbeth

VERDI *8 performances*

Macbeth	Marko Rothmüller (*Jugo-Slav*)
Banquo	Frederick Dalberg (*South African*)
Lady Macbeth	Dorothy Dow (*American*)
Gentlewoman	Patricia Bartlett (*Australian*)
Macduff	James Johnston (*Irish*)
Malcolm	John Kentish (*English*)
Doctor	Dennis Wicks (*English*)

Conductor	VITTORIO GUI
Producer	CARL EBERT
Designer	CASPAR NEHER

Così fan tutte

MOZART *3 performances*

Ferrando	Richard Lewis (*English*)
Guglielmo	Sesto Bruscantini (*Italian*)
Don Alfonso	Dezsö Ernster (*Hungarian*)
Fiordiligi	Sena Jurinac (*Jugo-Slav*)
Dorabella	Anna Pollak (*English*)
Despina	Alda Noni (*Italian*)

Conductor	VITTORIO GUI
Producer	CARL EBERT
Designer	ROLF GÉRARD

Artistic Director CARL EBERT

General Manager MORAN CAPLAT

Chief coach in charge of Musical Studies JANI STRASSER
Assistant Conductor BRYAN BALKWILL
Chorus Master LEO QUAYLE

MUSICAL STAFF

ERNA GAL, ROMEO OLIVIERI,
MAURITS SILLEM, THELMA STORY
Librarian HOWARD WICKS

PRODUCTION STAFF

Assistant Producers PETER EBERT, ANTHONY BESCH
Stage Director DOUGLAS CRAIG
Stage Managers JUNE DANDRIDGE, REGINALD CORNISH
Producers' Assistant GEORGE CHRISTIE
Wardrobe Manager ROSEMARY VERCOE
Property Manager HARRY KELLARD
Chief Technician R. W. GOUGH
Chief Electrician N. THORPE
Wardrobe Mistress NELLIE AYRE
Stage Assistant S. HUGGETT
Head Gardener F. HARVEY
Secretary to General Manager JANET MOORES
Box Office Manager PHYLLIS MAULE
Press Officer BERNARD MCNABB

THE ROYAL PHILHARMONIC ORCHESTRA

Alceste

GLUCK *8 performances*

Herald	Dennis Wicks	(*English*)
Evander	Alexander Young	(*English*)
Alceste	Magda Laszlo	(*Hungarian*)
High Priest	John Cameron	(*Australian*)
Admète	Richard Lewis	(*English*)
Hercules	Thomas Hemsley	(*English*)
Voice of Tanato	Hervey Alan	(*English*)
Apollo	John Cameron	(*Australian*)

Conductor VITTORIO GUI
Producer CARL EBERT
Scenery HUGH CASSON
Costumes ROSEMARY VERCOE
Statue of Apollo CHRISTOPHER IRONSIDE

La Cenerentola

ROSSINI *9 performances*

Don Ramiro	Juan Oncina	(*Spanish*)
Dandini	Sesto Bruscantini	(*Italian*)
Don Magnifico	Ian Wallace	(*Scottish*)
Clorinda	Alda Noni	(*Italian*)
Tisbe	Fernanda Cadoni	(*Italian*)
Cenerentola	Marina de Gabarain	(*Spanish*)
Alidoro	Hervey Alan	(*English*)

Conductor VITTORIO GUI
Producer CARL EBERT
Designer OLIVER MESSEL

Ariadne auf Naxos
(Second Version)

RICHARD STRAUSS *8 performances*

Composer	Sena Jurinac (*Jugo-Slav*)
Music Master	Sesto Bruscantini (*Italian*)
Dancing Master	Murray Dickie (*Scottish*)
Zerbinetta	Mattiwilda Dobbs (*American*)
Ariadne	Dorothy Dow (*American*)
Harlekin	Kurt Gester (*German*)
Scaramuccio	Alexander Young (*English*)
Truffaldin	Fritz Ollendorf (*German*)
Brighella	Murray Dickie (*Scottish*)
Najade	Edna Graham (*New Zealand*)
Dryade	Marjorie Thomas (*English*)
Echo	April Cantelo (*English*)
Bacchus	Carlos Guichandut (*Argentinian*)

Conductor JOHN PRITCHARD
Producer CARL EBERT
Designer OLIVER MESSEL

Die Entführung aus dem Serail

MOZART *6 performances*

Belmonte	Helmut Krebs (*German*)
Osmin	Fritz Ollendorf (*German*)
Pedrillo	Murray Dickie (*Scottish*)
Pasha Selim	Carl Ebert (*German*)
	David Franklin (*English*)
Constanze	Sari Barabas (*Hungarian*)
Blonde	Emmy Loose (*Czech*)
	April Cantelo (*English*)

Conductor ALFRED WALLENSTEIN
Producer CARL EBERT
Designer ROLF GÉRARD

Così fan tutte

MOZART *6 performances*

Ferrando	Juan Oncina (*Spanish*)
	Alexander Young (*English*)
Guglielmo	Geraint Evans (*Welsh*)
Don Alfonso	Sesto Bruscantini (*Italian*)
Fiordiligi	Sena Jurinac (*Jugo-Slav*)
	Rita McKerrow (*English*)
Dorabella	Anna Pollak (*English*)
Despina	Alda Noni (*Italian*)

Conductor JOHN PRITCHARD
Producer CARL EBERT
Designer ROLF GÉRARD

Edinburgh 23 viii - 12 ix: 18 performances

La Cenerentola

ROSSINI *7 performances*

Don Ramiro	Juan Oncina (*Spanish*)
Dandini	Sesto Bruscantini (*Italian*)
Don Magnifico	Ian Wallace (*Scottish*)
Clorinda	Alda Noni (*Italian*)
Tisbe	Fernanda Cadoni (*Italian*)
Cenerentola	Marina de Gabarain (*Spanish*)
Alidoro	Hervey Alan (*English*)

Conductor VITTORIO GUI
Producer CARL EBERT
Designer OLIVER MESSEL

The Rake's Progress

STRAVINSKY *5 performances*

First stage performance in Britain

Anne	Elsie Morison (*Australian*)
Tom Rakewell	Richard Lewis (*English*)
Trulove	Hervey Alan (*English*)
Nick Shadow	Jerome Hines (*American*)
Mother Goose	Mary Jarred (*English*)
Baba the Turk	Nan Merriman (*American*)
Sellem	Murray Dickie (*Scottish*)
Keeper of the Madhouse	Dennis Wicks (*English*)

Conductor ALFRED WALLENSTEIN
Producer CARL EBERT
Designer OSBERT LANCASTER

Idomeneo

MOZART *6 performances*

Ilia	Sena Jurinac (*Jugo-Slav*)
Idamante	Helmut Krebs (*German*)
Arbace	John Cameron (*Australian*)
Electra	Jennifer Vyvyan (*English*)
Idomeneo	Richard Lewis (*English*)
High Priest of Neptune	John Carolan (*Irish*)
Voice of Neptune	Hervey Alan (*English*)

Conductor JOHN PRITCHARD
Producer CARL EBERT
Designer OLIVER MESSEL

Artistic Director CARL EBERT

General Manager MORAN CAPLAT

Head of Music Staff JANI STRASSER

MUSICAL STAFF

Assistant Conductors PETER GELLHORN, ROMEO OLIVIERI,
MAURITS SILLEM
Coaches ERNA GAL, RAYMOND LEPPARD, THELMA STORY
Librarian HOWARD WICKS

PRODUCTION STAFF

Associate Producer PETER EBERT
Assistant Producers ANTHONY BESCH, DAVID MACDONALD
Producers' Assistant GEORGE CHRISTIE
Stage Director DOUGLAS CRAIG
Stage Managers JUNE DANDRIDGE, REGINALD CORNISH
Assistant Stage Managers ANN DUFFY, DAVID GAULD
Wardrobe Manager ROSEMARY VERCOE
Wardrobe Mistress NELLIE AYRE
Chief Wardrobe Assistants ROSEMARY WILKINS, JOAN PYLE
Property Manager HARRY KELLARD
Property Assistant R. COTCHER
Chief Technician R. W. GOUGH
Chief Electrician N. THORPE
Assistant Technician S. HUGGETT
Head Gardener F. HARVEY
Secretary to General Manager JANET MOORES
Box Officer Manager PHYLLIS MAULE
Press Officer BERNARD MCNABB

THE ROYAL PHILHARMONIC ORCHESTRA

The Barber of Seville

ROSSINI *9 performances*

Count Almaviva	Juan Oncina (*Spanish*)
Figaro	Sesto Bruscantini (*Italian*)
Rosina	Graziella Sciutti (*Italian*)
Bartolo	Ian Wallace (*Scottish*)
Basilio	Antonio Cassinelli (*Italian*)
Fiorello	Gwyn Griffiths (*Welsh*)
Berta	Noreen Berry (*South African*)
Ambrogio	Harold Williams (*English*)
Officer	David Kelly (*Scottish*)
Notary	Daniel McCoshan (*Scottish*)

Conductor VITTORIO GUI
Producer CARL EBERT
Designer OLIVER MESSEL

Alceste

GLUCK *6 performances*

Herald	Thomas Hemsley (*English*)
Evander	Paul Asciak (*Maltese*)
Alceste	Magda Laszlo (*Hungarian*)
High Priest	Raimundo Torres (*Spanish*)
Admète	Richard Lewis (*English*)
Hercules	Thomas Hemsley (*English*)
Voice of Tanato	James Atkins (*English*)
Apollo	Raimundo Torres (*Spanish*)

Conductors VITTORIO GUI
Bryan Balkwill
Producer CARL EBERT
Scenery HUGH CASSON
Costumes ROSEMARY VERCOE
Statue of Apollo CHRISTOPHER IRONSIDE

Arlecchino

BUSONI *6 performances*

First stage production in Britain

Ser Matteo	Ian Wallace (*Scottish*)
Arlecchino	Kurt Gester (*German*)
Abbate Cospicuo	Geraint Evans (*Welsh*)
Doctor Bombasto	Fritz Ollendorf (*German*)
Colombina	Elaine Malbin (*American*)
Leandro	Murray Dickie (*Scottish*)

Conductor JOHN PRITCHARD
Producer PETER EBERT
Designer PETER RICE

Don Giovanni

MOZART *9 performances*

Leporello	Benno Kusche (*German*)
Donna Anna	Margaret Harshaw (*American*)
Don Giovanni	James Pease (*American*)
The Commendatore	Hervey Alan (*English*)
Don Ottavio	Léopold Simoneau (*Canadian*)
Donna Elvira	Sena Jurinac (*Jugo-Slav*)
Zerlina	Anny Schlemm (*German*)
Masetto	Thomas Hemsley (*English*)

Conductor GEORG SOLTI
Producer CARL EBERT
Designer JOHN PIPER

Ariadne auf Naxos
(Second Version)

RICHARD STRAUSS *6 performances*

Composer	Sena Jurinac (*Jugo-Slav*)
Music Master	Geraint Evans (*Welsh*)
Dancing Master	Murray Dickie (*Scottish*)
Zerbinetta	Mattiwilda Dobbs (*American*)
	Ilse Hollweg (*German*)
Ariadne	Lucine Amara (*American*)
Harlekin	Kurt Gester (*German*)
Scaramuccio	Juan Oncina (*Spanish*)
Truffaldin	Fritz Ollendorf (*German*)
Brighella	Murray Dickie (*Scottish*)
Najade	Maureen Springer (*English*)
Dryade	Noreen Berry (*South African*)
Echo	Elaine Malbin (*American*)
Bacchus	Richard Lewis (*English*)

Conductor JOHN PRITCHARD
Producer CARL EBERT
Designer OLIVER MESSEL

The Rake's Progress

STRAVINSKY *6 performances*

Anne	Elsie Morison (*Australian*)
Tom Rakewell	Richard Lewis (*English*)
Trulove	Hervey Alan (*English*)
Nick Shadow	Marko Rothmüller (*Jugo-Slav*)
Mother Goose	Mary Jarred (*English*)
Baba the Turk	Marina de Gabarain (*Spanish*)
Sellem	Hugues Cuenod (*Swiss*)
Keeper of the Madhouse	David Kelly (*Scottish*)

Conductors PAUL SACHER
Bryan Balkwill
Producer CARL EBERT
Designer OSBERT LANCASTER

Le Comte Ory

ROSSINI *7 performances*

Raimbaud	Sesto Bruscantini (*Italian*)
Ory	Juan Oncina (*Spanish*)
Alice	Halinka de Tarczynska (*Australian*)
Ragonde	Monica Sinclair (*English*)
Isolier	Fernanda Cadoni (*Italian*)
Le Gouverneur	Ian Wallace (*Scottish*)
Adèle	Sari Barabas (*Hungarian*)

Conductor	VITTORIO GUI
Producer	CARL EBERT
Designer	OLIVER MESSEL

Così fan tutte

MOZART *5 performances*

Ferrando	Juan Oncina (*Spanish*)
	Richard Lewis (*English*)
Guglielmo	Geraint Evans (*Welsh*)
Don Alfonso	Sesto Bruscantini (*Italian*)
Fiordiligi	Sena Jurinac (*Jugo-Slav*)
Dorabella	Magda Laszlo (*Hungarian*)
Despina	Alda Noni (*Italian*)

Conductors	VITTORIO GUI
	John Pritchard
Producer	CARL EBERT
Scenery	ROLF GÉRARD
Costumes	ROSEMARY VERCOE

Ariadne auf Naxos
(Second Version)

RICHARD STRAUSS *6 performances*

Composer	Sena Jurinac (*Jugo-Slav*)
Music Master	Geraint Evans (*Welsh*)
Dancing Master	Murray Dickie (*Scottish*)
Zerbinetta	Mattiwilda Dobbs (*American*)
Ariadne	Lucine Amara (*American*)
Harlekin	Kurt Gester (*German*)
Scaramuccio	Juan Oncina (*Spanish*)
Truffaldin	Fritz Ollendorf (*German*)
Brighella	Murray Dickie (*Scottish*)
Najade	Maureen Springer (*English*)
Dryade	Noreen Berry (*South African*)
Echo	Elaine Malbin (*American*)
Bacchus	Richard Lewis (*English*)

Conductor	JOHN PRITCHARD
Producer	CARL EBERT
Designer	OLIVER MESSEL

Berlin 25 - 26 ix: 2 performances

La Cenerentola

ROSSINI *2 performances*

Don Ramiro	Juan Oncina (*Spanish*)
Dandini	Sesto Bruscantini (*Italian*)
Don Magnifico	Ian Wallace (*Scottish*)
Clorinda	Alda Noni (*Italian*)
	Halinka de Tarczynska (*Australian*)
Tisbe	Fernanda Cadoni (*Italian*)
Cenerentola	Marina de Gabarain (*Spanish*)
Alidoro	Hervey Alan (*English*)

Conductor	JOHN PRITCHARD
Producer	CARL EBERT
Designer	OLIVER MESSEL

Artistic Director CARL EBERT

General Manager MORAN CAPLAT

Head of Music Staff JANI STRASSER

MUSICAL STAFF

Chorus Master and Assistant Conductor PETER GELLHORN

Assistant Conductors and Coaches ROMEO OLIVIERI,
RAYMOND LEPPARD, DENIS VAUGHAN

Librarian HOWARD WICKS

PRODUCTION STAFF

Associate Producer PETER EBERT

Assistant Producers ANTHONY BESCH, RICHARD DAY

Stage Director DOUGLAS CRAIG

Stage Managers JUNE DANDRIDGE, GUY BLOOMER

Assistant Stage Managers ANN DUFFY, DAVID GAULD

Wardrobe Manager ROSEMARY VERCOE

Chief Wardrobe Assistants JOAN PYLE, ROSEMARY WILKINS

Chief Dresser NELLIE AYRE

Property Manager HARRY KELLARD

Chief Technician R. W. GOUGH

Chief Electrician N. THORPE

Assistant Technician S. HUGGETT

Head Gardener F. HARVEY

Secretary to General Manager JANET MOORES

Box Office Manager PHYLLIS MAULE

Press Officer BERNARD MCNABB

THE ROYAL PHILHARMONIC ORCHESTRA

Le nozze di Figaro

MOZART   *9 performances*

Figaro	Sesto Bruscantini (*Italian*)
Susanna	Elena Rizzieri (*Italian*)
Bartolo	Ian Wallace (*Scottish*)
Marcellina	Monica Sinclair (*English*)
Cherubino	Frances Bible (*American*)
	Risë Stevens (*American*)
Count Almaviva	Franco Calabrese (*Italian*)
Don Basilio	Hugues Cuenod (*Swiss*)
The Countess	Sena Jurinac (*Jugo-Slav*)
Antonio	Gwyn Griffiths (*Welsh*)
Barbarina	Jeannette Sinclair (*English*)
Don Curzio	Daniel McCoshan (*Scottish*)

Conductor   VITTORIO GUI
Producer   CARL EBERT
Designer   OLIVER MESSEL

Le Comte Ory

ROSSINI   *6 performances*

Raimbaud	Giuseppe Valdengo (*Italian*)
Ory	Juan Oncina (*Spanish*)
Alice	Halinka de Tarczynska (*Australian*)
Ragonde	Monica Sinclair (*English*)
Isolier	Fernanda Cadoni (*Italian*)
Le Gouverneur	Ian Wallace (*Scottish*)
Adèle	Sari Barabas (*Hungarian*)

Conductor   VITTORIO GUI
Producer   CARL EBERT
Designer   OLIVER MESSEL

Don Giovanni

MOZART   *9 performances*

Leporello	Geraint Evans (*Welsh*)
Donna Anna	Sena Jurinac (*Jugo-Slav*)
Don Giovanni	Giuseppe Valdengo (*Italian*)
The Commendatore	Hervey Alan (*English*)
Don Ottavio	Richard Lewis (*English*)
Donna Elvira	Lucine Amara (*American*)
Zerlina	Genevieve Warner (*American*)
Masetto	Thomas Hemsley (*English*)

Conductor   JOHN PRITCHARD
Producer   CARL EBERT
Designer   JOHN PIPER

The Barber of Seville

ROSSINI *9 performances*

Count Almaviva	Juan Oncina (*Spanish*)
Figaro	Sesto Bruscantini (*Italian*)
Rosina	Gianna d'Angelo (*American*)
Bartolo	Ian Wallace (*Scottish*)
Basilio	Cristiano Dalamangas (*Greek*)
Fiorello	Gwyn Griffiths (*Welsh*)
Berta	Monica Sinclair (*English*)
Ambrogio	Harold Williams (*English*)
Officer	David Kelly (*Scottish*)
Notary	Daniel McCoshan (*Scottish*)

Conductors VITTORIO GUI
Bryan Balkwill
Producer CARL EBERT
Designer OLIVER MESSEL

The Rake's Progress

STRAVINSKY *4 performances*

Anne	Elsie Morison (*Australian*)
Tom Rakewell	Richard Lewis (*English*)
Trulove	Hervey Alan (*English*)
Nick Shadow	Marko Rothmüller (*Jugo-Slav*)
Mother Goose	Mary Jarred (*English*)
Baba the Turk	Marina de Gabarain (*Spanish*)
Sellem	John Kentish (*English*)
Keeper of the Madhouse	David Kelly (*Scottish*)

Conductor PAUL SACHER
Producer CARL EBERT
Designer OSBERT LANCASTER

The Barber of Seville

ROSSINI *6 performances*

Count Almaviva	Juan Oncina (*Spanish*)
Figaro	Sesto Bruscantini (*Italian*)
Rosina	Gianna d'Angelo (*American*)
Bartolo	Ian Wallace (*Scottish*)
Basilio	Cristiano Dalamangas (*Greek*)
Fiorello	Gwyn Griffiths (*Welsh*)
Berta	Monica Sinclair (*English*)
Ambrogio	Harold Williams (*English*)
Officer	David Kelly (*Scottish*)
Notary	Daniel McCoshan (*Scottish*)

Conductor ALBERTO EREDE
Producer CARL EBERT
Designer OLIVER MESSEL

Falstaff

VERDI *6 performances*

Falstaff	Fernando Corena (*Swiss*)
Dr Caius	Dermot Troy (*Irish*)
Bardolph	Daniel McCoshan (*Scottish*)
Pistol	Marco Stefanoni (*Italian*)
Meg Page	Fernanda Cadoni (*Italian*)
Alice Ford	Anna Maria Rovere (*Italian*)
Mistress Quickly	Oralia Dominguez (*Mexican*)
Nannetta	Eugenia Ratti (*Italian*)
Fenton	Juan Oncina (*Spanish*)
	Kevin Miller (*Australian*)
Ford	Walter Monachesi (*Italian*)
Innkeeper	Harold Williams (*English*)

Conductor CARLO MARIA GIULINI
Producer CARL EBERT
Designer OSBERT LANCASTER

La forza del destino

VERDI *6 performances*

Marquis	David Kelly (*Scottish*)
Leonora	Sena Jurinac (*Jugo-Slav*)
Curra	Monica Sinclair (*English*)
Don Alvaro	David Poleri (*American*)
Don Carlo	Marko Rothmüller (*Jugo-Slav*)
An Alcade	James Atkins (*English*)
Trabuco	John Carolan (*Irish*)
Preziosilla	Marina de Gabarain (*Spanish*)
Fra Melitone	Ian Wallace (*Scottish*)
The Padre Guardiano	Hervey Alan (*English*)
Surgeon	Niven Miller (*Scottish*)

Conductor JOHN PRITCHARD
Producer PETER EBERT
Designer LESLIE HURRY

Artistic Director CARL EBERT

General Manager MORAN CAPLAT

Head of Music Staff JANI STRASSER

MUSICAL STAFF

Chorus Master PETER GELLHORN
Assistant Conductors and Coaches GEORGE COOP,
PAUL HAMBURGER, JOSEPH HOROVITZ
Librarian HOWARD WICKS

PRODUCTION STAFF

Assistant Producers ANTHONY BESCH, RICHARD DAY
Stage Director JUNE DANDRIDGE
Stage Managers REGINALD CORNISH, ANN DUFFY,
DAVID GAULD
Wardrobe Manager ROSEMARY VERCOE
Chief Dresser NELLIE AYRE
Property Manager HARRY KELLARD
Chief Technician R. W. GOUGH
Assistant S. HUGGETT
Chief Electrician N. THORPE
Assistant R. RICHARDS
Head Gardener F. HARVEY
Assistant General Manager DOUGLAS CRAIG
Personal Assistant to General Manager JANET MOORES
Box Office Manager SALLY MAYO
Press Officer BERNARD MCNABB

THE ROYAL PHILHARMONIC ORCHESTRA

Idomeneo

MOZART *7 performances*

Ilia	Elisabeth Grümmer (*German*)
Idamante	William McAlpine (*Scottish*)
Arbace	James Milligan (*Canadian*)
Electra	Lucille Udovick (*American*)
Idomeneo	Richard Lewis (*English*)
High Priest of Neptune	David Galliver (*Welsh*)
Voice of Neptune	Hervey Alan (*English*)

Conductor JOHN PRITCHARD
Producer CARL EBERT
Designer OLIVER MESSEL

Die Entführung aus dem Serail

MOZART *8 performances*

Belmonte	Ernst Haefliger (*Swiss*)
Osmin	Arnold van Mill (*Dutch*)
Pedrillo	Kevin Miller (*Australian*)
Pasha Selim	Leo Bieber (*German*)
Constanze	Mattiwilda Dobbs (*American*)
Blonde	Lisa Otto (*German*)
Sailor	James Atkins (*English*)
Dumb Slave	Harold Williams (*English*)

Conductors PAUL SACHER
          Peter Gellhorn
Producer CARL EBERT
Designer OLIVER MESSEL

Le nozze di Figaro

MOZART *9 performances*

Figaro	Sesto Bruscantini (*Italian*)
Susanna	Elena Rizzieri (*Italian*)
Bartolo	Ian Wallace (*Scottish*)
Marcellina	Monica Sinclair (*English*)
Cherubino	Cora Canne-Meijer (*Dutch*)
Count Almaviva	Michel Roux (*French*)
Don Basilio	Hugues Cuenod (*Swiss*)
The Countess	Elisabeth Grümmer (*German*)
	Joan Sutherland (*Australian*)
Antonio	Gwyn Griffiths (*Welsh*)
Barbarina	Jeannette Sinclair (*English*)
Don Curzio	Daniel McCoshan (*Scottish*)

Conductors	VITTORIO GUI
	Maurits Sillem
Producer	CARL EBERT
Designer	OLIVER MESSEL

The Magic Flute

MOZART *8 performances*

Tamino	Ernst Haefliger (*Swiss*)
Three Ladies	Joan Sutherland (*Australian*)
	Cora Canne-Meijer (*Dutch*)
	Monica Sinclair (*English*)
Papageno	Geraint Evans (*Welsh*)
Queen of the Night	Mattiwilda Dobbs (*American*)
Three Boys	Belva Boroditsky (*Canadian*)
	Jeannette Sinclair (*English*)
	Vera Kinrade (*English*)
Monostatos	Kevin Miller (*Australian*)
Pamina	Pilar Lorengar (*Spanish*)
The Speaker	Thomas Hemsley (*English*)
Sarastro	Frederick Guthrie (*American*)
	Drago Bernadic (*Jugo-Slav*)
Priests and Men in Armour	John Carolan (*Irish*)
	David Kelly (*Scottish*)
Papagena	Maureen Springer (*English*)
	Naida Labay (*Bulgarian*)

Conductor	VITTORIO GUI
Producer	CARL EBERT
Designer	OLIVER MESSEL

Don Giovanni

MOZART *9 performances*

Leporello	Geraint Evans (*Welsh*)
Donna Anna	Sena Jurinac (*Jugo-Slav*)
Don Giovanni	Kim Borg (*Finnish*)
The Commendatore	Hervey Alan (*English*)
Don Ottavio	Richard Lewis (*English*)
Donna Elvira	Elisabeth Lindermeier (*German*)
	Doreen Watts (*English*)
Zerlina	Elsie Morison (*Australian*)
Masetto	Thomas Hemsley (*English*)

Conductor	JOHN PRITCHARD
Producer	PETER EBERT
Designer	JOHN PIPER

Così fan tutte

MOZART *7 performances*

Ferrando	Richard Lewis (*English*)
	Juan Oncina (*Spanish*)
Guglielmo	Sesto Bruscantini (*Italian*)
Don Alfonso	Ivan Sardi (*Hungarian*)
Fiordiligi	Sena Jurinac (*Jugo-Slav*)
Dorabella	Nan Merriman (*American*)
Despina	Elena Rizzieri (*Italian*)

Conductors	VITTORIO GUI
	John Pritchard
Producer	CARL EBERT
Scenery	ROLF GÉRARD
Costumes	ROSEMARY VERCOE

Liverpool 10 ix - 22 ix: 12 performances

Le nozze di Figaro

MOZART *4 performances*

Figaro	Sesto Bruscantini (*Italian*)
Susanna	Elena Rizzieri (*Italian*)
Bartolo	Ian Wallace (*Scottish*)
Marcellina	Monica Sinclair (*English*)
Cherubino	Cora Canne-Meijer (*Dutch*)
Count Almaviva	Michel Roux (*French*)
Don Basilio	Hugues Cuenod (*Swiss*)
The Countess	Joan Sutherland (*Australian*)
Antonio	Gwyn Griffiths (*Welsh*)
Barbarina	Jeannette Sinclair (*English*)
Don Curzio	Daniel McCoshan (*Scottish*)

Conductors	VITTORIO GUI
	John Pritchard
Producer	CARL EBERT
Designer	OLIVER MESSEL

LIVERPOOL PHILHARMONIC ORCHESTRA

La Cenerentola

ROSSINI *4 performances*

Don Ramiro	Juan Oncina (*Spanish*)
Dandini	Sesto Bruscantini (*Italian*)
Don Magnifico	Ian Wallace (*Scottish*)
Clorinda	Cora Canne-Meijer (*Dutch*)
Tisbe	Gianna d'Angelo (*American*)
Cenerentola	Marina de Gabarain (*Spanish*)
Alidoro	Hervey Alan (*English*)

Conductors	VITTORIO GUI
	John Pritchard
Producer	CARL EBERT
Designer	OLIVER MESSEL

LIVERPOOL PHILHARMONIC ORCHESTRA

Don Giovanni

MOZART *4 performances*

Leporello	Geraint Evans (*Welsh*)
Donna Anna	Sena Jurinac (*Jugo-Slav*)
Don Giovanni	Kim Borg (*Finnish*)
The Commendatore	Hervey Alan (*English*)
Don Ottavio	Juan Oncina (*Spanish*)
Donna Elvira	Elisabeth Lindermeier (*German*)
Zerlina	Elsie Morison (*Australian*)
Masetto	Thomas Hemsley (*English*)

Conductors	JOHN PRITCHARD
	Bryan Balkwill
Producer	PETER EBERT
Designer	JOHN PIPER

LIVERPOOL PHILHARMONIC ORCHESTRA

1957

Glyndebourne 11 vi - 13 viii: 49 performances

Artistic Director CARL EBERT

General Manager MORAN CAPLAT

Head of Music Staff JANI STRASSER

MUSICAL STAFF

Chorus Master PETER GELLHORN

Assistant Conductors and Coaches GEORGE COOP,
PAUL HAMBURGER, LEONARD HANCOCK,
MARTIN ISEPP, JAMES LOCKHART

Librarian HOWARD WICKS

PRODUCTION STAFF

Associate Producer ANTHONY BESCH

Assistant Producer RICHARD DAY

Stage Director JUNE DANDRIDGE

Stage Managers ANN DUFFY, DAVID GAULD,
GEOFFREY GILBERTSON

Wardrobe Manager ROSEMARY WILKINS

Chief Dresser NELLIE AYRE

Maintenance BERTHA CUMMINS

Property Manager HARRY KELLARD

Chief Technician R. W. GOUGH

Assistant Technician S. HUGGETT

Chief Electrician N. THORPE

Assistant Electrician R. RICHARDS

Head Gardener F. HARVEY

Assistant General Manager DOUGLAS CRAIG

Personal Assistant to General Manager JANET MOORES

Regulating Secretary ELLEN MORGENTHAU

Press Officer BERNARD MCNABB

Box Office Manager SALLY MAYO

THE ROYAL PHILHARMONIC ORCHESTRA

L'italiana in Algeri

ROSSINI *8 performances*

Elvira Antonietta Pastori (*Italian*)
Zulma Josephine Veasey (*English*)
Mustafa Paolo Montarsolo (*Italian*)
Haly Thomas Hemsley (*English*)
Lindoro Juan Oncina (*Spanish*)
Isabella Oralia Dominguez (*Mexican*)
Taddeo Marcello Cortis (*Austrian*)

Conductor VITTORIO GUI
Producer PETER EBERT
Designer OSBERT LANCASTER

The Magic Flute

MOZART *8 performances*

Tamino David Lloyd (*American*)
Three Ladies Heather Harper (*Irish*)
Nancy Evans (*English*)
Monica Sinclair (*English*)
Papageno Geraint Evans (*Welsh*)
Heinz Blankenburg (*American*)
Queen of the Night Margareta Hallin (*Swedish*)
Three Boys Belva Boroditsky (*Canadian*)
Jeannette Sinclair (*English*)
Helen Watts (*English*)
Monostatos Kevin Miller (*Australian*)
Pamina Pilar Lorengar (*Spanish*)
The Speaker Thomas Hemsley (*English*)
Walter Hertner (*German*)
Sarastro Mihaly Szekely (*Hungarian*)
Priests and Men in Armour John Carolan (*Irish*)
James Atkins (*English*)
Papagena Rosl Schwaiger (*Austrian*)
Naida Labay (*Bulgarian*)

Conductors PAUL SACHER
Peter Gellhorn
Producer CARL EBERT
Designer OLIVER MESSEL

Falstaff

VERDI *9 performances*

Falstaff	Geraint Evans (*Welsh*)
Dr Caius	Hugues Cuenod (*Swiss*)
Bardolph	John Lewis (*Welsh*)
Pistol	Hervey Alan (*English*)
Meg Page	Fernanda Cadoni (*Italian*)
Alice Ford	Orietta Moscussi (*Italian*)
Mistress Quickly	Oralia Dominguez (*Mexican*)
Nannetta	Antonietta Pastori (*Italian*)
Fenton	Juan Oncina (*Spanish*)
Ford	Antonio Boyer (*Italian*)
Innkeeper	Harold Williams (*English*)

Conductor VITTORIO GUI
Producer CARL EBERT
Designer OSBERT LANCASTER

Der Schauspieldirektor

MOZART *8 performances*

Herr Frank	Peter Lagger (*Swiss*)
Herr Vogelsang	Alexander Young (*English*)
Mme Herz	Joan Sutherland (*Australian*)
Mlle Silberklang	Naida Labay (*Bulgarian*)
Herr Buff	Gwyn Griffiths (*Welsh*)

Conductor BRYAN BALKWILL
Producer ANTHONY BESCH
Designer PETER RICE

Ariadne auf Naxos
(Second Version)

RICHARD STRAUSS *8 performances*

Composer	Elisabeth Söderström (*Swedish*)
Music Master	Thomas Hemsley (*English*)
Dancing Master	Hugues Cuenod (*Swiss*)
Zerbinetta	Mimi Coertse (*South African*)
	Sari Barabas (*Hungarian*)
Ariadne	Lucine Amara (*American*)
Harlekin	Heinz Blankenburg (*American*)
Scaramuccio	Kevin Miller (*Australian*)
Truffaldin	Peter Lagger (*Swiss*)
Brighella	Edward Byles (*Welsh*)
Najade	Rosl Schwaiger (*Austrian*)
Dryade	Monica Sinclair (*English*)
Echo	Pilar Lorengar (*Spanish*)
Bacchus	David Lloyd (*American*)

Conductor JOHN PRITCHARD
Producer CARL EBERT
Designer OLIVER MESSEL

Le Comte Ory

ROSSINI *8 performances*

Raimbaud	Heinz Blankenburg (*American*)
Ory	Juan Oncina (*Spanish*)
Alice	Jeannette Sinclair (*English*)
Ragonde	Monica Sinclair (*English*)
Isolier	Fernanda Cadoni (*Italian*)
Le Gouverneur	Peter Lagger (*Swiss*)
Adèle	Sari Barabas (*Hungarian*)

Conductor VITTORIO GUI
Producer CARL EBERT
Designer OLIVER MESSEL

Die Entführung aus dem Serail

MOZART *8 performances*

Belmonte	Ernst Haefliger (*Swiss*)
Osmin	Mihaly Szekely (*Hungarian*)
Pedrillo	Kevin Miller (*Australian*)
Pasha Selim	Leo Bieber (*German*)
Constanze	Wilma Lipp (*Austrian*)
Blonde	Rosl Schwaiger (*Austrian*)
Sailor	James Atkins (*English*)
Dumb Slave	Harold Williams (*English*)

Conductor PAUL SACHER
Producer PETER EBERT
Designer OLIVER MESSEL

Artistic Director CARL EBERT

General Manager MORAN CAPLAT

Head of Music Staff JANI STRASSER

MUSICAL STAFF

Chorus Master PETER GELLHORN
Assistant Conductors and Coaches JOHN BARKER,
GEORGE COOP, PAUL HAMBURGER, MARTIN ISEPP,
JAMES LOCKHART, GEOFFREY PARSONS
Chorus Manager HAROLD WILLIAMS
Librarian HOWARD WICKS

PRODUCTION STAFF

Assistant Producer RICHARD DOUBLEDAY
Stage Director JUNE DANDRIDGE
Stage Managers ANN DUFFY, DAVID GAULD,
GEOFFREY GILBERTSON
Wardrobe Manager ROSEMARY WILKINS
Chief Dresser NELLIE AYRE
Maintenance BERTHA CUMMINS
Property Manager HARRY KELLARD
Chief Technician R. W. GOUGH
Assistant Technician S. HUGGETT
Chief Electrician N. THORPE
Assistant Electrician R. RICHARDS
Head Gardener F. HARVEY
Assistant General Manager DOUGLAS CRAIG
Personal Assistant to General Manager JANET MOORES
Regulating Secretary ELLEN MORGENTHAU
Press Officer BERNARD MCNABB
Box Office Manager FELICITY COZENS

THE ROYAL PHILHARMONIC ORCHESTRA

Le Comte Ory

ROSSINI *4 performances*

Raimbaud	Heinz Blankenburg (*American*)
Ory	Juan Oncina (*Spanish*)
Alice	Mary Illing (*English*)
Ragonde	Monica Sinclair (*English*)
Isolier	Fernanda Cadoni (*Italian*)
Le Gouverneur	Xavier Depraz (*French*)
Adèle	Sari Barabas (*Hungarian*)

Conductor VITTORIO GUI
Producer CARL EBERT
Designer OLIVER MESSEL

Falstaff

VERDI *4 performances*

Falstaff	Geraint Evans (*Welsh*)
Dr Caius	Hugues Cuenod (*Swiss*)
Bardolph	Mario Carlin (*Italian*)
Pistol	Marco Stefanoni (*Italian*)
Meg Page	Fernanda Cadoni (*Italian*)
Alice Ford	Ilva Ligabue (*Italian*)
Mistress Quickly	Oralia Dominguez (*Mexican*)
Nannetta	Graziella Sciutti (*Italian*)
Fenton	Juan Oncina (*Spanish*)
Ford	Mario Borriello (*Italian*)
Innkeeper	Harold Williams (*English*)

Conductor VITTORIO GUI
Producer CARL EBERT
Designer OSBERT LANCASTER

Falstaff

VERDI *9 performances*

Falstaff	Geraint Evans (*Welsh*)
Dr Caius	Hugues Cuenod (*Swiss*)
Bardolph	Mario Carlin (*Italian*)
Pistol	Marco Stefanoni (*Italian*)
Meg Page	Fernanda Cadoni (*Italian*)
Alice Ford	Ilva Ligabue (*Italian*)
Mistress Quickly	Oralia Dominguez (*Mexican*)
Nannetta	Graziella Sciutti (*Italian*)
Fenton	Juan Oncina (*Spanish*)
Ford	Mario Borriello (*Italian*)
Innkeeper	Harold Williams (*English*)

Conductor VITTORIO GUI
Producer CARL EBERT
Designer OSBERT LANCASTER

Le nozze di Figaro

MOZART *9 performances*

Figaro	Geraint Evans (*Welsh*)
Susanna	Graziella Sciutti (*Italian*)
Bartolo	Mihaly Szekely (*Hungarian*)
Marcellina	Monica Sinclair (*English*)
Cherubino	Teresa Berganza (*Spanish*)
	Josephine Veasey (*English*)
Count Almaviva	Michel Roux (*French*)
Don Basilio	Hugues Cuenod (*Swiss*)
The Countess	Pilar Lorengar (*Spanish*)
Antonio	Gwyn Griffiths (*Welsh*)
Barbarina	Mary Illing (*English*)
Don Curzio	John Kentish (*English*)

Conductor HANS SCHMIDT-ISSERSTEDT
Producer CARL EBERT
Designer OLIVER MESSEL

Alceste

GLUCK *8 performances*

Herald	Gwyn Griffiths (*Welsh*)
Evander	David Holman (*Canadian*)
Alceste	Consuelo Rubio (*Spanish*)
High Priest	Robert Massard (*French*)
Admète	Richard Lewis (*English*)
Hercules	Robert Massard (*French*)
Voice of Tanato	Dennis Wicks (*English*)
Apollo	Heinz Blankenburg (*American*)

Conductor VITTORIO GUI
Producer CARL EBERT
Scenery HUGH CASSON
Costumes ROSEMARY VERCOE
Statue of Apollo CHRISTOPHER IRONSIDE

The Rake's Progress

STRAVINSKY *7 performances*

Anne	Elsie Morison (*Australian*)
Tom Rakewell	Richard Lewis (*English*)
Trulove	David Ward (*English*)
Nick Shadow	Otakar Kraus (*Czech*)
Mother Goose	Tamara Chumakova (*Russian*)
Baba the Turk	Gloria Lane (*American*)
Sellem	Hugues Cuenod (*Swiss*)
	John Kentish (*English*)
Keeper of the Madhouse	Gwyn Griffiths (*Welsh*)

Conductor PAUL SACHER
Producer CARL EBERT
Designer OSBERT LANCASTER

1958 *continued*

Le Comte Ory

ROSSINI   *10 performances*

Raimbaud   Heinz Blankenburg (*American*)
Ory   Juan Oncina (*Spanish*)
Alice   Mary Illing (*English*)
Ragonde   Monica Sinclair (*English*)
Isolier   Fernanda Cadoni (*Italian*)
Le Gouverneur   Xavier Depraz (*French*)
Adèle   Sari Barabas (*Hungarian*)

Conductor   JOHN PRITCHARD
Producer   CARL EBERT
Designer   OLIVER MESSEL

Il segreto di Susanna

WOLF-FERRARI   *8 performances*

Gil   Michel Roux (*French*)
Countess   Mary Costa (*American*)
Sante   Heinz Blankenburg (*American*)

Conductor   JOHN PRITCHARD
Producer   PETER EBERT
Designer   CARL TOMS

Ariadne auf Naxos
(Second Version)

RICHARD STRAUSS   *8 performances*

Composer   Helga Pilarczyk (*German*)
Music Master   Geraint Evans (*Welsh*)
Dancing Master   Hugues Cuenod (*Swiss*)
Zerbinetta   Rita Streich (*German*)
Ariadne   Lucine Amara (*American*)
Harlekin   Heinz Blankenburg (*American*)
Scaramuccio   John Kentish (*English*)
Truffaldin   John Holmes (*English*)
Brighella   Duncan Robertson (*Scottish*)
Najade   Jacqueline Delman (*English*)
Dryade   Monica Sinclair (*English*)
Echo   Pilar Lorengar (*Spanish*)
Bacchus   Richard Lewis (*English*)

Conductor   JOHN PRITCHARD
Producer   CARL EBERT
Designer   OLIVER MESSEL

1959

Artistic Director CARL EBERT (1934)

General Manager MORAN CAPLAT (1945)

Conductors VITTORIO GUI (1948)
LEOPOLD LUDWIG (1959)
JOHN PRITCHARD (1947)
HANS SCHMIDT-ISSERSTEDT (1958)

Head of Music Staff JANI STRASSER (1934)

MUSICAL STAFF

Associate Conductor and Chorus Master
PETER GELLHORN (1954)
Assistant Conductors and Coaches JOHN BARKER (1958),
GEORGE COOP (1950), RHOSLYN DAVIES (1959),
MYER FREDMAN (1959), ERNA GAL (1950),
PAUL HAMBURGER (1956), MARTIN ISEPP (1957),
JAMES LOCKHART (1957), EVELYN TURNER INMAN (1951)
Chorus Manager HAROLD WILLIAMS (1938)
Librarian HOWARD WICKS (1951)

PRODUCTION STAFF

Producers CARL EBERT (1934), PETER EBERT (1947),
GÜNTHER RENNERT (1959)
Assistant Producers RICHARD DOUBLEDAY (1955),
JOHN COX (1959)
Assistant to GÜNTHER RENNERT: ANTHONY BESCH (1951)
Designers ROLF GÉRARD (1948), ITA MAXIMOWNA (1959),
OLIVER MESSEL (1950), ROSEMARY VERCOE (1951)
Choreographer ROBERT HARROLD (1951)
Ballet Mistress SILVIA ASHMOLE (1947)
Stage Director JUNE DANDRIDGE (1951)
Stage Managers ANN DUFFY (1954), DAVID GAULD (1953),
GEOFFREY GILBERTSON (1957)
Chief Technician R. W. (JOCK) GOUGH (1934)
Assistant Technician S. HUGGETT (1936)
Lighting Manager FRANCIS REID (1959)
Assistant Lighting T. FAULKNER (1959)
Wardrobe Manager ROSEMARY WILKINS (1951)
Cutters DOREEN BROWN (1957), HILARY CORBETT (1957)
Chief Dresser NELLIE AYRE (1947)
Maintenance BERTHA CUMMINS (1953)
Perruquière ALISON EDWARDS (1951)
Property Manager HARRY KELLARD (1947)
Head Gardener F. HARVEY (1934)
Assistant General Manager DOUGLAS CRAIG (1950)
Personal Assistant to the General Manager
JANET MOORES (1934)
Regulating Secretary ELLEN MORGENTHAU (1950)
Treasurer ERIC WHITEHORN (1953)
Press Officer BERNARD MCNABB (1953)
Box Office Manager FELICITY COZENS (1957)
Chief Telephonist KAY ARNOLD (1950)
Pianos maintained by HORACE JACKSON & SONS, LEWES (1934)
Transport by CARFAX, LEWES (1937) and
SOUTHDOWN MOTORS LTD, BRIGHTON (1946)
Catering by The Four Seasons Hotel & Catering Co Ltd,
under the direction of VERNON HERBERT (1956)

THE ROYAL PHILHARMONIC ORCHESTRA (1948)

Dates in parenthesis indicate the year of joining
Glyndebourne Opera

Glyndebourne 28 v - 16 viii: 68 performances

Der Rosenkavalier

RICHARD STRAUSS *13 performances*

Oktavian	Elisabeth Söderström (*Swedish*)
Feldmarschallin	Régine Crespin (*French*)
Ochs	Oscar Czerwenka (*Austrian*)
Valzacchi	John Kentish (*English*)
Annina	Nancy Evans (*English*)
Faninal	Willy Ferenz (*Austrian*)
Sophie	Anneliese Rothenberger (*German*)
Duenna	Elizabeth Crook (*English*)
Singer	William McAlpine (*Scottish*)
Landlord	Duncan Robertson (*Scottish*)
Police Inspector	Hervey Alan (*English*)

Conductor   LEOPOLD LUDWIG
Producer   CARL EBERT
Designer   OLIVER MESSEL

Idomeneo

MOZART   *9 performances*

Ilia	Sylvia Stahlman (*American*)
Idamante	William McAlpine (*Scottish*)
Arbace	Lauri Payne (*Australian*)
Electra	Angela Vercelli (*Italian*)
Idomeneo	Richard Lewis (*English*)
High Priest of Neptune	Duncan Robertson (*Scottish*)
Voice of Neptune	Hervey Alan (*English*)

Conductors   JOHN PRITCHARD
Peter Gellhorn
Producer   CARL EBERT
Designer   OLIVER MESSEL

Così fan tutte

MOZART   *12 performances*

Ferrando	Juan Oncina (*Spanish*)
Guglielmo	Geraint Evans (*Welsh*)
Don Alfonso	Carlos Feller (*Argentinian*)
Fiordiligi	Ilva Ligabue (*Italian*)
Dorabella	Gloria Lane (*American*)
Despina	Graziella Sciutti (*Italian*)

Conductor   JOHN PRITCHARD
Producer   CARL EBERT
Scenery   ROLF GÉRARD
Costumes   ROSEMARY VERCOE

Fidelio

BEETHOVEN   *12 performances*

Jaquino	Duncan Robertson (*Scottish*)
Marzelline	Elsie Morison (*Australian*)
Rocco	Mihaly Szekely (*Hungarian*)
Leonore	Gré Brouwenstijn (*Dutch*)
Pizarro	Kim Borg (*Finnish*)
First Prisoner	John Kentish (*English*)
Second Prisoner	Derick Davies (*Welsh*)
Florestan	Richard Lewis (*English*)
Don Fernando	David Kelly (*Scottish*)
	Lauri Payne (*Australian*)

Conductor   VITTORIO GUI
Producer   GÜNTHER RENNERT
Designer   ITA MAXIMOWNA

La Cenerentola

ROSSINI   *12 performances*

Don Ramiro	Juan Oncina (*Spanish*)
Dandini	Sesto Bruscantini (*Italian*)
Don Magnifico	Ian Wallace (*Scottish*)
Clorinda	Silvana Zanolli (*Italian*)
Tisbe	Miti Truccato Pace (*Italian*)
Cenerentola	Teresa Berganza (*Spanish*)
	Anna Maria Rota (*Italian*)
Alidoro	Hervey Alan (*English*)

Conductors   VITTORIO GUI
Peter Gellhorn
Producer   CARL EBERT
(Staged by Peter Ebert)
Designer   OLIVER MESSEL

Le nozze di Figaro

MOZART   *10 performances*

Figaro	Carlos Feller (*Argentinian*)
	Geraint Evans (*Welsh*)
Susanna	Elisabeth Söderström (*Swedish*)
Bartolo	Mihaly Szekely (*Hungarian*)
Marcellina	Johanna Peters (*Scottish*)
Cherubino	Josephine Veasey (*English*)
Count Almaviva	Michel Roux (*French*)
Don Basilio	Hugues Cuenod (*Swiss*)
The Countess	Pilar Lorengar (*Spanish*)
Antonio	Gwyn Griffiths (*Welsh*)
Barbarina	Mary Illing (*English*)
Don Curzio	John Kentish (*English*)

Conductor   PETER MAAG
Producer   CARL EBERT
Designer   OLIVER MESSEL

General Manager MORAN CAPLAT

Artistic Counsellors VITTORIO GUI, Head of Music

GÜNTHER RENNERT, Head of Production

MUSICAL STAFF

Director of Musical Preparation and Chief of Music Staff
JANI STRASSER

Chorus Master PETER GELLHORN

Assistant Conductors and Coaches GEORGE COOP,
MYER FREDMAN, ERNA GAL, PAUL HAMBURGER,
MARTIN ISEPP, COURTNEY KENNY, JOHN MATHESON,
GEOFFREY PARSONS, EVELYN TURNER INMAN

Chorus Manager HAROLD WILLIAMS

Librarian HOWARD WICKS

PRODUCTION STAFF

Assistant Producers JOHN COX, MICHAEL GELIOT

Production Manager JUNE DANDRIDGE

Stage Director GEOFFREY GILBERTSON

Stage Managers ANN DUFFY, DAVID GAULD

Assistant Stage Managers MICHAEL THOMSON,
SUSAN FRASER-ALLEN

Chief Theatre Technician and Director of Scenic Construction
R. W. (JOCK) GOUGH

Assistants S. HUGGETT, I. GREEN

Lighting under the supervision of ANTHONY BESCH

Lighting Manager FRANCIS REID

Wardrobe Manager ROSEMARY WILKINS

Cutters DOREEN BROWN, MARY QUEALLY

Chief Dresser NELLIE AYRE

Perruquière SHEILA DUNSDON

Property Manager HARRY KELLARD

Head Gardener F. HARVEY (retired), R. W. HILL

Assistant Manager JANET MOORES

Regulating Secretary ELLEN MORGENTHAU

Treasurer ERIC WHITEHORN

Press Officer BERNARD MCNABB

Box Office Manager PAMELA WILKINS

Appointed Photographer GUY GRAVETT

THE ROYAL PHILHARMONIC ORCHESTRA

I Puritani

BELLINI *11 performances*

Sir Bruno Robertson	John Kentish (*English*)
Elvira	Joan Sutherland (*Australian*)
Arturo	Nicola Filacuridi (*Italian*)
Giorgio	Giuseppe Modesti (*Italian*)
Riccardo	Ernest Blanc (*French*)
Lord Walton	David Ward (*English*)
Queen Henrietta	Monica Sinclair (*English*)

Conductors VITTORIO GUI
Bryan Balkwill
Producer GIANFRANCO ENRIQUEZ
Designer DESMOND HEELEY

Falstaff

VERDI *11 performances*

Falstaff	Geraint Evans (*Welsh*)
Dr Caius	Hugues Cuenod (*Swiss*)
Bardolph	Mario Carlin (*Italian*)
Pistol	Marco Stefanoni (*Italian*)
Meg Page	Anna Maria Rota (*Italian*)
Alice Ford	Ilva Ligabue (*Italian*)
Mistress Quickly	Oralia Dominguez (*Mexican*)
Nannetta	Mariella Adani (*Italian*)
Fenton	Juan Oncina (*Spanish*)
Ford	Sesto Bruscantini (*Italian*)
Innkeeper	Harold Williams (*English*)

Conductor VITTORIO GUI
Producer CARL EBERT
Designer OSBERT LANCASTER

Der Rosenkavalier

RICHARD STRAUSS   *13 performances*

Oktavian	Regina Sarfaty (*American*)
Feldmarschallin	Régine Crespin (*French*)
	Claire Watson (*American*)
Ochs	Oscar Czerwenka (*Austrian*)
Valzacchi	John Kentish (*English*)
Annina	Nancy Evans (*English*)
Faninal	Willy Ferenz (*Austrian*)
Sophie	Anneliese Rothenberger (*German*)
Duenna	Elizabeth Crook (*English*)
Singer	William McAlpine (*Scottish*)
Landlord	Duncan Robertson (*Scottish*)
Police Inspector	Hervey Alan (*English*)

Conductor   LEOPOLD LUDWIG
Producer   CARL EBERT
(Rehearsed by Richard Doubleday)
Designer   OLIVER MESSEL

La Cenerentola

ROSSINI   *12 performances*

Don Ramiro	Juan Oncina (*Spanish*)
Dandini	Sesto Bruscantini (*Italian*)
Don Magnifico	Ian Wallace (*Scottish*)
Clorinda	Silvana Zanolli (*Italian*)
Tisbe	Miti Truccato Pace (*Italian*)
Cenerentola	Anna Maria Rota (*Italian*)
Alidoro	Hervey Alan (*English*)

Conductors   VITTORIO GUI
Peter Gellhorn
Producer   CARL EBERT
(Staged by Peter Ebert)
Designer   OLIVER MESSEL

Don Giovanni

MOZART   *13 performances*

Leporello	Geraint Evans (*Welsh*)
	Sesto Bruscantini (*Italian*)
Donna Anna	Joan Sutherland (*Australian*)
Don Giovanni	Ernest Blanc (*French*)
The Commendatore	Marco Stefanoni (*Italian*)
Don Ottavio	Richard Lewis (*English*)
Donna Elvira	Ilva Ligabue (*Italian*)
Zerlina	Mirella Freni (*Italian*)
Masetto	Leonardo Monreale (*Italian*)

Conductors   JOHN PRITCHARD
Peter Gellhorn
Producer   GÜNTHER RENNERT
Designer   ITA MAXIMOWNA

The Magic Flute

MOZART   *10 performances*

Tamino	Richard Lewis (*English*)
Three Ladies	Heather Harper (*Irish*)
	Catherine Wilson (*English*)
	Monica Sinclair (*English*)
Papageno	Geraint Evans (*Welsh*)
Queen of the Night	Margareta Hallin (*Swedish*)
Three Boys	Emily Maire (*Scottish*)
	Elizabeth Harwood (*English*)
	Theresia Bester (*South African*)
Monostatos	Gwyn Griffiths (*Welsh*)
Pamina	Pilar Lorengar (*Spanish*)
The Speaker	Carlos Feller (*Argentinian*)
Sarastro	Mihaly Szekely (*Hungarian*)
Priests and Men in Armour	James Conrad (*South African*)
	David Read (*English*)
Papagena	Dodi Protero (*Canadian*)

Conductor   COLIN DAVIS
Producer   CARL EBERT
(Staged by Anthony Besch)
Designer   OLIVER MESSEL

Falstaff

VERDI *7 performances*

Falstaff	Geraint Evans (*Welsh*)
Dr Caius	Hugues Cuenod (*Swiss*)
Bardolph	Mario Carlin (*Italian*)
Pistol	Marco Stafanoni (*Italian*)
Meg Page	Anna Maria Rota (*Italian*)
Alice Ford	Ilva Ligabue (*Italian*)
Mistress Quickly	Oralia Dominguez (*Mexican*)
Nannetta	Mariella Adani (*Italian*)
Fenton	Juan Oncina (*Spanish*)
Ford	Sesto Bruscantini (*Italian*)
Innkeeper	Harold Williams (*English*)

Conductor VITTORIO GUI
Producer CARL EBERT
(Directed by Peter Ebert)
Designer OSBERT LANCASTER

I Puritani

BELLINI *6 performances*

Sir Bruno Robertson	John Kentish (*English*)
Elvira	Joan Sutherland (*Australian*)
Arturo	Nicola Filacuridi (*Italian*)
Giorgio	Giuseppe Modesti (*Italian*)
Riccardo	Ernest Blanc (*French*)
Lord Walton	David Ward (*English*)
Queen Henrietta	Monica Sinclair (*English*)

Conductors VITTORIO GUI
Bryan Balkwill
Producer GIANFRANCO ENRIQUEZ
Designer DESMOND HEELEY

Il segreto di Susanna

WOLF-FERRARI *4 performances*

Gil	Sesto Bruscantini (*Italian*)
Countess	Mariella Adani (*Italian*)
Sante	Heinz Blankenburg (*American*)

Conductor JOHN PRITCHARD
Producer PETER EBERT
Designer CARL TOMS

La Voix Humaine

POULENC *4 performances*

Elle	Denise Duval (*French*)

Conductor JOHN PRITCHARD
Producer and Designer JEAN COCTEAU

Arlecchino

BUSONI *4 performances*

Ser Matteo	Ian Wallace (*Scottish*)
Arlecchino	Heinz Blankenburg (*American*)
Abbate Cospicuo	Gwyn Griffiths (*Welsh*)
Doctor Bombasto	Carlos Feller (*Argentinian*)
Colombina	Helga Pilarczyk (*German*)
Leandro	Dermot Troy (*Irish*)

Conductor JOHN PRITCHARD
Producer PETER EBERT
Designer PETER RICE

General Manager MORAN CAPLAT

Artistic Counsellors VITTORIO GUI, Head of Music
GÜNTHER RENNERT, Head of Production

MUSICAL STAFF

Director of Musical Preparation and Chief of Music Staff
JANI STRASSER
Chorus Master PETER GELLHORN
Music Staff GEORGE COOP, MYER FREDMAN, ERNA GAL,
GERALD GOVER, PAUL HAMBURGER, MARTIN ISEPP,
JOHN MATHESON, GEOFFREY PARSONS, FRANK SHIPWAY,
EVELYN TURNER INMAN
Chorus Manager HAROLD WILLIAMS
Librarian HOWARD WICKS

PRODUCTION STAFF

Assistant Producers JOHN BARTON, JOHN COX,
MICHAEL GELIOT, ROWLAND HOLT WILSON
Production Manager JUNE DANDRIDGE
Stage Director GEOFFREY GILBERTSON
Stage Managers ANN DUFFY, STEPHEN WEBBER
Assistant Stage Managers MICHAEL THOMSON,
SUSAN FRASER-ALLEN
Chief Theatre Technician and Director of Scenic Construction
R. W. (JOCK) GOUGH
Assistants I. GREEN, S. HUGGETT
Lighting Manager FRANCIS REID
Wardrobe Manager ROSEMARY WILKINS
Cutters DOREEN BROWN, MARY QUEALLY
Chief Dresser GLADYS CHISHOLM
Perruquière SHEILA DUNSDON
Property Manager HARRY KELLARD
Head Gardener R. W. HILL
Assistant Manager JANET MOORES
Regulating Secretary ELLEN THURMAN
Treasurer ERIC WHITEHORN
Press Officer BERNARD MCNABB
Box Office Manager PAMELA WILKINS
Appointed Photographer GUY GRAVETT

THE ROYAL PHILHARMONIC ORCHESTRA

L'elisir d'amore

DONIZETTI *14 performances*

Adina Eugenia Ratti (*Italian*)
Nemorino Luigi Alva (*Peruvian*)
Belcore Enzo Sordello (*Italian*)
Dulcamara Carlo Badioli (*Italian*)
Giannetta Emily Maire (*Scottish*)

Conductor CARLO FELICE CILLARIO
Producer and Designer FRANCO ZEFFIRELLI

Die Entführung aus dem Serail

MOZART *15 performances*

Belmonte Heinz Hoppe (*German*)
Osmin Mihaly Szekely (*Hungarian*)
  Michael Langdon (*English*)
Pedrillo Duncan Robertson (*Scottish*)
Pasha Selim Robert Speaight (*English*)
Constanze Mattiwilda Dobbs (*American*)
Blonde Dorit Hanak (*Austrian*)
Sailor Derick Davies (*Welsh*)
Dumb Slave Harold Williams (*English*)

Conductor PETER GELLHORN
Producer PETER EBERT
Designer OLIVER MESSEL

Fidelio

BEETHOVEN *12 performances*

Jaquino Duncan Robertson (*Scottish*)
Marzelline Elsie Morison (*Australian*)
Rocco Mihaly Szekely (*Hungarian*)
Leonore Gré Brouwenstijn (*Dutch*)
Pizarro Herbert Fliether (*German*)
First Prisoner John Kentish (*English*)
Second Prisoner Derick Davies (*Welsh*)
Florestan Richard Lewis (*English*)
Don Fernando Hugh Beresford (*English*)

Conductor VITTORIO GUI
Producer GÜNTHER RENNERT
Assistant Producer ANTHONY BESCH
Designer ITA MAXIMOWNA

Don Giovanni

MOZART *13 performances*

Leporello Geraint Evans (*Welsh*)
Donna Anna Gerda Scheyrer (*Austrian*)
Don Giovanni György Melis (*Hungarian*)
The Commendatore Michael Langdon (*English*)
Don Ottavio Richard Lewis (*English*)
Donna Elvira Ilva Ligabue (*Italian*)
Zerlina Mirella Freni (*Italian*)
Masetto Leonardo Monreale (*Italian*)

Conductors JOHN PRITCHARD
Peter Gellhorn
Producer GÜNTHER RENNERT
Associate Producer ANTHONY BESCH
Designer ITA MAXIMOWNA

Elegy for Young Lovers

HANS WERNER HENZE *8 performances*

World Première in Original Language
Libretto by W. H. Auden and Chester Kallman

Hilda Mack Dorothy Dorow (*English*)
Carolina Kerstin Meyer (*Swedish*)
Dr Reischmann Thomas Hemsley (*English*)
Toni Reischmann André Turp (*Canadian*)
Gregor Mittenhofer Carlos Alexander (*American*)
Elizabeth Zimmer Elisabeth Söderström (*Swedish*)
Josef Mauer John Kentish (*English*)

Conductors JOHN PRITCHARD
Hans Werner Henze
Producer GÜNTHER RENNERT
Designer LILA DE NOBILI

The Barber of Seville

ROSSINI *10 performances*

Count Almaviva Juan Oncina (*Spanish*)
Figaro Sesto Bruscantini (*Italian*)
Rosina Alberta Valentini (*Italian*)
Bartolo Ian Wallace (*Scottish*)
Basilio Carlo Cava (*Italian*)
Fiorello Duncan Robertson (*Scottish*)
Berta Laura Sarti (*Italian*)
Ambrogio Harold Williams (*English*)
Officer John Evans (*Welsh*)

Conductor VITTORIO GUI
Producer CARL EBERT
(Staged by Peter Ebert)
Designer OLIVER MESSEL

General Manager MORAN CAPLAT

Artistic Counsellors VITTORIO GUI

GÜNTHER RENNERT (Head of Production)

MUSICAL STAFF
Director of Musical Preparation and Chief of
Music Staff JANI STRASSER
Chorus Master MYER FREDMAN
Music Staff GEORGE COOP, MYER FREDMAN, ERNA GAL,
GERALD GOVER, PAUL HAMBURGER, MARTIN ISEPP,
ROBERT JONES, COURTNEY KENNY, LEONE MAGIERA,
JOHN MATHESON, GEOFFREY PARSONS,
FRANK SHIPWAY, EVELYN TURNER INMAN
Chorus Manager HAROLD WILLIAMS
Librarian HOWARD WICKS

PRODUCTION STAFF
Assistant Producers JOHN COX, MICHAEL GELIOT,
ROWLAND HOLT WILSON, STEPHEN WEBBER
Production Manager JUNE DANDRIDGE
Stage Director GEOFFREY GILBERTSON
Stage Managers ANN DUFFY, STEPHEN WEBBER
Assistant Stage Managers DAVID BIGGS, DON AITKEN
Chief Theatre Technician and Director of
Scenic Construction R. W. (JOCK) GOUGH
Assistants I. GREEN, S. HUGGETT
Lighting Manager FRANCIS REID
Wardrobe Manager ROSEMARY WILKINS
Assistant PHYLLIS HAWLING
Cutters DOREEN BROWN, MARY QUEALLY
Wardrobe Mistress GLADYS CHISHOLM
Perruquière SHEILA DUNSDON
Property Manager HARRY KELLARD
Head Gardener R. W. HILL
Assistant Manager JANET MOORES
Regulating Secretary ELLEN THURMAN
Treasurer ERIC WHITEHORN
Press Officer BERNARD MCNABB
Box Office Manager PAMELA WILKINS
Appointed Photographer GUY GRAVETT

THE ROYAL PHILHARMONIC ORCHESTRA

Pelléas et Mélisande

DEBUSSY *10 performances*

Pelléas Henri Gui (*French*)
Mélisande Denise Duval (*French*)
Golaud Michel Roux (*French*)
Geneviève Kerstin Meyer (*Swedish*)
Anna Reynolds (*English*)
Arkel Guus Hoekman (*Dutch*)
Yniold Rosine Brédy (*French*)
Doctor John Shirley-Quirk (*English*)

Conductor VITTORIO GUI
Producer CARL EBERT
Designer BENI MONTRESOR

Le nozze di Figaro

MOZART *16 performances*

Figaro Heinz Blankenburg (*American*)
Susanna Mirella Freni (*Italian*)
Bartolo Carlo Cava (*Italian*)
Marcellina Johanna Peters (*Scottish*)
Cherubino Edith Mathis (*Swiss*)
Maureen Keetch (*English*)
Count Almaviva Gabriel Bacquier (*French*)
Don Basilio Hugues Cuenod (*Swiss*)
The Countess Leyla Gencer (*Turkish*)
Antonio Derick Davies (*Welsh*)
Barbarina Maria Zeri (*Greek*)
Don Curzio John Kentish (*English*)

Conductors SILVIO VARVISO
John Pritchard
Producer CARL EBERT
Designer OLIVER MESSEL

Così fan tutte

MOZART *15 performances*

Ferrando Loren Driscoll (*American*)
Guglielmo Ingvar Wixell (*Swedish*)
Don Alfonso Michel Roux (*French*)
Fiordiligi Antigone Sgourda (*Greek*)
Dorabella Stefania Malagù (*Italian*)
Despina Reri Grist (*American*)

Conductor JOHN PRITCHARD
Producer CARL EBERT
Scenery ROLF GÉRARD
Costumes BERNARD NEVILL

L'incoronazione di Poppea

MONTEVERDI *12 performances*

(arr Raymond Leppard)

First professional production in England

Ottone Walter Alberti (*Italian*)
Poppea Magda Laszlo (*Hungarian*)
Nerone Richard Lewis (*English*)
Arnalta Oralia Dominguez (*Mexican*)
Jean Allister (*Irish*)
Ottavia Frances Bible (*American*)
Damigella Soo-Bee Lee (*Chinese*)
Seneca Carlo Cava (*Italian*)
Valetto Duncan Robertson (*Scottish*)
Drusilla Lydia Marimpietri (*Italian*)
Lucano Hugues Cuenod (*Swiss*)
First Soldier Dennis Brandt (*English*)
Second Soldier Gerald English (*English*)
Pallade Josephine Allen (*English*)
Liberto John Shirley-Quirk (*English*)
Amor Marta Sellas (*Scottish*)
Lictor Dennis Wicks (*English*)

Conductor JOHN PRITCHARD
Producer GÜNTHER RENNERT
Scenery HUGH CASSON
Costumes CONWY EVANS

Ariadne auf Naxos
(First Version)

RICHARD STRAUSS *11 performances*

Le Bourgeois Gentilhomme

M. Jourdain Miles Malleson
Dorante Richard Gale
Dorimène Marion Mathie
Professor of Philosophy Walter Hudd

Ariadne auf Naxos

Najade Day McAusland (*Scottish*)
Dryade Jean Allister (*Irish*)
Echo Morag Noble (*Scottish*)
Ariadne Enriqueta Tarrés (*Spanish*)
Harlekin Heinz Blankenburg (*American*)
Zerbinetta Gianna d'Angelo (*American*)
Reri Grist (*American*)
Brighella Duncan Robertson (*Scottish*)
Truffaldin Dennis Wicks (*English*)
Scaramuccio Adrian de Peyer (*English*)
Bacchus Richard Lewis (*English*)
William McAlpine (*Scottish*)

Conductor SILVIO VARVISO
Producer CARL EBERT
(Staged by Peter Ebert)
Designer OLIVER MESSEL

L'elisir d'amore

DONIZETTI *6 performances*

Adina Mirella Freni (*Italian*)
Nemorino Luigi Alva (*Peruvian*)
Belcore Enzo Sordello (*Italian*)
Dulcamara Sesto Bruscantini (*Italian*)
Giannetta Emily Maire (*Scottish*)

Conductor CARLO FELICE CILLARIO
Producer and Designer FRANCO ZEFFIRELLI
Assistant Producer MICHAEL GELIOT

General Manager MORAN CAPLAT

Artistic Counsellors VITTORIO GUI
GÜNTHER RENNERT (Head of Production)

Music Counsellor JOHN PRITCHARD

MUSICAL STAFF

Director of Musical Preparation and Chief of
Music Staff JANI STRASSER

Chorus Master MYER FREDMAN

Music Staff JOHN BACON, GEORGE COOP,
MYER FREDMAN, ERNA GAL, THOMAS GLIGOROFF,
GERALD GOVER, PAUL HAMBURGER, MARTIN ISEPP,
ROBERT JONES, COURTNEY KENNY,
GEOFFREY PARSONS, EVELYN TURNER INMAN

Chorus Manager HAROLD WILLIAMS

Librarian HOWARD WICKS

PRODUCTION STAFF

Assistant Producers JOHN COX, DENNIS MAUNDER

Production Manager JUNE DANDRIDGE

Stage Director GEOFFREY GILBERTSON

Stage Managers MALCOLM FRASER, WILLIAM LAWFORD,
JOAN WESTON

Assistant Stage Manager DON AITKEN

Chief Theatre Technician and Director of
Scenic Construction R. W. (JOCK) GOUGH

Assistants I. GREEN, H. JACKSON, B. PULLEN

Lighting Manager FRANCIS REID

Wardrobe Manager KEGAN SMITH

Assistant EILEEN HETIGIN

Cutters DAVID HARVEY-JONES, JEAN HUNNISETT

Wardrobe Mistress GLADYS CHISHOLM

Perruquière SHEILA DUNSDON

Property Manager HARRY KELLARD

Head Gardener R. W. HILL

Assistant Manager JANET MOORES

Regulating Secretary ELLEN THURMAN

Treasurer ERIC WHITEHORN

Press Officer BERNARD MCNABB

Box Office Manager PAMELA WILKINS

Appointed Photographer GUY GRAVETT

THE ROYAL PHILHARMONIC ORCHESTRA

Capriccio

RICHARD STRAUSS *10 performances*

Flamand	Horst Wilhelm (*German*)
Olivier	Raymond Wolansky (*American*)
La Roche	Benno Kusche (*German*)
The Countess	Elisabeth Söderström (*Swedish*)
The Count	Tom Krause (*Finnish*)
Clairon	Sona Cervena (*Czech*)
Italian Tenor	Pierre Duval (*Canadian*)
Italian Soprano	Alberta Valentini (*Italian*)
Major-Domo	John Shirley-Quirk (*English*)
Monsieur Taupe	Hugues Cuenod (*Swiss*)

Conductors	JOHN PRITCHARD
	Bryan Balkwill
Producer	GÜNTHER RENNERT
Scenery	DENNIS LENNON
Costumes	ANTHONY POWELL

Fidelio

BEETHOVEN *8 performances*

Jaquino	Duncan Robertson (*Scottish*)
Marzelline	April Cantelo (*English*)
	Maureen Keetch (*English*)
Rocco	Victor de Narké (*Argentinian*)
Leonore	Gré Brouwenstijn (*Dutch*)
Pizarro	Herbert Fliether (*German*)
First Prisoner	John Kentish (*English*)
Second Prisoner	Derick Davies (*Welsh*)
Florestan	Richard Lewis (*English*)
Don Fernando	Benno Kusche (*German*)

Conductor	BRYAN BALKWILL
Producer	GÜNTHER RENNERT
Assistant Producer	JOHN COX
Designer	ITA MAXIMOWNA

Pelléas et Mélisande

DEBUSSY *10 performances*

Pelléas	Hans Wilbrink (*Dutch*)
Mélisande	Denise Duval (*French*)
Golaud	Michel Roux (*French*)
Geneviève	Anna Reynolds (*English*)
Arkel	Guus Hoekman (*Dutch*)
Yniold	Rosine Brédy (*French*)
Doctor	John Shirley-Quirk (*English*)

Conductor	VITTORIO GUI
Producer	CARL EBERT
Designer	BENI MONTRESOR

L'incoronazione di Poppea

MONTEVERDI *10 performances*

(arr Raymond Leppard)

Ottone	Walter Alberti (*Italian*)
Poppea	Magda Laszlo (*Hungarian*)
Nerone	Richard Lewis (*English*)
Arnalta	Oralia Dominguez (*Mexican*)
	Jean Allister (*Irish*)
Ottavia	Frances Bible (*American*)
Damigella	Soo-Bee Lee (*Chinese*)
Seneca	Carlo Cava (*Italian*)
Valetto	Duncan Robertson (*Scottish*)
Drusilla	Lydia Marimpietri (*Italian*)
Lucano	Hugues Cuenod (*Swiss*)
	Gerald English (*English*)
First Soldier	Dennis Brandt (*English*)
Second Soldier	Gerald English (*English*)
Pallade	Elizabeth Bainbridge (*English*)
Liberto	John Shirley-Quirk (*English*)
Amor	Annon Lee Silver (*Canadian*)
Lictor	Dennis Wicks (*English*)

Conductor JOHN PRITCHARD
Producer GÜNTHER RENNERT
Scenery HUGH CASSON
Costumes CONWY EVANS

Le nozze di Figaro

MOZART *10 performances*

Figaro	Heinz Blankenburg (*American*)
Susanna	Liliane Berton (*French*)
Bartolo	Carlo Cava (*Italian*)
	Michael Langdon (*English*)
Marcellina	Rosa Laghezza (*Italian*)
Cherubino	Edith Mathis (*Swiss*)
Count Almaviva	Michel Roux (*French*)
Don Basilio	Hugues Cuenod (*Swiss*)
The Countess	Leyla Gencer (*Turkish*)
Antonio	Derick Davies (*Welsh*)
Don Curzio	John Kentish (*English*)
Barbarina	Maria Zeri (*Greek*)

Conductors SILVIO VARVISO
Myer Fredman
Producer PETER EBERT
(Based on the original production by Carl Ebert)
Designer OLIVER MESSEL

The Magic Flute

MOZART *13 performances*

Tamino	Ragnar Ulfung (*Norwegian*)
Three Ladies	Antigone Sgourda (*Greek*)
	Maureen Keetch (*English*)
	Elizabeth Bainbridge (*English*)
Papageno	Heinz Blankenburg (*American*)
Queen of the Night	Claudine Arnaud (*Belgian*)
Three Boys	Margaret Neville (*English*)
	Anne Pashley (*English*)
	Pauline Darroll (*English*)
Monostatos	Duncan Robertson (*Scottish*)
Pamina	Judith Raskin (*American*)
The Speaker	Donald Bell (*Canadian*)
Sarastro	Carlo Cava (*Italian*)
Priests and Men in Armour	Dennis Brandt (*English*)
	Dennis Wicks (*English*)
Papagena	Maria Zeri (*Greek*)

Conductor VITTORIO GUI
Producer FRANCO ENRIQUEZ
Designer EMANUELE LUZZATI

The Rake's Progress

STRAVINSKY *9 performances*

Anne	Heather Harper (*Irish*)
Tom Rakewell	Richard Lewis (*English*)
Trulove	Dennis Wicks (*English*)
Nick Shadow	Delme Bryn Jones (*Welsh*)
	Hermann Uhde (*German*)
Mother Goose	Tamara Chumakova (*Russian*)
Baba the Turk	Gloria Lane (*American*)
Sellem	Hugues Cuenod (*Swiss*)
Keeper of the Madhouse	Derick Davies (*Welsh*)

Conductor PAUL SACHER
Producer PETER EBERT
(Original by Carl Ebert)
Designer OSBERT LANCASTER

General Manager MORAN CAPLAT

Artistic Counsellor GÜNTHER RENNERT
(Head of Production)

Music Counsellor JOHN PRITCHARD

MUSICAL STAFF
Conductors BRYAN BALKWILL, MYER FREDMAN,
LAMBERTO GARDELLI, VITTORIO GUI,
RAYMOND LEPPARD, JOHN PRITCHARD
Director of Musical Preparation and Chief of
Music Staff JANI STRASSER
Chorus Master MYER FREDMAN
Music Staff JOHN BACON, GEORGE COOP,
MYER FREDMAN, ERNA GAL, GERALD GOVER,
MARTIN ISEPP, ROBERT JONES, COURTNEY KENNY,
KENNETH MONTGOMERY, GEOFFREY PARSONS,
EVELYN TURNER INMAN
Chorus Manager HAROLD WILLIAMS
Librarian HOWARD WICKS

PRODUCTION STAFF
Producers PETER EBERT, FRANCO ENRIQUEZ,
GÜNTHER RENNERT
Associate Producer JOHN COX
Assistant Producers DENNIS MAUNDER, JOAN WESTON
Production Manager JUNE DANDRIDGE
Stage Director GEOFFREY GILBERTSON
Stage Managers DON AITKEN, ALISOUN BROWNE,
DAVID NEAL
Assistant Stage Managers CHARLES HAMILTON,
STEPHEN MUMFORD
Chief Technician DESMOND COLLINS
Assistant I. GREEN
Staff Carpenter B. PULLEN
Lighting Manager FRANCIS REID
Wardrobe Manager ROSEMARY WILKINS
Assistant JEAN HUNNISETT
Cutter DAVID HARVEY-JONES
Assistant NUALA WILLIS
Dyer MAURICE CONNELL
Wardrobe Mistress GLADYS CHISHOLM
Make-up supervised by TONY WILSON
Property Manager HARRY KELLARD
Property Mistress BELINDA CADBURY
Head Gardener R. W. HILL
Assistant Manager JANET MOORES
Regulating Secretary UNA MARCHETTI
Treasurer ERIC WHITEHORN
Press Officer BERNARD MCNABB
Chief Telephonist KAY ARNOLD
Transport Officer REX ROGERS
Appointed Photographer GUY GRAVETT
Honorary Acoustic Adviser F. W. ALEXANDER, PH.D
Honorary Electronic Engineering Consultant
JOHN D. BARNES, M.A.

GLYNDEBOURNE FESTIVAL ORCHESTRA

Macbeth

VERDI *12 performances*

Macbeth	Kostas Paskalis (*Greek*)
Banquo	Plinio Clabassi (*Italian*)
Lady Macbeth	Marta Pender (*American*)
Gentlewoman	Rae Woodland (*English*)
Macduff	John Wakefield (*English*)
Malcolm	Dennis Brandt (*English*)
Doctor	Derick Davies (*Welsh*)
	Emyr Green (*Welsh*)
Servant	Peter Lehmann Bedford (*English*)
Murderer	Erich Vietheer (*Australian*)

Conductor LAMBERTO GARDELLI
Producer FRANCO ENRIQUEZ
Designer EMANUELE LUZZATI

L'incoronazione di Poppea

MONTEVERDI *12 performances*

(*arr Raymond Leppard*)

Ottone	Walter Alberti (*Italian*)
Poppea	Saramae Endich (*American*)
Nerone	Richard Lewis (*English*)
Arnalta	Oralia Dominguez (*Mexican*)
Ottavia	Kerstin Meyer (*Swedish*)
	Dorothy Wilson (*English*)
Damigella	Soo-Bee Lee (*Chinese*)
Seneca	Carlo Cava (*Italian*)
Valetto	Duncan Robertson (*Scottish*)
Drusilla	Margaret Neville (*English*)
Lucano	Hugues Cuenod (*Swiss*)
	Gerald English (*English*)
First Soldier	Dennis Brandt (*English*)
Second Soldier	Gerald English (*English*)
Pallade	Elizabeth Bainbridge (*English*)
Liberto	Neilson Taylor (*English*)
Amor	Annon Lee Silver (*Canadian*)
Lictor	Stafford Dean (*English*)

Conductor RAYMOND LEPPARD
Producer GÜNTHER RENNERT
Associate Producer JOHN COX
Scenery HUGH CASSON
Costumes CONWY EVANS

La pietra del paragone

ROSSINI *13 performances*

Fabrizio	David Hartley (*English*)
Pacuvio	Heinz Blankenburg (*American*)
Ortensia	Anna Reynolds (*English*)
Fulvia	Alberta Valentini (*Italian*)
Asdrubale	Ugo Trama (*Italian*)
Giocondo	Umberto Grilli (*Italian*)
Clarice	Josephine Veasey (*English*)
Macrobio	Michel Roux (*French*)

Conductors	JOHN PRITCHARD
	Myer Fredman
Producer	GÜNTHER RENNERT
Designer	OSBERT LANCASTER

Capriccio

RICHARD STRAUSS *11 performances*

Flamand	Horst Wilhelm (*German*)
Olivier	Raymond Wolansky (*American*)
La Roche	Benno Kusche (*German*)
	Derick Davies (*Welsh*)
	Otto Wiener (*Austrian*)
The Countess	Elisabeth Söderström (*Swedish*)
The Count	George Fortune (*American*)
Clairon	Sona Cervena (*Czech*)
Italian Tenor	Amadeo Casanovas (*Spanish*)
Italian Soprano	Alberta Valentini (*Italian*)
Major-Domo	Stafford Dean (*English*)
Monsieur Taupe	Hugues Cuenod (*Swiss*)

Conductors	JOHN PRITCHARD
	Bryan Balkwill
Producer	GÜNTHER RENNERT
Assistant Producer	DENNIS MAUNDER
Scenery	DENNIS LENNON
Costumes	ANTHONY POWELL

The Magic Flute

MOZART *12 performances*

Tamino	Ragnar Ulfung (*Norwegian*)
Three Ladies	Margherita Kalmus (*English*)
	Anna Reynolds (*English*)
	Elizabeth Bainbridge (*English*)
Papageno	Heinz Blankenburg (*American*)
Queen of the Night	Claudine Arnaud (*Belgian*)
Three Boys	Margaret Neville (*English*)
	Dorothy Wilson (*English*)
	Pauline Darroll (*English*)
Monostatos	Duncan Robertson (*Scottish*)
Pamina	Judith Raskin (*American*)
The Speaker	Delme Bryn Jones (*Welsh*)
Sarastro	Carlo Cava (*Italian*)
Priests and Men in Armour	Dennis Brandt (*English*)
	Dennis Wicks (*English*)
Papagena	Maria Zeri (*Greek*)

Conductors	VITTORIO GUI
	Bryan Balkwill
Producer	FRANCO ENRIQUEZ
Associate Producer	JOHN COX
Designer	EMANUELE LUZZATI

Idomeneo

MOZART *12 performances*

Ilia	Gundula Janowitz (*Austrian*)
	Lorna Elias (*Welsh*)
Idamante	Luciano Pavarotti (*Italian*)
Arbace	Neilson Taylor (*English*)
Electra	Enriqueta Tarrés (*Spanish*)
Idomeneo	Richard Lewis (*English*)
High Priest of Neptune	David Hughes (*Welsh*)
Voice of Neptune	Dennis Wicks (*English*)

Conductor	JOHN PRITCHARD
Producer	PETER EBERT
	(Original by Carl Ebert)
Designer	OLIVER MESSEL

Appendix B *List of Artists in principal roles 1934-64*

A	Arlecchino	
AL	Alceste	
AN–1	Ariadne auf Naxos (1st version)	
AN	Ariadne auf Naxos (2nd version)	
BM	Ballo in maschera, Un	
BO	Beggar's Opera, The	
BS	Barber of Seville, The	
C	Cenerentola, La	
CAP	Capriccio	
CO	Comte Ory, Le	
CT	Così fan tutte	
DG	Don Giovanni	
DP	Don Pasquale	
E	Entführung aus dem Serail, Die	
EA	Elisir d'amore, L'	
EY	Elegy for Young Lovers	
F	Falstaff	
FD	Forza del destino, La	
FI	Fidelio	
I	Idomeneo	
IA	Italiana in Algeri, L'	
IP	Incoronazione di Poppea, L'	
M	Macbeth	
NF	Nozze di Figaro, Le	
O	Orpheus	
P	Puritani, I	
PM	Pelléas et Mélisande	
PP	Pietra del paragone, La	
R	Rosenkavalier, Der	
RL	Rape of Lucretia, The	
RP	Rake's Progress, The	
S	Schauspieldirektor, Der	
SS	Segreto di Susanna, Il	
VH	Voix Humaine, La	
Z	Magic Flute, The (Die Zauberflöte)	

Abercrombie,
  Elisabeth 1938. *Gentlewoman (M)*
Adani, Mariella 1960. *Nannetta (F)*
  1960. *Susanna (SS)*
Alan, Hervey 1949. *Tommaso (BM)*
  1952, 53, 56, 59. *Neptune (I)*
  1952, 53, 54, 56, 59, 60. *Alidore (C)*
  1953, 54, 55. *Trulove (RP)*
  1954, 55, 56. *Commendatore (DG)*
  1955. *Guardiano (FD)*
  1957. *Pistol (F)*
  1959, 60. *Police Inspector (R)*
Alarie, Pierrette 1951. *Zerlina (DG)*
Alberti, Walter 1962, 63, 64. *Ottone (IP)*
Alexander, Carlos 1961. *Gregor Mittenhofer (EY)*
Allin, Norman 1934. *Bartolo (NF)*
Allister, Jean 1962, 63. *Arnalta (IP)*
  1962. *Dryade (AN–1)*
Alnar, Ayhan 1947. *Susanna (NF)*
Alsen, Herbert 1937. *Osmin (E)*
  1937. *Sarastro (Z)*
Alva, Luigi 1961, 62. *Nemorino (EA)*
Amara, Lucine 1954, 57, 58. *Ariadne (AN)*
  1955. *Donna Elvira (DG)*
Anders, Peter 1950. *Bacchus (AN–1)*
Andrésen, Ivar 1935. *Osmin (E)*
  1935. *Sarastro (Z)*
Arnaud, Claudine 1963, 64. *Queen of the Night (Z)*
Atkins, James 1954. *Major Domo (AN)*
  1955. *Alcade (FD)*
  1956. *Priest and Man in Armour (Z)*
Ayars, Ann 1947. *Eurydice*
  1948. *Zerlina (DG)*

Baccaloni, Salvatore 1936, 37, 38, 39. *Leporello (DG)*
  1936, 37, 38, 39. *Bartolo (NF)*
  1936. *Osmin (E)*
  1937. *Don Alfonso (CT)*
  1938, 39. *Don Pasquale (DP)*
Bacquier, Gabriel 1962. *Count (NF)*
Badioli, Carlo 1961. *Dr Dulcamara (EA)*
Bainbridge, Elizabeth 1963, 64. *Pallade (IP)*
  1963, 64. *Third Lady (Z)*
Barabas, Sari 1953. *Constanze (E)*
  1954, 55, 57, 58. *Countess Adèle (CO)*
  1957. *Zerbinetta (AN)*
Bartlett, Patricia 1952. *Gentlewoman (M)*
Beckwith, Jean 1935, 36, 37. *Second Boy (Z)*
Bedford, Peter
  Lehmann 1964. *Soldier (M)*
Beilke, Irma 1936. *Blonde (E)*
Bell, Donald 1963. *Speaker (Z)*
Berganza, Teresa 1958. *Cherubino (NF)*
  1959. *Cenerentola (C)*
Bernardic, Drago 1956. *Sarastro (Z)*
Berry, Noreen 1954. *Berta (BS)*
Berton, Liliane 1963. *Susanna (NF)*

Bester, Theresia 1960. *Third Boy (Z)*

Bettoni, Vincenzo 1934. *Alfonso (CT)*

Bible, Frances 1955. *Cherubino (NF)*
1962, 63. *Ottavia (IP)*

Bieber, Leo 1956, 57. *Pasha Selim (E)*

Blanc, Ernest 1960. *Sir Richard Forth (P)*
1960. *Don Giovanni (DG)*

Blankenburg, Heinz 1957, 63, 64. *Papageno (Z)*
1957, 58. *Harlekin (AN)*
1957, 58. *Raimbaud (CO)*
1958. *Apollo (AL)*
1958, 60. *Sante (SS)*
1960. *Arlecchino (A)*
1962. *Harlekin (AN–1)*
1962, 63. *Figaro (NF)*
1964. *Pacuvio (PP)*

Borg, Kim 1956. *Don Giovanni (DG)*
1959. *Pizarro (FI)*

Borgioli, Dino 1937, 38, 39. *Don Ottavio (DG)*
1938. *Ernesto (DP)*

Boroditsky, Belva 1956, 57. *First Boy (Z)*

Borriello, Mario 1950. *Alfonso (CT)*
1958. *Ford (F)*

Boyer, Antonio 1957. *Ford (F)*

Brandt, Dennis 1962, 63, 64. *First Soldier (IP)*
1963, 64. *Priest and Man in Armour (Z)*
1964. *Malcolm (M)*

Brannigan, Owen 1946. *Collatinus (RL)*
1947, 51. *Bartolo (NF)*
1947. *Banquo (M)*
1951. *Melitone (FD)*
1951. *Leporello (DG)*

Brédy, Rosine 1962, 63. *Yniold (PM)*

Brouwenstijn, Gré 1959, 61, 63. *Leonore (FI)*

Brownlee, John 1935, 36, 37, 38, 39, 49. *Alfonso (CT)*
1935. *Speaker (Z)*
1936, 37, 38, 39. *Don Giovanni (DG)*
1936, 37, 38, 39, 47. *Count (NF)*

Bruscantini, Sesto 1951, 53. *Alfonso (CT)*
1952, 56, 59. *Guglielmo (CT)*
1952, 53, 54, 56, 59, 60. *Dandini (C)*
1953, *Music Master (AN)*
1954, 55, 61. *Figaro (BS)*
1954. *Raimbaud (CO)*
1955, 56. *Figaro (NF)*
1960. *Ford (F)*
1960. *Leporello (DG)*

Bryn Jones, Delme 1963. *Nick Shadow (RP)*
1964. *Speaker (Z)*

Byles, Edward 1957. *Brighella (AN)*

Cadoni, Fernanda 1952, 53, 54. *Tisbe (C)*
1954, 55, 57, 58. *Isolier (CO)*
1955, 57, 58. *Mrs Page (Meg) (F)*

Calabrese, Franco 1955. *Count (NF)*

Cameron, John 1952, 53. *Arbace (I)*
1953. *High Priest (AL)*
1953. *Apollo (AL)*

Canne-Meijer, Cora 1956. *Cherubino (NF)*
1956. *Second Lady (Z)*
1956. *Tisbe (C)*

Cantelo, April 1950, 51. *Barbarina (NF)*
1950. *Echo (AN–1)*
1953. *Echo (AN)*
1953. *Blonde (E)*
1963. *Marzelline (FI)*

Carlin, Mario 1958, 60. *Bardolph (F)*

Carolan, John 1953. *High Priest (I)*
1955. *Trabuco (FD)*
1956, 57. *Priest and Man in Armour (Z)*

Carroll, Christina 1948. *Donna Elvira (DG)*

Casanovas, Amadeo 1964. *Italian Tenor (CAP)*

Cassinelli, Antonio 1954. *Basilio (BS)*

Cava, Carlo 1961. *Basilio (BS)*
1962, 63. *Bartolo (NF)*
1962, 63, 64. *Seneca (IP)*
1963, 64. *Sarastro (Z)*

Cervena, Sona 1963, 64. *Clairon (CAP)*

Chumakova, Tamara 1958, 63. *Mother Goose (RP)*

Clabassi, Plinio 1964. *Banquo (M)*

Coertse, Mimi 1957. *Zerbinetta (AN)*

Conrad, James 1960. *Priest and Man in Armour (Z)*

Corena, Fernando 1955. *Falstaff (F)*

Cortis, Marcello 1957. *Taddeo (IA)*

Costa, Mary 1958. *Susanna (SS)*

Craig, Douglas 1950. *Harlekin (AN–1)*

Crespin, Régine 1959, 60. *Marschallin (R)*

Crook, Elizabeth 1959, 60. *Duenna (R)*

Cross, Joan 1946. *Female Chorus (RL)*

Cuenod, Hugues 1954, 58, 63. *Sellem (RP)*
1955, 56, 58, 59, 62, 63. *Basilio (NF)*
1957, 58, 60. *Dr Caius (F)*
1957, 58. *Dancing Master (AN)*
1962, 63, 64. *Lucano (IP)*
1963, 64. *Monsieur Taupe (CAP)*

Czerwenka, Oscar 1959, 60. *Baron Ochs (R)*

Dalamangas,
Cristiano 1955. *Basilio (BS)*

Dalberg, Frederick 1952. *Banquo (M)*

Danco, Suzanne 1948, 49. *Fiordiligi (CT)*
1951. *Donna Elvira (DG)*

D'Angelo, Gianna 1955. *Rosina (BS)*
1956. *Clorinda (C)*
1962. *Zerbinetta (AN–1)*

Dargavel, Bruce 1950. *Truffaldin (AN–1)*
1951. *Commendatore (DG)*
1951. *Neptune (I)*
1951. *Guardiano (FD)*

Darroll, Pauline 1963, 64. *Third Boy (Z)*

Davies, Derick 1959, 61, 63. *Second Prisoner (FI)*
1962, 63. *Antonio (NF)*
1963. *Keeper of the Madhouse (R1)*
1964. *Doctor (M)*
1964. *La Roche (CAP)*

Dean, Stafford 1964. *Lictor (IP)*
1964. *Major Domo (CAP)*

De Gabarain, Marina 1952, 53, 54, 56. *Cenerentola (C)*
1954, 55. *Baba the Turk (RP)*
1955. *Preziosilla (FD)*

Della Casa, Lisa 1951. *Countess (NF)*

Delman, Jacqueline 1958. *Najade (AN)*

Del Signore, Gino 1939. *Ferrando (CT)*

de Narké, Victor 1963. *Rocco (FI)*

de Peyer, Adrian 1962. *Scaramuccio (AN–1)*

Depraz, Xavier 1958. *Le Gouverneur (CO)*

Dickie, Murray 1950, 53. *Pedrillo (E)*
1950, 51. *Basilio (NF)*
1950. *Brighella (AN–1)*

Dickie, Murray	1953, 54. *Brighella (AN)*
	1953. *Sellem (RP)*
	1953, 54. *Dancing Master (AN)*
	1954. *Leandro (A)*
Dobbs, Mattiwilda	1953, 54. *Zerbinetta (AN)*
	1956, 61. *Constanze (E)*
	1956. *Queen of the Night (Z)*
Domgraf-	1934, 35, 37. *Figaro (NF)*
Fassbaender, Willi	1934, 35, 37. *Guglielmo (CT)*
	1935. *Papageno (Z)*
	1935. *Pasha Selim (E)*
Dominguez, Oralia	1955, 57, 58, 60. *Mistress Quickly* **(F)**
	1957. *Isabella (IA)*
	1962, 63, 64. *Arnalta (IP)*
Donlevy, Edmund	1946. *Junius (RL)*
Dorow, Dorothy	1961. *Hilda Mack (EY)*
Dow, Dorothy	1952. *Lady Macbeth (M)*
	1953. *Ariadne (AN)*
Driscoll, Loren	1962. *Ferrando (CT)*
Duff, Lesley	1946. *Lucia (RL)*
Dunlop, Fergus	1934, 35, 36, 37, 38, 39. *Antonio (NF)*
Duval, Denise	1960. *Elle (VH)*
	1962, 63. *Mélisande (PM)*
Duval, Pierre	1963. *Italian Tenor (CAP)*
Eadie, Noel	1935. *Constanze (E)*
	1935, 36. *Queen of the Night (Z)*
Ebers, Clara	1950. *Countess (NF)*
Ebert, Carl	1935, 36, 37, 53. *Pasha Selim* **(E)**
	1935, 36, 37. *Speaker (Z)*
Eisinger, Irene	1934, 35, 37, 38, 39, 49. *Despina* **(CT)**
	1935, 37. *Papagena (Z)*
	1935, 37. *Blonde (E)*
	1937, 38, 39. *Susanna (NF)*
	1938, 39. *Barbarina (NF)*
	1940. *Polly Peachum (BO)*
Endrich, Saramae	1964. *Poppea (IP)*
English, Gerald	1962, 63. *Second Soldier (IP)*
	1964. *Lucano (IP)*
Ernster, Dezsö	1952. *Alfonso (CT)*
Evans, Geraint	1950, 53, 54, 59. *Guglielmo (CT)*
	1951. *Masetto (DG)*
	1954. *Cospicuo (A)*
	1954. *Music Master (AN)*
	1955, 56, 60, 61. *Leporello (DG)*
	1956, 57, 60. *Papageno (Z)*
	1957, 58, 60. *Falstaff (F)*
	1958, 59. *Figaro (NF)*
Evans, John	1961. *Officer (BS)*
Evans, Nancy	1946. *Lucretia (RL)*
	1957. *Second Lady (Z)*
	1959, 60. *Annina (R)*
Farell, Marita	1937. *Zerlina (DG)*
	1937, 38. *Cherubino (NF)*
	1937. *Second Lady (Z)*
Farrington, Joseph	1940. *Lockit (BO)*
Feller, Carlos	1959. *Alfonso (CT)*
	1959. *Figaro (NF)*
	1960. *Speaker (Z)*
	1960. *Dr Bombasto (A)*
Ferenz, Willy	1959, 60. *Faninal (R)*
Ferrier, Kathleen	1946, 47. *Lucretia (RL)*
	1947. *Orpheus (O)*

Field-Hyde, Margaret	1937. *Papagena (Z)*
Filacuridi, Nicola	1960. *Lord Arthur Talbot (P)*
Flegg, Bruce	1940. *Filch (BO)*
	1947. *Basilio (NF)*
Fliether, Herbert	1961, 63. *Pizzaro (FI)*
Fort, Luigi	1939. *Ernesto (DP)*
Fortune, George	1964. *Count (CAP)*
Frank, Ernest	1937. *Monostatos (Z)*
	1947. *Antonio (NF)*
Franklin, David	1936, 38, 39, 48. *Commendatore (DG)*
	1937. *Sarastro (Z)*
	1938, 39. *Banquo (M)*
	1939. *Notary (DP)*
	1953, 54, 58. *Major Domo (AN*
	1953. *Bassa Selim (E)*
Freni, Mirella	1960, 61. *Zerlina (DG)*
	1962. *Susanna (NF)*
	1962. *Adina (EA)*
Fyson, Leslie	1950, 51. *Don Curzio (NF)*
Galliver, David	1956. *High Priest (I)*
Gencer, Leyla	1962, 63. *Countess (NF)*
Gester, Kurt	1953, 54. *Harlekin (AN)*
	1954. *Arlecchino (A)*
Graham, Edna	1953. *Najade (AN)*
	1957. *Zerbinetta (AN)*
Grandi, Margherita	1939, 47. *Lady Macbeth (M)*
	1949. *Amelia (BM)*
Gray, Linda	1940. *Lucy Lockit (BO)*
Griffiths, Gwyn	1954, 55. *Fiorella (BS)*
	1955, 56, 58, 59. *Antonio (NF)*
	1957. *Buff (S)*
	1958. *The Herald (AL)*
	1958. *The Oracle (AL)*
	1958. *Keeper of the Madhouse (RP)*
	1960. *Monostatos (Z)*
	1960. *Cospicuo (A)*
Grilli, Umberto	1964. *Giocondo (PP)*
Grist, Reri	1962. *Despina (CT)*
	1962. *Zerbinetta (AN–1)*
Grümmer, Elisabeth	1956. *Ilia (I)*
	1956. *Countess (NF)*
Güden, Hilde	1948. *Despina (CT)*
	1948. *Zerlina (DG)*
Gui, Henri	1962. *Pelléas (PM)*
Guichandut, Carlos	1953. *Bacchus (AN)*
Guthrie, Frederick	1956. *Sarastro (Z)*
Haefliger, Ernst	1956, 57. *Belmonte (E)*
	1956. *Tamino (Z)*
Hallin, Margareta	1957, 60. *Queen of the Night* **(Z)**
Hanak, Dorit	1961. *Blonde (E)*
Hancock, George	1936. *Speaker (Z)*
Harper, Heather	1957, 60. *First Lady (Z)*
	1963. *Anne (RP)*
Harshaw, Margaret	1954. *Donna Anna (DG)*
Hartley, David	1964. *Fabrizio (PP)*
Harwood, Elizabeth	1960. *Second Boy (Z)*
Heinemann, Lili	1936. *Papagena (Z)*
Helletsgruber, Luise	1934, 35, 36, 37, 38. *Dorabella (CT)*
	1934, 35, 36. *Cherubino (NF)*
	1935, 37. *First Lady (Z)*
	1936, 37, 38. *Donna Elvira (DG)*

Hemsley, Thomas 1953, 54. *Hercules (AL)*
1954. *The Herald (AL)*
1954, 55, 56. *Masetto (DG)*
1956, 57. *Speaker (Z)*
1957. *Haly (IA)*
1957, 58. *Music Master (AN)*
1961. *Don Fernando (FI)*
1961. *Dr Reischmann (EY)*

Henderson, Roy 1934, 35. *Count (NF)*
1936, 37, 38, 39. *Masetto (DG)*
1935, 36, 37. *Papageno (Z)*
1936, 37, 38, 39. *Guglielmo (CT)*
1940. *Peachum (BO)*

Hertner, Walter 1957. *Speaker (Z)*
Hill, Rose 1939. *Barbarina (NF)*
Hines, Jerome 1953. *Nick Shadow (RP)*
Hoekman, Guus 1962, 63. *Arkel (PM)*
Hollweg, Ilse 1950. *Constanze (E)*
1950. *Zerbinetta (AN–1)*
1954. *Zerbinetta (AN)*

Holm, Richard 1950. *Belmonte (E)*
Holman, David 1958. *Evandre (AL)*
Holmes, John 1958. *Truffaldin (AN)*
Hoppe, Heinz 1961. *Belmonte (E)*
Horne, William 1949. *Riccardo (BM)*
Houston, Roxane 1951. *Zerlina (DG)*
Howe, Janet 1951. *Marcellina (NF)*
Howland, Alice 1951. *Dorabella (CT)*
Hughes, David 1964. *High Priest (I)*

Illing, Mary 1958. *Alice (CO)*
1958, 59. *Barbarina (NF)*

Janowitz, Gundula 1964. *Ilia (I)*
Jarred, Mary 1953, 54, 55. *Mother Goose (RP)*
Johnston, James 1952. *Macduff (M)*
Jones, Morgan 1934, 35, 36, 37. *Don Curzio (NF)*
1935, 36, 37. *Man in Armour (Z)*
Jurinac, Sena 1949. *Dorabella (CT)*
1950, 51, 52, 53, 54, 56. *Fiordiligi (CT)*
1950. *Cherubino (NF)*
1951, 52, 53. *Ilia (I)*
1953, 54. *The Composer (AN)*
1954. *Donna Elvira (DG)*
1955, 56. *Donna Anna (DG)*
1955. *Countess (NF)*
1955. *Donna Leonora (FD)*

Kalmus, Margherita 1964. *First Lady (Z)*
Kassen, Gerald 1935. *Man in Armour (Z)*
Keetch, Maureen 1962. *Cherubino (NF)*
1963. *Marzelline (FI)*
1963. *Second Lady (Z)*
Kelly, David 1954, 55. *Keeper of the Madhouse (RP)*
1956. *Priest and Man in Armour (Z)*
1959. *Don Fernando (FI)*
Kentish, John 1952. *Malcolm (M)*
1955, 58. *Sellem (RP)*
1958, 59, 62, 63. *Don Curzio (NF)*
1958. *Scaramuccio (AN)*
1959, 60. *Valzacchi (R)*
1959, 61, 63. *First Prisoner (FI)*
1960. *Sir Bruno Robertson (P)*
1961. *Mauer (EY)*

Kinasiewicz, Maria 1952. *Electra (I)*
Kinrade, Vera 1956. *Third Boy (Z)*
Kipnis, Alexander 1936. *Sarastro (Z)*
Kočová, Míla 1935. *Queen of the Night (Z)*
Konetzni, Hilde 1938. *Donna Elvira (DG)*
Koréh, Endre 1950. *Osmin (E)*
Kraus, Otakar 1946. *Tarquinius (RL)*
1958. *Nick Shadow (RP)*
Krause, Tom 1963. *Count (CAP)*
Krebs, Helmut 1953. *Belmonte (E)*
1953. *Idamante (I)*
Kunz, Erich 1936. *Pasha Selim (E)*
1948, 50. *Guglielmo (CT)*
Kusche, Benno 1954. *Leporello (DG)*
1963, 64. *La Roche (CAP)*
1963. *Don Fernando (FI)*

Labay, Naida 1956, 57. *Papagena (Z)*
1957. *Mlle Silberklang (S)*
Lagger, Peter 1957. *Frank (S)*
1957. *Truffaldin (AN)*
1957. *Le Gouverneur (CO)*
Laghezza, Rosa 1963. *Marcellina (NF)*
Lane, Gloria 1958, 63. *Baba the Turk (RP)*
1959. *Dorabella (CT)*
Langdon, Michael 1961. *Osmin (E)*
1961. *Commendatore (DG)*
1963. *Bartolo (NF)*
Laszlo, Magda 1953, 54. *Alceste (AL)*
1954. *Dorabella (CT)*
1962, 63. *Poppea (IP)*
Lawson, Catherine 1946. *Bianca (RL)*
1947. *Marcellina (NF)*
Lee, Soo-Bee 1962, 63, 64. *Damigella (IP)*
Lewis, Gwent 1947. *Don Curzio (NF)*
Lewis, John 1957. *Bardolph (F)*
Lewis, Richard 1948, 55, 56, 60, 61. *Don Ottavio (DG)*
1950, 51, 52, 54, 56. *Ferrando (CT)*
1951, 52, 53, 56, 59, 64. *Idomeneo (I)*
1953, 54, 58. *Admète (AL)*
1953, 54, 58, 62. *Bacchus (AN)*
1953, 54, 55, 58, 63. *Tom Rakewell (RP)*
1959, 61, 63. *Florestan (FI)*
1960. *Tamino (Z)*
1962, 63, 64. *Nerone (IP)*
Ligabue, Ilva 1958, 60. *Mrs Ford (Alice) (F)*
1959. *Fiordiligi (CT)*
1960, 61. *Donna Elvira (DG)*
Lindermeier, Elisabeth 1956. *Donna Elvira (DG)*
Lipp, Wilma 1957. *Constanze (E)*
Lissitschkina,
Sinaida 1937. *Queen of the Night (Z)*
Lloyd, David 1938, 39. *Macduff (M)*
1939. *Don Ottavio (DG)*
Lloyd, David 1957. *Tamino (Z)*
1957. *Bacchus (AN)*
London, George 1950. *Figaro (NF)*
Loose, Emmy 1953. *Blonde (E)*
Lorengar, Pilar 1956, 57, 60. *Pamina (Z)*
1957, 58. *Echo (AN)*
1958, 59. *Countess (NF)*
Loring, Francis 1949. *Silvano (BM)*
Ludwig, Walther 1935. *Tamino (Z)*
1935. *Belmonte (E)*

Maclean, Bruna	1951. *Curra (FD)*
MacNeil, Dorothy	1951. *Donna Elvira (DG)*
	1951. *Cherubino (NF)*
Maire, Emily	1960. *First Boy (Z)*
	1961, 62. *Giannetta (EA)*
Malagù, Stefania	1962. *Dorabella (CT)*
Malbin, Elaine	1954. *Echo (AN)*
	1954. *Colombina (A)*
Manén, Lucie	1934. *Cherubino (NF)*
Marimpietri, Lydia	1962, 63. *Drusilla (IP)*
Markan, Maria	1939. *The Countess (NF)*
Mason, Stanley	1951. *Calatrava (FD)*
Massard, Robert	1958. *High Priest (AL)*
	1958. *Hercules (AL)*
Mathis, Edith	1962, 63. *Cherubino (NF)*
McAlpine, William	1956, 59. *Idamante (I)*
	1959, 60. *The Singer (R)*
	1962. *Bacchus (AN-1)*
McAusland, Day	1962. *Najade (AN-1)*
McCoshan, Daniel	1954, 55. *Notary (BS)*
	1955, 56. *Don Curzio (NF)*
	1955. *Bardolph (F)*
McKerrow, Rita	1953. *Fiordiligi (CT)*
McKinley, Andrew	1947. *Malcolm (M)*
Melis, György	1961. *Don Giovanni (DG)*
Menotti, Tatiana	1936. *Despina (CT)*
	1947. *Susanna (NF)*
Merriman, Nan	1953. *Baba the Turk (RP)*
	1956. *Dorabella (CT)*
Meyer, Kerstin	1961. *Carolina (EY)*
	1962. *Geneviève (PM)*
	1964. *Ottavia (IP)*
Midgley, Walter	1947. *Macduff (M)*
Mildmay, Audrey	1934, 35, 36, 38, 39. *Susanna (NF)*
	1936, 38, 39. *Zerlina (DG)*
	1938, 39. *Norina (DP)*
	1940. *Polly Peachum (BO)*
Miller, Kevin	1955. *Fenton (F)*
	1956, 57. *Pedrillo (E)*
	1956, 57. *Monostatos (Z)*
	1957. *Scaramuccio (AN)*
Miller, Mildred	1951. *Preziosilla (FD)*
Milligan, James	1956. *Arbace (I)*
Mitchell, Molly	1935, 36, 37. *Third Boy (Z)*
Modesti, Giuseppe	1960. *Sir George Walton (P*
Monachesi, Walter	1955. *Ford (F)*
Monreale, Leonardo	1960, 61. *Masetto (DG)*
Montarsolo, Paolo	1957. *Mustafa (IA)*
Moor, Julia	1936. *Queen of the Night (Z)*
	1936. *Constanze (E)*
Morison, Elsie	1953, 54, 55, 58. *Anne (RP)*
	1956. *Zerlina (DG)*
	1959. *Marzelline (FI)*
Moscucci, Orietta	1957. *Mrs Ford (Alice) (F)*
Munteanu, Petre	1948, 49. *Ferrando (CT)*
Nash, Heddle	1934, 35, 36, 37, 38, *Basilio (NF)*
	1934, 35, 36, 37, 38. *Ferrando (CT)*
	1935, 36, 37. *Pedrillo (E)*
Neville, Margaret	1963, 64. *First Boy (Z)*
	1964. *Drusilla (IP)*
Newton, Joyce	1937. *Third Lady (Z)*
Nielsen, Flora	1946. *Female Chorus (RL)*

Nilsson, Birgit	1951. *Electra (I)*
Noble, Morag	1962. *Echo (AN-1)*
Noni, Alda	1949. *Oscar (BM)*
	1950. *Blonde (E)*
	1950, 52, 53, 54. *Despina (CT)*
	1952, 53, 54. *Clorinda (C)*
Noval, Thorkild	1936, 37. *Tamino (Z)*
Ollendorff, Fritz	1953, 54. *Truffaldin (AN)*
	1953. *Osmin (E)*
	1954. *Dr Bombasto (A)*
Oncina, Juan	1952, 53, 54, 56, 59, 60. *Don Ramiro (C)*
	1953, 56, 59. *Ferrando (CT)*
	1954, 55, 57, 58. *Comte Ory (O)*
	1954. *Scaramuccio (AN)*
	1954, 55, 61. *Almaviva (BS)*
	1955, 57, 58, 60. *Fenton (F)*
	1956. *Don Ottavio (DG)*
	1957. *Lindoro (IA)*
Otto, Lisa	1956. *Blonde (E)*
Pashley, Anne	1962. *Second Boy (Z)*
Paskalis, Kostas	1964. *Macbeth (M)*
Pastori, Antonietta	1957. *Elvira (IA)*
	1957. *Nannetta (F)*
Pataky,	1936. *Don Ottavio (DG)*
Koloman von	1936. *Belmonte (E)*
Pavarotti, Luciano	1964. *Idamante (I)*
Payne, Lauri	1959. *Arbace (I)*
	1959. *Don Fernando (F)*
Pears, Peter	1946. *Male Chorus (RL)*
Pease, James	1954. *Don Giovanni (DG)*
Pender, Marta	1964. *Lady Macbeth (M)*
Pernerstorfer, Alois	1951. *Leporello (DG)*
	1951. *Figaro (NF)*
Perras, Margherita	1937. *Constanze (E)*
Peters, Johanna	1959, 62. *Marcellina (NF)*
Petri, Mario	1951. *Don Giovanni (DG)*
Picchi, Mirto	1949. *Riccardo (BM)*
Pilarczyk, Helga	1958. *The Composer (AN)*
	1960. *Colombina (A)*
Pini, Amalia	1949. *Ulrica (BM)*
Poell, Alfred	1951. *Arbace (I)*
	1951. *Count (NF)*
Poleri, David	1951, 55. *Alvaro (FD)*
Pollak, Anna	1946. *Bianca (RL)*
	1952, 53. *Dorabella (CT)*
Porte, Betsy de la	1935, 36. *Third Lady (Z)*
Protero, Dodi	1960. *Papagena (Z)*
Quensel, Isa	1951. *Despina (CT)*
Radford, Winifred	1934, 35, 36, 37, 38. *Barbarina (NF)*
	1935, 36, 37. *First Boy (Z)*
	1938. *Zerlina (DG)*
Raskin, Judith	1963, 64. *Pamina (Z)*
Ratti, Eugenia	1955. *Nannetta (F)*
	1961. *Adina (EA)*
Rautawaara, Aulikki	1934, 35, 36, 37, 38. *Countess (NF)*
	1935, 36, 37. *Pamina (Z)*
Read, David	1960. *Priest and Man in Armour (Z)*

Redgrave, Michael 1940. *Macheath (BO)*
Reynolds, Anna 1962, 63. *Geneviève (PM)*
    1964. *Ortensia (PP)*
    1964. *Second Lady (Z)*
Ritchie, Margaret 1946. *Lucia (RL)*
Rizzieri, Elena 1955, 56. *Susanna (NF)*
    1956. *Despina (CT)*
Robertson, Duncan 1958. *Brighella (AN)*
    1959. *High Priest (I)*
    1959, 61, 63. *Jaquino (FI)*
    1961. *Pedrillo (E)*
    1961. *Fiorello (BS)*
    1962, 63, 64. *Valetto (IP)*
    1962. *Brighella (AN–1)*
    1963, 64. *Monostatos (Z)*
Rogier, Frank 1946. *Tarquinius (RL)*
Rota, Anna Maria 1959, 60. *Cenerentola (C)*
    1960. *Mrs Page (Meg) (F)*
Rothenberger,
    Anneliese 1959, 60. *Sophie (R)*
Rothmüller, Marko 1949, 51, 52. *Guglielmo (CT)*
    1950. *Count (NF)*
    1951. *Don Carlo (FD)*
    1952. *Macbeth (M)*
    1954, 55. *Nick Shadow (RP)*
Roux, Michel 1956, 58, 59, 63. *Count (NF)*
    1958. *The Count (SS)*
    1962, 63. *Golaud (PM)*
    1962. *Don Alfonso (CT)*
    1964. *Macrobio (PP)*
Rovere, Anna Maria 1955. *Mrs Ford (Alice) (F)*
Rubio, Consuelo 1958. *Alceste (AL)*

Sardi, Ivan 1956. *Don Alfonso (CT)*
Sarfaty, Regina 1960. *Oktavian (R)*
Sarti, Laura 1961. *Berta (BS)*
Scheyrer, Gerda 1961. *Donna Anna (DG)*
Schiötz, Aksel 1946. *Male Chorus (RL)*
Schlemm, Anny 1954. *Zerlina (DG)*
Schönning, Sophie 1935, 36. *Second Lady (Z)*
Schwaiger, Rosl 1957. *Papagena (Z)*
    1957. *Blonde (E)*
Schwarz, Paul 1936. *Monostatos (Z)*
Schwarz, Vera 1938. *Lady Macbeth (M)*
Sciutti, Graziella 1954. *Rosina (BS)*
    1958. *Nannetta (F)*
    1958. *Susanna (NF)*
    1959. *Despina (CT)*
Sellas, Marta 1962. *Amor (IP)*
Sgourda, Antigone 1962. *Fiordiligi (CT)*
    1963. *First Lady (Z)*
Sharp, Frederick 1946. *Junius (RL)*
Shirley-Quirk, John 1962, 63. *Doctor (PM)*
    1962, 63. *Liberto (IP)*
    1963. *Major Domo (CAP)*
Silver, Annon Lee 1963, 64. *Amor (IP)*
Silveri, Paolo 1948. *Don Giovanni (DG)*
    1949. *Renato (BM)*
Simionato, Giulietta 1947. *Cherubino (NF)*
Simoneau, Leopold 1951, 54. *Don Ottavio (DG)*
    1951, 52. *Idamante (I)*
Sinclair, Jeannette 1955, 56. *Barbarina (NF)*
    1956, 57. *Second Boy (Z)*
    1957. *Alice (CO)*
Sinclair, Monica 1954, 55, 57, 58. *Ragonde (CO)*

    1955, 56, 58. *Marcellina (NF)*
    1955. *Berta (BS)*
    1955. *Curra (FD)*
    1956, 57, 60. *Third Lady (Z)*
    1957, 58. *Dryade (AN)*
    1960. *Queen Henrietta (P)*
Söderström, 1957. *The Composer (AN)*
    Elisabeth 1959, 61. *Oktavian (R)*
    1959. *Susanna (NF)*
    1961. *Elizabeth (EY)*
    1963, 64. *The Countess (CAP)*
Sordello, Enzo 1961, 62. *Belcore (EA)*
Souez, Ina 1934, 35, 36, 37, 38, 39. *Fiordiligi (CT)*
    1936, 37, 38, 39. *Donna Anna (DG)*
Speaight, Robert 1961. *Pasha Selim (E)*
Springer, Maureen 1950. *Najade (AN–1)*
    1954. *Najade (AN)*
Stabile, Mariano 1936, 38, 39. *Figaro (NF)*
    1938, 39. *Malatesta (DP)*
    1948. *Don Alfonso (CT)*
Stahlman, Sylvia 1959. *Ilia (I)*
Starling, Eric 1937. *Belmonte (E)*
    1938, 39. *Malcolm (M)*
    1938. *Don Curzio (NF)*
    1939. *Basilio (NF)*
Stear, Ronald 1935. *Bartolo (NF)*
    1935. *Speaker (Z)*
Steber, Eleanor 1947. *Countess (NF)*
Stefanoni, Marco 1955, 58, 60. *Pistol (F)*
    1960. *Commendatore (DG)*
Stevens, Risë 1939, 55. *Cherubino (NF)*
    1939. *Dorabella (CT)*
Storm, Erika 1936. *First Lady (Z)*
Streich, Rita 1958. *Zerbinetta (AN)*
Sutherland, Joan 1956. *Countess (NF)*
    1956. *First Lady (Z)*
    1957. *Madame Herz (S)*
    1960. *Elvira (P)*
    1960. *Donna Anna (DG)*
Szekely, Mihaly 1957, 60. *Sarastro (Z)*
    1957, 61. *Osmin (E)*
    1958, 59. *Dr Bartolo (NF)*
    1959, 61. *Rocco (FI)*

Tajo, Italo 1947. *Figaro (NF)*
    1947. *Banquo (M)*
Taranto, Vito de 1948. *Leporello (DG)*
Tarczynska, 1954, 55. *Alice (CO)*
    Halinka de 1954. *Clorinda (C)*
Tarrés, Enriqueta 1962. *Ariadne (AN–1)*
    1964. *Electra (I)*
Taylor, Neilson 1964. *Liberto (IP)*
    1964. *Arbace (I)*
Terry, Vera 1947. *Gentlewoman (M)*
Thebom, Blanche 1950. *Dorabella (CT)*
Thomas, Maldwyn 1939. *Don Curzio (NF)*
Thomas, Marjorie 1950. *Dryade (AN–1)*
    1953. *Dryade (AN)*
Thomas, Robert 1951. *Trabuco (FD)*
Toros, Hella 1939. *Donna Elvira (DG)*
Torres, Raimundo 1954. *High Priest (AL)*
Trama, Ugo 1964. *Asdrubale (PP)*
Trent, Barbara 1947. *Barbarina (NF)*
Troetschel, Elfride 1950. *Susanna (NF)*
Troy, Dermot 1954. *Evandre (AL)*

Troy, Dermot 1955. *Dr Caius (F)*
1960. *Leandro (A)*
Truccato Pace, Miti 1959, 60. *Tisbe (C)*
Turp, André, 1961. *Toni Reischmann (EY)*

Udovick, Lucille 1956. *Electra (I)*
Uhde, Hermann 1963. *Nick Shadow (RP)*
Ulfung, Ragnar 1963, 64. *Tamino (Z)*

Valdengo, Giuseppe 1955. *Raimbaud (CO)*
1955. *Don Giovanni (DG)*
Valentini, Alberta 1961. *Rosina (BS)*
1963, 64. *Italian Soprano (CAP)*
1964. *Fulvia (PP)*
Valentino, Francesco 1938, 39, 47. *Macbeth (M)*
Van Mill, Arnold 1956. *Osmin (E)*
Veasey, Josephine 1957. *Zulma (IA)*
1958, 59. *Cherubino (NF)*
1964. *Clarice (PP)*
Vercelli, Angela 1959. *Electra (I)*
Vietheer, Erich 1964. *Murderer (M)*
Vlachopoulos, Zoë 1947. *Amor (O)*
Vyvyan, Jennifer 1953. *Electra (I)*

Wakefield, John 1964. *Macduff (M)*
Walbrook, Anton 1950. *Pasha Selim (E)*
Walker, Norman 1937. *Commendatore (DG)*
1937. *Speaker (Z)*
1946. *Collatinus (RL)*
Wallace, Ian 1948. *Masetto (DG)*
1949. *Samuele (BM)*
1950, 55, 56, 61. *Bartolo (NF)*
1952, 53, 54, 56, 59, 60. *Don Magnifico (C)*
1954, 55. *Dr Bartolo (BS)*
1954, 60. *Ser Matteo (A)*
1954, 55. *Le Gouverneur (CO)*
Ward, David 1958. *Trulove (RP)*
1960. *Lord Walton (P)*
Warner, Genevieve 1951, 55. *Zerlina (DG)*
1951. *Susanna (NF)*
Watson, Claire 1960. *Marschallin (R)*
Watson, Jean 1949. *Ulrica (BM)*
1950. *Marcellina (NF)*
Watts, Doreen 1956. *Donna Elvira (DG)*
Watts, Helen 1957. *Third Boy (Z)*
Wegner, Walburga 1951. *Leonora (FD)*
Welitsch, Ljuba 1948. *Donna Anna (DG)*
1949. *Amelia (BM)*
Wicks, Dennis 1950. *Antonio (NF)*
1951. *Alcade (FD)*
1952. *Doctor (M)*
1953. *The Herald (AL)*
1953. *Keeper of the Madhouse (RP)*
1962, 63. *Lictor (IP)*
1962. *Truffaldin (AN–1)*
1963, 64. *Priest and Man in Armour (Z)*
1963. *Trulove (RP)*
1964. *Voice of Neptune (I)*
Wiener, Otto 1964. *La Roche (CAP)*
Wilbrink, Hans 1963. *Pelléas (PM)*
Wilhelm, Horst 1963, 64. *Flamand (CAP)*
Williams, Harold 1954, 55, 61. *Ambrogio (BS)*
1955, 57, 58, 60. *The Inn Keeper (F)*
1961. *Dumb Slave (E)*

Willis, Constance 1934, 35, 36, 37, 38, 39. *Marcellina (NF)*
1939. *Gentlewoman (M)*
1940. *Mrs Peachum (BO)*
Wilson, Catherine 1960. *Second Lady (Z)*
Wilson, Dorothy 1964. *Ottavia (IP)*
1964. *Second Boy (Z)*
Wixell, Ingvar 1962. *Guglielmo (CT)*
Wolansky, Raymond 1963, 64. *Olivier (CAP)*
Woodland, Rae 1964. *Gentlewoman (M)*

Young, Alexander 1950. *Scaramuccio (AN–1)*
1951, 52. *High Priest (I)*
1951. *Don Curzio (NF)*
1951. *Basilio (NF)*
1953. *Scaramuccio (AN)*
1953. *Evandre (AL)*
1953. *Ferrando (CT)*
1957. *Vogelsang (S)*

Zadek, Hilde 1950. *Ariadne (AN–1)*
1951. *Donna Anna (DG)*
Zanolli, Silvana 1959, 60. *Clorinda (C)*
Zareska, Eugenia 1948. *Dorabella (CT)*
Zeri, Maria 1962, 63. *Barbarina (NF)*
1963, 64. *Papagena (Z)*
Ziegler, Edwin 1935. *Monostatos (Z)*

Conductors

Ansermet, Ernest 1946. *The Rape of Lucretia*
Austin, Frederic 1940. *The Beggar's Opera*
Balkwill, Bryan 1954. *Alceste*
1954. *The Rake's Progress*
1955. *The Barber of Seville*
1956. *Don Giovanni*
1957. *Der Schauspieldirektor*
1958. *Le Comte Ory*
1960. *I Puritani*
1963. *Fidelio*
1964. *Capriccio*
Beecham, Sir Thomas 1950. *Ariadne auf Naxos (first version)*
Bernard, Anthony 1940. *The Beggar's Opera*
Busch, Fritz 1934, 35, 36, 37, 38, 39, 51. *Le nozze di Figaro*
1934, 35, 36, 37, 38, 39, 50, 51. *Così fan tutte*
1935, 36, 37. *The Magic Flute*
1935, 36, 37, 50. *Die Entführung aus dem Serail*
1936, 37, 38, 39, 51. *Don Giovanni*
1938, 39. *Macbeth*
1938, 39. *Don Pasquale*
1951. *Idomeneo*
1951. *La forza del destino*
Cellini, Renato 1947. *Le nozze di Figaro*
Cillario, Carlo Felice 1961, 62. *L'elisir d'amore*
Davis, Colin 1960. *The Magic Flute*
Erede, Alberto 1938, 39. *Le nozze di Figaro*
1938, 39. *Don Giovanni*
1955. *The Barber of Seville*
Fredman, Myer 1963. *Le nozze di Figaro*
1964. *La pietra del paragone*

333

Fricsay, Ferenç	1950. *Le nozze di Figaro*
Gardelli, Lamberto	1964. *Macbeth*
Gellhorn, Peter	1956. *Die Entführung aus dem Serail*
	1957, 60. *The Magic Flute*
	1958. *Alceste*
	1959. *Idomeneo*
	1959, 60. *La Cenerentola*
	1959. *Le nozze di Figaro*
	1960, 61. *Don Giovanni*
Goodall, Reginald	1946. *The Rape of Lucretia*
Giulini, Carlo Maria	1955. *Falstaff*
Goldschmidt, Berthold	1947. *Macbeth*
Gui, Vittorio	1948, 49, 52, 54, 56. *Così fan tutte*
	1949. *Un ballo in maschera*
	1952. *Macbeth*
	1952, 53, 56, 59. *La Cenerentola*
	1953, 54, 58. *Alceste*
	1954, 55, 61. *The Barber of Seville*
	1954, 55, 57, 58. *Le Comte Ory*
	1955, 56. *Le nozze di Figaro*
	1956, 63, 64. *The Magic Flute*
	1957. *L'italiana in Algeri*
	1957, 58, 60. *Falstaff*
	1959, 61. *Fidelio*
	1960. *I Puritani*
	1962, 63. *Pelléas et Mélisande*
Henze, Hans Werner	1961. *Elegy for Young Lovers*
Kubelik, Rafael	1948. *Don Giovanni*
Leppard, Raymond	1964. *L'incoronazione di Poppea*
Ludwig, Leopold	1959, 60. *Der Rosenkavalier*
Maag, Peter	1959. *Le nozze di Figaro*
Mudie, Michael	1940. *The Beggar's Opera*
Oppenheim, Hans	1935. *Le nozze di Figaro*
	1935. *Die Entführung aus dem Serail*
	1936. *The Magic Flute*
	1946. *The Rape of Lucretia*
	1949. *Così fan tutte*
	1949. *Un ballo in maschera*
Pritchard, John	1951, 56, 62. *Le nozze di Figaro*
	1951, 53, 54, 56, 59, 62. *Così fan tutte*
	1951, 55, 56, 60, 61. *Don Giovanni*
	1952, 53, 56, 59, 64. *Idomeneo*
	1953, 54, 57, 58. *Ariadne auf Naxos*
	1954. *Arlecchino*
	1954, 56, 60. *La Cenerentola*
	1955. *La forza del destino*
	1958. *Le Comte Ory*
	1958, 60. *Il segreto di Susanna*
	1960. *La Voix Humaine*
	1961. *Elegy for Young Lovers*
	1962, 63. *L'incoronazione di Poppea*
	1963, 64. *Capriccio*
	1964. *La pietra del paragone*
Sacher, Paul	1954, 55, 58, 63. *The Rake's Progress*
	1956, 57. *Die Entführung aus dem Serail*
	1957. *The Magic Flute*
Schmidt-Isserstedt, Hans	1958. *Le nozze di Figaro*
Sillem, Maurits	1956. *Le nozze di Figaro*
Solti, Georg	1954. *Don Giovanni*
Stiedry, Fritz	1947. *Orpheus*
Susskind, Walter	1947. *Le nozze di Figaro*
Varviso, Silvio	1962, 63. *Le nozze di Figaro*
	1962. *Ariadne auf Naxos* (*first version*)
Wallenstein, Alfred	1953. *Die Entführung aus dem Serail*
	1953. *The Rake's Progress*

Producers

Besch, Anthony	1957. *Der Schauspieldirektor*
Cocteau, Jean	1960. *La Voix Humaine*
Crozier, Eric	1946. *The Rape of Lucretia*
Ebert, Carl	All operas up to and including 1939. Subsequently:
	1947. *Orpheus*
	1947, 50, 51, 55, 56, 58, 59, 62. *Le nozze de Figaro*
	1947, 52. *Macbeth*
	1948, 51, 54. *Don Giovanni*
	1948, 49, 50, 51, 52, 53, 54, 56, 59, 62. *Così fan tutte*
	1949. *Un ballo in maschera*
	1950, 53. *Die Entführung aus dem Serail*
	1950, 62. *Ariadne auf Naxos* (*first version*)
	1953, 54, 57, 58. *Ariadne auf Naxos* (*second version*)
	1951, 52, 53, 56, 59. *Idomeneo*
	1951. *La forza del destino*
	1952, 53, 54, 56, 59, 60. *La Cenerentola*
	1953, 54, 58. *Alceste*
	1953, 54, 55, 58, 63. *The Rake's Progress*
	1954, 55, 61. *The Barber of Seville*
	1954, 55, 57, 58. *Le Comte Ory*
	1955, 57, 58, 60. *Falstaff*
	1956, 57. *The Magic Flute*
	1959, 60. *Der Rosenkavalier*
	1962, 63. *Pelléas et Mélisande*
Ebert, Peter	1954, 60. *Arlecchino*
	1955, 56. *Don Giovanni*
	1955. *La forza del destino*
	1956, 57, 61. *Die Entführung aus dem Serail*
	1957. *L'italiana in Algeri*
	1958, 60. *Il segreto di Susanna*
	1963. *Le nozze di Figaro*
	1963. *The Rake's Progress*
Enriquez, Franco	1960. *I Puritani*
	1963, 64. *The Magic Flute*
	1964. *Macbeth*
Gielgud, John	1940. *The Beggar's Opera*
Rennert, Günther	1959, 61, 63. *Fidelio*
	1960, 61. *Don Giovanni*
	1961. *Elegy for Young Lovers*
	1962, 63, 64. *L'incoronazione di Poppea*
	1963, 64. *Capriccio*
	1964. *La pietra del paragone*
Zeffirelli, Franco	1961, 62. *L'elisir d'amore*

Designers

Carl, Joseph	1947. *Orpheus*
Casson, Hugh	1953, 54, 58. *Alceste*
	1962, 63, 64. *L'incoronazione di Poppea*
Cocteau, Jean	1960. *La Voix Humaine*
Gérard, Rolf	1948, 49, 50, 51, 52, 53, 56, 59, 62. *Così fan tutte*
	1950. *Le nozze di Figaro*
	1950, 53. *Die Entführung aus dem Serail*
Heeley, Desmond	1960. *I Puritani*
Hurry, Leslie	1951, 55. *La forza del destino*

Lancaster, Osbert	1953, 54, 55, 58, 63. *The Rake's Progress*
	1955, 57, 58, 60. *Falstaff*
	1957. *L'italiana in Algeri*
	1964. *La pietra del paragone*
Lennon, Dennis	1963, 64. *Capriccio*
Luzzati, Emanuele	1963, 64. *The Magic Flute*
	1964. *Macbeth*
Maximowna, Ita	1959, 61, 63. *Fidelio*
	1960, 61. *Don Giovanni*
Messel, Oliver	1950, 53, 54, 55, 58, 62. *Ariadne auf Naxos*
	1951, 52, 53, 56, 59, 64. *Idomeneo*
	1952, 53, 54, 56, 59, 60. *La Cenerentola*
	1954, 55, 61. *The Barber of Seville*
	1954, 55, 57, 58. *Le Comte Ory*
	1955, 56, 58, 59, 62, 63. *Le nozze di Figaro*
	1956, 57, 61. *Die Entführung aus dem Serail*
	1956, 57, 60. *The Magic Flute*
	1959, 60. *Der Rosenkavalier*
Montresor, Beni	1962, 63. *Pelléas et Mélisande*
Motley	1940. *The Beggar's Opera*
Neher, Caspar	1938, 39, 47, 52. *Macbeth*
	1949. *Un ballo in maschera*
Nobili, Lila de	1961. *Elegy for Young Lovers*
Piper, John	1946, *The Rape of Lucretia*
	1951, 54, 55, 56. *Don Giovanni*
Rice, Peter	1954, 60. *Arlecchino*
	1957. *Der Schauspieldirektor*
Scott, Hutchinson	1951. *Le nozze di Figaro*
Toms, Carl	1958, 60. *Il segreto di Susanna*
Wilson, Hamish	1934, 35, 36, 37, 38, 39, 47. *Le nozze di Figaro*
	1934, 35, 36, 37, 38, 39. *Così fan tutte*
	1935, 36, 37. *The Magic Flute*
	1935, 36, 37. *Die Entführung aus dem Serail*
	1936, 37, 38, 39, 48. *Don Giovanni*
	1938, 39. *Don Pasquale*
Zeffirelli, Franco	1961, 62. *L'elisir d'amore*

Designers—Costumes only

Evans, Conwy	1962, 63, 64. *L'incoronazione di Poppea*
Gérard, Rolf	1951. *Le nozze di Figaro*
Green, Kenneth	1938, 39. *Don Pasquale*
Heckroth, Hein	1936, 37, 38, 39, 48. *Don Giovanni*
Litherland, Ann	1934, 35, 36, 37, 38, 39, 47. *Le nozze di Figaro*
	1934, 35, 36, 37, 38, 39. *Così fan tutte*
	1935, 36, 37. *Die Entführung aus dem Serail*
Nevill, Bernard	1962. *Così fan tutte*
Powell, Anthony	1963, 64. *Capriccio*
Vercoe, Rosemary	1953, 54, 58. *Alceste*
	1954, 56, 59. *Così fan tutte*

General Managers

Nightingale, Alfred	1934–35
Bing, Rudolf	1936–48
Caplat, Moran	since 1949

Le nozze di Figaro

(1934 production)

Figaro	Willi Domgraf-Fassbaender
Susanna	Audrey Mildmay
Don Basilio	Heddle Nash
Marcellina	Constance Willis
Cherubino	Luise Helletsgruber
Count Almaviva	Roy Henderson
The Countess	Aulikki Rautawaara
Bartolo	Norman Allin
	Italo Tajo
Antonio	Fergus Dunlop
Barbarina	Winifred Radford
Don Curzio	Morgan Jones

Conductor FRITZ BUSCH

Deleted in USA and Great Britain

Così fan tutte

(1935 production)

Ferrando	Heddle Nash
Guglielmo	Willi Domgraf-Fassbaender
Don Alfonso	John Brownlee
Fiordiligi	Ina Souez
Dorabella	Luise Helletsgruber
Despina	Irene Eisinger

Conductor FRITZ BUSCH

Deleted in USA and Great Britain

Available as an import:
Capitol-Odeon (Electrola) E 80681/3 (3 LPs)

Don Giovanni

(1936 production)

Leporello	Salvatore Baccaloni
Donna Anna	Ina Souez
Don Giovanni	John Brownlee
The Commendatore	David Franklin
Don Ottavio	Koloman von Pataky
Donna Elvira	Luise Helletsgruber
Zerlina	Audrey Mildmay
Masetto	Roy Henderson

Conductor FRITZ BUSCH

Deleted in USA and Great Britain

Available as an import:
Capitol-Odeon (Electrola) E 80598/600 (3 LPs)

Orpheus

(Abridged version of 1947 production)

Orpheus	Kathleen Ferrier
Eurydice	Ann Ayars
Amor	Zoë Vlachopoulos

Conductor FRITZ STIEDRY

Great Britain: Decca LXT 2893
USA: London 5103

Così fan tutte

(Excerpts from 1950 production)

Ferrando	Richard Lewis
Guglielmo	Erich Kunz
Don Alfonso	Mario Borriello
Fiordiligi	Sena Jurinac
Dorabella	Blanche Thebom

Conductor FRITZ BUSCH

Deleted in USA and Great Britain

Idomeneo

(Excerpts from 1951 production)

Ilia	Sena Jurinac
Idamante	Alexander Young
Electra	Dorothy MacNeil
Idomeneo	Richard Lewis

Conductor FRITZ BUSCH

Deleted in USA and Great Britain

Available as an import: Electrola E80722

La Cenerentola

(1953 production)

Don Ramiro	Juan Oncina
Dandini	Sesto Bruscantini
Don Magnifico	Ian Wallace
Clorinda	Alda Noni
Tisbe	Fernanda Cadoni
Cenerentola	Marina de Gabarain
Alidoro	Hervey Alan

Conductor VITTORIO GUI

Deleted in USA and Great Britain

Le nozze di Figaro

(1955 production)

Figaro	Sesto Bruscantini
Susanna	Graziella Sciutti
Don Basilio	Hugues Cuenod
Marcellina	Monica Sinclair
Cherubino	Risë Stevens
Count Almaviva	Franco Calabrese
The Countess	Sena Jurinac
Bartolo	Ian Wallace
Antonio	Gwyn Griffiths
Barbarina	Jeannette Sinclair
Don Curzio	Daniel McCoshan

Conductor VITTORIO GUI

Great Britain: On tape only
SAT 1006/7. SAT 1003/4, SAT 1009/11 (7½ i.p.s.)

Deleted in USA

Le Comte Ory

(1955 production)

Raimbaud	Michel Roux
Alice	Jeannette Sinclair
Ory	Juan Oncina
Ragonde	Monica Sinclair
Le Gouverneur	Ian Wallace
Isolier	Cora Canne-Meijer
Adèle	Sari Barabas

Conductor VITTORIO GUI

In Great Britain on TH 2,
from Tillet and Holt, 122 Wigmore Street, W1

Available in USA: Angel 3565 B/L (2 LPS)

Idomeneo

(1956 production)

Ilia   Sena Jurinac
Idamante   Léopold Simoneau
Electra   Lucille Udovick
Idomeneo   Richard Lewis
Arbace   James Milligan

Conductor   JOHN PRITCHARD

Great Britain: HMV ALP 1515/7 (3 LPs)
USA: Angel 3574 C/L (3 LPs)

Arlecchino

(1954 production)

Ser Matteo   Ian Wallace
Arlecchino   Kurt Gester
Abbate Cospicuo   Geraint Evans
Doctor Bombasto   Fritz Ollendorf
Colombina   Elaine Malbin
Leandro   Murray Dickie

Conductor   JOHN PRITCHARD

Great Britain: On tape only HTA 14 (7½ i.p.s.)
Deleted in USA

The Barber of Seville

(1962)

Rosina   Victoria de los Angeles
Count Almaviva   Luigi Alva
Figaro   Sesto Bruscantini
Basilio   Carlo Cava
Bartolo   Ian Wallace

Conductor   VITTORIO GUI

Great Britain: Angel AN 114/6 (mono)
SAN 114/6 (stereo – 3 LPs)
USA: Angel 3638 C/L (mono – 3 LPs)
Angel S 3638 C/L (stereo)

L'incoronazione di Poppea

(Abridged version of 1963 production)

Poppea   Magda Laszlo
Nerone   Richard Lewis
Ottavia   Frances Bible
Arnalta   Oralia Dominguez
Ottone   Walter Alberti
Drusilla   Lydia Marimpietri
Seneca   Carlo Cava
Lucano   Hugues Cuenod

Conductor   JOHN PRITCHARD

Great Britain: HMV AN 126/7 (mono – 2 LPs)
SAN 126/7 (stereo)
USA: Angel 3644 B/L (mono)
Angel S3644 B/L (stereo)

Appendix D   *Operas and casts in chronological order*   1965-80

General Manager MORAN CAPLAT

Music Counsellor JOHN PRITCHARD

Artistic Counsellor GÜNTHER RENNERT

Head of Music Staff and Preparation JANI STRASSER

Conductors LAMBERTO GARDELLI, GIANANDREA GAVAZZENI, VITTORIO GUI, JOHN PRITCHARD, MYER FREDMAN
Chorus Master MYER FREDMAN
Music Staff STEUART BEDFORD, VALENTINO BARCELLESI, FRANCES COLLINS, GEORGE COOP, ERNA GAL, GERALD GOVER, MARTIN ISEPP, ROY JESSON, COURTNEY KENNY, KENNETH MONTGOMERY
Chorus Manager HAROLD WILLIAMS
Librarian HOWARD WICKS
Assistant to Head of Music Staff BRIAN DICKIE

Producers FRANCO ENRIQUEZ, FRANK HAUSER, DANIEL LEVEUGLE, HANS NEUGEBAUER, GÜNTHER RENNERT
Assistant Producers ALISOUN BROWNE, JOAN DOWNES, DENNIS MAUNDER
Lighting FRANCIS REID
Production Manager JUNE DANDRIDGE
Stage Director GEOFFREY GILBERTSON
Stage Manager ALISOUN BROWNE
Deputy Stage Managers CHARLES HAMILTON, BARRY ILES
Chief Technician DESMOND COLLINS
Assistant IVOR GREEN
Staff Carpenter BERT PULLEN
Wardrobe Manager ROSEMARY WILKINS
Cutters DAVID HARVEY-JONES, JOAN MINTO
Wardrobe Mistress GLADYS CHISHOLM
Assistant to Wardrobe Manager TONY LEDELL
Wigs SHEILA DUNSDON
Property Manager ANNABELLE HAWTREY
Assistant Manager JANET MOORES
Regulating Secretary UNA MARCHETTI
Treasurer ERIC WHITEHORN
Press Officer BERNARD MCNABB
Transport REX ROGERS
Box Office Manager CAROLINE ARTHUR
Appointed Photographer GUY GRAVETT
Catering by VERNON HERBERT

LONDON PHILHARMONIC ORCHESTRA

Il matrimonio segreto

CIMAROSA   *13 performances*

Paolino	Pietro Bottazzo (*Italian*)
Carolina	Margherita Rinaldi (*Italian*)
Geronimo	Carlo Badioli (*Italian*)
Elisetta	Alberta Valentini (*Italian*)
Fidalma	Rosa Laghezza (*Italian*)
Count Robinson	Federico Davià (*Italian*)

Conductors	VITTORIO GUI
	Myer Fredman
Producer	FRANK HAUSER
Designer	DESMOND HEELEY

Der Rosenkavalier

RICHARD STRAUSS   *15 performances*

Oktavian	Teresa Zylis-Gara (*Polish*)
	Josephine Veasey (*English*)
Feldmarschallin	Montserrat Caballé (*Spanish*)
	Erika Schmidt (*German*)
Ochs	Manfred Jungwirth (*Austrian*)
	Otto Edelmann (*Austrian*)
Valzacchi	David Hughes (*Welsh*)
Annina	Anna Reynolds (*English*)
Faninal	John Modenos (*American*)
Sophie	Edith Mathis (*Swiss*)
	Liselotte Hammes (*German*)
Duenna	Angela Jenkins (*English*)
Singer	Jon Andrews (*New Zealand*)
Landlord	David Lennox (*English*)
Police Inspector	Richard Golding (*English*)

Conductor	JOHN PRITCHARD
Producer	HANS NEUGEBAUER
Designer	OLIVER MESSEL

Anna Bolena

DONIZETTI   *12 performances*

Giovanna (Jane Seymour)	Patricia Johnson (*English*)
Anna (Anne Boleyn)	Leyla Gencer (*Turkish*)
	Gwenyth Annear (*Australian*)
Smeton	Maureen Morelle (*English*)
Enrico (Henry VIII)	Carlo Cava (*Italian*)
Rochefort (Lord Rochford)	Don Garrard (*Canadian*)
Riccardo (Lord Richard Percy)	Juan Oncina (*Spanish*)
Hervey	Lloyd Strauss Smith (*English*)

Conductors	GIANANDREA GAVAZZENI
	Myer Fredman
Producer	FRANCO ENRIQUEZ
Designer	LORENZO GHIGLIA

Le nozze di Figaro

MOZART   *13 performances*

Figaro	Walter Alberti (*Italian*)
Susanna	Lydia Marimpietri (*Italian*)
Bartolo	Federico Davià (*Italian*)
Marcellina	Rosa Laghezza (*Italian*)
Cherubino	Biancamaria Casoni (*Italian*)
Count Almaviva	Gérard Souzay (*French*)
	John Kitchiner (*English*)
	Michel Roux (*French*)
Don Basilio	Hugues Cuenod (*Swiss*)
The Countess	Montserrat Caballé (*Spanish*)
	Lorna Elias (*Welsh*)
	Josephine Veasey (*English*)
Antonio	Derick Davies (*Welsh*)
Barbarina	Audrey Attwood (*English*)
Don Curzio	David Lennox (*English*)

Conductors	VITTORIO GUI
	Myer Fredman
Producer	DANIEL LEVEUGLE
Designer	OLIVER MESSEL

Macbeth

VERDI   *9 performances*

Macbeth	Kostas Paskalis (*Greek*)
Banquo	Michael Langdon (*English*)
Lady Macbeth	Gunilla af Malmborg (*Swedish*)
Gentlewoman	Margaret Curphey (*English*)
Macduff	David Hughes (*Welsh*)
Malcolm	Lloyd Strauss Smith (*English*)
Doctor	Derick Davies (*Welsh*)
Servant	Peter Lehmann Bedford (*English*)
Murderer	Paschal Allen (*English*)

Conductor	LAMBERTO GARDELLI
Producer	FRANCO ENRIQUEZ
Associate Producer	Dennis Maunder
Designer	EMANUELE LUZZATI

La pietra del paragone

ROSSINI   *12 performances*

Fabrizio	David Hartley (*English*)
Pacuvio	Heinz Blankenburg (*American*)
Ortensia	Anna Reynolds (*English*)
Fulvia	Alberta Valentini (*Italian*)
Asdrubale	Ugo Trama (*Italian*)
Giocondo	Umberto Grilli (*Italian*)
Clarice	Josephine Veasey (*English*)
Macrobio	Michel Roux (*French*)

Conductor	JOHN PRITCHARD
Producer	GÜNTHER RENNERT
Associate Producer	Joan Downes
Designer	OSBERT LANCASTER

General Manager MORAN CAPLAT

Music Counsellor JOHN PRITCHARD

Artistic Counsellor GÜNTHER RENNERT

Head of Music Staff and Preparation JANI STRASSER

Conductors CARLO FELICE CILLARIO, MYER FREDMAN,
HANS GIERSTER, LEOPOLD LUDWIG, JOHN PRITCHARD
Music Staff STEUART BEDFORD, MICHAEL FREYHAN, ERNA GAL,
GERALD GOVER, JONATHAN HINDEN, ANTHONY HOSE, MARTIN ISEPP,
ROY JESSON, COURTNEY KENNY, JEAN MALLANDAINE,
KENNETH MONTGOMERY
Chorus Manager HAROLD WILLIAMS
Librarian HOWARD WICKS

Producers FRANCO ENRIQUEZ, DENNIS MAUNDER,
MICHAEL REDGRAVE, GÜNTHER RENNERT
Assistant Producers ALISOUN BROWNE, CHARLES HAMILTON
Lighting FRANCIS REID
Production Manager JUNE DANDRIDGE
Stage Director GEOFFREY GILBERTSON
Stage Manager ALISOUN BROWNE
Deputy Stage Managers CHARLES HAMILTON, ANDREW PAGE
Chief Technician ALBERT PULLEN
Assistant IVOR GREEN
Staff Carpenter REX CARTER
Wardrobe Manager ROSEMARY WILKINS
Cutters DAVID HARVEY-JONES, JOAN MINTO
Wardrobe Mistress GLADYS CHISHOLM
Wigs SHEILA DUNSDON
Property Manager ANNABELLE HAWTREY
Assistant Manager JANET MOORES
Regulating Secretary UNA MARCHETTI
Administrative Assistant BRIAN DICKIE
Treasurer ERIC WHITEHORN
Press Secretary HELEN O'NEILL
Appointed Photographer GUY GRAVETT
Transport REX ROGERS
Box Office Manager CAROLINE ARTHUR
Catering by VERNON HERBERT

LONDON PHILHARMONIC ORCHESTRA

DOUBLE BILL
Dido and Aeneas

PURCELL   *13 performances*
(arr Benjamin Britten, Imogen Holst)

Belinda	Sheila Armstrong	(*English*)
Dido	Janet Baker	(*English*)
Second Lady in Waiting	Angela Hickey	(*English*)
Aeneas	Thomas Hemsley	(*English*)
Sorceress	Patricia Johnson	(*English*)
First Witch and voice of Mercury	Clare Walmesley	(*English*)
Second Witch	Jean Allister	(*Irish*)
	Pamela Bowden	(*English*)
Sailor	Ryland Davies	(*Welsh*)

Conductor   JOHN PRITCHARD
Producer   FRANCO ENRIQUEZ
Assistant Producer   Alisoun Browne
Designer   LORENZO GHIGLIA
Choreographer   PAULINE GRANT

L'Heure espagnole

RAVEL   *13 performances*

Ramiro	Pierre Le Hémonet	(*French*)
Torquemada	Hugues Cuenod	(*Swiss*)
Concepcion	Isabel Garcisanz	(*Spanish*)
Gonzalve	Michel Sénéchal	(*French*)
Gomez	Victor Autran	(*French*)

Conductor   JOHN PRITCHARD
Producer   DENNIS MAUNDER
Designer   OSBERT LANCASTER

Werther

MASSENET   *13 performances*

The Bailiff	Stafford Dean (*English*)
Johann	Anthony Raffell (*English*)
Schmidt	Adrian de Peyer (*English*)
Sophie	Françoise Doué (*French*)
Werther	Jean Brazzi (*French*)
Charlotte	Hélia T'Hezan (*French*)
Albert	Peter Gottlieb (*Brazilian*)
	Pierre Le Hémonet (*French*)

Conductor	CARLO FELICE CILLARIO
Producer	MICHAEL REDGRAVE
Scenery	HENRY BARDON
Costumes	DAVID WALKER

Jephtha

HANDEL   *12 performances*
*(Oratorio in two parts realized for
scenic performance by Caspar Neher and
Günther Rennert)*

Zebul	Don Garrard (*Canadian*)
Jephtha	Richard Lewis (*English*)
Storgè	Patricia Johnson (*English*)
Hamor	Calvin Marsh (*American*)
Iphis	Heather Harper (*Irish*)
Angel	Margaret Price (*Welsh*)

Conductors	LEOPOLD LUDWIG
	Myer Fredman
Producer and Choreographer	GÜNTHER RENNERT
Original designs	CASPAR NEHER
	(*realized by Erich Kondrak*)

Sponsored by the Peter Stuyvesant Foundation

The Magic Flute

MOZART   *16 performances*

Tamino	George Shirley (*American*)
Three Ladies	Margaret Kingsley (*English*)
	Anne Pashley (*English*)
	Ann Cooper (*English*)
Papageno	Peter-Christoph Runge (*German*)
	Heinz Blankenburg (*American*)
Queen of the Night	Rae Woodland (*English*)
Three Boys	Annon Lee Silver (*Canadian*)
	Anne Howells (*English*)
	Janet Kenny (*New Zealand*)
Monostatos	Hugues Cuenod (*Swiss*)
Pamina	Arlene Saunders (*American*)
The Speaker	Thomas Hemsley (*English*)
	Brian Donlan (*English*)
Sarastro	Victor de Narké (*Argentinian*)
Priests and Men in Armour	Ryland Davies (*Welsh*)
	Richard Van Allan (*English*)
Papagena	Sheila Armstrong (*English*)

Conductors	HANS GIERSTER
	Myer Fredman
Producer	FRANCO ENRIQUEZ
Designer	EMANUELE LUZZATI

General Manager MORAN CAPLAT

Music Counsellor JOHN PRITCHARD

Artistic Counsellor GÜNTHER RENNERT

Head of Music Staff and Preparation JANI STRASSER

Conductors CARLO FELICE CILLARIO, MYER FREDMAN,
KENNETH MONTGOMERY, RAYMOND LEPPARD, JOHN PRITCHARD
Music Staff UBALDO GARDINI, JONATHAN HINDEN, ANTHONY HOSE,
MARTIN ISEPP, ROY JESSON, GORDON KEMBER, COURTNEY KENNY,
JEAN MALLANDAINE, KENNETH MONTGOMERY
Chorus Manager HAROLD WILLIAMS
Librarian HOWARD WICKS

Producers FRANCO ENRIQUEZ, DENNIS MAUNDER,
MICHAEL REDGRAVE, GÜNTHER RENNERT
Assistant Producers ALISOUN BROWNE, GEOFFREY GILBERTSON,
CHARLES HAMILTON
Lighting FRANCIS READ
Production Manager JUNE DANDRIDGE
Stage Director GEOFFREY GILBERTSON
Stage Manager ALISOUN BROWNE
Deputy Stage Managers CHARLES HAMILTON, ANDREW PAGE
Chief Technician ALBERT PULLEN
Assistant IVOR GREEN
Staff Carpenters REX CARTER, A. FOORD
Wardrobe Manager ROSEMARY WILKINS
Assistant TONY LEDELL
Cutter DAVID HARVEY-JONES
Wardrobe Mistress GLADYS CHISHOLM
Wigs SHEILA DUNSDON
Property Manager ANNABELLE HAWTREY
Assistant Manager JANET MOORES
Regulating Secretary UNA MARCHETTI
Treasurer ERIC WHITEHORN
Press Secretary HELEN O'NEILL
Appointed Photographer GUY GRAVETT
Transport REX ROGERS
Box Office Manager CAROLINE ARTHUR
Catering by VERNON HERBERT

LONDON PHILHARMONIC ORCHESTRA

La Bohème

PUCCINI   *16 performances*

Marcello	Attilio D'Orazi (*Italian*)
Rodolfo	Ottavio Garaventa (*Italian*)
Colline	Federico Davià (*Italian*)
Schaunard	Enrico Fissore (*Italian*)
Benoît/Alcindoro	Carlo Badioli (*Italian*)
Mimì	Anna Novelli (*Italian*)
Musetta	Alberta Valentini (*Italian*)
Parpignol	Alastair Newlands (*Scottish*)
Sergeant	Brian Donlan (*English*)
Customs Officer	James Christiansen (*English*)

Conductors	JOHN PRITCHARD
	Myer Fredman
Producer	MICHAEL REDGRAVE
Scenery	HENRY BARDON
Costumes	DAVID WALKER

L'elisir d'amore

DONIZETTI   *15 performances*

Adina	Adriana Maliponte (*Italian*)
Nemorino	Ugo Benelli (*Italian*)
Belcore	Zsolt Bende (*Hungarian*)
Dulcamara	Carlo Badioli (*Italian*)
Giannetta	Sheila Armstrong (*English*)

Conductors	CARLO FELICE CILLARIO
	Kenneth Montgomery
Producer	DENNIS MAUNDER
Designer	FRANCO ZEFFIRELLI

L'Ormindo

CAVALLI   *15 performances*
(arr Raymond Leppard)

Ormindo	John Wakefield (*English*)
Amida	Peter-Christoph Runge (*German*)
Nerillo	Isabel Garcisanz (*Spanish*)
Sicle	Irmgard Stadler (*German*)
Melide	Maureen Lehane (*English*)
Erice	Hugues Cuenod (*Swiss*)
Erisbe	Anne Howells (*English*)
Mirinda	Jane Berbié (*French*)
King Ariadeno	Federico Davià (*Italian*)
Osmano	Richard Van Allan (*English*)

Conductor	RAYMOND LEPPARD
Producer	GÜNTHER RENNERT
Designer	ERICH KONDRAK

Don Giovanni

MOZART   *14 performances*

Leporello	Paolo Montarsolo (*Italian*)
Donna Anna	Althea Bridges (*Australian*)
Don Giovanni	Kostas Paskalis (*Greek*)
The Commendatore	Marius Rintzler (*Rumanian*)
Don Ottavio	Sven Olof Eliasson (*Norwegian*)
	Richard Lewis (*English*)
Donna Elvira	Teresa Zylis-Gara (*Polish*)
Zerlina	Sheila Armstrong (*English*)
Masetto	Leonardo Monreale (*Italian*)

Conductors	JOHN PRITCHARD
	Myer Fredman
Producer	FRANCO ENRIQUEZ
Associate Producer	Dennis Maunder
Designer	EMANUELE LUZZATI

Sponsored by the Peter Stuyvesant Foundation

General Administrator MORAN CAPLAT

Music Counsellor and Principal Conductor
JOHN PRITCHARD

Adviser on Production FRANCO ENRIQUEZ

Head of Music Staff and Preparation JANI STRASSER

Conductors MYER FREDMAN, LAMBERTO GARDELLI,
RAYMOND LEPPARD, KENNETH MONTGOMERY, JOHN PRITCHARD
Music Staff ATHANAS ATHANASOV, UBALDO GARDINI, MARY HILL,
JONATHAN HINDEN, ANTHONY HOSE, MARTIN ISEPP, GORDON KEMBER,
JEAN MALLANDAINE, KENNETH MONTGOMERY, EVELYN TURNER-INMAN
Chorus Manager HAROLD WILLIAMS
Librarian HOWARD WICKS
Assistant to Head of Music Staff NICHOLAS SNOWMAN

Producers FRANCO ENRIQUEZ, MICHAEL HADJIMISCHEV,
GÜNTHER RENNERT
Associate Producer CHARLES HAMILTON
Assistant Producers GEOFFREY CONNOR, RICHARD HUGHES
Lighting FRANCIS REID
Production Manager JUNE DANDRIDGE
Stage Director GEOFFREY GILBERTSON
Stage Management RITA GUENIGAULT, IAN STORROW,
OLIVER BOUCHIER, IAIN MCLEAN, TOM REDMAN
Chief Technician ALBERT PULLEN
Assistant IVOR GREEN
Staff Carpenters REX CARTER, FRANK EADE
Chief Electrician JIM THOMAS
Wardrobe Manager TONY LEDELL
Cutter GARY DAHMS
Wardrobe Mistress GLADYS CHISHOLM
Wigs SHEILA DUNSDON
Property Manager ANNABELLE HAWTREY
Assistant Manager JANET MOORES
Regulating Secretary DIANA HEPBURNE-SCOTT
Treasurer ERIC WHITEHORN
Press Secretary HELEN O'NEILL
Appointed Photographer GUY GRAVETT
Transport REX ROGERS
Box Office Manager JANET WOODS
Catering by VERNON HERBERT

LONDON PHILHARMONIC ORCHESTRA

Eugene Onegin

TCHAIKOVSKY   *17 performances*

Larina	Pamela Bowden (*English*)
Tatyana	Elisabeth Söderström (*Swedish*)
Olga	Gertrude Jahn (*German*)
Filippyevna	Virginia Popova (*Bulgarian*)
Onegin	Assen Selimsky (*Bulgarian*)
Lensky	Wieslaw Ochman (*Polish*)
Prince Gremin	Kim Borg (*Finnish*)
Petrovich	Anthony Williams (*English*)
Zaretsky	Richard Van Allan (*English*)
Monsieur Triquet	Hugues Cuenod (*Swiss*)

Conductors	JOHN PRITCHARD Myer Fredman
Producer	MICHAEL HADJIMISCHEV
Designer	PIER LUIGI PIZZI
Choreographer	PAULINE GRANT

L'Ormindo

CAVALLI   *12 performances*
(arr Raymond Leppard)

Ormindo	John Wakefield (*English*)
Amida	Peter-Christoph Runge (*German*)
Nerillo	Isabel Garcisanz (*Spanish*)
Sicle	Hanneke van Bork (*Dutch*) Elizabeth Tippett (*Australian*)
Melide	Jean Allister (*Irish*)
Erice	Hugues Cuenod (*Swiss*)
Erisbe	Anne Howells (*English*)
Mirinda	Jane Berbié (*French*)
King Ariadeno	Federico Davià (*Italian*)
Osmano	Richard Van Allan (*English*)

Conductors	RAYMOND LEPPARD Kenneth Montgomery
Producer	GÜNTHER RENNERT
Associate Producer	Charles Hamilton
Designer	ERICH KONDRAK

Die Entführung aus dem Serail

MOZART   *17 performances*

Belmonte	Richard Van Vrooman (*American*)
	Ryland Davies (*Welsh*)
Osmin	Paolo Montarsolo (*Italian*)
	Dimiter Petkov (*Bulgarian*)
Pedrillo	Karl-Ernst Mercker (*German*)
Pasha Selim	Otakar Kraus (*Czech*)
Constanze	Margaret Price (*Welsh*)
Blonde	Birgit Nordin (*Swedish*)

Conductors	JOHN PRITCHARD
	Myer Fredman
Producer	FRANCO ENRIQUEZ
Designer	EMANUELE LUZZATI

Sponsored by the Peter Stuyvesant Foundation

Anna Bolena

DONIZETTI   *12 performances*

Giovanna (*Jane Seymour*)	Patricia Johnson (*English*)
Anna (*Anne Boleyn*)	Milla Andrew (*Canadian*)
Smeton	Janet Coster (*English*)
Enrico (*Henry VIII*)	Marius Rintzler (*Rumanian*)
Rochefort (*Lord Rochford*)	Stafford Dean (*English*)
Riccardo (*Lord Richard Percy*)	George Shirley (*American*)
Hervey	Peter Baillie (*New Zealand*)

Conductor	LAMBERTO GARDELLI
Producer	FRANCO ENRIQUEZ
Designer	LORENZO GHIGLIA

347

General Administrator MORAN CAPLAT

Musical Director JOHN PRITCHARD

Adviser on Production FRANCO ENRIQUEZ

Head of Music Staff and Preparation JANI STRASSER

Conductors MYER FREDMAN, REINHARD PETERS, JOHN PRITCHARD
Music Staff JOHN BYRT, JEAN DATTAS, LIONEL FRIEND,
UBALDO GARDINI, GERALD GOVER, MARY HILL, JONATHAN HINDEN,
MARTIN ISEPP, COURTNEY KENNY, JEAN MALLANDAINE,
HENRY WARD
Chorus Manager HAROLD WILLIAMS
Librarian HOWARD WICKS
Assistant to Head of Music Staff NICHOLAS SNOWMAN

Producers FRANCO ENRIQUEZ, PIERRE MÉDECIN,
SIR MICHAEL REDGRAVE
Assistant Producers ROGER BRUNYATE, GEOFFREY GILBERTSON,
PATRICK LIBBY
Lighting ROBERT ORNBO, FRANCIS REID
Production Manager JUNE DANDRIDGE
Stage Director GEOFFREY GILBERTSON
Stage Management RITA GUENIGAULT, IAN STORROW,
OLIVER BOUCHIER, IAIN MCLEAN, TOM REDMAN
Chief Technician ALBERT PULLEN
Assistant IVOR GREEN
Staff Carpenters REX CARTER, FRANK EADE
Chief Electrician JIM THOMAS
Wardrobe Manager TONY LEDELL
Cutter GARY DAHMS
Wardrobe Mistress GLADYS CHISHOLM
Wigs SHEILA DUNSDON
Property Manager ANNABELLE HAWTREY
Assistant Manager JANET MOORES
Regulating Secretary DIANA HEPBURNE-SCOTT
Treasurer ERIC WHITEHORN
Press GILLIAN WIDDICOMBE
Appointed Photographer GUY GRAVETT
Transport REX ROGERS
Box Office Manager JANET WOODS
Catering by VERNON HERBERT

LONDON PHILHARMONIC ORCHESTRA

Werther

MASSENET *17 performances*

The Bailiff	Stafford Dean (*English*)
Johann	Richard Van Allan (*English*)
Schmidt	Hugues Cuenod (*Swiss*)
Sophie	Annon Lee Silver (*Canadian*)
	Wendy Eathorne (*English*)
Werther	Jean Brazzi (*French*)
Charlotte	Josephine Veasey (*English*)
Albert	Peter Gottlieb (*French*)

Conductor	MYER FREDMAN
Producer	MICHAEL REDGRAVE
Scenery	HENRY BARDON
Costumes	DAVID WALKER

Così fan tutte

MOZART *19 performances*

Ferrando	Ryland Davies (*Welsh*)
Guglielmo	Knut Skram (*Norwegian*)
Don Alfonso	Paolo Montarsolo (*Italian*)
	Michel Roux (*French*)
Fiordiligi	Hanneke van Bork (*Dutch*)
Dorabella	Anne Howells (*English*)
	Rosanna Creffield (*English*)
Despina	Jane Berbié (*French*)
	Maria Casula (*Italian*)

Conductors	JOHN PRITCHARD
	Myer Fredman
Producer	FRANCO ENRIQUEZ
Designer	EMANUELE LUZZATI

Sponsored by the Peter Stuyvesant Foundation

Pelléas et Mélisande

DEBUSSY   *9 performances*

Pelléas	Peter-Christoph Runge (*German*)
Mélisande	Ileana Cotrubas (*Rumanian*)
	Jill Gomez (*Trinidadian*)
Golaud	Jacques Mars (*French*)
Geneviève	Jocelyn Taillon (*French*)
	Margaret Lensky (*English*)
Arkel	Guus Hoekman (*Dutch*)
Yniold	Anne-Marie Blanzat (*French*)
Doctor	Richard Van Allan (*English*)

Conductor	JOHN PRITCHARD
Producer	PIERRE MÉDECIN
Designer	BENI MONTRESOR

Don Giovanni

MOZART   *15 performances*

Leporello	Paolo Montarsolo (*Italian*)
	Richard Van Allan (*English*)
Donna Anna	Phyllis Curtin (*American*)
Don Giovanni	Ruggero Raimondi (*Italian*)
The Commendatore	Marius Rintzler (*Rumanian*)
Don Ottavio	Wieslaw Ochman (*Polish*)
Donna Elvira	Irmgard Stadler (*German*)
Zerlina	Sheila Armstrong (*English*)
Masetto	Leonardo Monreale (*Italian*)

Conductor	REINHARD PETERS
Producer	FRANCO ENRIQUEZ
Designer	EMANUELE LUZZATI

Sponsored by the Peter Stuyvesant Foundation

General Administrator MORAN CAPLAT

Musical Director JOHN PRITCHARD

Head of Music Staff and Preparation JANI STRASSER

Conductors MYER FREDMAN, RAYMOND LEPPARD, REINHARD PETERS,
JOHN PRITCHARD

Music Staff ATHANAS ATHANASOV, NICHOLAS BRAITHWAITE,
KENNETH CLEVELAND, MARK ELDER, LIONEL FRIEND, ERNA GAL,
UBALDO GARDINI, MARY HILL, JONATHAN HINDEN, MARTIN ISEPP,
COURTNEY KENNY, JEAN MALLANDAINE, SERGEI NOLBANDOV,
EVELYN TURNER-INMAN, HENRY WARD

Chorus Manager HAROLD WILLIAMS

Librarian HOWARD WICKS

Producers JOHN COX, FRANCO ENRIQUEZ, COLIN GRAHAM,
MICHAEL HADJIMISCHEV, PETER HALL

Assistant Producers ALISOUN BROWNE, CHARLES HAMILTON
PATRICK LIBBY, ADRIAN SLACK

Lighting ROBERT ORNBO

Production Manager JUNE DANDRIDGE

Stage Director GEOFFREY GILBERTSON

Stage Management RITA GUENIGAULT, IAN STORROW,
TOM REDMAN, NICHOLAS RIDEAL, CHRISTOPHER BARRON

Chief Technician ALBERT PULLEN

Assistant IVOR GREEN

Staff Carpenters REX CARTER, FRANK EADE

Chief Electrical Technician JIM THOMAS

Chief Stage Electrician ROBERT MACKAY

Wardrobe Manager TONY LEDELL

Cutter GARY DAHMS

Wardrobe Mistress GLADYS CHISHOLM

Wigs SHEILA DUNSDON

Property Manager ANNABELLE HAWTREY

Assistant Manager JANET MOORES

Regulating Secretary DIANA SCOTT

Treasurer JOHN BARDEN

Press GILLIAN WIDDICOMBE

Publicity HELEN O'NEILL

Appointed Photographer GUY GRAVETT

Chief Telephonist BRENDA HERMITAGE

Transport REX ROGERS

Box Office Manager JANET WOODS

Catering by VERNON HERBERT

LONDON PHILHARMONIC ORCHESTRA

The Magic Flute

MOZART   *17 performances*

Tamino	Wieslaw Ochman (*Polish*)
Three Ladies	Teresa Cahill (*English*)
	Rosanna Creffield (*English*)
	Patricia Conti (*English*)
	Gwenyth Annear (*Australian*)
	Yvonne Fuller (*English*)
	Marjory McMichael (*Scottish*)
Papageno	Heinz Blankenburg (*American*)
	Knut Skram (*Norwegian*)
	John Gibbs (*English*)
Queen of the Night	Urszula Koszut (*Polish*)
	Louise Lebrun (*Canadian*)
Three Boys	Wendy Eathorne (*English*)
	Valerie Baulard (*English*)
	Sylvia Eaves (*English*)
Monostatos	Alexander Oliver (*Scottish*)
Pamina	Sheila Armstrong (*English*)
	Ileana Cotrubas (*Rumanian*)
The Speaker	Richard Van Allan (*English*)
Sarastro	Hans Sotin (*German*)
Priests and Men in Armour	Keith Erwen (*Welsh*)
	Michael Rippon (*English*)
Papagena	Norma Burrowes (*Irish*)
Conductors	REINHARD PETERS
	Myer Fredman
Producer	FRANCO ENRIQUEZ
Designer	EMANUELE LUZZATI

La Calisto

CAVALLI   *9 performances*
(arr Raymond Leppard)

La Natura	Enid Hartle (*English*)
L'Eternità	Margaret Lensky (*English*)
Il Destino	Louise Lebrun (*Canadian*)
Giove	Ugo Trama (*Italian*)
Mercurio	Peter Gottlieb (*French*)
Calisto	Ileana Cotrubas (*Rumanian*)
	Jill Gomez (*Trinidadian*)
Endimione	James Bowman (*English*)
Diana	Janet Baker (*English*)
	Sarah Walker (*English*)
Linfea	Hugues Cuenod (*Swiss*)
Satirino	Janet Hughes (*English*)
Pane	Federico Davià (*Italian*)
Silvano	Owen Brannigan (*English*)
Giunone	Irmgard Stadler (*German*)
Conductor	RAYMOND LEPPARD
Producer	PETER HALL
Designer	JOHN BURY

Il turco in Italia

ROSSINI   *16 performances*

Zaida	Isabel Garcisanz (*Spanish*)
Albazar	John Fryatt (*English*)
The Poet	Michel Roux (*French*)
Don Geronio	Elfego Esparza (*American*)
Fiorilla	Graziella Sciutti (*Italian*)
	Sheila Armstrong (*English*)
Selim	Paolo Montarsolo (*Italian*)
Narciso	Ugo Benelli (*Italian*)

Conductors	JOHN PRITCHARD
	Myer Fredman
Producer	JOHN COX
Designer	EMANUELE LUZZATI

Sponsored by the Peter Stuyvesant Foundation

The Rising of the Moon

NICHOLAS MAW   *8 performances*
World première

Brother Timothy	Alexander Oliver (*Scottish*)
Cathleen Sweeney	Anne Howells (*English*)
Donal O'Dowd	John Gibbs (*English*)
Lord Francis Jowler	Richard Van Allan (*English*)
Captain Lillywhite	John Fryatt (*English*)
Major Max von Zastrow	Peter Gottlieb (*French*)
Lady Eugenie Jowler	Rae Woodland (*English*)
Frau Elisabeth von Zastrow	Kerstin Meyer (*Swedish*)
Miss Atalanta Lillywhite	Annon Lee Silver (*Canadian*)
Corporal Haywood	Brian Donlan (*English*)
Cornet John Stephen Beaumont	John Wakefield (*English*)
Widow Sweeney	Johanna Peters (*English*)
Mr Lynch	Dennis Wicks (*English*)

Conductor	RAYMOND LEPPARD
Producer	COLIN GRAHAM
Designer	OSBERT LANCASTER

Eugene Onegin

TCHAIKOVSKY   *16 performances*

Larina	Pamela Bowden (*English*)
Tatyana	Katja Usunov (*Austro-Bulgarian*)
Olga	Alexandrina Milcheva (*Bulgarian*)
Filippyevna	Virginia Popova (*Bulgarian*)
Onegin	Nikola Vassilev (*Bulgarian*)
Lensky	Wieslaw Ochman (*Polish*)
Prince Gremin	Dimiter Petkov (*Bulgarian*)
Petrovich	William Elvin (*Scottish*)
Zaretsky	Richard Van Allan (*English*)
Monsieur Triquet	Hugues Cuenod (*Swiss*)

Conductors	JOHN PRITCHARD
	Myer Fredman
Producer	MICHAEL HADJIMISCHEV
Designer	PIER LUIGI PIZZI
Choreographer	PAULINE GRANT

General Administrator MORAN CAPLAT

Musical Director JOHN PRITCHARD

Conductors ALDO CECCATO, MYER FREDMAN, RAYMOND LEPPARD, JOHN PRITCHARD

First Conductor and Head of Music Staff MYER FREDMAN

Music Staff ATHANAS ATHANASOV, KENNETH CLEVELAND, MARK ELDER, CHRISTOPHER FIFIELD, LIONEL FRIEND, ERNA GAL, UBALDO GARDINI, ARTHUR HAMMOND, JONATHAN HINDEN, MARTIN ISEPP, JEAN MALLANDAINE, SERGEI NOLBANDOV, EVELYN TURNER–INMAN, HENRY WARD

Chorus Master KENNETH CLEVELAND

Chorus Manager HAROLD WILLIAMS

Librarian HOWARD WICKS

Producers JOHN COX, COLIN GRAHAM, MICHAEL HADJIMICHEV, PETER HALL, PAOLO MONTARSOLO

Associate Producer PATRICK LIBBY

Assistant Producers ROGER BRUNYATE, ADRIAN SLACK

Lighting ROBERT ORNBO

Production Manager JUNE DANDRIDGE

Stage Director GEOFFREY GILBERTSON

Stage Management RITA GUENIGAULT, IAN STORROW, TOM REDMAN, NICHOLAS RIDEAL, CHRISTOPHER BARRON, TIM VAUGHAN–HUGHES

Chief Technician ALBERT PULLEN

Assistant IVOR GREEN

Staff Carpenters REX CARTER, FRANK EADE

Chief Electrical Technician JIM THOMAS

Chief Stage Electrician ROBERT MACKAY

Wardrobe Manager TONY LEDELL

Cutter GARY DAHMS

Wardrobe Mistress GLADYS CHISHOLM

Wigs SHEILA DUNSDON

Property Manager ANNABELLE HAWTREY

Opera Manager BRIAN DICKIE

Front of House Manager JANET MOORES

Regulating Secretary DIANA SCOTT

Treasurer JOHN BARDEN

Press and Publicity HELEN O'NEILL

Appointed Photographer GUY GRAVETT

Transport REX ROGERS

Box Office Manager JANET WOODS

Catering by VERNON HERBERT

LONDON PHILHARMONIC ORCHESTRA

The Queen of Spades

TCHAIKOVSKY   *16 performances*

Hermann	Maurice Maievsky (*French*)
	Gheorghi Sapoundjiev (*Bulgarian*)
Count Tomsky	Pavel Guerdjikov (*Bulgarian*)
Prince Yeletsky	Assen Selimsky (*Bulgarian*)
Officers	Anthony Roden (*Australian*)
	Michael Rippon (*English*)
	Gavin Walton (*English*)
Chaplitsky	Maurice Arthur (*English*)
Narumov	Brian Donlan (*English*)
The Countess	Virginia Popova (*Bulgarian*)
Lisa	Teresa Kubiak (*Polish*)
Pauline	Reni Penkova (*Bulgarian*)
Governess	Enid Hartle (*English*)
Prilepa	Angela Bostock (*English*)
Master of Ceremonies	Terry Jenkins (*English*)
Masha	Kathleen Smales (*English*)

Conductor	JOHN PRITCHARD
Producer	MICHAEL HADJIMISCHEV
Designer	PIER LUIGI PIZZI
Choreographer	PAULINE GRANT

The Rising of the Moon

NICHOLAS MAW   *8 performances*

Brother Timothy	Alexander Oliver (*Scottish*)
Cathleen Sweeney	Anne Howells (*English*)
	Delia Wallis (*English*)
Donal O'Dowd	John Gibbs (*English*)
Lord Francis Jowler	Richard Van Allan (*English*)
Captain Lillywhite	John Fryatt (*English*)
Major Max von Zastrow	Peter Gottlieb (*French*)
Lady Eugenie Jowler	Rae Woodland (*English*)
Frau Elisabeth von Zastrow	Kerstin Meyer (*Sweden*)
Miss Atalanta Lillywhite	Annon Lee Silver (*Canadian*)
	Sara de Javelin (*English*)
	Wendy Eathorne (*English*)
Corporal Haywood	Brian Donlan (*English*)
Cornet John Stephen Beaumont	John Wakefield (*English*)
Widow Sweeney	Johanna Peters (*English*)
Mr Lynch	Dennis Wicks (*English*)

Conductor	MYER FREDMAN
Producer	COLIN GRAHAM
Associate Producer	Patrick Libby
Designer	OSBERT LANCASTER

Ariadne auf Naxos

RICHARD STRAUSS   *16 performances*

Major Domo	Richard Van Allan (*English*)
Music Master	Thomas Hemsley (*English*)
The Composer	Anne Howells (*English*)
	Delia Wallis (*English*)
Bacchus	Helge Brilioth (*Swedish*)
	Wilmer Neufeld (*Canadian*)
An Officer	Terry Jenkins (*English*)
Dancing Master	Alexander Oliver (*Scottish*)
Wig Maker	William Elvin (*Scottish*)
Lackey	Thomas Lawlor (*Irish*)
Zerbinetta	Sylvia Geszty (*Hungarian*)
Ariadne	Helen Vanni (*American*)
Harlekin	John Gibbs (*English*)
Scaramuccio	Maurice Arthur (*English*)
Truffaldino	Dennis Wicks (*English*)
Brighella	John Fryatt (*English*)
Najade	Teresa Cahill (*English*)
Dryade	Enid Hartle (*English*)
Echo	Yvonne Fuller (*English*)

Conductor	ALDO CECCATO
Producer	JOHN COX
Designer	MICHAEL ANNALS

Così fan tutte

MOZART   *12 performances*

Ferrando	Jerry Jennings (*American*)
Guglielmo	Knut Skram (*Norwegian*)
Don Alfonso	Paolo Montarsolo (*Italian*)
Fiordiligi	Margaret Price (*Welsh*)
	Elizabeth Harwood (*English*)
Dorabella	Edith Thallaug (*Norwegian*)
Despina	Jane Berbié (*French*)

Conductor	JOHN PRITCHARD
Producer	FRANCO ENRIQUEZ
Revival produced by	PAOLO MONTARSOLO
Associate Producer	Roger Brunyate
Designer	EMANUELE LUZZATI

Sponsored by the Peter Stuyvesant Foundation

La Calisto

CAVALLI   *8 performances*
(arr Raymond Leppard)

La Natura	Marjorie Biggar (*Canadian*)
L'Eternità	Enid Hartle (*English*)
Il Destino	Teresa Cahill (*English*)
Giove	Ugo Trama (*Italian*)
Mercurio	Peter Gottlieb (*French*)
Calisto	Ileana Cotrubas (*Rumanian*)
Endimione	James Bowman (*English*)
Diana	Janet Baker (*English*)
Linfea	Hugues Cuenod (*Swiss*)
Satirino	Janet Hughes (*English*)
Pane	Federico Davià (*Italian*)
Silvano	Owen Brannigan (*English*)
Giunone	Teresa Kubiak (*Polish*)
The Echo	Isla Brodie (*Scottish*)

Conductor	RAYMOND LEPPARD
Producer	PETER HALL
Associate Producer	Patrick Libby
Designer and Lighting	JOHN BURY

General Administrator MORAN CAPLAT

Musical Director JOHN PRITCHARD

Consultant Specialist in Singing and Interpretation
JANI STRASSER

Director of Production JOHN COX

First Conductor and Head of Music Staff
MYER FREDMAN

Conductors ALDO CECCATO, MYER FREDMAN, BERNARD HAITINK,
RAYMOND LEPPARD, JOHN PRITCHARD
Music Staff CHRISTOPHER FIFIELD, ISOBEL FLINN, LIONEL FRIEND,
ERNA GAL, UBALDO GARDINI, JONATHAN HINDEN, MARTIN ISEPP
EUGENE KOHN, JEAN MALLANDAINE, PETER ROBINSON,
EVELYN TURNER-INMAN, HENRY WARD
Librarian HOWARD WICKS
Music Secretary ELAINE STEABLER

Producers JOHN COX, MICHAEL HADJIMICHEV, PETER HALL
Associate Producer PATRICK LIBBY
Assistant Producers ADRIAN SLACK, CONWAY WILSON-YOUNG
Lighting ROBERT BRYAN, ROBERT ORNBO
Production Manager JUNE DANDRIDGE
Stage Director GEOFFREY GILBERTSON
Stage Management IAN STORROW, TOM REDMAN, NICHOLAS RIDEAL,
MICHAEL BEAUCHAMP, NOEL STAUNTON
Chief Technician ALBERT PULLEN
Assistant IVOR GREEN
Staff Carpenters REX CARTER, FRANK EADE
Chief Electrical Technician JIM THOMAS
Wardrobe Manager TONY LEDELL
Cutter GARY DAHMS
Wardrobe Mistress GLADYS CHISHOLM
Wigs SHEILA DUNSDON
Property Manager ANNABELLE HAWTREY
Opera Manager BRIAN DICKIE
Front of House Manager JANET MOORES
Regulating Secretary DIANA SCOTT
Treasurer JOHN BARDEN
Press and Publicity HELEN O'NEILL
Appointed Photographer GUY GRAVETT
Transport REX ROGERS
Box Office Manager JANET WOODS
Catering by VERNON HERBERT

LONDON PHILHARMONIC ORCHESTRA

Ariadne auf Naxos

RICHARD STRAUSS   *17 performances (two series)*

Major Domo	Richard Van Allan (*English*)
	James Atkins (*English*)
Music Master	Thomas Hemsley (*English*)
The Composer (I)	Irmgard Stadler (*German*)
(II)	Delia Wallis (*English*)
Bacchus (I)	Maurice Maievsky (*French*)
(II)	Wilmer Neufeld (*Canadian*)
An Officer	James Anderson (*Scottish*)
Dancing Master	Alexander Oliver (*Scottish*)
Wig Maker	William Elvin (*Scottish*)
Lackey	Thomas Lawlor (*Irish*)
Zerbinetta	Sylvia Geszty (*Hungarian*)
	Patricia Wise (*American*)
Ariadne (I)	Gloria Lane (*American*)
(II)	Helen Vanni (*American*)
Harlekin	John Gibbs (*English*)
Scaramuccio	Terry Jenkins (*English*)
Truffaldino	Dennis Wicks (*English*)
Brighella	John Fryatt (*English*)
Najade	Janet Price (*Welsh*)
Dryade	Enid Hartle (*English*)
Echo	Yvonne Fuller (*English*)

Conductors	MYER FREDMAN (*Series I*)
	ALDO CECCATO (*Series II*)
Producer	JOHN COX
Designer	MICHAEL ANNALS

Il ritorno d'Ulisse in patria

MONTEVERDI   *14 performances*
(arr Raymond Leppard)

L'humana fragilità	Annabel Hunt (*English*)
Tempo	Ugo Trama (*Italian*)
Fortuna	Patricia Greig (*Scottish*)
Amore	Laureen Livingstone (*Scottish*)
Penelope	Janet Baker (*English*)
Ericlea	Virginia Popova (*Bulgarian*)
Melanto	Janet Hughes (*English*)
Eurimaco	John Wakefield (*English*)
Nettuno	Clifford Grant (*Australian*)
	Robert Lloyd (*English*)
Giove	David Hughes (*Welsh*)
	Brian Burrows (*English*)
Ulisse	Benjamin Luxon (*English*)
Minerva	Anne Howells (*English*)
Eumete	Richard Lewis (*English*)
Iro	Alexander Oliver (*Scottish*)
Telemaco	Ian Caley (*English*)
Antinöo	Ugo Trama (*Italian*)
Anfimono	Bernard Dickerson (*English*)
Pisandro	John Fryatt (*English*)
Giunone	Vivien Townley (*English*)

Conductor	RAYMOND LEPPARD
Producer	PETER HALL
Designer	JOHN BURY

Die Entführung aus dem Serail

MOZART   *18 performances (two series)*

Belmonte (I)	Horst Laubenthal (*German*)
(II)	Ryland Davies (*Welsh*)
	Anthony Roden (*Australian*)
Osmin (I)	Marius Rintzler (*Rumanian*)
(II)	Noel Mangin (*New Zealand*)
	Richard Van Allan (*English*)
Pedrillo	Kimmo Lappalainen (*Finnish*)
Pasha Selim	Richard Van Allan (*English*)
	James Atkins (*English*)
Constanze (I)	Sylvia Geszty (*Hungarian*)
(II)	Margaret Price (*Welsh*)
Blonde	Danièle Perriers (*French*)
Conductors	BERNARD HAITINK (*Series I*)
	JOHN PRITCHARD (*Series II*)
Producer	JOHN COX
Designer	EMANUELE LUZZATI

Macbeth

VERDI   *15 performances*

Macbeth	Kostas Paskalis (*Greek*)
	Delme Bryn-Jones (*Welsh*)
Banquo	James Morris (*American*)
Lady Macbeth	Joyce Barker (*South African*)
	Gloria Lane (*American*)
Gentlewoman	Rae Woodland (*English*)
Macduff	Keith Erwen (*Welsh*)
Malcolm	Ian Caley (*English*)
Doctor	Brian Donlan (*English*)
Servant	Ian Caddy (*English*)
Murderer	John Tomlinson (*English*)
Conductors	JOHN PRITCHARD
	Myer Fredman
Producer	MICHAEL HADJIMISCHEV
Designer	EMANUELE LUZZATI
Choreographer	PAULINE GRANT

355

General Administrator MORAN CAPLAT

Musical Director JOHN PRITCHARD

Director of Production JOHN COX

Conductors ANDREW DAVIS, MYER FREDMAN, BERNARD HAITINK, RAYMOND LEPPARD, JOHN PRITCHARD, HENRY WARD
Music Staff ERNA GAL, UBALDO GARDINI, JONATHAN HINDEN, MARTIN ISEPP, JAN LATHAM-KOENIG, JEAN MALLANDAINE, DAVID PARRY, PETER ROBINSON, ROBIN STAPLETON, GILES SWAYNE, EVELYN TURNER-INMAN, HENRY WARD
Librarian CHARMIAN HUGHES
Music Secretary CELIA HARDING

Producers JOHN COX, PETER HALL
Associate Producers PATRICK LIBBY, ADRIAN SLACK
Assistant Producers MICHAEL BEAUCHAMP, JOHN HOPE MASON
Lighting ROBERT BRYAN
Production Manager JUNE DANDRIDGE
General Stage Manager GEOFFREY GILBERTSON
Stage Management GABRIELLE BRIDGES, TOM REDMAN, NICHOLAS RIDEAL, TREVOR TWENTYMAN, PHILIP JENKINS, NOEL STAUNTON
Chief Technician ALBERT PULLEN
Assistant IVOR GREEN
Staff Carpenters REX CARTER, FRANK EADE
Chief Electrical Technician JIM THOMAS
Wardrobe Manager TONY LEDELL
Cutter GARY DAHMS
Wardrobe Mistress RUTH FEATHERSTONE
Wigs SHEILA DUNSDON
Property Manager ANNABELLE HAWTREY
Opera Manager BRIAN DICKIE
Front of House Manager JANET MOORES
Regulating Secretary DIANA SCOTT
Treasurer JOHN BARDEN
Press and Publicity HELEN O'NEILL
Appointed Photographer GUY GRAVETT
Transport DESMOND WORSFOLD
Box Office Manager JANET WOODS
Catering by VERNON HERBERT

LONDON PHILHARMONIC ORCHESTRA

The Magic Flute

MOZART   *18 performances (two series)*

Tamino (I)	George Shirley (*American*)
(II)	Anthony Roden (*Australian*)
Three Ladies (I)	Linda Esther Gray (*Scottish*)
	Doreen Cryer (*English*)
	Enid Hartle (*English*)
(II)	Gwenyth Annear (*Australian*)
	Patricia Greig (*Scottish*)
	Angela Vernon Bates (*English*)
Papageno (I)	Thomas Allen (*English*)
(II)	Peter-Christoph Runge (*German*)
Queen of the Night	Edita Gruberova (*Czech*)
Three Boys	Joy Roberts (*English*)
	Annabel Hunt (*English*)
	Susan Lees (*English*)
Monostatos (I)	Brian Burrows (*English*)
(II)	Alexander Oliver (*Scottish*)
Pamina (I)	Sheila Armstrong (*English*)
(II)	Elisabeth Speiser (*Swiss*)
The Speaker (I)	Michael Rippon (*English*)
(II)	Thomas Hemsley (*English*)
Sarastro (I)	Robert Lloyd (*English*)
(II)	Manfred Schenk (*German*)
Priests and Men in Armour	
(I)	Anthony Roden (*Australian*)
(II)	Athole Still (*Scottish*)
	John Tomlinson (*English*)
Papagena	Elizabeth Gale (*English*)
Conductors	BERNARD HAITINK (*Series I*)
	MYER FREDMAN (*Series II*)
Associate Producers	JOHN COX, ADRIAN SLACK
Designer	EMANUELE LUZZATI

The Visit of the Old Lady

GOTTFRIED VON EINEM   *8 performances*
First performance in England

Claire Zachanassian	Kerstin Meyer (*Swedish*)
Her Butler	Edgar Evans (*Welsh*)
Koby	Duncan Robertson (*Scottish*)
Loby	Ian Caley (*English*)
Alfred Ill	Donald Bell (*Canadian*)
His Wife	Rae Woodland (*English*)
His Daughter	Sara de Javelin (*Canadian*)
His Son	Roderic Keating (*English*)
The Mayor	Alan Crofoot (*Canadian*)
The Pastor	Don Garrard (*Canadian*)
The Schoolmaster	Derek Hammond-Stroud (*English*)
The Doctor	Brian Donlan (*English*)
Police Chief	Michael Rippon (*English*)
First Woman	Isla Brodie (*Scottish*)
Second Woman	Lorna Brindley (*Scottish*)
Hofbauer	Anthony Bremner (*Australian*)
Helmesberger	Edward Sadler (*English*)
Station Master	Keith Brookes (*English*)
Ticket Inspector	John Carr (*English*)
Guard	Thomas Lawlor (*Irish*)
Cameraman	John Tomlinson (*English*)

Conductors	JOHN PRITCHARD
	Myer Fredman
Producer	JOHN COX
Designer	MICHAEL ANNALS

Le nozze di Figaro

MOZART   *17 performances*

Figaro	Knut Skram (*Norwegian*)
Susanna	Ileana Cotrubas (*Rumanian*)
	Britta Möllerström (*Swedish*)
Bartolo	Marius Rintzler (*Rumanian*)
	Michael Rippon (*English*)
Marcellina	Nucci Condò (*Italian*)
Cherubino	Frederica von Stade (*American*)
Count Almaviva	Benjamin Luxon (*English*)
Don Basilio	John Fryatt (*English*)
The Countess	Elizabeth Harwood (*English*)
	Kiri Te Kanawa (*New Zealand*)
Antonio	Thomas Lawlor (*Irish*)
Barbarina	Elizabeth Gale (*English*)
Don Curzio	Bernard Dickerson (*English*)

Conductors	JOHN PRITCHARD
	Myer Fredman
Producer	PETER HALL
Designer	JOHN BURY

Sponsored by the Peter Stuyvesant Foundation

Il ritorno d'Ulisse in patria

MONTEVERDI   *11 performances*
(arr Raymond Leppard)

L'humana fragiltà	Annabel Hunt (*English*)
Tempo	Ugo Trama (*Italian*)
Fortuna	Patricia Greig (*Scottish*)
Amore	Laureen Livingstone (*Scottish*)
Penelope	Janet Baker (*English*)
Ericlea	Virginia Popova (*Bulgarian*)
Melanto	Janet Hughes (*English*)
Eurimaco	John Wakefield (*English*)
Nettuno	Robert Lloyd (*English*)
Giove	Brian Burrows (*English*)
Ulisse	Benjamin Luxon (*English*)
	Richard Stilwell (*American*)
Minerva	Anne Howells (*English*)
Eumete	Richard Lewis (*English*)
Iro	Alexander Oliver (*Scottish*)
Telemaco	Ian Caley (*English*)
Antinöo	Ugo Trama (*Italian*)
Anfimono	Bernard Dickerson (*English*)
Pisandro	John Fryatt (*English*)
Giunone	Rae Woodland (*English*)

Conductors	RAYMOND LEPPARD
	Henry Ward
Producer	PETER HALL
Associate Producer	Patrick Libby
Designer	JOHN BURY

Capriccio

RICHARD STRAUSS   *10 performances*

Flamand	Leo Goeke (*American*)
Olivier	Richard Stilwell (*American*)
La Roche	Marius Rintzler (*Rumanian*)
The Countess	Elisabeth Söderström (*Swedish*)
The Count	Håkan Hagegård (*Swedish*)
Clairon	Kerstin Meyer (*Swedish*)
Italian Tenor	Ricardo Cassinelli (*Argentinian*)
Italian Soprano	Eugenia Ratti (*Italian*)
Major Domo	Thomas Lawlor (*Irish*)
Monsieur Taupe	Hugues Cuenod (*Swiss*)

Conductors	JOHN PRITCHARD
	Andrew Davis
Producer	JOHN COX
Scenery	DENNIS LENNON
Costumes	MARTIN BATTERSBY
Choreographer	PAULINE GRANT

General Administrator MORAN CAPLAT

Musical Director JOHN PRITCHARD

Director of Production JOHN COX

Conductors MYER FREDMAN, RAYMOND LEPPARD,
KENNETH MONTGOMERY, JOHN PRITCHARD
Music Staff JULIAN DAWSON, JONATHAN HINDEN, MARTIN ISEPP,
JAN LATHAM-KOENIG, JEAN MALLANDAINE, GWYN MORRIS,
DAVID PARRY, CALVIN SIMMONS, INGRID SURGENOR, GILES SWAYNE,
EVELYN TURNER-INMAN, HENRY WARD
Chorus Director PETER GELLHORN
Librarian CHARMIAN HUGHES
Music Secretary CELIA HARDING

Producers JOHN COX, PETER HALL, PATRICK LIBBY
Associate Producer ADRIAN SLACK
Assistant Producers JOHN HOPE MASON, CHRISTOPHER RENSHAW
Lighting ROBERT BRYAN
Production Manager JUNE DANDRIDGE
General Stage Manager GEOFFREY GILBERTSON
Stage Management TOM REDMAN, GABRIELLE BRIDGES,
NOEL STAUNTON, TIMOTHY TYRREL, MICHAEL ANDREWS,
RICHARD LOVEGROVE
Chief Technician ALBERT PULLEN
Stage Foreman IVOR GREEN
Staff Carpenters REX CARTER, FRANK EADE
Chief Electrical Technician JIM THOMAS
Wardrobe Manager TONY LEDELL
Cutter JOHN KING
Wardrobe Mistress RUTH FEATHERSTONE
Wigs SHEILA DUNSDON
Property Manager ANNABELLE HAWTREY
Opera Manager BRIAN DICKIE
Front of House Manager JANET MOORES
Regulating Secretary DIANA SCOTT
Treasurer JOHN BARDEN
Press and Publicity HELEN O'NEILL
Appointed Photographer GUY GRAVETT
Transport DESMOND WORSFOLD
Box Office Manager JANET WOODS
Catering by VERNON HERBERT

LONDON PHILHARMONIC ORCHESTRA

La Calisto

CAVALLI	*12 performances* *(arr Raymond Leppard)*
La Natura	Cynthia Buchan (*Scottish*)
L'Eternità	Linda Esther Gray (*Scottish*) Jillian Crowe (*English*)
Il Destino	Patricia Greig (*Scottish*) Miriam Bowen (*Welsh*)
Giove	Ugo Trama (*Italian*)
Mercurio	John Fryatt (*English*)
Calisto	Barbara Hendricks (*American*)
Endimione	James Bowman (*English*)
Diana	Anne Howells (*English*)
Linfea	Hugues Cuenod (*Swiss*)
Satirino	Janet Hughes (*English*)
Pane	Ugo Trama (*Italian*)
Silvano	John Tomlinson (*English*)
Giunone	Janet Jacques (*English*)
The Echo	Isla Brodie (*Scottish*)
Conductors	RAYMOND LEPPARD Kenneth Montgomery
Original Production by	PETER HALL
Re-produced by	Patrick Libby
Designer	JOHN BURY

Idomeneo

MOZART	*17 performances (two series)*
Ilia (I)	Glenys Fowles (*Australian*)
(II)	Bozena Betley (*Polish*)
Idamante (I)	Kimmo Lappalainen (*Finnish*)
(II)	Leo Goeke (*American*)
Arbace	Alexander Oliver (*Scottish*) James Anderson (*Scottish*)
Electra (I)	Krysztina Kujawinska (*Polish*) Linda Esther Gray (*Scottish*)
(II)	Josephine Barstow (*English*)
Idomeneo (I)	George Shirley (*American*)
(II)	Richard Lewis (*English*)
High Priest of Neptune	John Fryatt (*English*)
Voice of Neptune	Dennis Wicks (*English*)
Conductor	JOHN PRITCHARD
Producer	JOHN COX
Designer	ROGER BUTLIN
Sponsored by the Peter Stuyvesant Foundation	

Intermezzo

RICHARD STRAUSS   *12 performances*

Christine	Elisabeth Söderström (*Swedish*)
Robert Storch	Marco Bakker (*Dutch*)
Anna	Elizabeth Gale (*English*)
Franzl	Richard Allfrey (*English*)
Therese	Angela Whittingham (*English*)
Fanny	Barbara Dix (*English*)
Marie	Susan Varley (*English*)
Baron Lummer	Alexander Oliver (*Scottish*)
The Lawyer's Wife	Rae Woodland (*English*)
Resi	Cynthia Buchan (*Scottish*)
The Commercial Counsellor	Donald Bell (*Canadian*)
The Opera Singer	Dennis Wicks (*English*)
Stroh, the Conductor	Anthony Rolfe Johnson (*English*)
The Legal Counsellor	Brian Donlan (*English*)
The Lawyer	Thomas Lawlor (*Irish*)

Conductor	JOHN PRITCHARD
Producer	JOHN COX
Designer	MARTIN BATTERSBY
Choreographer	PAULINE GRANT
Sponsored by the Fred Kobler Trust	

The Visit of the Old Lady

GOTTFRIED VON EINEM   *6 performances*

Claire Zachanassian	Kerstin Meyer (*Swedish*)
Her Butler	Edgar Evans (*Welsh*)
Koby	Duncan Robertson (*Scottish*)
Loby	Ian Caley (*English*)
Alfred Ill	Donald Bell (*Canadian*)
His Wife	Rae Woodland (*English*)
His Daughter	Cynthia Buchan (*Scottish*)
His Son	Philip Griffiths (*Welsh*)
The Mayor	Alan Crofoot (*Canadian*)
The Pastor	Dennis Wicks (*English*)
The Schoolmaster	Derek Hammond-Stroud (*English*)
The Doctor	Brian Donlan (*English*)
Police Chief	Thomas Lawlor (*Irish*)
First Woman	Isla Brodie (*Scottish*)
Second Woman	Lorna Brindley (*Scottish*)
Hofbauer	Anthony Bremner (*Australian*)
Helmesberger	Alan Watt (*Scottish*)
Station Master	Keith Brooks (*English*)
Cameraman	Powell Harrison (*English*)

Conductor	MYER FREDMAN
Producer	JOHN COX
Designer	MICHAEL ANNALS

Le nozze di Figaro

MOZART   *18 performances*

Figaro	Knut Skram (*Norwegian*)
	Thomas Allen (*English*)
Susanna	Evelyn Mandac (*Philippine*)
	Elizabeth Gale (*English*)
Bartolo	Ugo Trama (*Italian*)
Marcellina	Nucci Condò (*Italian*)
Cherubino	Helena Jungwirth-Ahnsjö (*Swedish*)
	Joy Roberts (*English*)
Count Almaviva	Michael Devlin (*American*)
	Håkan Hagegård (*Swedish*)
Don Basilio	John Fryatt (*English*)
The Countess	Kiri Te Kanawa (*New Zealand*)
	Helena Döse (*Swedish*)
Antonio	Thomas Lawlor (*Irish*)
Barbarina	Elizabeth Gale (*English*)
	Susanna Ross (*English*)
Don Curzio	Bernard Dickerson (*English*)

Conductors	JOHN PRITCHARD
	Kenneth Montgomery
	Peter Gellhorn
Producer	PETER HALL
Associate Producer	Adrian Slack
Designer	JOHN BURY
Choreographer	PAULINE GRANT
Sponsored by the Peter Stuyvesant Foundation	

General Administrator MORAN CAPLAT

Musical Director JOHN PRITCHARD

Director of Production JOHN COX

Conductors ANDREW DAVIS, BERNARD HAITINK, RAYMOND LEPPARD,
KENNETH MONTGOMERY, JOHN PRITCHARD
Music Staff MARTIN ISEPP (Chief Festival Coach), JULIAN DAWSON,
UBALDO GARDINI, JONATHAN HINDEN, DIMITRI MAKAROFF,
JEAN MALLANDAINE, DAVID PARRY, SIMON RATTLE,
CALVIN SIMMONS, INGRID SURGENOR, ANIKO PETER-SZABO,
EVELYN TURNER-INMAN, HENRY WARD
Chorus Director PETER GELLHORN
Librarian CHARMIAN HUGHES

Producers JOHN COX, MICHAEL HADJIMISCHEV, JONATHAN MILLER,
ADRIAN SLACK
Assistant Producers JULIAN HOPE, CHRISTOPHER RENSHAW
Lighting ROBERT BRYAN
Production Manager JUNE DANDRIDGE
General Stage Manager GEOFFREY GILBERTSON
Senior Stage Manager TOM REDMAN
Stage Management GABRIELLE BRIDGES, DAVID EDY,
RICHARD LOVEGROVE, COLIN MOSSMAN
Chief Technician ALBERT PULLEN
Stage Foreman IVOR GREEN
Staff Carpenters REX CARTER, FRANK EADE
Chief Electrical Technician JIM THOMAS
Wardrobe Manager TONY LEDELL
Cutter JOHN KING
Wardrobe Mistress RUTH FEATHERSTONE
Wigs SHEILA DUNSDON
Property Manager ANNABELLE HAWTREY
Opera Manager BRIAN DICKIE
Assistant and Music Secretary CELIA HARDING
Front of House Manager JANET MOORES
Regulating Secretary DIANA SCOTT
Treasurer JOHN BARDEN
Press and Publicity HELEN O'NEILL
Appointed Photographer GUY GRAVETT
Transport DESMOND WORSFOLD
Box Office Manager JANET WOODS
Catering by VERNON HERBERT

LONDON PHILHARMONIC ORCHESTRA

The Cunning Little Vixen

JANÁČEK　　*13 performances*

The Forester	Benjamin Luxon (*English*)
The Vixen	Norma Burrowes (*Irish*)
The Forester's Wife	Enid Hartle (*English*)
The Dog	Alan Watt (*Scottish*)
The Cock	Hugues Cuenod (*Swiss*)
The Hen	Isla Brodie (*Scottish*)
The Badger	Richard Robson (*English*)
The Parson	Brian Donlan (*English*)
The Schoolmaster	Bernard Dickerson (*English*)
The Innkeeper	John Michael Flanagan (*English*)
The Fox	Robert Hoyem (*American*)
The Owl⎫ The Woodpecker⎭	Enid Hartle (*English*)
The Poacher	Thomas Lawlor (*Irish*)
The Innkeeper's Wife	Barbara Dix (*English*)

Conductor	RAYMOND LEPPARD
Producer	JONATHAN MILLER
Scenery	PATRICK ROBERTSON
Costumes	ROSEMARY VERCOE

Eugene Onegin

TCHAIKOVSKY　　*16 performances*

Larina	Pamela Bowden (*English*)
Tatyana	Elizabeth Tippett (*Australian*) Galia Yoncheva (*Bulgarian*)
Olga	Reni Penkova (*Bulgarian*) Cynthia Buchan (*Scottish*)
Filippyevna	Virginia Popova (*Bulgarian*)
Lensky	Ryland Davies (*Welsh*) Anthony Rolfe Johnson (*English*)
Onegin	Richard Stilwell (*American*)
Prince Gremin	Don Garrard (*Canadian*)
Petrovich	Alan Watt (*Scottish*)
Zaretsky	Thomas Lawlor (*Irish*)
Monsieur Triquet	Hugues Cuenod (*Swiss*)

Conductor	ANDREW DAVIS
Producer	MICHAEL HADJIMISCHEV
Designer	PIER LUIGI PIZZI

The Rake's Progress

STRAVINSKY   *13 performances*

Anne	Jill Gomez (*Trinidadian*)
Tom Rakewell	Leo Goeke (*American*)
Trulove	Don Garrard (*Canadian*)
Nick Shadow	Donald Gramm (*American*)
Mother Goose	Thetis Blacker (*English*)
Baba the Turk	Rosalind Elias (*American*)
Sellem	John Fryatt (*English*)
Keeper of the Madhouse	Malcolm King (*English*)

Conductor   BERNARD HAITINK
Producer   JOHN COX
Designer   DAVID HOCKNEY

Così fan tutte

MOZART   *16 performances*

Ferrando	Robert Johnson (*American*)
	Anson Austin (*Australian*)
Guglielmo	Knut Skram (*Norwegian*)
	Thomas Allen (*English*)
Don Alfonso	Michael Devlin (*American*)
	Frantz Petri (*French*)
Fiordiligi	Bozena Betley (*Polish*)
	Helena Döse (*Swedish*)
Dorabella	Reni Penkova (*Bulgarian*)
	Sylvia Lindenstrand (*Swedish*)
Despina	Evelyn Mandac (*Philippine*)
	Danièle Perriers (*French*)

Conductors   JOHN PRITCHARD
                     Kenneth Montgomery
Producer   ADRIAN SLACK
Designer   EMANUELE LUZZATI
Sponsored by the Peter Stuyvesant Foundation

Intermezzo

RICHARD STRAUSS   *10 performances*

Christine	Elisabeth Söderström (*Swedish*)
Robert Storch	Marco Bakker (*Dutch*)
Anna	Elizabeth Gale (*English*)
Franzl	James Baker (*English*)
Therese	Catherine McCord (*Scottish*)
Fanny	Jean Williams (*New Zealand*)
Marie	Susan Varley (*English*)
Baron Lummer	Alexander Oliver (*Scottish*)
The Lawyer's Wife	Isla Brodie (*Scottish*)
Resi	Cynthia Buchan (*Scottish*)
The Commercial Counsellor	Alan Watt (*Scottish*)
	Donald Bell (*Canadian*)
The Opera Singer	Dennis Wicks (*English*)
Stroh, the Conductor	Anthony Rolfe Johnson (*English*)
The Legal Counsellor	Brian Donlan (*English*)
The Lawyer	Thomas Lawlor (*Irish*)

Conductor   JOHN PRITCHARD
Producer   JOHN COX
Designer   MARTIN BATTERSBY
Choreographer   PAULINE GRANT
Sponsored by the Fred Kobler Trust

General Administrator MORAN CAPLAT

Musical Director JOHN PRITCHARD

Director of Production JOHN COX

Conductors ANDREW DAVIS, BERNARD HAITINK,
KENNETH MONTGOMERY, JOHN PRITCHARD, CALVIN SIMMONS
Music Staff MARTIN ISEPP (Chief Festival Coach), ROBIN BOWMAN,
RICHARD BRADSHAW, ROSETTA ELY, JONATHAN HINDEN,
GRAHAM JOHNSON, JEAN MALLANDAINE, DAVID PARRY,
FRANÇOISE PETRO-MAROTEL, SIMON RATTLE, INGRID SURGENOR,
ANIKO PETER-SZABO, EVELYN TURNER-INMAN, HENRY WARD,
STEPHEN WILDER
Librarian CHARMIAN HUGHES

Producers JOHN COX, PETER HALL, JEAN-PIERRE PONNELLE,
ADRIAN SLACK, RENÉ TERRASSON
Assistant Producers JULIAN HOPE, CHRISTOPHER RENSHAW,
TIMOTHY TYRREL
Lighting ROBERT BRYAN
Production Manager JUNE DANDRIDGE
General Stage Manager GEOFFREY GILBERTSON
Stage Management SUSAN USHER, ALAN HATTON, COLIN MOSSMAN,
PETER STENNING, SIMON ASH, ANTHONY RUSSELL-ROBERTS
Chief Technician ALBERT PULLEN
Stage Foreman IVOR GREEN
Staff Carpenters REX CARTER, FRANK EADE
Chief Electrical Technician JIM THOMAS
Wardrobe Manager TONY LEDELL
Senior Cutter JOHN KING
Wardrobe Mistress RUTH FEATHERSTONE
Wigs SHEILA DUNSDON
Property Manager ANNABELLE HAWTREY
Opera Manager BRIAN DICKIE
Front of House Manager JANET MOORES
Regulating Secretary CELIA HARDING
Treasurer JOHN BARDEN
Press and Publicity HELEN O'NEILL
Information JOYCE AKINS
Transport DESMOND WORSFOLD
Box Office Manager HELEN STEPHENSON
Catering by VERNON HERBERT

LONDON PHILHARMONIC ORCHESTRA

Falstaff

VERDI   *15 performances*

Falstaff	Donald Gramm (*American*) Richard Cross (*American*)
Dr Caius	John Fryatt (*English*)
Bardolph	Bernard Dickerson (*English*)
Pistol	Ugo Trama (*Italian*)
Meg Page	Reni Penkova (*Bulgarian*)
Alice Ford	Kay Griffel (*American*)
Mistress Quickly	Nucci Condò (*Italian*)
Nannetta	Elizabeth Gale (*English*)
Fenton	Max-René Cosotti (*Italian*) Anthony Rolfe Johnson (*English*)
Ford	Richard Stilwell (*American*) Benjamin Luxon (*English*)

Conductors   JOHN PRITCHARD
Kenneth Montgomery

Producer and Designer   JEAN-PIERRE PONNELLE

*Sponsored by the Fred Kobler Trust and the Corbett Foundation of
Cincinnati, Ohio*

Pelléas et Mélisande

DEBUSSY   *9 performances*

Pelléas	André Jobin (*French*)
Mélisande	Anne-Marie Blanzat (*French*)
Golaud	Michael Devlin (*American*)
Geneviève	Jocelyne Taillon (*French*)
Arkel	Don Garrard (*Canadian*)
Yniold	Elisabeth Conquet (*French*)
Doctor	Malcolm King (*English*)

Conductor   BERNARD HAITINK
Producer   RENÉ TERRASSON
Scenery   PATRICK ROBERTSON
Costumes   ROSEMARY VERCOE

Sponsored by the Lily and Henry Davis Charitable Trust

Le nozze di Figaro

MOZART   *19 performances*

Figaro	Knut Skram (*Norwegian*)
	Samuel Ramey (*American*)
Susanna	Adrienne Csengery (*Hungarian*)
	Lillian Watson (*English*)
Bartolo	Ugo Trama (*Italian*)
Marcellina	Nucci Condò (*Italian*)
	Joyce McCrindle (*Scottish*)
Cherubino	Cynthia Buchan (*Scottish*)
	Delia Wallis (*English*)
Count Almaviva	Hans Helm (*German*)
	Michael Devlin (*American*)
Don Basilio	John Fryatt (*English*)
The Countess	Bozena Betley (*Polish*)
	Helena Döse (*Swedish*)
Antonio	Thomas Lawlor (*Irish*)
Barbarina	Susanna Ross (*English*)
Don Curzio	Bernard Dickerson (*English*)

Conductors	JOHN PRITCHARD
	Calvin Simmons
Producer	PETER HALL
Associate Producer	Adrian Slack
Designer	JOHN BURY
Choreographer	PAULINE GRANT

Sponsored by the Peter Stuyvesant Foundation

Così fan tutte

MOZART   *10 performances*

Ferrando	David Kuebler (*American*)
	David Rendall (*English*)
Guglielmo	Knut Skram (*Norwegian*)
Don Alfonso	Frantz Petri (*French*)
Fiordiligi	Bozena Betley (*Polish*)
Dorabella	Trudeliese Schmidt (*German*)
Despina	Lillian Watson (*English*)
	Danièle Perriers (*French*)

Conductor	KENNETH MONTGOMERY
Producer	ADRIAN SLACK
Designer	EMANUELE LUZZATI

Sponsored by the Peter Stuyvesant Foundation

Capriccio

RICHARD STRAUSS   *9 performances*

Flamand	Ryland Davies (*Welsh*)
Olivier	Dale Duesing (*American*)
La Roche	Marius Rintzler (*Rumanian*)
The Countess	Elisabeth Söderström (*Swedish*)
The Count	Håkan Hagegård (*Swedish*)
Clairon	Kerstin Meyer (*Swedish*)
Italian Tenor	Ricardo Cassinelli (*Argentinian*)
Italian Soprano	Eugenia Ratti (*Italian*)
Major Domo	Thomas Lawlor (*Irish*)
Monsieur Taupe	Hugues Cuenod (*Swiss*)

Conductor	ANDREW DAVIS
Producer	JOHN COX
Scenery	DENNIS LENNON
Costumes and Furniture	MARTIN BATTERSBY
Choreographer	PAULINE GRANT

General Administrator MORAN CAPLAT

Musical Director JOHN PRITCHARD

Director of Production JOHN COX

Conductors ANDREW DAVIS, BERNARD HAITINK, JOHN PRITCHARD, SIMON RATTLE, CALVIN SIMMONS

Music Staff MARTIN ISEPP (Chief Festival Coach), STEPHEN BARLOW, ROBIN BOWMAN, NICHOLAS BRAITHWAITE, RICHARD BRADSHAW, HILDE BEAL, NICHOLAS CLEOBURY, ROSETTA FLY, CHRISTOPHER FIFIELD, JOHN FRASER, JONATHAN HINDEN, JEAN MALLANDAINE, ANIKO PETER-SZABO, HENRY WARD, STEPHEN WILDER

Librarian CHARMIAN HUGHES

Assistant JONATHAN BURTON

Producers JOHN COX, PETER HALL, JONATHAN MILLER, JEAN-PIERRE PONNELLE, GRAZIELLA SCIUTTI

Staff Producers JULIAN HOPE, GUUS MOSTART, STEWART TROTTER, TIMOTHY TYRREL, GRAHAM VICK

Lighting ROBERT BRYAN

Production Manager JUNE DANDRIDGE

General Stage Manager GEOFFREY GILBERTSON

Stage Management SUSAN USHER, ALAN HATTON, DAVID PENN, SUSAN FORTESCUE, PHILIP HESELTON, STEPHEN LAWLESS, PHILIP MACDONALD

Chief Technician ALBERT PULLEN

Stage Foreman IVOR GREEN

Staff Carpenters REX CARTER, FRANK EADE

Chief Electrical Technician JIM THOMAS

Wardrobe Manager TONY LEDELL

Senior Cutter JOHN KING

Wardrobe Mistress RUTH FEATHERSTONE

Wigs SHEILA DUNSDON

Property Manager ANNABELLE HAWTREY

Opera Manager BRIAN DICKIE

Secretary to General Administrator VICTORIA WALSH

Front of House Manager JANET MOORES

Treasurer JOHN BARDEN

Press and Publicity HELEN O'NEILL

Information JOYCE AKINS

Transport DESMOND WORSFOLD

Box Office Manager HELEN STEPHENSON

Catering by VERNON HERBERT

LONDON PHILHARMONIC ORCHESTRA

Don Giovanni

MOZART *18 performances*

Leporello	Stafford Dean (*English*)
	Richard Van Allan (*English*)
Donna Anna	Joan Carden (*Australian*)
	Horiana Branisteanu (*Rumanian*)
Don Giovanni	Benjamin Luxon (*English*)
	Thomas Allen (*English*)
The Commendatore	Pierre Thau (*French*)
Don Ottavio	Leo Goeke (*American*)
	Philip Langridge (*English*)
Donna Elvira	Rosario Andrade (*Mexican*)
	Rachel Yakar (*French*)
Zerlina	Elizabeth Gale (*English*)
	Adrienne Csengery (*Hungarian*)
Masetto	John Rawnsley (*English*)
Conductors	JOHN PRITCHARD
	BERNARD HAITINK
	Calvin Simmons
Producer	PETER HALL
Designer	JOHN BURY
Choreographer	PAULINE GRANT
	Sponsored by Imperial Tobacco Ltd

DOUBLE BILL
La Voix Humaine

POULENC *9 performances*

Elle	Graziella Sciutti (*Italian*)
Conductor	GALVIN SIMMONS
Producer	GRAZIELLA SCIUTTI
Designer	MARTIN BATTERSBY

The Cunning Little Vixen

JANÁČEK   *9 performances*

The Forester	Thomas Allen (*English*)
The Vixen	Norma Burrowes (*Irish*)
	Eilene Hannan (*Australian*)
The Forester's Wife	Enid Hartle (*English*)
The Dog	Alan Watt (*Scottish*)
The Cock	Hugues Cuenod (*Swiss*)
The Hen	Isla Brodie (*Scottish*)
The Badger	Michael Lewis (*English*)
The Parson	Brian Donlan (*English*)
The Schoolmaster	Bernard Dickerson (*English*)
The Innkeeper	John Michael Flanagan (*English*)
The Fox	Robert Hoyem (*American*)
The Owl ⎫	Enid Hartle (*English*)
The Woodpecker ⎭	
The Poacher	Thomas Lawlor (*Irish*)
The Innkeeper's Wife	Phyllis Cannan (*Scottish*)

Conductor	SIMON RATTLE
Producer	JONATHAN MILLER
Scenery	PATRICK ROBERTSON
Costumes	ROSEMARY VERCOE

Die schweigsame Frau

RICHARD STRAUSS   *10 performances*

Morosus	Richard Cross (*American*)
Theodosia	Johanna Peters (*English*)
Schneidebart	Peter Gottlieb (*French*)
Henry	Jerome Pruett (*American*)
Aminta	Janet Perry (*American*)
Isotta	Nan Christie (*Scottish*)
Carlotta	Enid Hartle (*English*)
Morbio	Alan Watt (*Scottish*)
Vanuzzi	Federico Davià (*Italian*)
Farfallo	Ugo Trama (*Italian*)

Conductor	ANDREW DAVIS
Producer	JOHN COX
Designer	MICHAEL ANNALS

Falstaff

VERDI   *17 performances*

Falstaff	Renato Capecchi (*Italian*)
	Richard Cross (*American*)
Dr Caius	John Fryatt (*English*)
Bardolph	Bernard Dickerson (*English*)
Pistol	Ugo Trama (*Italian*)
Meg Page	Reni Penkova (*Bulgarian*)
Alice Ford	Teresa Cahill (*English*)
	Kay Griffel (*American*)
Mistress Quickly	Nucci Condò (*Italian*)
Nannetta	Elizabeth Gale (*English*)
Fenton	Max-René Cosotti (*Italian*)
Ford	Brent Ellis (*American*)
	Benjamin Luxon (*English*)

Conductors	JOHN PRITCHARD
	Calvin Simmons
Produced and designed by	JEAN-PIERRE PONNELLE
Rehearsed by	Julian Hope
Sponsored by the Fred Kobler Trust and the Corbett Foundation of Cincinnati, Ohio	

The Rake's Progress

STRAVINSKY   *8 performances*

Anne	Felicity Lott (*English*)
Tom Rakewell	Leo Goeke (*American*)
Trulove	Richard Van Allan (*English*)
Nick Shadow	Samuel Ramey (*American*)
Mother Goose	Nuala Willis (*Irish*)
Baba the Turk	Rosalind Elias (*American*)
Sellem	John Fryatt (*English*)
Keeper of the Madhouse	Thomas Lawlor (*Irish*)

Conductor	BERNARD HAITINK
Producer	JOHN COX
Designer	DAVID HOCKNEY

General Administrator MORAN CAPLAT

Musical Director BERNARD HAITINK

Director of Production JOHN COX

Conductors NICHOLAS BRAITHWAITE, ANDREW DAVIS, BERNARD HAITINK, KENNETH MONTGOMERY, NICOLA RESCIGNO, ED SPANJAARD

Music Staff MARTIN ISEPP (Head of Music Staff), STEPHEN BARLOW, HILDE BEAL, ROBIN BOWMAN, NICHOLAS CLEOBURY (Chorus Master), ROSETTA ELY, CHRISTOPHER FIFIELD, HAL FRANCE, THOMAS FULTON, JONATHAN HINDEN, JEAN MALLANDAINE, DAVID PARRY, ANIKO PETER-SZABO, ED SPANJAARD, STEPHEN WILDER

Librarian CHARMIAN HUGHES

Assistant JONATHAN BURTON

Producers JOHN COX, PETER HALL

Associate Producers JULIAN HOPE, GUUS MOSTART, STEWART TROTTER

Staff Producers IAN ANGUS, DAVID PENN

Lighting ROBERT BRYAN

Production Manager JUNE DANDRIDGE

General Stage Manager GEOFFREY GILBERTSON

Stage Mangement SUSAN USHER, ALAN HATTON, STEPHEN LAWLESS, DAVID MAYO, JULIE CROCKER, ROBERT JONES, JANE RANDALL

Technical Manager ALBERT PULLEN

Stage Foreman IVOR GREEN

Staff Carpenters REX CARTER, FRANK EADE

Electrical Manager JIM THOMAS

Wardrobe Manager TONY LEDELL

Senior Cutter JOHN KING

Wardrobe Mistress RUTH FEATHERSTONE

Wigs PATRICIA CAMERON

Property Manager ANNABELLE HAWTREY

Opera Manager BRIAN DICKIE

Secretary to General Administrator VICTORIA WALSH

Front of House Manager JANET MOORES

Treasurer JOHN BARDEN

Press and Publicity HELEN O'NEILL

Information JOYCE AKINS

Transport DESMOND WORSFOLD

Box Office Manager HELEN STEPHENSON

Catering by VERNON HERBERT

LONDON PHILHARMONIC ORCHESTRA

The Magic Flute

MOZART   *16 performances*

Tamino	Leo Goeke (*American*)
Three Ladies	Mani Mekler (*Israeli*)
	Patricia Parker (*English*)
	Nucci Condò (*Italian*)
Papageno	Benjamin Luxon (*English*)
Queen of the Night	May Sandoz (*American*)
	Sylvia Greenberg (*Israeli*)
Three Boys	Kate Flowers (*English*)
	Lindsay John (*English*)
	Elizabeth Stokes (*English*)
Monostatos	John Fryatt (*English*)
Pamina	Isobel Buchanan (*Scottish*)
	Felicity Lott (*English*)
The Speaker	Willard White (*Jamaican*)
	Henry Herford (*English*)
Sarastro	Thomas Thomaschke (*German*)
	Kolos Kovats (*Hungarian*)
Priest	Richard Berkeley Steele (*English*)
Men in Armour	Neil McKinnon (*Scottish*)
	John Rath (*English*)
Papagena	Elisabeth Conquet (*French*)
Conductors	ANDREW DAVIS
	BERNARD HAITINK
Producer	JOHN COX
Associate Producer	Guus Mostart
Designer	DAVID HOCKNEY
Sponsored by	Imperial Tobacco Ltd

Don Giovanni

MOZART   *9 performances*

Leporello	Stafford Dean (*English*)
	Malcolm King (*English*)
Donna Anna	Norma Sharp (*American*)
Don Giovanni	Brent Ellis (*American*)
The Commendatore	Leonard Mroz (*Polish*)
Don Ottavio	Philip Langridge (*English*)
	Keith Lewis (*New Zealand*)
Donna Elvira	Rosario Andrade (*Mexican*)
Zerlina	Elizabeth Gale (*English*)
Masetto	John Rawnsley (*English*)
Conductors	KENNETH MONTGOMERY
	Nicholas Braithwaite
Original Producer	PETER HALL
Rehearsed by	Stewart Trotter
Designer	JOHN BURY
Choreographer	PAULINE GRANT
Sponsored by	Imperial Tobacco Ltd

La Bohème

PUCCINI   *16 performances*

Marcello	Brent Ellis (*American*)
	John Rawnsley (*English*)
Rodolfo	Alberto Cupido (*Italian*)
Colline	Willard White (*Jamaican*)
Schaunard	Alan Charles (*Welsh*)
Benoît	Thomas Lawlor (*Irish*)
Mimì	Linda Zoghby (*American*)
Musetta	Ashley Putnam (*American*)
Alcindoro	Federico Davià (*Italian*)
Parpignol	Neil McKinnon (*Scottish*)
Sergeant	Brian Donlan (*English*)
Customs Officer	Paul Nemeer (*English*)

Conductors	NICOLA RESCIGNO
	Nicholas Braithwaite
Producer	JOHN COX
Associate Producer	Julian Hope
Scenery	HENRY BARDON
Costumes	DAVID WALKER

Sponsored by the Peter Stuyvesant Foundation

The Rake's Progress

STRAVINSKY   *6 performances*

Anne	Felicity Lott (*English*)
Tom Rakewell	Leo Goeke (*American*)
Trulove	John Michael Flanagan (*English*)
Nick Shadow	Samuel Ramey (*American*)
Mother Goose	Nuala Willis (*Irish*)
Baba the Turk	Katherine Pring (*English*)
Sellem	John Fryatt (*English*)
Keeper of the Madhouse	Brian Donlan (*English*)

Conductor	BERNARD HAITINK
Producer	JOHN COX
Associate Producer	Julian Hope
Designer	DAVID HOCKNEY

Così fan tutte

MOZART   *15 performances*

Ferrando	Max-René Cosotti (*Italian*)
Guglielmo	Håkan Hagegård (*Swedish*)
Don Alfonso	Stafford Dean (*English*)
Fiordiligi	Bozena Betley (*Polish*)
	Helen Walker (*English*)
Dorabella	Maria Ewing (*American*)
	Patricia Parker (*English*)
Despina	Nan Christie (*Scottish*)

Conductors	BERNARD HAITINK
	Ed Spanjaard
Producer	PETER HALL
Designer	JOHN BURY

Sponsored by National Westminster Bank

General Administrator MORAN CAPLAT

Musical Director BERNARD HAITINK

Director of Production JOHN COX

Conductors STEPHEN BARLOW, NICHOLAS BRAITHWAITE,
ANDREW DAVIS, BERNARD HAITINK
Music Staff MARTIN ISEPP (Head of Music Staff), STEPHEN BARLOW,
HILDE BEAL, ROBIN BOWMAN, NICHOLAS CLEOBURY (Chorus Master),
ROSETTA ELY, CHRISTOPHER FIFIELD, JANE GLOVER,
JONATHAN HINDEN, JEAN MALLANDAINE, ANIKO PETER-SZABO,
CRAIG RUTENBERG, STEPHEN WILDER, CHRISTOPHER WILLIS
Librarian CHARMIAN HUGHES
Associate JONATHAN BURTON

Producers JOHN COX, PETER HALL, PATRICK LIBBY,
GUUS MOSTART
Associate Producers JEREMY JAMES TAYLOR, DAVE HEATHER
Staff Producers STEFAN JANSKI, STEPHEN LAWLESS,
NIGEL WARRINGTON
Lighting ROBERT BRYAN
Production Manager JUNE DANDRIDGE
General Stage Manager TOM REDMAN
Stage Management JULIE CROCKER, JANE RANDALL,
TREFOR GLYN-JONES, BENJAMIN HAYES,
STUART DORNFORD-MAY, NICK MURRAY
Technical Manager ALBERT PULLEN
Stage Foreman IVOR GREEN
Staff Carpenters REX CARTER, FRANK EADE
Electrical Department KEITH BENSON, HUGH CHINNICK, PAUL PYANT,
PAUL HANRAHAN
Wardrobe Manager TONY LEDELL
Senior Cutter JOHN KING
Wardrobe Mistress RUTH FEATHERSTONE
Wigs PATRICIA CAMERON
Property Manager ANNABELLE HAWTREY
Opera Manager BRIAN DICKIE
Assistant SUSAN DIXON
Music Secretary NATALIA BYRNE
Personal Assistant to General Administrator VICTORIA WALSH
House Manager GEOFFREY GILBERTSON
Treasurer JOHN BARDEN
Accommodation Manager JANET MOORES
Press and Publicity HELEN O'NEILL
Information JOYCE AKINS
Transport DESMOND WORSFOLD
Box Office Manager HELEN STEPHENSON
Catering by VERNON HERBERT

LONDON PHILHARMONIC ORCHESTRA

Fidelio

BEETHOVEN   *12 performances*

Jaquino	Ian Caley (*English*)
Marzelline	Elizabeth Gale (*English*)
Rocco	Curt Appelgren (*Swedish*)
Leonore	Elisabeth Söderström (*Swedish*)
Pizarro	Robert Allman (*Australian*)
Florestan	Anton de Ridder (*Dutch*)
Don Fernando	Michael Langdon (*English*)

Conductor	BERNARD HAITINK
Producer	PETER HALL
Associate Producer	Guus Mostart
Design and Lighting	JOHN BURY
	Sponsored by Imperial Tobacco Ltd.

Il ritorno d'Ulisse in patria

MONTEVERDI   *10 performances*
             (*arr Raymond Leppard*)

L'humana fragiltà	Diana Montague (*English*)
Tempo	Ugo Trama (*Italian*)
Fortuna	Lynda Russell (*English*)
Amore	Kate Flowers (*English*)
Penelope	Frederica von Stade (*American*)
Ericlea	Nucci Condò (*Italian*)
Melanto	Patricia Parker (*English*)
Eurimaco	Max-René Cosotti (*Italian*)
Nettuno	Roger Bryson (*English*)
Giove	Keith Lewis (*New Zealand*)
	Kevin John (*Welsh*)
Ulisse	Richard Stilwell (*American*)
Minerva	Ann Murray (*Irish*)
Eumete	Richard Lewis (*English*)
Iro	Alexander Oliver (*Scottish*)
Telemaco	Patrick Power (*New Zealand*)
Antinöo	Ugo Trama (*Italian*)
Anfimono	Bernard Dickerson (*English*)
Pisandro	John Fryatt (*English*)
Giunone	Claire Powell (*English*)

Conductor	RAYMOND LEPPARD
Original Production	PETER HALL
Revived by	Patrick Libby
Associate	Dave Heather
Designer	JOHN BURY

Die schweigsame Frau

RICHARD STRAUSS   *11 performances*

Morosus	Marius Rintzler (*Rumanian*)
Theodosia	Johanna Peters (*English*)
Schneidebart	Peter Gottlieb (*French*)
Henry	Jerome Pruett (*American*)
Aminta	Krisztina Laki (*Hungarian*)
Isotta	Kate Flowers (*English*)
Carlotta	Enid Hartle (*English*)
Morbio	Alan Watt (*Scottish*)
Vanuzzi	Joseph Rouleau (*Canadian*)
Farfallo	Ugo Trama (*Italian*)

Conductors	ANDREW DAVIS
	Stephen Barlow
Producer	JOHN COX
Designer	MICHAEL ANNALS

Sponsored by the Peter Stuyvesant Foundation

Così fan tutte

MOZART   *17 performances*

Ferrando	John Aler (*American*)
Guglielmo	Alan Titus (*American*)
Don Alfonso	Stafford Dean (*English*)
	Brian Donlan (*English*)
Fiordiligi	Bozena Betley (*Polish*)
Dorabella	Patricia Parker (*English*)
Despina	Nan Christie (*Scottish*)

Conductors	BERNARD HAITINK
	Nicholas Braithwaite
Original Production by	PETER HALL
Rehearsed by	Guus Mostart
Designer	JOHN BURY

Sponsored by National Westminster Bank

La fedeltà premiata

HAYDN   *12 performances*

Nerina	Kathleen Battle (*American*)
Lindoro	James Atherton (*American*)
Melibeo	Richard Van Allan (*English*)
Amaranta	Sylvia Lindenstrand (*Swedish*)
Perrucchetto	Thomas Allen (*English*)
Fileno	Max-René Cosotti (*Italian*)
Celia	Julia Hamari (*Hungarian*)
Diana	Eiddwen Harrhy (*Welsh*)

Conductors	BERNARD HAITINK
	Nicholas Braithwaite
Producer	JOHN COX
Designer	HUGH CASSON

Sponsored by the Fred Kobler Trust

General Administrator MORAN CAPLAT

Musical Director BERNARD HAITINK

Director of Production JOHN COX

Conductors STEPHEN BARLOW, ANDREW DAVIS,
BERNARD HAITINK, GUSTAV KUHN, SIMON RATTLE
Music Staff MARTIN ISEPP (Head of Music Staff), STEPHEN BARLOW,
ROBIN BOWMAN, ROSETTA ELY, CHRISTOPHER FIFIELD,
GERALDINE FRANK, JANE GLOVER (Chorus Director),
JONATHAN HINDEN, NICHOLAS KRAEMER, ANIKO PETER-SZABO,
CRAIG RUTENBERG, GEOFFREY TOZER, STEPHEN WILDER,
CHRISTOPHER WILLIS
Librarian JONATHAN BURTON
Associate CHARMIAN HUGHES

Producers JOHN COX, JEAN-PIERRE PONNELLE, PETER WOOD,
JULIAN HOPE, GUUS MOSTART
Associate Producer ROBERT CARSEN
Staff Producers DAFFYD BURNE-JONES, STEPHEN LAWLESS,
NIGEL WARRINGTON
Lighting ROBERT BRYAN
Production Manager JUNE DANDRIDGE
General Stage Manager TOM REDMAN
Stage Management JULIE CROCKER, TREFOR GLYN-JONES
NICK MURRAY, SIMON DODSON, BENJAMIN HAYES, PAUL JUDGES,
PHILIP TICEHURST
Technical Manager ALBERT PULLEN
Stage Foreman IVOR GREEN
Staff Carpenters REX CARTER, FRANK EADE
Electrical Department KEITH BENSON, GERRY AMIES,
HUGH CHINNICK, PAUL PYANT, PAUL HANRAHAN
Wardrobe Manager TONY LEDELL
Senior Cutter JOHN KING
Wardrobe Mistress RUTH FEATHERSTONE
Wigs PATRICIA CAMERON
Property Manager ANNABELLE HAWTREY
Opera Manager BRIAN DICKIE
Assistant SUSAN DIXON
Personal Assistant to General Administrator VICTORIA WALSH
House Manager GEOFFREY GILBERTSON
Treasurer JOHN BARDEN
Accommodation Manager JANET MOORES
Chief Telephonists BRENDA HERMITAGE, JOAN PULLEN
Press and Publicity HELEN O'NEILL
Information JOYCE AKINS
Transport DESMOND WORSFOLD
Box Office Manager HELEN STEPHENSON
Catering by VERNON HERBERT

LONDON PHILHARMONIC ORCHESTRA

Die Entführung aus dem Serail

MOZART   *12 performances*

Belmonte	Gösta Winbergh (*Swedish*)
Osmin	Willard White (*Jamaican*)
Pedrillo	James Hoback (*American*)
Pasha Selim	Thomas Thomaschke (*German*)
Constanze	Valerie Masterson (*English*)
Blonde	Lillian Watson (*English*)

Conductor	GUSTAV KUHN
Producer	PETER WOOD
Associate Producer	Guus Mostart
Designer	WILLIAM DUDLEY

Sponsored by Dredsner Bank and Deutsche BP A.G.

Falstaff

VERDI   *14 performances*

Falstaff	Renato Capecchi (*Italian*)
Dr Caius	John Fryatt (*English*)
Bardolph	Bernard Dickerson (*English*)
Pistol	Ugo Trama (*Italian*)
Meg Page	Claire Powell (*English*)
Alice Ford	Teresa Cahill (*English*)
Mistress Quickly	Nucci Condò (*Italian*)
Nannetta	Lucia Aliberti (*Italian*)
Fenton	Max-René Cosotti (*Italian*)
Ford	Alberto Rinaldi (*Italian*)

Conductor	ANDREW DAVIS
Original Production and Designs by	JEAN-PIERRE PONNELLE
Rehearsed by	Julian Hope

Revival sponsored by the Peter Stuyvesant Foundation

The Magic Flute

MOZART   *14 performances*

Tamino	Ryland Davies (*Welsh*)
Three Ladies	Catherine McCord (*Scottish*)
	Maria Moll (*English*)
	Fiona Kimm (*English*)
Papageno	Stephen Dickson (*American*)
	Benjamin Luxon (*English*)
Queen of the Night	Rita Shane (*American*)
Three Boys	Deborah Rees (*Welsh*)
	Yvonne Lea (*English*)
	Jane Findlay (*English*)
Monostatos	Francis Egerton (*Irish*)
Pamina	Norma Burrowes (*Irish*)
	Isobel Buchanan (*Scottish*)
The Speaker	Willard White (*Jamaican*)
Sarastro	Thomas Thomaschke (*German*)
Priest	Adrian Thompson (*English*)
Men in Armour	David Johnston (*English*)
	Roger Bryson (*English*)
Papagena	Meryl Drower (*Welsh*)

Conductors	ANDREW DAVIS
	BERNARD HAITINK
Original Production by	JOHN COX
Rehearsed by	JOHN COX and GUUS MOSTART
Designer	DAVID HOCKNEY
Sponsored by Imperial Tobacco Ltd	

Der Rosenkavalier

RICHARD STRAUSS   *16 performances*

Oktavian	Felicity Lott (*English*)
Feldmarschallin	Rachel Yakar (*French*)
	Elizabeth Harwood (*English*)
Ochs	Donald Gramm (*American*)
	Artur Korn (*Austrian*)
Valzacchi	John Fryatt (*English*)
Annina	Nucci Condò (*Italian*)
Faninal	Derek Hammond-Stroud (*English*)
Sophie	Krisztina Laki (*Hungarian*)
Duenna	Rae Woodland (*English*)
Singer	Dennis O'Neill (*Welsh*)
Landlord	Bernard Dickerson (*English*)
Police Inspector	David Wilson-Johnson (*English*)

Conductor	BERNARD HAITINK
Producer	JOHN COX
Designer	ERTÉ
Sponsored by Imperial Tobacco Ltd	

La fedeltà premiata

HAYDN   *8 performances*

Nerina	Kate Flowers (*English*)
Lindoro	James Atherton (*American*)
Melibeo	Ferruccio Furlanetto (*Italian*)
Amaranta	Linda Zoghby (*American*)
Perrucchetto	John Rawnsley (*English*)
Fileno	Max-René Cosotti (*Italian*)
Celia	Evelyn Petros (*American*)
Diana	Elizabeth Ritchie (*English*)

Conductor	SIMON RATTLE
Producer	JOHN COX
Designer	HUGH CASSON
Sponsored by the Fred Kobler Trust	

AB	Anna Bolena
AN	Ariadne auf Naxos
B	Bohème, La
CAL	Calisto, La
CAP	Capriccio
CT	Così fan tutte
CV	Cunning Little Vixen, The
D	Dido and Aeneas
DG	Don Giovanni
E	Entführung aus dem Serail, Die
EA	Elisir d'amore, L'
EO	Eugene Onegin
F	Falstaff
FED	Fedeltà premiata, La
FI	Fidelio
HE	Heure espagnole, L'
I	Idomeneo
INT	Intermezzo
J	Jephtha
LO	Ormindo, L'
M	Macbeth
MS	Matrimonio segreto, Il
NF	Nozze di Figaro, Le
PM	Pelléas et Mélisande
PP	Pietra del paragone, La
QS	Queen of Spades, The
R	Rosenkavalier, Der
RM	Rising of the Moon, The
RP	Rake's Progress, The
RU	Ritorno d'Ulisse in patria, Il
SF	Schweigsame Frau, Die
T	Turco in Italia, Il
V	Visit of the Old Lady, The
VH	Voix humaine, La
W	Werther
Z	Magic Flute, The (Die Zauberflöte)

Alberti, Walter	1965. *Figaro (NF)*
Aler, John	1979. *Ferrando (CT)*
Aliberti, Lucia	1980. *Nannetta (F)*
Allen, Paschal	1965. *Murderer (M)*
Allen, Thomas	1973. *Papageno (Z)*
	1974. *Figaro (NF)*
	1975. *Guglielmo (CT)*
	1977. *Don Giovanni (DG)*
	1977. *The Forester (CV)*
	1979. *Perrucchetto (FED)*
Allister, Jean	1966. *Witch (D)*
	1968. *Melide (LO)*
Allman, Robert	1979. *Pizarro (FI)*
Andrade, Rosario	1977, 78. *Donna Elvira (DG)*
Andrew, Milla	1968. *Anna (AB)*
Annear, Gwenyth	1965. *Anna (AB)*
	1970, 73. *First Lady (Z)*
Appelgren, Curt	1979. *Rocco (FI)*
Armstrong, Sheila	1966. *Belinda (D)*
	1966. *Papagena (Z)*
	1967. *Giannetta (EA)*
	1967, 69. *Zerlina (DG)*
	1970, 73. *Pamina (Z)*
	1970. *Fiorilla (T)*
Arthur, Maurice	1971. *Chaplitsky (QS)*
	1971. *Scaramuccio (AN)*
Atherton, James	1979, 80. *Lindoro (FED)*
Atkins, James	1971. *Major Domo (AN)*
	1972. *Pasha Selim (E)*
Attwood, Audrey	1965. *Barbarina (NF)*
Austin, Anson	1975. *Ferrando (CT)*
Autran, Victor	1966. *Gomez (HE)*
Badioli, Carlo	1965. *Geronimo (MS)*
	1967. *Benoît, Alcindoro (B)*
Baillie, Peter	1968. *Hervey (AB)*
Baker, Janet	1966. *Dido (D)*
	1970, 71. *Diana (CAL)*
	1972, 73. *Penelope (RU)*
Bakker, Marco	1974, 75. *Robert (INT)*
Barker, Joyce	1972. *Lady Macbeth (M)*
Barstow, Josephine	1974. *Electra (I)*
Battle, Kathleen	1979. *Nerina (FED)*
Baulard, Valerie	1970. *Third Boy (Z)*
Bedford, Peter Lehmann	1965. *Servant (M)*
Bell, Donald	1973, 74. *Alfred Ill (V)*
	1974, 76. *Commercial Counsellor (INT)*
Bende, Zsolt	1967. *Belcore (EA)*
Benelli, Ugo	1967. *Nemorino (EA)*
	1970. *Narciso (T)*
Berbié, Jane	1968, 69. *Miranda (LO)*
	1969, 71. *Despina (CT)*
Berkeley Steele, Richard	1978. *Priest (Z)*
Betley, Bozena	1974. *Ilia (I)*
	1975, 76, 78, 79. *Fiordiligi (CT)*
	1976. *Countess (NF)*
Biggar, Marjorie	1971, 72, 73. *Natura (CAL)*
Blacker, Thetis	1975. *Mother Goose (RP)*
Blankenburg, Heinz	1965. *Pacuvio (PP)*
	1966, 70. *Papageno (Z)*
Blanzat, Anne-Marie	1969. *Yniold (PM)*
	1976. *Mélisande (PM)*
Borg, Kim	1968. *Gremin (EO)*
Bork, Hanneke van	1968. *Sicle (LO)*
	1969. *Fiordiligi (CT)*
Bostock, Angela	1971. *Prilepa (QS)*
Bottazzo, Pietro	1965. *Paolino (MS)*
Bowden, Pamela	1966. *Witch (D)*
	1968, 70, 75. *Larina (EO)*
Bowen, Miriam	1974. *Destino (CAL)*

Bowman, James 1970, 71, 74. *Endimione* (CAL)
Branisteanu, Horiana 1977. *Donna Anna* (DG)
Brannigan, Owen 1970, 71. *Silvano* (CAL)
Brazzi, Jean 1966, 69. *Werther* (W)
Bremner, Anthony 1973, 74. *Hofbauer* (V)
1974. *Endimione* (CAL)
Bridges, Althea 1967. *Donna Anna* (DG)
Brilioth, Helge 1971. *Bacchus* (AN)
Brindley, Lorna 1973. *Second Lady* (Z)
1973, 74. *Second Woman* (V)
Brodie, Isla 1971, 74. *Echo* (CAL)
1973, 74. *First Woman* (V)
1975, 77. *The Hen* (CV)
1975. *Lawyer's Wife* (INT)
Brookes, Keith 1973, 74. *Station Master* (V)
Bryn-Jones, Delme 1972. *Macbeth* (M)
Bryson, Roger 1979. *Nettuno* (RU)
1980. *Man in Armour* (Z)
Buchan, Cynthia 1974. *Natura* (CAL)
1974. *Resi* (INT)
1974. *Ill's Daughter* (V)
1975. *Olga* (EO)
1976. *Cherubino* (NF)
Buchanan, Isobel 1978, 80. *Pamina* (Z)
Burrowes, Norma 1970. *Papagena* (Z)
1975, 77. *The Vixen* (CV)
1980. *Pamina* (Z)
Burrows, Brian 1972, 73. *Giove* (RU)
1973. *Monostatos* (Z)

Caballé, Montserrat 1965. *Marschallin* (R)
1965. *Countess* (NF)
Caddy, Ian 1972. *Servant* (M)
Cahill, Teresa 1970. *First Lady* (Z)
1971. *Najade* (AN)
1971. *Il Destino* (CAL)
1977, 80. *Alice Ford* (F)
Caley, Ian 1972, 73. *Telemaco* (RU)
1972. *Malcolm* (M)
1973, 74. *Loby* (V)
1979. *Jaquino* (FI)
Cannan, Phyllis 1977. *Innkeeper's Wife* (CV)
Capecchi, Renato 1977, 80. *Falstaff* (F)
Carlyle, Joan 1965. *Countess* (NF)
Casoni, Biancamaria 1965. *Cherubino* (NF)
Cassinelli, Ricardo 1973, 76. *The Italian Tenor* (CAP)
Casula, Maria 1969. *Despina* (CT)
Cava, Carlo 1965. *Enrico* (AB)
Channing, Lynn 1972. *Echo* (AN)
Charles, Alan 1978. *Schaunard* (B)
Christie, Nan 1977. *Isotta* (SF)
1978, 79. *Despina* (CT)
Condò, Nucci 1973, 74, 76. *Marcellina* (NF)
1976, 77, 80. *Mistress Quickly* (F)
1979. *Ericlea* (RU)
1980. *Annina* (R)
Conquet, Elisabeth 1976. *Yniold* (PM)
1977, 78. *Papagena* (Z)
Conti, Patricia 1970. *Third Lady* (Z)
Cooper, Ann 1966. *Third Lady* (Z)
Cosotti, Max-René 1976, 77, 80. *Fenton* (F)
1978. *Ferrando* (CT)
1979, 80. *Fileno* (FED)
1979. *Eurimaco* (RU)
Coster, Janet 1968. *Smeton* (AB)
Cotrubas, Ileana 1969. *Mélisande* (PM)
1970, 71. *Calisto* (CAL)
1970. *Pamina* (Z)
1973. *Susanna* (NF)

Creffield, Rosanne 1969. *Dorabella* (CT)
1970. *Second Lady* (Z)
Crofoot, Alan 1973, 74. *The Mayor* (V)
Cross, Richard 1976, 77. *Falstaff* (F)
1977. *Morosus* (SF)
Crowe, Jillian 1974. *L'Eternità* (CAL)
Cryer, Doreen 1973. *Second Lady* (Z)
Csengery, Adrienne 1976. *Susanna* (NF)
1977. *Zerlina* (DG)
Cuenod, Hugues 1965. *Torquemada* (HE)
1966. *Monostatos* (Z)
1967, 68. *Erice* (LO)
1968, 70, 75. *Triquet* (EO)
1969. *Schmidt* (W)
1970, 71. *Linfea* (CAL)
1973, 76. *M. Taupe* (CAP)
1975, 77. *The Cock* (CV)
Cupido, Alberto 1978. *Rodolfo* (B)
Curphey, Margaret 1965. *Gentlewoman* (M)
Curtin, Phyllis 1969. *Donna Anna* (DG)

Davià, Federico 1965. *Count Robinson* (MS)
1965. *Bartolo* (NF)
1967. *Colline* (B)
1967, 68. *Ariadeno* (LO)
1970, 71. *Pane* (CAL)
1977. *Vanuzzi* (SF)
1978. *Alcindoro* (B)
Davies, Derek 1965. *Antonio* (NF)
1965. *Doctor* (M)
Davies, Ryland 1965. *Major Domo* (R)
1966. *Sailor* (D)
1966. *Priest and Man in Armour* (Z)
1968, 72. *Belmonte* (E)
1969. *Ferrando* (CT)
1975. *Lensky* (EO)
1976. *Flamand* (CAP)
1980. *Tamino* (Z)
Dean, Stafford 1966, 69. *Bailiff* (W)
1968. *Rochefort* (AB)
1977, 78. *Leporello* (DG)
1978, 79. *Don Alfonso* (CT)
de Javelin, Sara 1971. *Atalanta* (RM)
1973. *Ill's Daughter* (V)
de Peyer, Adrian 1966. *Bailiff* (W)
de Ridder, Anton 1979. *Florestan* (FI)
Devlin, Michael 1974, 76. *The Count* (NF)
1975. *Don Alfonso* (CT)
1976. *Golaud* (PM)
Dickerson, Bernard 1972, 73, 79. *Anfinomo* (RU)
1973, 74, 76. *Don Curzio* (NF)
1975, 77. *Schoolmaster* (CV)
1976, 77, 80. *Bardolph* (F)
Dickson, Stephen 1980. *Papageno* (Z)
Dix, Barbara 1973, 74. *The Mayor's Wife* (V)
1974. *Fanny* (INT)
1975. *Innkeeper's Wife* (CV)
Donlan, Brian 1970, 71. *Haywood* (RM)
1971. *Narumov* (QS)
1972. *Doctor* (M)
1973, 74. *Doctor* (V)
1974, 75. *Legal Counsellor* (INT)
1975, 77. *The Parson* (CV)
1967, 78. *Sergeant* (B)
1978. *Keeper of the Madhouse* (RP)
1979. *Don Alfonso* (CT)
Döse, Helena 1974, 76. *Countess* (NF)
1975. *Fiordiligi* (CT)
Drower, Meryl 1980. *Papagena* (Z)
Duesing, Dale 1976. *Olivier* (CAP)

373

Eathorne, Wendy   1969. *Sophie* (W)
1970. *First Boy* (Z)
1971. *Atalanta* (RM)
Eaves, Sylvia   1970. *Second Boy* (Z)
Edelmann, Otto   1965. *Baron Ochs* (R)
Egerton, Francis   1980. *Monostatos* (Z)
Elias, Lorna   1965. *Countess* (NF)
Elias, Rosalind   1975, 77. *Baba the Turk* (RP)
Eliasson, Sven Olof   1967. *Don Ottavio* (DG)
Ellis, Brent   1977. *Ford* (F)
1978. *Don Giovanni* (DG)
1978. *Marcello* (B)
Elvin, William   1970. *Petrovich* (EO)
1971, 72. *Wigmaker* (AN)
Erwen, Keith   1970. *Priest and Man in Armour* (Z)
1972. *Macduff* (M)
Esparza, Elfego   1970. *Don Geronio* (T)
Evans, Edgar   1973, 74. *Butler* (V)
Ewing, Maria   1978. *Dorabella* (CT)

Findlay, Jane   1980. *Third Boy* (Z)
Fissore, Enrico   1967. *Schaunard* (B)
Flanagan, John Michael   1975, 77. *Innkeeper* (CV)
Flowers, Kate   1978. *First Boy* (Z)
1979. *Amore* (RU)
1979. *Isotta* (SF)
1980. *Nerina* (FED)
Fowles, Gladys   1974. *Ilia* (I)
Fryatt, John   1970. *Albazar* (T)
1970, 71. *Lillywhite* (RM)
1971, 72. *Brighella* (AN)
1972, 73, 79. *Pisandro* (RU)
1973, 74, 76. *Don Basilio* (NF)
1974. *Mercurio* (CAL)
1974. *High Priest* (I)
1975, 77, 78. *Sellem* (RP)
1976, 77, 80. *Dr Caius* (F)
1978. *Monostatos* (Z)
1980. *Valzacchi* (R)
Fuller, Yvonne   1970. *Second Lady* (Z)
1971, 72. *Echo* (AN)
Furlanetto, Ferruccio   1980. *Melibeo* (FED)

Gale, Elizabeth   1973. *Papagena* (Z)
1973, 74. *Barbarina* (NF)
1974. *Susanna* (NF)
1974, 75. *Anna* (INT)
1976, 77. *Nannetta* (F)
1977, 78. *Zerlina* (DG)
1979. *Marzelline* (FI)
Garavanta, Ottavio   1967. *Rodolfo* (B)
Garcisanz, Isabel   1966. *Concepcion* (HE)
1967, 68. *Nerillo* (LO)
1970. *Zaida* (T)
Garrard, Don   1965. *Rochefort* (AB)
1973. *Pastor* (V)
1975. *Gremin* (EO)
1975. *Trulove* (RP)
1976. *Arkel* (PM)
Gencer, Leyla   1965. *Anna* (AB)
Geszty, Sylvia   1971, 72. *Zerbinetta* (AN)
1972. *Constanze* (E)
Gibbs, John   1970. *Papageno* (Z)
1970, 71. *Donal O'Dowd* (RM)
1971, 72. *Harlekin* (AN)
Goeke, Leo   1973. *Flamand* (CAP)
1974. *Idamante* (I)
1975, 77, 78. *Tom Rakewell* (RP)
1977. *Don Ottavio* (DG)
1978. *Tamino* (Z)

Golding, Richard   1965. *Police Inspector* (R)
Gomez, Jill   1969. *Mélisande* (PM)
1970. *Calisto* (CAL)
1975. *Anne* (RP)
Gottlieb, Peter   1966, 69. *Albert* (W)
1970, 71. *Zastrow* (RM)
1970, 71. *Mercurio* (CAL)
1977, 79. *Schneidebart* (SF)
Gramm, Donald   1975. *Nick Shadow* (RP)
1976. *Falstaff* (F)
1980. *Baron Ochs* (R)
Grant, Clifford   1972. *Nettuno* (RU)
Gray, Linda Esther   1973. *First Lady* (Z)
1974. *L'Eternità* (CAL)
1974. *Electra* (I)
Greenberg, Sylvia   1978. *Queen of the Night* (Z)
Greig, Patricia   1972, 73. *Fortuna* (RU)
1972. *Gentlewoman* (M)
1973. *Second Lady* (Z)
1974. *Il Destino* (CAL)
1976, 77. *Alice Ford* (F)
Griffel, Kay   1974. *Ill's Son* (V)
Griffiths, Philip   1965. *Giocondo* (PP)
Grilli, Umberto   1973. *Queen of the Night* (Z)
Gruberova, Edita   1971. *Count Tomsky* (QS)
Guerdjikov, Pavel   1973, 76. *Count* (CAP)
Hagegård, Håkan   1974. *Count* (NF)
1978. *Guglielmo* (CT)
Hamari, Julia   1979. *Celia* (FED)
Hammes, Liselotte   1965. *Sophie* (R)
Hammond-Stroud, Derek   1973, 74. *Schoolmaster* (V)
1980. *Faninal* (R)
Hannan, Eilene   1977. *The Vixen* (CV)
Harper, Heather   1966. *Iphis* (J)
Harrhy, Eiddwen   1979. *Diana* (FED)
Harrison, Powell   1974. *Cameraman* (V)
Hartle, Enid   1970. *Natura* (CAL)
1971. *Governess* (QS)
1971, 72. *Dryade* (AN)
1973. *Third Lady* (Z)
1975, 77. *Forester's Wife, Owl, Woodpecker* (CV)
1977, 79. *Carlotta* (SF)
Hartley, David   1965. *Fabrizio* (PP)
Harwood, Elizabeth   1971. *Fiordiligi* (CT)
1973. *Countess* (NF)
1980. *Marschallin* (R)
Helm, Hans   1976. *Count* (NF)
Hemsley, Thomas   1966. *Aeneas* (D)
1966, 73. *Speaker* (Z)
1971, 72. *Music Master* (AN)
Hendricks, Barbara   1974. *Calisto* (CAL)
Herford, Henry   1978. *Speaker* (Z)
Hickey, Angela   1966. *Second Lady* (Z)
Hoback, James   1980. *Pedrillo* (E)
Hoekman, Guus   1969. *Arkel* (PM)
Howells, Anne   1966. *Second Boy* (Z)
1967, 68. *Erisbe* (LO)
1969. *Dorabella* (CT)
1970, 71. *Cathleen* (RM)
1971. *Composer* (AN)
1972, 73. *Minerva* (RU)
1974. *Diana* (CAL)
Hoyem, Robert   1975, 77. *The Fox* (CV)
Hughes, David   1965. *Valzacchi* (R)
1965. *Macduff* (M)
1972. *Giove* (RU)
Hughes, Janet   1970, 71, 74. *Satirino* (CAL)
1972, 73. *Melanto* (RU)

Hunt, Annabel	1972, 73. *L'humana fragiltà (RU)*
	1973. *Second Boy (Z)*
Jahn, Gertrude	1968. *Olga (EO)*
Jenkins, Angela	1965. *Duenna (R)*
Jenkins, Terry	1971. *Master of Ceremonies (QS)*
	1971. *Officer (AN)*
	1972. *Scaramuccio (AN)*
Jennings, Jerry	1971. *Ferrando (CT)*
Jobin, André	1976. *Pelléas (PM)*
John, Kevin	1979. *Giove (RU)*
John, Lindsay	1978. *Second Boy (Z)*
Johnson, Patricia	1965, 68. *Giovanna (AB)*
	1966. *Sorceress (D)*
	1966. *Storge (J)*
Johnson, Robert	1975. *Ferrando (CT)*
Johnston, David	1980. *Man in Armour (Z)*
Jungwirth, Manfred	1965. *Baron Ochs (R)*
Jungwirth-Ahnsjö, Helena	1974. *Cherubino (NF)*
Keating, Roderic	1973. *Ill's Son (V)*
Kenny, Janet	1966. *Third Boy (Z)*
Kimm, Fiona	1980. *Third Lady (Z)*
King, Malcolm	1975. *Keeper of the Madhouse (RP)*
	1976. *Doctor (PM)*
	1978. *Leporello (DG)*
Kingsley, Margaret	1966. *First Lady (Z)*
Kitchiner, John	1965. *Count (NF)*
Korn, Artur	1980. *Baron Ochs (R)*
Koszut, Urszula	1970. *Queen of the Night (Z)*
Kovats, Kolos	1978. *Sarastro (Z)*
Kraus, Otakar	1968. *Pasha Selim (E)*
Kubiak, Teresa	1971. *Lisa (QS)*
	1971. *Giunone (CAL)*
Kuebler, David	1976. *Ferrando (CT)*
Kujawinska, Krystyna	1974. *Electra (I)*
Laghezza, Rosa	1965. *Fidalma (MS)*
	1965. *Marcellina (NF)*
Laki, Krisztina	1979. *Aminta (SF)*
	1980. *Sophie (R)*
Lane, Gloria	1972. *Ariadne (AN)*
	1972. *Lady Macbeth (M)*
Langdon, Michael	1965. *Banquo (M)*
	1979. *Don Fernando (FI)*
Langridge, Philip	1977, 78. *Don Ottavio (DG)*
Lappalainen, Kimmo	1972, 73. *Pedrillo (E)*
	1974. *Idamante (I)*
Laubenthal, Horst	1972. *Belmonte (E)*
Lawlor, Thomas	1971, 72. *Lackey (AN)*
	1973, 76. *Major Domo (CAP)*
	1973. *Guard (V)*
	1973, 74, 76. *Antonio (NF)*
	1974, 75. *Lawyer (INT)*
	1974. *Police Chief (V)*
	1975. *Zaretsky (EO)*
	1975, 77. *The Poacher (CV)*
	1977. *Keeper of the Madhouse (RP)*
Lea, Yvonne	1980. *Second Boy (Z)*
Lebrun, Louise	1970. *Queen of the Night (Z)*
	1970. *Il Destino (CAL)*
Lees, Susan	1970. *Third Boy (Z)*
Lehane, Maureen	1967. *Melide (LO)*
Le Hémonet, Pierre	1966. *Ramiro (HE)*
	1966. *Albert (W)*
Lennox, David	1965. *Landlord (R)*
	1965. *Don Curzio (NF)*
Lensky, Margaret	1969. *Geneviève (PM)*
	1970. *L'Eternità (CAL)*

Lewis, Keith	1978. *Don Ottavio (DG)*
	1979. *Giove (RU)*
Lewis, Michael	1977. *The Badger (CV)*
Lewis, Richard	1966. *Jephtha (J)*
	1967. *Don Ottavio (DG)*
	1972, 73, 79. *Eumete (RU)*
	1974. *Idomeneo (I)*
Lindenstrand, Sylvia	1975. *Dorabella (CT)*
	1979. *Amaranta (FED)*
Livingstone, Laureen	1972, 73. *Amore (RU)*
Lloyd, Robert	1972, 73. *Nettuno (RU)*
	1973. *Sarastro (Z)*
Lott, Felicity	1977, 78. *Anne (RP)*
	1978. *Pamina (Z)*
	1980. *Oktavian (R)*
Luxon, Benjamin	1972, 73. *Ulisse (RU)*
	1974. *Count (NF)*
	1975. *The Forester (CV)*
	1976, 77. *Ford (F)*
	1977. *Don Giovanni (DG)*
	1978, 80. *Papageno (Z)*
McCord, Catherine	1975. *Therese (INT)*
	1980. *First Lady (Z)*
McCrindle, Joyce	1976. *Marcellina (NF)*
McKinnon, Neil	1978. *Man in Armour (Z)*
	1978. *Parpignol (B)*
Maievsky, Maurice	1971. *Hermann (QS)*
	1972. *Bacchus (AN)*
Maliponte, Adriana	1967. *Adina (EA)*
Malmborg, Gunilla af	1965. *Lady Macbeth (M)*
Mandac, Evelyn	1974. *Susanna (NF)*
	1975. *Despina (CT)*
Mangin, Noel	1972. *Osmin (E)*
Marimpietri, Lydia	1965. *Susanna (NF)*
Mars, Jacques	1969, 70. *Golaud (PM)*
Marsh, Calvin	1966. *Hamor (J)*
Masterson, Valerie	1980. *Constanze (E)*
Mathis, Edith	1965. *Sophie (R)*
Mekler, Mani	1978. *First Lady (Z)*
Mercker, Karl-Ernst	1969. *Pedrillo (E)*
Meyer, Kerstin	1970, 71. *Elisabeth (RM)*
	1973, 74. *Claire Zachanassian (V)*
	1973, 76. *Clairon (CAP)*
Modenos, John	1965. *Faninal (R)*
Moll, Maria	1980. *Second Lady (Z)*
Möllerström, Britta	1973. *Susanna (NF)*
Monreale, Leonardo	1967. *Masetto (DG)*
Montague, Diana	1979. *L'humana fragiltà (RU)*
Montarsolo, Paolo	1967, 69. *Leporello (DG)*
	1968. *Osmin (E)*
	1969, 71. *Don Alfonso (CT)*
	1970. *Selim (T)*
Morelle, Maureen	1965. *Smeton (AB)*
Moreno, Myrna	1972. *Melanto (RU)*
Morris, James	1972. *Banquo (M)*
Mroz, Leonard	1978. *Commendatore (DG)*
Murray, Ann	1979. *Minerva (RU)*
Nemeer, Paul	1978. *Customs Officer (B)*
Neufeld, Wilmer	1971, 72. *Bacchus (AN)*
Nordin, Birgit	1968. *Blonde (E)*
Novelli, Anna	1967. *Mimì (B)*
Ochman, Wieslaw	1968, 70. *Lensky (EO)*
	1969. *Don Ottavio (DG)*
	1970. *Tamino (Z)*

Oliver, Alexander   1970, 73, *Monostatos (Z)*
1970, 71. *Brother Timothy (RM)*
1971, 72. *Dancing Master (AN)*
1972, 73, 79. *Iro (RU)*
1974. *Arbace (I)*
1974, 75. *Baron Lummer (INT)*
Oncina, Juan   1965. *Riccardo (AB)*
O'Neill, Dennis   1980. *Singer (R)*

Parker, Patricia   1978. *Second Lady (Z)*
1978, 79. *Dorabella (CT)*
1979. *Melanto (RU)*
Pashley, Anne   1966. *Second Lady (Z)*
Paskalis, Kostas   1965, 72. *Macbeth (M)*
1967. *Don Giovanni (DG)*
Pender, Marta   1965. *Lady Macbeth (M)*
Penkova, Reni   1971. *Pauline (QS)*
1975. *Olga (EO)*
1975. *Dorabella (CT)*
1976, 77. *Meg Page (F)*
Perriers, Danièle   1972. *Blonde (E)*
1975, 76. *Despina (CT)*
Perry, Janet   1977. *Aminta (SF)*
Peters, Johanna   1970, 71. *Widow Sweeney (RM)*
1977, 1979. *Theodosia (SF)*
Petkov, Dimiter   1968. *Osmin (E)*
1970. *Gremin (EO)*
Petri, Frantz   1975, 76. *Don Alfonso (CT)*
Petros, Evelyn   1980. *Celia (FED)*
Popova, Virginia   1968, 70. *Filippyevna (EO)*
1971. *Countess (QS)*
1972, 73. *Ericlea (RU)*
Powell, Claire   1979. *Giunone (RU)*
1980. *Meg Page (F)*
Power, Patrick   1979. *Telemaco (RU)*
Price, Janet   1972. *Najade (AN)*
Price, Margaret   1966. *Angel (J)*
1968, 72. *Constanze (E)*
1971. *Fiordiligi (CT)*
Pring, Katherine   1978. *Baba the Turk (RP)*
Pruett, Jerome   1977, 79. *Henry (SF)*
Putnam, Ashley   1978. *Musetta (B)*

Raffell, Anthony   1966. *Johann (W)*
Raimondi, Ruggero   1969. *Don Giovanni (DG)*
Ramey, Samuel   1976. *Figaro (NF)*
1977, 78. *Nick Shadow (RP)*
Rath, John   1978. *Man in Armour (Z)*
Ratti, Eugenia   1973, 76. *Italian Soprano (CAP)*
Rawnsley, John   1977, 78. *Masetto (DG)*
1978. *Marcello (B)*
1980. *Perrucchetto (FED)*
Rees, Deborah   1980. *First Boy (Z)*
Reynolds, Anna   1965. *Annina (R)*
Rinaldi, Alberto   1980. *Ford (F)*
Rinaldi, Margherita   1966. *Carolina (MS)*
Rintzler, Marius   1967, 69. *Commendatore (DG)*
1968. *Enrico (AB)*
1972. *Osmin (E)*
1973. *Bartolo (NF)*
1973, 76. *La Roche (CAP)*
1979. *Morosus (SF)*
Rippon, Michael   1970. *Priest and Man in Armour (Z)*
1971. *Surin (QS)*
1973. *Speaker (Z)*
1973. *Bartolo (NF)*
1973. *Police Chief (V)*
Ritchie, Elizabeth   1980. *Diana (FED)*
Roberts, Joy   1973. *First Boy (Z)*
1974. *Cherubino (NF)*

Robson, Richard   1975. *The Badger (CV)*
Roden, Anthony   1971. *Chekalinsky (QS)*
1972. *Belmonte (E)*
1973. *Tamino (Z)*
1973. *Man in Armour (Z)*
Rolfe Johnson, Anthony   1974, 75. *Stroh (INT)*
1975. *Lensky (EO)*
1976. *Fenton (F)*
Ross, Susanna   1974, 76. *Barbarina (NF)*
Rouleau, Joseph   1979. *Vanuzzi (SF)*
Roux, Michel   1965. *Count (NF)*
1965. *Macrobio (PP)*
1969. *Don Alfonso (CT)*
1970. *The Poet (T)*
Runge, Peter-Christoph   1966, 73. *Papageno (Z)*
1967. *Amida (LO)*
1969. *Pelléas (PM)*
Russell, Lynda   1979. *Fortuna (RU)*

Sandoz, May   1978. *Queen of the Night (Z)*
Sapoundjiev, Gheorgi   1971. *Hermann (QS)*
Saunders, Arlene   1966. *Pamina (Z)*
Schenk, Manfred   1973. *Sarastro (Z)*
Schmidt, Erika   1965. *Marschallin (R)*
Schmidt, Trudeliese   1976. *Dorabella (CT)*
Sciutti, Graziella   1970. *Fiorilla (T)*
1977. *Elle (VH)*
Selimsky, Assen   1968. *Onegin (EO)*
1971. *Yeletsky (QS)*
Sénéchal, Michel   1966. *Gonzalve (HE)*
Sharp, Norma   1978. *Donna Anna (DG)*
Shirley, George   1966, 73. *Tamino (Z)*
1974. *Idomeneo (I)*
Silver, Annon Lee   1969. *Sophie (W)*
1970. *Atalanta (RM)*
Skram, Knut   1969, 71, 75, 76. *Guglielmo (CT)*
1970. *Papageno (Z)*
1973, 74, 76. *Figaro (NF)*
Smales, Kathleen   1971. *Masha (QS)*
Söderström, Elisabeth   1968. *Tatyana (EO)*
1973, 76. *Countess (CAP)*
1974, 75. *Christine (INT)*
1979. *Leonore (FI)*
Sotin, Hans   1970. *Sarastro (Z)*
Souzay, Gérard   1965. *Count (NF)*
Speiser, Elisabeth   1973. *Pamina (Z)*
Stade, Frederica von   1973. *Cherubino (NF)*
1979. *Penelope (RU)*
Stadler, Irmgard   1967. *Sicle (LO)*
1969. *Donna Elvira (DG)*
1970. *Giunone (CAL)*
1972. *Composer (AN)*
Still, Athole   1973. *Man in Armour (Z)*
Stilwell, Richard   1973, 79. *Ulisse (RU)*
1973. *Olivier (CAP)*
1975. *Onegin (EO)*
1976. *Ford (F)*
Stokes, Elizabeth   1978. *Third Boy (Z)*
Strauss Smith, Lloyd   1965. *Hervey (AB)*
1965. *Malcolm (M)*

Te Kanawa, Kiri   1973, 74. *Countess (NF)*
Thallaug, Edith   1971. *Dorabella (CT)*
T'Hezan, Hélia   1966. *Charlotte (W)*
Thomaschke, Thomas   1978, 80. *Sarastro (Z)*
1980. *Pasha Selim (E)*
Thompson, Adrian   1980. *Priest (Z)*
Tippett, Elizabeth   1968. *Sicle (LO)*
Titus, Alan   1979. *Guglielmo (CT)*

Tomlinson, John	1972. *Murderer (M)*
	1973. *Cameraman (V)*
	1973. *Man in Armour (Z)*
	1974. *Silvano (CAL)*
Townley, Vivien	1979. *Giunone (RU)*
Trama, Ugo	1965. *Asdrubale (PP)*
	1970, 71, 74. *Giove (CAL)*
	1972, 73, 79. *Antinöo (RU)*
	1972, 73, 79. *Tempo (RU)*
	1974. *Pane (CAL)*
	1974, 76. *Bartolo (NF)*
	1976, 77, 80. *Pistol (F)*
	1977, 79. *Farfallo (SF)*
Usanov, Katja	1970. *Tatyana (EO)*
Valentini, Alberta	1965. *Elisetta (MS)*
	1965. *Fulvia (PP)*
	1967. *Musetta (B)*
Van Allan, Richard	1966. *Priest and Man in Armour (Z)*
	1966, 68. *Osmano (LO)*
	1968, 70. *Zaretsky (EO)*
	1969. *Johann (W)*
	1969. *Doctor (PM)*
	1969, 77. *Leporello (DG)*
	1970. *The Speaker (Z)*
	1970, 71. *Jowler (RM)*
	1971, 72. *Major Domo (AN)*
	1972. *Osmin (E)*
	1972. *Pasha Selim (E)*
	1977. *Trulove (RP)*
	1979. *Melibeo (FED)*
Vanni, Helen	1971, 72. *Ariadne (AN)*
Van Vrooman, Richard	1968. *Belmonte (E)*
Varley, Susan	1974. *Marie (INT)*
Vassiliev, Nikola	1970. *Onegin (EO)*
Veasey, Josephine	1965. *Oktavian (R)*
	1965. *Clarice (PP)*
	1969. *Charlotte (W)*
Vernon Bates, Angela	1973. *Third Lady (Z)*
Wakefield, John	1967, 68. *Ormindo (LO)*
	1970, 71. *Beaumont (RM)*
	1972, 73. *Eurimaco (RU)*
Walker, Helen	1978. *Fiordiligi (CT)*
Walker, Sarah	1970. *L'Eternità (CAL)*
	1970. *Diana (CAL)*
Wallis, Delia	1971. *Cathleen (RM)*
	1971, 72. *Composer (AN)*
	1976. *Cherubino (NF)*
Walmesley, Clare	1966. *Witch (D)*
Walton, Gavin	1971. *Surin (QS)*
Watson, Lillian	1976. *Susanna (NF)*
	1976. *Despina (CT)*
	1980. *Blonde (E)*
Watt, Alan	1974. *Helmesberger (V)*
	1975, 77. *The Dog (CV)*
	1975. *Petrovich (EO)*
	1975. *Commercial Counsellor (INT)*
	1977, 79. *Morbio (SF)*
White, Willard	1978, 80. *The Speaker (Z)*
	1978. *Colline (B)*
	1980. *Osmin (E)*
Wicks, Dennis	1970, 71. *Lynch (RM)*
	1971, 72. *Truffaldino (AN)*
	1974, 75. *Opera Singer (IN)*
Williams, Jean	1975. *Fanny (INT)*
Willis, Nuala	1977, 78. *Mother Goose (RP)*
Wilson-Johnson, David	1980. *Police Inspector (R)*
Winbergh, Gösta	1980. *Belmonte (E)*

Wise, Patricia	1972. *Zerbinetta (AN)*
Woodland, Rae	1966. *Queen of the Night (Z)*
	1970, 71. *Lady Jowler (RM)*
	1972. *Gentlewoman (M)*
	1973, 74. *Mrs Ill (V)*
	1973. *Giunone (RU)*
	1974. *Lawyer's Wife (INT)*
	1980. *Duenna (R)*
Yakar, Rachel	1977. *Donna Elvira (DG)*
	1980. *Marschallin (R)*
Yoncheva, Galia	1975. *Tatyana (EO)*
Zoghby, Linda	1978. *Mimì (B)*
	1980. *Amaranta (FED)*
Zylis-Gara, Teresa	1965. *Oktavian (R)*
	1967. *Donna Elvira (DG)*

Conductors

Barlow, Stephen	1979. *Die schweigsame Frau*
	1980. *Der Rosenkavalier*
Braithwaite, Nicholas	1978. *La Bohème*
	1978. *The Magic Flute*
	1979. *Così fan tutte*
	1979. *La fedeltà premiata*
Ceccato, Aldo	1971, 72. *Ariadne auf Naxos*
Cillario, Carlo Felice	1966. *Werther*
	1967. *L'elisir d'amore*
Davis, Andrew	1973, 76. *Capriccio*
	1975. *Eugene Onegin*
	1977, 79. *Die schweigsame Frau*
	1978, 80. *The Magic Flute*
	1980. *Falstaff*
Fredman, Myer	1965, 67. *Il matrimonio segreto*
	1965. *Anna Bolena*
	1966, 70, 73. *The Magic Flute*
	1966. *Jephtha*
	1967. *La Bohème*
	1967. *Don Giovanni*
	1968, 70. *Eugene Onegin*
	1968, 73. *Die Entführung aus dem Serail*
	1969. *Così fan tutte*
	1969. *Werther*
	1970. *Il turco in Italia*
	1971. *The Rising of the Moon*
	1972. *Ariadne auf Naxos*
	1972. *Macbeth*
	1973, 74. *The Visit of the Old Lady*
	1973. *Le nozze di Figaro*
Gardelli, Lamberto	1965. *Macbeth*
	1968. *Anna Bolena*
Gavazzeni, Gianandrea	1965. *Anna Bolena*
Gellhorn, Peter	1974. *Le nozze di Figaro*
Gierster, Hans	1966. *The Magic Flute*
Gui, Vittorio	1965. *Il matrimonio segreto*
	1965. *Le nozze di Figaro*
Haitink, Bernard	1972. *Die Entführung aus dem Serail*
	1973, 78, 80. *The Magic Flute*
	1975, 77, 78. *The Rake's Progress*
	1976. *Pélleas et Mélisande*
	1977. *Don Giovanni*
	1978, 79. *Così fan tutte*
	1979. *Fidelio*
	1979. *La fedeltà premiata*
	1980. *Der Rosenkavalier*
Kuhn, Gustav	1980. *Die Entführung aus dem Serail*

Producers

Designers

Designers—Costumes only

Le nozze di Figaro

(1934 production)

Cast as in Appendix C page 336
Available from USA only on Turnabout THS 65081–3

Così fan tutte

(1935 production)

Cast as in Appendix C page 336
Available from USA only on Turnabout THS 65126–8

Don Giovanni

(1936 production)

Cast as in Appendix C page 336
Available from USA only on Turnabout THS 65084–6

Idomeneo

(Excerpts from 1951 production)

Cast as in Appendix C page 337
World Records SH 294

Le Comte Ory

(1955 production)

Cast as in Appendix C page 337
EMI recording re-issued in 1980—RLS 744

The Barber of Seville

(1962)

Cast as in Appendix C page 338
HMV—SLS 5165

L'Ormindo

(1968 production)

Ormindo	John Wakefield
Amida	Peter-Christoph Runge
Nerillo	Isabel Garcisanz
Sicle	Hanneke van Bork
Melide	Jean Allister
Erice	Hugues Cuenod
Erisbe	Anne Howells
Mirinda	Jane Berbié
Ariadeno	Federico Davià
Osmano	Richard Van Allan

Conductor   RAYMOND LEPPARD
Argo ZNF 8–10

La Calisto

(1971 production)

Diana	Janet Baker
Calisto	Ileana Cotrubas
Endimione	James Bowman
Mercurio	Peter Gottlieb
Satirino	Janet Hughes
Linfea	Hugues Cuenod
Giove	Ugo Trama
Pane	Federico Davià
Giunone	Teresa Kubiak
Silvano	Owen Brannigan
La Natura	Marjorie Biggar
L'Eternità	Enid Hartle
Il Destino	Teresa Cahill

Conductor   RAYMOND LEPPARD
Argo ZNF 11-12

Die Entführung aus dem Serail

(Excerpts from 1972 production)

Belmonte	Ryland Davies
Constanze	Margaret Price
Blonde	Danièle Perriers
Pedrillo	Kimmo Lappalainen
Osmin	Noel Mangin

Conductor   JOHN PRITCHARD
Classics for Pleasure 40032

Il ritorno d'Ulisse in patria

(1979 production)

Ulisse	Richard Stilwell
Penelope	Frederica von Stade
Ericlea	Nucci Condò
Eurimaco	Max-René Cosotti
Melanto	Patricia Parker
Minerva	Ann Murray
Eumete	Richard Lewis
Iro	Alexander Oliver
Telemaco	Patrick Power
Antinöo	Ugo Trama
Anfimono	Bernard Dickerson
Pisandro	John Fryatt
Giunone	Claire Powell
Giove	Keith Lewis
Nettuno	Roger Bryson

Conductor   RAYMOND LEPPARD
CBS Masterworks 79332

Index